LEGACY
GENERATIONS OF CREATIVES IN DIALOGUE

Lukas Feireiss

FRAME

LEGACY GENERATIONS OF CREATIVES IN DIALOGUE

Lukas Feireiss

Jonathan Lethem and Bob Dylan engaging in lingering conversation over music and the legacy of the 1960s in a Santa Monica seaside hotel suite. Olafur Eliasson and his mentor architect Einar Thorstein talking about the creative process of model making. Star architects Rem Koolhaas and Daniel Libeskind critically questioning the concept of legacy with their respective artist daughters Charlie Koolhaas and Rachel Libeskind. Reading between the lines with Ahmir Questlove Thompson and George Clinton. Exploring a family's legacy in the woods of Cape Cod with three generations of Chermayeffs. Reflecting upon Le Corbusier with Tom Sachs. These are but a few of the numerous conversations between generations of creatives featured in the book you're holding.

What is this phenomenon we call 'legacy'? This intangible inheritance that we eventually leave for our posterity? Is it the creative and intellectual heritage that one generation passes on to the next? Is it art for an artist; a building for an architect; for a writer, is it the words; for a musician, is it music; for a parent, is it children? Is it asset or accident? Is it deliberate or random? Is it our choices and actions, our words and deeds? Is it something entirely different?

Whatever it may be, this book tries to probe this open question by engaging—in critical dialogue—different generations of creatives, connectors and thinkers alike. In some cases, between inherent legacy of parent and child, in many cases between mentor and students, or simply between friends. The illustrious contributors to this dialogue derive from an array of fields of knowledge and experience. Their stories often provide very personal insights, not only into their work and life, but while investigating a wider perspective on the overall realm of art, design, architecture, music, literature, photography and curation in the 20th and 21st century.

My objective with this collection is to look more closely at what has been handed down from preceding generations. I wish to examine the original responses of the succeeding generations to these influences and explore how they have been used and reinterpreted. The cross-generational exchange of ideas obviously lies at the heart of this publication. I'd like to note that I don't regard the legacy of an individual person or predecessor as an end-point, but rather a simple moment in an eternal interplay of contributions, inspirations and conversations that naturally extends, transforms and reshapes over time.

The various texts in this book range from classical interviews, to essayistic narratives as well as more experimental formats. Some of the contributions are based on existing, previously published texts, while others are sourced transcripts of never-before published interviews. Most of the contributions are unique and have been purposely conceived for this book. With that in mind, I would like to express my heartfelt gratitude to all of the contributing authors for their generous support in finally bringing this book to life. It is only thanks to their diverse pieces that this book has become so rich and multi-layered in form and content. Additionally, the unintentional intertextuality that occurs between many of the present texts generates an intertwined thematic undercurrent in these separate works. Given this correlation, each contribution creates layers of depth for the next one. From an editorial perspective, this is more than I had ever hoped for.

This book is intended to stimulate intensive reflection about life, love, and creativity across generations and professional boundaries. It has been my explicit intention to create a source of inspiration for creatives beyond established etiquette. I sincerely hope that my personal enthusiasm for the subject will also spread to the reader. If this book inspires some of its readers to survey their own legacy or to reach out to those whose legacy had an impact on their lives, it will have more than served its purpose. No final conclusion is offered on what legacy means, except for encouraging the next generation to work towards realizing their own greatness.

Meet the Chermayeffs. Work in Progress

Lukas Feireiss

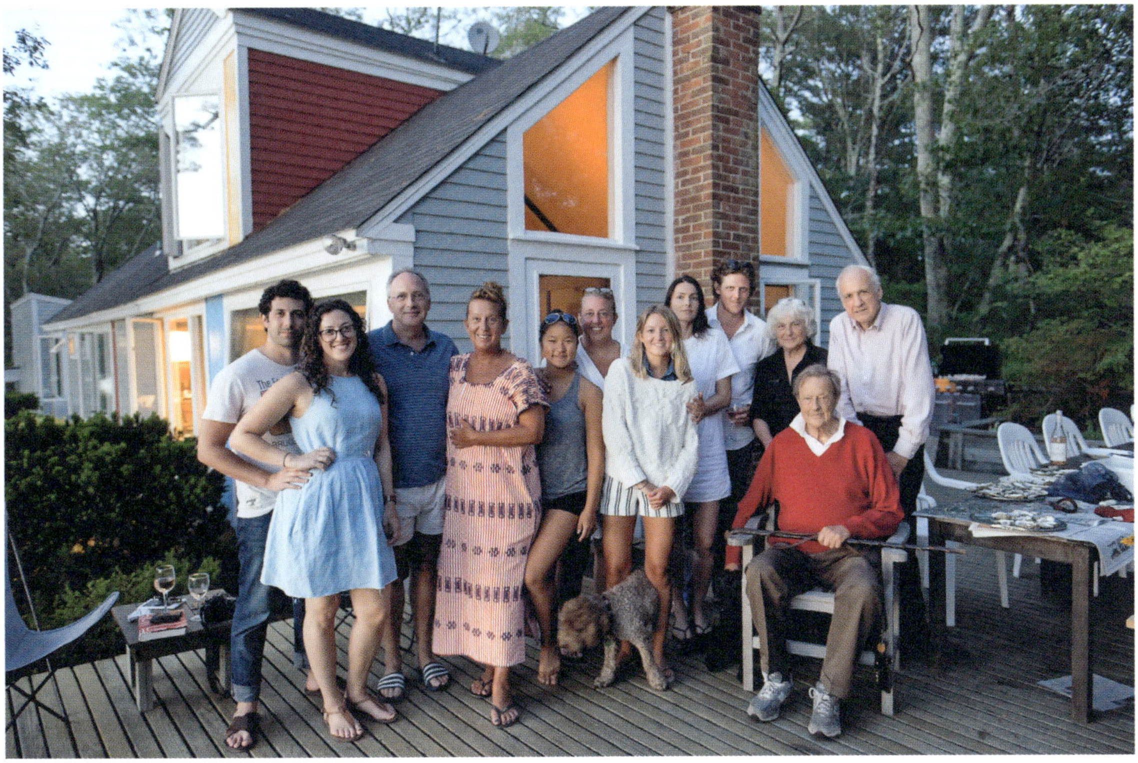

LUKAS FEIREISS spends a long summer day talking to three generations of CHERMAYEFFS, trying to wrap his head around this extraordinary family and its exceptional legacy of creativity, intelligence and ambition.

IN THE WOODS

Little did I know what adventure I was about to embark on, when in the summer of 2016 I was invited by my friend, the Berlin-based architect Sam Chermayeff, to his yearly family reunion near Wellfleet in Outer Cape Cod, Massachusetts. A good five hour drive from New York on Route six, deep among the pine trees, black oak, and sand dunes, his grandfather, Serge Chermayeff—professional tango dancer-turned interior designer-turned architect-turned academic and founding father of the family's legacy—bought a plot of land in the 1940s next to a small glacial kettle pond to build his own studio vacation home. This secluded area would become the destination for artists, intellectuals, bohemians and many European émigrés between the 1940s and 1970s. In direct vicinity to the Chermayeff cabin, just across the small pond, Hungarian designer and architect Marcel Breuer, artists György Kepes, as well as Finnish-American architect and designer Eero Saarinen all built small vacation homes for their families. Leading figures from the country's top art, architecture, and design institutions, like Florence and Hans Knoll, Arshile Gorky, Max Ernst, and Peggy Guggenheim were regular guests in this unusual setting amidst obscure rutted sand roads, rustic cabins and wild natural surroundings. Hidden away in the woods, the modest Chermayeff cabin made from inexpensive and salvaged materials expanded and grew non-cohesively over the decades along with the family, and eventually became the main residence for Serge and his wife Barbara for more than 20 years after his retirement. To this day, it serves as family domicile to his children and progeny. It is here, set deep in the woods and overlooking the pristine pond, where I get to spend a long summer day talking to three generations of Chermayeffs, sliding down a neck breaking zip-line into the pond, sipping chilled white wine and barbecuing fresh lobster and local oysters in Bourbon-Chipotle-Butter at sunset whilst trying to wrap my head around this extraordinary family and its exceptional legacy of creativity, intelligence and ambition.

THE HERO'S JOURNEY

The Chermayeff saga begins with Serge (1900-1996), the supreme patriarch of the family, at the beginning of the 20th century. The one person that everyone in the family refers to, in one way or another. Born in 1900 to a highly cultivated and rich Jewish family in the Russian Empire, Serge is educated abroad from an early age (at the age of ten he is sent alone to a preparatory school in England). The Russian Revolution then removes a substantial amount of the family fortune and forces his family to escape to Berlin, and later Paris. Well-versed in five languages, Serge begins a career as journalist, and professional dandy in London during this time. Short of money, he finds employment as a waiter on board of the steamship ocean liner Queen Elizabeth II and travels to Argentina, where he then spends a year working as a gaucho and learning tango. After his return from Argentina, he wins the World Tango Championship in London in 1927, marries his wife Barbara (1904-2000) and becomes a British citizen. Shortly after he starts his career as an interior designer.

↰ The Chermayeffs and friends in front of the family cabin in Cape Cod, Massachusetts, USA, 2016. All images © 2016 Daniel Salemi.

↗ The original Chermayeff cabin extended over time. Additional cabins for the family were built alongside.

→ Lukas Feireiss in conversation with Peter Chermayeff in front of his cabin.

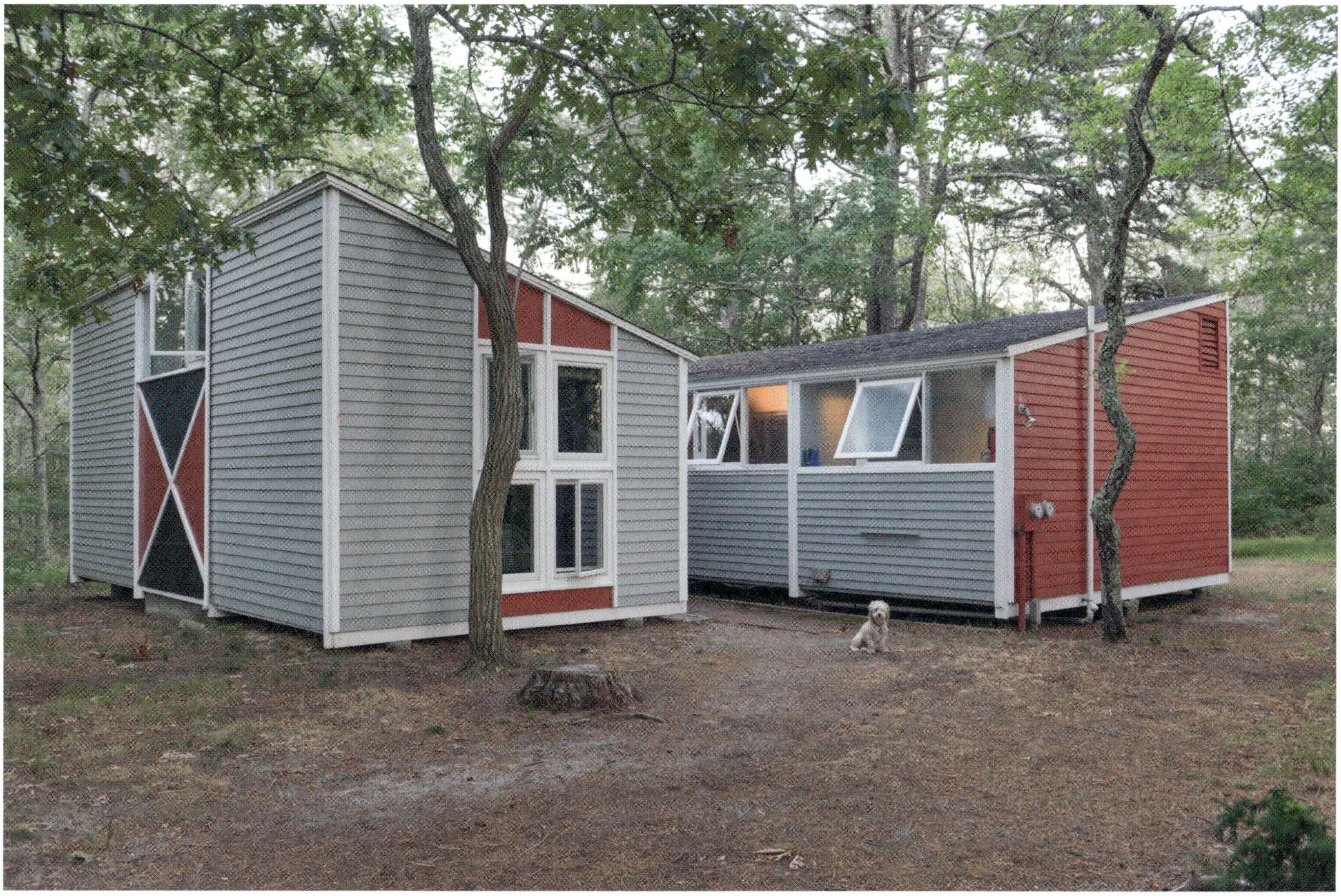

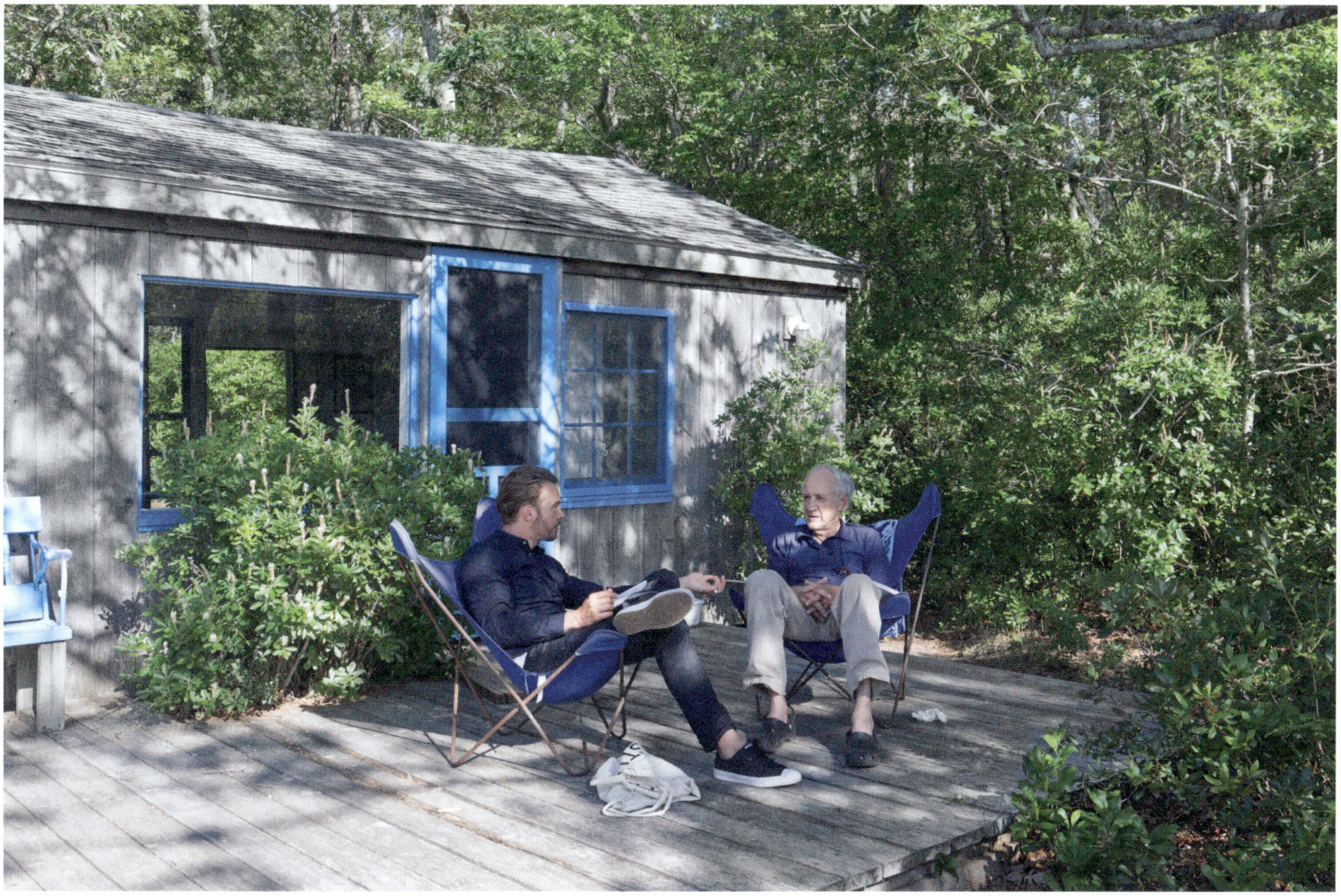

By 1933, Chermayeff completes his first building and opens an office with his friend the distinguished German architect Erich Mendelsohn, who had fled from Nazi Germany. Soon after the outbreak of the Second World War, Mendelsohn moves to Israel, while Serge and Barbara, along with their two sons Ivan and Peter, leave for the United States via Canada. Having built a handful of small houses on the West coast and teaching at Brooklyn College in the

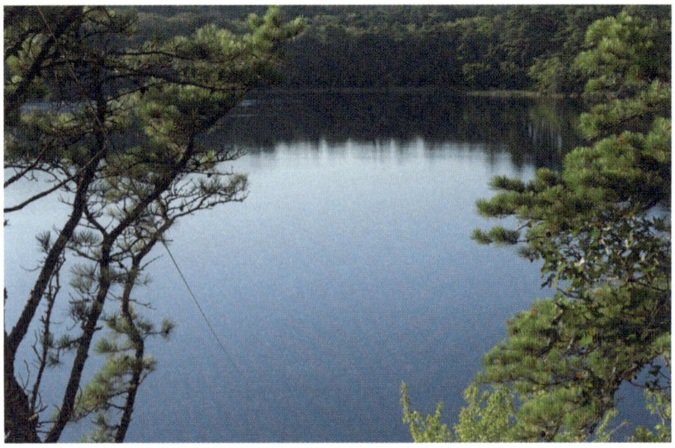

first years, Serge becomes an American citizen and is eventually appointed as president of the Chicago Institute of Design in 1946 (on recommendation of Walter Gropius, founder of the Bauhaus school), where he introduces architecture in the context of environmental design which he regards as the total scope of architecture, design and planning. In 1952 he becomes Professor at Harvard and in 1963 he takes up a post at Yale until his retirement as Professor Emeritus in 1969. Withdrawing almost entirely from public life after his retirement, the summer cottage in Cape Cod becomes his main residence. Here he resides with his wife from 1972 onwards and endures old age while drinking martinis and producing countless abstract drawings and paintings until his death in 1996.

THE SAGA CONTINUES

During my day here in Wellfleet, I am told numerous stories by various family members about Serge's intimidating and entertaining, fearsome and charming, terrifying and inspiring personality. He surely seemed to have been the king of his world. I am told of summers of unbridled celebration, cocktail nights, never-ending discussions and mesmerizing story telling in the cabin, of his two fierce and free-roaming German shepherd dogs, his shotgun rifle chases of intruders, his recurring citizen's arrests and his loud voice that, famously, could be heard across the pond. Serge was known for his ferocious temper. 'Everything was high drama. That was his way of holding the conversation', his granddaughter Maro tells me casually as she passes by in the open kitchen in search of her teenage daughter Su Huai (2002). Maro

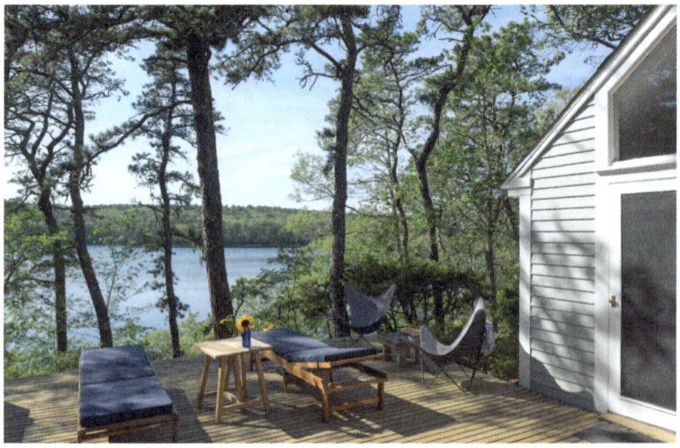

(1962) herself is the third daughter of Serge's son Ivan (1932-2017) and his first wife Sara (1934-2016). Maro is an internationally accomplished and Emmy nominated producer of numerous films and television programs (including the Maria Abramovic documentary *The Artist is Present* (2012) and department chair of social documentary film at the School of Visual Arts in New York.

Despite his seemingly overpowering and menacing character, Serge was extremely supportive of his two sons, Peter and Ivan, and always full of praise for them. 'With regards to my brother and me, he was totally encouraging all the time. No matter what we did. Even if it was complete rubbish.' Ivan, the oldest of Serge's sons and a design icon in his own right, tells me. As one of the eminent graphic designers of his era, Ivan forged some of the most recognizable corporate logos of the second half of the 20th century (including those of the cable channel Showtime, the publisher HarperCollins, the Museum of Modern Art, Mobil Oil, Chase Bank, and the Smithsonian Institution). 'My father simply helped you make it better,' he adds. It's at this point that I start noticing some patterns in the inherited Chermayeff family traits—the nurturing of individual interests, the sense of sharing and collaboration, as well as the personal and public acknowledgment through creative achievement, and the constant possibility of aesthetic improvement.

Serge's quest for infinite improvement often showed in brutal and unfiltered criticism outside of the family. Peter's wife, Andrea Peterson (a descendant of Felix Mendelssohn Bartholdy and childhood neighbour to the Chermayeffs) tells me of a class reunion at Harvard Graduate School of Design at which Serge (as always, dressed to kill in a white linen suit with a red handkerchief in his breast pocket, despite his advanced age at the time) listens to numerous speeches made in his honour before slowly getting up and saying: 'I look around the room and I am ashamed I ever taught any of you architecture. There hasn't been anyone worthy of the name in the last 40 years.' There was a dead silence for half a minute and then everybody just went on as if he hadn't said it. Amongst his students were the likes of Sir Norman Foster and Sir Richard Rogers, to mention but a few. Serge was equally feared and loved by his students and it was not uncommon for him to call former students, and by then, accomplished architects, to ask them if they ever considered taking up another line of work. When Serge finally left Yale, he still spend more than two decades in correspondence with many of his former graduates from all over the world who sent in their work for him to comment. 'That was his morning job for three to four hours a day,' Ivan remembers. 'They were not lightheaded letters but real thoughts. That was so great about him. He was involved in it and cared about it.'

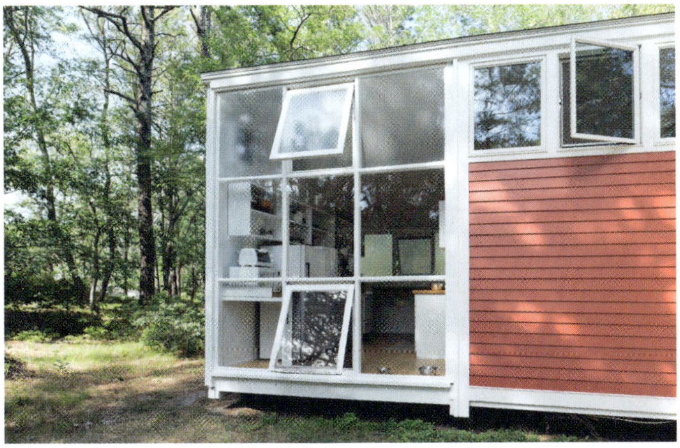

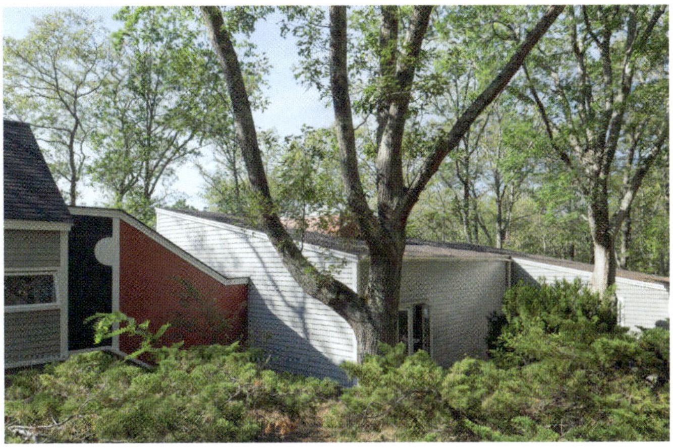

But Ivan never studied under his father. He decided very early not to become an architect, and avoided being at the same place as his father: 'I thought that architecture was fraught with failure and I don't like failure, so I became a graphic designer.' Peter (1936), Serge's second son, however took it on, and studied under his father at Harvard. 'It was fun. Even though he was tough with me. He said, I had to work hard and won't get any privilege, and I didn't expect any other treatment,' he tells me on the small wooden porch of his little cabin further down along the pond where he lives with his second wife Andrea, an old friend of the family. 'There was this sense of pleasure in his toughness' Peter says reminiscing how his class-mates complained bitterly about the cruelty of his old man, while at the same time enjoying it. A still practicing architect himself at the age of 81, Peter has become one of the world's foremost designers of aquariums in Boston, Osaka, Lisbon, Chattanooga, Genoa, and Baltimore. Together with his brother Ivan, he co-founded the Cambridge Seven Associates (C7A) in the early 1960s—a multi-disciplinary design firm whose work ranged from architecture, planning, exhibit design, graphics, industrial design, and filmmaking, and included such projects as the modernization of the MBTA, Boston's urban transportation system, the United States Exhibition at Expo'67 and the design of many diverse building types. During his studies at Harvard, Peter also started making films. While taking sabbaticals from architectural work at regular intervals, he actually shot animal documentaries for The Encyclopædia Britannica in Tanzania (using the Land Rover, camera, and cook of his friend the Dutch wildlife filmmaker Hugo von Lawick, who was married at the time to famous British primatologist and expert

↖ Various impressions of the Chermayeff family cabin with view on the glacial pond.

↱ Entrance situation of the main cabin.

↱↱ Interior view of the main cabin.

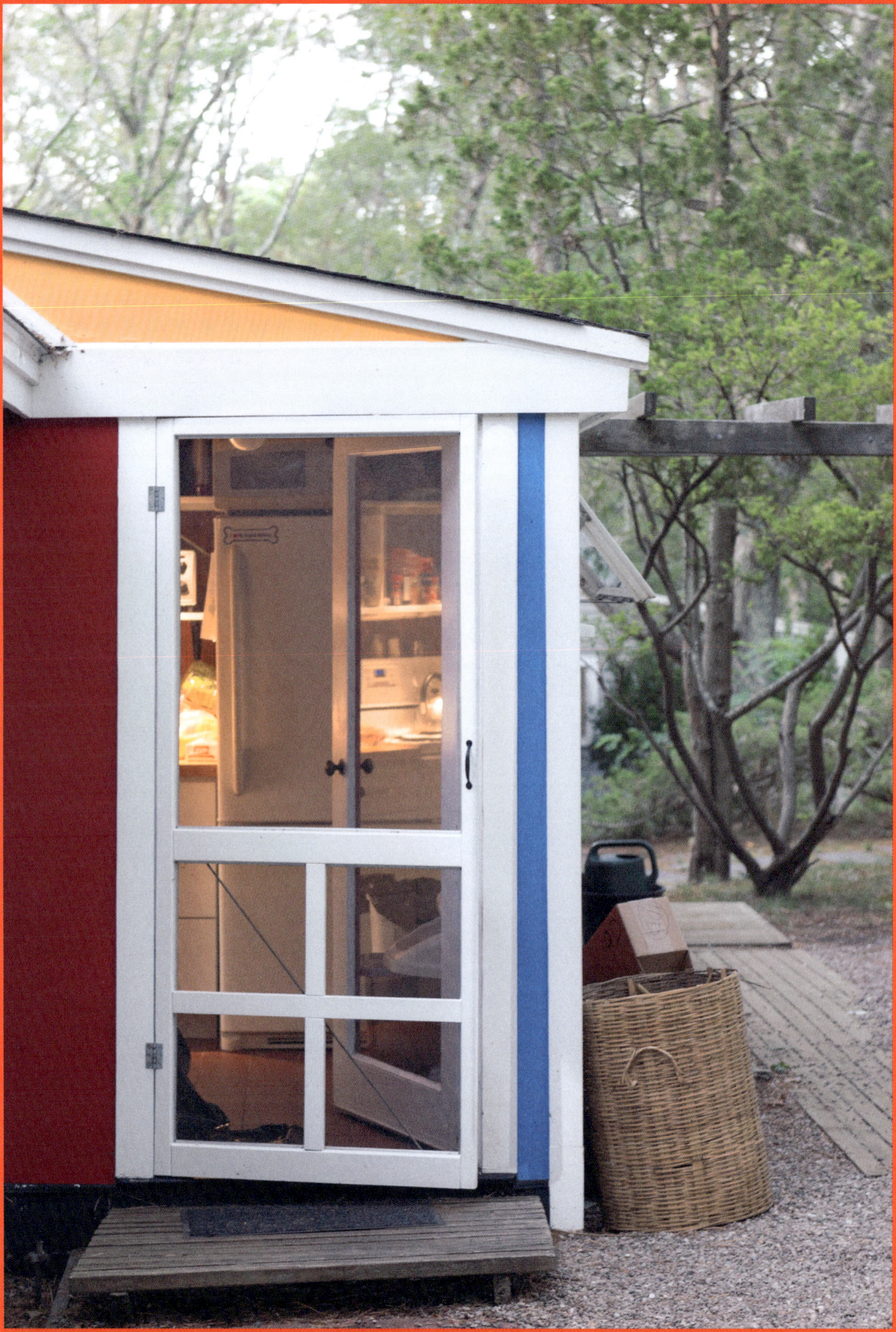

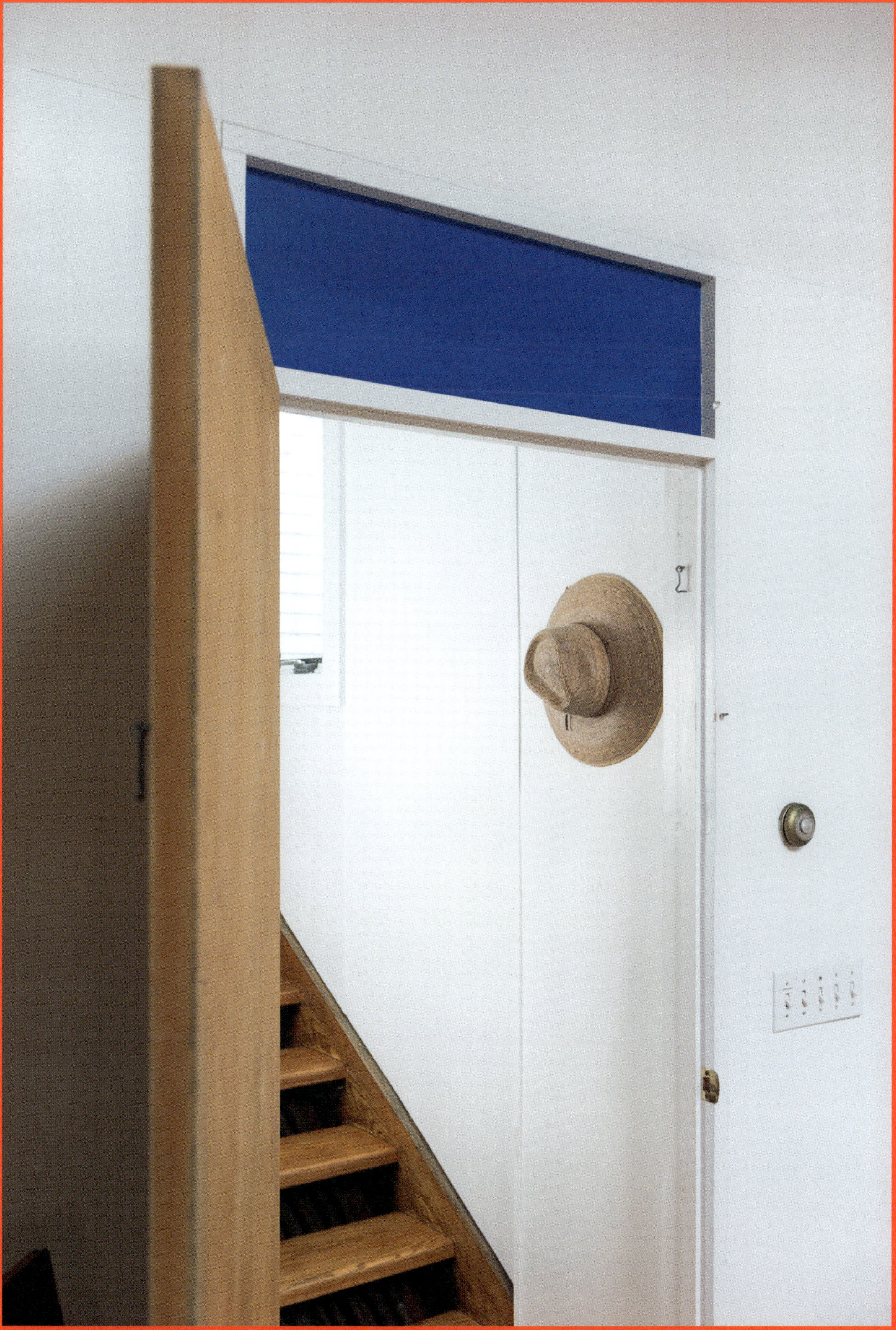

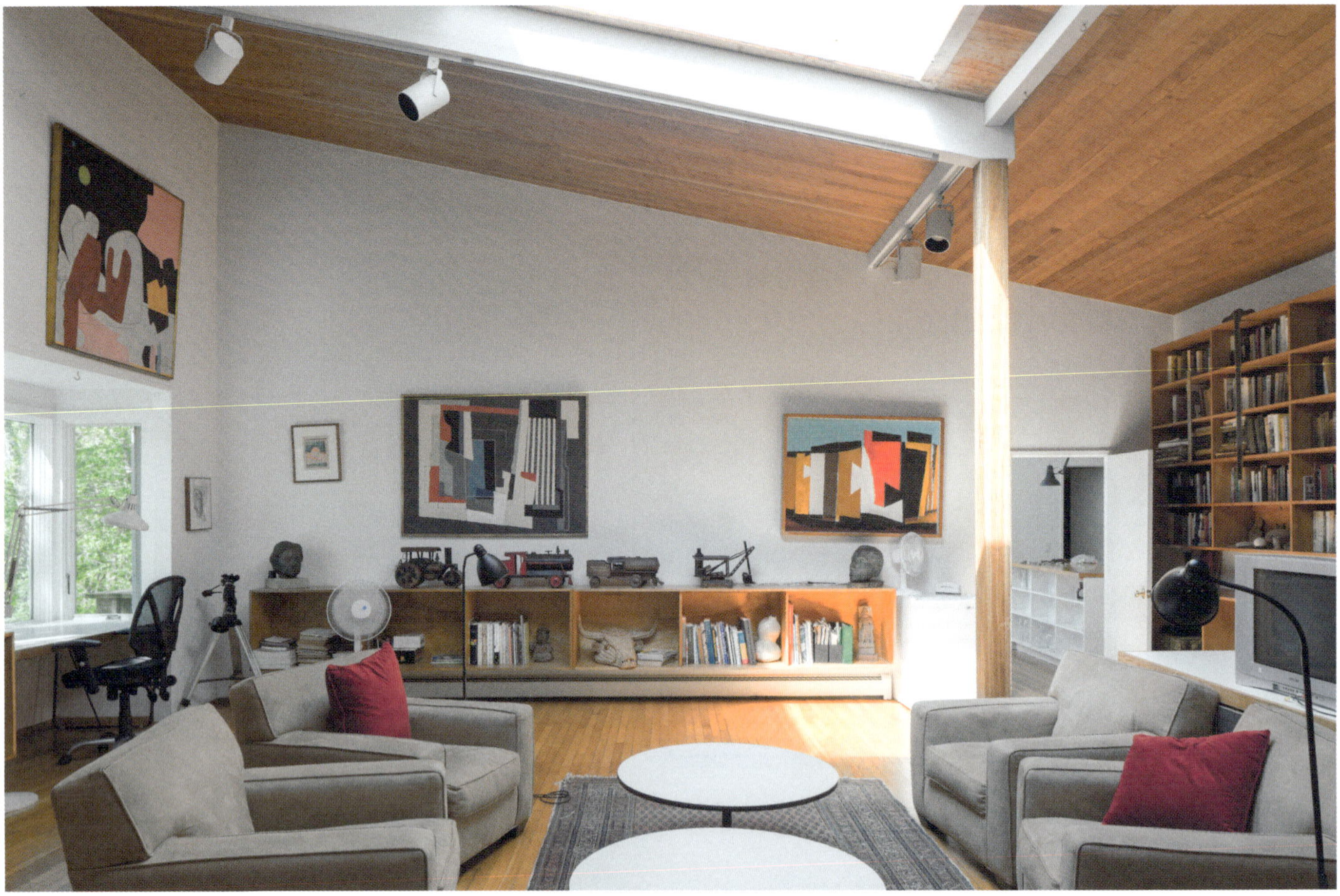

on chimpanzees, Jane Goodall). Reflecting upon his father's ways of teaching him he says: 'Whenever he suggested ideas for me to explore that I had not already begun to explore, I would resist. I would like him to refine or help me think about a problem, but in a path I was already on, not to steer me.' The ability to let a persons' own ideas mature, even when they were moving slower than one might have liked, was what kept a healthy dynamic between them. 'It was that level of independence and separation that I needed, but it was not different from what I felt growing up here on the pond.'

THE COMPANY YOU KEEP

Both Ivan and Peter grew up surrounded by extraordinary people of talent and special quality, going to Phillips Academy Andover (another Chermayeff trademark: three generations and nine family members went to this boarding school in Massachusetts, that is pegged as the best high school in America with a legacy of academic excellence, but also as one of the world's most expensive. John C Phillips, whose ancestors founded the academy and who inherited 800 acres in Cape Cod in his early 20s, was also the one who sold the land and the small cabin to Serge Chermayeff near Wellfleet), regularly spending the weekends at their surrogate grandparents Isa and Walter Gropius, or babysitting for the kids of their surrogate uncles Marcel Breuer and György Kepes just across the pond, and having the likes of Frank Lloyd Wright and Buckminster Fuller as regular house guests for dinner. Dinners, I am told, where everyone was treated equally, and the children's opinions were always taken seriously, no matter their age. Here another Chermayeff trademark comes to the fore: a genuine, almost omnivorous curiosity in everything and everyone. This is closely followed by another family trademark (that Maro self-mockingly brings to my attention) that comes along with the almost natural understanding that the party only starts when the Chermayeffs arrive and that they are the most interesting people in the room: an almost supernatural self-confidence.

This remarkable life of exceptional intensity continues in the generations to come. Ivan and his first wife Sara, were allegedly hanging out at their friend Miles Davis' house the night before their first daughter Catherine was born. Catherine (1957) studied photography and became the picture editor

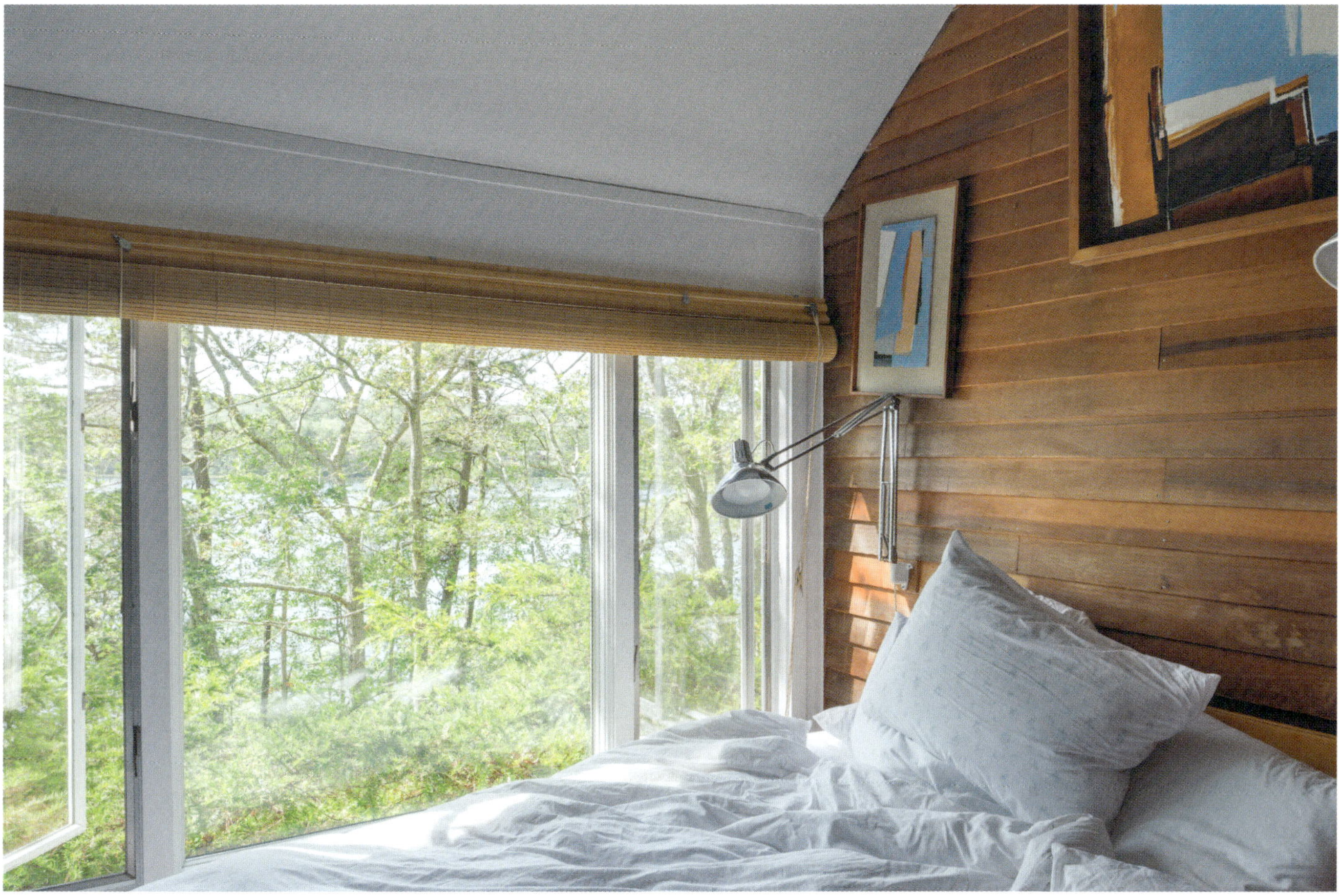

of *Fortune Magazine* at age of 23 (on invitation of Milton Glaser, one of the most celebrated graphic designers in the United States, and creator of the iconic logo for I love NY) hiring the likes of Irving Penn and Nan Golden. Eventually, she takes up the position of special projects director of Magnum Photos, the famous photo agency founded by Henri Cartier-Bresson, whose foundation she is involved with until this day. Apart from the afore-mentioned strong work ethic that runs in the family, ('We never stop working.'), it is also this combination of art and commerce that Catherine has learned from her father Ivan. 'He did not choose to go out and be a painter. He's very driven by the success of commerce,' she says. To no surprise, one of her two daughters, Loulou (1991), works in the advertising world, while the other, Fanny (1993), makes jewelry. 'Creative life has a great value in our family. We have all been fed that and we bought it.' Catherine says with a smile. Everything in the Chermayeff universe evolves around ideas, design and their accomplishment in one way or another. Almost everyone in the family is somehow involved in the creative industries. Creativity reigns supreme, here constitutes another Chermayeff credo, as well as deep-rooted sense of aestheticism. Nobody in this family seems to take the way things look lightly. Sam (1981), Ivan's youngest son with his second wife, Jane (1950-2014), shares another poignant family anecdote of how his sister Catherine, as a young girl, asked for a bicycle for her birthday. Secretly climbing up into the closet the day before the big day, she's excited to find this pink Barbie bicycle. The next day, however, she received that same bicycle wrapped neatly in red, but completely painted over in a matt black radiator colour.

Sam, an architect and designer himself, earned his spurs after his studies with Japanese architecture office SANAA in Tokyo, where he designed and realized SANAA's Serpentine Pavilion, and organized the 12th Venice Architecture Biennial, People Meet in Architecture, before starting his own practice June14 Meyer-Grohbrügge & Chermayeff in Berlin and New York in 2010. Since then, he has been collaborating with artist like **Olafur Eliasson** **(page → 30)** and Thomas Demand, whilst also teaching at Bauhaus Dessau, Columbia University and Cornell. Notwithstanding the fact that Sam remembers his grandfather mainly as a rather mean and scary person that was constantly

↖ Inside the living room and former studio of Serge Chermayeff with his paintings on the walls.

↑ View from bedroom into the woods towards the pond.

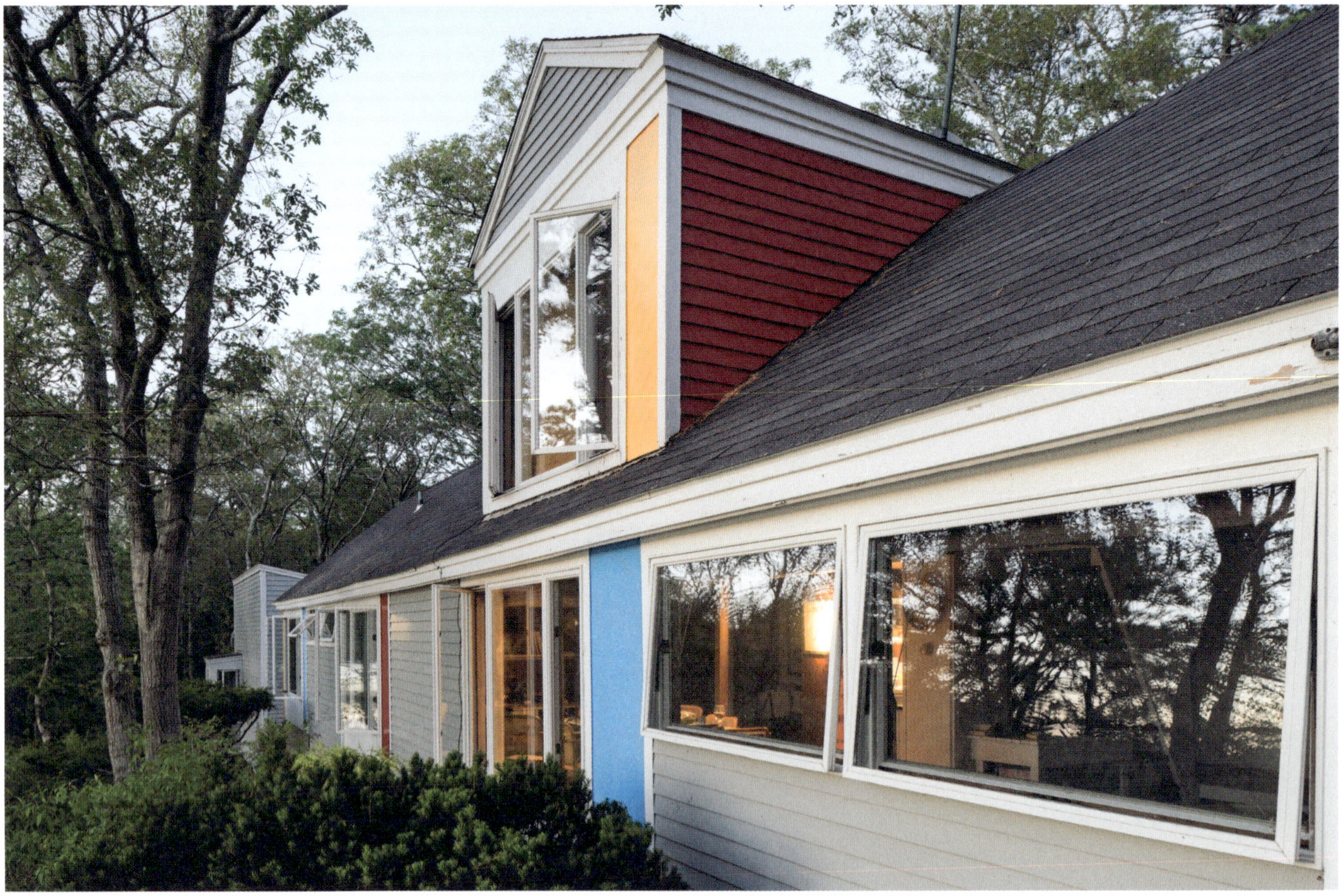

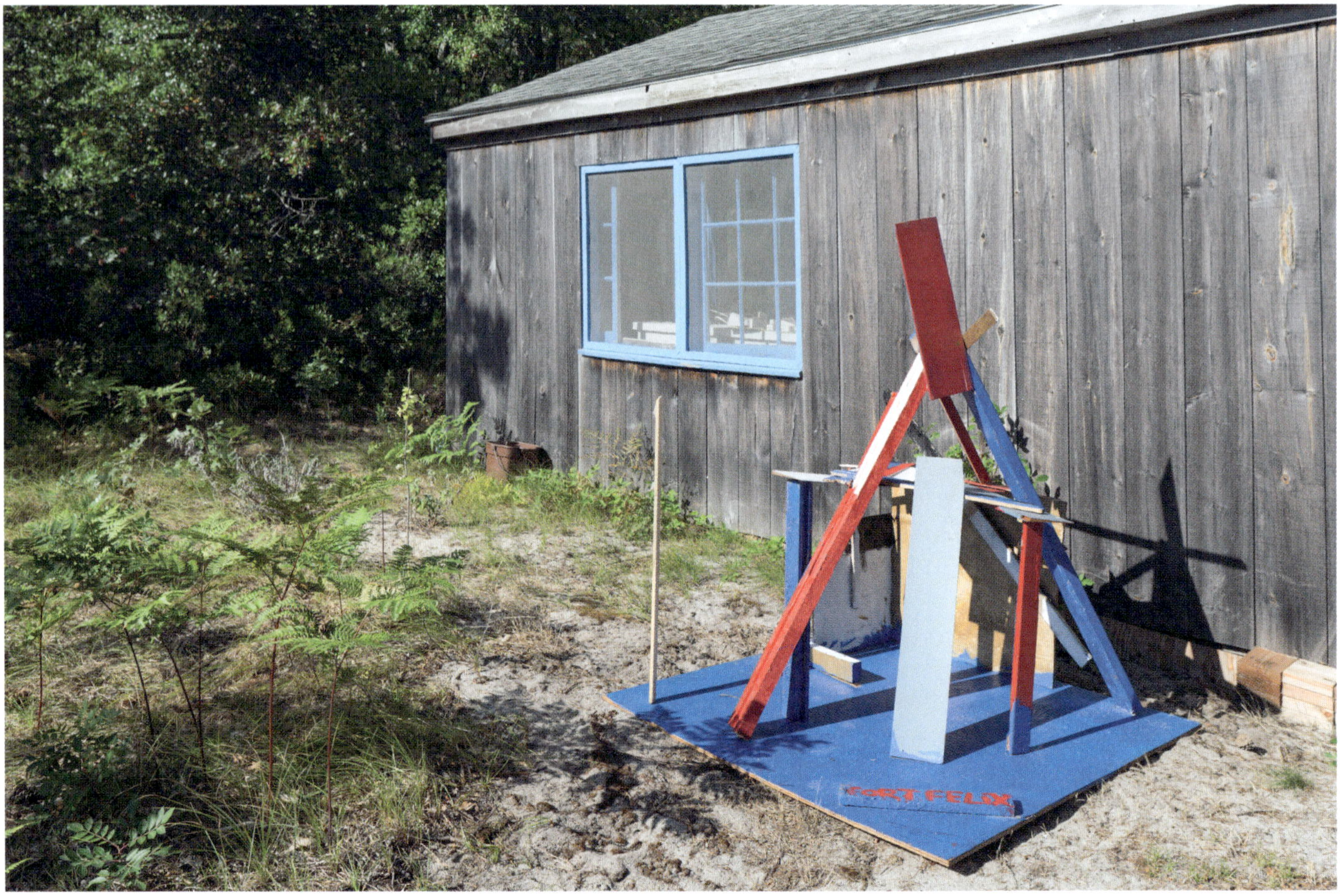
FORT FELIX

screaming and yelling, Sam somewhat instinctively seems to follow a similar approach in his practice as an architect. One of opening things up and questioning what is private and what is public. Serge's entire professional life was about finding these limits as well. Together with Christopher Alexander, he co-authored *Community and Privacy: Toward a New Architecture of Humanism* (1965), a seminal book on the topic.

Against this backdrop, one can imagine that not following a creative path appears almost unnatural for a Chermayeff, and as a downright rebellious move. Peter's son Nicolas (1969), a successful investment banker, is for example one of the rare exceptions from this Chermayeff rule. Having watched his father's and uncle's volatile world of creativity with its tremendous fluctuations of great highs and deep lows, he deliberately decided for another, more stable career path. Maro tells me that Nicolas, nonetheless, half-jokingly says 'I'm not the real winner here, because I'm not in the arts.' Nicolas' sister Jessica (1984), a producer and director working closely with her aunt Maro, didn't stray so far however.

ENLIGHTENED AMATEURISM

To Peter, the Chermayeff way, however, is less about a creative practice and more generally about the pursuit of any enterprise of value, whether it's artistic or in any another realm: 'It's the notion of doing things at the highest level we can, while solving problems and having a worthwhile purpose to the exercise.' This also means risk-taking and testing things out that one maybe knows nothing about. 'A kind of enlightened amateurism in parts,' as Peter calls it. 'Not to be too safe. Give it a shot. You can sort it out, and if things don't work out, not to be discouraged,' he tells me with genuine belief, before politely excusing himself, as he needs to get ready for afternoon cocktails at prominent architectural theorist and designer Charles Jencks' place somewhere further down the sandy road. Here are two more for the Chermayeff creed: No fear, just do it. Literally everyone in the family can attest to it. One of Catherine's early childhood memories is maybe the most telling examples of this fearless attitude: 'When I was not even three years old, my grandfather (who was the age I am now) took me out on the row boat in the middle of the pond and told me: 'Now you are going to swim.' Then he threw me over board. "I'm here in the boat. If you need me, come here." What was I to do—I swam.' In a way, the numerous Ben Nicholson, Picasso and Le Corbusier copy-paintings that Serge produced during his retirement, and are now primary pieces in the house corroborate to that artistic do-it-yourself-and better-spirit as well (and thereby appear cooler than the originals).

↖ Frontside of the Chermayeff cabin facing the pond.

← Installation by Peter Chermayeff's grand children in front of his cabin.

FAMILY FIRST

Later that day I also get to talk to Catherine's visiting friend Adam Bellow about the bonds between children and parents and the transmission of family legacies. Adam not only happens to be a well-known neo-conservative intellectual and editor of many controversial and notorious right-wing books of our era (which seems oddly off and at the same time strangely natural in the overall leftist and liberal family environment of the Chermayeffs) but also the son of Pulitzer and Nobel Prize winning writer Saul Bellow, who allegedly once visited Serge and Barbara with fellow writer and New York Intellectual Alfred Kazin here at the pond in the 1950s.

To top it off, Adam is also the author of a book in praise of nepotism—the favoured treatment of one's relatives—in which he explores the trend toward dynasticism and family branding at the heart of the American elite. Whilst sometimes a family's legacy can be a burden or an obligation, he argues, in the creatives arts it's often times different—it's a privilege. 'There is a sense of having an opportunity to participate in a creative legacy.' Thereby a cycle of generosity and gratitude knits the whole family together, enables, protects and enriches them. For the Chermayeff's this legacy is very plastic and collaborative. 'It's about what they can make and what they can do in the world, and about being involved in a common enterprise'. There's obviously a great joy in being a parent whose child chooses freely to extend the legacy into the next generation. Impressively, the Chermayeffs all found a way to continue this tradition as unique and strong individuals.

I am sitting in this cabin in the woods, three generations after Serge Chermayeff first arrived. The sun is setting, it's getting dark inside and I am being called out to dinner at a large table on the wooden terrace. I have the feeling that when Serge laid the foundation of this prolific lineage of unconventional creatives and thinkers, he probably didn't think of himself as being the creator of a family legacy. He was just doing his thing.

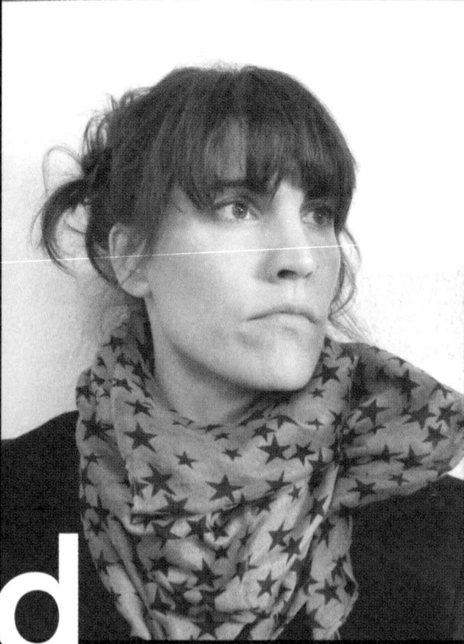

A Kind of Legacy

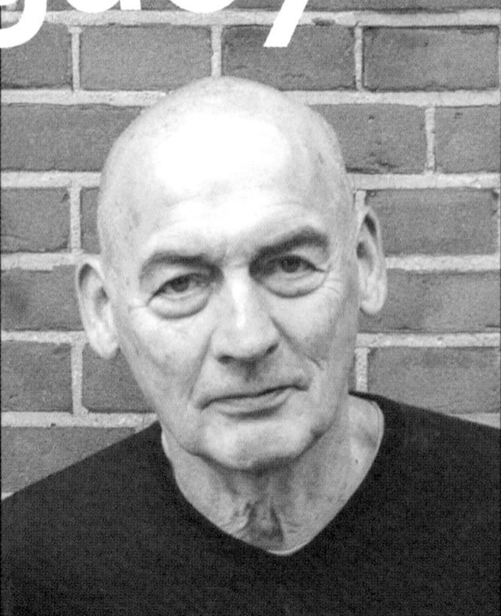

Charlie Koolhaas and Rem Koolhaas

Beyond simply passing down values from father to daughter, Dutch photographer CHARLIE KOOLHAAS and architect REM KOOLHAAS critically question the concept of creative legacy as the beginning of something new that naturally extends and transforms through its successors. Here, the notion of legacy is explored in the sense of development rather than preservation.

CHARLIE KOOLHAAS How much of your legacy is enforcing what you have done, and how much is it about dismantling the rules that you have created. Rather, is the concept of legacy more complicated than just simply passing down your values?

REM KOOLHAAS I can say several things about legacy. I don't think of it in terms of protecting your legacy, or seeing legacy as something that consists of a whole that needs to somehow be continued. The way in which I think about legacy is doing things as well as possible in the moment, and then to trying to animate them with complete freedom by anyone who is the user. Although I am interested in what happens after, I feel neither responsible nor interested in maintaining a connection. I see legacy, to some extent, as a launching of something that then triggers other things by other people.

CK When you think about a building or any work, are you thinking about it solely in the present, and not about how it will date or age?

RK I think that buildings don't date in the traditional way. Of course there's wear and tear, but the dating of buildings is also part of the pleasure of history. It would be terrible if they didn't date, otherwise one would get stuck in a kind of permanent principle. I think dating is part of the warmth that buildings have, but I've never been sentimental in adjusting, if necessary, after a certain while. When we switch to look at conservation, it is very interesting to discover that in almost any kind of configuration or building, there are still potential elements that can be continuously used. I really think of it in terms of respecting the—

↖ Portrait of Charlie Koolhaas. Photo by Jan Suklennik.

← Portrait of Rem Koolhaas. Photo by Charlie Koolhaas.

CK The legacy?

RK The legacy, or respecting the areas.

CK When you talk about when you are doing work on preservation, is it preservation of someone else's work that you are focused on?

RK Yes, but usually in terms of how much more use there is, and how much more potential there can be invoked or reinvented. Legacy is, typically, connected to an idea of stability and, in my case, more connected to further development, rather than stagnation.

CK Okay, so it's about avoiding a kind of nostalgia towards something that relates to a past moment or achievement. I've noticed that a lot with your dance theatre, how unsentimental you were about them tearing it down. You logically thought it was a kind of strange, silly thing to do. That didn't seem to be a personal feeling, or was it? Did that feel like a tearing down of legacy?

RK No. I thought it was particularly stupid, but it's part of a kind of rape of stupidity that we have to deal with in general.

CK Do you think that now, in a way, because buildings come down so much quicker and are built with such different materials, that the concept of legacy changes?

RK No, no, no.

CK Is that because you are not expecting a building to last 200 years anymore?

RK Absolutely. Part of our preservation exhibition

in Venice was a potential argument for this. It has also come up in certain architectural projects, that legacy has fundamentally changed; simply in the sense that almost every building is conceived with a limited lifespan, which is mostly defined by financial calculations, and has therefore become much more provisional.

I've become really deeply aware of that, and also in a way I've been supporting it, because I think that very few buildings deserve eternal life—very few programs or arguments deserve eternal life. Another fact that I find so fascinating in other cultures is that they are really able to experience what an entire community feels and thinks.

'I think that buildings don't date in the traditional way. Of course there's wear and tear, but the dating of buildings is also part of the pleasure of history.'

REM KOOLHAAS

CK In a way we see the legacy of human civilization being destroyed constantly on television. What do you see happening, for instance, in Syria?

RK Well, that is really something I feel incredible pain about.

CK Why is that different?

RK Maybe it's simply a kind of optical difference, but of course in Syria you have a sense of incredible richness—in Italy as well—an incredible richness, simply because the whole country is a kind of conflict carpet of different remnants that all have extremely eloquent remnants of other value systems—of religions—and are also a testimony to the fact that all of those could happen at the same place. Now we are faced with an incredible abundance, and also seemingly richness, but with considerably less value; so it's maybe simply a matter of quantity. I mean, there is so little that is left and so much of it present, so—

→ Rem Koolhaas at the CCTV building in the Beijing Central Business District, China. Photo by Charlie Koolhaas.

↳ Prada Foundation in Milan, Italy. Photo by Charlie Koolhaas.

CK You're saying that in those sorts of moments, histories are important just because they say something about the possibilities for the present moment and the future—possibilities for different systems and ideologies living together, whereas somehow, right now, it's unimaginable.

RK Yes, but in that sense I guess I am nostalgic about the possibility of things lasting 2000 years. Also about the possibility of making architecture that is on the one hand extremely compelling, but not necessarily original, and that is clearly not an expression of individuals but rather an expression of a collective. In a way, I think that every architect is imprinted with that ambition, and that you can read every architects' career in terms of how remote that ambition inevitably is, and maybe how and at what moments it approximates that origin. Even today.

CK That's because now, in a way, it's about an expression of a virtual system rather than a—

RK I think it's also hard to tell what it is now. Maybe it always was hard to tell what it was, so I am not excluding the possibility that in retrospect you have got a similar kind of moment.

CK What about your personal legacy? When you drive around Rotterdam for example, do you see the results of your legacy? What do you see in the architecture?

RK No.

CK You don't see any influences of you work?

RK Yes, of course I see my influence, but usually I find these moments very confronting. Inevitably they don't have the depth of including your own work, they don't have the depth of what your original ambition tried to inspire, basically.

CK Are you saying that legacies are then just a series of failures, to a certain extent?

RK Yes, to some extent, but I don't mean it in its totality. Take De Rotterdam for instance, I think it has a kind of single experience that is really amazing, and I am very happy with it. I feel the same with CCTV, too. It's not that I am unhappy with what we did.

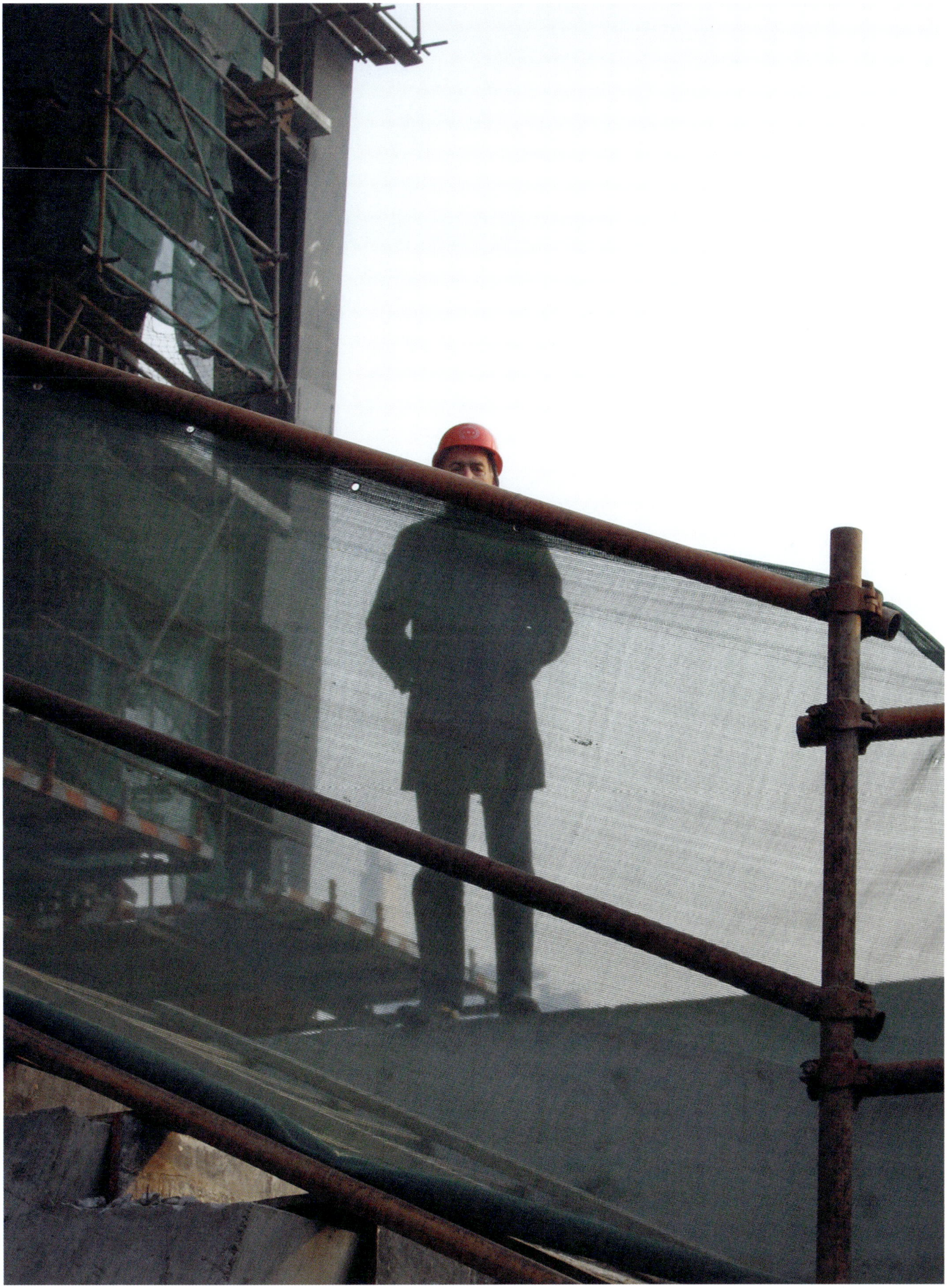

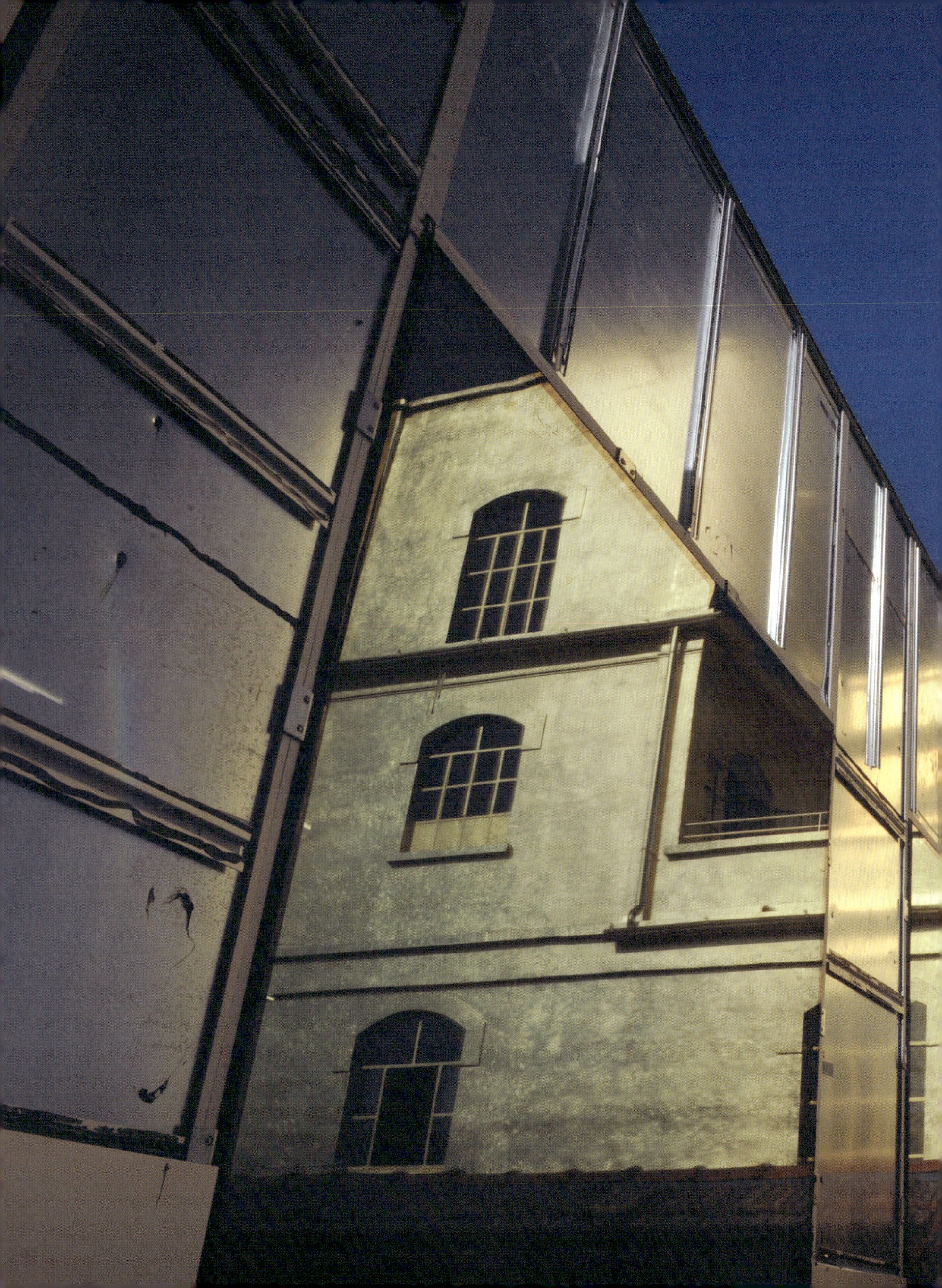

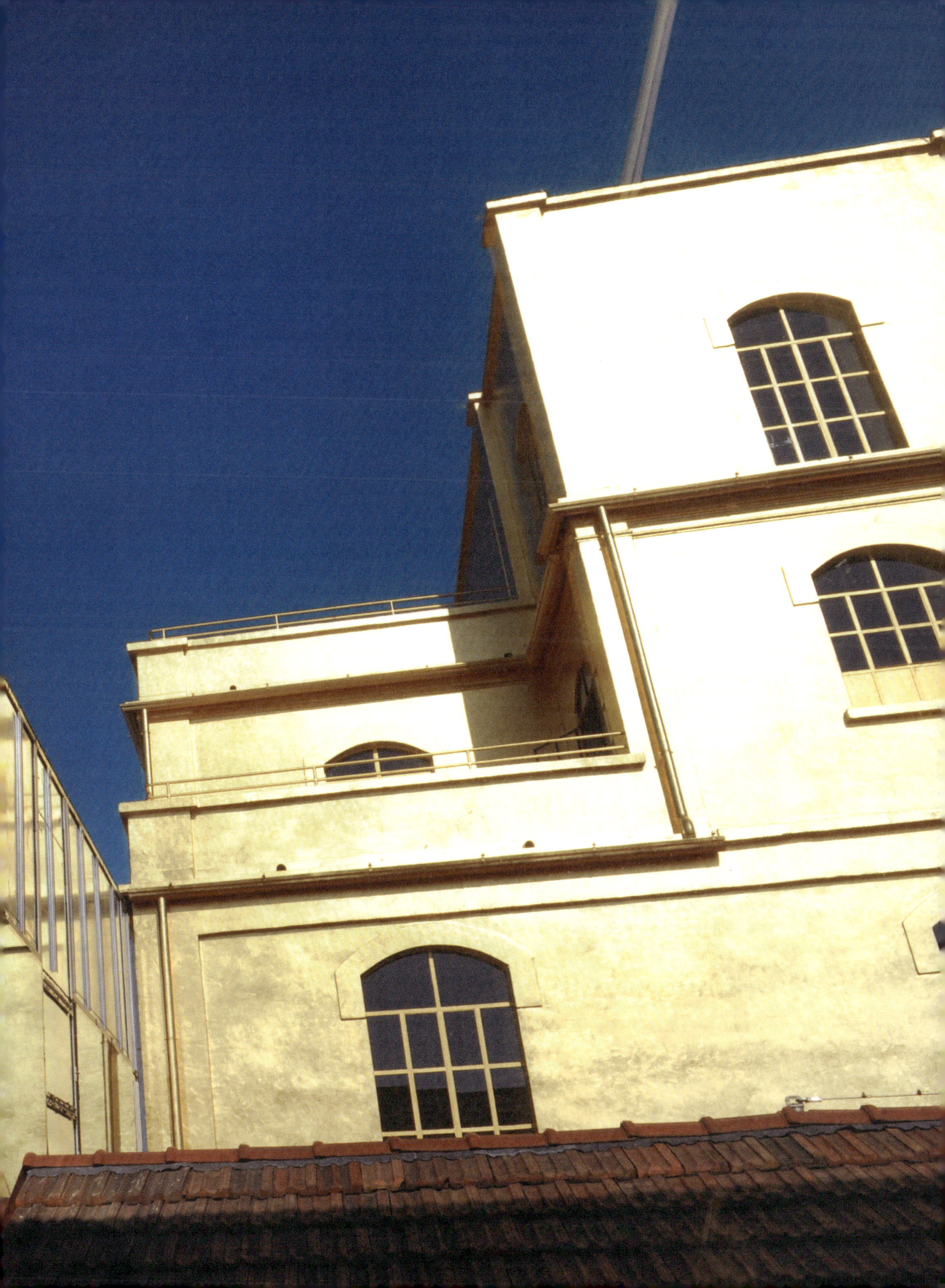

'I'm trying to work against the apparent: the apparent success or the apparent imposition of the language that we created.'

REM KOOLHAAS

CK In both those instances the buildings have come to represent the cities, actually,

RK More than me, then.

CK Well, very much the expression of the new identity for both those cities, anyway.

RK I think that is actually an interesting point, because maybe both of them are general enough not to be associated with me, but with other things, and it will be a kind of ideal legacy, or articulating a particular moment. What I found in retrospect is that perhaps one of the most successful things about CCTV that it introduced—in a country that is totally obsessed with stability—a building that is totally unstable in terms of its perception.

CK In a way de Rotterdam as well—it's implying that there is a tension or fragility.

RK No, it's very clear that both of them don't only the express their strength but also their weakness. 'Legacy,' the word, seems to imply a kind of masculine incentive, and I'm becoming much more inclined to relativize that too.

CK Okay then, legacy is of course a male thing, in that traditionally heirs have always been male.

RK Yeah, yeah.

CK OMA is often referred to as a kind of school, and you have definitely sent hundreds of architects into the world after they've been part of OMA, and they are now making now buildings, a lot of buildings. Is that part of your legacy, or what's the connection to that?

RK No, I honestly don't, but I guess it is. I don't have a very mature or considered relationship with it. My relationship is mostly between the kind of sympathy and—not quite embarrassment—but with disconnecting; but then that's really a great kind of inconsistency there.

CK What about when you see—

RK Do you know who this singer is? Dalida, an Egyptian singer in France. It's so incredible.

CK Rem, so what about when you go to an architectural bookstore and you see this type of aesthetic that there's no doubt you helped create, the kind of architectural language—what do you think about that, is that again just something in the present moment?

RK I really try not to think about that. I mean, it's a really lame answer, but I try not to think about it. I also don't have a feeling that I created the language. I have the feeling that I operated within a certain envelope of what is possible today, and I would say, in general, that there are so many arguments to be humbled by today. One of them, for instance, is that buildings don't last nearly that long, but the second one—and that is what I was shown with elements of architecture—is that you live in a certain incredibly reduced repertoire of what you can actually do. It's such a compelling definition of what is possible, and also such a limited actual choice of how you can source certain things, and what issues you can raise. For instance—even if I wanted to—I couldn't suddenly start decorating any kind of interior that we are creating with allegorical statements. The whole idea of creating a language, if that was ever valuable, or even possible—which I doubt anyway—is really dubious. That's a consolation. I'm trying to work against the apparent: the apparent success or the apparent imposition of the language that we created. In other words, we are, I think, in a profound way, the expression of what is possible today. Maybe we express that whether they did it, but nevertheless, I think the word 'creation' is entirely misplaced; it's more than that.

CK The word 'creation'?

RK It's entirely misplaced, or rather; it's a manipulation of possibilities.

CK Is it like pushing to the end of the boundaries and that's what happens?

RK Not even the end.

CK Why do you think that you have been criticised, for example, for the Biennale? It was described as an ego-maniacal exhibition, when in fact, you were just showing all the technologies that were available that you didn't create.

RK I think that it's probably really unwise to analyse that in detail but I think that the whole point of the office now is that it's really a genuine project. The other partners are doing things, manifestly doing things, and are being credited for doing said things. That is a very logical outcome. It's what we always wanted to do, and at the same time, it is very welcome to me, because it also enables me to do things that are, let's say, more myself again.

CK Is it with legacy in mind that you've attempted to, over the last ten years, create an office that can run without you, at some point?

RK It's not so much running without me, but that it is, to some extent, independent of me.

CK Is that for the sake of the continuity into the future?

RK No, it's not for the sake of the continuity. I think it's because we all like to work in Zurich. I guess it's a plan, and that is one of the motivations behind it, but that's

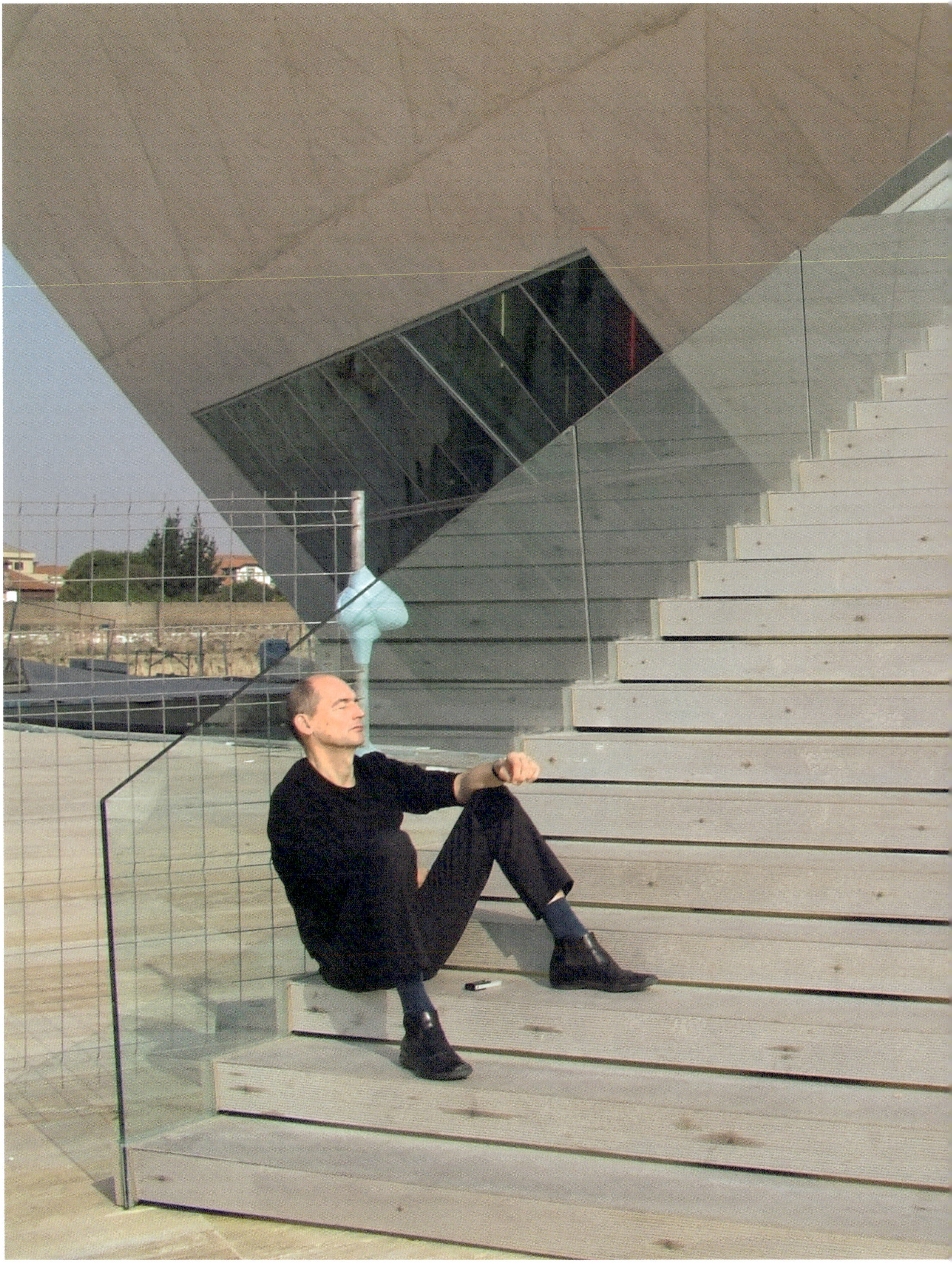

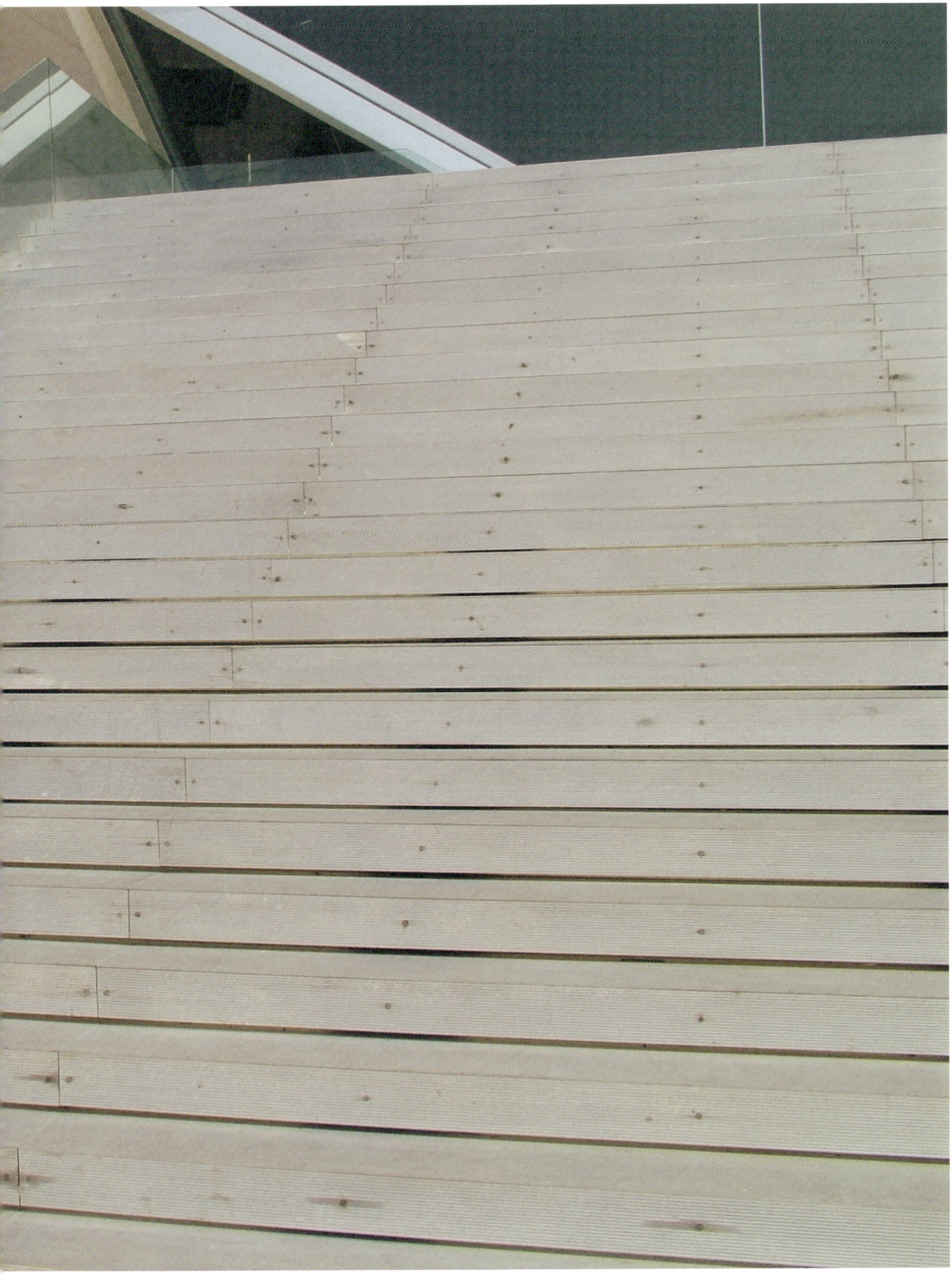

not the ultimate plan—to create a situation where this can continue. That's because I think there is no ultimate plan—it's consistently contingent, influenced by forces that we cannot control and cannot predict, so it would be a kind of useless ambition.

CK Again, are you not thinking about a legacy of any kind?

RK No.

CK Past your own life, do you think about the moment after?

RK Well—

CK When you die, do you ever think about what will happen afterwards? Do you think about how you go down in history?

RK No, really, honestly I do not. I only think about it in terms of those close to me; but that's really the only scale in which I think about it.

CK Okay, so in that vein, what does a legacy mean in terms of being a father, or a grandfather or any of these things?

RK Well, you hope that people are intelligent and doing well, and doing things that you can recognize and relate to; I mean, that's turning out to be a really big pleasure. I think it would also be very exciting to have children that do things well that you totally do not understand. I would enjoy if my child went into banking.

CK Yes, you were grooming me for that. I'm still open. What you seem to be saying is that one's personal legacy continues not through people, or in their buildings or their work but that a legacy is something completely outside of oneself.

RK We are talking about work so far. Of course I think there's a huge amount of legacy that comes through DNA and, in a personal sense, that is a big preoccupation. Also in terms of time and energy—it's taking a lot of my overall effort, but I mean, that's not something to talk about on the record, you know?

CK No, because that's a biological feeling.

RK Incentive, yes—a beautiful one. That's also the incredible thing—we still have this biological programming, no matter how everything around us totally changes.

CK When you said—

RK Do you want something else?

CK No, so you basically you're not taking responsibility—

RK Yes, I'm not taking responsibility.

CK —for anything that's happened in Architecture with your work or your reactions to you work?

RK I can see that in this discipline, I am responsible for certain things, or that certain things have had effects, but I am not taking responsibility.

CK Does that mean that you are also not claiming it?

RK I'm also not claiming it, no absolutely not. I don't know why not, but it's really a temperamental issue. I think it would be a fantastic burden if you claimed it. I don't want to be burdened by something that is not oriented on either the present day or the future.

CK How have you impacted the world?

RK I think that one impact has been to a kind of openness to another definition of perfection, and another definition of the city. When we started, the whole ideology of architecture was incredibly Euro centric, Western centric. From the very beginning I think I've been very active in trying to undermine and change that, and I think that, but of course you cannot just say it wouldn't have happened anyway, because the whole orientation in China is completely independent of me. On the other hand, I've been the first to claim that there was something architecturally relevant happening there, you know, or a warning that our whole position was unsustainable, and so that's also why, as I said, the entire current civilisation really encourages humility because you can see in almost every kind of sense, or every moment, that at the most you are acting in parallel or maybe slightly in front of insights that are general anyway.

CK Okay. I think that's good.

↰ Rem Koolhaas at Casa de Musica in Porto, Portugal. Photo by Charlie Koolhaas.

↗ Rem Koolhaas near the CCTV building in Beijing, China. Photo by Charlie Koolhaas.

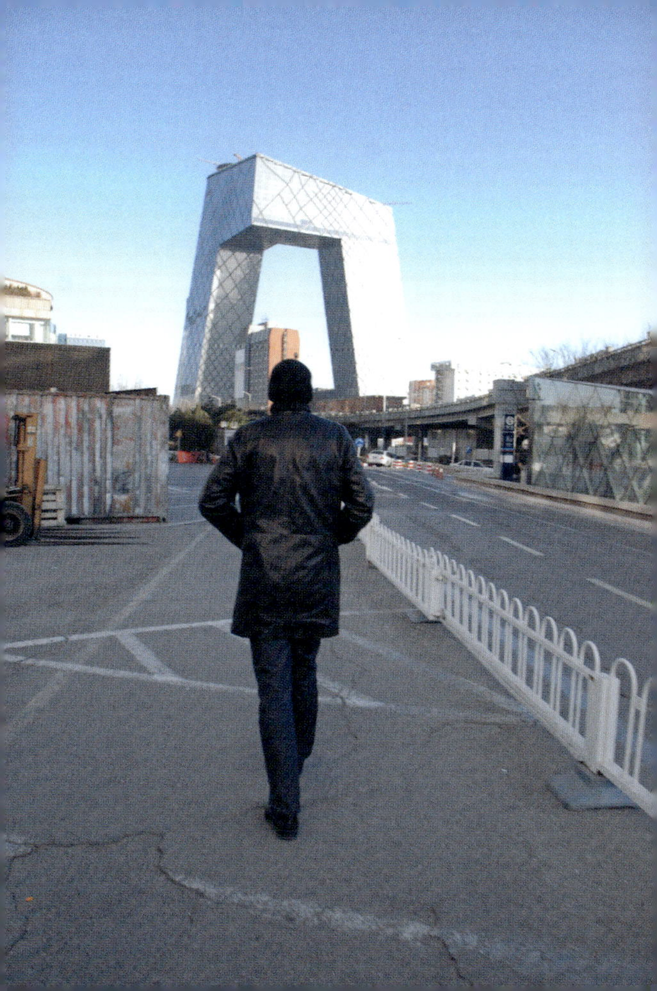

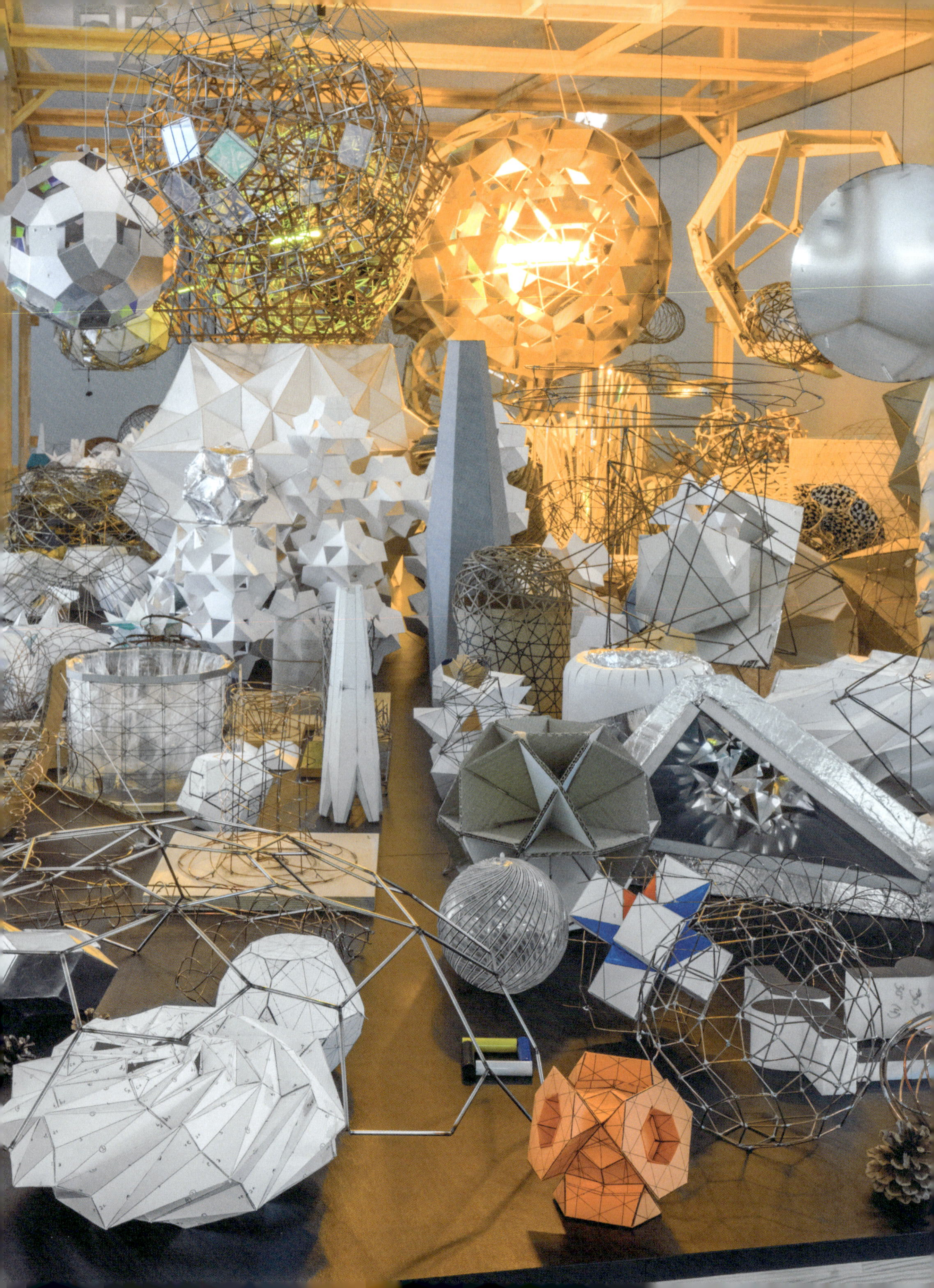

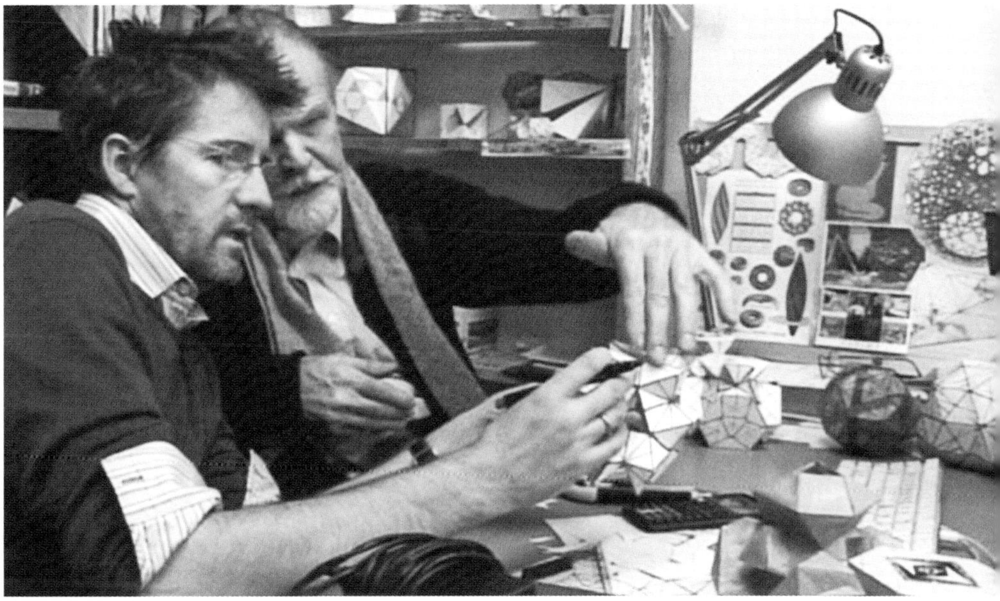

The Legacy of The Model Room

Olafur Eliasson and Einar Thorsteinn

Danish-Icelandic artist OLAFUR ELIASSON speaks with his friend and mentor, the late Icelandic architect EINAR THORSTEINN, about the creative process of model making in the studio. A protégé of Buckminster Fuller, Einar Thorsteinn is the mad scientist behind Olafur's most elaborate works over the course of two decades.

OLAFUR ELIASSON I heard about Einar while studying at architectural school in Denmark. A structural engineer pointed out to me that someone who specialized in the topic I was interested in at the time—which was sort of a Buckminster Fuller dome structure—was this Icelandic person who was much more talented and better able to help me than the architecture school in Denmark was at the time.

We met for the first time in Iceland in 1996. I came to your house and I was very impressed with the exciting environment and the fantastic workspace. We started talking about the problem that I had: I was about to create a sculpture which looked very much like a Buckminster Fuller dome. It was something between a sculpture and a play-scaffold or something like that in a landscape outside, for a landscaping project in Denmark. I simply couldn't find anybody who could crunch that Buckminster Fuller mathematical principle, and Einar turned out to be very capable of doing that. When we met, I was very non-mystical and pragmatic, saying that there is no doubt that Einar has a kind of toolbox which is very unique and exceptionally useful for me. It was not about me trying to learn what Einar could do; it was just a huge chance for me to actually express some of the ideas that I was working on with greater precision.

↰↰ The Model room at Studio Olafur Eliasson in Berlin, 2003. All images by Carol Diehl and Terry Perk.

↰ Olafur Elliasson and Einar Thorsteinn in conversation.

→ Einar Thorsteinn, 2008.

Einar, I think, has an unbelievable ability to imagine a space without having to draw it out; he can speak about it with a certain efficiency that makes it tangible for me. That is something very unique. A lot of polyphonic shapes are very hard to talk about, since the language in which we speak doesn't embrace those shapes.

EINAR THORSTEINN All my life I have been bumping into people like **Frei Otto** **(page → 170)**. He was a kind of hero for us young architects in the old days in Germany. Then Buckminster Fuller, and finally I became close to Linus Pauling. The difference between these people and Olafur Eliasson is that I never had such a close relationship with them as with Olafur. When we met the first time, I sensed what he was saying. He was into experimentation, and this was good for me—experimentation is good. At the beginning Olafur had a very small studio and maybe—how many?—three, four, or five people. We would actually go into the basis of things and look into new ideas. We were

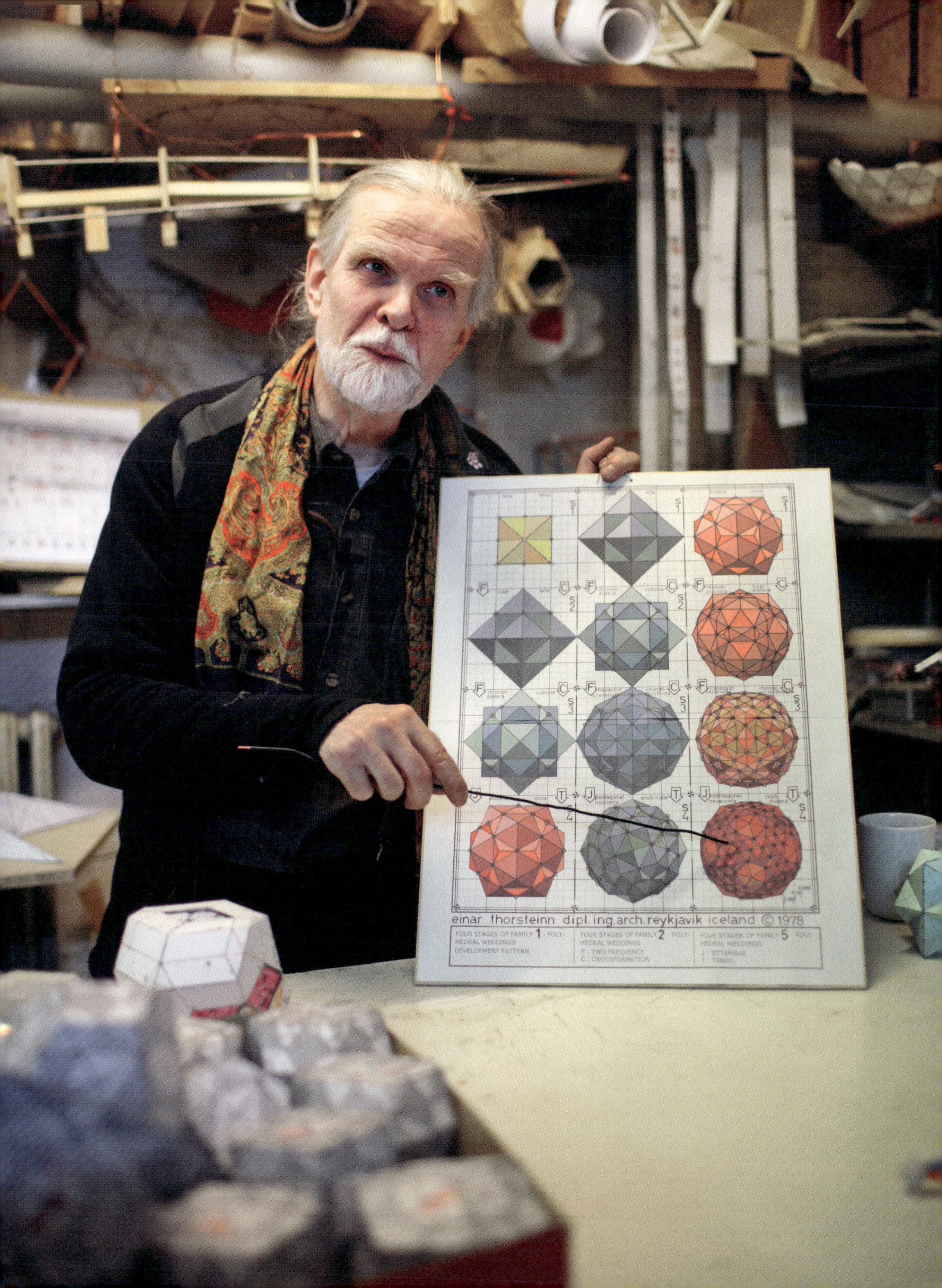
einar thorsteinn dipl.ing.arch.reykjavik iceland © 1978
FOUR STAGES OF FAMILY 1 - POLY-HEDRAL WEDDINGS
DEVELOPMENT PATTERN
FOUR STAGES OF FAMILY 2 - POLY-HEDRAL WEDDINGS
F : TWO FREQUENCY
C : CROSSFORMATION
FOUR STAGES OF FAMILY 5 - POLY-HEDRAL WEDDINGS
J : JITTERBUG
T : TANGO

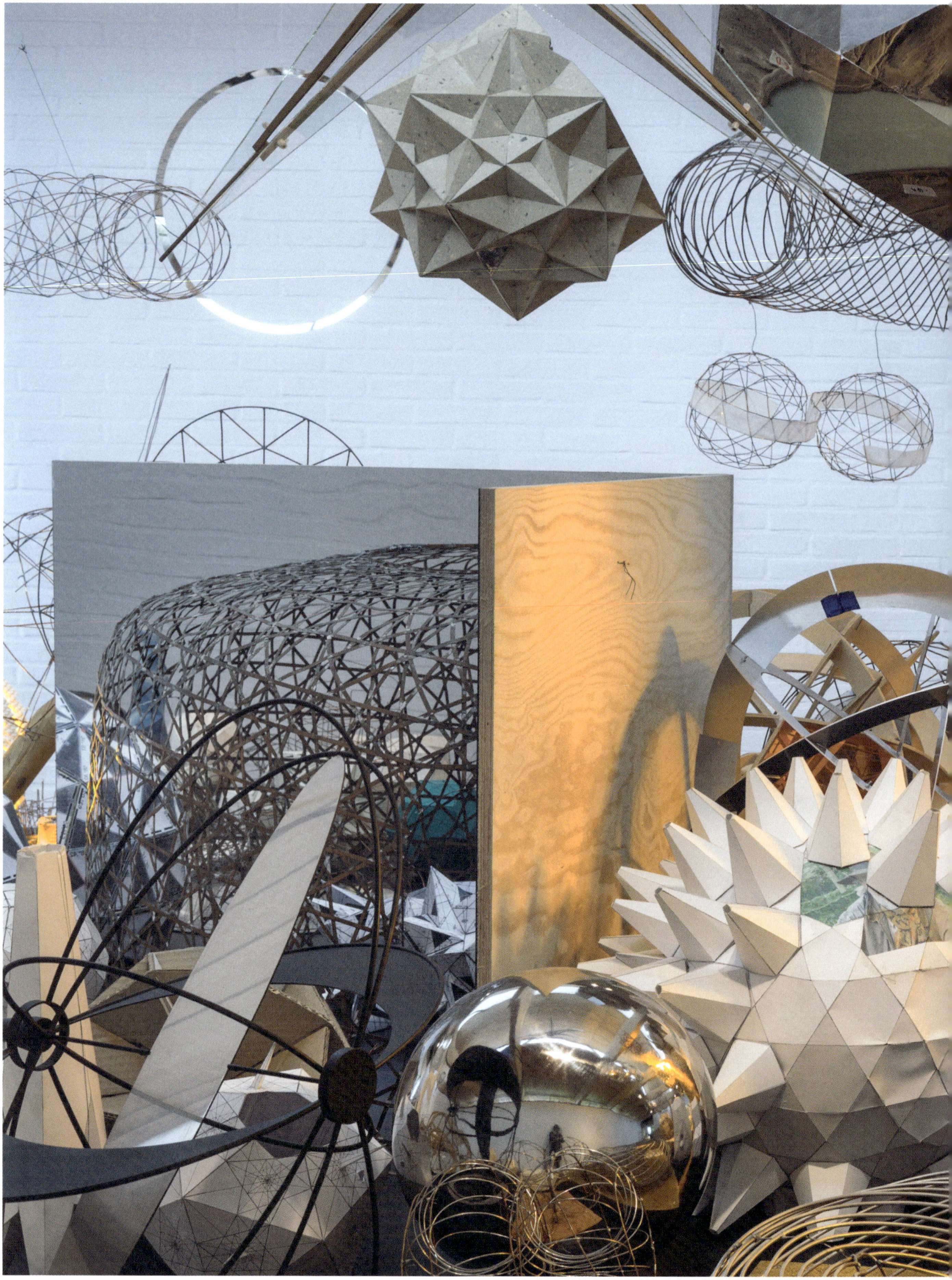

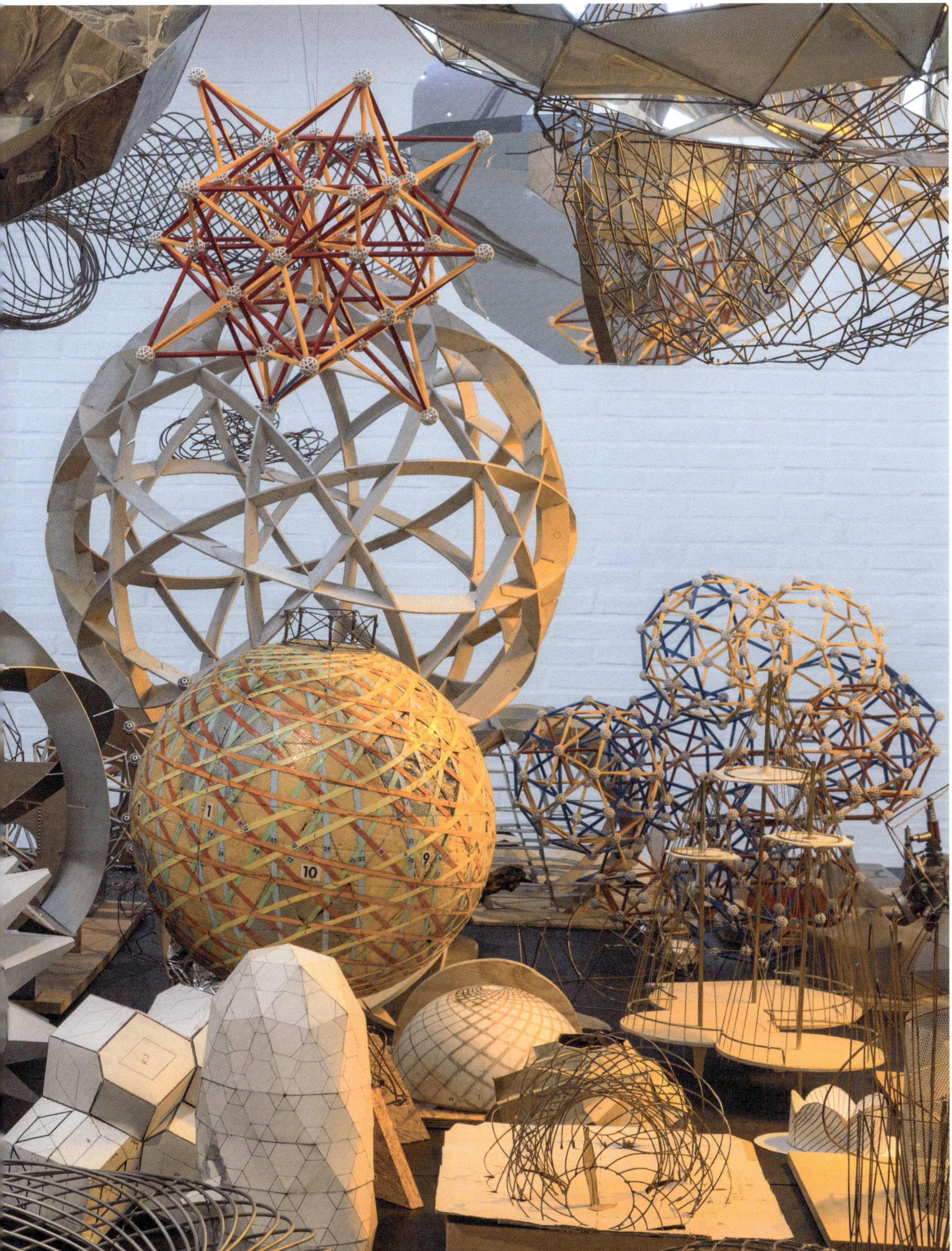

looking into ideas that we had at our disposal, that we might be able to use in this or that. This was totally different from today—now I am some kind of authority or something, and people come to me and ask me about things I don't even know about. I try to answer! This is different, you know. It is not what I saw coming, but it has happened. As a private person, you are always working for yourself. You are working on something that you believe in, that you believe is correct.

The cooperation turned out to be about how much you give to the other person, and how much he gives back. You know? You kind of come together, and Olafur and I found a way to come together. I think, today, it's very straightforward.

OE If you look at the studio, there is a palette of skills: a map of competences which makes the studio perform. I'm not really good at anything, but I'm okay at everything. I would not have so many people working with me if I were particularly good at something, right? I could have chosen to keep this studio completely secret, very closed, and could have claimed that I was working more or less alone. That would have satisfied a certain market mechanism, but of course it would have been rather irresponsible and would probably have caused a lot of frustration within the studio. Of course, it was never even a question.

I think what a place like the studio does has to do with the extent to which people know what will happen, how well they can predict it. Something unpredictable can actually be the carrier of criticism in a certain way—by being unpredictable, you're not exactly a psychopath, but you are in the way that there's that little psychopathic element, in that people are looking at you and they just don't know what you're going to do. Until the moment it becomes predictable, which is when you lose a degree of friction with your surroundings. Compared to the real world, the studio is pretty experimental. Compared to something really experimental, we are probably a little more pragmatic. But we are also a little bit unpredictable.

↰ The Model room at Studio Olafur Eliasson in Berlin, 2003.

ET I think *Model room* (2003) is the legacy of our cooperation, so to speak. *Model room* was not built on purpose. We didn't say, 'Oh, let's build a model room!' It just happened that there were so many models piling up from different kinds of projects. One day Olafur had the genius idea to make an art piece out of it. In *Model room* there are many, many models that never became any art pieces. There are maybe three groups of models: there are models of pieces that are already art pieces, there is a second group of models that are studies of art pieces that are now being made, and there is a third group of models that are proposals for something that hasn't been executed.

If you do a model, you do it to better understand what you're talking about. You talk about something, you have an idea, and this idea in your head is maybe not three-dimensional. It's just an idea; you have a feeling about something. The 3D study is basically to make the idea physical. Only then you can say, 'No, this is not what I meant; I meant something else.' And then you can go on from that.

OE When one asks about a model in *Model room*, the tendency in the language with which one asks is to suggest that the model has a rather conserva-

> 'It was not about me trying to learn what Einar could do; it was just a huge chance for me to actually express some of the ideas that I was working on with greater precision.'
>
> OLAFUR ELIASSON

tive purpose as a little sculpture. It's very important to fight against this sense of nice little objects in a 'Wunderkammer'. I think that what is exciting about the models is that each of them, in one way or the other, presents an attempt to solve a problem—a problem not as an autonomous configuration of time and space, but as a way to tie time and society together. Every model somehow represents a conflict with society or with the time in which we live. Each was an attempt, in one way or another, to present a sort of non-formalistic or non-modern or non-utopic or very utopic or very formal or very modern dialogue with the time in which it took place. That means the potential of the model is not in the intrinsic proportional quality within the model; it is in how this intrinsic proportional quality performs on a much larger scale.

What we normally would call the finished object is also a model, is also an experiment. It is also temporal, in the sense that it performs over time and might collapse physically or ideologically. I have come to like every stage of a model more by acknowledging that it will never not be a model.

If you look at a model, you see that there is a kind of geometric language inside it. This geometric language does different things. We are in a society which is pretty much organized around a certain spatial language, a spatial language that has some kind of cultural and political history.

People make the mistake, generally speaking, of taking this for granted as being a set of truths. And what a successful geometric or spatial language can do is to break this paradigm of truthfulness by showing that the values with which we live today are also, in fact, constructions. Some geometric spatial experiments do this quite efficiently by introducing a set of rules or principles as a criticism. Not necessarily replacing one truth with another truth—I'm afraid of that—but, essentially, showing that what we consider to be true, what we take for granted as being reality, is, in fact, relative to our engagement. This is where I think alternative spatial principles such as different geometric models or ideas or mathematical, spatial, or scientific ways of defining space hold so much potential. One of the greatest potentials is the way you actually introduce them to the world, and I think one should be careful not to repeat the same mistake that we are currently surrounded by—namely, to claim that we have the right answers for everything.

For the time being, at least, it's more interesting for me to use this alternative spatial language to show that what we take for granted as being reality is not at all real. A geometric language of the principles of phenomena can have a highly productive impact on the surroundings. Anybody who has a non-Euclidean way of seeing things, like Einar, is capable of producing consequences that go beyond geometric questions and are very much linked to the world. It's only a question of how one puts it into the world. How does one take an idea and translate it into a frictional phenomenon that actually produces time?

This conversation between Olafur Eliasson and Einar Thorsteinn was originally recorded in Berlin, 2016. Directed by Terry Perk. Produced by Carol Diehl.

Reports on the State of Bob Dylan

Jonathan Lethem

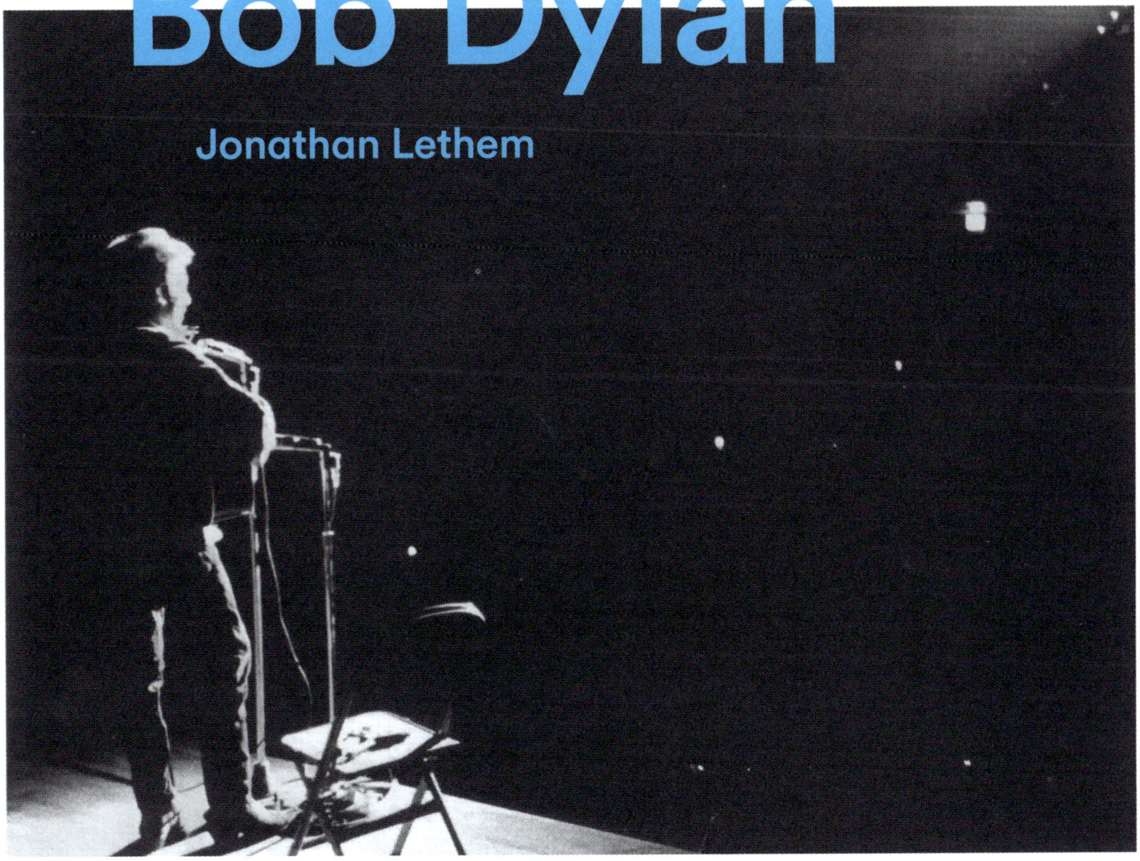

Acclaimed American writer and novelist JONATHAN LETHEM sits down with BOB DYLAN to linger over songs as artefacts of music. They examine the process of their making, the power and impact of paintings and books, and non-existence of retirement plans for the legend of the 1960s.

'Did I ever want to acquire the 1960s? No. But I own the 1960s—who's going to argue with me?'

BOB DYLAN

'I don't really have a herd of astrologers telling me what's going to happen. I just make one move after the other, this leads to that.' Is the voice familiar? I'm sitting in a Santa Monica seaside hotel suite, ignoring a tray of sliced pineapple and sugar dust cookies, while Bob Dylan sits across from my tape recorder, giving his best to my questions. The man before me is fitful in his chair, not impatient, but keenly alive to the moment, and ready on a dime to make me laugh and to laugh himself. The expressions on Dylan's face, in person, seem to compress and encompass versions of his persona across time—a sixty-five-year-old with a nineteen-year-old cavorting somewhere inside. Above all, though, it is the tones of his speaking voice that seem to kaleidoscope through time: the yelp of the folk pup, or the sarcastic rim-shot timing of the hounded hipster-idol, the beguilement of the 1970s sex symbol and—always—the gravel of the elder statesman, that antediluvian bluesman's voice, the young aspirant so legendarily invoked at the very outset of his work, and then ever so gradually aged into.

It's that voice, the voice of a rogue ageless in decrepitude, that grounds the paradox of the achievement of Dylan's late work. Are these our 'modern tunes,' or some ancient, silent-movie dream, a fugue in black-and-white? They seem to survey a broken world through the prism of a heart that's worn and worldly, yet decidedly unbroken itself. Dylan offers us nourishment from the root cellar of American cultural life. For an amnesiac society, that's arguably as mind-expanding an offering as anything in his 1960s work. With each succeeding record, Dylan's convergence with his muses effortlessly grows increasingly natural.

Rather than analyzing lyrics, Dylan prefers to linger over songs as artifacts of music and describes the process of their making. The singer and performer known for his love-hate affair with the recording studio tells me simply 'I don't like to make records. I do it reluctantly.' Dylan himself is his records' producer since his 1993 album *World Gone Wrong*, often credited under the nom-de-studio Jack Frost. 'I didn't feel like I wanted to be overproduced any more,' he tells me. 'I felt like I've always produced my own records anyway, except I just had someone there, in the way. I feel like nobody's gonna know how I should sound except me, anyway. Nobody knows what they want out of players except me, nobody can tell a player what he's doing wrong, nobody can find a player who can play but he's not playing, like I can. I can do that in my sleep.'

As ever, Dylan is circling, defining what he is first by what he isn't, by what he doesn't want, doesn't like, doesn't need, locating meaning by a process of elimination. This rhetorical strategy goes back at least as far as *It Ain't Me, Babe* (1964) and All *I Really Want to Do* (1965) 'I ain't looking to compete with you,' etc. and it still has plenty of real juice in it.

'The records I used to listen to and still love, you can't make a record that sounds that way,' he explains. It is as if having taken his new material down to the crossroads of the recording studio, Dylan isn't wholly sure the deal struck with the devil there was worth it. 'Brian Wilson made all his records with four tracks, but you couldn't make his records if you had a hundred tracks today. We all like records that are played on record players, but let's face it, those days are gon-n-n-e. You do the best you can, you fight that technology in all kinds of ways, but I don't know anybody who's made a record that sounds decent in the past 20 years, really. You listen to these modern records, they're atrocious, they have sound all over them. There's no definition of nothing, no vocal, no nothing, just like static. Even these songs probably sounded ten times better in the studio when we recorded 'em. CDs are small. There's no stature to it. I remember when that Napster guy came up across, it was like, "Everybody's gettin' music for free.' I was like, 'Well, why not? It ain't worth nothing anyway."

Hearing the word 'Napster' come from Bob Dylan's mouth, I venture a question about bootleg recordings. In my own wishful thinking, The Bootleg Series, a sequence of superb archival retrospectives, sanctioned by Dylan and released by Columbia, represents a kind of unspoken consent to the tradition of pirate scholarship—an acknowledgment that Dylan's outtakes, alternate takes, rejected album tracks and live performances are themselves a towering body of work that faith-

↰ Bob Dylan performing at St. Lawrence University in New York, 1963. Source: St. Lawrence University Yearbook 1964

↖ Bob Dylan in Barcelona, 1984. Photo by F. Antolín Hernandez Con.

ful listeners deserve to hear. As Michael Gray says in The Bob Dylan Encyclopedia, the first three-disc release of outtakes 'could, of itself, establish Dylan's place as the pre-eminent songwriter and performer of the age and as one of the great artists of the 20th century.' *On Love and Theft's Sugar Baby* (2001), the line 'Some of these bootleggers, they make pretty good stuff' was taken by some as a shout-out to this viewpoint. Today, at least, that line seems to have had only moonshine whiskey as its subject. 'I still don't like bootleg records. There was a period of time when people were just bootlegging anything on me, because there was never anyone in charge of the recording sessions. All my stuff was being bootlegged high and low, far and wide. They were never intended to be released, but everybody was buying them. My record company said, 'Well, everybody else is buying these records, we might as well put them out.' Dylan can't possibly be sorry that the world has had the benefit of hearing, for instance, Blind Willie McTell—an outtake from 1983's *Infidels* that has subsequently risen as high in most people's Dylan pantheon as a song can rise, and that he himself has played live since. Can he? 'I started playing it live because I heard the Band doing it. Most likely it was a demo, probably showing the musicians how it should go. It was never developed fully, I never got around to completing it. There wouldn't have been any other reasons for leaving it off the record. It's like taking a painting by Manet or Picasso—goin' to his house and lookin' at a half-finished painting and grabbing it and selling it to people who are 'Picasso fans.' The only fans I know I have are the people who I'm looking at when I play, night after night.'

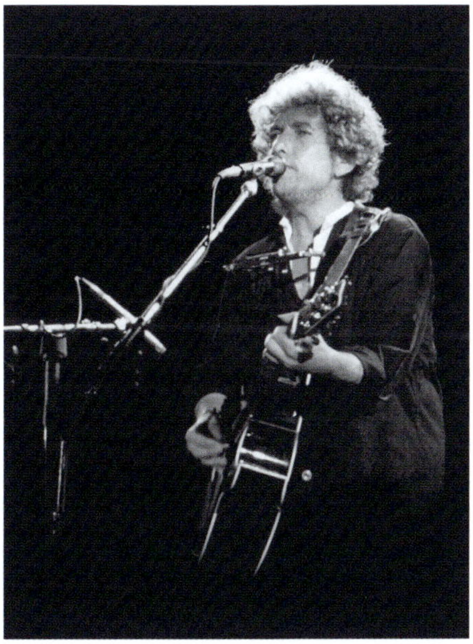

I've always wanted to ask: when a song suddenly appears on a given evening's set list, retrieved from among the hundreds in his back catalog, is it because Dylan's been listening to his old records? 'I don't listen to any of my records. When you're inside of it, all you're listening to is a replica. I don't know why somebody would look at the movies they make—you don't read your books, do you?' Point taken. He expands on the explanation he offered for Blind Willie McTell: 'Strangely enough, sometimes we'll hear a cover of a song and figure we can do it just as well. If somebody else thought so highly of it, why don't I? Some of these arrangements I just take. The Dead did a lot of my songs, and we'd just take the whole arrangement, because they did it better than me. Jerry Garcia could hear the song in all my bad recordings, the song that was buried there. If I want to sing something different, I just bring out one of them Dead records and see which one I wanna do. I never do that with my records.' Speaking of which: 'I've heard it said, you've probably heard it said, that all the arrangements change night after night. Well, that's a bunch of bullshit, they don't know what they're talkin' about. The arrangements don't change night after night. The rhythmic structures are different, that's all. You can't change the arrangement night after night—it's impossible.'

Let me take a moment to reintroduce myself, your interviewer and guide here. I'm a 42-year old moonlighting novelist, and a lifelong Dylan fan, but one who, it must be emphasized, doesn't remember the 1960s. I'm no longer a young man, but I am young for the job I'm doing here. My parents were Dylan fans, and my first taste of his music came through their LPs—I settled on *Nashville Skyline* (1969), because it looked friendly. The first Dylan record I was able to respond to as new—to witness its arrival in stores and reception in magazines, and therefore to make my own—was *Slow Train Coming* (1979). As a fan in my early twenties, I digested Dylan's catalog to that point and concluded that its panoply of styles and stances was itself the truest measure of his genius—call us the Biograph generation, if you like. In other words, the struggle to capture Dylan and his art-like smoke in one particular bottle or another seemed laughable to me. A mistaken skirmish fought before it had become clear that mercurial responsiveness—anchored only by the existential commitment to the act of connection in the present moment—was the gift of freedom his songs had promised all along. To deny it

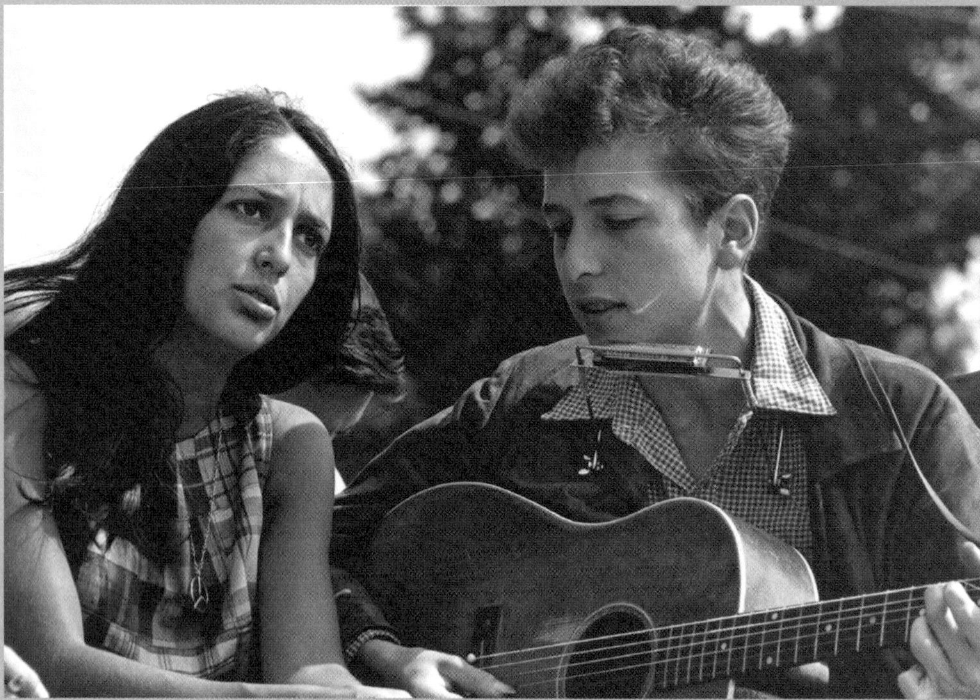

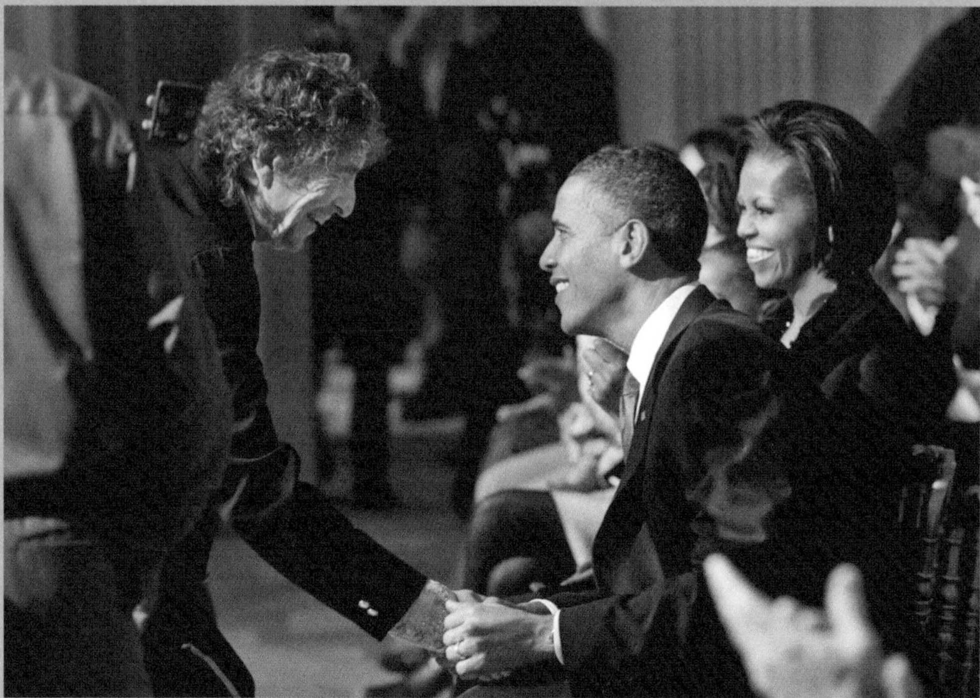

to the man himself would be absurd. By the time I required anything of Bob Dylan, it was the mid-1980s, and I merely required him to be good. Which, in the mid-1980s, Dylan kind of wasn't. I recall taking home *Empire Burlesque* (1985) and struggling to discern songwriting greatness under the glittery murk of Arthur Baker's production, a struggle I lost. The first time I saw Dylan in concert, it was, yes, in a football stadium in Oakland, with the Grateful Dead. By the time of *Down in the Groove* (1988), the album's worst song might have seemed to describe my plight as fan; I was in love with the ugliest girl in the world.

Nevertheless, 1980s Dylan was my Dylan, and I bore down hard on what was there. Contrary to what you may have heard (in Chronicles, Volume One, among other detractors), there was water in that desert. From scattered tracks like *Rank Strangers to Me* (1988), *The Groom's Still Waiting at the Altar* (1981) and *Brownsville Girl* (1986), to cassette-tape miracles like *Lord Protect My Child* (1991) and *Foot of Pride* (1991), both later to surface on The Bootleg Series, to a version of *San Francisco Bay Blues* (1992) I was lucky enough to catch live in Berkeley, to a blistering take on Sonny Boy Williamson's *Don't Start Me to Talkin'* (1984) on Late Night With David Letterman, the irony is not only that 'bad' Dylan was often astonishingly good; it is that his then-seemingly-rudderless exploration of roots-music sources can now be seen to point unerringly to the triumphs to come—I mean, the triumphs of now. Not that Dylan himself would care to retrace those steps. When I gushed about the Sonny Boy Williamson moment on Letterman, he gaped, plainly amazed, and asked, 'I played that?'

The drama of my projected relationship to my hero, thin as it may seem to those steeped in the 1960s or 1970s listeners' sense of multiple betrayals—

← Joan Baez and Bob Dylan at Civil Rights March on Washington, D.C., 1963. Photo by Rowland Scherman. Source: U.S. National Archives and Records Administration.

↙ Bob Dylan shakes President Obama's hand following his performance at the *In Performance At The White House: A Celebration Of Music From The Civil Rights Movement* concert in the East Room of the White House, 2010. Official White House photo by Pete Souza.

'Most people who write about music have no idea what it feels like to play it.'

BOB DYLAN

he's gone Electric! Country-Domestic-Unavailable! Christian!—was the one Dylan described to David Gates of Newsweek in 1997, and in the *Oh Mercy* (1989) chapter of his memoir, *Chronicles* (2004)—the relocation and repossession of his voice and of his will to compose and perform, as enacted gradually through the 1990s. Early in that decade it might have seemed that he'd quit, or at least taken refuge or solace in the solo acoustic folk records he'd begun making in his garage: *Good as I Been to You* (1992) and *World Gone Wrong* (1993). Live shows in what had become The Never Ending Tour were stronger and stronger in those years, but new songs were scarce. Then came *Time Out of Mind* (2014), an album as cohesive—and ample—as any he'd ever recorded. When that was followed by *Love and Theft* (2001), and then *Chronicles*, a reasonable Dylan fan might conclude he was living in the best of all possible worlds. In fact, with the satellite radio show beaming into our homes—Dylan promised to do 50 of the things!—Dylan can be said to have delivered more of his voice and his heart to his audience in the past decade than ever before, and more than anyone might have reasonably dared to hope. 'Well, isn't that funny,' Dylan snorts when I mention 'the myth of inaccessibility.' 'I've just seen that Wenner Books published a book of interviews with me that's that big.' He stretches out his hands to show me. 'What happened to this inaccessibility? Isn't there a dichotomy there?' Yet it's awfully easy, taking the role of Dylan's interviewer, to feel oneself playing surrogate for an audience that has never quit holding its hero to an impossible standard—the more he offers, the more we want. The greatest artist of my lifetime has given me anything I could ever have thought to ask, and yet here I sit, somehow brokering between him and the expectations neither of us can pretend don't exist. 'If I've got any kind of attitude about me—or about what I do, what I perform, what I sing, on any level, my attitude is, compare it to somebody else! Don't compare it to me. Are you going to compare Neil Young to Neil Young? Compare it to somebody else, compare it to Beck—whom I like—or whoever else is on his level. This record should be compared to the artists who are working on the same ground. I'll take it any way it comes but compare it to that. That's what everybody's record should be—if they're really serious about what they're doing. Let's face it, you're either serious about what you're doing or you're not serious about what you're doing. You can't mix the two. Life is short.'

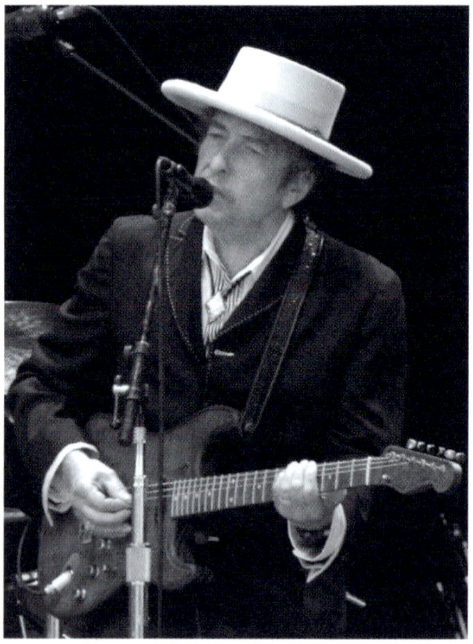

↗ Bob Dylan, onstage in Victoria-Gasteiz, at the Azkena Rock Festival, 2010. Photo by Alberto Cabello from Vitoria Gasteiz.

→ Portrait of Jonathan Lethem. Photo by Adrian Cook.

I can't help but wonder if he's lately been reconditioned by the success of Martin Scorsese's documentary *No Direction Home* (2005), to feel again the vivid discomfort of his unwanted savior's role. 'You know, everybody makes a big deal about the 1960s. The 1960s, it's like the Civil War days. I mean, you're talking to a person who owns the 1960s. Did I ever want to acquire the 1960s? No. But I own the 1960s—who's going to argue with me?' He charms me with another joke: 'I'll give 'em to you if you want 'em. You can have 'em.' For Dylan, as ever, what matters is the work, not in some archival sense, but in its present life. 'My old songs, they've got something—I agree, they've got something! I think my songs have been covered—maybe not as much as White *Christmas* (1942) or *Stardust* (1927), but there's a list of over 5000 recordings. That's a lot of people covering your songs, they must have something. If I was me, I'd cover my songs too. A lot of these songs I wrote in 1961 and 1962 and 1964, and 1973, and 1985, I can still play a lot of those songs well, how many other artists made songs during that time? How many do you hear today? I love Marvin Gaye, I love all that stuff. But how often are you gonna hear *What's Going On*? (1971) I mean, who sings it? Who sings *Tracks of My Tears* (1978)? Where is that being sung tonight?' He's still working to plumb the fullest truth in the matter of his adventures in the recording studio. 'I've had a rough time recording. I've managed to come up with songs, but I've had a rough time recording. But maybe it should be that way. Other stuff which sounds incredible, that can move you to tears—for all those who were knocked off our feet by listening to music from yesteryear, how many of those songs are really good? Was it just the record that was great? Well, the record was great. The record was an art form. You know, when all's said and done, maybe I was never part of that art form, because my records really weren't artistic at all. They were just documentation. Maybe bad players playing bad changes, but still something coming through. The something that's coming through, for me today, was to make it just as real. To show you how it's real.' Dylan muses on the fate of art in posterity. 'How many people can look at the Mona Lisa? You ever been there? I mean, maybe three people can see it at once. Yet, how long has that painting been around? More people have seen that painting than have ever listened to, let's name somebody—I don't want to say Alicia Keys—say, Michael Jackson. More people have ever seen the Mona Lisa than ever listened to Michael Jackson, and only three people can see it at once. Talk about impact.'

Conversation about painting leads to conversation about other forms. 'That's what I like about books, there's no noise in it. Whatever you put on the page, it's like making a painting. Nobody can change it. Writing a book is the same way, it's written in stone—it might as well be! It's never gonna change. One's not gonna be different in tone than another, you're not gonna have to turn this one up louder to read it.' Dylan savored the reception of *Chronicles*. 'Most people who write about music, they have no idea what it feels like to play it. With the book I wrote, I thought—the people who are writing reviews of this book, man, they know what the hell they're talking about—It spoils you. They know how to write a book, they know more about it than me. The reviews of this book, some of 'em almost made me cry—in a good way. I'd never felt that from a music critic, ever.'

While my private guess would have been that Dylan had satisfied the scribbling impulse (or as he says on *Modern Times* (2006), 'I've already confessed/No need to confess again'), in fact he seems to be deep into planning for a *Chronicles, Volume Two*. Unlike me however, he claims no familiarity with The Bob Dylan Encyclopedia. 'Those are not the circles I really move around in,' he chuckles when I ask. 'That's not something that would overlap with my life.' I've come to feel that Dylan's sweeping simplifications of his own journey's story are outstandingly healthy ones. Puncturing myths, boycotting analysis and ignoring chronology are likely part of a long and lately quite successful campaign not to be incarcerated within his own legend. Dylan's greatest accomplishment since his Sixties apotheosis may simply be that he has claimed his story as his own. Think of him howling the first line of *Most Likely You'll Go Your Way and I'll Go Mine* (1966) upon his return to the stage during the 1974 tour: 'You say you love me and you're thinkin' of me/But you know you could be wroooonngg!'). I take our conversation today the way I took *Chronicles*, and the long journal-song *Highlands* (1997): as vivid and generous reports on the state of Bob Dylan and his feelings in the present moment.

When all is said and done, Bob Dylan is keen that I understand where he's coming from, and in order for me to understand that, I have to grasp what he saw in the artists who preceded him. 'If you think about all the artists that recorded in the 1940s and the 1930s, and in the 1950s, you had big bands, sure, but they were the vision of one man—I mean, the Duke Ellington band was the vision of one man, the Louis Armstrong band, it was the individual voice of Louis Armstrong. Going into all the rhythm & blues stuff, and the rockabilly stuff, the stuff that trained me to do what I do, that was all individually based. That was what you heard—the individual crying in the wilderness. That's kind of lost too. I mean, who's the last individual performer that you can think of—Elton John, maybe? I'm talking about artists with the willpower not to conform to anybody's reality but their own. Patsy Cline and Billy Lee Riley. Plato and Socrates, Whitman and Emerson. Slim Harpo and Donald Trump. It's a lost art form. I don't know who else does it beside myself, to tell you the truth.' Is he satisfied? 'I always wanted to stop when I was on tap. I didn't want to fade away. I didn't want to be a has-been, I wanted to be somebody who'd never be forgotten. I feel that, one way or another, it's OK now, I've done what I wanted for myself.' These remarks, it should be noted, are yet another occasion for laughter. 'I see that I could stop touring at any time, but then, I don't really feel like it right now.' May the Never Ending Tour never end. 'I think I'm in my middle years now,' Bob Dylan tells me. 'I've got no retirement plans.'

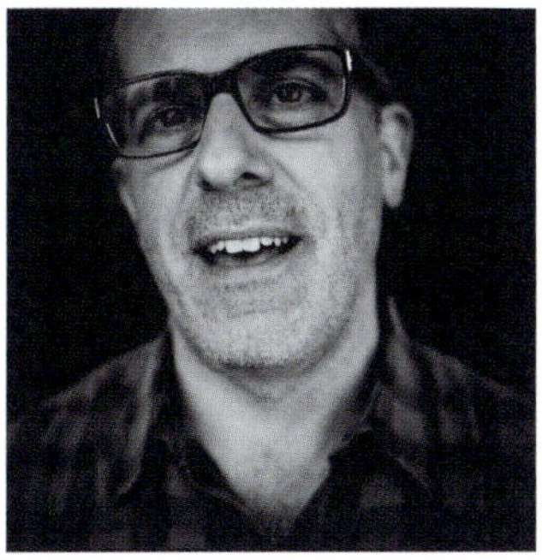

An extended version of this text by Jonathan Lethem was originally published under the title The Genius and Modern Times of Bob Dylan in Rolling Stone Magazine in September 2006.

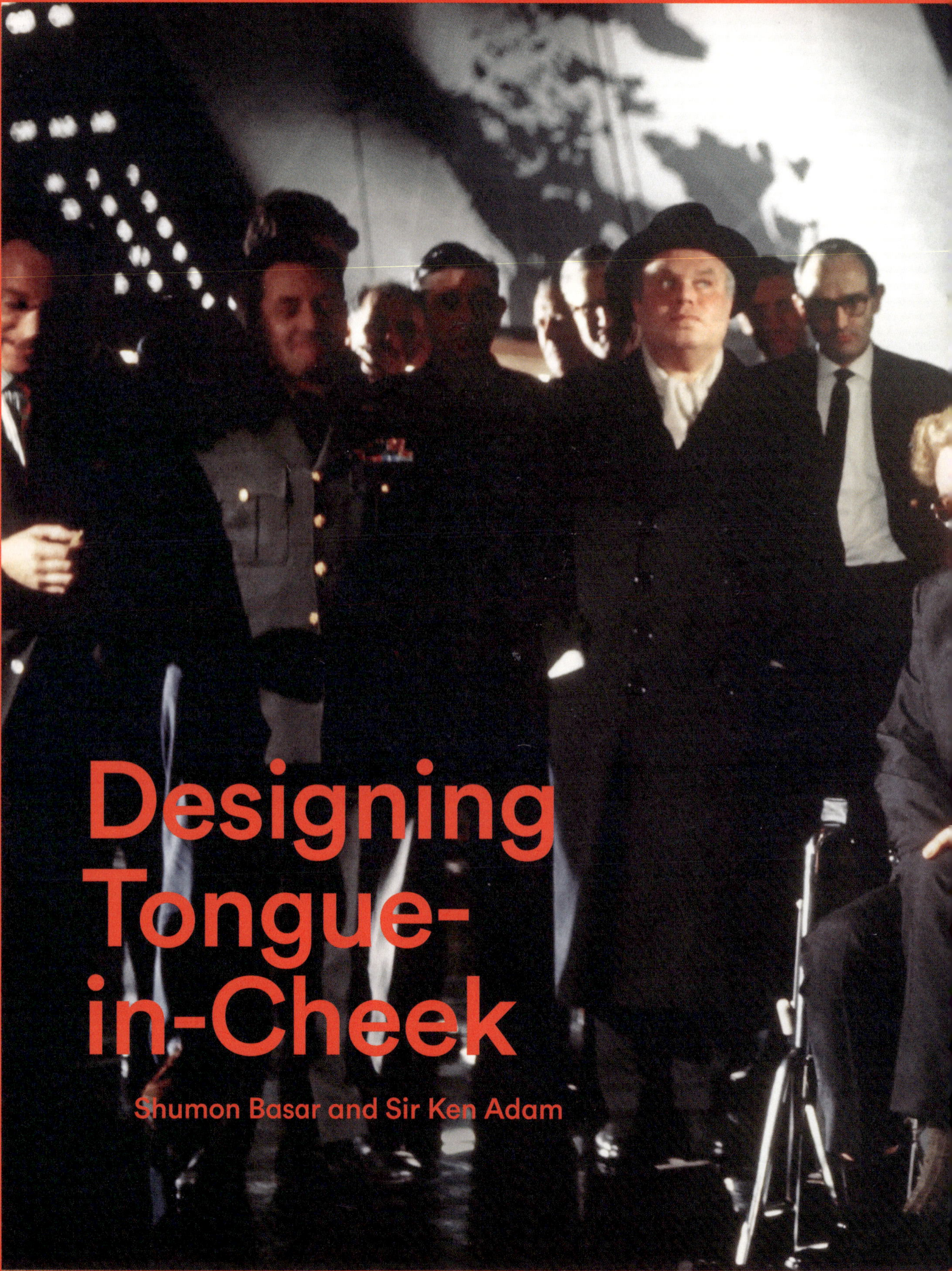

Designing Tongue-in-Cheek

Shumon Basar and Sir Ken Adam

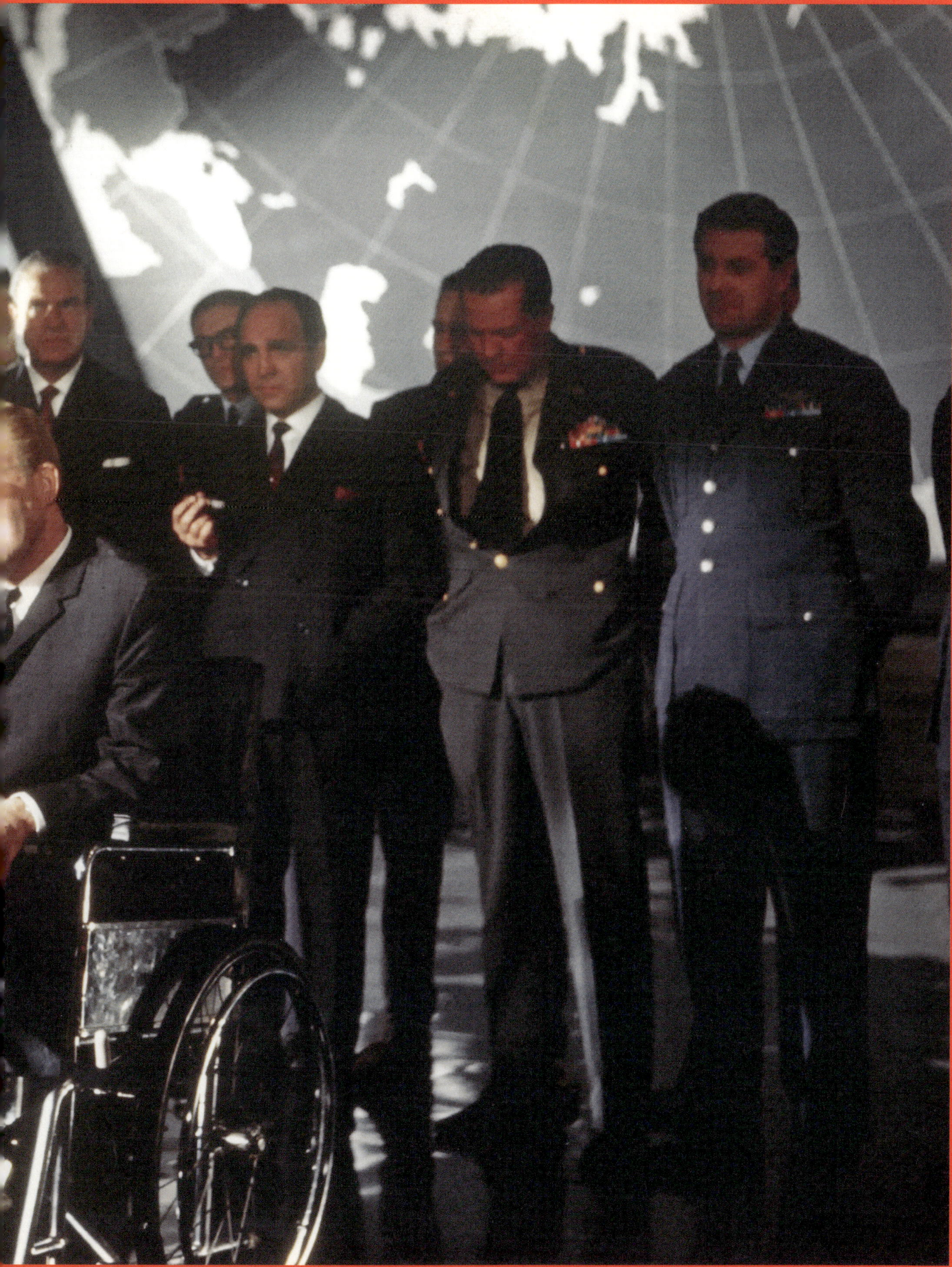

SIR KEN ADAM was one of the most outstanding production designers of the 20th century. Together with writer, thinker and cultural critic SHUMON BASAR he talks, among many other things, about his early influences and inspirations, his training as an architect, his work for the James Bond movies, working with Stanley Kubrick, and the power of imagination.

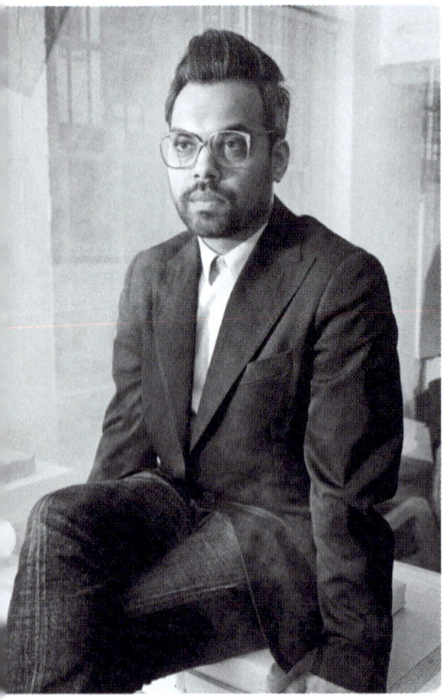

SHUMON BASAR Your personal biography is not only a mirror of the 20th century, but your professional legacy is also that of the history of production design and of film-making in the 20th century. In over 75 films you've managed to create worlds that have somehow become embedded in our imagination; worlds that are not necessarily of the past, the present or the future but are a magical combination of all three. I was wondering which films, from a visual perspective, had an impact on you when you were young?

KEN ADAM Well, in those early years of my life in Berlin I wasn't actually allowed to go to the cinema. Only theatre and opera. Once, however, I was allowed to go. It was a nature film, and I remember that there was a fight between a tiger and a python. The images influenced me for the rest of my life, really. I still have nightmares about it. However, the first time I saw real films was maybe at the age of 13 when we relocated to London: *The Cabinet of Dr. Caligari* (1920) by Robert Wiene and *Dr. Mabuse* (1922) by Fritz Lang. These films just blew me away. From the age of 14 or 15 I knew that I wanted to design for either theatre or film. The stylized Expressionist cinema of the time actually inspires me to this day.

SB In 1933 Hitler came to power in Germany and, in a sense, Germany ceased to be what it had been up till that point. A year later, you and your family, moved to London. Obviously you weren't the only ones to become refugees here. Many German artists and architects who were involved in the Bauhaus also moved to London at that time. It was almost like a first wave of Modernism to hit Britain.

KA Right. It was very popular in England. By this time, I was studying architecture at the Bartlett and we were, strangely enough, terribly traditional. In my spare time, however, I used to draft for the Modern Architectural Research Society (MARS), which was a splinter group of the Bauhaus. The first time I really came into contact with modern design was through a former assistant of Erich Mendelsohn who was one my bosses at an architectural firm that I was working for.

SB I understand that you didn't study architecture to become an architect, and that you had an interesting encounter with Vincent Korda, who, at the time, was one of the most progressive movie art directors. He made films like *Things to Come* (1936), and later *The Thief of Bagdad* (1940), for which he won an Academy Award.

KA Yes, when I met Korda he was already much older, and he told me: 'If you want to design for films, I advise you to have a grounding in architecture. I started as a painter, but I think that an architectural background is more useful.' That's why I studied architecture, even though I never completed my studies, because the war started.

SB Is it true that one of the distinctions at that time between art directors who were working on cinema and those who were working in the theatre was that often those working in the theatre came from more of a fine arts background?

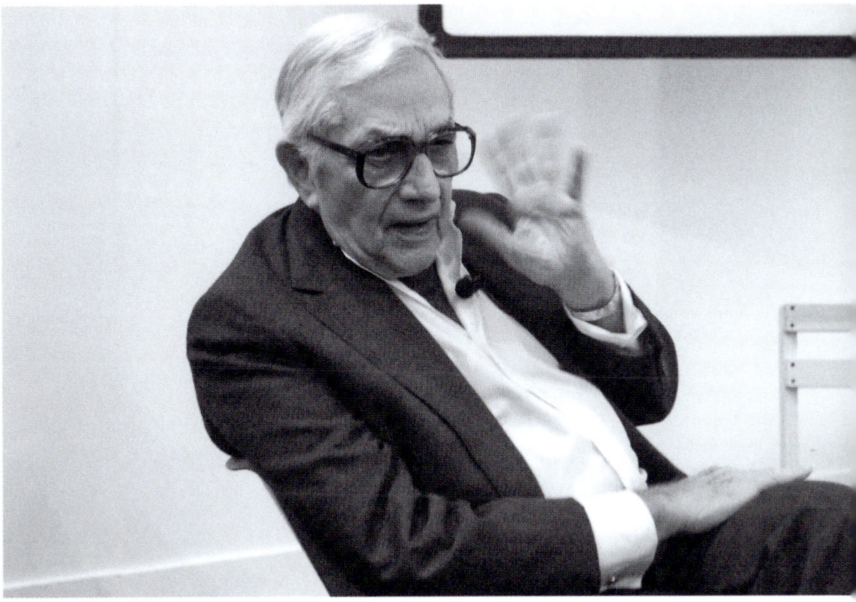

KA Yes, absolutely. In a way, theatrical designers had to me more imaginative, because all you had was a stage. You were bound by the limitations of the side lines and the live public. This imaginative aspect very much appealed to me, and I tried to translate it in the context of film as well, like I did in the infamous war room I created for Stanley Kubrick's *Dr Strangelove* (1964). *How I Learned to Stop Worrying and Love the Bomb* (1964) was a completely imaginary set that the public accepted as reality. When Ronald Reagan became president of the United States, he allegedly asked his Chief of Staff to have a look at the war room. I did this also in many of my designs for the James Bond films. For *Goldfinger* (1965), for example, I designed the entire interior of Fort Knox, the biggest gold depository, in a full-size 60 feet high set design.

SB You said at one point, that you were, in a way, delighted that you didn't get permission to get inside Fort Knox?

KA Right. Nobody, including the president of the United States, is allowed inside. At the same time, I thought that the audience still wants to see the biggest gold depository in the world. I piled up gold 60-feet high, which is completely impractical, because gold is far too heavy, but in film you get away with these impracticalities, and people believe it. After the film, United Artists got over 300 letters from irate Americans about how it was possible that a British film unit and director were allowed inside Fort Knox when their own president isn't even allowed in.

SB Let us return to London at the beginning of World War II for a moment. You said you never finished your architecture studies because the war started. Initially, one of the partners at the architecture office you were working for helped you avoid internment but eventually you were enlisted, and you became the only German national at the time flying for the Royal Air Force. I'm wondering whether flying, and that sense of space and imagining the world that you saw from the airplane, somehow subsequently contributed to your imagination?

KA Well, I was a born pilot, but war-time flying was a different kettle of fish. I was very scared at that time. Particularly when we became rocket typhoons, which meant that we used to dive at speeds between 500mph and 600mph onto German positions and release our rockets. At first, we thought it was going to be a piece of cake, but we found out soon that it wasn't at all. I think if you have a lot of imagination, you also know fear. In the act of doing something, attacking something, the fear leaves you because you concentrate really on what you're doing, but afterwards the fear sets in. Fear manifests itself in different ways. My greatest war time friend, an Australian with whom I shared the same tent, and who was eventually killed, always insisted that he was never afraid when we were flying, but

↰ Scene from Stanley Kubrick's *Dr. Strangelove or: How I Learned to Stop Worrying and Love the Bomb*, 1964. Source: Deutsche Kinemathek - Ken Adam Archiv.

↑ Sir Ken Adam, 2009. Photo by Valerie Bennet. Source: Architectural Assocation, London.

← Portrait of Shumon Basar. Photo by Leon Chew.

‘Kubrick was like a computer, really. I mean, he had an unbelievable brain and a lot of imagination.’

KEN ADAM

when I introduced him to a girlfriend of mine, he fell in love with her and he was shit scared. (Laughs)

SB I'd like to talk a little bit about the 1950s. It was quite an important decade for you, as you made the transition from art director to production designer, and you received your first Oscar nomination for *Around the World in Eighty Days* (1956), but you also got to work with the legendary director and production designer William Cameron Menzies.

KA Yes, Menzies was actually the first person to be ever called a production designer. I adored Menzies, who was associate producer on Around the World in Eighty Days, but poor Menzies had become an alcoholic at the time and he was extremely nervous. Every time Menzies would come by our little apartment a bottle of Scotch went missing. But he helped me enormously in terms of not being afraid of stylization in film design, and of the use of colours, too. I'm very grateful to him.

SB Just one last thing about the 1950s which I find very interesting. One of the things that you also did to make some money was design a number of interiors—particularly of coffee bars in Oxford.

KA Oh yes. Coffee bars were just taking off at the time. Keep in mind, nobody in England, or in London went to a cafe. I mean, that was Paris—people on the other side of the channel. I designed some of the first coffee bars in London and in Oxford, and in Richmond to earn some money and making ends meet.

SB Coming back to the movies—you once told me that Terence Young, the director of the first Bond Film *Dr. No* (1962) gave you a huge amount of freedom in sculpting the vision of the first Bond.

KA Yes, there's no question about that. The first Bond was a low-budget film. My set budget, originally, was only 12,000 GBP. Somehow, they had some money stashed away, and they gave me another 6000 GPB—but that was it. Nobody expected the success of this film. One of the sets that critics later hailed as style-setting for all future Bond movies, was actually invented on the spot, because I completely forgot about it. I had only 570 GBP left, so I came up with this minimalistic set built in perspective on a sloping platform.

SB To me, it seems to be one of the films that is most clearly influenced by the Expressionist films that we were talking about before. Your influences were—whether consciously or unconsciously—really started surfacing.

KA Yes, indeed.

SB Did the very modest budget of *Dr. No* force you to make do with a bricolage of things that you already had? From what I understand, certain objects in the movie even belonged to you and your wife at the time.

KA Yes. (Laughs) I sort of mixed all sorts of things. I liked it because what I did on the first Bond was to really experiment with new materials, too. Real wooden floors, copper or gun metal doors, and things like that. I strongly felt that it was about time that in film design one expresses our technical age. Remember, it was in the early 1960s. I think it was an age of invention. On top of that, Terence had complete confidence in me. He left the style completely to me, and I got away with it. I was all by myself at Pinewood Studios, with nobody looking over my shoulder while the whole unit was shooting in Jamaica.

SB After the next Bond film with Terence Young called *From Russia With Love* (1963) you also started working with Stanley Kubrick, with whom you established a very close relationship. I imagine Kubrick to have been a very different director to Young.

KA Yes, of course. Kubrick was like a computer, really. I mean, he had an unbelievable brain and a lot of imagination. He was brilliant but very difficult to work with—but we got on very well. I think he was probably the director I had the closest relationship ever with. At the same time, he became very destructive, and I didn't really want to do another film for him. I got out of doing *2001: A Space Odyssey* (1968) and originally also out of Barry Lyndon (1975) but then Stanley got me back on board. Looking back, I realise that it was a mistake.

SB From your early sketches of the war room for *Dr. Strangelove*, it looks like it was originally imagined on two levels, is that correct?

KA Yes. Kubrick loved the idea, and I had it built over the course of three weeks. Then one day, on our daily commute to the studio in my Jaguar E-type, he suddenly told me that he didn't know what to do with the second level anymore and that I had to come up with something else. I nearly flipped out, but I didn't have the confidence in those days—yet. I walked in the gardens of Shepperton Studios and took a double dose of Valium to calm down. Then I started scribbling on this design whilst he was standing behind me, saying: 'Gee, Ken, it looks like a triangle. Isn't that the strongest geometric form?' I said: 'Absolutely, Stanley.' 'And what are you going

↱ Archive picture of stage design by Sir Ken Adam for *James Bond: You Only Live Twice*, 1967. Source: Deutsche Kinemathek - Ken Adam Archiv.

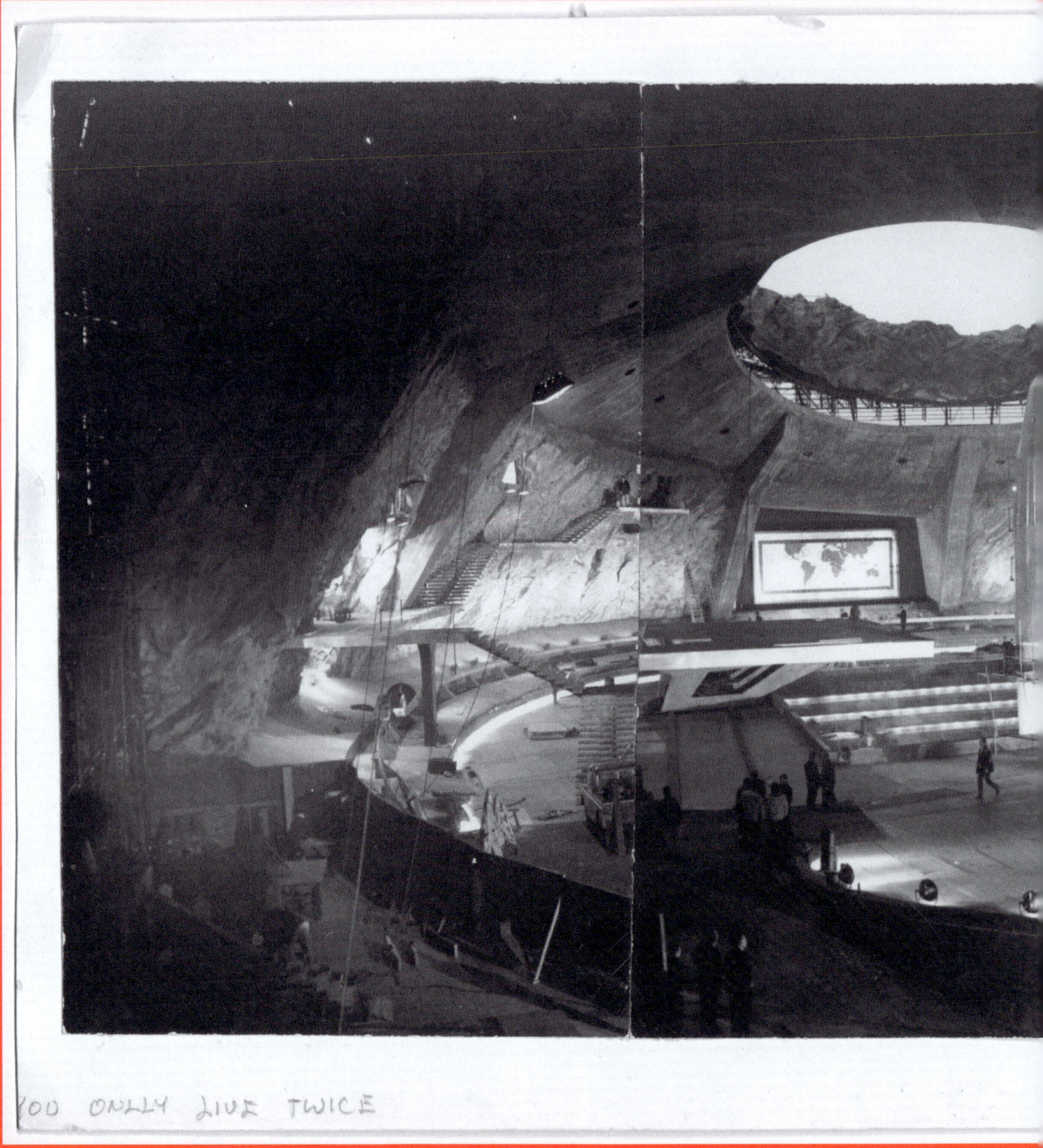
YOU ONLLY LIVE TWICE

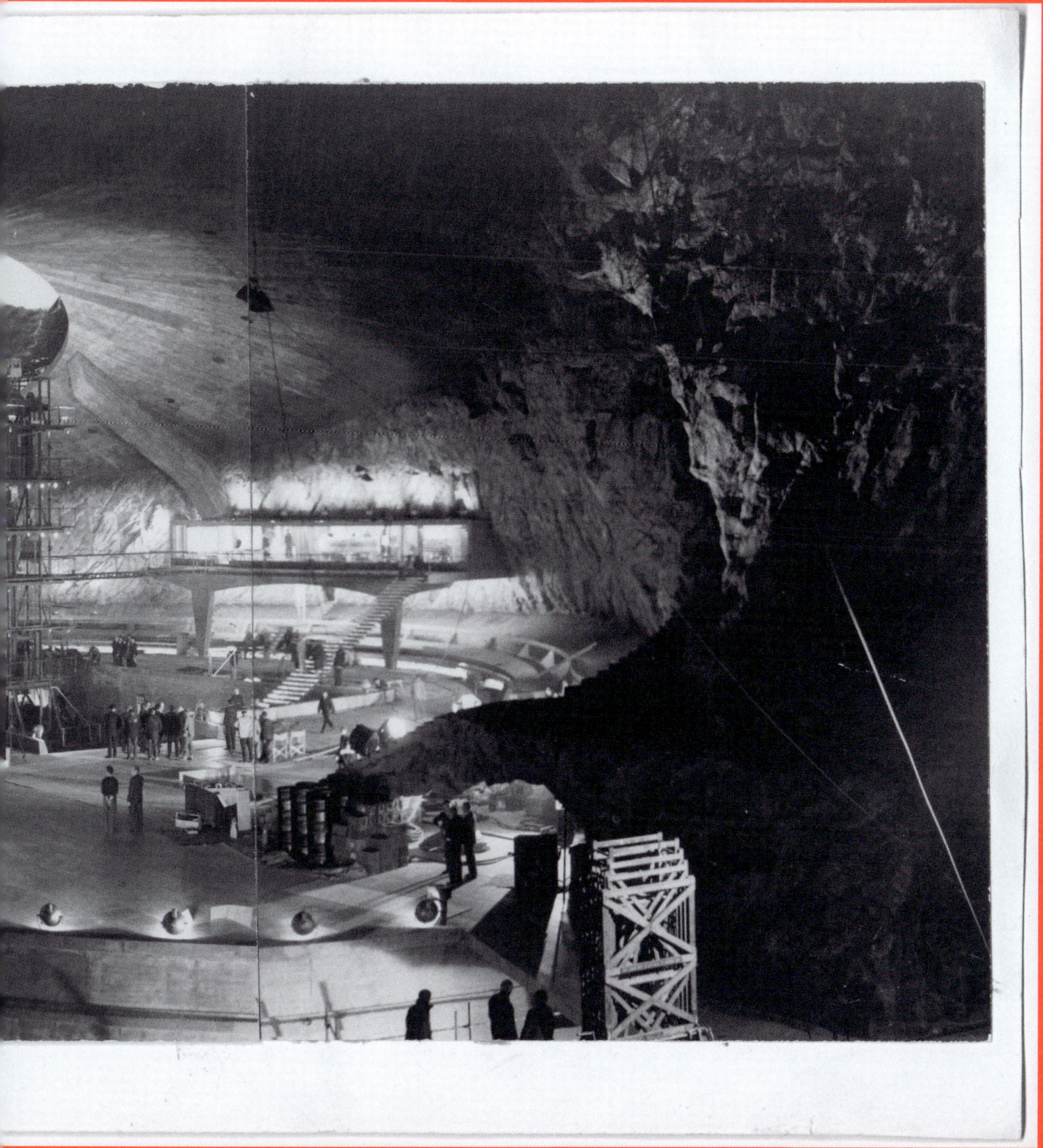

> 'In a way, theatrical designers had to be more imaginative, because all you had was a stage.'
>
> KEN ADAM

to use for material?' I said: Reinforced concrete. 'So, like a giant bomb shelter?' I said: 'Yes.' That's how I sold the idea. Then he never used that angle in the movie at all!

SB Whilst you avoided working with Kubrick again, you obviously continued to design the Bond films for many years. Since you just mentioned your Jaguar E-Type, and I know that you have quite a fancy for cars in general, I was wondering if you could say a few words about the gadget-wielding cars in the Bond movies?

KA Yes. It was a very easy way for me to get rid of my frustrations with having a sports car at the same time—in particular the Jaguar E-type, with that long nose. Every time I parked it somewhere, somebody bashed in part of the nose, you see. For Bond, I put machine guns in the front of the car. It was a wonderful way for me to deal with road rage. (Laughs) Aston Martins sales shot up, unsurprisingly. I believe it was by 47 per cent after the release of the film.

SB What was the biggest set you've built?

KA That's probably *James Bond - You Only Live Twice* (1967). During the making of the movie, we found out that Ian Fleming had never been to Japan, because after two helicopters had flown over Japan for three weeks, we still hadn't found any of the locations that Fleming wrote about. As a result, in desperation, we flew over Kyushu, a Southern island, and we luckily found this area of actual volcanoes. Incredible. That triggered the idea: Wouldn't it be fun if the villain has his headquarters inside this big volcano crater? I did a quick scribble and Albert R 'Cubby' Broccoli, the producer of the Bond movies, asked me: 'How much is it going to cost?' I said: 'Cubby, don't ask me how much it's going to cost, I have no idea.' He said: 'If I give you a million dollars, can you do it?' To which I said: 'Yes.' Then, of course, all my worries started, because even though a million dollars in 1966 was a fortune, the ideas I had were rather grandiose, and I thought I was actually going crazy. A lot of my assistants thought so, too. We had a great team, though, and we managed everything in time. From my experience, fewer things go wrong on the most difficult and large-scale sets than with a corner set of a room.

SB I have noticed that in many of the Bond movies you play with the contrast between things that are hyper-modern, almost space-age, and traditional, neo-classical interiors. Do you consider this a rather anti-modernist idea?

KA Well, remember that I designed all those things tongue-in-cheek. That was a saving grace, you know. So many people tried to analyse it and say that it's about my past, but I don't think it had anything to do with my past.

SB How do you feel about all these extraordinary sets and temporary architectures you've created throughout your career being either taken down or even blown-up spectacularly at the end of the Bond movies? Nothing is built to last. There's no physical residue.

KA I don't agree with your analysis there. In films the most important thing for me is that if I design something, that it is well photographed and well-acted. It's not like I'm creating architecture that remains for history. That is a very important distinction. If the scene works in the set I've designed, then I'm happy.

SB Lastly, you once said that no design is worth doing, if you just reproduce reality—that you don't believe that you can get a sense of reality by copying. Fantasy is more acceptable and believable to the public. Would you say this perhaps encapsulates your approach to the cinema?

KA Yes, absolutely, but I'm not the originator of this idea. Just think of all these incredible early Hollywood films designed by Cecil Gibbons, for example. Art Deco interiors with women in Balenciaga dresses and men in tails and so forth. This was completely unreal for the American public, but they loved it as a form of escapism. In a way, that's just what I have given the public. They accepted my ideas as reality even though they were a complete departure from reality. I think that's what a designer has to be able to do.

This conversation between Shumon Basar and Sir Ken Adam was originally recorded at the Architectural Assocation, London, 2015.

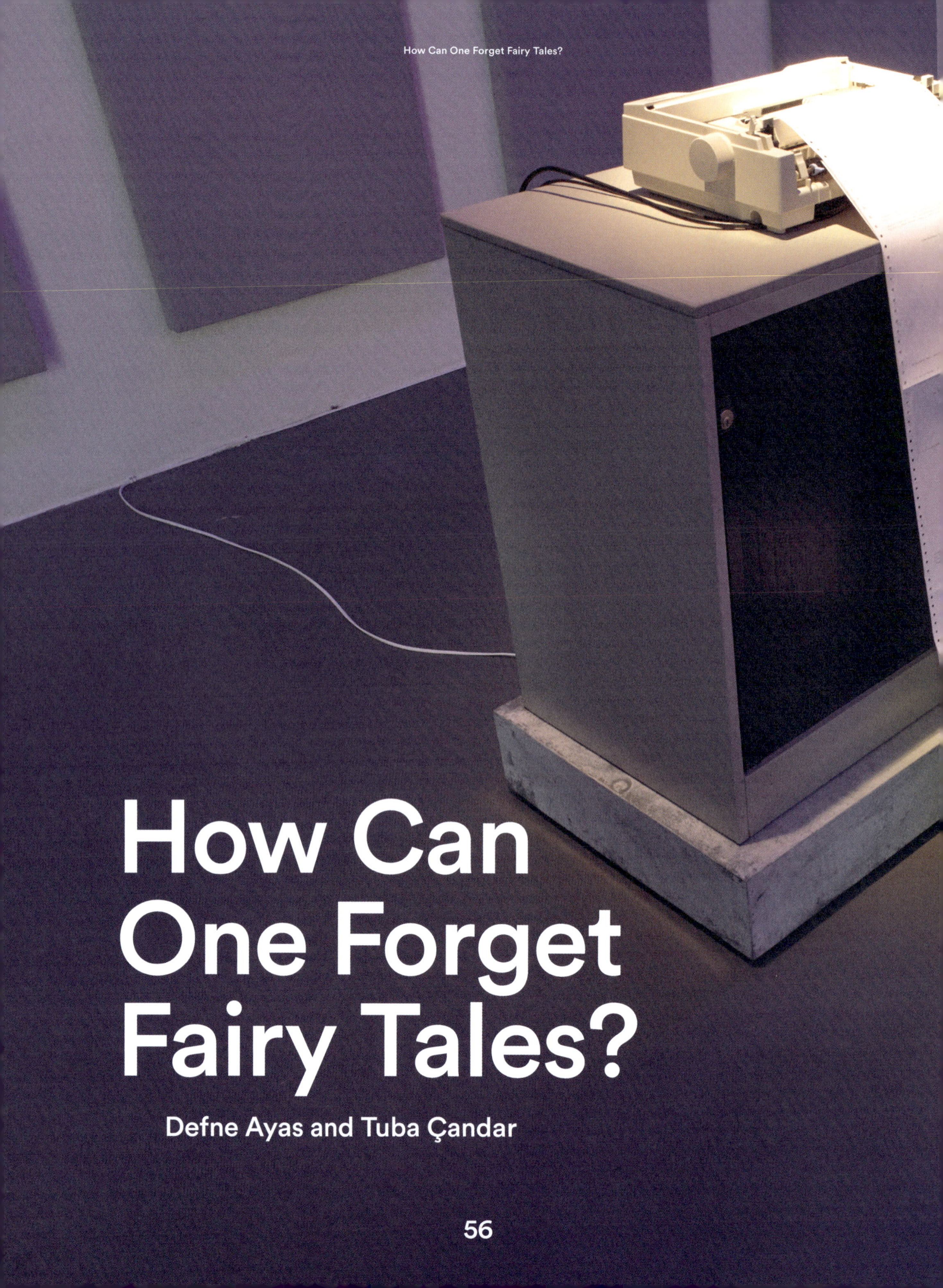

How Can One Forget Fairy Tales?

Defne Ayas and Tuba Çandar

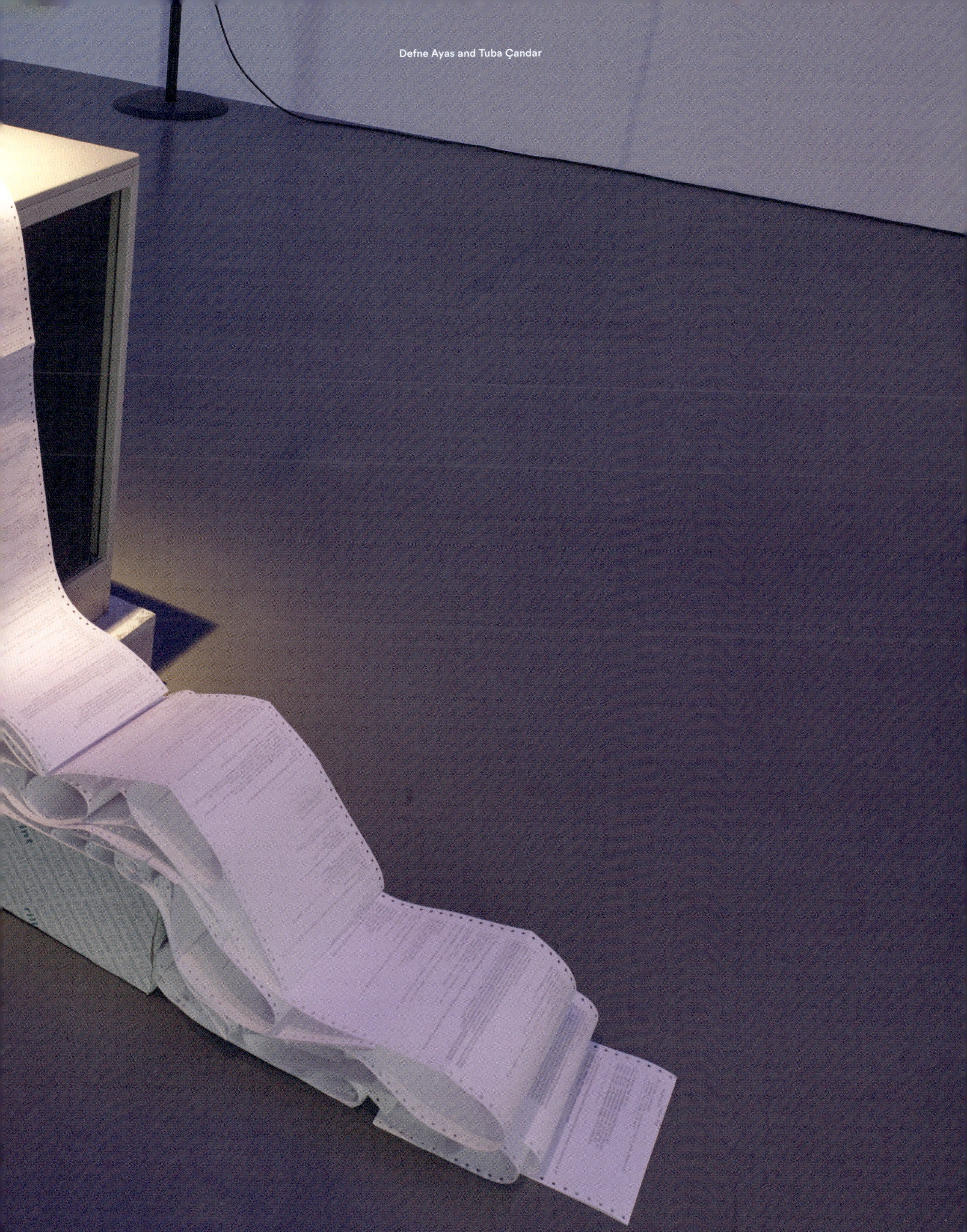

This deeply personal conversation takes place between Turkish curator DEFNE AYAS and her mother, the Turkish writer and editor TUBA ÇANDAR. In this dialogue, mother and daughter take us on stroll down memory lane, reflecting on their personal family history as well as key political moments of 20th century history.

DEFNE AYAS You read a lot of fiction growing up. What was it like being so immersed in books?

TUBA ÇANDAR I swallowed all the Turkish translations of Sartre, Camus, and Beauvoir. It was the time of existentialist literature. I read to the point that there was a small resistance in our household. I would just lock myself indoors and devour these books for hours. My parents were absolutely fine with me doing my homework studiously but not with my 'dabbling' in literature. I had to pretend to read schoolbooks while folding my fiction books inside them.

DA I remember how late artist Chen Shaoxiong would read Sartre in the mid-1980s, but only because it was cool, and this way he could get 'chicks'. This wave was also taking China by storm, impacting an entire generation of artists and intellectuals.

TÇ There's something generational, no doubt. This was what was translated into Turkish at the time, starting in the 1960s onward.

DA Growing up in the household of a navy officer's family during this existentialist wave, was there a strong emphasis on power or reference to some imaginary military legacy?

TÇ My dad had political aspirations and was involved in two military coups over the years. I was twelve years old when the first military coup took place, on the 27th of May 1960. The coup was interpreted as a progressive revolution rather than anti-democratic or oppressive, since it paved the way for a democratic constitution. The prosecution of the overthrown party members was regularly broadcast live on the radio. Their anxious voices are still in my ear, along with the intimidating accusations of the prosecutors. My mother would defend the civilian politicians, and my father would be on the side of the military prosecutors. He would just discredit my mother for 'not understanding the situation' well.

DA What else do you remember from that period?

TÇ Arrested party members were imprisoned and tried on a military island half an hour boat ride away from Heybeliada, the island on which I grew up. On trial days, there would be 'shuttle boats' organized by the military for the relatives. I remember all these families waiting on the deck of my favorite hotel on the seaside, the Panorama Hotel. Their agony is certainly carved into my memory. I didn't understand it all at the time, but something was not instinctively quite right. It was an early sense for justice for me—something archetypical.

I also recall the pogroms of 6th-7th September 1955. I was seven years old at the time. The ruling Demokrat Parti together with the Turkish Intelligence Service had provoked a bunch of thugs and rioters to assault Istanbul's minorities and plunder their properties. I was staying in Beyoğlu at my grandfather's apartment. He held my hand and led me through the main shopping street İstiklâl Avenue, which was all littered with broken shards from the smashed store windows and merchandise from the looted shops. He said: 'Don't ever forget this!' I never did. It took me a while to piece it all together, until I started studying political science in Ankara.

DA Before university, you spent a year in the United States on an exchange scholarship, even attending a speech by Martin Luther King Jr.

TÇ Staying with an American family in a suburb of Cleveland with five kids was a learning curve,

↖ Exhibition overview Rana Hamadeh, *The Ten Murders of Josephine*, Witte de With Center for Contemporary Art Rotterdam, 2017. Variable dimensions. Photo by Kristien Daem.

→ *Triple Goddess*, Elâ Tara, Defne and Tuba at the Museum of Natural History Berlin, 2015. Photo by Christoph Loeffler.

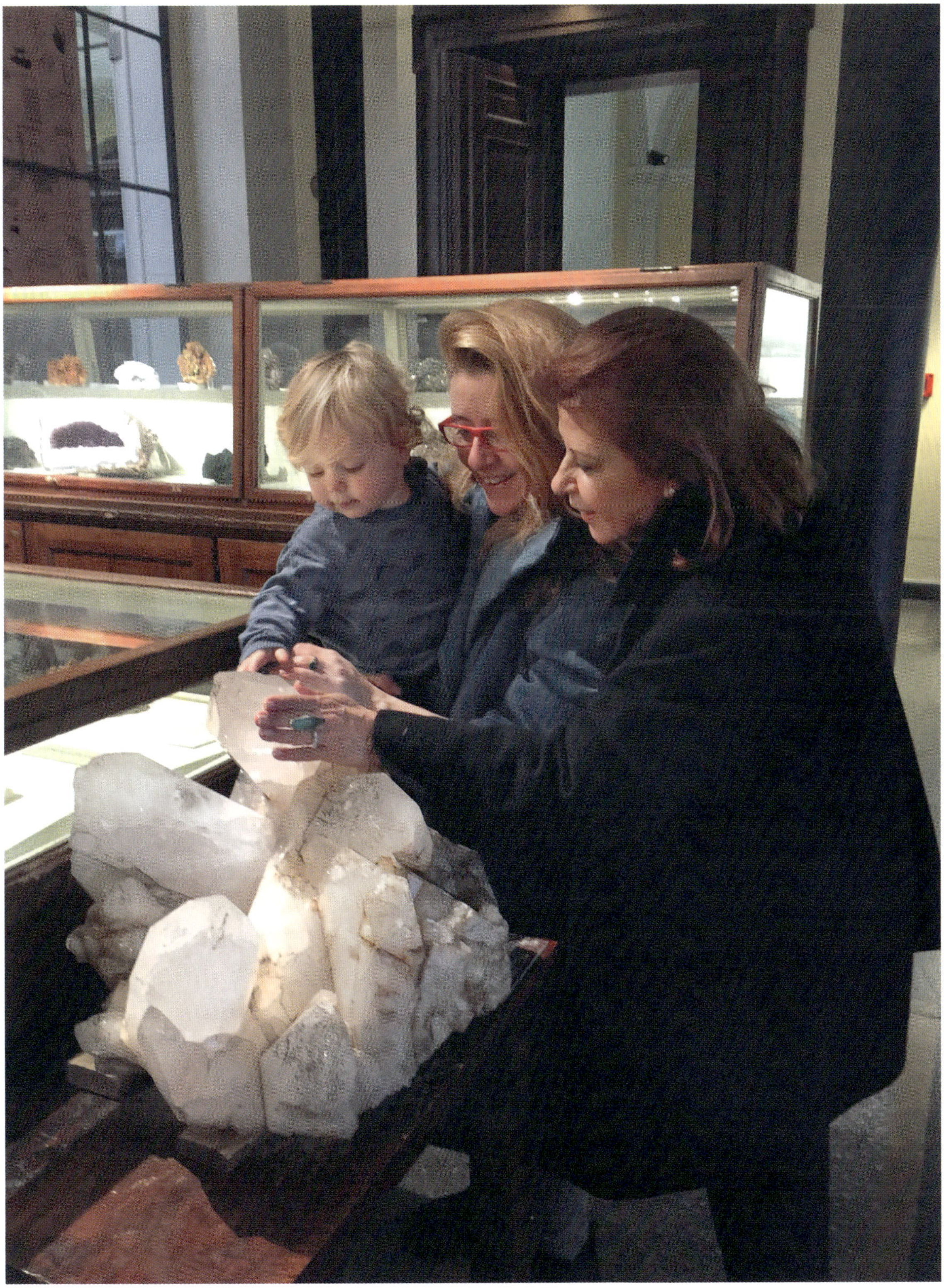

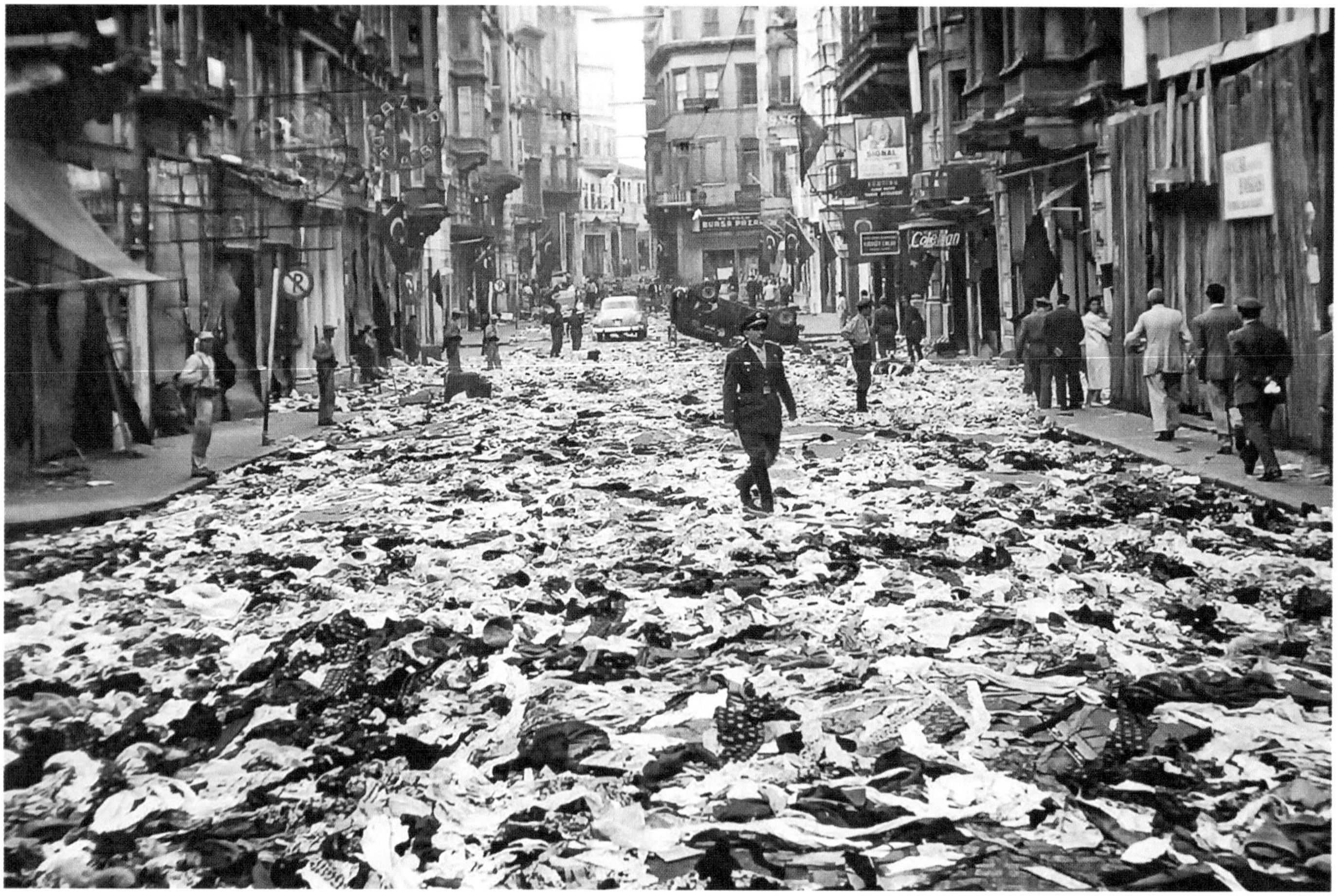
SIGNAL
BURSA PAZARI

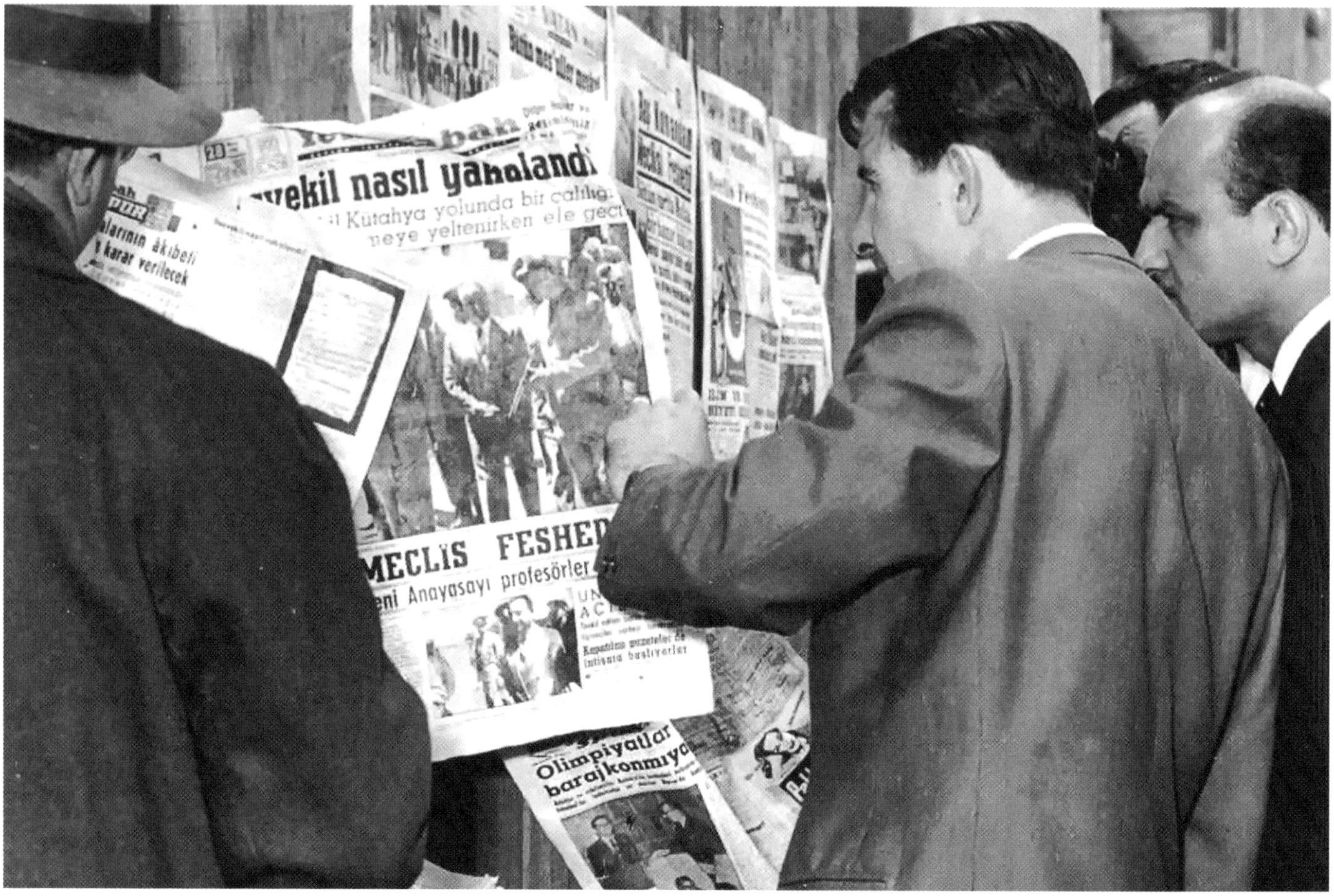
nasıl yakalandı
Kutahya yolunda bir
karar verilecek
MECLİS
Anayasayı profesörler
Olimpiyatlar

← Greeks targeted at Istanbul Pogrom in 1955. Photo by Thari Vakfi.

→ Dr Martin Luther King giving his *I Have A Dream* speech during the March on Washington in Washington, D.C., on 28 August 1963. Credit: National Archives and Records Administration, NAID 542069.

↙ Citizens at a newsstand read of the arrest of Prime Minister Menderes after the coup in 1960 in Istanbul, Turkey. Source: AP Photo.

especially coming from Istanbul's grandeur. In 1967, the city was in flames with black riots. I listened to Dr Martin Luther King Jr in a church and really woke up to the idea of what charisma is—both in a linguistic and physical sense. Years later, even after meeting many leaders including Yasser Arafat, there was nothing like it for me. I didn't come back from the States an awe-struck fan of white America but more as someone who believed in some fundamentals and values of democracy. The period was also so rife with anti-war sentiments because of the Vietnam War—the Flower Generation, with the anti-war demonstrators placing carnations into the barrels of soldiers' rifles, and so on. In the spring of that same year, I visited Oberlin College over a weekend and witnessed the students' lively discussions—even though I didn't understand half of what was discussed. A year later, Martin Luther King Jr was assassinated, and the Faculty of Political Sciences where I started studying turned into a platform for organizing strikes and boycotts.

'I listened to Dr Martin Luther King Jr in a church and really woke up to the idea of what charisma is—both in a linguistic and physical sense.'

TUBA ÇANDAR

DA At the university, you became involved with the student movement and translated Chairman Mao's *Little Red Book* (1964) into Turkish. What dream were you after? Marx, Mao, saving the proletariat, communist theory, ethics, your boyfriend? Was it because you read *Das Kapital* (1867)?

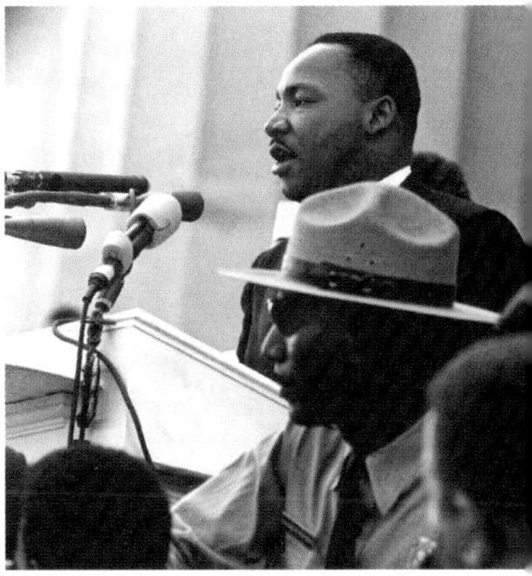

TÇ I didn't become a 'revolutionary' because I read Das Kapital. Let me confess: I even fell asleep once trying to decipher that book. We were more concerned with the 'how' of making a revolution. We read more Lenin, Stalin and Mao, and how to apply theory to practice.

I translated not only the *Little Red Book* but also his four-volume *Selected Works* (1961)! As a reward for my labor, the Maoist movement decided to send me to Beijing for the Xinhua News Agency to be a translator. China then and China now are obviously very different. The cultural Revolution was happening, and the place was boiling over with purges and lynchings, intellectuals sent to labor camps. I was not aware of all this then. I was naively getting excited looking at the photos of the revolutionary women peasants in the pages of *Beijing Review*. We were just happy singing 'The Internationale' in Turkish. In the end, the trip did not work out, and I am glad it didn't!

DA Obviously, I didn't have the same ideals you had when I went to China three decades later. I surfed the liberal wave, not the communist one. Why did you choose the route through China rather than the Soviet Union? Why did you decide to reject America?

TÇ China was more like Turkey, with its semi-feudal structure. It was not capitalist like the West, with its strong bourgeoisie and developed working class. The Chinese revolution seemed a better fit for our movement.

My position was that the workers should have equal rights, and I was ready to put myself to that struggle. I wasn't alone; all my friends fostered the same idealism. Those of us from urban elite families, who studied at foreign, private schools, took a sudden leftist and 'internationalist' turn. We were all ready to defend the rights of 'all the oppressed classes and peoples.' The irony was that I had no experience of working-class culture, apart from the limited contact I had with the cleaner that came to our house. Those who came from lower economic classes became ultranationalists in the meantime. A contradictory picture, no?

'I did not write that book, I just lived the book. Sometimes I think I may have created a 'karma' without knowing it.'

TUBA ÇANDAR

DA Your university department was a springboard for diplomats-in-waiting. What happened to the 'movement'?

TÇ At the university I met with students from Anatolia, from Kurdish and Alevite backgrounds. This was a different kind of diversity than the one I knew in Istanbul. There were more than 500 people in those classes, including PKK founder Abdullah Öcalan, but also the former prime minister Mesut Yılmaz, who was a friend from high school, though he chose the right-wing path and stood at a distance from our staged events. What began as protests against university administration turned into demonstrations against the government, which all came to an end to with the military coup of 12th March 1970. The military regime targeted us with a period of imprisonment and torture. We turned from a space of legality to illegality. It was in this period that the movement wanted to send me to China. I was about to be sent there in 1972 from Switzerland, as it was the only country that had diplomatic ties to China.

DA With the first Swiss ambassador to China being the now-famed Chinese art collector Uli Sigg, a dear friend—

TÇ I was in Bern at the Chinese Embassy drinking green tea with the first Chinese person I had seen in my life. I was 24 years old and had passed the translation exams, but this wasn't enough. I also had to be married, because the Chinese were concerned about the 'mixing of the races,' if I were to remain unmarried.

In the meantime, the space for Maoists was narrowing in Turkey, with the leadership arrested. When I returned to Istanbul without my Chinese permit in hand, the remaining movement tasked me with 'raising the class consciousness of fellow workers,' and sent me to a shantytown in the outskirts of the city. Who knew that I would be sexually harassed while on my mission? I ran away from that household and found refuge again in my parents' home. It was my family that helped me escape Turkey again. I ended up with some relative of mine in Germany because I spoke the language, and this was where I ended up with your dad, and you were born.

↘ *Hitit Güneşi Mualla Eyüboğlu Anhegger* by Tuba Çandar, 2003. Published by Doğan Kitap.

DA Was this movement strictly intellectual and idealistic? What about romance?

TÇ The one and only love story during this period was my fiancé. He spotted me at a conference of a famed leftist author and said, 'She is the one!' Then he used all sorts of tricks to 'hunt' me. He was the president of the student association at the time, and he mobilized mutual friends, so he could come to Istanbul to find me. Everything seemed right at the beginning, all according to parental expectations. He graduated from the Faculty of Political Sciences and began his academic career at the Middle East Technical University, already earning his living as a T.A. His parents were lawyers, so my parents were pleased. Within a year of our 'dating', I found myself engaged to him.

We would only talk about the revolution, singing international revolutionary songs like *Bella Ciao* (1993) etc. No clubbing whatsoever. I meant to say this to you before, I danced with him for the first time at our engagement party at the Dedeman Hotel, and I was shocked to find out that he did not know how to dance!

DA What?!

TÇ He was a good young man, full of humor and love. Then we both fled Turkey after the coup. He went to the Palestinian refugee camps in Beirut; a year later I found myself in Germany. We lost track of each other. Then your father entered my life, and another meandering story began. He was a dentist and had done his military service under my father's command. As soon as he heard that I was in Germany, he applied to the German Chamber of Dentists, and, with not a word of German, found a job in a tiny town in the Nordrhein-Westfalen near the Dutch border, settled there, and jumped in his secondhand Volkswagen Hässliche Ente to find me in Frankfurt. He was very handsome. Now, how do you not get dragged behind such a man? We got married. Marriage was very frustrating and upsetting to me. We had no common references, and he was not like any man I knew, rather cynical and extremely jealous.

DA After divorcing my father, you went back to marry Cengiz, your first fiancé, who also became my adopted father. You were his intellectual sparring partner, but you also continued to write, also about the lives of others. Why not write more, since your work is so lucid? Why not write about your life when it is so rich? You barely have any family records of your own and no organized photo albums of our family, yet you made it your cause to record other people's lives.

TÇ This is the most fundamental question of my life. Especially in the last few years.

Yes, I worked as editor of many cultural monthlies. I had a stormy divorce and married my ex-fiancé. Whether I liked it or not, I tried to create a family of three independent personalities. I believe I succeeded in this!

I devoted many hours to my husband, who became an important public figure in Turkey as a result. This was not a sacrifice or a compromise for me but a pleasure. There has always been a high voltage of intellectual exchange between us. I joined him on his work travels from Bosnia during the war to Berlin during the fall of the Wall to the Middle East. I met presidents and foreign ministers of different countries. I continued to write travel impressions for magazines and profiles of cultural figures for weekly newspapers. If I said that I did not have the time to write because of this hectic pace of life, it would just be an excuse. After I turned 50, I wrote three biographies. When it comes to writing my own life, however, in our country, where politics swing back and forth at an insane pace, it is not easy to keep a record like normal people living calm lives do. That's why I always use interviews with people to write biographies.

DA How did the subjects of your three biographies act as projection board for you or your interests?

TÇ Turkey's first female architect and the restorer of the Topkapı Palace Imperial Harem, Mualla Eyüboğlu, was 69—my age now—when I first met her. She was a monumental figure—her appearance, her house, her personality—but also extremely humble. I fell in love with her. I have always admired Murat Belge and his books as a left-wing intellectual with his individualistic stand 'far from the crowd.' Hrant Dink is a different story, of course. I knew and loved him in person, and when he was killed, it was as if we were killed. It was a task; a duty; an obligation for me to write his story, and I did so with great commitment and devotion. I wrote his life as well as the anguish of Armenians in Turkey, which became a story about our shared country and their removal from their roots. I did not write that book, I just lived the book. Sometimes I think I may have created a 'karma' without knowing it. Look what our life has become in recent years! We've lost our home, our city, and our country. Our friends have lost their jobs, have been detained and jailed. We had to leave the country. Like Diaspora Armenians, we have become a minority. Now we are all in exile, both inside and outside the country.

It took time to establish a new life in Stockholm at this age. Now I am reading plenty again. I have written nothing but an article for the Swedish PEN's special issue on Turkey. Am I lazy, really? If I look at you and what you do, it's easy to think so, but with this little interview we're having, perhaps you've directed me to think about my own life. You're really applying to me—to a lesser extent—my biography writing method.

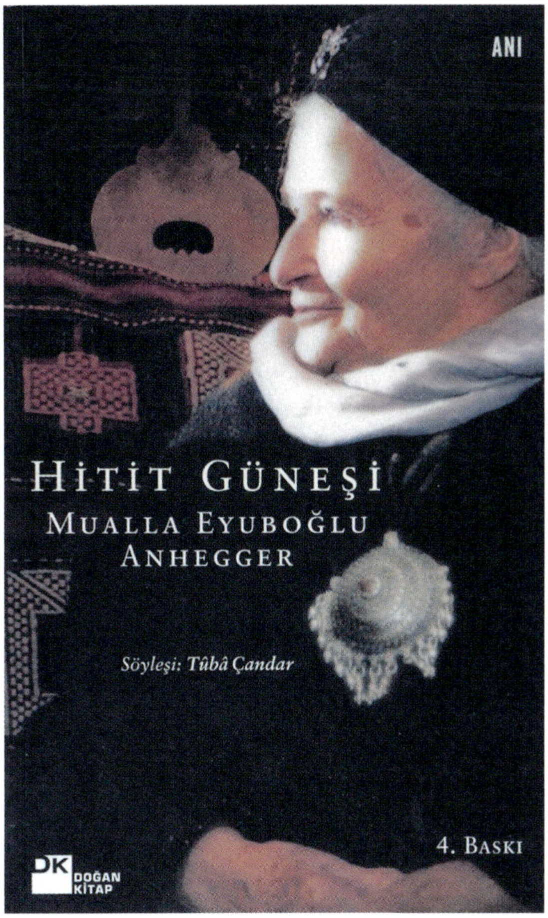

DA Someone said that I'm your blonde carbon copy. How does it feel to see your (occasional) mirror in me?

TÇ I'm always surprised that our friends think that we're so similar. Physically, you look completely like your father, and more so everyday really. Some people think our voices are similar on the phone, but I really do not think we're so alike. I am not a managerial type like you are, which became more visible during your time at Witte de With. I prefer to work independently. I see you super busy and productive—I'm not like that. We are also such different mothers, at least until now. I stopped working and became a housewife when I became a mother. You have not allowed this extremely demanding work life to stop your motherhood. When I had a bit of spare time, I would find a babysitter and go out. You spend your entire free time according to your child's schedule. We are also different as partners. I have always shared my husband's life; you and your husband live independent lives. Of course, our characters might look alike, as well as our temperaments and our discussion styles. This is why we might misunderstand each other.

DA There is that saying in Turkish: 'Mothers and daughters fight, and neighbors think it is real.' The constant push-and-pull to enhance, devour, and appropriate each other—

TÇ I thought that the stormy mother-daughter dynamic between us would pass when you became a mother, but it did not, nor when you went abroad for college. All of this is a tiring aspect of our mother-daughter relationship. Nothing is more rewarding and satisfying to me than when we catch each other thinking the same thing at the same time. Our observations and perceptions of a new person or situation—even if you are a little faster than me—are quite similar though.

DA Maybe it's also in the stars, Mum. Gemini I (Week of Freedom) versus Cancer I (Week of the Empath). You know my bible, my obsession, The Secret Language of Birthdays, which even led me to work with artist Willem de Rooij to publish the English translation of Mondrian's horoscope.

TÇ When I try like amateur psychiatrist to understand this, I come to the conclusion that it is about my divorce from your father rather than our similarities or differences. We might have had a cooler

↓ Marina Abramovic, *Transitory Objects: Bed(s) For Human Use*, 2012. Wood, black quartz crystals, headphones, pillows. Six sets, each 80 × 200 × 65 cm. Courtesy of the artist. Photo by Aad Hoogendoorn. Courtesy of Witte de With Center for Contemporary Art, 2013.

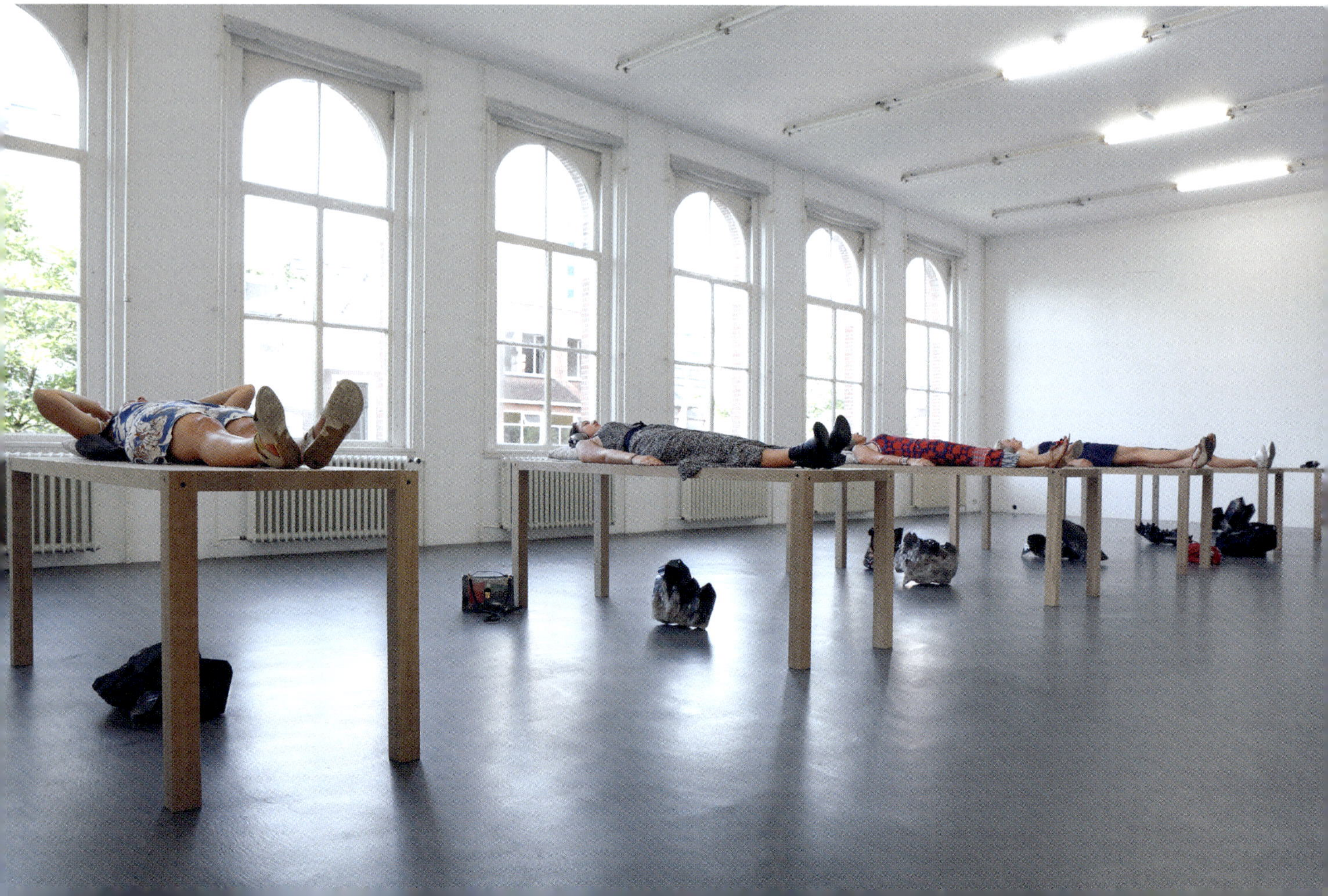

relationship because a mother always feels guilty for some reason.

DA I feel like I might be picking up where you left off, from the Austrian high school to US, China, and Germany. Is divorce and Sweden next for me? Hope not!

TÇ Never thought of this, but you are right! This cannot be just coincidence, no? Then again, these are all the things your life gives you: we have no way to make sense of all this. Should we call it 'destiny'? I'm not sure. Divorce is not half-hearted in my life, so you cannot complete that. We do not know how Sweden will develop. It's too early to say much. If I die here, for example, it may not be necessary to complete it!

I wonder how it will all proceed with you and Elâ Tara, as you two look a lot like each other. You two are like carbon copies: your leadership skills, your inability to lose, the way you do not want to share your parents with others. From your point of departure, you share Germany as your birthplace. After you married Christoph, you lived in cities all over: New York, Amsterdam, Shanghai, Rotterdam. Your daughter chose to be born in Berlin. She is growing up with Turkish, German, and English like you and I did. When I think about it, I feel like my mother feels you look at me from above. How uncanny!

DA Didn't you have a dream recently, waking up you were convinced your role was to be a full grandmother? What knowledge as a woman should my daughter Elâ cherish from her amazing anane (grandmother) most? What do you think she will think of your life and your period of Turkey?

TÇ Both of my grandmothers were dead by the time I was born, so perhaps that's why I want to leave my granddaughter a lot. I do not want to sell the house in Istanbul, because it is where she took her first steps. I do not even know if I will be able to return and live there, but I want the house to represent some sort of continuity for her. I certainly would not want to be known only as a grandmother living in Stockholm. I wish that she would remember me in my own space, in my own habitat, in my own language. It's too heavy to acknowledge that it may never be possible. Language is so very important, and your efforts to teach Turkish to Elâ are so precious to me! It is the only condition that my granddaughter can get to know me as my daughter knows me. Otherwise, she will never know her grandmother fully.

DA Now that I am struggling to even teach her our mother tongue, which she refuses to speak, I want to know how she should be able to make sense of it all when she grows up. I am still at loss for words to understand how the very context, which I took as my spiritual blanket in my work (which is also losing its roof) is being wiped out. Elâ, mind you, received the a-circumflex letter in your name to her name, the hat as we say it in Turkish, which is also vanishing from Turkish grammar.

TÇ It's very difficult for all of us to understand the period we live in, and it will be hard for her to understand all this and the time I had lived in. Difficult to transmit it all to her in words. I have come to understand that this is only possible through my own writing. I should perhaps write for my one and only grandchild from now on; after all, this is all that matters. Perhaps later in her life she would want to find out about this life of mine, a life that is very different in time and place from her own reality, something that would read like a fairy tale, which she would most likely love. This way she would remember me. How can one forget fairy tales?

How many times have you told me to write my life? I've forgotten just how many. I won't forget this one. It's because it is being recorded now; in fact, I started writing it now, as we are speaking, exactly what you wanted me to do with my own writing. Isn't it? I thank you for that.

> 'I should perhaps write for my one and only grandchild from now on; after all, this is all that matters.'
>
> DEFNE AYAS

Multi-instrumentalist, drummer and joint frontman for the Grammy Award-winning band The Roots and New York Times Best-selling author AHMIR QUESTLOVE THOMPSON sits down with GEORGE CLINTON, the mastermind behind the highly influential Parliament and Funkadelic collective to talk about the 1970s and how everything began.

Between the Lines

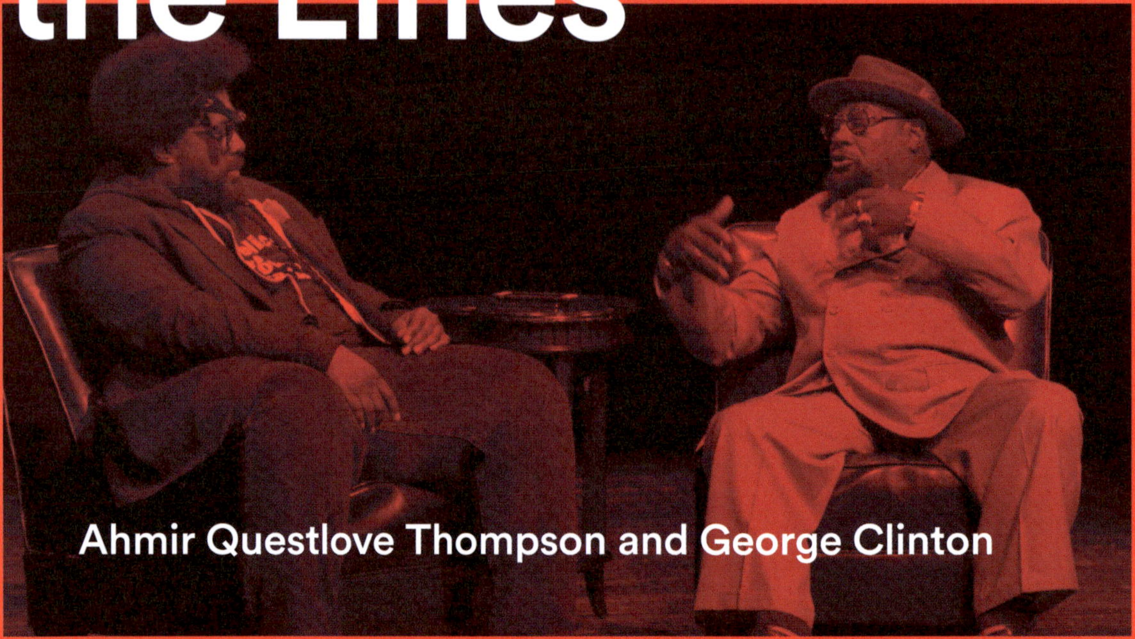

Ahmir Questlove Thompson and George Clinton

AHMIR QUESTLOVE THOMPSON This is an incredible moment for me. In all the years that I've known you, I never had the chance to talk to you like this—one on one—about your legacy. I would like to talk to you about the early years of Funkadelic and Parliament. I guess what I want to start with is your time in Detroit.

GEORGE CLINTON What made me go to Detroit originally was Motown. We thought we was all that, but they already had The Temptations. When we made a hit record in 1967 with The Parliament's *(I Wanna) Testify* with a Motown rival company, that's when we migrated to Detroit for real. We became part of both the Motown scene of the time but also of the upcoming rock scene with Iggy Pop, MC5 and all the others. It was also the time that the Beatles got all trippy with St. Pepper's Lonely Hearts Club Band. So we was able to switch to a more psychedelic attitude, which was Funkadelic.

AQT How radical was the idea of Funkadelic's heavier, psychedelic rock-oriented sound?

GC It wasn't radical at all to me. I just took the mid-tempo music and called it funk and vowed to never let anybody change it. When it came time to be called 'R'n'B', 'urban', 'black' or whatever, we were always all of that. No matter what they were saying, we would call it funk and 'funkadelic' and 'supergroovalistic.' We were gonna say it every way you can possibly say it, and doing it any way you possibly could. It's really about how you can trend something. If you know how to trend it, you can hang in there with everybody. You can't go against the kids though. That's the one thing. If they come up with something new, you might as well bow your head because they got it. It's their term.

AQT You once told me one of the smartest things I ever heard anyone tell me. You said 'Always trust the taste of a nine year old.'

GC Yeah, from nine to thirteen. That's bubble gum; teeny bopping. They are the ones that gonna be tweeting and talking about it. Even today with Youtube, I go to my great-grand kids—they call me grand dude—and they show me short video clips. This is what it is. If you come home and see somebody new who ain't doing what you are doing, you might feel threatened, but you better go hurry up and learn what it is. Don't get mad. If you get mad, you're counting yourself out. Don't react too fast and give it a little bit of time. It'll start sounding good to you.

AQT I'm glad that you are saying this because my father and me, we had these musical clashes that started in 1988. Every year before we were cool, but in 1988 Public Enemy came out and he just hated it. He just thought it was the worst noise he had ever heard. For me, Public Enemy was revelation. I love the fact that you always put your best foot forward as far as embracing the culture.

✓ Ahmir Questlove Thompson in conversation with George Clinton at Schomburg Center for Research in Black Culture, The New York Public Library, 2015.

GC When I heard Chuck D of Public Enemy say 'Bring the noise' I knew that he knew the theory of it. People love anything that you are convinced of yourself. Even if it is you admitting that you are being noisy. When Public Enemy came on, they knew what the concept was: 'Let's be noisy, we're Public Enemy. We are going to wreck shit.' That's the way they felt about it, and that's the way they did it. Chuck was serious, and Flav was the hype man. They gave you both sides of it. What Chuck was saying was serious, but you can't be that kind of serious 24/7, and you won't get but one record out.

AQT One of my favourite samples of Funkadelic is actually on Public Enemy's *Bring the Noise.*

GC Yeah, Public Enemy was always my favourite style of sampling. They used it so creatively. All those different samples that they made real arrangements with.

AQT For *Bring the Noise* they used this 10-second guitar intro from *Get Off Your Ass and Jam* on Funkadelic's *Lets Take It to the Stage* (1975). I assume that guitar solo was Eddie Hazel?

GC No, it was actually this little homeless looking white kid that had the nerve to walk in the studio while we were finishing up. He said: 'Let me put a solo down and if you like it, you give me 25 dollars.' This little kid, maybe 16 or 17 years old, plugged his guitar in when the song came on, and he just didn't stop. He went through the whole song like that and everybody was just looking at him, thinking 'What did just happen?'

AQT Were you guys actually laughing? I ask, because I can hear laughter in the background on that track.

GC Yes, we were laughing. You know he looked really strung out. Nobody expected that. So right when he put the song down I gave him 50 dollars. By the time we actually listened to half of the song, I was getting ready to give him another 50 dollars, but he was gone. We never found out who he was. We talked about it lots of times. I think he didn't even know who we were. I think he was just trying his luck.

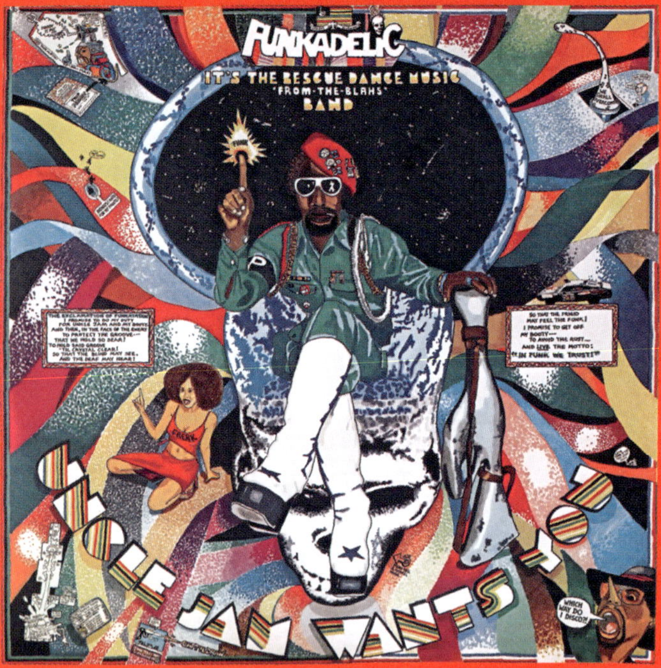

AQT Did you ever feel any kind of disillusionment about life in the 1970s after the flower-power movement had passed?

GC Well, the money came back into the game and I got into it winning. If it's going to be about money, well, let's spend some money then. At the same we did a record with Funkadelic in 1972 called *America Eats Its Young*. You couldn't say that now under any circumstances. That's probably a terrorist term now. At that time, though, people was in agreement. The Vietnam War had to stop. Women had to have their rights. People of colour had to have their rights. Gays had to have their rights. Everybody was in agreement.

AQT Did you feel at the time that funk could have been watered down and that you needed to make a statement - like this is the absolute uncut funk, this is our declaration?

GC We felt we had to 'refunkatize' it. We went in with the psychedelic funk but it was pure funk. We were calling it dope, uncut funk, the bomb—the street terms for drugs. We knew to communicate through routes so people would hear you. If you got something to offer, that they can get off on, they are going to be hooked on funk. It's a good thing to be hooked on.

AQT Did you have some kind of master plan that you would sort of multi-task these different acts like Parliament and Funkadelic and artists like Bootsy Collins before you started with all this?

GC No. It just unfolded as we went along. I ain't got nothing to do with that. I feel lucky as hell.

AQT Alright, let's talk Funkadelic's s second album *Maggot Brain* (1971) which you recorded with the likes of Eddie Hazel and Billy Bass Nelson. What were the dynamics like working with these younger musicians at the time?

GC They were maybe five to six years younger than us. They were just young enough for us to have missed the concept of shooting heroin. We've seen a few older people do it but we missed it as a concept. By then everybody was shooting dope though. It was strange to see these kids in our band—maybe 15 years old—doing it. They were not snorting, they were banging. To deal with that as being older and being their boss was difficult. Eventually they became Funkadelic and they became the boss and we caught hell from them. At least the rest of the band did. I never did. We had to protect them too. I mean, their parents gave us guardianship over them when we went up. We all went out there when the acid came. Believe it or not that was the most beautiful time because everyone quit everything else, you know. When that ended everyone went back to drinking. (Laughs)

AQT So acid was what affected the first Funkadelic records?

GC Oh yes. I think we maybe started making sense on *Cosmic Slop* (1973). *Standing on the Verge of Getting It On* (1974) was even a bit clearer. After *One Nation Under a Groove* (1978) we were cleaner than we had ever been.

AQT How many takes did it usually take for a song?

GC You didn't do but one take of that, because you wouldn't know what to listen for. I mean, what are you going to compare it to? As a matter of fact, on *Maggot Brain* I had to turn the band off, because they were not where it's at. I did the mixing all live. Like when Jimi Hendrix played with the live feedback of his Stratocaster, I kind of did the same on the mixing board. The engineers didn't even want their name on the record - they said, it's distorted. They just got up and left, saying 'You're a fool, you're messing up money'.

AQT I tell you a funny story about *Cosmic Slop*. At the time when I was growing up, my dad had about 5000 records. We had a lot of Funkadelic records too, like *Lets Take It to the Stage* (1975) and *Standing on the Verge of Getting It On* (1974) but we didn't have *Cosmic Slop* (1973). The first time I ever heard *Cosmic Slop* was, of all places, on The Cosby Show. Do you remember the episode in which Cliff Huxtable couldn't get any sleep because all the kids were watching TV and listening to the radio? In one scene, Cliff is in the kitchen with Vanessa and Robert and they are listening to *Cosmic Slop*. After getting the meaning of the song, I was always wondering who was so progressive at The Cosby Show, that a song about a woman who has to prostitute herself, and is negotiating her life with the devil while justifying herself to her kids, ends up on a sitcom that is supposed to be one of the cleanest. I thought that was such a perfect irony, because the song is so deep.

GC You know, everybody was trying to hustle to take care of their kids. Everywhere you looked. Nobody was hustling for the sake of hustling. They had to justify it in their own mind.

AQT In most black narratives, it's never that humanized. In *Cosmic Slop* there is such a vulnerability in the narrative.

GC I hear you coming, but I gotta tell you, we were on acid, man (Laughs). I do believe it was the acid talking because I'm not like that. I come from the streets. Believing in peace and love was corny to me. I mean, we all became hippies but I was out there chasing skirt. I'm sorry to say that, but that's where we were at the time. That type of story came from me looking around what was going on in the streets. Don't hide it. Say it. The story ain't mine but it is somebody's. I just paint the picture of what's going around me every day. I had this conversation with Ice Cube when he wanted to do a version of *One Nation Under a Groove*, I said: 'Man, you just did this record saying horrible things.' He replied: 'No, Mr Clinton. I'm just mirroring what I see on the street.' That's what he was doing. If you lie about it, you perpetrate it even more. That's the way I feel about it.

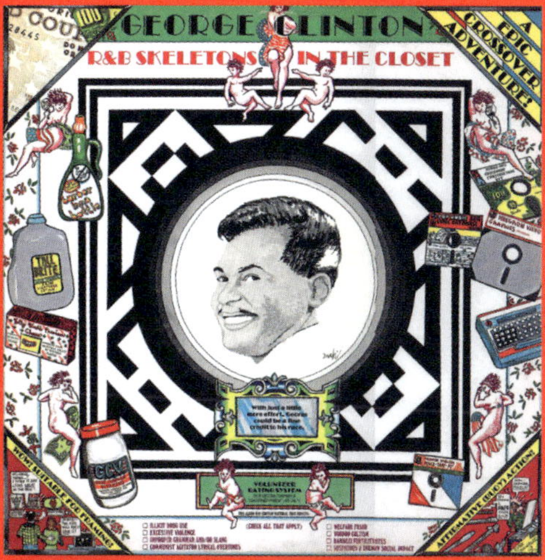

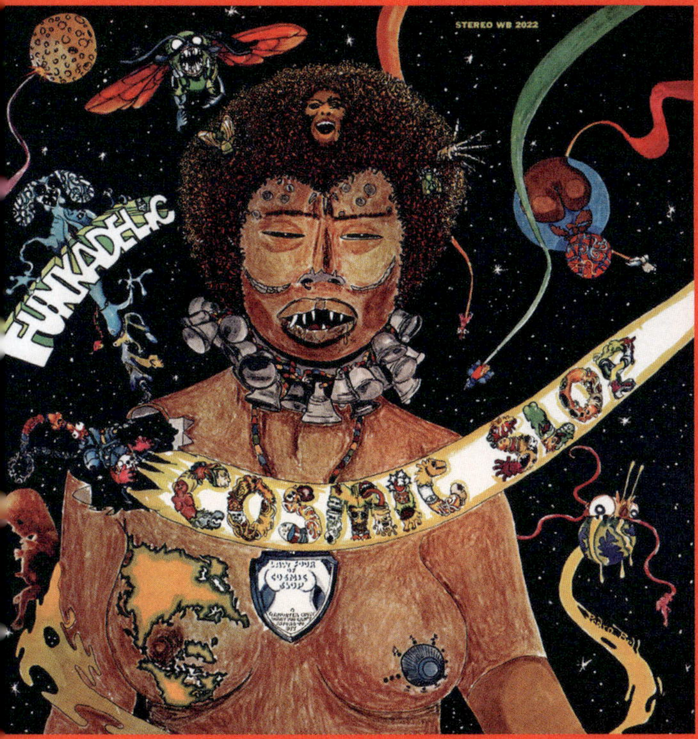

AQT Around the time of *Cosmic Slop* your relationship with artist and illustrator Pedro Bell started, who's best known for the elaborate cover designs and artworks for numerous Funkadelic and George Clinton solo albums. So much work and detail went into the actual artwork of the record sleeves. The Funkadelic artwork became quintessential for my understanding of the band and the music. It was almost like watching a video.

GC Yeah, you can take it to the bathroom and read it for weeks.

AQT How did you meet Pedro Bell?

GC He used to write me letters. All the envelopes were covered with his drawings of these creatures and concepts. One day the Postmaster General came to my house because he wanted to know what kind of organization I was involved in. I mean, they had an eye on us at the time anyway. I thought that if Pedro's drawings are that powerful I should ask him to do the album cover. I told him about *Cosmic Slop* and what the album was about. You see, he had alien pimps and cosmic hoes. That was Pedro's theme. We're still working together. He's legally blind now, but he still illustrated my last album.

↑ *R&B Skeletons in the Closet*, George Clinton, 1986. Art by Pedro Bell.

↖ *Uncle Jam Wants You*, Funkadelic, 1979. Art by Pedro Bell.

← *Cosmic Slop*, Funkadelic, 1973. Art by Pedro Bell.

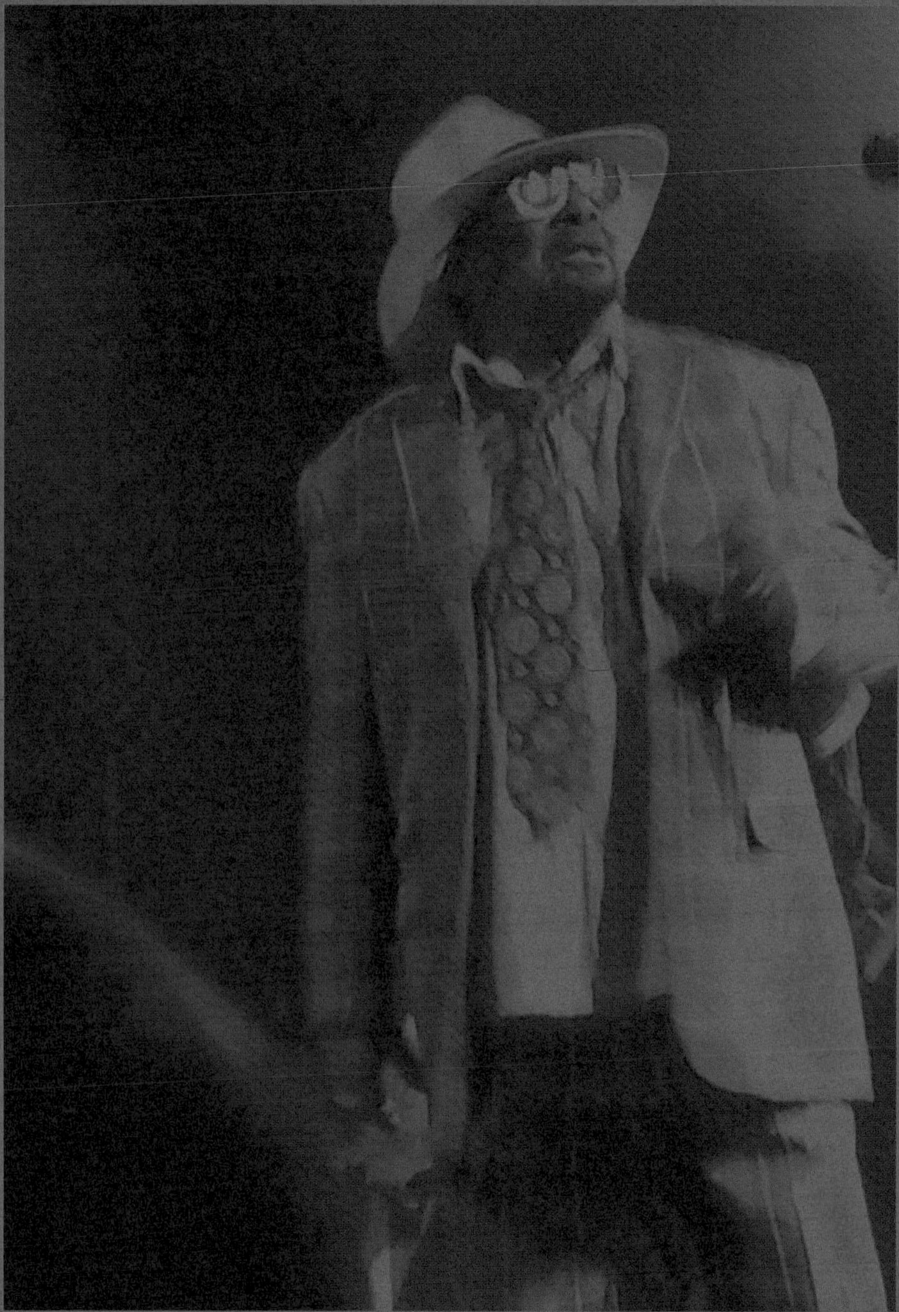

↖ George Clinton performing in Auckland, New Zealand, 2015. Photo by Corry Harris.

→ Ahmir Questlove Thompsone in Sao Paulo, Brazil, 2011. Source: Flickr. Author: maissoma.

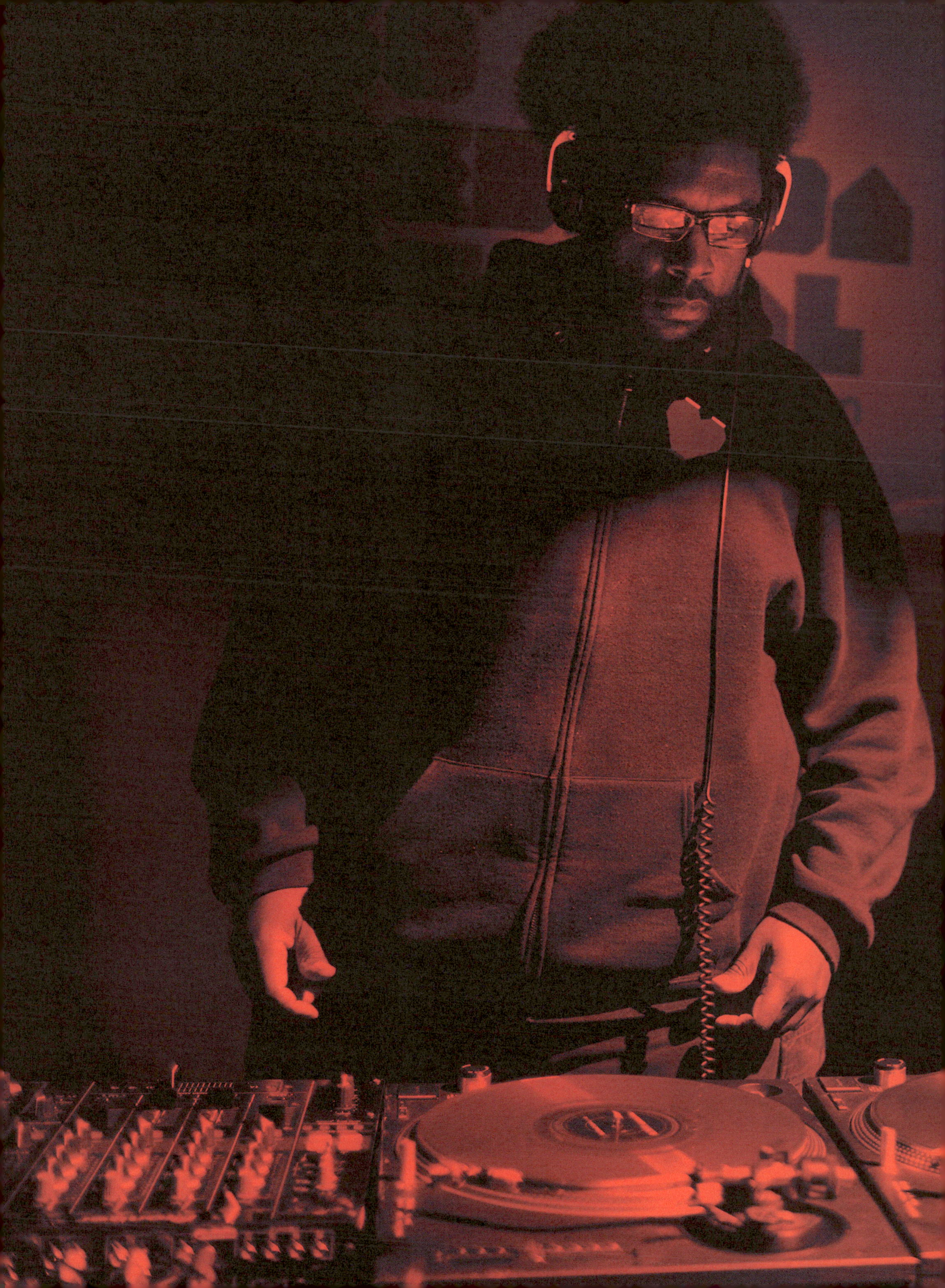

‘Everybody was trying to hustle to take care of their kids. Everywhere you looked. Nobody was hustling for the sake of hustling.’

GEORGE CLINTON

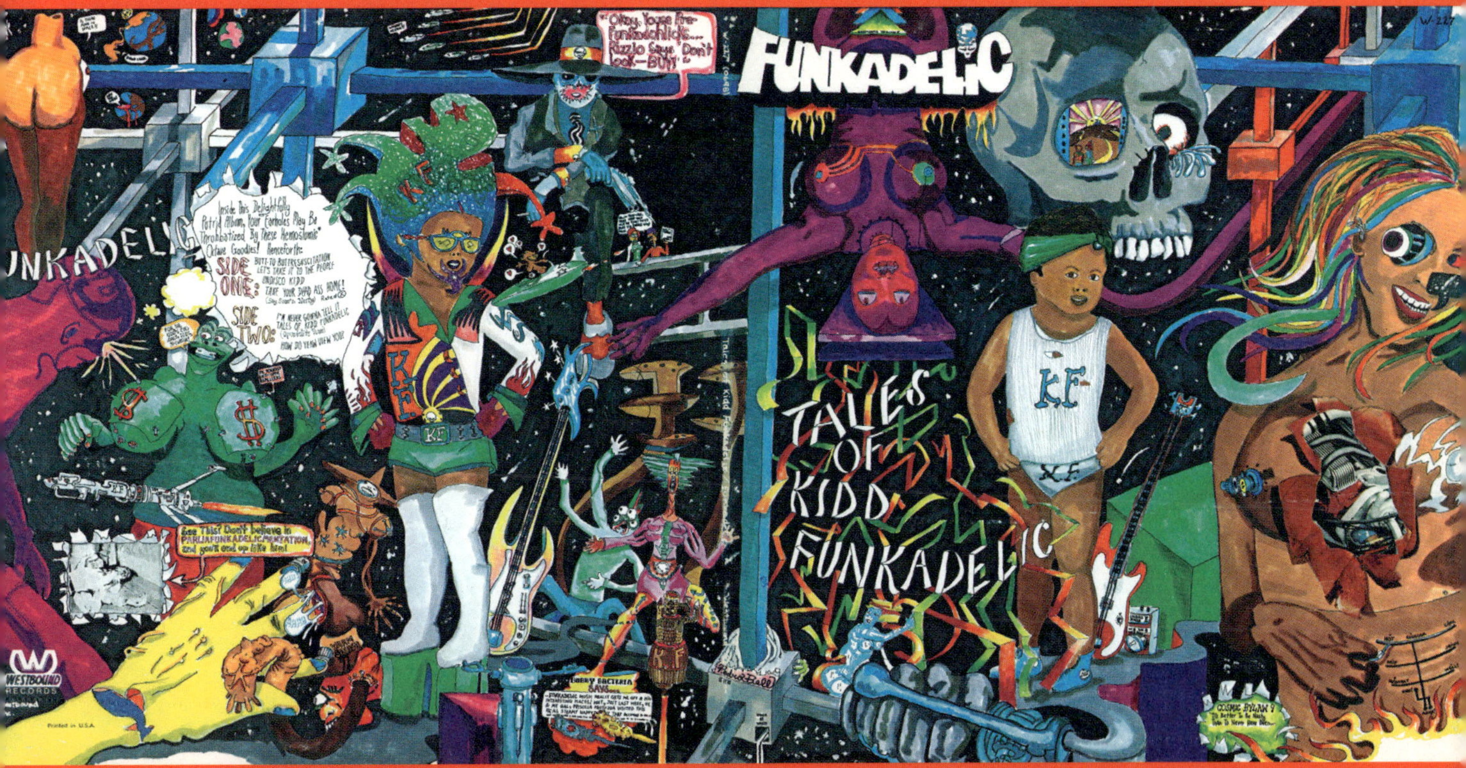

↑ Funkadelic, *Tales of Kidd*, 1976. Art by Pedro Bell.

AQT I noticed that on Funkadelic's *Let's Take it to the Stage* (1974) you are playfully calling out your peers of the moment: Snufus, James Clown, Earth, Hot Air and No Fire, Fool and the Gang. What was that about?

GC It's the same theory as in hip hop, when they diss each other knowing that it's a game. The first one who gets mad is the loser. We did it really playfully, we tried to nudge only at people we liked.

AQT Was there never any friction about it?

GC I think only Earth, Wind and Fire felt some sort of way about it. They even put us off the show once and sent us home. When they started to include some pyramids and things like that in their design they were straight biting off us. I felt good. I felt some kind of way too. (Laughs)

AQT Where did the whole Funkadelic P-Funk sci-fi afro-futuristic mythology and mysticism stem from? Are you going to say acid again? (Laughs)

GC I could, but I was into these things ever since Star Trek. It was probably just some weed, no acid. You know what I'm saying. This is early sixties.

AQT I read in your book *Brothas Be, Yo Like George, Ain't That Funkin' Kinda Hard On You?: A Memoir* (2014) that you had some kind of a close encounter of a third kind. Is that true?

GC Yeah, that happened for real, and we wasn't on drugs. Bootsy Collins and myself, we were on our way to Toronto, where I was living at the time, when we saw a light come out of the clouds - a straight beam, like a laser. First, neither one of us said anything but when we were driving home to my place, we saw the same light coming right down through the trees a block and a half in front of us; like a live-wire. Electricity sparkling. Bam. A second later, on the other side of the street, in the block we were in, and a third one right on the hood of the car. When that happened, we noticed all of the streetlights started coming on. It was suddenly getting dark. When we arrived at my place, my daughter came out of the house and said: 'You guys look like you've seen a ghost!' Man, we were just sitting there. That was around the time when we just finished the Parliament's *Mothership Connection* (1975) album. When that record came out and became a hit and Bootsy's debut album *Stretchin' Out in Bootsy's Rubber Band* (1976) came out and became a hit too, we knew it was on.

This conversation between Ahmir Questlove Thompson and George Clinton was originally recorded upon the release of Clinton's latest book, "Brothas Be, Yo Like George, Ain't That Funkin' Kinda Hard on You?: A Memoir." at Schomburg Center for Research in Black Culture in New York. Courtesy of Schomburg Center for Research in Black Culture, The New York Public Library, 2015.

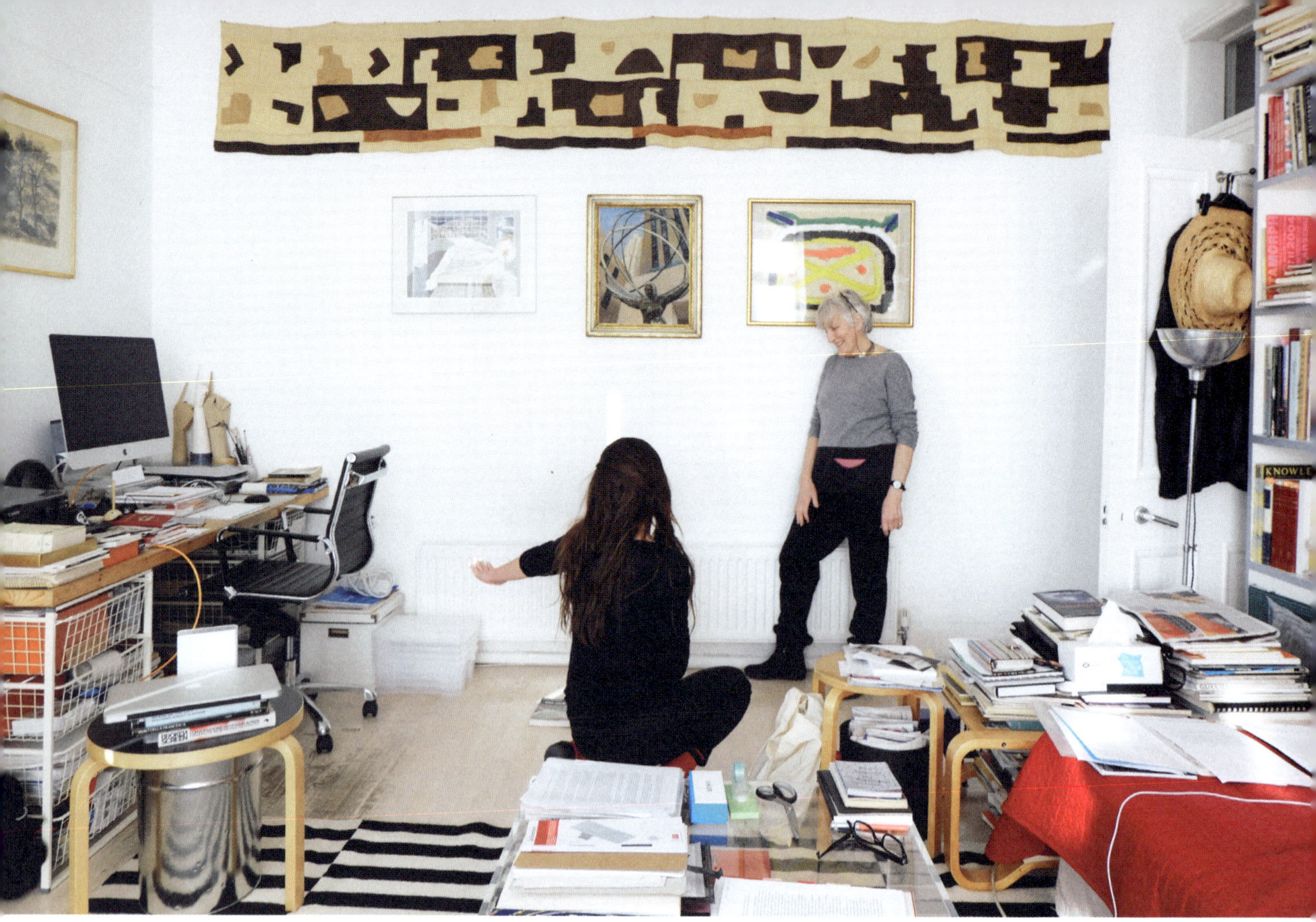

I've Just Never Learned to Say No

Diana Ibáñez López and Madelon Vriesendorp

Two similar minds, Spanish architect DIANA IBÁNEZ LÓPEZ and Dutch artist MADELON VRIESENDORP, engage in a free-form conversation, sharing stories and territories and their mutual love of hybridity.

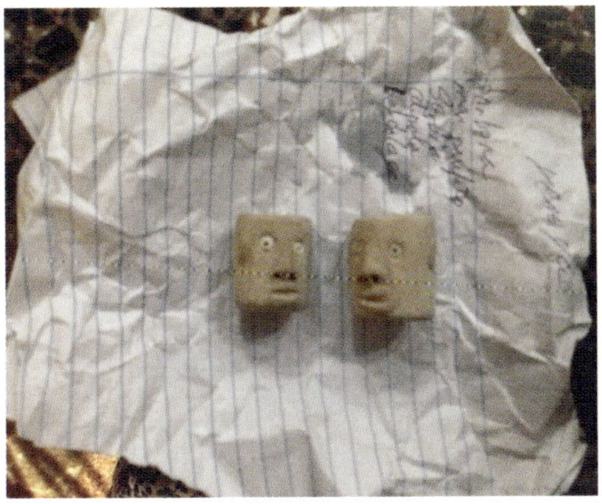

Skirting around the port of Havana in search of the pre-fab housing blocks shipped from Russia as ballast during the missile crisis and hastily thrown up by the docks, I come across a shop counter piled with two-faced, shocked mud heads, their expressions carved with a pin and punctuated by beady staring eyes. It is *Elegua*, spirit-messenger of roads. I buy two—one for myself, the other for Madelon Vriesendorp's collection of *Exus*, a Yoruba-Christian hybrid spirit-form. In her kitchen, she picks hers out with precision. 'It looks just like a friend', she says, without saying whom. She accepts her head with the same kinetic delight she accepted this article: 'Career? I have no career! It's just that I've never learnt to say no.'

I recognize that resistance to being defined as any one thing, as a logical progression of projects. The ever-tedious question 'What do you do?' triggers in me a guttural 'a—' as I gauge if it's worth diving in, or whether '—architecture' will do.

OUTSIDER ART, OUTSIDE ARCHITECTURE

In her living room, one of the 'bad paintings' that Maddie and **Rem (Koolhaas)** **(page → 18)** collected for *Delirious New York* hangs in the central spot, barging aside *Flagrant Délit*, Maddie's best-known work. I notice that the words 'bad', 'stupid' and 'ugly' are lavished on a number of objects around us with an immense amount of care.

In the kitchen sits A collection of 70 model chairs, constructed and amassed throughout a lifetime. The smallest of them measures 12.5mm, and the largest 30cm in height. They have just come home from the exhibition in Lina Bo Bardi's home—where they were installed in the Bo Bardi fireplace—having been plucked from Maddie's wider collection especially for it.

As we talk, a long yellow chair is taken from the set and placed back into its other place in the collection—under a gift-shop figurine from *The Garden of Earthly Delights*. The chair and the figurine appear as a duo in Maddie's frieze of Dutch, Belgian and French cultural icons that decorated the Thalys fast train buffet car.

I find it liberating that her collection has this kind of fluidity. It affirms my own experience of how different bits of work tie together over time, with

↖ Diana Ibáñez López and Madelon Vriesendorp, 2018 Photo by Gili Merin.

← *Exus* bought in Havana 2018.Photo by Diana Ibáñez López.

↓ Madelon Vriesendorp's collection of model chairs, just returned from the Bo Bardi fireplace. Photo by Gili Merin.

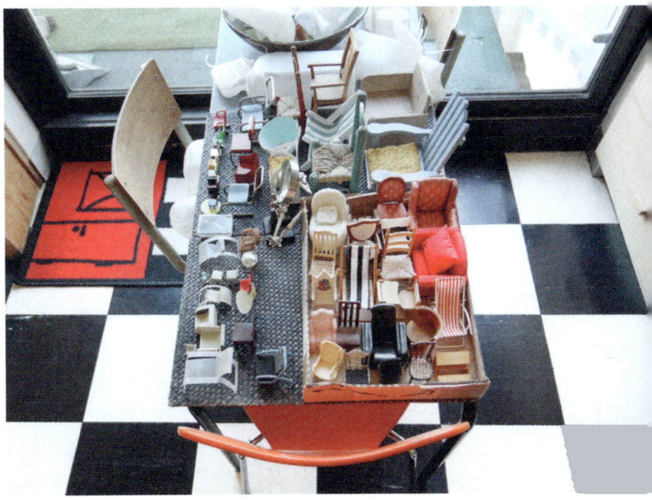

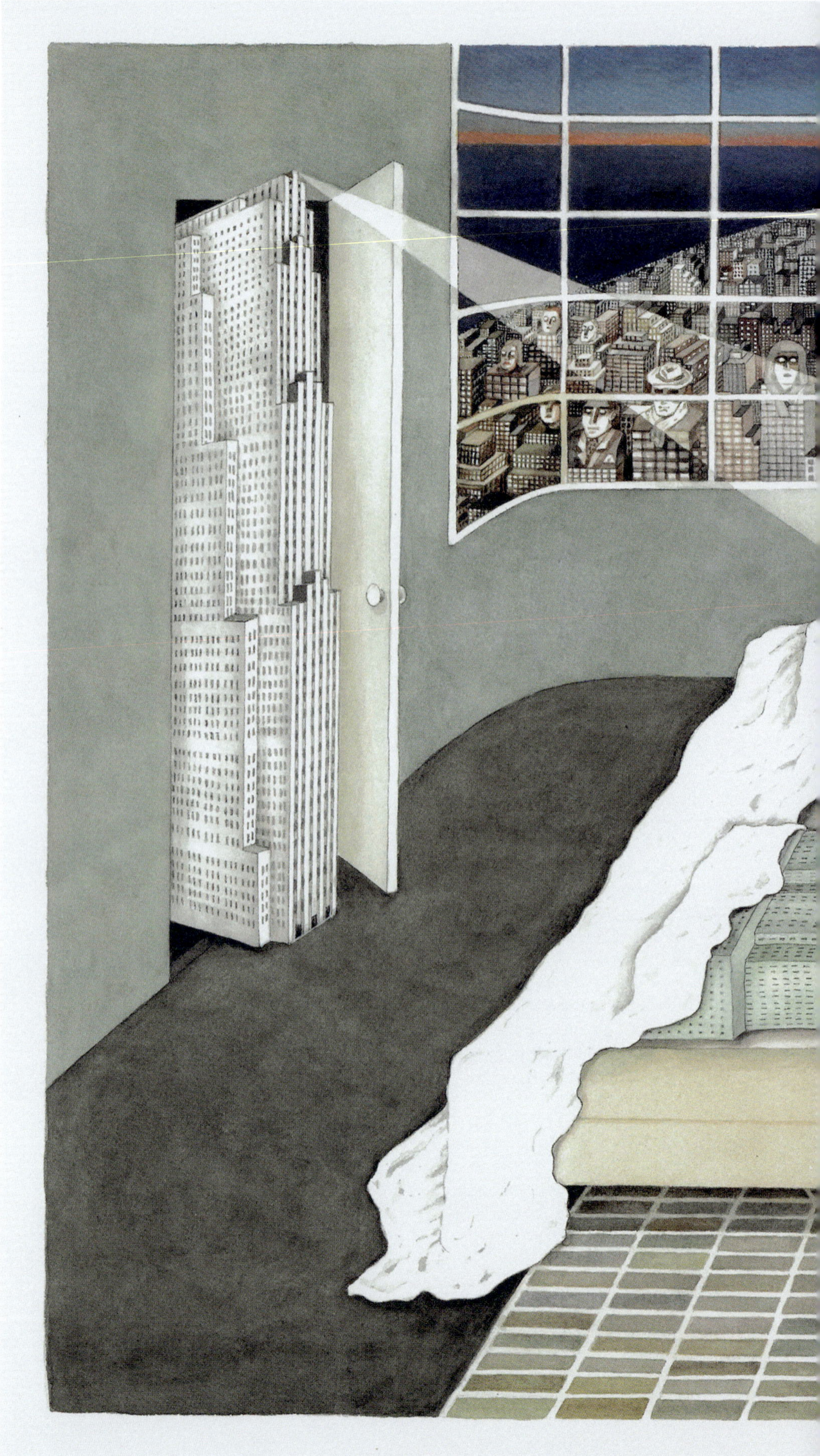

→ Madelon Vriesendorp
Flagrant Delit, Version II, 1975.

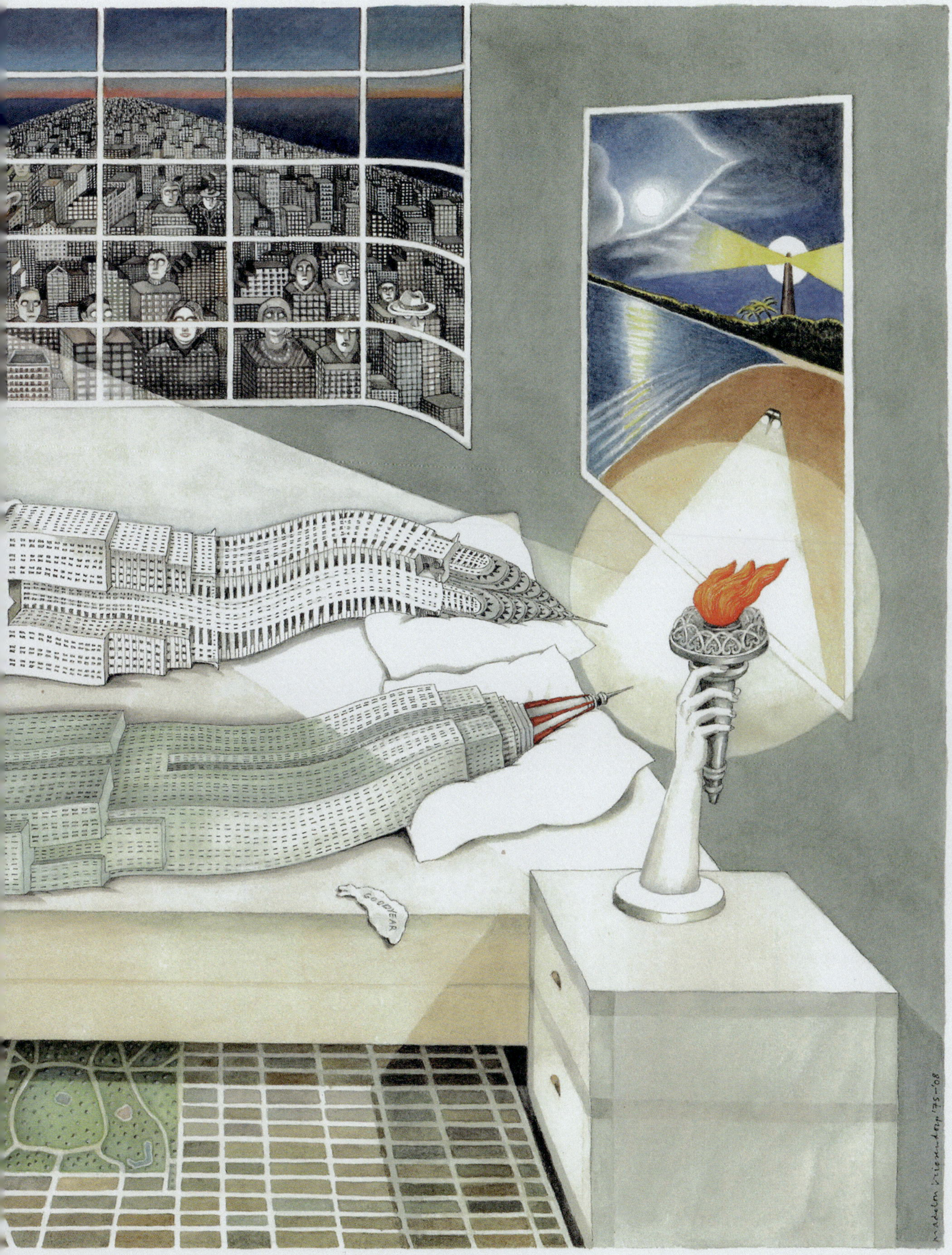
GOODYEAR

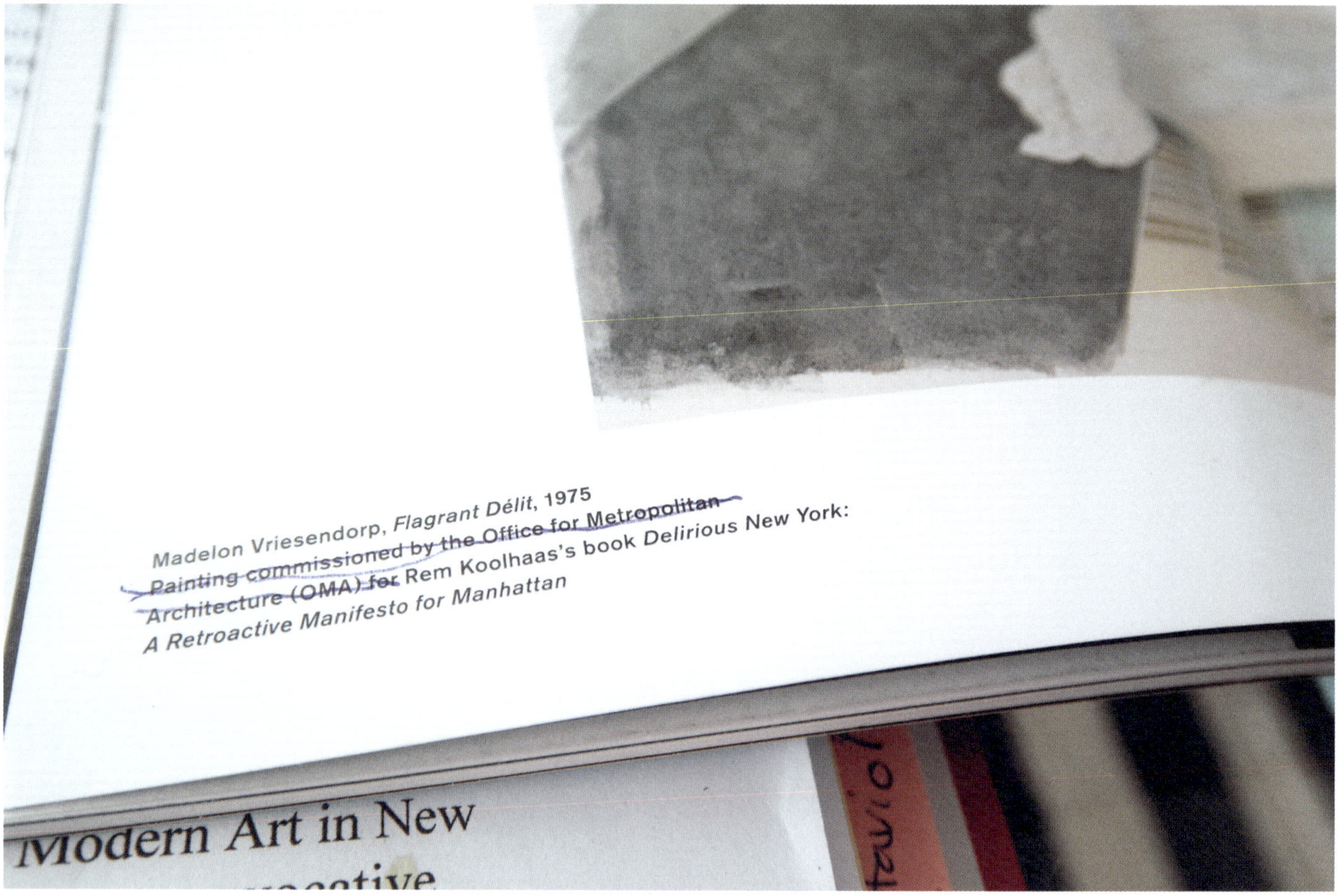
Madelon Vriesendorp, Flagrant Délit, 1975
Painting commissioned by the Office for Metropolitan
Architecture (OMA) for Rem Koolhaas's book Delirious New York:
A Retroactive Manifesto for Manhattan
Modern Art in New

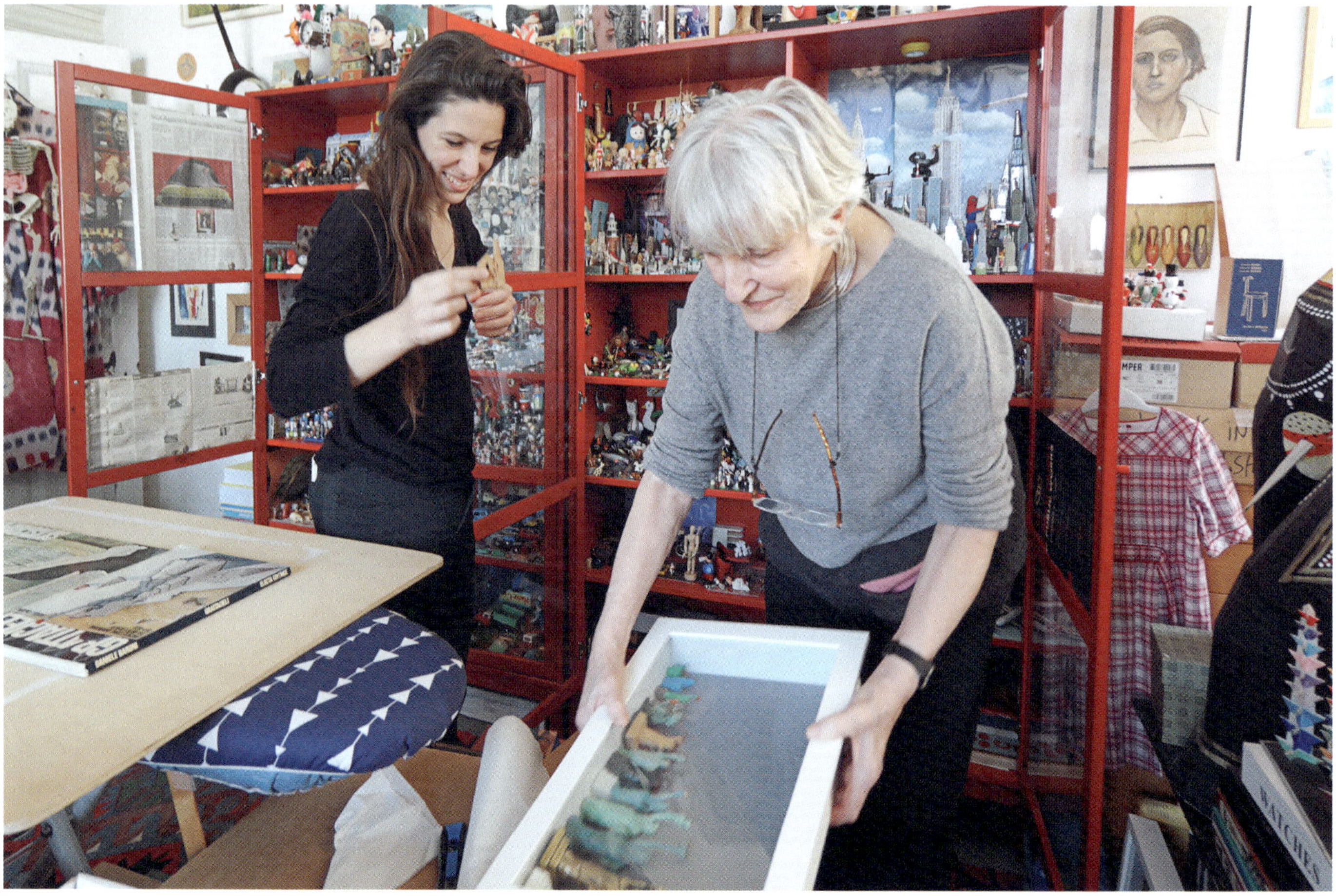
WATCHES

changes and disjunctions not making sense until years later: MVRDV (architecture); Cairo (editorial, research, design); Phaidon Press (editorial, research, architecture); Münster University (literature research on blank space); Timeline.com (app start-up, journalism); The Why Factory (editorial, research, architecture, teaching); Regeneration at a London local authority (commissioning architecture, strategy); UCL (urbanism, teaching); Royal College of Art (architecture, teaching); HfG Karlsruhe (product design, teaching); and Create London (arts, charity, architecture, commissioning, research, outreach, policy).

In summary, I'm not an 'architect.' I find myself nodding forcefully as Maddie summarises her practice as an instinctual involvement with the people around her:

> 'Whatever people asked me, I just did it.' (Laughs)
>
> This is an old-fashioned way of working. It's not just doing one thing that you repeat and repeat. A lot of people do that, things get bigger and bigger and they get a reputation. I become smaller.'

#MENEITHER

A few days before we meet, Maddie is awarded the Ada Louise Huxtable Prize for women working in the wider architecture industry, in recognition of her significant contribution to architecture and the built environment.

> 'I have to prepare the talk for this prize. I'm going to start a movement of #meneither instead of #metoo, for all those women who have not been recognised for the things they have done.'
>
> 'Like this: "Painting commissioned by the Office"—which didn't exist yet—"for Rem Koolhaas's book!" It's so annoying!'
>
> 'They haven't even cropped the edges. It's the same hysterical quest for authenticity, like the way they stripped the colour off Sienna to make it authentic. Now people say 'All that stone, lovely', but it's not lovely, it's completely wrong!
>
> Reinier de Graaf wrote a book lately and my watercolour of the *City of the Captive Globe* is again credited to Zoe. The mistake was never noticed in the back of the original *Delirious New York* and every edition was credited wrongly thereafter.'

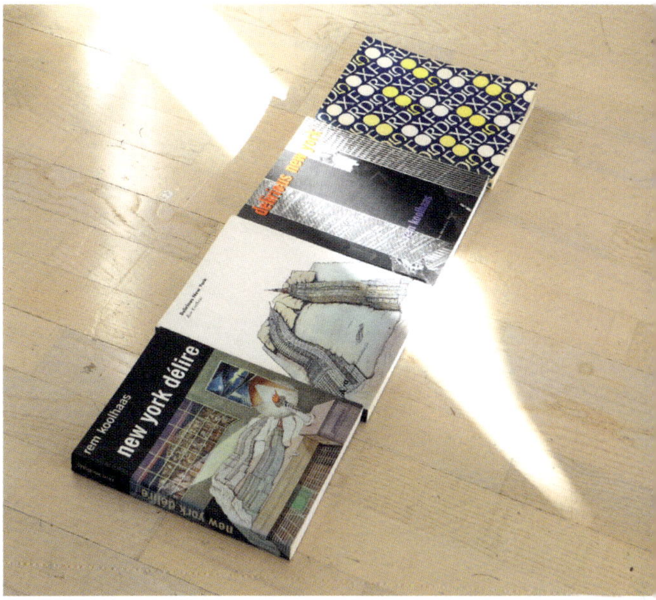

↖ Erroneous caption for *Flagrant Délit*. Photo by Gili Merin.

↙ In Madelon Vriesendorp's studio. Photo by Gili Merin.

↑ *The Gradual, Inevitable March Towards Amnesia*. Photo by Gili Merin.

↱ Madelon Vriesendorp, *Atelier HSL: Thalys Frieze Project*, Paris, 2011.

To illustrate the point, Maddie lays out four editions of *Delirious New York*, and tracks the use, blurring, then gradual erasure of *Flagrant Délit* from its cover, a process of editorial attrition and disregard she has titled *The Gradual, Inevitable March Towards Amnesia*.

I ask about the origins of *Flagrant Délit*, before it became part of *The Inevitable March* series.

> 'While we collected postcards I did a series of paintings. It wasn't really meant for this cover at all. I was just doing my own thing.
>
> 'Then, a man called Baroni put it on the cover of a book he presented at the Frankfurt Book Fair. He never asked me for permission to use my work. We had sent some pictures to a publisher, and he just gave out my paintings. Then an editor said to Rem, "You're crazy, everybody was intrigued by the cover at the fair, why don't you use it?"'

Maddie has added the Baroni cover to her collection, arranged on a drawing board, so that the painting is whole again.

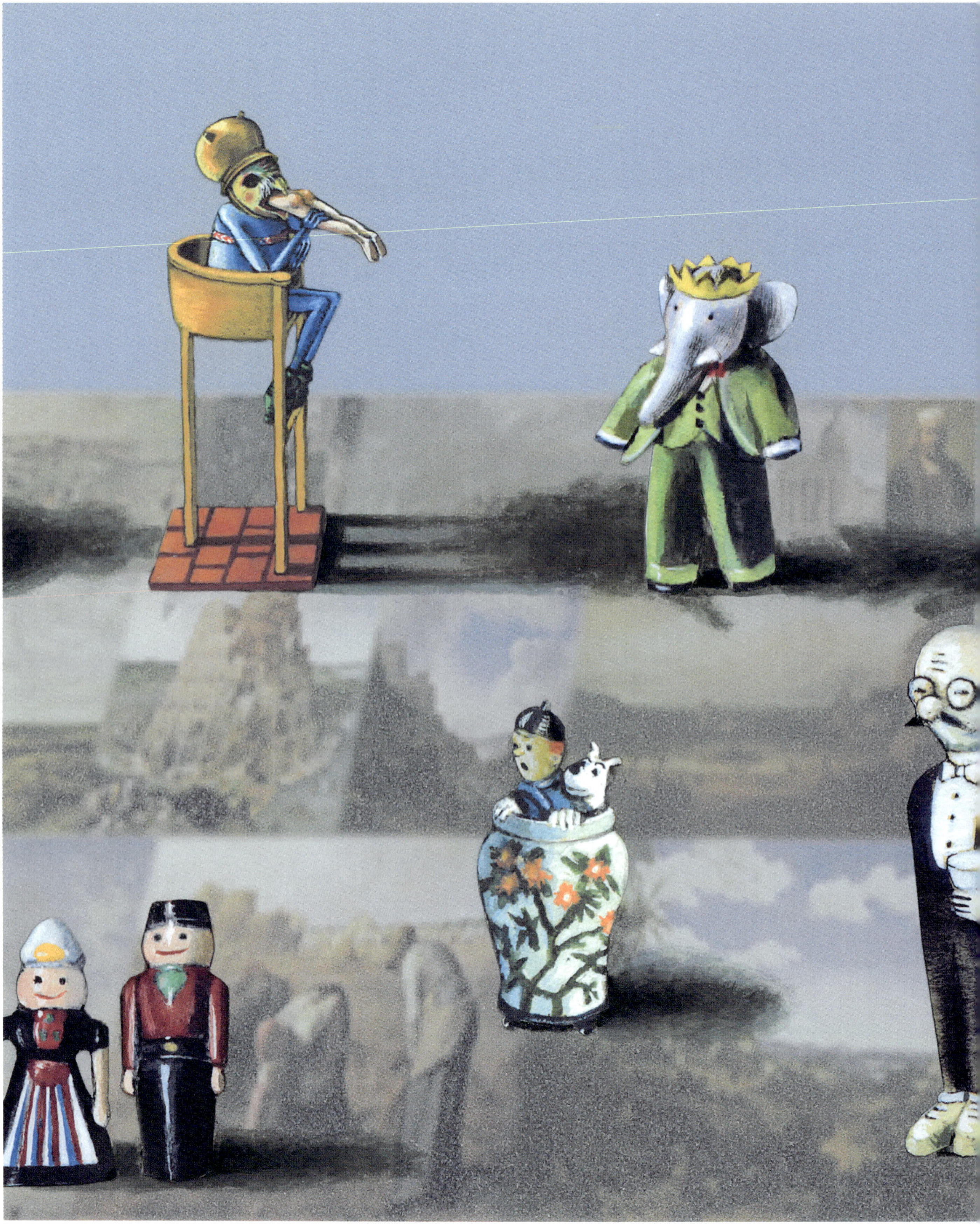

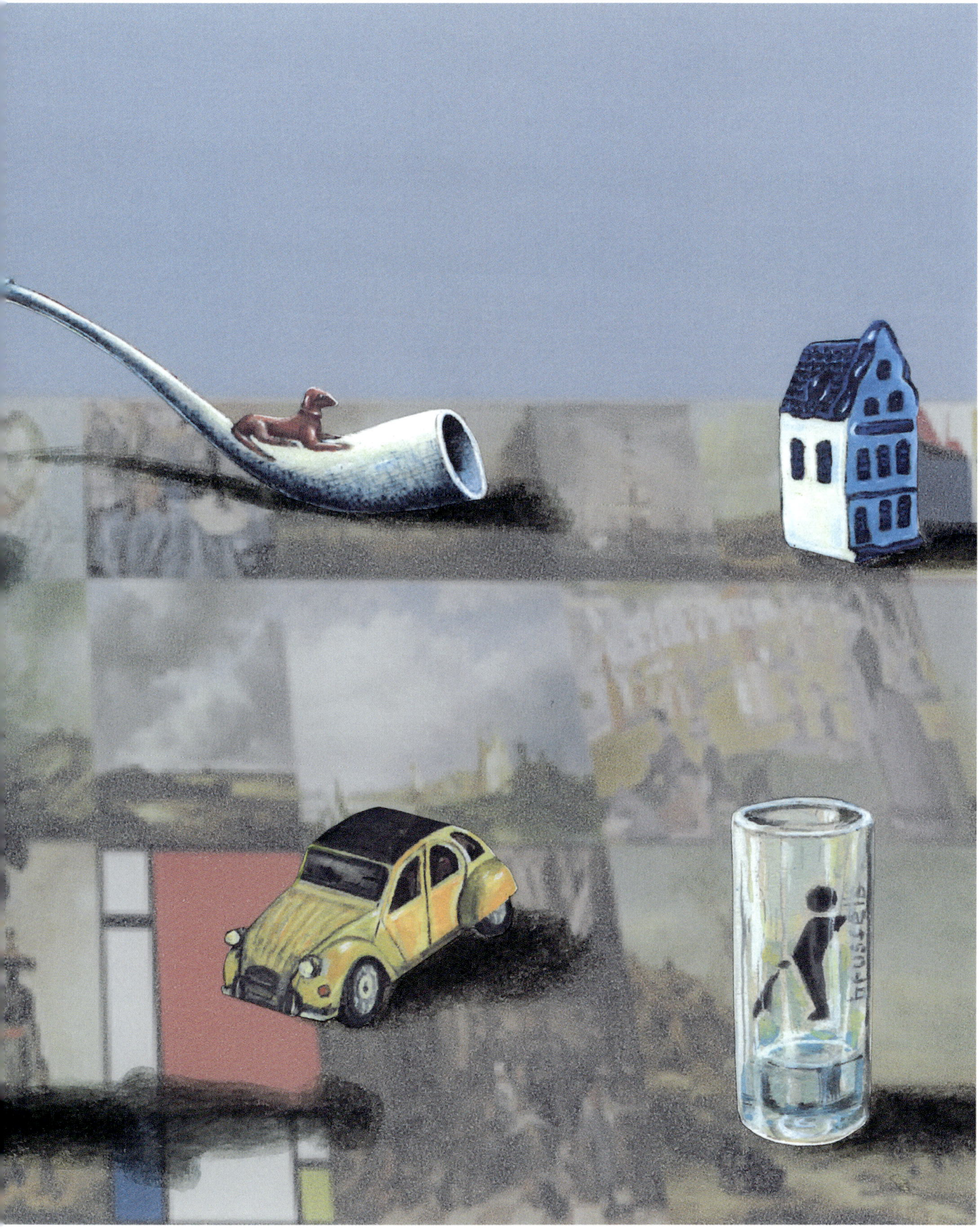

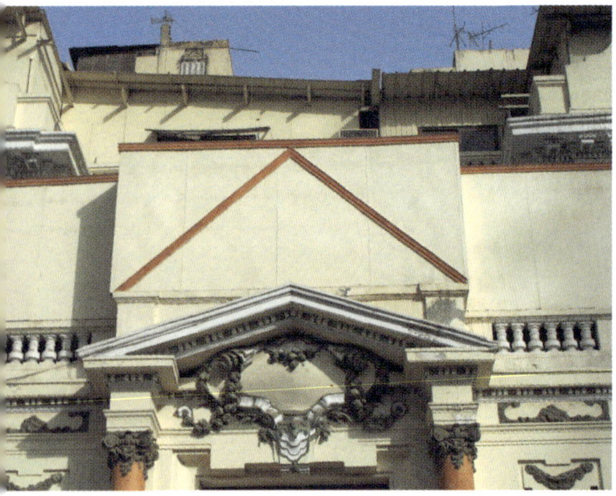

'...I don't want the prize acceptance speech to be some sort of enormous lament. Lots of positive stuff came out of it.'

IRRESISTIBLE AMBIGUITY

Like *Délit* and *Exodus*, the teasing cityscape of Maddie's cabinets twists our understanding of normality. This perspective of the city, the future city, gives utterance to the approximate, to the unknown and the uncomfortable. It's a space of ambiguity that is very fertile for design.

The photo above is one of my favourites from my time in Cairo. It is the confused façade of a police station near where I lived. It reminds me of The Why Factory, which I had helped design the year before. Both of these buildings tease the rules of the system without merely breaking them.

← Police station in Cairo's Mounira district, 2009 Photo by Diana Ibáñez López.

↙ MVRDV The Why Factory, Delft, 2009. Photo by Rob 't Hart.

→ Diana's collection of 99 names of Allah laid out in Madelon's living room. Photo by Gili Merin.

What excites me about the police station is the middle storey. It samples the colonial-era villa architecture with some respect, but not too much. It is just as respectful of the crinkly-tin extension above, and its flimsy material only manages to feign formality through the approximate mimicking of a pediment. The informal-looking third storey is also implicit in this ambiguous hybridity—it is an informal build, but formal in use, and is careful to match itself to the official beige below. As Maddie writes in *Freaks of Culture*, an article published in *Bidoun 14* to accompany The World of Madelon Vriesendorp exhibition at the AA,

> 'The objects that miss their target most are often the most irresistible.'

This blurred line between the official and unofficial drove the design of The Why Factory tribune. The

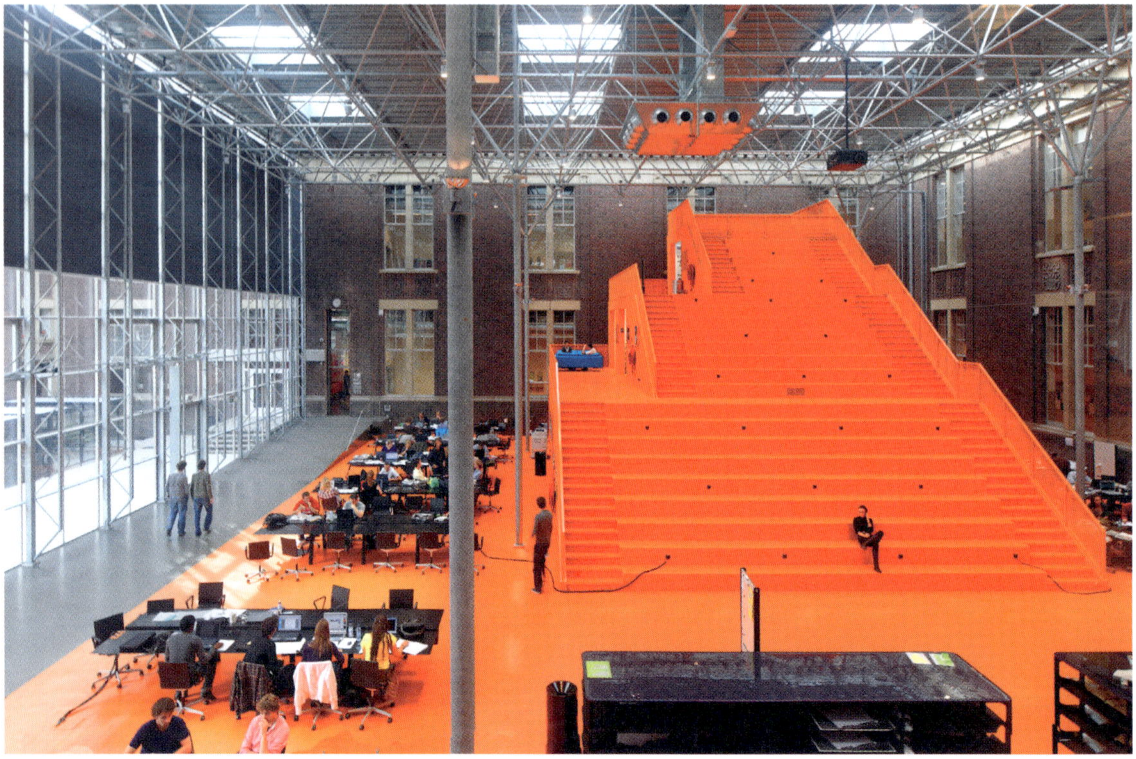

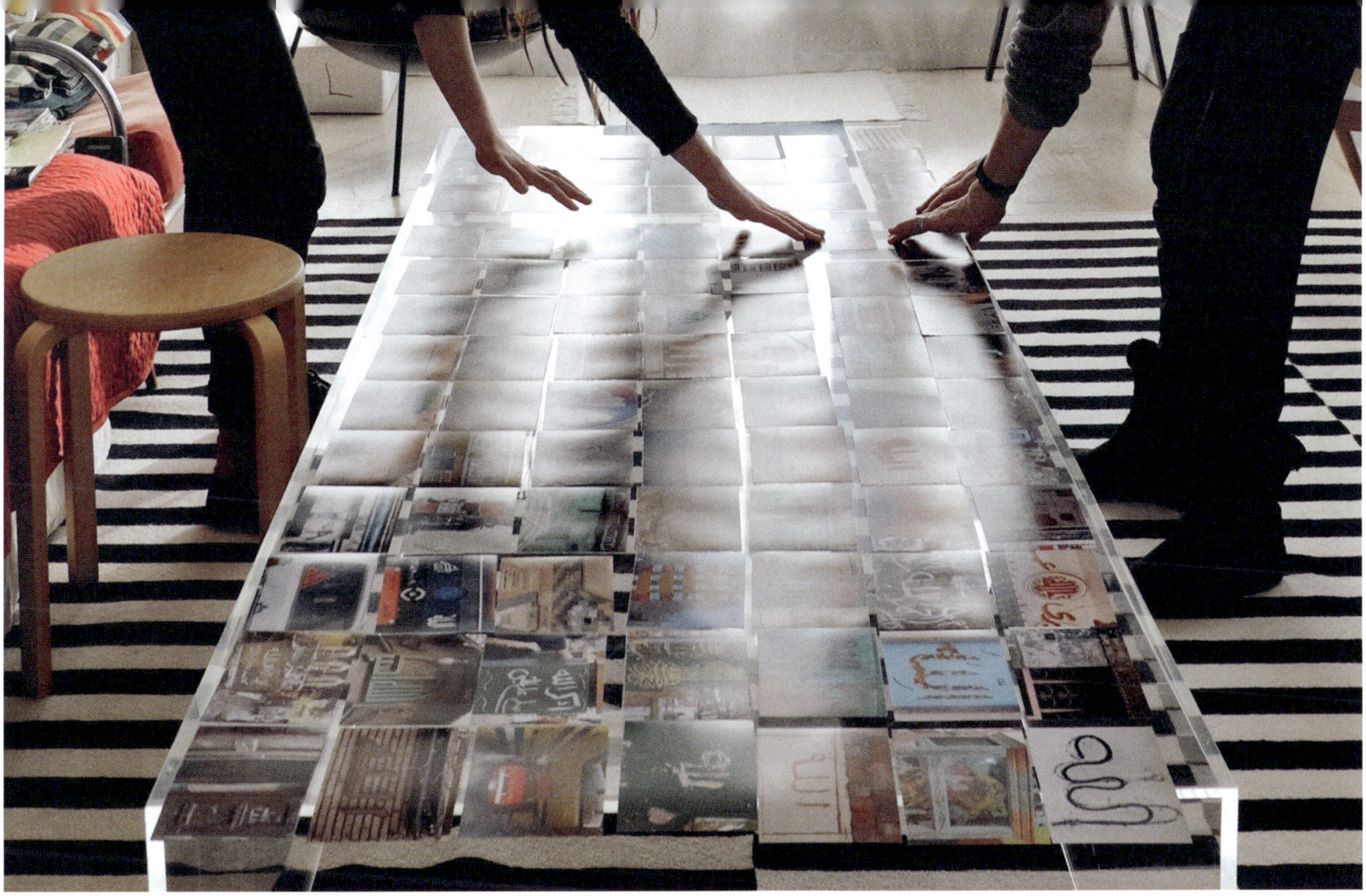

original brief for the building strictly capped it at two storeys due to fire risk, and asked, simply, for four bland faculty offices with studio space around them. We tweaked the brief by negotiating a little extra height above the fire regulation, for a little room seldom used (housing a photocopier)—to create an immense lecture hall on the outside of the stacked rooms, which places the students, literally, above the tutors: a deliberately 'pop', official accident of the design process.

Together the building I made and the one I found make a pair in my collection; they showcase this 'irresistible ambiguity.' They are also tripartite, temple-like and orange.

OBSESSIVE COLLECTING

In Islam, Allah has 99 names or attributes—known as the *Most Beautiful Names*—that scholars learn by rote. According to Hadith, anyone who memorises them will enter paradise. I spread 99 across Maddie's living room table. They're a collection of the name of God inscribed into the built environment, the opposite of a scholarly, laboured process of inscription into the mind. In a semi-literate city the promised paradise seems a world away, but, in a popular twist, the one 'original' name of Allah appears again and again as decoration, blessing, securing a profane and often inconsequential space. On Cairo's streets, I collected the *Name manifest* as glue residue, manicured hedge, chip-fat, stick-on stained glass, plaster ventilation bricks, gold bubble writing, neon cable and more: the divine in the wider architecture industry.

The celebration of hybrid, weird, 'low' culture manifestations forms the heart of both our collections. The *Names* may seem to say only one thing—unlike the official scholarly attributes—but they are, if anything, less repetitive, because each is intensively and materially descript. Each *Name* has a voice. Like the chair of the Hieronymus Bosch figure, each *Name* can simultaneously belong to a number of sub-collections of the cultures of Cairo.

Together, of course, they make a paradisiacal set. I lay them out on an empty vitrine, originally made to hold Maddie's collection for her solo retrospective at the AA, and which she rescued after the show, loathe to see anything thrown away. In the spirit of giving each object individual voice, she resisted an initial temptation to install a cityscape inside, because removed from the exhibition she discovered the uncanny beauty of the thick Perspex and the space it holds when empty.

> 'There's one too many to fit on the table—it's a sign!'

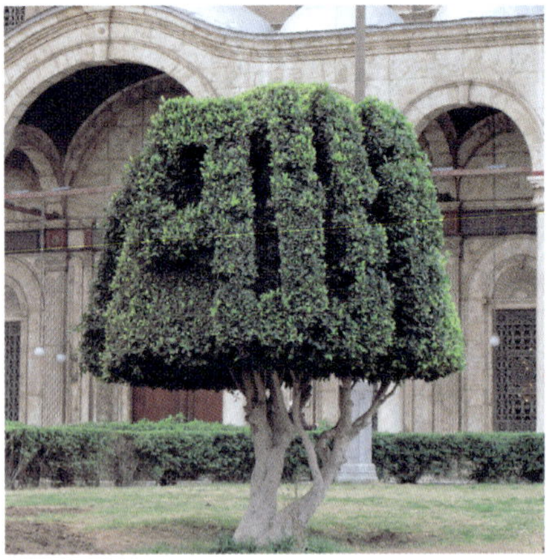

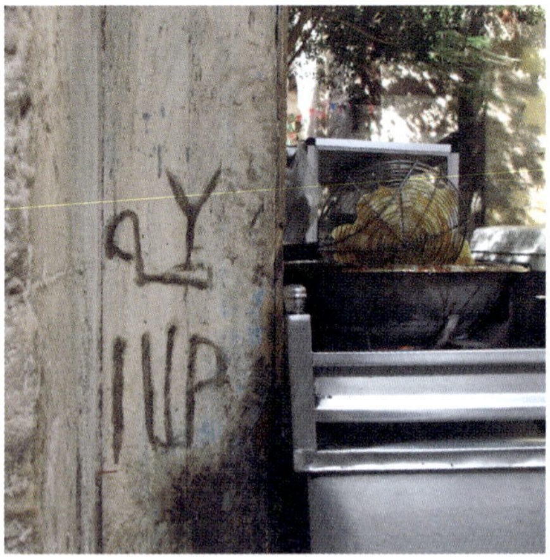

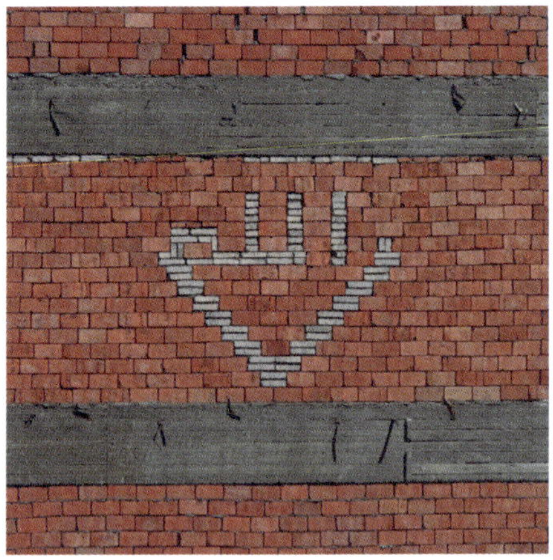

SIGNS AND INTUITION

Before I leave I play *The Mind Game*, and Maddie ends her reading of my psyche by checking an old book of Chinese horoscopes, to better decipher my placement of the art object, the fish and snake, dangling off the wall by its tail, in her stage set.

DIL I was due to be born on April fools', but I was characteristically late.

MV You are born in the week of the star! I have an amazing birthdate, 1-2-3-4-5. (12th March 1945… at 6am). I must have told you because I can't stop telling everybody.

Do you have music around you when you work? I have radio or music. There has to be something to distract my mind, something outside of it.

DIL I spent a couple of months working on the window grid for the Rotterdam Markethall, hundreds of iterations. That was when I started listening to Radio 4. Now, when I see the Rotterdam Market Hall's facade, I see spoken word radio.

What's your memory of what your horoscope says?

MV Mine is horrendously exact. It's so painful.

DIL It says you've got some great 'weaknesses': reckless and foolhardy!

MV Yes, taking unnecessary risks and still surviving. (laughs)

DIL And that you're prone to wanderlust?

MV I like to go to places. I don't have this thing you do of moving around, but I love to go to the not-so-glamorous places.

Visit the Pitt Rivers Museum. You'll love it, it has everything in it.

I don't like museums that show all the work of just one person; it's boring and the artist would have probably thought 'this is not good enough' about most of it. Better the collection of some crazy collector who sought out certain things: if they're all different things, not more of the same, then it is interesting.

DIL The great thing about collections is that whatever else the collector was doing or making, this was their way of thinking through the world.

MV Exactly, they collected all these things not to have to travel again. *(looks back at my arrangement of The Mind Game)*

'...Ahhh: you're an outsider.'

From Madelon Vriesendorp, that's a big compliment.

END

Photographs of the conversation by Gili Merin, an architect and photographer who writes about the fabrication of sacred landscapes.

↑ 6 of 99 names from the Allah series. Photos by Diana Ibáñez López.

↘ Madelon's studio. Photo by Gili Merin.

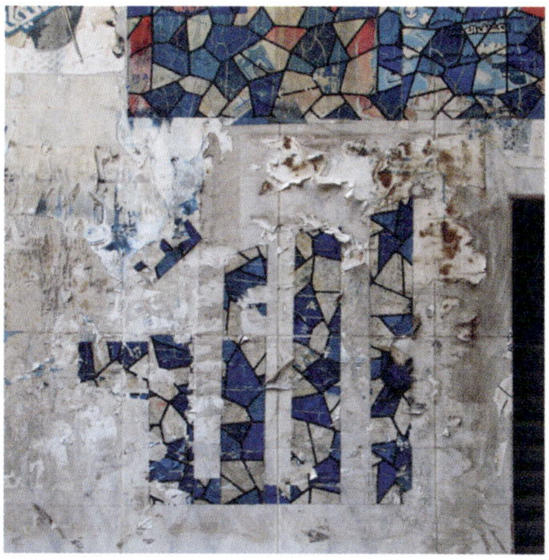

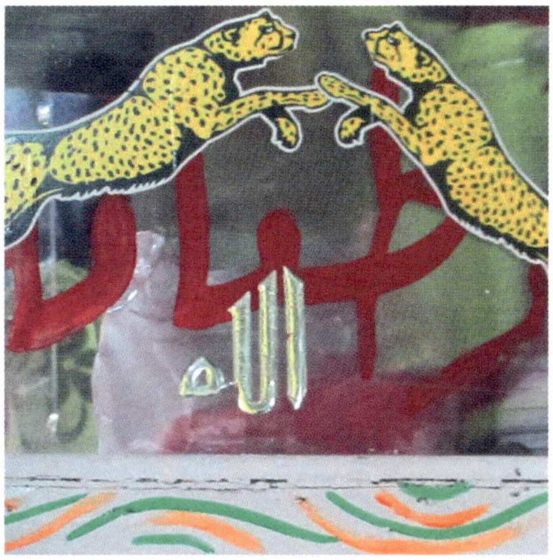

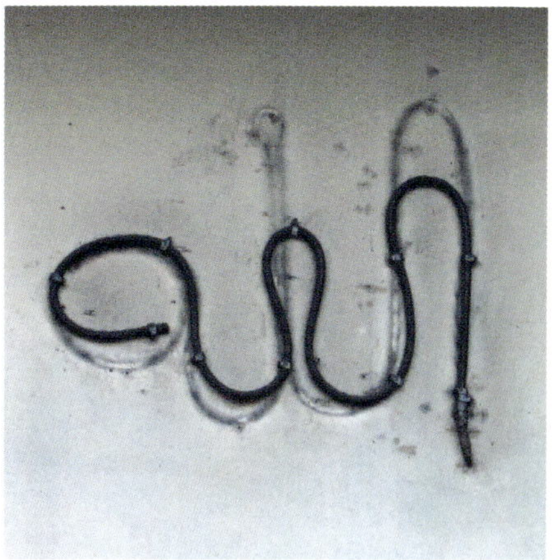

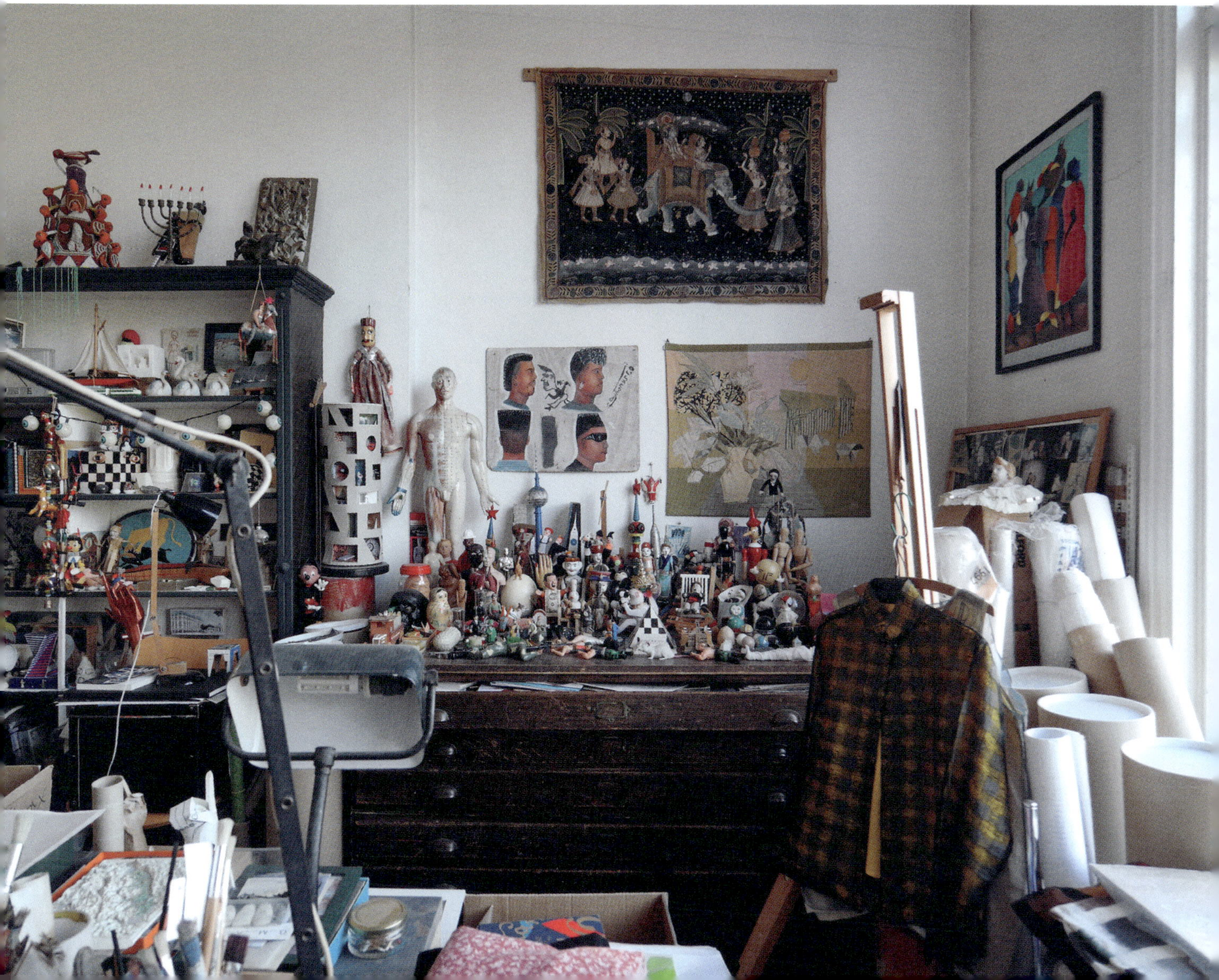

Dimensions of Imagination and Creativity

Rachel Libeskind and Daniel Libeskind

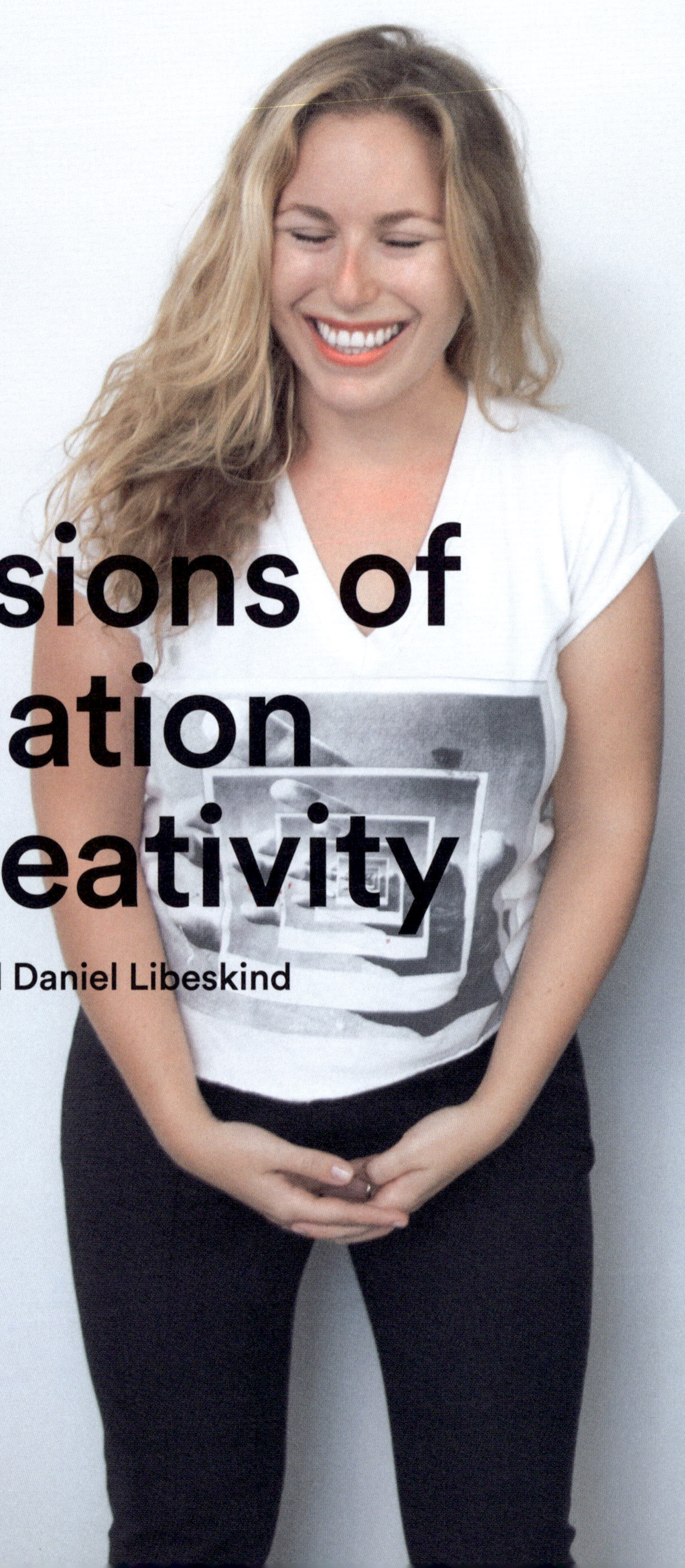

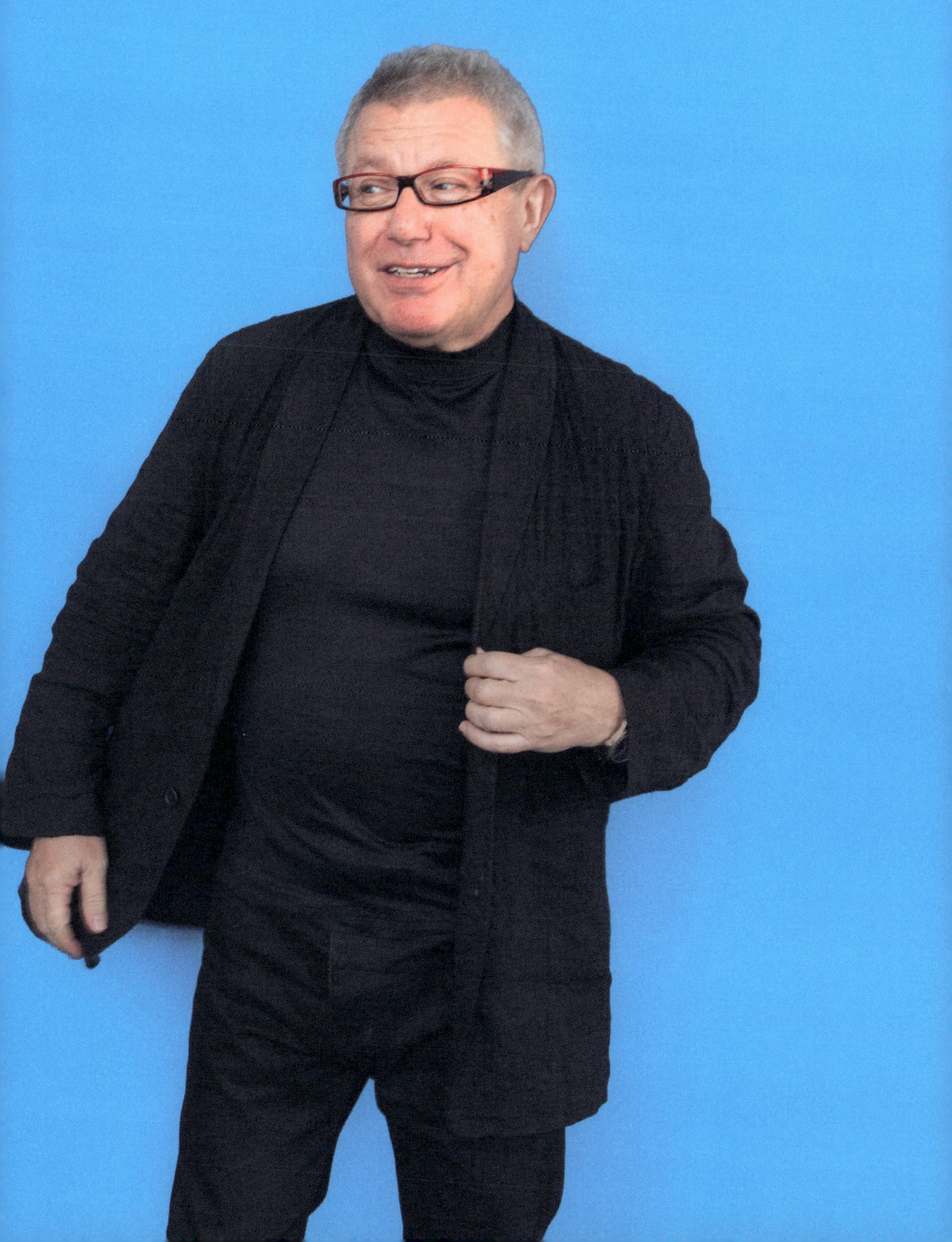

In an intellectual tour-de-force, artist RACHEL LIBESKIND and architect DANIEL LIBESKIND engage in a lively philosophical discussion on the notion of legacy in the arts in the past, present and future as well as the ultimate legacy of the Holocaust in the 20th century and beyond.

DANIEL LIBESKIND Legacy is a gift, passed through time, and so it's not something minor; it's really the dimension that includes imagination and creativity.

RACHEL LIBESKIND It's also something that one inherits, but in the inheriting, there is actually a burden because it's not a formally inherited object or title. It's actually something that has to be continually worked on, in order to be passed on in terms of a continued generational legacy.

DL The giver of this gift is unknown.

RL No, you are the giver of the gift!

DL No, you are the giver of the gift; the gift is coming from the future and the past simultaneously.

RL That's true—legacy is not something that goes from past to future but is actually something going in both directions.

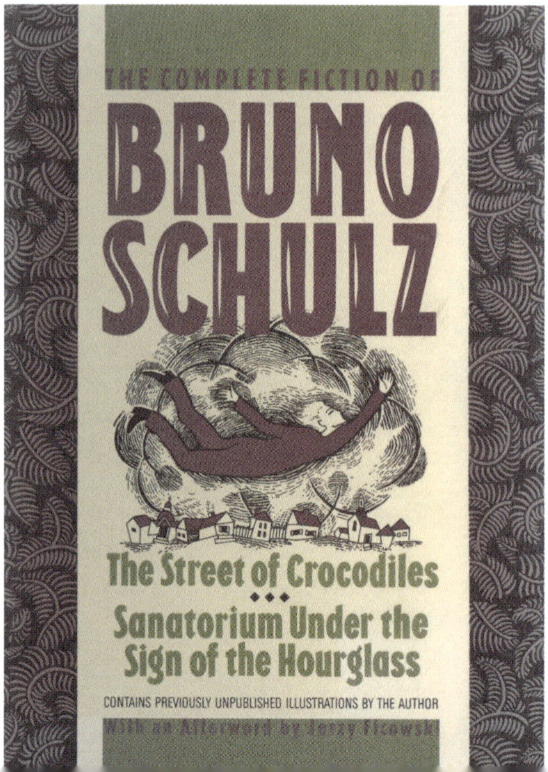

DL Bruno Schulz—whom I also read in Polish—particularly his essay *Treatise on Tailors' Dummies*, is to me a fundamental piece of a legacy that brings together deep Jewish roots with the world that has vanished and is coming into being. Very closely connected to it, as a part of this legacy, is *Hypnerotomachia Poliphili* by Francesco Colonna, which is a Renaissance narration of an impossible dream that is illustrated as a treatise for future architecture. I bring these books together as a part of a specific legacy, even though they have nothing explicitly to do with my work, they have always been lurking in the dreams I've had.

RL Bruno Schulz, specifically, comes out of a legacy that is very close to us genetically and geographically—a Jew of Ashkenazi descent living in Galicia, which is the area between Poland and Germany.

DL Drohobycz, where Schulz was born, was a centre of Jewish life. He suffered the fate of many Jews: they killed him like a dog. He was murdered on the street by a Schutzstaffel (SS) officer, who knew him well and kept him like a dog. That is also part of that book.

RL I discovered in reading the essays of Bruno Schulz, (which are less known than his books of short stories) that he refers to the image from Goethe's *Erlkonig* of the man who, on horseback, in the dead of night, carries a boy to help and safety. Every German child in elementary school in Berlin is made to learn this epic poem by heart. He says in the essay that we have a 'fixed fund of capital' when it comes to

↰ Rachel and Daniel Libeskind, 2016. Photo by Christopher Lane.

← Image of the cover of *The Complete Ficiton of Bruno Schulz*.

↗ View of Staten Island and World Trade Center, 2014. Photo by Joe Woolhead.

→ Aerial viewo of Jewish Museum Berlin. Photo by Guenter Schneider.

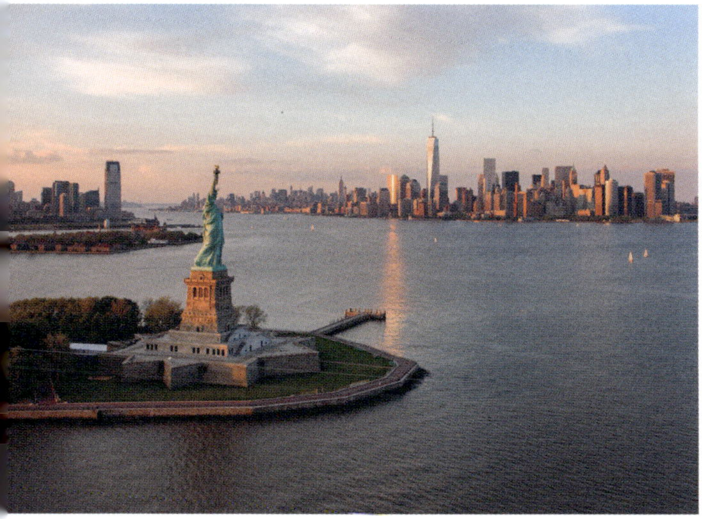

images that are destined to us, and us alone,[1] and that for the rest of your life, you spend time trying to understand why these images are so pertinent to your creative work.

DL Isn't the word 'Liebeskind' mentioned in the Goethe poem?

RL Yes! 'Du liebes Kind, komm geh mit mir' (Dear child, come with me) which is what Death says to the little boy. It really is very interconnected. I would say that Bruno Schulz is, in a lot of ways, haunting us.

DL Agreed. This notion of a fixed fund of capital of images—I've always connected with the first view I saw at Mount of Olives when I came to Israel in 1957, when Jerusalem was divided. We had to kneel on a rooftop of a building, overlooking the old city as we couldn't get to it. Seeing in the background the true picture of Jerusalem with the golden dome and feeling that—even though we were being shot at by Jordanian snipers—this was always going to be the Jerusalem of the heart. To me, that view of Jerusalem is very close to another paradisiacal view, which is the view of Manhattan skyline. I remember arriving to New York by boat and being met with that amazing skyline. Those two views are definitely part of what I would call the legacy of the world, of my life, of my history.

RL It's funny, when I think about views that are early in the horizon of my memory—of space and time—I think about the view from the roof of the Jewish Museum, looking onto the East. In my early memories of the 1990s, I see a low, grey sky hanging over Berlin, and I think about how that is my Mount of Olives view, from the top of the Jewish Museum! Looking out onto East Berlin—unchartered territory.

DL That makes complete sense, because you were looking towards Oranienburger Strasse, which was written about by Paul Celan, but also where Humboldt had his library, everything comes full circle—the olives of history.

RL Actually, I remember my bedroom in New York City, when I moved there from Berlin; my bedroom window looked very adjacently south, at the site of the World Trade Centre (WTC), and I could see the edge of the site where the One World Trade was being built. That's a legacy of the changing landscape in my history—of our history. The Freedom Tower.

DL 'Now with the drops of this most balmy time My love looks fresh, and Death to me subscribes, Since, spite of him, I'll live in this poor rhyme, While he insults o'er dull and speechless tribes'[2] That's Shakespeare.

RL That's beautiful.

DL The drops! What does that mean?

RL I have an idea! You know, scientifically, we are inhaling the same molecules of oxygen that Shakespeare inhaled, that Christopher Columbus—that thief!—inhaled, that Homer inhaled. We are drinking the same molecules of hydrogen and oxygen in our water, the same molecules that Lincoln drank, or Hitler drank.

DL They were all exhaled by God!

RL Well, that depends on who you ask. (Laughs)

DL We are breathing the exhalations of God!

RL Well, of the universe. Of Gaia, of God —I don't know.

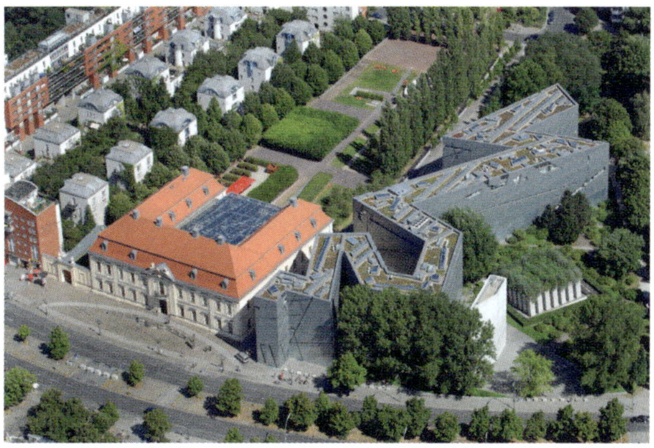

1

'I do not know just how in childhood we arrive at certain images, images of crucial significance to us. They are like filaments in a solution around which the sense of the world crystallizes for us...They are meanings that seem predestined for us, ready and waiting at the very entrance of our life...such images constitute a program, establish our soul's fixed capital, which is allotted to us very early in the form of inklings and half-conscious feelings. It seems to me that the rest of our life passes in the interpretation of those insights, in the attempt to master them with all the range of intellect we have in our possession. These early images mark the boundaries of an artist's creativity. His creativity is a deduction from assumptions already made. He cannot now discover anything new, he learns only to understand more and more the secret entrusted to him at the beginning, and his art is a constant exegesis, a commentary on that single verse that was assigned him. But art will never unravel that knot completely. The secret remains insoluble. The knot in which the soul was bound is no trick knot, coming apart with a tug at its end. On the contrary, it grows tighter and tighter. We work at it, untying, tracing the path of the string, seeking the end, and out of this manipulating comes art.'

BRUNO SCHULZ

2

'Not mine own fears, nor the prophetic soul
Of the wide world dreaming on things to come,
Can yet the lease of my true love control,
Suppos'd as forfeit to a confin'd doom.
The mortal moon hath her eclipse endur'd
And the sad augurs mock their own presage;
Incertainties now crown themselves assur'd
And peace proclaims olives of endless age.
Now with the drops of this most balmy time
My love looks fresh, and Death to me subscribes,
Since, spite of him, I'll live in this poor rhyme,
While he insults o'er dull and speechless tribes;
And thou in this shalt find thy monument,
When tyrants' crests and tombs of brass are spent.'

WILLIAM SHAKESPEARE
Sonnet 107: Not mine own fears, nor the prophetic soul

DL I think it's true that our legacy is very clear: number one—the world was created out of nothing. Two—that there is free will. Number three—that there is a divinity in us, that shapes us. Roughly hewn, as Shakespeare says.

RL Is that your life philosophy? Is that your spiritual philosophy?

DL I think it's the spiritual philosophy of every modern thinker, starting with Descartes. Descartes is not so different from Rabbi Nachman of Bratslav. I love Rabbi Nachman, first of all because my father carried his name—Nachman. Rabbi Nachman had this great questioning—first and foremost a questioning of God. As did Descartes. Descartes' radical doubt as a method of thinking is the first real accounting of thought. I don't think any other philosopher—not Nietzsche, not Heidegger, not Derrida, no one has ever surpassed Descartes, because he had the boldest scheme: the scheme of throwing the gauntlet with the Cogito as his captive.

RL It's very integral to the way you see the world.

DL It's integral to the way you see the world! You have the cogito also!

RL Okay, the next image you brought me is the Moai sculptures, the incredible heads from Easter Island, which I know you actually visited a few years ago for your sixty fifth birthday.

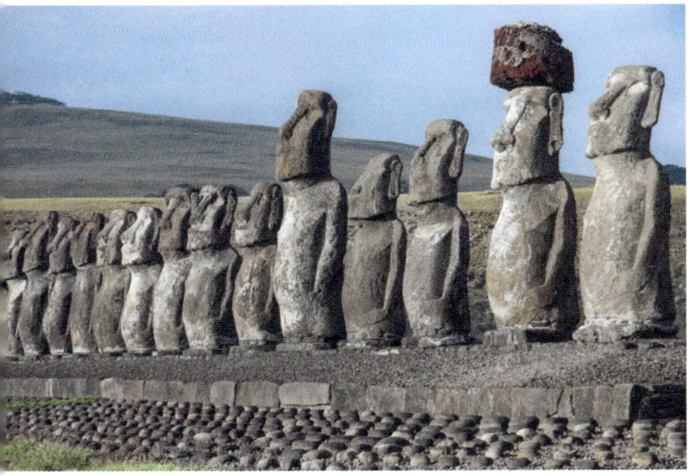

DL I never thought that I would see something like this—a civilization that died because of its' love of art. They spent all their resources destroying the island, to carve these gigantic figures. As far as I am aware, nobody has been able to figure out how they even made them or transported them to the edge of the islands.

RL It's one of the great mysteries. This goes back to this idea that it wasn't art as we understand it—the art itself was their belief. In the premodern era, civilizations had no separation between art or culture or religion—it was all one and the same. It was actually a Gesamtkunstwerk (a total artwork).

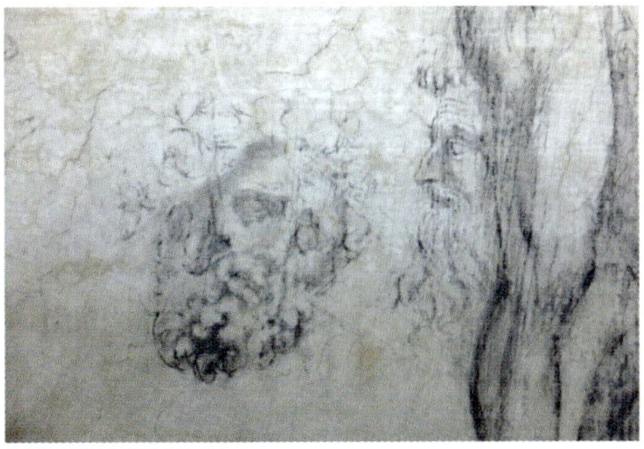

↑ Michelangelo doodles in Medici Chapel of the Basilica di San Lorenzo, Florence. Source: Ministry of Cultural Heritage and Activities and Tourism (Public Domain).

↙ Moai statues at Ahu Tongariki on Easter Island, 2008. Photo by Itanart.

DL What I love about them is that all the sculptures are arranged in lines, looking outwards onto the sea. Why are they looking out there? What are they looking for? Then of course, on the centre of the island, there are these incredible bird-like figure drawings. They remind me so much of Max Ernst's *Oiseaux en peril* (Birds in peril, 1975), the eggs and the birds—somehow this is part of our visual legacy.

RL That reminds me of a few years ago, when on a family vacation in Florence, because of a great gesture courtesy of the Florentine government, we were allowed to enter the basement of the San Lorenzo Cathedral. They had discovered, behind a large wooden armoire which had been unmoved for several hundreds of years, a trap door that led to a very small room, no bigger than two meters by three meters. This tiny room was where Michelangelo hid for just over a year during the revolution in Florence. The most incredible thing was that the walls of this tiny space bore the traces of the sketches he made directly onto the walls! Of David, of Medusa, of many works he had not yet even created.

DL To my knowledge, this has not been reproduced in any books, nor is it accessible to the public.

RL Honestly that was one of the greatest gifts you ever gave me—being able to see this.

'Scientifically, we are inhaling the same molecules of oxygen that Shakespeare inhaled, that Christopher Columbus—that thief!—inhaled, that Homer inhaled.'

DANIEL LIBESKIND

I don't think there will be another experience to see something as magical and untouched as that.

DL Don't you think that that whole experience was a passage out of *Cinnamon Shops (and Other Stories, 2016)* by Schulz? Possibly even of *Hypnerotomachia Poliphili (The Strife of Love in a Dream, 1499)* by Francesco Colonna.

RL The thing that shook me, and really stays with me from that experience, is that drawing on the wall, or cave paintings—when you think about the earliest forms of what we call art, an edifice of human creation—were already being made 30,000 years ago. These paintings are just pigment on a surface at eye level. The mystery remains whether they were representing reality or a dream. What is incredible to me is that there is very little difference between the cave paintings and Michelangelo's sketches on the walls of the hidden room in San Lorenzo.

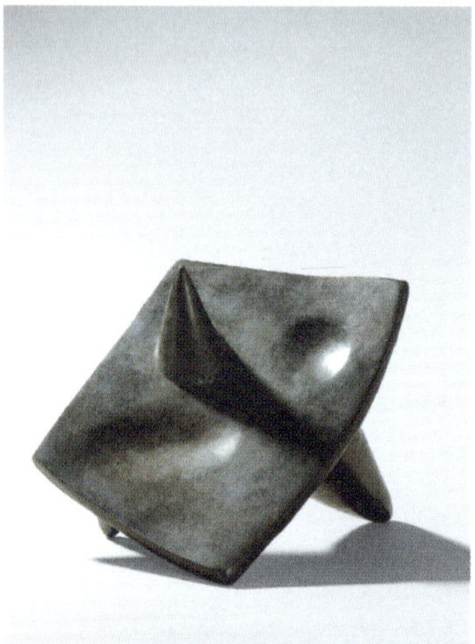

DL This is why I love, in this context, Giacometti's *Objet désagréable à jeter, (Disagreeable object to be thrown away, 1931)* which is one of his greatest sculptures. It speaks about the destruction, in time, of the idea of art—which coincides with the Moai

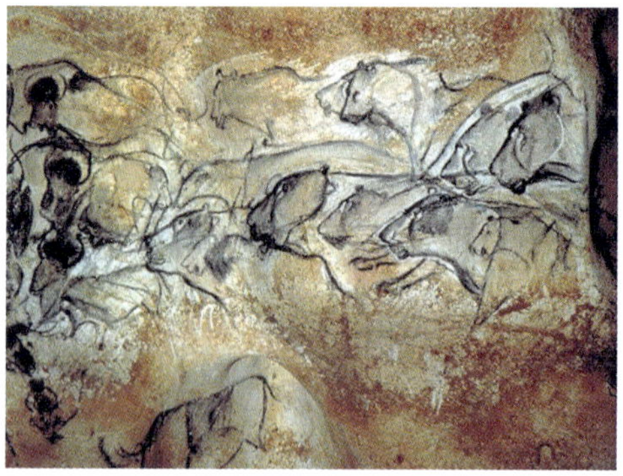

as well. Perhaps they actually knew that they were self-immolating, through art. It didn't bother them, they may have willed it. The way, as you have spoken about it, the death of Gaia is a self-destruction of the planet in our time.

RL All things must come to an end. Giacometti has always fascinated me because, according to the brilliant Benjamin Buchloh, with whom I studied at Harvard, Giacometti's figures were actually representations of the post-war body—the survivors of death. It was this idea that people had been reduced to the indexicality of the vertical.

DL Well, that brings us to a fundamental point, which is that the Holocaust has changed everything, for everyone—sometimes even without someone knowing about it.

RL That's the ultimate legacy.

DL Well, the world has been altered completely, no matter if someone is building a vernacular house in India, or someone is cutting a piece of wood somewhere in Africa, they have been inhaling the air of the Holocaust.

RL Not only the Holocaust. Obviously the holocaust is a hugely emblematic historical event for us, since both of us only exist because of the Holocaust. In Derrida's words 'The enabling violation of the Holocaust, is the only reason we are here today,' and obviously it is an event that touches us more closely than maybe any other historical event on that scale. The Holocaust represents something more than just an event in

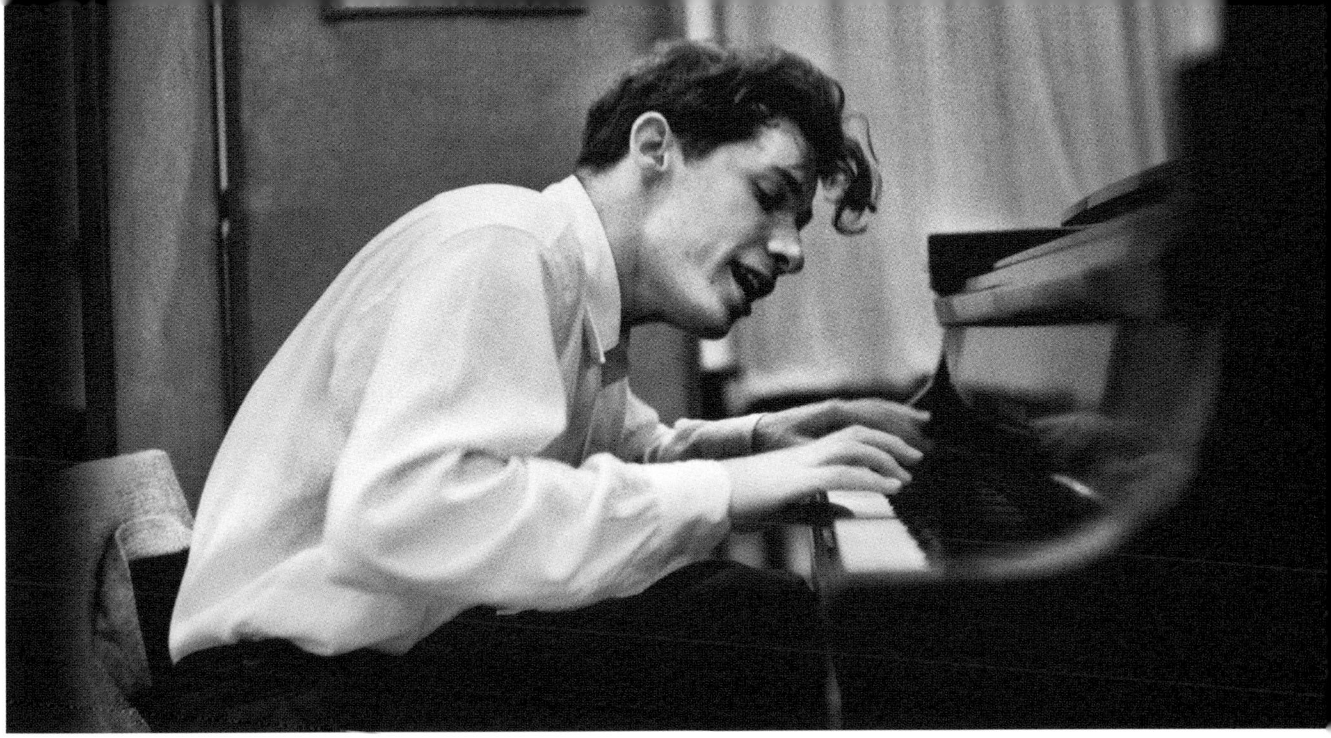

time and space; it also represents an idea that we see being played around by many different forces on our earth.

DL Especially in our time, where we see Holocaust denial, and the tendencies towards a fascist right-wing perspective.

RL It's a denial of truth itself! It's no coincidence that the survivors of the horrible shooting at the high school in Parkland, Florida adopted the hashtag #neveragain—which is a phrase used often in referring to the horrors of the Holocaust.

DL I want to talk about Bach, the greatest architect of all time! Nobody refers to his music as old. It is always contemporary. In fact, he was popularized by a Jew—by Mendelsohn. Mendelsohn was the first one to play Bach in the 19th century. Bach, who at the time was considered a medieval composer, was brought back into the light of the court. Of course, Mendelsohn himself was excised from the canon of German music by Hitler.

RL It is amazing to think about how much music is a part of both of our lives. I mean, for me it is a result of being your offspring, your spawn, and my upbringing which involved playing an instrument or singing, and learning music, a lesser version of your childhood where you were actually a professional musician!

DL If you think about my father, who had no education and taught himself, and created his own musical notation in order to transcribe the music of his childhood to the piano—

RL Necessity is the mother of invention! Let no lack of education stop you from making and creating music. It reminds me of that Schiller quote you used in your book, 'Architecture is Frozen Music'—possibly one of the most important metaphors ever spoken. I just think about how much time you spend listening to music now—how much of your youth you spent actually playing music, it always shocks me that you're not a composer!

DL Especially on the instrument that I played! The accordion—which is like carrying an entire orchestra around on your back. It's not light! It's not a violin or a flute, or even a piano, which you don't have to carry. You carry an entire house, which you have to compress to make it come alive! It's why people associate it with gypsies or beggars—sleeping with your own house wherever you go.

RL It is actually such a cumbersome performance, it transcends the lightness of music—a micro-technosphere!

DL In a way, it's the instrument of the future, since you don't need an orchestra, you have everything you need on your back. Didn't Ambrose Bierce say in the Devil's Dictionary that the accordion was 'an instrument in harmony with the sentiments of an assassin'?

RL It makes me think of how much Bach we actually listened to in our household,

↑ Glenn Gould. Photo by Bettmann/Corbis.

↖ Chauvet Cave, Ardèche,-France. Dated to 30,000 to 28,000 B.C. Courtesy of DRAC Rhone-Alpes, Ministre de la Culture / AP Images.

↙ Alberto Giacometti, Objet désagréable à jeter, (Disagreeable object to be thrown away, 1931. © The Estate of Alberto Giacometti (Fondation Giacometti, Paris and ADAGP, Paris).

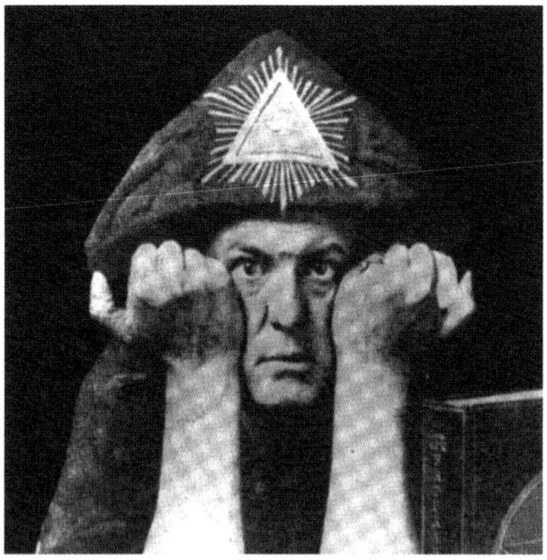

← Aleister Crowley, The Evil Beast.

↓ Portrait of Rachel Libeskind in her studio in New York. Photo by Vera Comploj.

→ Daniel Libeskind holding his daughter Rachel in his arm, Berlin, ca. 1991. From the Libeskind family archive.

and how you used to test me to see whether I knew the difference in playing styles between Glenn Gould and Rosalyn Tureck!

DL I was kind of a sadist! What a difficult test. She almost created Glenn Gould's own interpretation!

RL What I'm getting at about Glenn Gould is that the power of music is a very specific, impactful memory. You showed me the film about Gould, *Thirty Two Short Films About Glenn Gould* (1993). In the film, they shoot him playing the piano in his home, and he truly looks possessed! Deranged, and truly possessed by a spirit. We have discussed this before, but I feel it's important to restate, that someone like Gould is less than some kind of technical genius, but more a man who was perhaps channelling, in the words of Aleister Crowley, the spirit of Bach himself.

DL I think that is the legacy emblem, because what is legacy? Nobody reinvents themselves, and that's why all those who claim that they created their own aesthetic, their own language—that is fraudulent. The work always comes from somewhere, the sphere of both family, and the rejection of the family. It comes from the society in which you live. Think about it: how lucky I am to have lived not as an architect in the post-war era, where I would have been compelled to work on the reconstruction of building, but in a time where there was a revolution against the establishment, and an alternative life, and a reality of available resources.

RL I'm saddled with the opposite. I'm saddled in a time where there is less freedom. We have such a sense of urgency, on every single level of life in society.

DL With it comes a decrease in economic viability. That's why so much great art was created in Holland, in the time of Vermeer and Rembrandt. They had wealthy patrons! They had resources. They had peace!

RL I want to just quickly go back to the idea that great artists of all kind are like mediums. I know the terminology you use when you speak about your work often implies, and I know as your daughter you often use the word, haunting. Now, we have very different definitions of this word. I remember, as a child, but also still now, you used to tell me that you didn't think that ghosts existed. Yet the words that you would use to talk about space, buildings, etc. were often referring to as 'haunting,' that the void itself is a presence of the dead—itself a kind of haunting.

DL Etymologically, the word ghost, is related to the word host. So, to host, to be hospitable, in your space, in a space of welcoming, can be said as in Hamlet, Horatio says, 'There are more things in heaven and earth, Horatio, Than are dreamt of in your philosophy.'[3] I would say that the things that are 'more' in heaven and earth' is the strangeness of life itself, and that's a kind of legacy—every legacy is both a stranger, and something to be welcomed.

RL Both a ghost and a host.

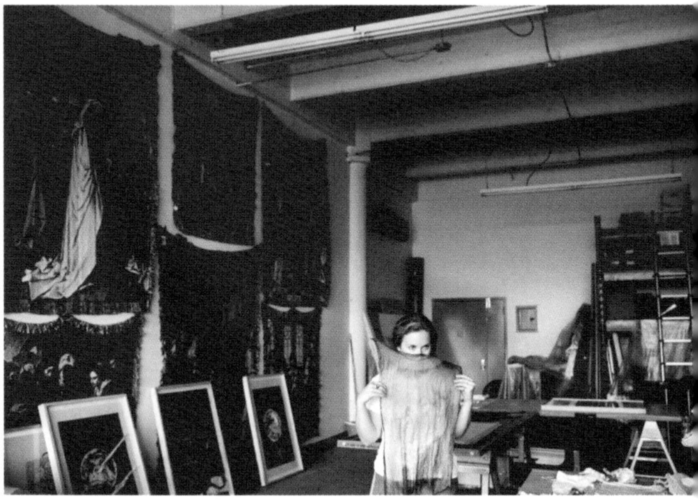

3
Hamlet (1.5.167-8), Hamlet to Horatio

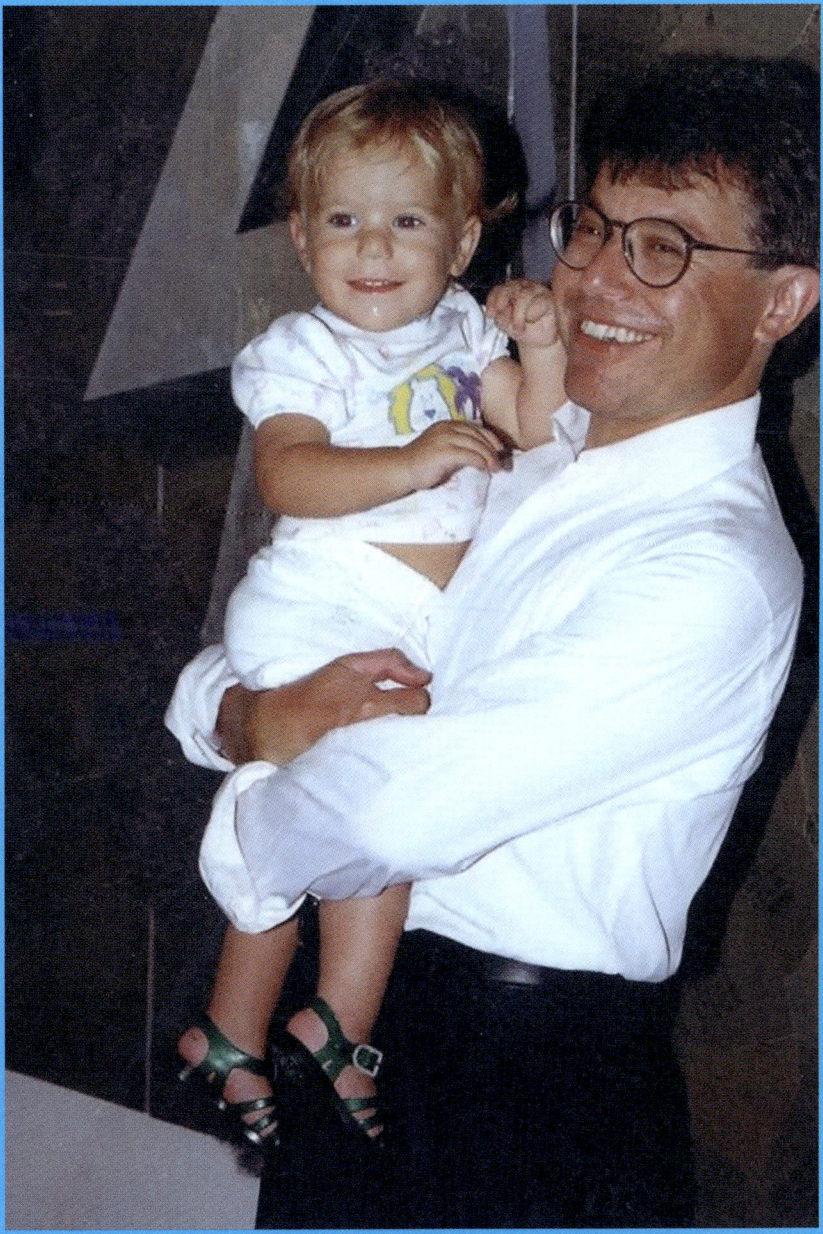

London-based curator and writer FRANCESCA GAVIN sits down with American painter KERRY JAMES MARSHALL to talk about aesthetic regimes in the history of art and his exploration of the concept of blackness in his three decade-spanning work.

The Perfect Blackness

Francesca Gavin and Kerry James Marshall

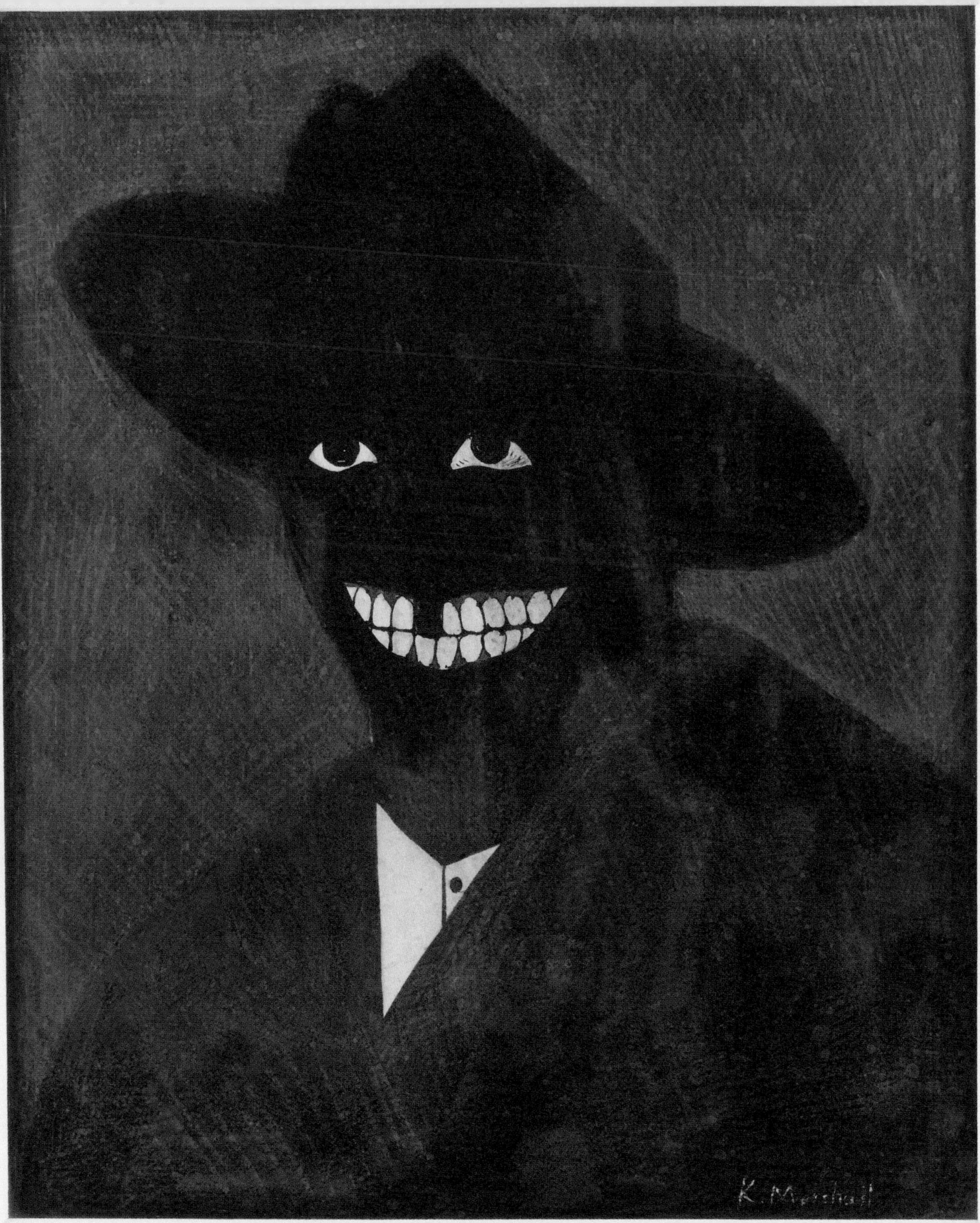
K. Marshall

How do you make art that speaks to people beyond the rigid walls of the art world? Kerry James Marshall has an exceptionally unique visual language and approach to making 'stuff' that juggles a deep understanding of the history of art with a pop accessibility that can be read by anyone. The style and approach of his work has changed dramatically throughout this career - from early collage pieces, through text works and comic-strip influenced narratives, to paintings which have veered from 18th romantic scenes to intense portraiture. At the crux of his work is a redefinition and exploration of the concept of blackness. The results are fascinating, confrontational, emotional and say something about contemporary society in its entirety.

His personal path has echoed the African American experience—born in Birmingham, Alabama; raised in South Central LA during the height of the civil rights movement; based in Chicago for much of his working life. Now in his sixties, he has shown in the Whitney Biennial, Documenta, at the Museum of Contemporary Art (MOCA) in LA and Vienna Secession. It is now that Marshall has harnessed the kind of attention that is getting him magazine covers and serious establishment presence. It isn't over the top to describe him as one of the most technically skilled and politically articulate artists alive today. James Marshall talked to me about coming in to your own and how he approaches the body, magic and the perfect blackness.

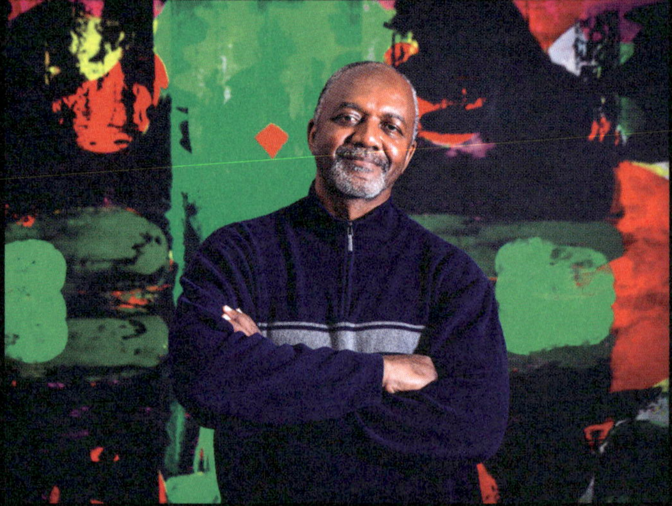

FRANCESCA GAVIN Throughout your work you have referenced the history of art, but I find it particularly fascinating to be reworking, rethinking, addressing those big American white abstract painters.

KERRY JAMES MARSHALL The challenge for black artists in general, I would argue, is trying to find a place for themselves in an aesthetic regime or aesthetic system, and a history that did not include them as participants in the formulation of its authorizing idea. Here we are operating within a class structure that, in the main, large number of black artists don't come from. The challenge has been trying to figure out a way to get inside, but to come in with imagery that has black subject matter or black subjects by a person who is black. People felt like that particular specificity set limitations on how people were able to perceive the work because there is the notion that the black body can never really be a universal body. If you come with the black body in a picture, then people automatically tend to limit their perception of it, believing it is only relevant to black people. A remedy to that marginalization for African American artists who wanted to be seen as just artists and not 'black artists' was to do abstract work.

FG Would you say that abstraction allowed freedom?

KJM This was the belief. The problem with doing abstract work is this notion of belatedness. When you come late, and you are outside the specific discourse that articulates the parameters of a genre, even of abstraction, then the work is always seen as derivative. Black people who did abstract work weren't any more likely to break into the mainstream as people who did figurative work. My thing is that, well, it's difficult for any artist to get recognition. You might as well do what you want and address the issues that are important to you; but try and do it in a way that on some level forces the issue, compels attention.

FG Your approach to the physical body, in particular the nudes, can be weirdly confrontational in a wonderful way. Was that part of your intention?

KJM Yes. Painting the figures as I do, black with a black colour is a part of that. It is unavoidable. They're not brown skinned in all those different shades; they are none of those things. They are black. That in itself is confrontational you can argue—it demands to be identified as what it is.

↰ Kerry James Marshall, *A Portrait of the Artist as a Shadow of His Former Self*, 1980. © Kerry James Marshall, Courtesy the artist and David Zwirner.

↑ Portrait of Kerry James Marshall. © Kerry James Marshall. Photo by Felix Clay. Courtesy the artist and David Zwirner.

→ Kerry James Marshall, *Souvenir I*, 1997. © Kerry James Marshall, Courtesy the artist and David Zwirner.

FG There is also this incredible richness to the kind of black paint which you use.

KJM I hope so. Being black should not be completely reductive. Within that extreme black, there can be richness and variety. Black becomes chromatic.

FG Some of your pieces bring to mind Renaissance portraiture—the depiction of figures against these flat background colours, in a kind of non-space. Was that a reference you were striving for?

KJM I'm nothing if I'm not a child of art history—really, in the end that's all I have to go on. My idea of art was formed around Italian Renaissance and Flemish paintings. That's the stuff that I, in some ways, wanted to match in terms of the authority of those pictures. That no-space, that no-place is really important because that may be one of the things that allow the figures to exist out of time. Then the images are more of a phenomenal representation.

FG Why have you begun to depict figures full length, rather than the closer portraiture you explored in your Lost Boys series?

KJM History painting, multi-figure narrative pictures, was supposed to be the most challenging thing to do. The Lost Boys was my most sustained attempt at making a big history painting. If you study the history of western painting, it's divided into a handful of genres, portraiture, history paintings, allegories, landscape and interiors, and still-lifes. Some of (my) full figure pictures are sort of allegorical. In particular, the two paintings of Frankenstein and the Bride of Frankenstein.

FG If you think about stereotypes within the representation of black culture, was it part of your aim to come up with a redefine of ideas of sexuality and romance?

KJM The absence of those kinds of images as a common place could, perhaps, suggest that black people really don't like each other because carefree love is not reflected in the imagery we produce. A lot of what I am doing, really, is just to provide images of this sort. I think the absence of this kind of image is psychologically damaging. If you always see images of pleasure, images of desire and beauty that are represented using other people, then your longing and desire for pleasure will always be embodied in another. You can't help it.

I have often talked about something tha

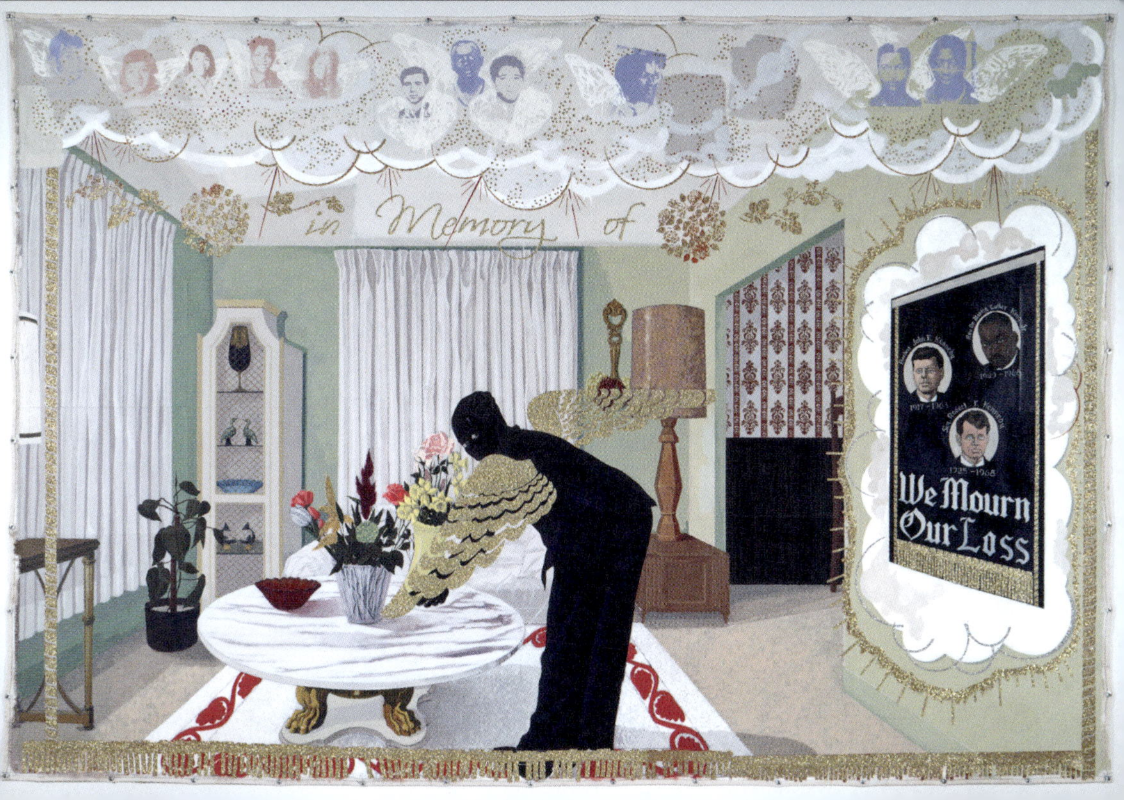

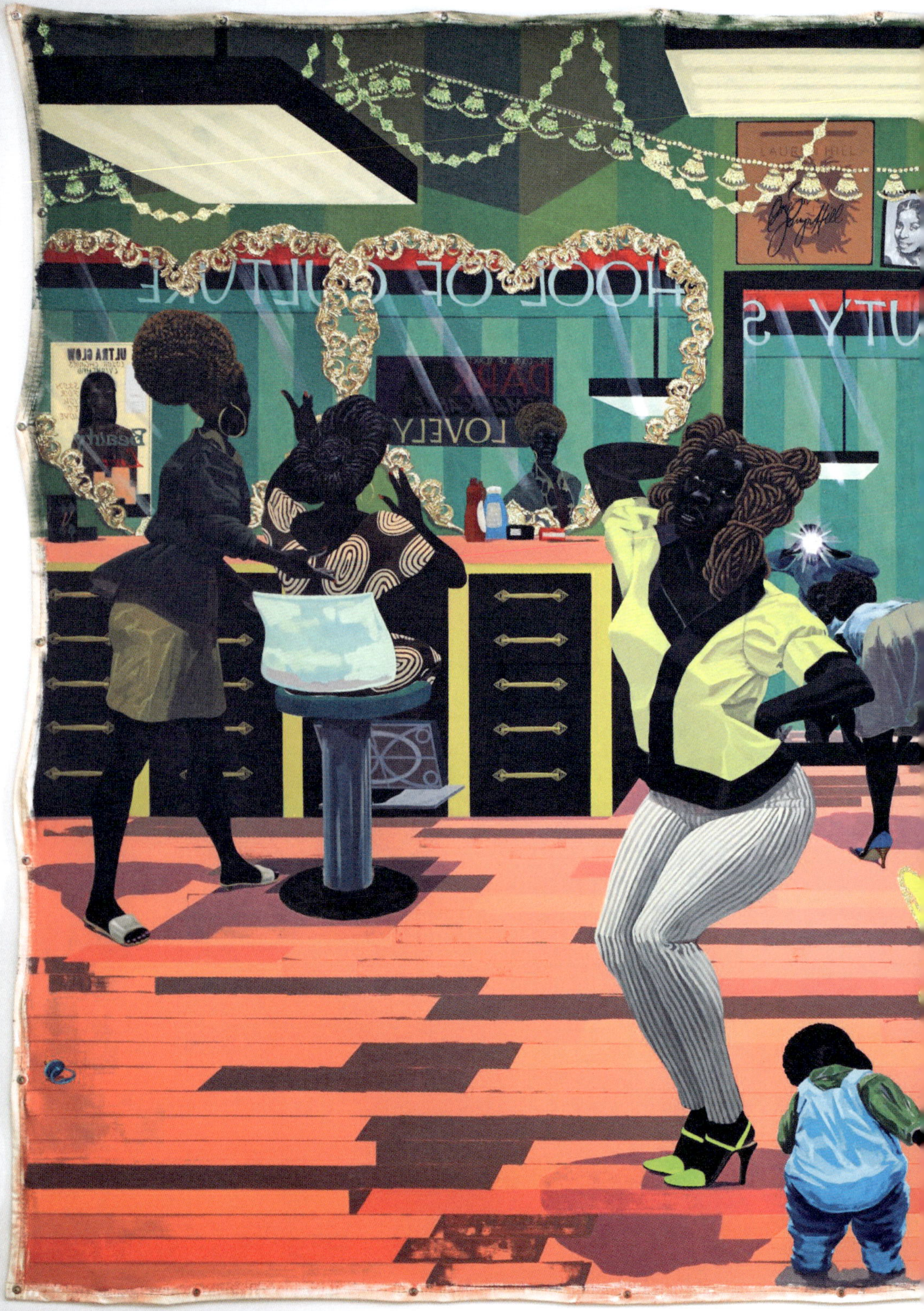
LOVELY

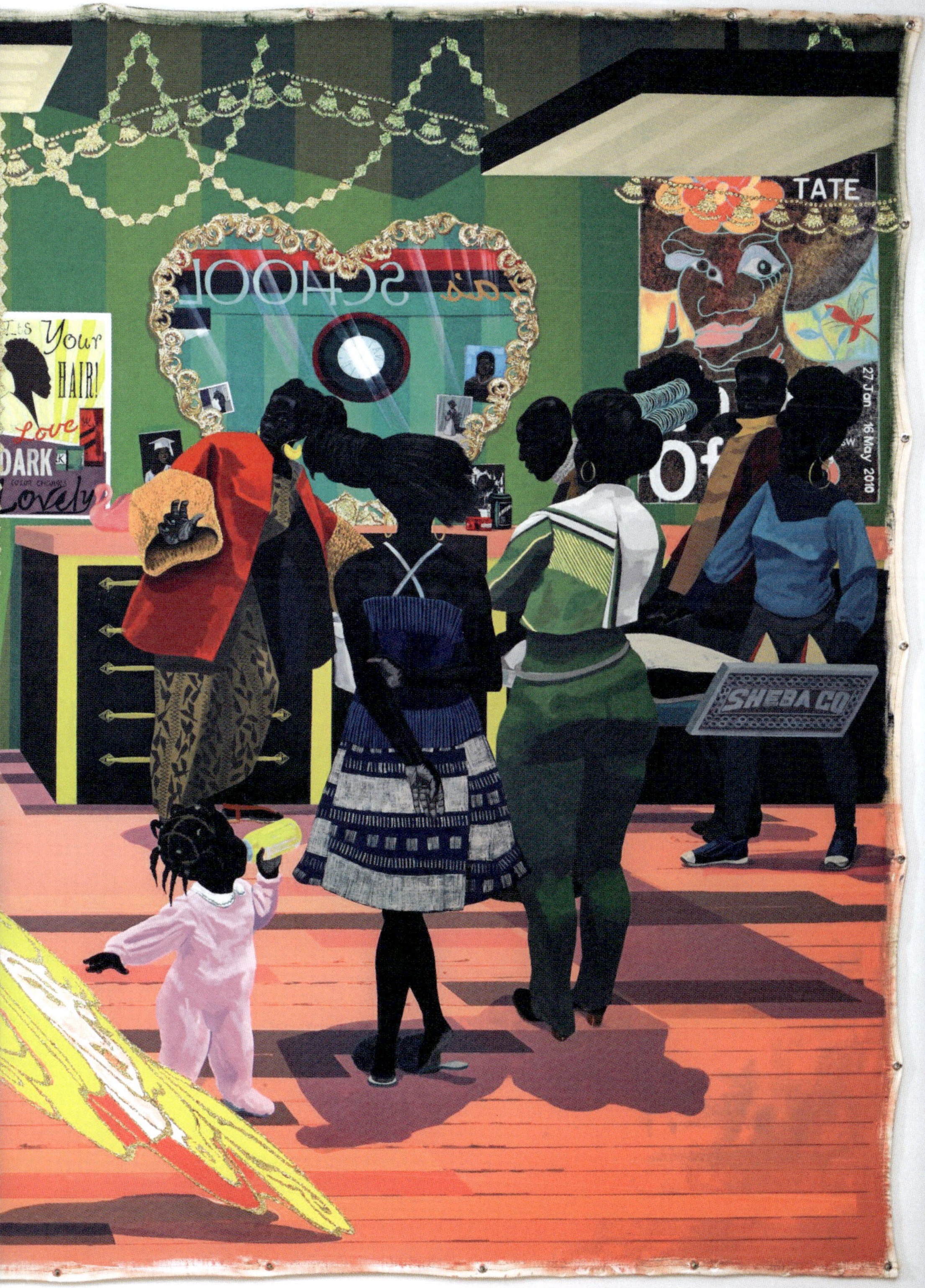
SCHOOL
TATE
It's Your HAIR!
Love
DARK
Lovely
27 Jan 16 May 2010
SHEBA CO

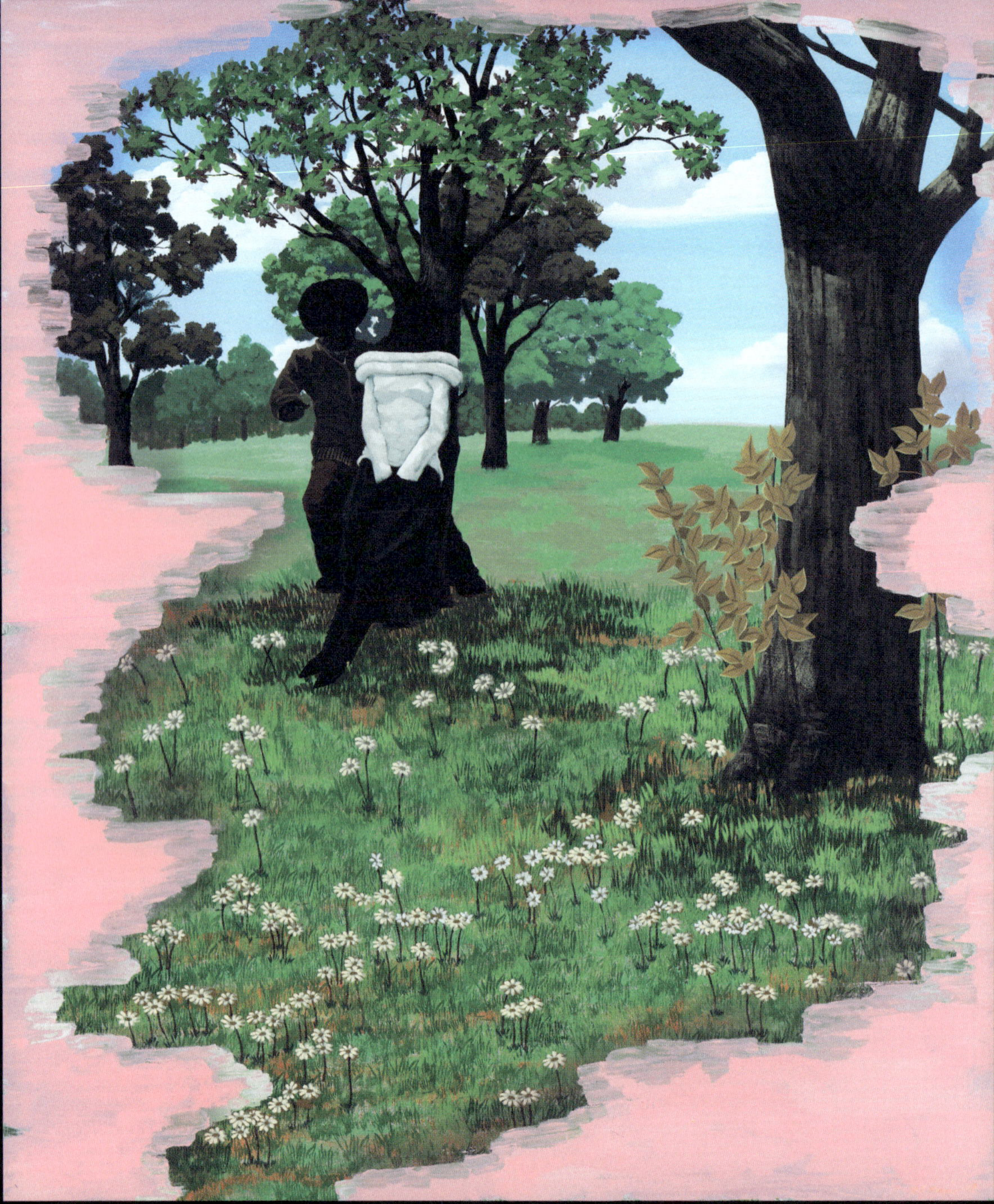

another writer noted in one of his essays. The Harry Potter empire—how many movies did they make? Seven? Then you have the Tolkien books, Lord of the Rings and then there is all the sword and sorcery dragon movies, all the Robin Hood movies. These are movies that say white people do magic. There were no black hobbits. There were no black knights. In all of the King Arthur movies, they're no black wizards; it appears that we don't have a rich enough fantasy life to produce this kind of material.

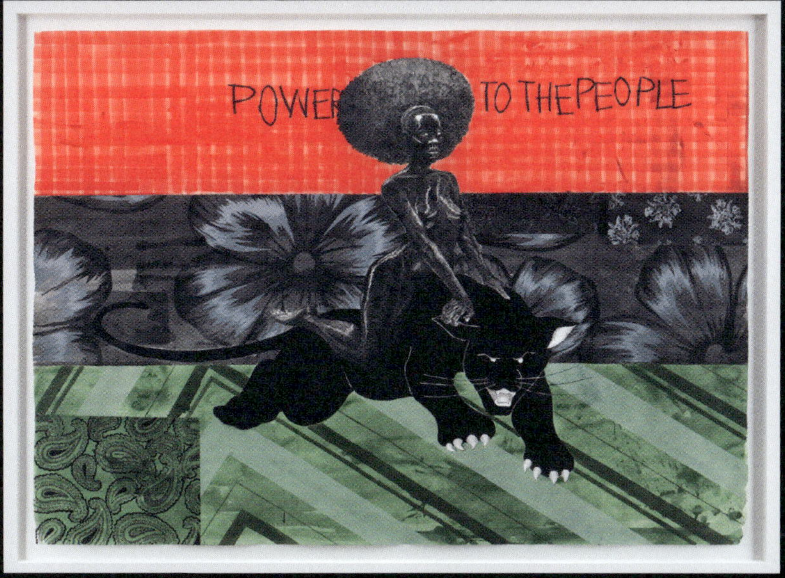

FG You have a collection of images of how black people were represented throughout popular culture? How does that collection of imagery play into your forms of representation?

KJM A show of mine in Antwerp was kind of organised around this idea of a counter archive. It's amassing images of black people in every kind of way that you can find. On the one hand there is one way in which black people can be represented that I find too problematic to exist - structured around ideas of positive representations of black people. If you operate on a philosophy that says that the only worthwhile representation of black people are positive representations, then that means it cuts off whole layers of complexity that need to be represented to demonstrate just how fully complex black people actually are.

Part of that thing of collecting all those images is to collect everything. If all your trying to do is find positive images then you end up allowing for the stereotypes, the negative stereotypes of what black people are, as some sort of rule. You're constantly trapped in this cycle of criticising other people for the way they represent black people. Which means if you're running around trying to police people - and it probably means that you're not engaged in the image production that you need to in order to offset it. That's one of the reasons I collected images the way that I did.

The other thing is collecting all those images you start to get a sense for the kinds of images you see the least and that sort of tells you in some ways what kind of images you might want to fill in some of the gaps. You don't see a lot of pastoral representations of black people. You just don't see a lot of rural representations of black people. There is a certain type of black body that occupies the space. It's either an anthropological body or it's a sociological body — so it's black people engaged in the struggle for liberation/freedom, or black people admired in some kind of pre-modern state.

FG That is what makes the everyday context of your history paintings so interesting.

KJM I'm almost trying to make images of black people where they are not really doing anything, really not doing much, they are just there but they seem to be enjoying themselves because they are not under any particular stress. They're just chilling.

FG You have been making work for decades, but it feels like you're coming into your own now. How do you about the concept of aging and growing as an artist?

KJM One should always believe they can get better, do better work next time. Otherwise, what would be the reason to continue? I am always trying to make a perfect picture. A prefect manifestation of blackness.

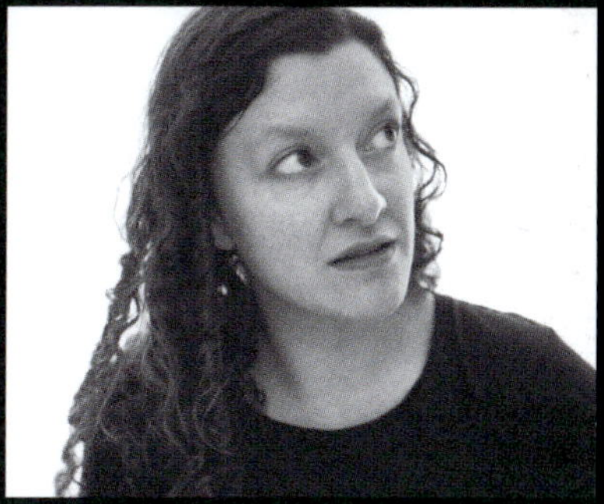

FG That is an interesting thing to be striving for as a concept—the perfect blackness.

KJM Especially at a time when people are retreating from various identity formations and notions of what people will call essentialist representations and identities. This is not a moment in which looking for absolutes seems to be particularly celebrated. I don't have a problem with the pursuit.

An extended version of this interview was originally published in Twin Magazine.

↰ Kerry James Marshall *School of Beauty, School of Culture*, 2012. © Kerry James Marshall, Courtesy the artist and David Zwirner.

↖ Kerry James Marshall *Vignette #12*, 2008. © Kerry James Marshall, Courtesy the artist and David Zwirner.

↗ Kerry James Marshall *Untitled*, 2009. © Kerry James Marshall, Courtesy the artist and David Zwirner.

→ Portrait of Francesca Gavin. Photo by Jez Tozer.

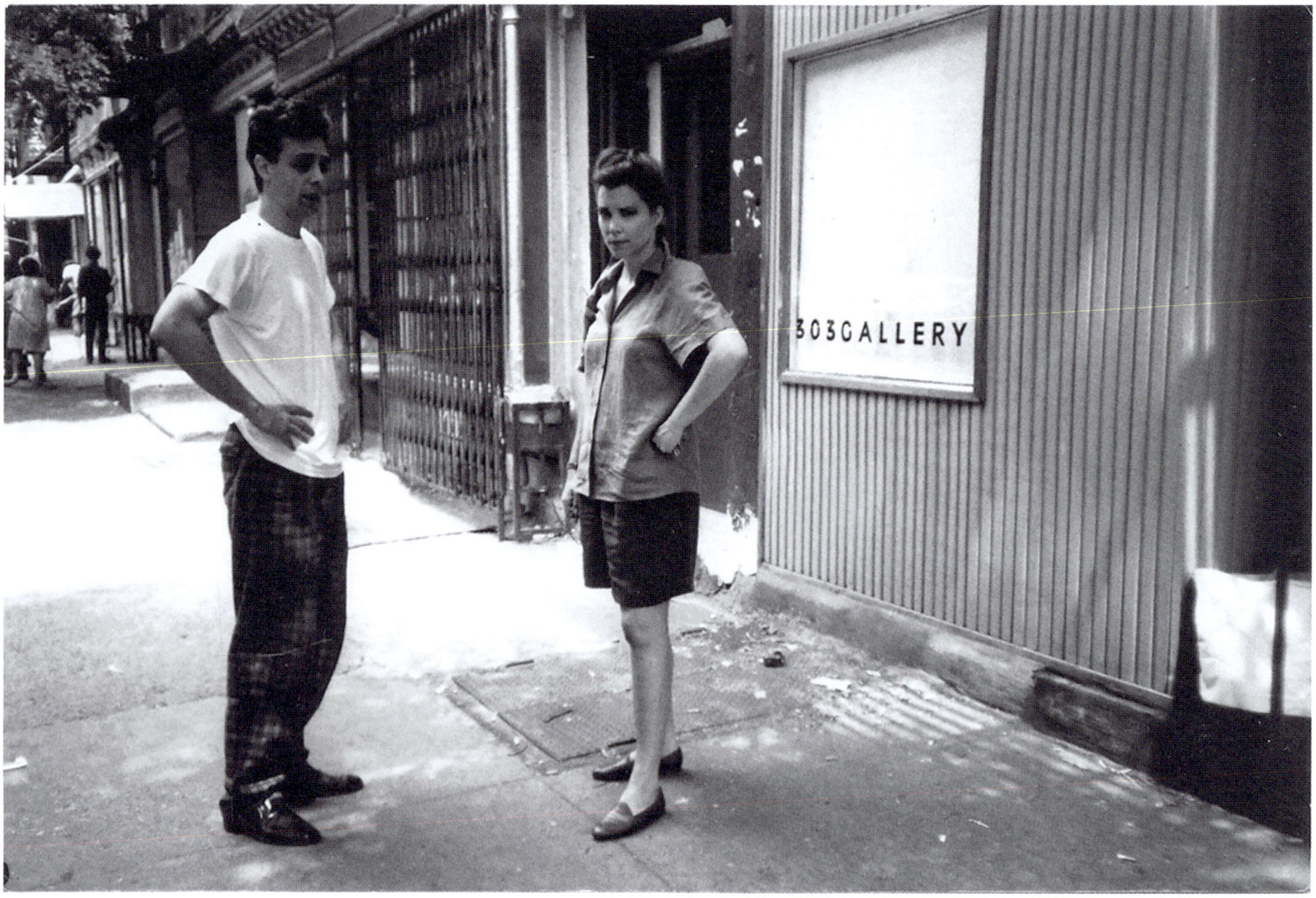

Structures for Creative Acts to Take Place

Fabiola Alondra and Lisa Spellman

Fortnight Institute's New York-based founder FABIOLA ALONDRA from Mexico City talks to 303 Gallery founder LISA SPELLMAN in New York City on how to run a gallery space for contemporary art with passion and personality.

FABIOLA ALONDRA Let's go back to the beginning. Your beginning.

We all have a tale to tell. As humans, one reason why we have been able to survive is because of our ability to tell stories. How do our unique stories shape us? Our shared experiences and individual paths lead us to unexpected places leaving behind a trail of influence. In your case, a legacy of your own creation that started 34 years ago and counting. Before we begin to talk about your inspiring 303 Gallery, founded in 1984 in New York City, I would like to learn more about your story. When did you know you wanted to become a gallery owner and dealer? What led to the opening of 303 Gallery in 1984?

LISA SPELLMAN I moved to New York in the late 1970s to attend the School of Visual Arts (SVA). While I was attending SVA for photography, I realized then that I wanted to open a gallery. I started walking around the SVA neighbourhood looking for spaces and found this old rent-controlled loft on the top floor of 303 Park Ave South.

Photography was too isolating a medium for me. Back then you would be in the dark room, day and night. I wasn't only doing it for my own work, but also working for other photographers. I really missed talking with other artists, that was the most exciting part. This was around 1982-1983 I had the idea to open a gallery, and it took a year or so to organize and open it.

FA What do you think is most challenging about owning a gallery? What are your favorite aspects of running a gallery? Your least favorite?

LS I think it's really easy running a gallery. The most challenging part is finding good artists. The first few shows were group shows because I wanted to train my eye.

One of my favorite things about the gallery is that it is a creation that you can build together with the artists and staff and then you can take it almost anywhere, like an organism that keeps growing. Working side by side with my colleagues and artists each day is inspiring. I really like running the gallery in all its aspects, from the business side to the creative. In so many ways, it is the perfect business: it is your own vision, but it is also a shared vision, a brick and mortar business that is creative!

My least favorite thing is bills and paying rent! More seriously, though, if you actually let it, becoming an art production machine. You have to know when to stop and find a source of inspiration, something external to ground you. For me, that would be a connection to an actual, natural landscape not a manufactured one. I find it through surfing, being in the water, seeing the horizon line.

FA My gallery is almost 3 years old, yours 35. What is your advice to me? What makes a gallery last so long? There are so many spaces already. How does a gallery stand out?

LS Don't take anyone's advice.

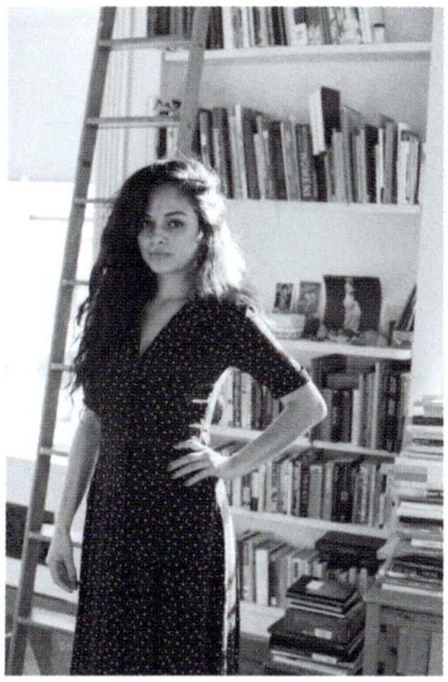

↑ Fabiola Alondra in front of her book collection. Photo by Rafael Rios.

↖ Lisa Spellman with Colin de Land in front of 303 Gallery, East 6th Street, 1986. Courtesy of 303 Gallery, New York.

‘Don’t take anyone’s advice.’

LISA SPELLMAN

‘We need art and creative energy in order to thrive.’

FABIOLA ALONDRA

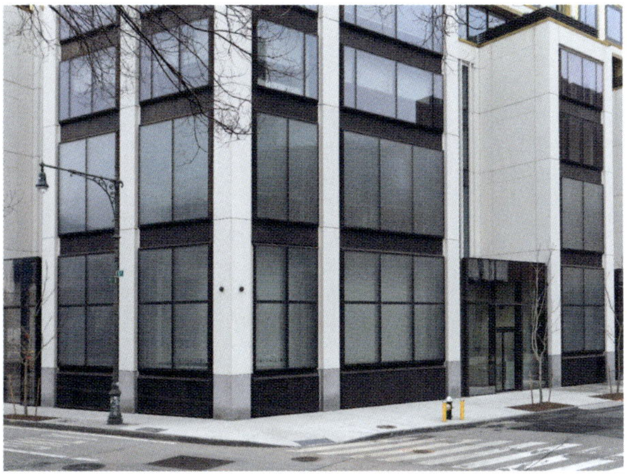

← Exterior of 303 Gallery, 2018. Courtesy of 303 Gallery, New York.

When galleries feel like an extension of the owner's passions and interests, that individuality comes through and it feels very sincere. Like Fortnight Institute!

FA My space today is on 60 East 4th St. I love the East Village. When we decided to open a gallery, we knew we wanted to be in the East Village. We like how authentic it feels, we love the sense of community and that it is not over saturated with galleries. What was the East Village like when 303 was there?

LS When I moved to the East Village, it turned out to be the last year of the East Village gallery scene. Pat Hearn, Colin de Land, and myself were the only holdouts, but there was still a vibrant collecting atmosphere. Things were well reviewed, and there was huge support. It was a close-knit community back then. I got to know artists from visiting their studios. You'd meet them at an opening, get their phone number, and send a fax to set up a visit. It was very analogue in those days, and approaching new artists was fairly straightforward.

The East Village freed art from the straight-jacket mentality that said a gallery could only be on 57th Street or in Soho. It was an amazing, fertile time, with a great degree of flexibility on the part of both artists and galleries.

FA That spirit of community and support continues, and it really keeps us going. I hope and aim for collaboration and a continued network of support between galleries and artists. From the big to medium and small galleries, we all need each other. It is all connected. I find it most inspiring when people work together. We need art and creative energy in order to thrive.

LS I've never viewed the act of putting together a gallery as a creative act in itself, but I do still hold to the belief that it can, when all the right ingredients are there, provide a structure in which creative acts can take place.

↓ *Summer Reading* group exhibition at Fortnight Institute, June-August 2016. Courtesy of Fortnight Institute, New York.

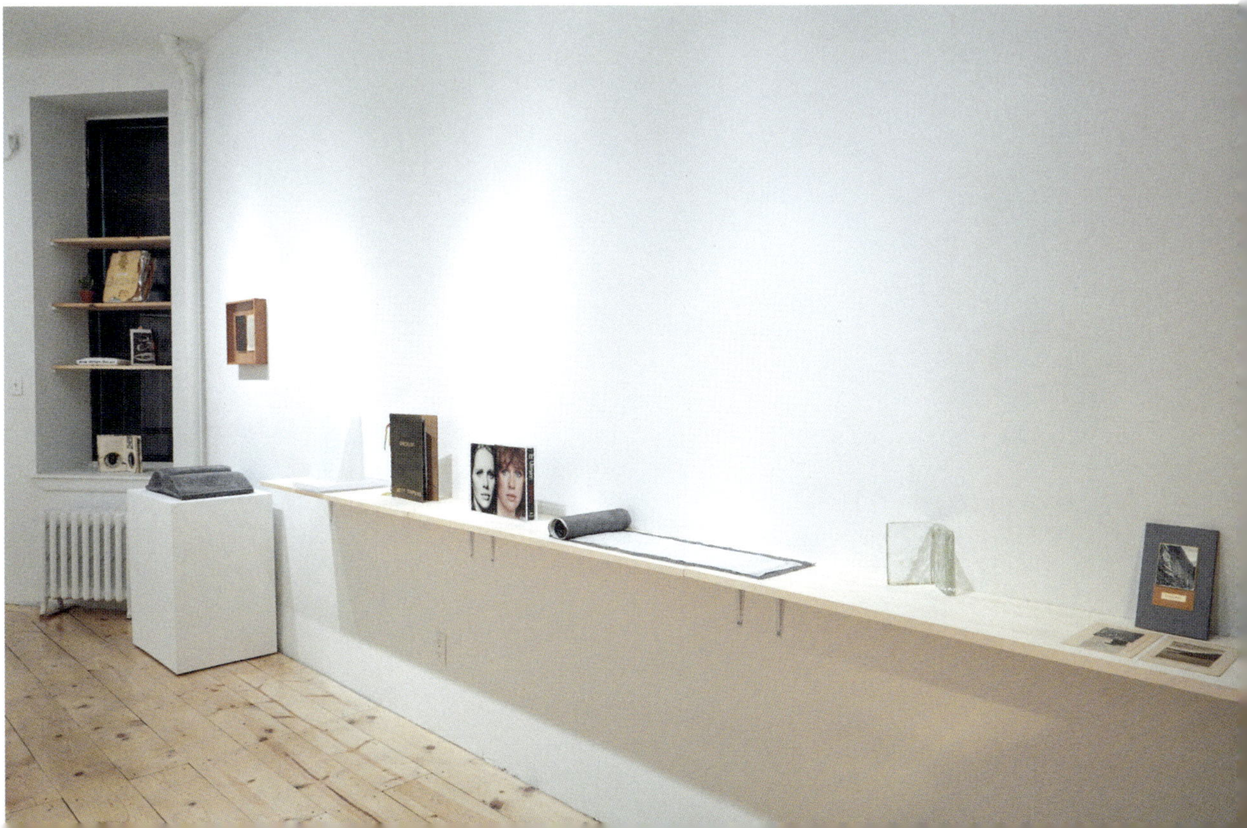

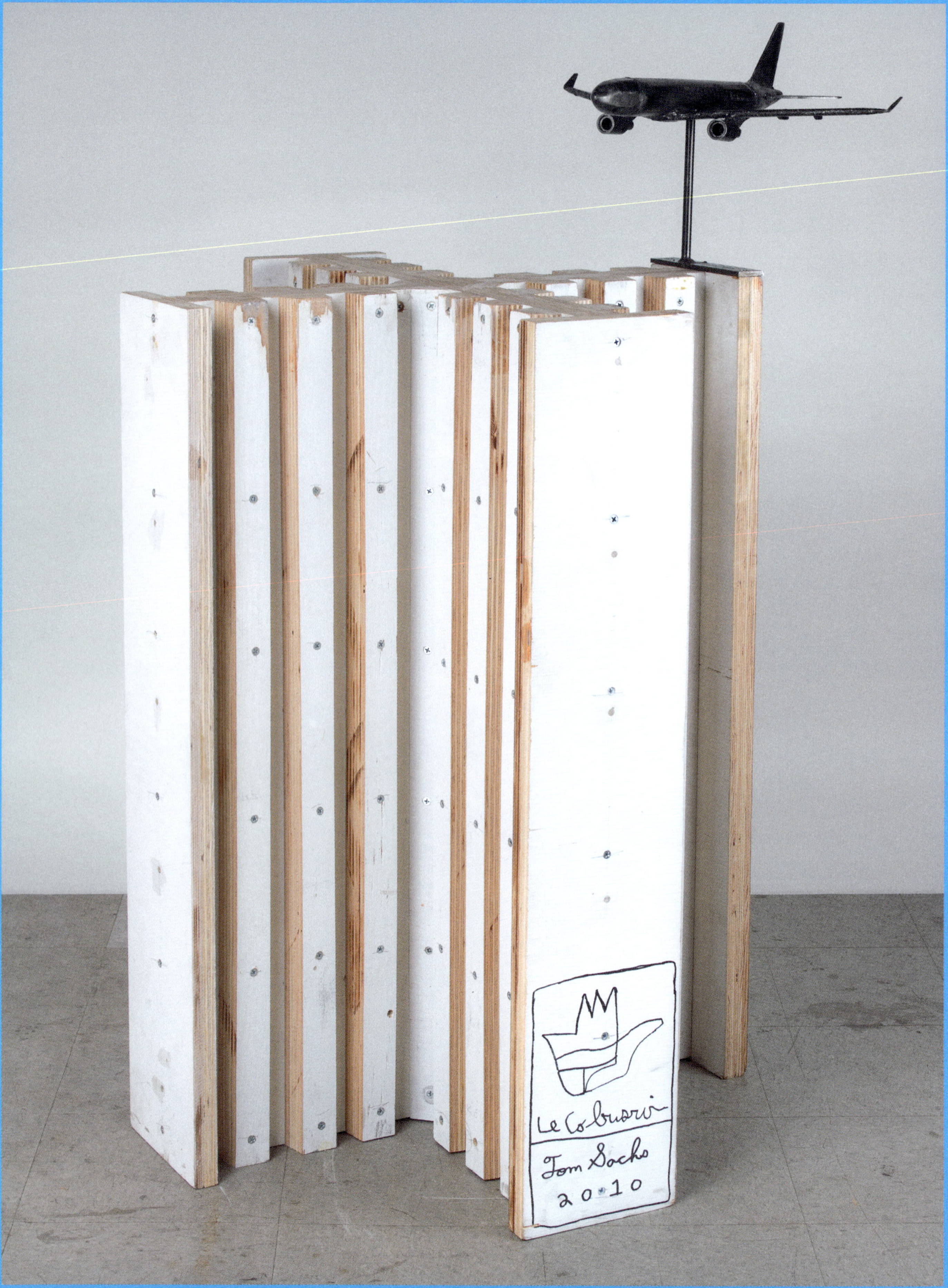
Tom Sachs
2010

American artist TOM SACHS builds models, drawings, and paintings exploring the legacy of Swiss-French pioneer of modern architecture Le Corbusier. Together with LUKAS FEIREISS, Sachs engages in inspiring conversation about his life-long fascination with Modernism in architecture in general, and with Le Corbusier in particular.

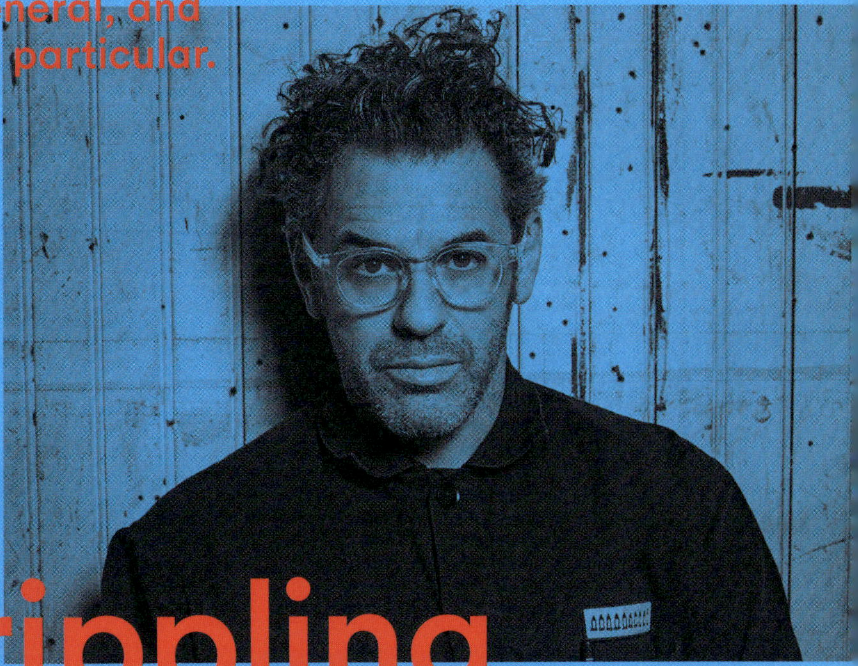

The Crippling Legacy of Le Corbusier

Lukas Feireiss and Tom Sachs

LUKAS FEIREISS From your exhibition *Nutsy's* (2003) at the Deutsche Guggenheim in Berlin, to your Le Corbusier Installation at the Venice Biennale of Architecture (2010), you've been exploring the legacy of Swiss-French architect, designer, painter, urban planner Le Corubiser. What is it about this pioneer of Modern architecture that you are so fascinated by?

TOM SACHS To me, Le Corbusier is one of the most important artists of the 20th century (not including his paintings and sculptures), and certainly the most important architect. He was not only a great sculptor of concrete, but also a utopian visionary. No other architect has been copied more than him, and no other architects' work has been expanded upon more than his. We are talking about a guy who really tried to solve the housing problems of the time, in particular in the post-war era through projects like Unite d'Habitation (1952).

LF Unité d'Habitation is arguably one of the most influential Brutalist building of all time, and what Le Corbusier called a house is 'A machine for living in'. You recreated Le Corbusier's massive housing block that was intended as a universal solution for better living conditions as foam core model.

TS Unité, or any other project by Le Corbusier that embodied his architectural principles, his five points of architecture (pilotis or concrete columns, a free design of the ground plan and the facade, horizontal windows and roof gardens) are a combination of humanism and the embrace of the machine. Today, we live in a polarized world. There are very few forces in place that embrace the mechanical age as well as humanity. Le Corbusier, as an individual, and of course through his work, was a champion of both. It's not about good or evil, God or the devil. It's always about both. The Greeks had it right. (Laughs) We are all part Dionysus, part Apollo. Le Corbusier was a great humanist who embraced nature. He swam every day, he even died because he swam in the Mediterranean Sea against his doctor's orders and had a heart attack. At the same time, there was nobody around that was more high-tech than him. I think he and Elon Musk would have gotten along really well. Musk's crazy vision of launching a settlement on Mars is also truly humanist.

LF It's a certain kind of universalism that both of them have.

TS Yes. The great utopians aren't the autocratic people that have only one way to live. The great utopians have a larger vision for humanity.

LF One could argue, however, that the entire Modern and utopian project failed completely. Architects' zealous, but misled systematization, mechanization and automatization of social and urban problems in utopian grand schemes contributed to the creation of many cheerless places around the world. Your artistic examination of Le Corbusier's legacy appears to be both a homage and a critique of Modernism. To pick up your analogy from before, a creative tension between the Apollonian and Dionysian opposites is palpable here.

TS Absolutely. The core idea in *Nutsy*'s was the contrast of the vision of Le Corbusier, one of the pioneers of Modern architecture, versus the vision of Ray Kroc, the inventor of McDonald's and how they each, in different ways, formed modernism.

LF The iconography of the McDonald's fast-food chain is indeed a common revenant in your oeuvre. Your installation *McBusier* merges a McDonald's Drive-In with Le Corbusier's Villa Savoye (1931). Both are connected by a street. Here, we are looking at two building typologies that incorporate the automobile in the architecture.

TS Both buildings, Villa Savoye and the McDonalds Drive-In look at the automobile in different ways. It might be a bit of a heavy-handed comparison but in this context, but Kroc represents the success of Modernism and Le Corbusier—its failure. Le Corbusier failed, because there is practically only one Villa Savoye. McDonalds, on the other hand, succeeded. There are a million Drive-In's around the world. Kroc obviously didn't invent the Drive-In, but he certainly maximized it.

LF I believe that the space for parking under the pilotis of Le Corbusier's Villa Savoye is even based on the curve radius of the Citroën Traction Avant.

TS Yes. When I was in college in Europe, I was so obsessed with Villa Savoye that I actually got a Citroën Traction Avant. The uncle of my friend Joel Fitzpatrick owned one that we were able to borrow. We got the car and we drove it all the way to Poissy, in the outskirts of Paris. They didn't let us drive the car underneath Villa Savoye but we got pretty close. We also really got to enjoy the drive. The view out of the window of the car was in a way what Le Corbusier was always trying to mimic in the horizontal strip windows of Villa Savoye.

↰↰ Tom Sachs, *The Radiant City*, 2010. Image courtesy of the artist. © Tom Sachs.

↰ Tom Sachs Portrait, New York, USA. Photo by Mario Sorrenti.

→ Tom Sachs, *The Radiant City*, 2010. Photo by Genevieve Hanson. © Tom Sachs.

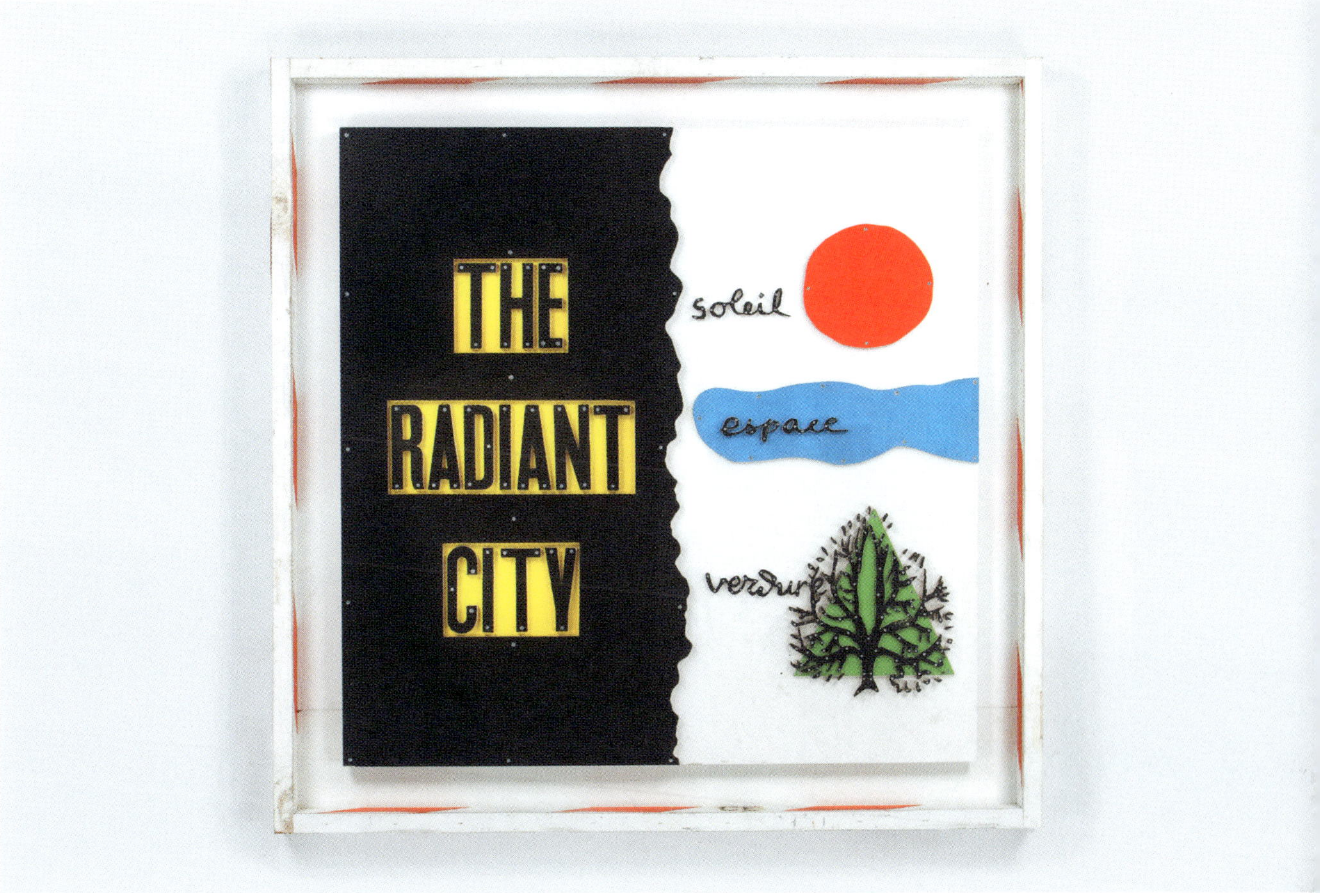

LF I understand you studied architecture, is that correct?

TS I went to the Architectural Association School of Architecture (AA) in London. Architecture was actually one of the first subjects that really inspired me. My science teacher in high-school already introduced me to Le Corbusier's Villa Savoye as a building and as a phenomenon. The town I grew up in, Westport, Connecticut, had a lot of amazing Bauhaus architecture, too. I witnessed too many of these beautiful buildings sacrificed by greedy developers. A couple of buildings by Marcel Breuer were eventually bulldozed to make room for McMansions (houses built to the maximum allowable size per lot, according to local building code).

LF It seems that you also hint at the disillusionment of the Modern project in your model of Le Corbusier's Radiant City (1930). It's maybe the most megalomaniac of Le Corbusier's urbanist proposals: 60 storey tall skyscrapers that separate all aspects of life, work and production.

TS Oh yes, Le Corbusier was a crazy person and a total megalomaniac. Recently it came out that at one point he was even sympathetic to Adolf Hitler's visions, which is sort of surprising at first. When you think about it, you realize that someone like Le Corbusier just wanted to be on the side of who's wining, so that he could built more and fulfil his visions. He knew that he wasn't going to change the tides of the war.

LF Kind of like Wernher von Braun, the dubious mastermind behind who exploited the military and forced labour prisoners in Nazi Germany to further his covert vision of traveling to the Moon. I mean, he devoted his entire life to reaching the Moon and became the leading figure in the development of rocket technology in Nazi Germany during World War II and, subsequently, for the NASA in the United States.

TS Exactly, 100 per cent. Very similar characters. Ultimately von Braun or Le Corbusier only cared about their vision and they did what whatever it took. You can easily despise them for their mercenary position, but they were also totally committed. That's inspiration!

LF Let's come back to your model of Le Corbusier's Radiant City. You added an airplane model that seems to reference both Le Corbusier's original idea of a defence system against aerial attacks but also eerily calls to mind 9/11 and the World Trade Centre. This

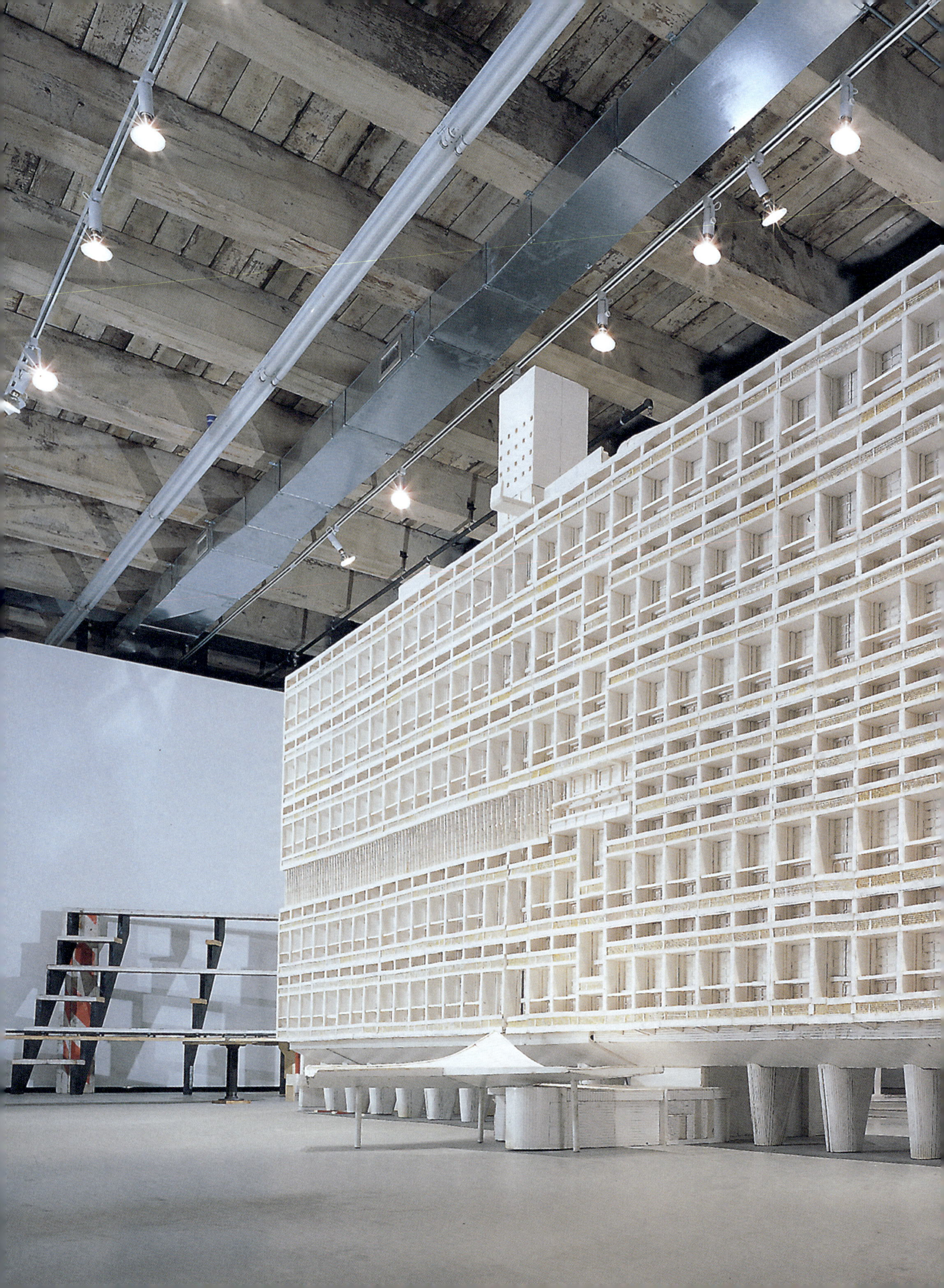

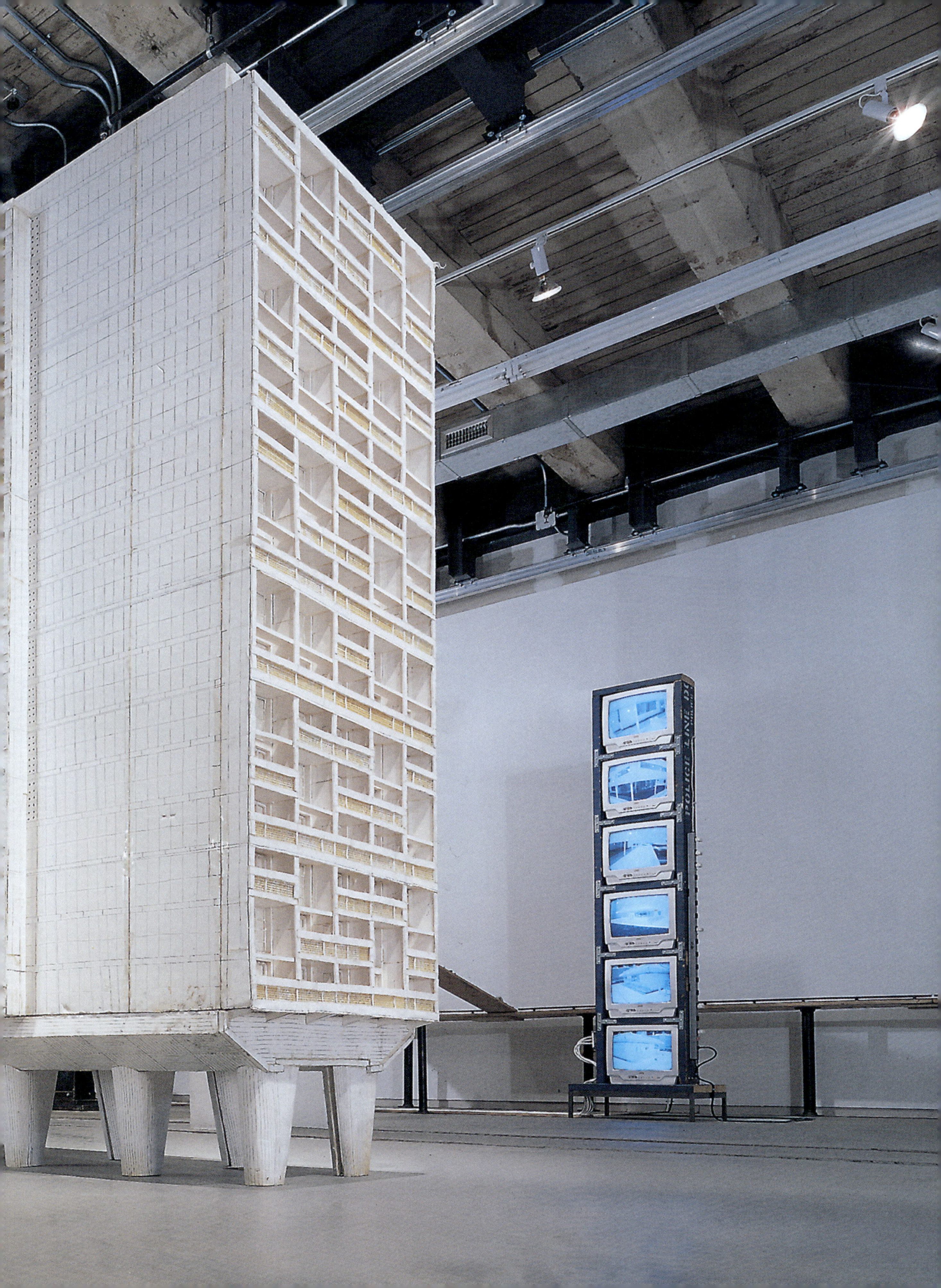

‘In this short life, I intend to do all I can, to leave my finger prints on things.’

TOM SACHS

made me think of Minoru Yamasaki, the architect of the World Trade Centre (1973-2001) who was also the architect of the infamous Pruitt-Igoe (1955-1977) housing project in St. Louis, Missouri. With its publicly televised implosion in 1972, Pruitt-Igoe became an immortal icon of failure. American architecture theorist, Charles Jencks even called it the death of Modern architecture in his seminal book *The Language of Post-Modern Architecture* (1977). Did you intend this analogy, or is this too far-fetched now?

TS This is absolutely intended. Just think of it, Yamazaki was a super prolific architect and one of Le Corbusier's greatest disciples. Of all the numerous, giant Modernist projects he built during his life time that ranged from airports, to universities and office towers, his two most famous buildings were the ones that were destroyed. It was more infamy than fame.

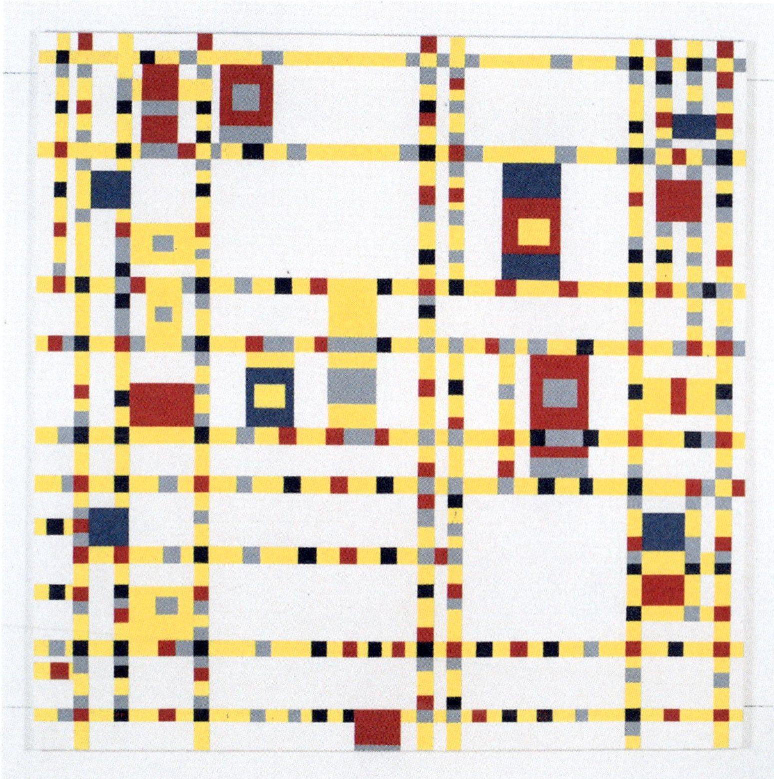

LF What a tragic legacy—to unwillingly become the enigmatic composer of Modern architecture's requiem!

TS Yes, unimaginable. With regards to Pruitt-Igoe, there is even a pre-construction interview with Yamazaki about the essential problem of high density dwelling, in which he prophesied the demise of Pruitt-Igoe. He explicitly says that low-rise buildings are better for living and more satisfactory than high-rise multi-story living. Man is a ground animal, he says, and it's quite natural for him to live near the earth. Yamasaki understands what's humane, safe, and dignified; yet he subjects himself to economic and political conditioning that prevents him from achieving the ideal. As Le Corbusier's disciple, Minoru basically sold out the idealistic goals of Unité so gratuitously that Pruitt-Igoe was demolished within 16 years of its construction.

LF You've also recreated the image of Le Corbusier's Modulor—his standard model of the human form for the scale of architectural proportions. Having watched your ingenious studio manual Ten Bullets about working to code, you must just love the idea of having your very own measurement system, don't you?

TS I do. (Laughs) I love the idea behind it. Feet and inches are basically impossible, because it's so much harder to do the maths with, than with the metric system, but then again feet and inches are much more related to the human body and nature. Le Corbusier's idea was that his Modulor system would be so easy, that even the rustic people who would built Unité could apply it, without being educated whilst at the same time being harmonious with nature. I went to college and I couldn't figure out how to build anything with the Modulor system. I don't know how anyone would understand it on the spot. I think it's totally stupid but the megalomaniac idea that you could create your own measuring system is fantastic. It's my favourite thing ever.

LF You once said about your gaffer's tape version of a Mondrian painting: 'Making is a way of having it.' Is your exploration of Le Corbusier's legacy then maybe a form of artistic co-ownership?

TS I always made things that I wanted to own. I always wanted a Mondrian of my own, but I knew

↰ Tom Sachs, *Unite*, 2001, Astrup Fearnley Museum of Modern Art, Norway. Photo by Tom Powel. © Tom Sachs.

↑ Tom Sachs, *165 Broadway Boogie Woogie (Mondrian)*, 1996, Image courtesy of Fondazione Prada. © Tom Sachs.

'Today, we live in a polarized world. There are very few forces in place that embrace the mechanical age as well as humanity. Le Corbusier, as an individual, and of course through his work, was a champion of both.'

TOM SACHS

that I would have to go into the finance business to be able to afford one. That, however, never appeared to me as an authentic use of my time. I made my own out of gaffer tape and possessed it in that way. I probably spend more time with *Broadway Boogie Woogie* (1942-43), Piet Mondrian's greatest work, than Si Newhouse who bought and then gave it to the museum. Even though mine wasn't made by Mondrian, but by myself, I know I spend more time with it than Si did. That's a good lesson that I continue to teach myself over and over again. With Le Corbusier it's the same. I always wanted to live in Villa Savoye. I remember talking to Patrick Beale, my architecture professor, about it when I was in college. He said: 'Come on, Tom. You can do better than Villa Savoye. Don't copy Le Corbusier. Take it to the next level. Don't settle!' I thought that was a very beautiful, enlightening and encouraging thing to say to a young student who's not sure where he was going to go with his work, whether it was architecture or sculpture. Making sculptures of these different things and engaging with them in their ideological ways is a way of owning them.

↗ Tom Sachs, *Le Corbusier Installation: The Radiant City zine*, 2010. Image courtesy of the artist. © Tom Sachs.

LF You've mastered the practice of bricolage—of creating something new out of already existing materials. Each recreation and appropriation thereby shows your unique and personal traces.

TS Bricolage is a way of putting my hand into something. We're living in a time where there is almost no evidence of any human involvement in the production of things anymore. Take an iPhone for example, it's the best made device but there is no evidence what so ever that a human was involved in the making of it. I think bricolage in general—and putting hand-evident elements into sculpture in particular—is an important advantage that artists have today. It is an opportunity of the individual to show his or her mark. In this short life, I intend to do all I can, to leave my finger prints on things. That's why I am making ceramics. The way I do ceramics is through bricolage. There is a lot of failure, there's a lot of repair there are a lot of fingerprints. That's what I do best.

LF Looking at your artistic exploration of Le Corbusier, I find it very inspiring that you don't seem to regard his legacy as an end-point but rather as a simple moment in an infinite chain of contributions that naturally extends and transforms in your work. Do you see yourself following a legacy?

TS I consider my work as well as Le Corbusier's, and actually almost anybody's work to be part of a long chain of history. Thereby I don't look at my work in one direct succession. However, one could easily draw some sort of a line starting with Auguste Rodin, whose student was Constantin Brancusi whose student was Isamu Noguchi who worked with Charles and Ray Eames, who were an inspiration for a lot of things that **Frank Gehry** **(page → 198)** was doing, for whom I once worked. That's one possible line or path but there are many others. Take for example architecture and bricolage: Here I'm also looking at the work of Gordon Matta-Clark and his notion of Anarchitecture—a combination of anarchy and architecture. At the same time, I'm looking at people that are nameless. Nutsy for example—after whom I named my exhibition at the Deutsche Guggenheim in Berlin—is a bike mechanic that I met in Jamaica, who practices bricolage with pure mastery. He is also a leader in his community, because his wife ran the local post office. If you wanted your mail you wouldn't mess around with Nutsy, the bike mechanic, because he was married to the boss and she would screw up your mail delivery. I think there are so many paths to follow. Even Le Corbusier is in a path. His work continues in so many ways until this day.

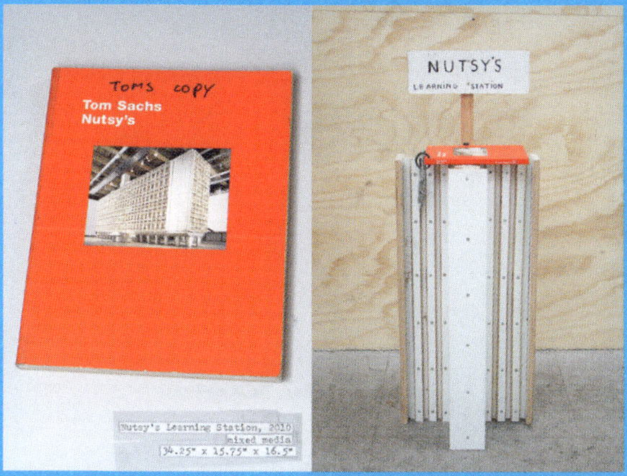
TOMS COPY
Tom Sachs
Nutsy's
NUTSY'S
LEARNING STATION
Nutsy's Learning Station, 2010
mixed media
34.25" x 15.75" x 16.5"

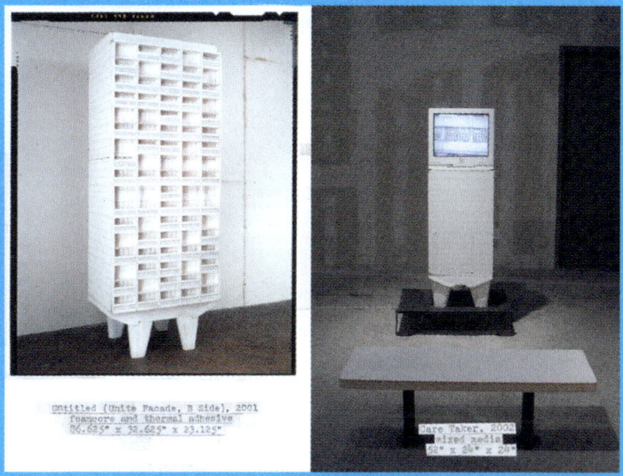
Untitled (Unite Facade, B Side), 2001
foamcore and thermal adhesive
86.625" x 32.625" x 23.125"
Care Taker, 2002
mixed media
52" x 24" x 24"

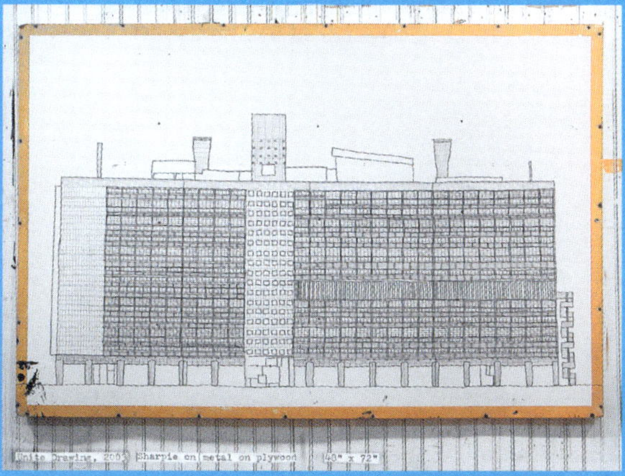
Unite Drawing, 2003 Sharpie on metal on plywood 48" x 72"

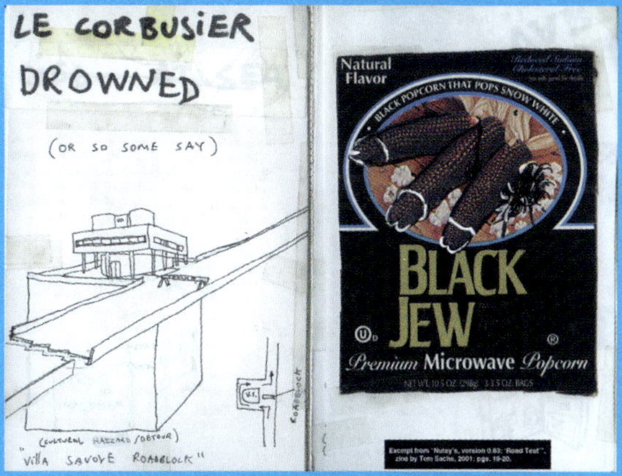
LE CORBUSIER
DROWNED
(OR SO SOME SAY)
VILLA SAVOYE ROADBLOCK
Natural Flavor
BLACK POPCORN THAT POPS SNOW WHITE
BLACK JEW
Premium Microwave Popcorn
Excerpt from "Nutsy's, version 0.83: 'Road Test'", zine by Tom Sachs, 2001: pgs. 19-20.

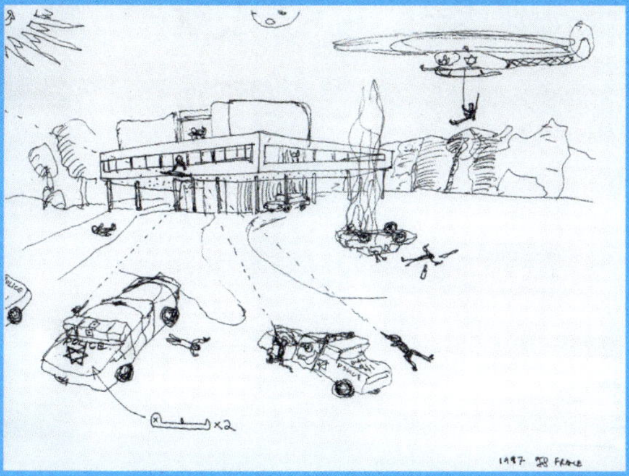
1997 TS FRANCE

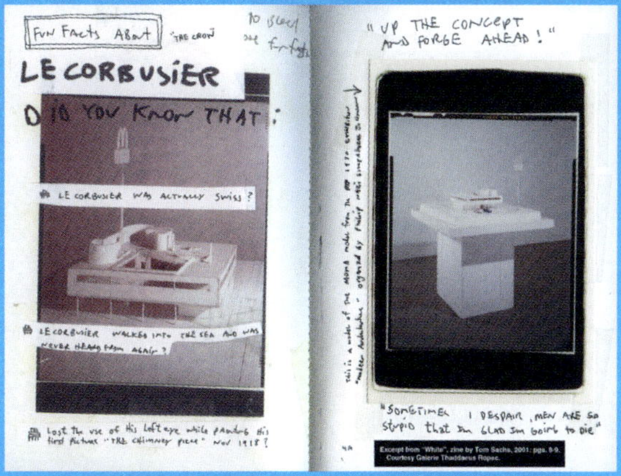
FUN FACTS ABOUT
LE CORBUSIER
DID YOU KNOW THAT:
LE CORBUSIER WAS ACTUALLY SWISS?
LE CORBUSIER WALKED INTO THE SEA AND WAS NEVER HEARD FROM AGAIN?
"UP THE CONCEPT AND FORGE AHEAD!"
"SOMETIMES I DESPAIR, MEN ARE SO STUPID THAT I'M GLAD I'M GOING TO DIE"
Excerpt from "White", zine by Tom Sachs, 2001: pgs. 8-9.
Courtesy Galerie Thaddaeus Ropac.

For Others to Define

Aric Chen and Arata Isozaki

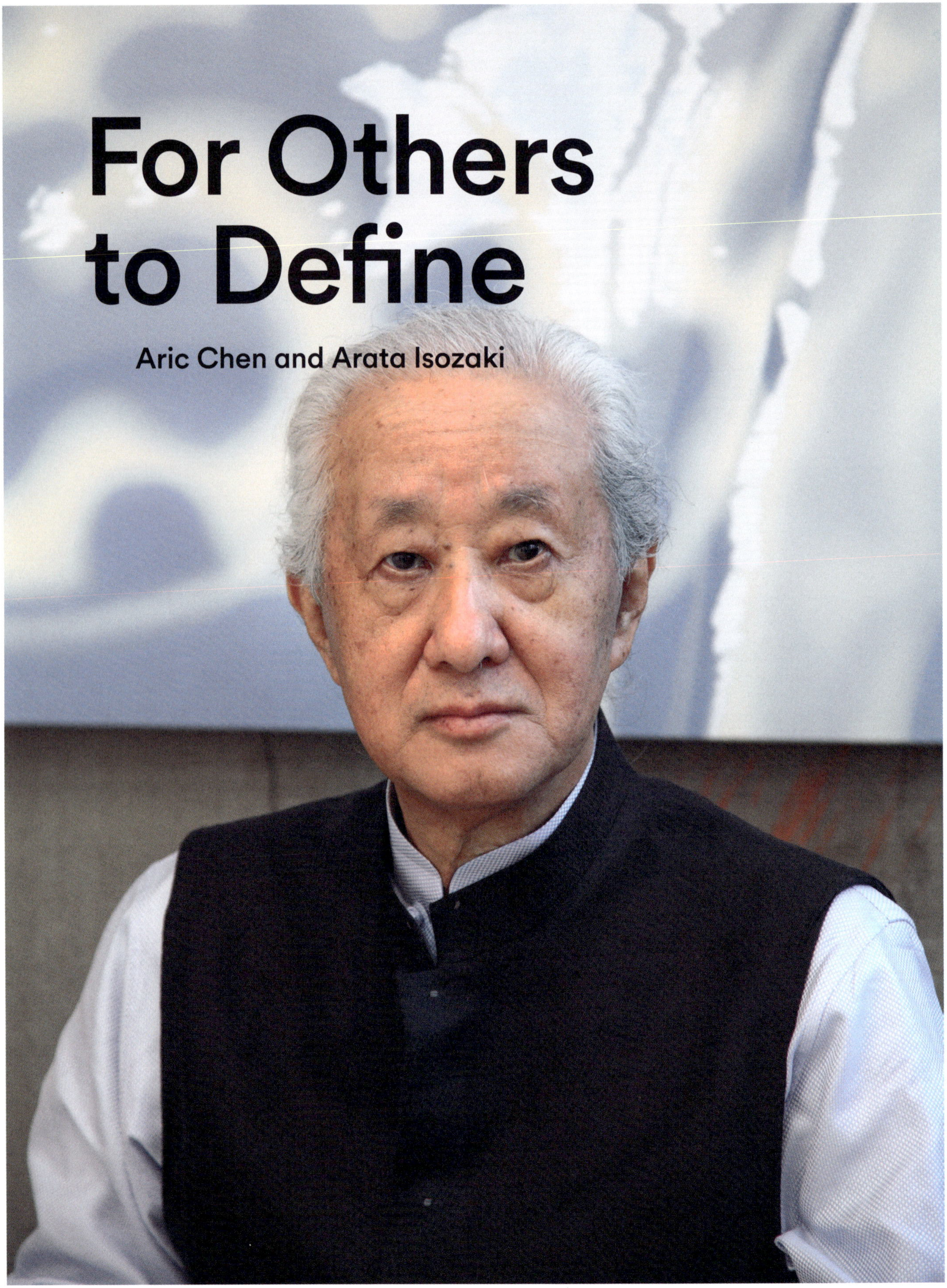

Hong Kong-based curator ARIC CHEN meets with Japanese architect ARATA ISOZAKI to question the notion of legacy and to discuss the importance of independence and diversity as well as the ability to adapt in the field of architecture and design.

Since 1980, Arata Isozaki has spent his summers at a house he built in the Japanese mountain retreat of Karuizawa where, like many others, he goes to escape the heat of Tokyo. On a wooded, sloping site, the property actually consists of two clapboard houses and a small hut on stilts—a 'Tree-House' where the architect withdraws, it's been said, to 'disavow his occupation as an architect.'

In 2016, Isozaki, then 84, had extended his stay at the house well into the autumn, as he was recovering from a neck affliction that made it difficult for him to stand, or even sit, for prolonged periods of time. (He would soon recover.) As such, it was to Karuizawa that I went to see him on October 8.

ARIC CHEN Isozaki, it's a privilege to be speaking about legacies with someone who has such an imposing one. You've operated at the centre of architectural discourse, whether in Japan or globally, for nearly six decades. Yet in thinking about our talk today, I was immediately reminded of the time you told me about your refusal to accept honours, awards, even the Pritzker—all the conventional trappings of a legacy in architecture. Clearly, these things are unimportant to you. Perhaps your rejection of them is, in fact, part of your legacy.

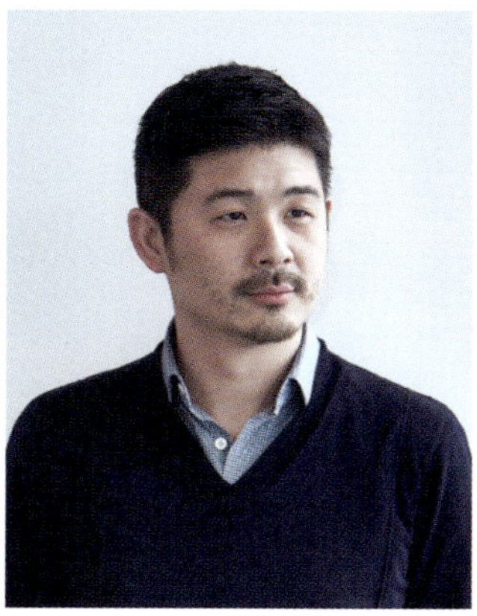

ARATA ISOZAKI One can't talk about one's own legacy. That's for others to define. I can answer any other question you ask, but it's difficult for me to talk about the legacy of my architecture. However, I can speak a little about the Pritzker Prize, since you mention it.

When I turned 60, I decided not to own any property or accept any positions, titles, or other signs of power and authority, including prizes, honours, and so on. Of course, you need influence in order to get work, but anything formal I decided to decline. In Zen Buddhism, there's a saying, 'muichimotsu'. It means 'having nothing,' or 'the whole universe is nothing.' I decided not to own anything—I didn't have any property anyway (the house in Karuizawa is not technically his)—and to be free of possessions. I was offered prizes and honours, but I didn't want them.

AC What prompted this?

AI It's a bit personal, perhaps even rebellious. People are too obsessed with status and position. I've been on the jury for many prizes, including the Pritzker. I was on its jury for its first eight years. Other architects of course knew this, and they would lobby me for the prize. It created some uncomfortable situations for me and became very complicated, like a comedy. People send you their portfolios, documents, other materials. They want to see you surreptitiously. It's like they're running an election campaign. I became tired of it and decided I didn't want to be involved.

However, this tendency of mine started even earlier. In the 1960s, it was thought that in order to be a good designer, you had to be a professor at a good university. I was offered several

← ← Arata Isozaki. Photo by Keizo Kioku.

← Portrait of Aric Chen. Photo by M+, Honk Kong.

professorships, but I refused them. I saw things in opposite terms: in order to make good design, you have to be independent.

AC You've always had an independent streak. Looking back at the 1960s, many people assume you were part of the Metabolism group—it's easy to think that you were—but in fact, you weren't. Legacy is in many ways about defining a person, whereas you've always been notoriously hard to define. Perhaps your legacy is an anti-legacy?

AI I agree. I don't want to be a part of a legacy. I don't want a legacy in the conventional sense.

AC You seem drawn to the idea of being an outsider.

AI In 1996, I went to Philip Johnson's 90th birthday in New York. Philip invited a lot of people, though he excluded all the critics. (Laughs) Of course, there were a lot of events, but for the main birthday party, he invited only a few people. There's a well-known group photo from that day. **Phyllis Lambert (page → 178)** is seated on one side of Philip, and I'm on the other. There are quite a number of architects in the picture (among them, Michael Graves, Robert A M Stern, Richard Meier, Peter Eisenman, **Frank Gehry (page → 198)**, and **Rem Koolhaas (page → 18)**). Zaha Hadid stood behind me. At the time, she felt excluded from this boys' club. I was the only one she felt comfortable with.

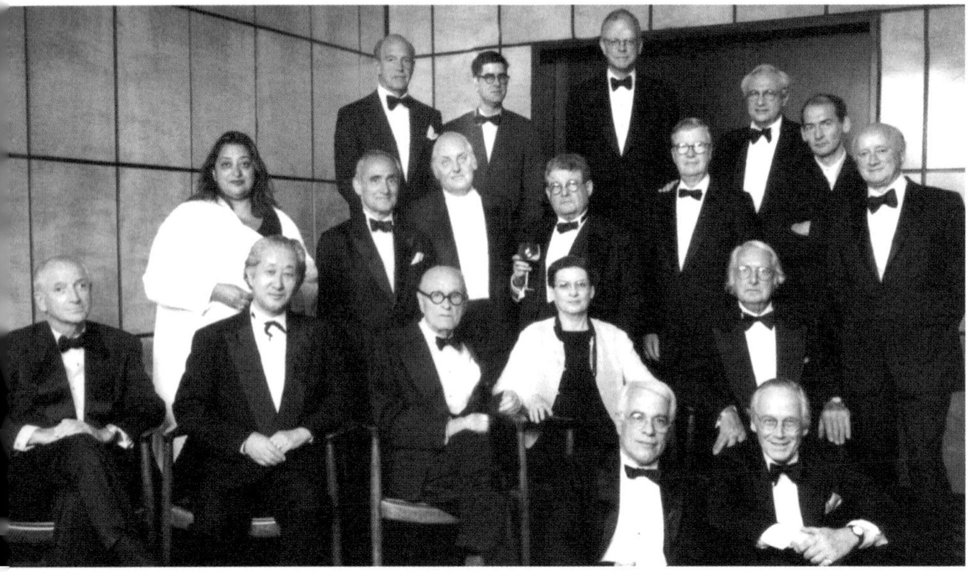

AC You're also perhaps the only one in that photo whose work has been so wide-ranging. There's no Isozaki manifesto, theory, or 'school of Isozaki.' Instead, there are many. You weren't part of a movement, you were part of all of them. I believe Maki once referred to you as a 'chameleon.'

→ *Suki, MA Space-Time* in Japan, Musée des Arts Décoratifs, Paris, 1978. Photo by Shuji Yamada.

↙ Philip Johnson's 90th birthday, 1996. Photo by Timothy Greenfield-Sanders.

AI If you have nothing new, you have nothing special. People change, circumstances change, society changes. If you stay with the same approach or position, it becomes a conceit, and that leads to rot. My work is diverse because, for me, doing something once is enough. What's constant is change. However, I don't set out to change course on purpose, or just for the sake of it; it comes naturally.

AC Maybe I can make a proposition. The Japanese concept of 'ma', the notion of 'space-time' that refers to the in-between, or the interstitial, often comes up with you. It was the subject of an exhibition you curated in Paris in 1978, and that travelled to New York and Sweden. 'Ma' suggests a state of constant change, and also a state of being that is neither here nor there but, as such, achieves a presence nonetheless. Perhaps you're a 'ma' architect.

AI In Paris, I applied 'ma' to architecture by looking at boundaries dividing space, at shadows, at sites of ceremony and ritual. It was a different interpretation of 'ma', and nobody agreed with me. No scholars accepted my argument. I also included some of my own buildings, and I was criticized at a symposium by French architects who said my work simply borrowed from 18th century France, from Ledoux and Boullée and their Platonic forms. Peter Cook was there, and he stood up and made the argument that, like the United Kingdom, Japan is an island country. We're always on the edge, on the periphery, and so we see and do things differently. This difference expresses itself in the UK as eccentricity; in Japan, it becomes 'ma'. That stands in contrast with the logo-centrism you find in the Continental European tradition, which relies on the literal interpretation of words and meanings, and which Derrida critiqued. Derrida tried to turn logo-centrism inside-

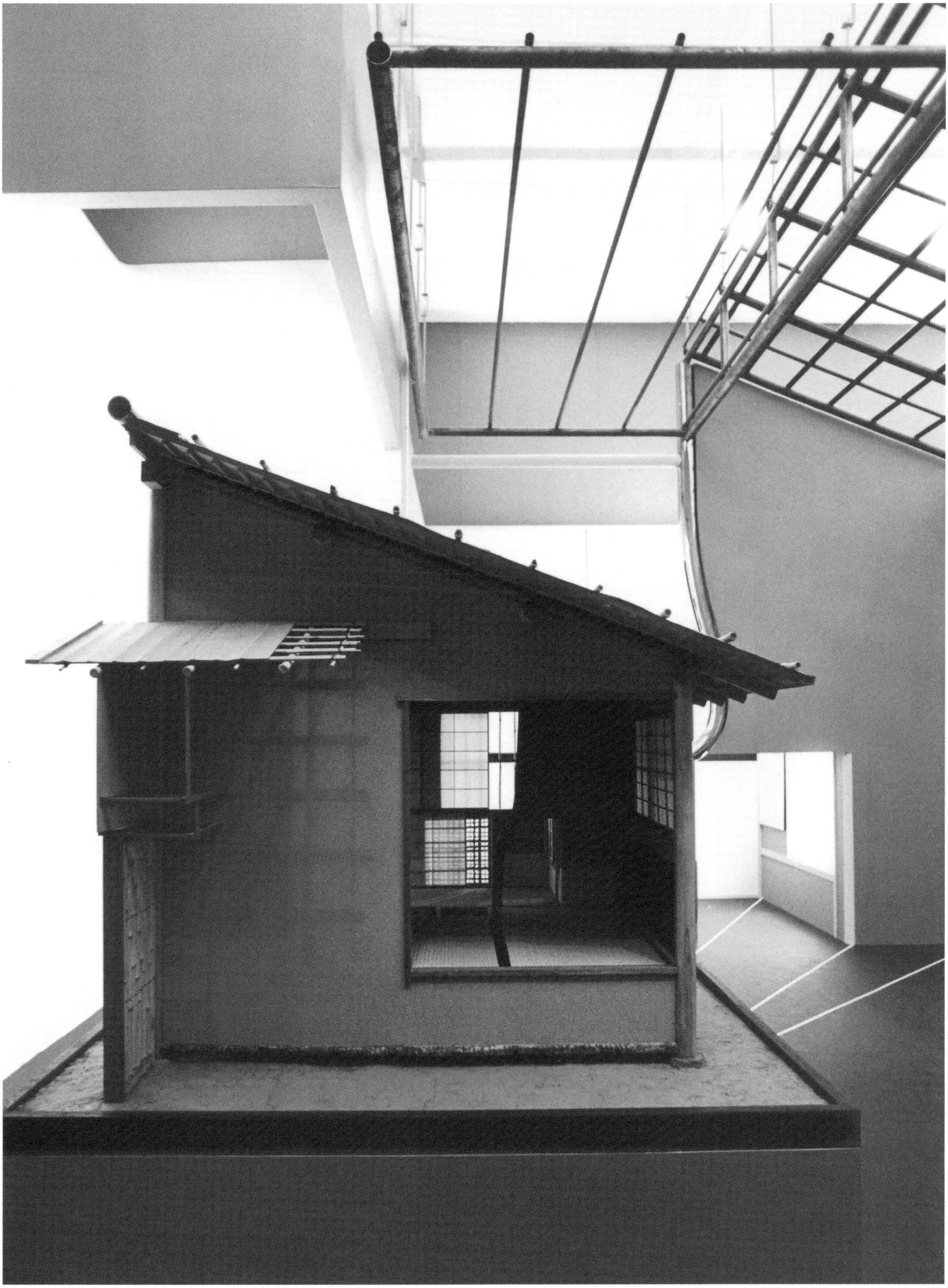

‘If you stay with one design style, then that style becomes the end. It’s not a beginning.’

ARATA ISOZAKI

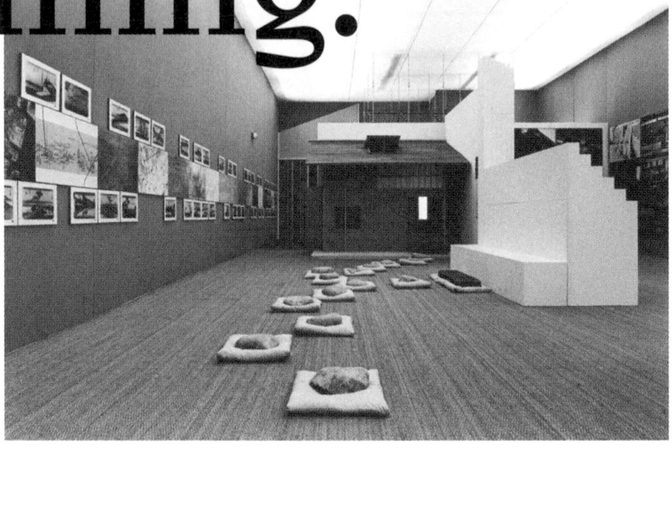

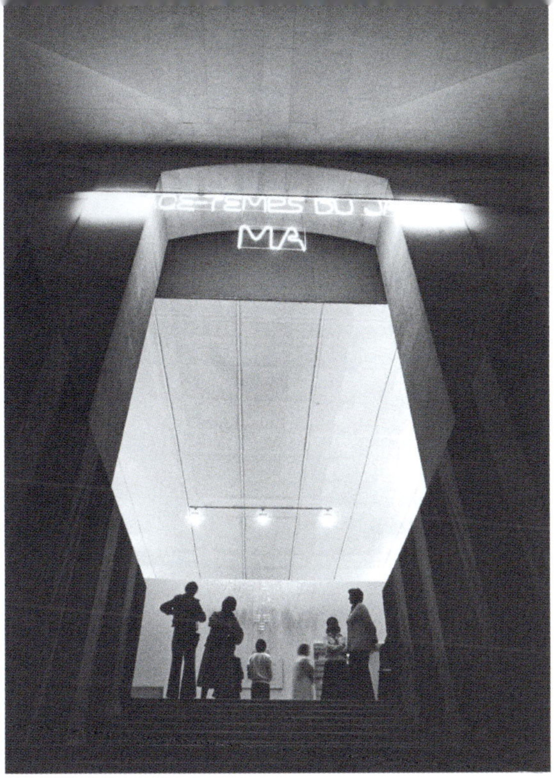

← Entrance, *MA Space-Time* in Japan, Musée des Arts Décoratifs, Paris, 1978. Photo by Shuji Yamada.

↙ *Michiyuki, MA Space-Time* in Japan, Musée des Arts Décoratifs, Paris, 1978. Photo by Shuji Yamada.

out, but Japan had already done that. I was trying to show that through 'ma'.

AC It wasn't that you were misquoting the French; it was the French who were misreading you.

AI Correct. For example, in Europe, time and space are separately defined entities, but in Japan, they are one concept: 'ma'. Gideon wrote about time, space, and architecture in a strictly divided and periodized way. I wanted to deconstruct this idea of modernism. Of course, time and space exist, but in what sense? I was questioning this by looking at artefacts and architecture that embody their simultaneity. Derrida understood this. When he came to Japan in 1984, we did a public talk about this. I think Zaha also understood this. She was not a logo-centric architect.

AC It was around this time, in 1983, that you served on the jury that awarded Zaha the first prize in the Peak competition in Hong Kong. While her proposal was never built, it's often considered her breakthrough project. You were an early supporter of hers, along with numerous other architects who are now quite well-known. This is another way of looking at your legacy.

AI Zaha was a shaman. After MoMA did its Deconstructivist Architecture exhibition, in 1988, Zaha was lumped in with the Deconstructivists. The big mistake was that Deconstructivism became associated with forms and compositions, not the ideas behind them. Zaha was not a Deconstructivist at all. Neither was Rem, though he didn't care if he was called one. Zaha was totally different from Deconstructivism, but people couldn't explain how. Since she died, I've realized she was a shaman, a conduit for something almost supernatural. Building construction and technology have only logic; you have to be logical or else you can't build—but Zaha was not logical. For me, she connects to the idea of 'ma'—something outside, more intuitive.

AC You've been as prolific with your writings as with your buildings. There's always a palpable sense of history in your texts. I was reading on the train here an essay you wrote that schematized a 'new world system' layered atop Japan's Edo and 'modern' periods. Sometimes, you insert yourself in the third person. In *City Demolition Industry, Inc* (1962), you present a sort of fictionalized internal dialogue. The narrator, named

↓ Arata Isozaki, The Museum of Contemporary Art, Los Angeles, 1983. Silkscreen print.

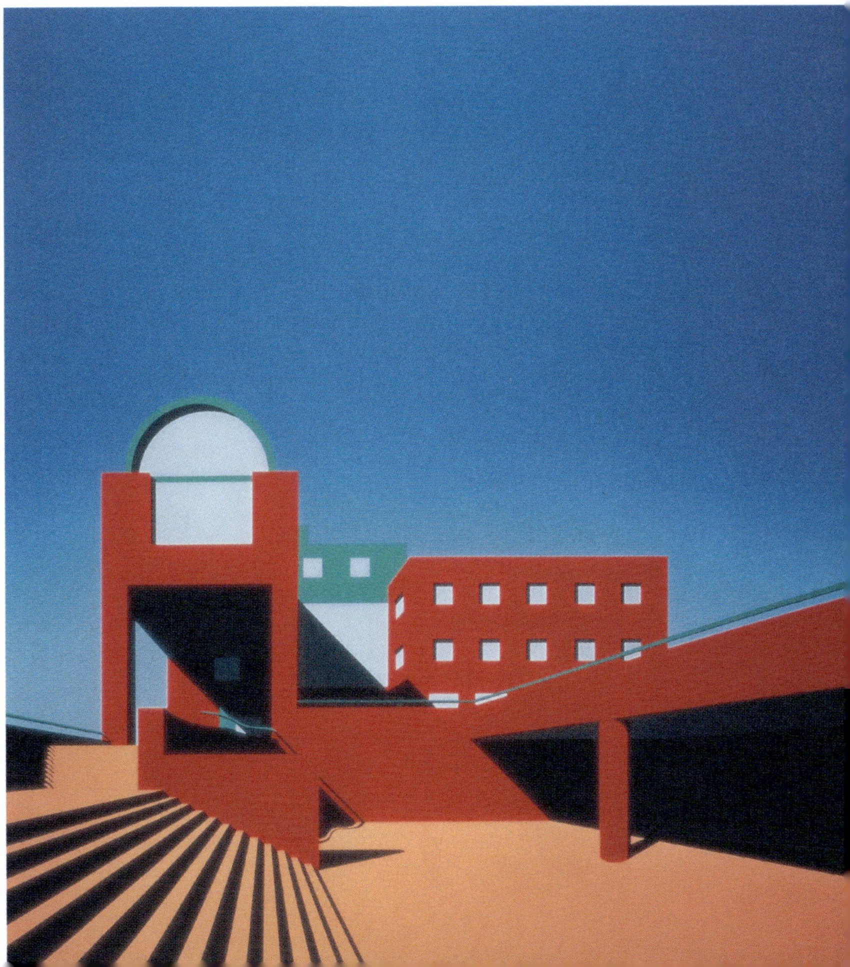

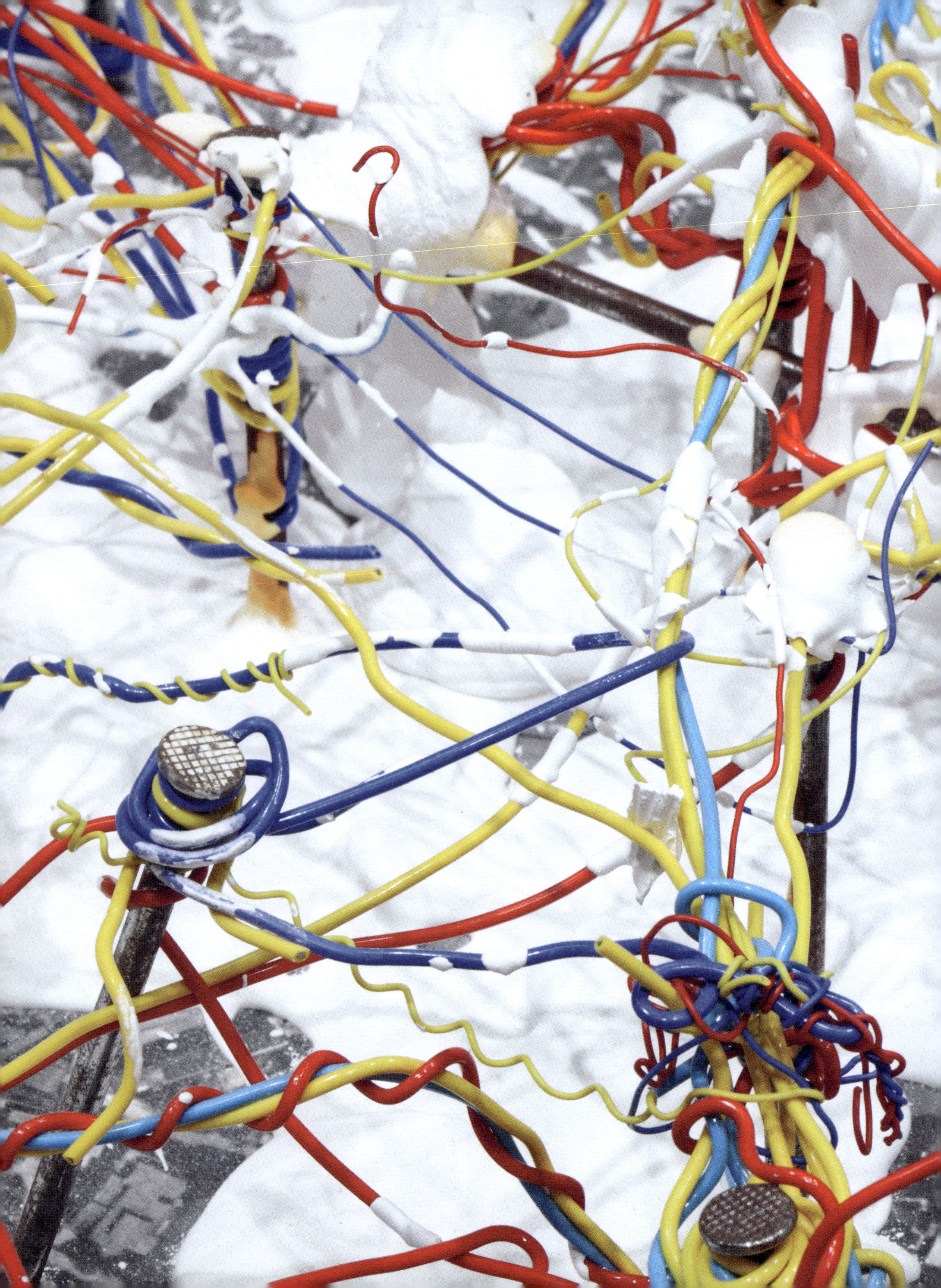

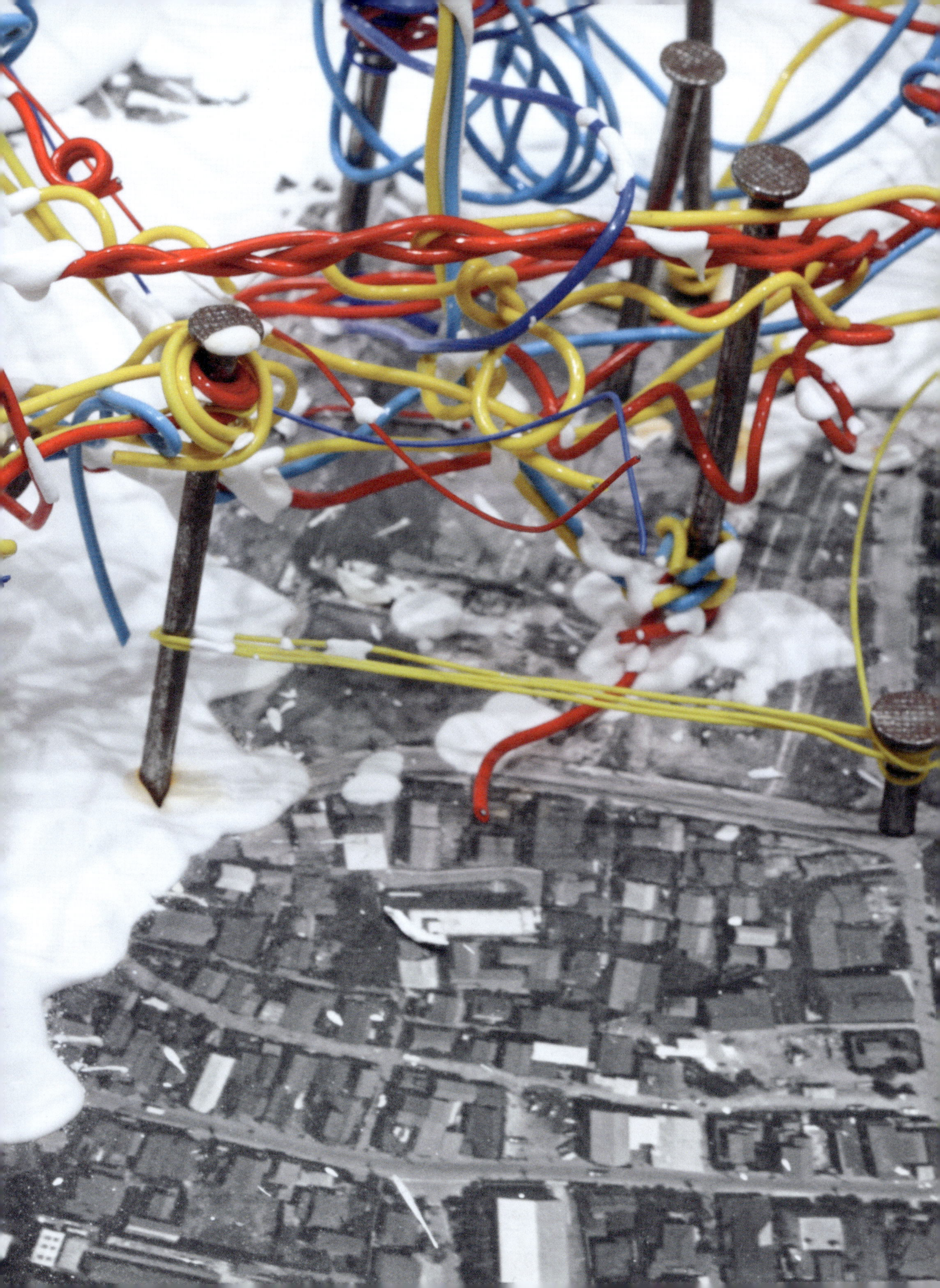

'One can't talk about one's own legacy. That's for others to define.'

ARATA ISOZAKI

Arata, is recalling his encounter with a friend, named Shin, who acts as a kind of alter-ego, a cynical 'killer' who believes that the only way to save cities is to destroy them. Arata, however, is somewhat more circumspect. It's a very aesthetic critique of utopianism, technocracy, bureaucracy, and market capitalism, but I'm wondering to what extent it reflects your own struggles as an architect.

AI Everybody has two sides, many sides, and Shin and Arata are at extremes. One is trying to construct, the other is trying to deconstruct. Maybe I'm a bit schizophrenic.

AC Almost 40 years later, in 2001, you wrote *Rumour City* (2007), a follow-up to City Demolition Industry Inc in which, among other things, Arata reflects on the current state of things and comes to the conclusion that Shin has succeeded in destroying the city. One can sense the powerlessness of the architect here, and then you end the text with: 'By the way, in mainland China, Isozaki Arata is called Ji Qi Xin (it is spelled Shin in Japan). In other words, over there, Isozaki Arata does not exist.' Again, you become elusive.

Moving along, this prompted me to also think about how active you've been in China in recent years, and how I've heard that one of the things you most enjoy about China is how you and your work are often mis-interpreted there. Could you give an example?

AI Once, in Chengdu, I was invited to give a keynote and was joined by Chinese architects who spoke about my work. One of them introduced me as the 'Che Guevara of Japanese architecture'.

AC You mention Guevara in *Rumour City*, but what was this architect referring to?

AI I think he was calling me a provocateur. Che Guevara was always making revolution. That was the difference between him and Castro, as with Trotsky and Stalin. Guevara didn't want to govern, he wanted continuous revolution. In that sense, I suppose I'm more like Guevara and Trotsky.

AC Revolutions have beginnings, but it's much more difficult to determine where they end.

AI That's true. Earlier, we were talking about design styles. If you stay with one design style, then that style becomes the end. It's not a beginning. I'm interested in beginnings, the starting point and genesis, and how something is created. Of course, the beginning is always dangerous; you don't know how things will go, whether it will become gold or garbage.

I'm constantly questioning, though, which is why my interest lies in beginnings. I want to know how questions arise, and I'm always reflecting on this. I try to make—not to express, not to persuade, but to make a project that then generates something else. Samuel Beckett said that it doesn't matter who creates, as long as someone is creating. Otherwise, you're waiting for God, but he never comes.

↰ Arata Isozaki, Incubation Process (detail), 1962/2011, mixed media. Courtesy of Misa Shin Gallery.

↓ Arata Isozaki, New Tokyo City Hall, 1986, silkscreen print.

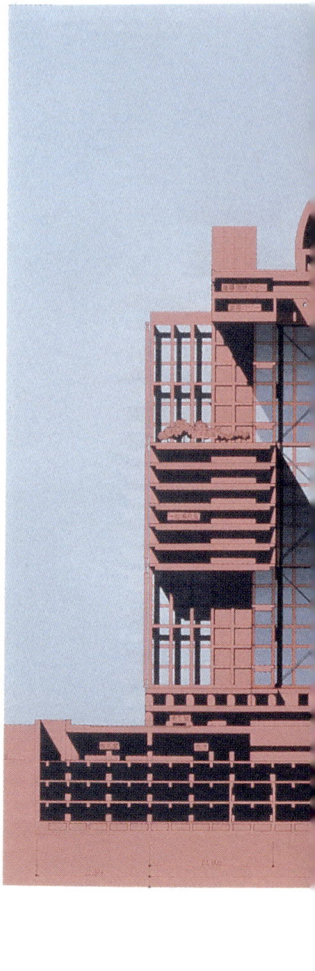

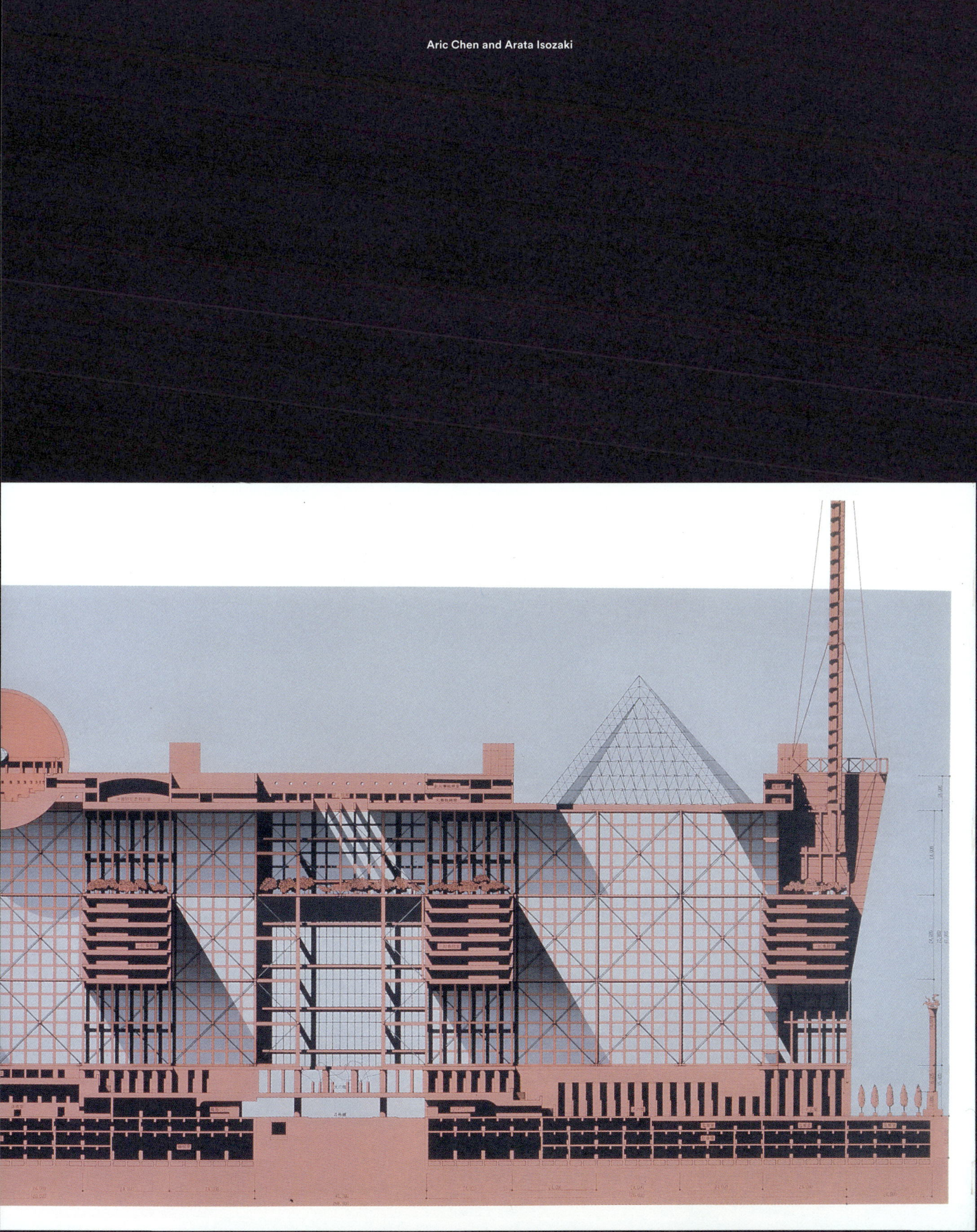

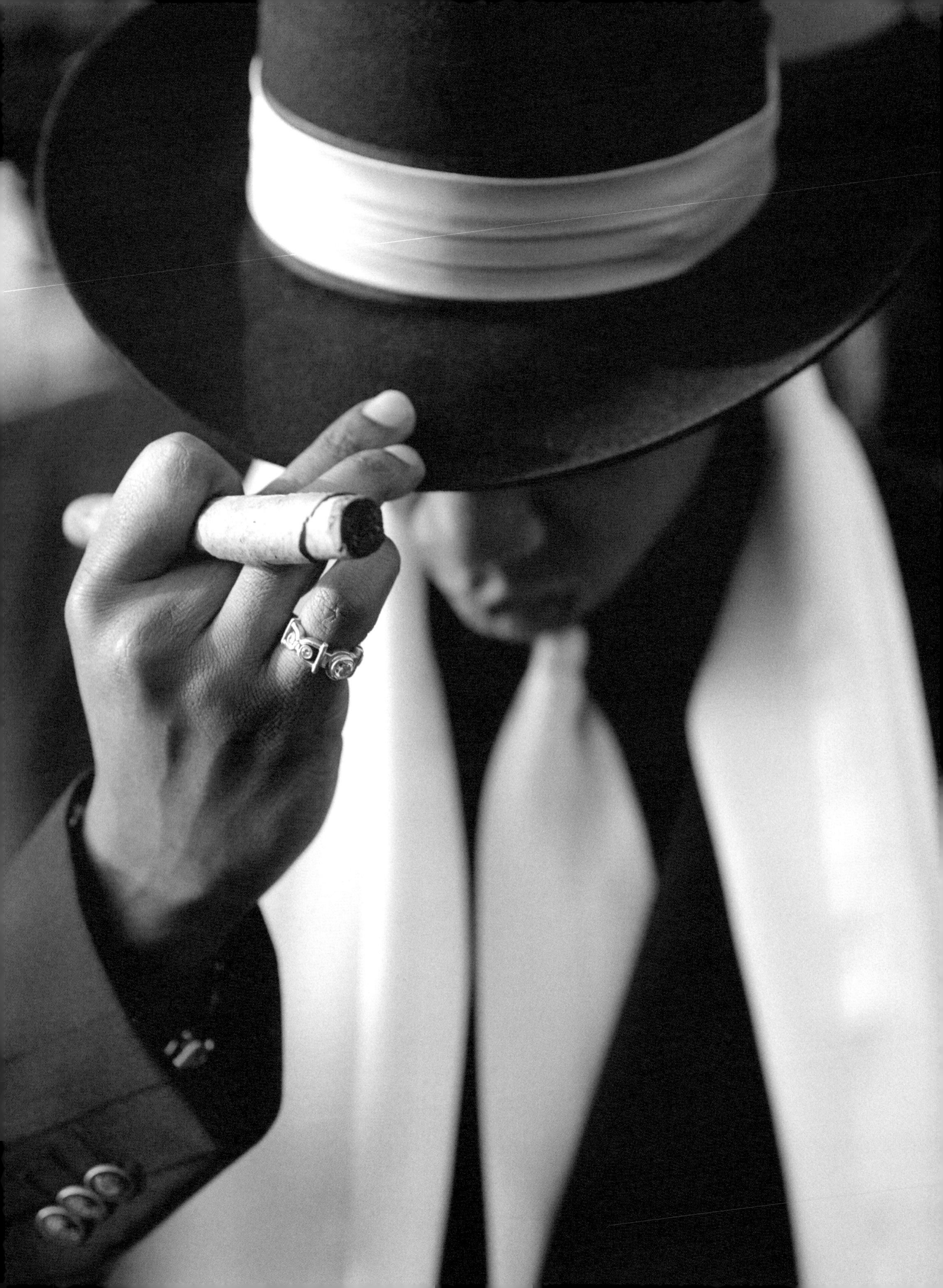

Maintaining Legacy

Lukas Feireiss and Jonathan Mannion

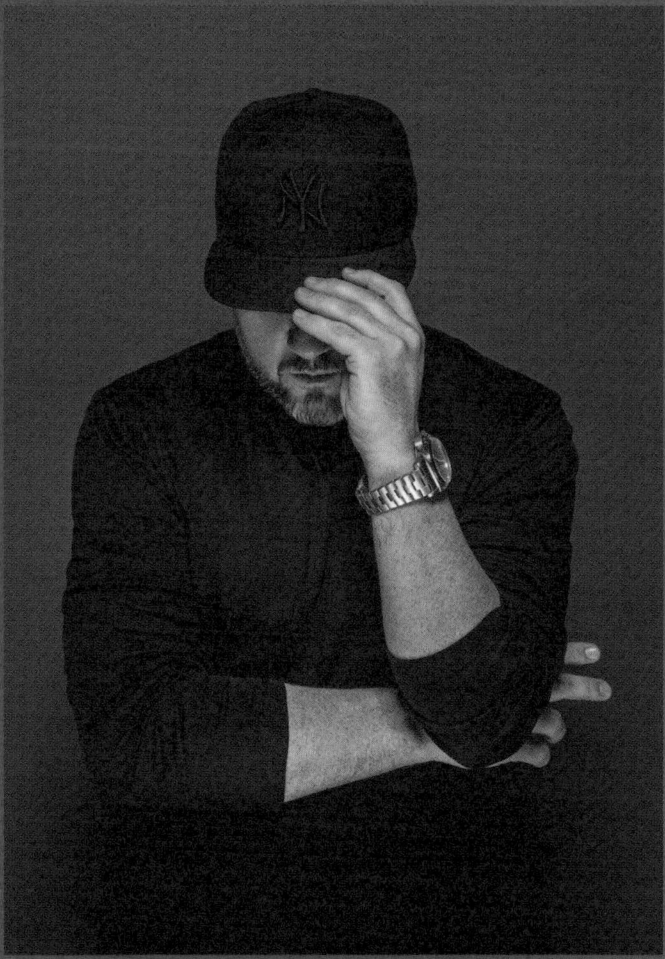

← Jay Z by Jonathan Mannion for his debut album, *Reasonable Doubt*, 1996.

→ Portrait of Jonathan Mannion, 2016. Photo by Zach Wolfe.

JONATHAN MANNION has been the photographer whose lens has defined hip-hop. In conversation with LUKAS FEIREISS, the New York City based photographer talks about being present, unlocking the potential in your subject, and the visual legacy he created in collaboration with some of the greatest artists to ever hold the mic.

Several years ago, Jonathan Mannion and I met in Berlin. It was during the making of an exhibition for which different artists were invited to recreate and reinterpret a selection of some of his iconic photographs, based on his anecdotal input. I was one of these artists at the time. Ever since then, an ongoing dialogue and friendship has been developing between the two of us that now extends to my teenage son. A signed photograph of Notorious BIG at the Palladium by Jonathan hangs above my son's bed. It's also thanks to Jonathan that, at this aforementioned exhibition, I was introduced to the woman who would become my wife.

LUKAS FEIREISS I am thrilled to talk to you in the context of this book on creative legacies, since you have been instrumental in creating the visual legacy for some of the most outstanding hip hop artist over the course of more than two decades—from the late Aaliyah to Jay Z, Nas, DMX, Eminem, Outkast, The Game, to mention but a few. In a way, your legacy can be viewed through the visual legacy of all the album covers that you shot throughout your career.

JONATHAN MANNION I'm blessed to be aligned with these great people through the visuals we have created for any one of these projects. I understood the connection between music and image very early. Take, for example, the cover art of Bob Marley's *Kaya* (1978) album. Whoever took that picture of Bob Marley is now forever linked to that music and that artist. That's always been understood by me, growing up looking at an album covers by Bob Marley, John Coltrane or KISS. These are images that sear into your brain when they are done properly. It makes the artist memorable, and others forgettable. That is something that I have chased on the highest level with all of the artists I worked with.

LF How did it all start for you?

JM It has always been about the music for me. Music is the soundtrack of our lives. I think almost everybody has a connection to music, but I enjoyed it from a very early age. Maybe that's because music was played in the house all the time when I grew up, but it was also something that I have discovered gradually over time—different people telling me to listen to this or that. Music has always been part of my soul, but I also knew that I didn't want to be a musician. Being the son of two visual artists, painters, I wanted to make a contribution to music in another way. Eventually, I found what my contribution could be. I meant to elevate the visuals for a body of music that I loved: Hip Hop, R'n'B, Reggae. I wanted to get to the heart of this music and tell the story about how rich that music and its creators were. It's also important to say—this is my connection. I want to be forever attached to the biggest version or presentation of this music. Initially it was about record covers, the tapes, then CDs and now it's become almost more of an entire visual campaign. Music is not digested in the same way that it always has been. It's changing all the time. That was where it really began. I wanted to do album covers. I want to spend quality time with people. I want to present an entire project and the storytelling behind to find that iconic image that represents the whole project and became the cover. The indelible mark that is connected to the music forever.

→ DMX by Jonathan Mannion for his 2nd studio album *Flesh of My Flesh, Blood of My Blood*, 1998

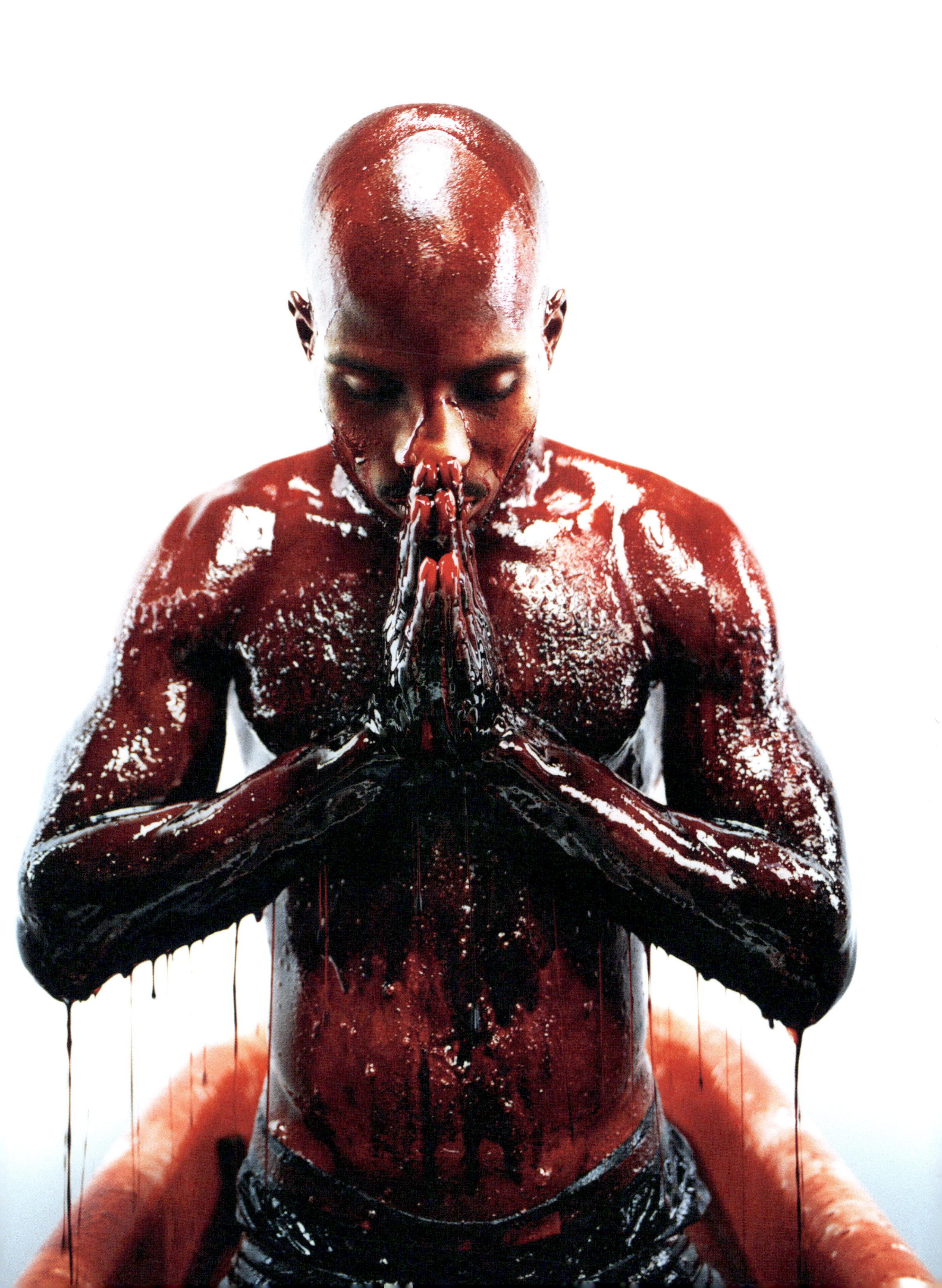

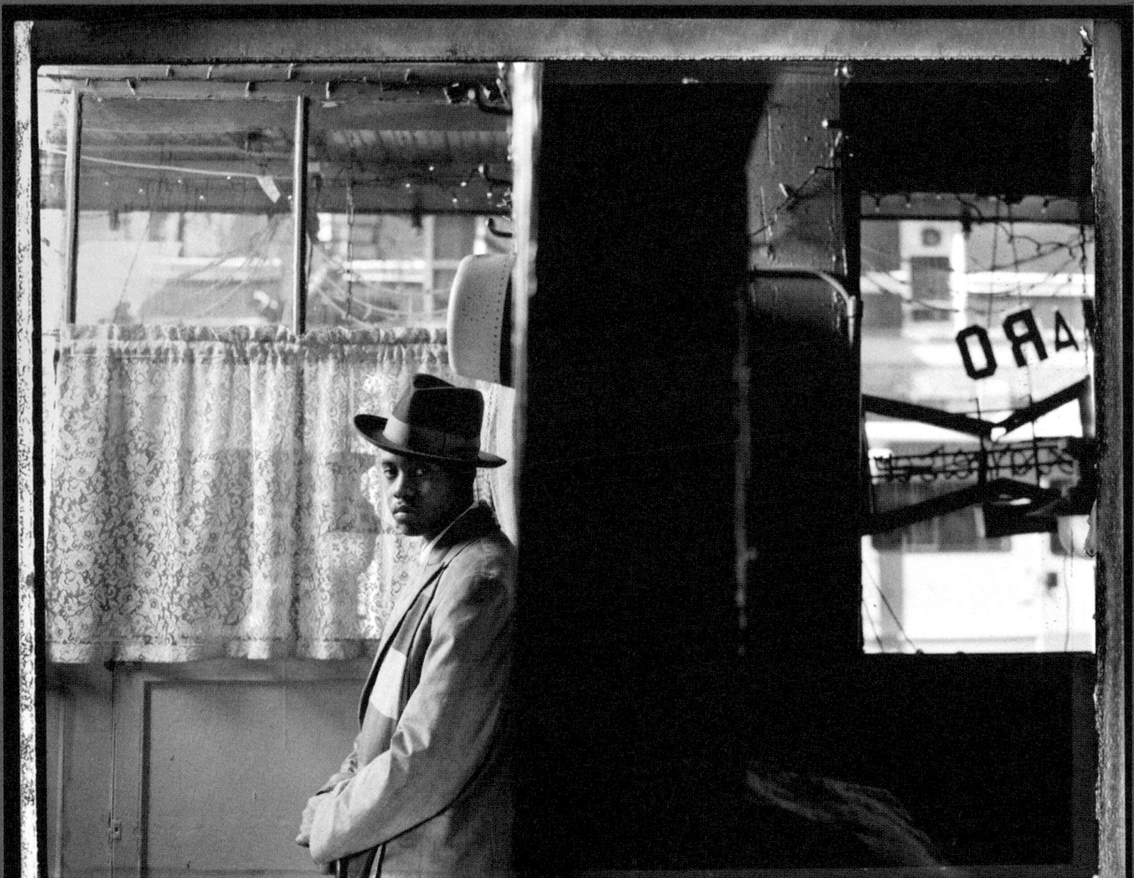

'It's not the loudest voice, but the most pure and truest voice that breaks through the noise.'

JONATHAN MANNION

LF You have worked with so many living legends and have been instrumental in shaping their visual identity over years and even decades. In a way, you have to become almost the medium for the artist's visual expression. This must demand an enormous amount of trust and respect from both sides. Do you develop a visual scheme together or do they trust that you come up with something?

JM Every artist and every project is different. I had an artist tell me: 'Look, I don't want you tell me how to rap in the booth. That's what I do masterfully, so I don't want to tell you how you do your pictures. You just show up and tell me what you want me to do, and it's on.' I would say that that's 80 per cent of the time. 80 per cent of the work I've created has been just out of my head based on listening to the music or getting the album title or talking to the artists, or just following an artist's journey over time. I think that's a pretty accurate number. Even art directors, when I ask them: 'So what are we going to do today?' they often say: 'I hired you, my job is done. I'm not art directing anymore.' The 20 per cent of the collaborative work where artist walk in with an idea—a genius like Eminem, for example, has these special things he definitely wants to do, a photograph on his mother's steps were he grew up or whatever it is. I think it is great artists, like Nas, Eminem or Outkast that attach to a deeper level of their own work, because their mind is so expansive and they can think about visuals and music at the same time. They make the time to think about how they we want to be perceived. Attaching to these moments and having discussions, that's the gift of really working collaboratively with an artist to make the magic happen.

LF Talking about being able to translate an artist's ideas and music into images, I believe, you were 25 years old when you shot the now iconic album cover for Jay-Z's debut album *Reasonable Doubt* (1996).

JM Yes, that was actually the very first album cover I shot. That cover will stand the test of time. It's part of people's own musical journey. It's because of that effort and execution for Reasonable Doubt that I was asked to do it again for I*n My Lifetime, Vol. I*, then *Volume 2*, then *Dynasty*, then *Again, The Black Album*—eight albums in total. I think it is the most epic run a photographer has had with an artist in history. Everyone is always looking for what's next, but if something is working and feels right, you go with it. I was fortunate; I had a decade with Jay. Those projects and images established a true foundation for what he was going to grow to become. I'm quiet around Jay, which is kind of funny because I'm rarely quiet, but there is something about that light he carries when he walks into a room. He's someone I really admire and respect for his talents, his composure and his personality.

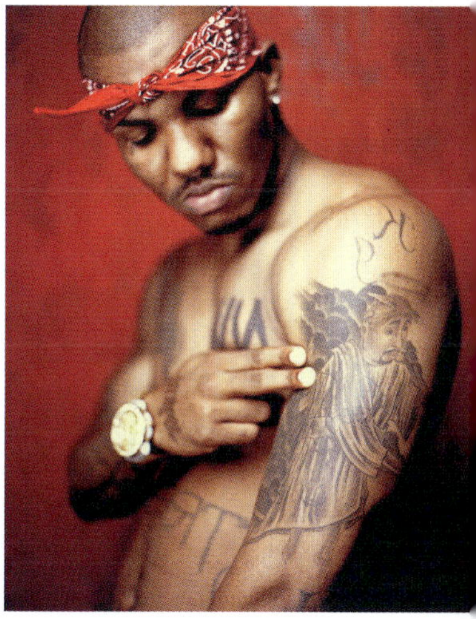

Reasonable Doubt (2016) marked twenty years of my first album cover. It's interesting to think that for the next two decades I will be celebrating anniversaries of every album cover that I have ever done. We're entering a moment of celebration of the work I have created over these last 20-something years of my life. It's an exciting time.

LF You've literally created the portraits for so many legendary artists' albums that have become as you called it earlier the 'soundtrack' to any hip hop fan's lives.

JM I can't tell you how many times people have approached me and thanked me for that Jay Z *Reasonable Doubt* cover or the DMX *Flesh of My Flesh, Blood of My Blood* cover, or the Alliyah pictures. They tell me that they had these posters all over their room. I feel very blessed. The thriving of the entire genre has also contributed to my success. You are only as successful as the company that you keep and how well surrounded are you by people with a similar vision who are also rising and want to continue to rise. Ultimately, I just wanted to make the definitive picture of the person in the moment. I say it all the time, and it's the clearest way that

↑ The Game by Jonathan Mannion for his debut album, The Documentary, 2004.

← Nas by Jonathan Mannion for Complex Magazine, 2002.

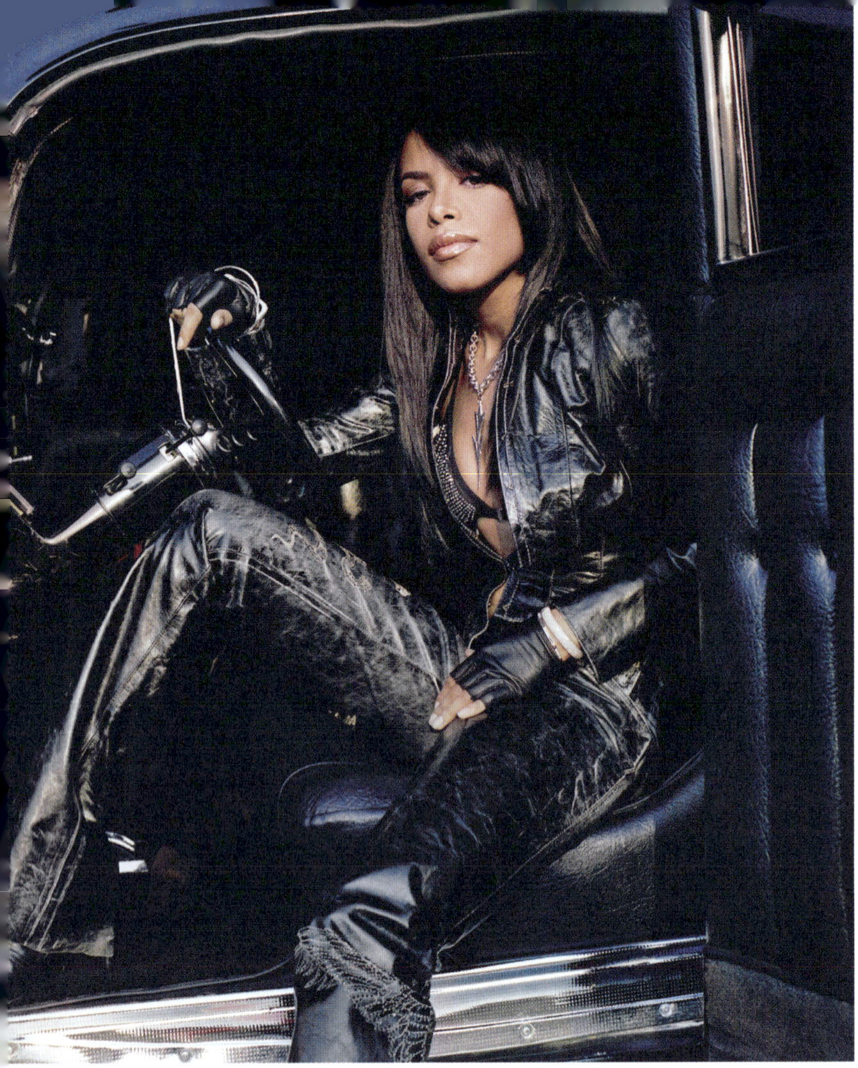

I can describe what I do: when you close your eyes and think of a picture of DMX, I want it to be mine. When you close your eyes and think of a picture of Jay Z, I want it to be mine. I want it to be mine for Nelly, Ludacris, for Outkast—'Outkast with the flag? Oh, yeah I know that one.' DMX in the blood, 'Yeah, I know that one.' Aaliyah against the background with the fur for *I Care 4 U*, "I know that one." We - the photographers - are the unsung heroes of what many people have said is that final stage in the artistic process in the making of an album. Once there is a visual to it, it becomes a real thing. It forces the artist to deliver the project. The visuals are almost the exclamation point for the music.

LF I imagine the dynamic between the artist and the photographer on the set of a photoshoot to be very delicate and intimate. What's your secret trick?

JM The photographer's dynamic with an artist—in my case, with some of the greatest MCs who have ever touched a microphone—has been a rewarding job and a personal dream come true. Ultimately, you have to allow the subject to let their guard down in order to help to guide the session in the right direction. Sometimes the image calls for laughter, other times strength, it just depends. I'm prepared to capture any moment. I want a full range of emotion from my subjects. It's when all of these elements come together that epic photographs are made.

I walk into every shoot with the perspective that I have to do everything that I possibly can to maneuver through the situation, even if it's tense and awkward, in order to deliver high level images. I may walk in with my agenda, my checklist of twelve things that I want on any given day, but that almost always changes. Those twelve things have literally never happened in my career. On any shoot, scratch, 1,4,6,7,8, 10. Ok, so now we need to fill in the gaps. I think that being supremely adaptable has allowed me to react to any set of circumstances with ease.

I basically break it down to two components: photography and psychology. I studied studio art, painting, graphic design for four years, but I am also a psychology major and earned two degrees from Kenyon College. The art degree was sort of my play-time, but I didn't want to go away with something that came so naturally to me. I wanted to come away with something I knew would be beneficial in anything that I decided to do—and that was understanding people. It's a gift to have the ability to navigate interactions with ease in order to break down someone's guard and get to the truth.

LF Has this been further reinforced in the photography world by working with iconic portrait photographer Richard Avedon after college?

JM Yes, absolutely. Avedon is known for his psychological portraits. These images are sometimes uncomfortable ones, because they reveal an honesty within that subject in that moment or what his version of the reality was that he wanted to portray. He created environments that could make someone incredibly tense or incredibly comfortable and feel like a million bucks or as if they could fly.

The psychology mixed with the knowledge of photography is to me the perfect blend of that intimacy between the artist and the photographer's ability to achieve a brilliant image.

↖ Aaliyah by Jonathan Mannion for her 3rd studio album *I Care 4 U*, 2001

→ Eminem by Jonathan Mannion for his 3rd studio album *The Marshall Mather's* LP, 2001.

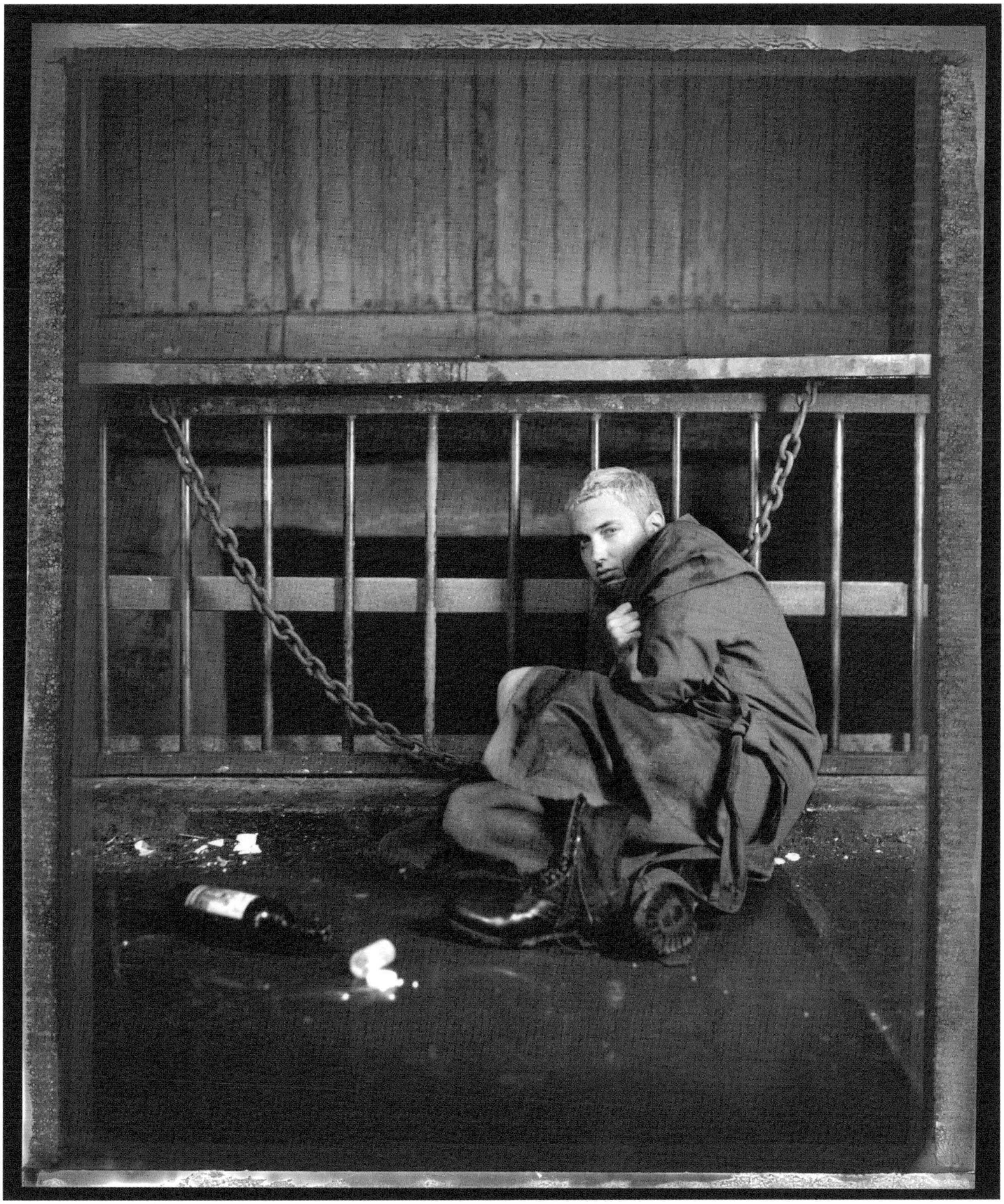

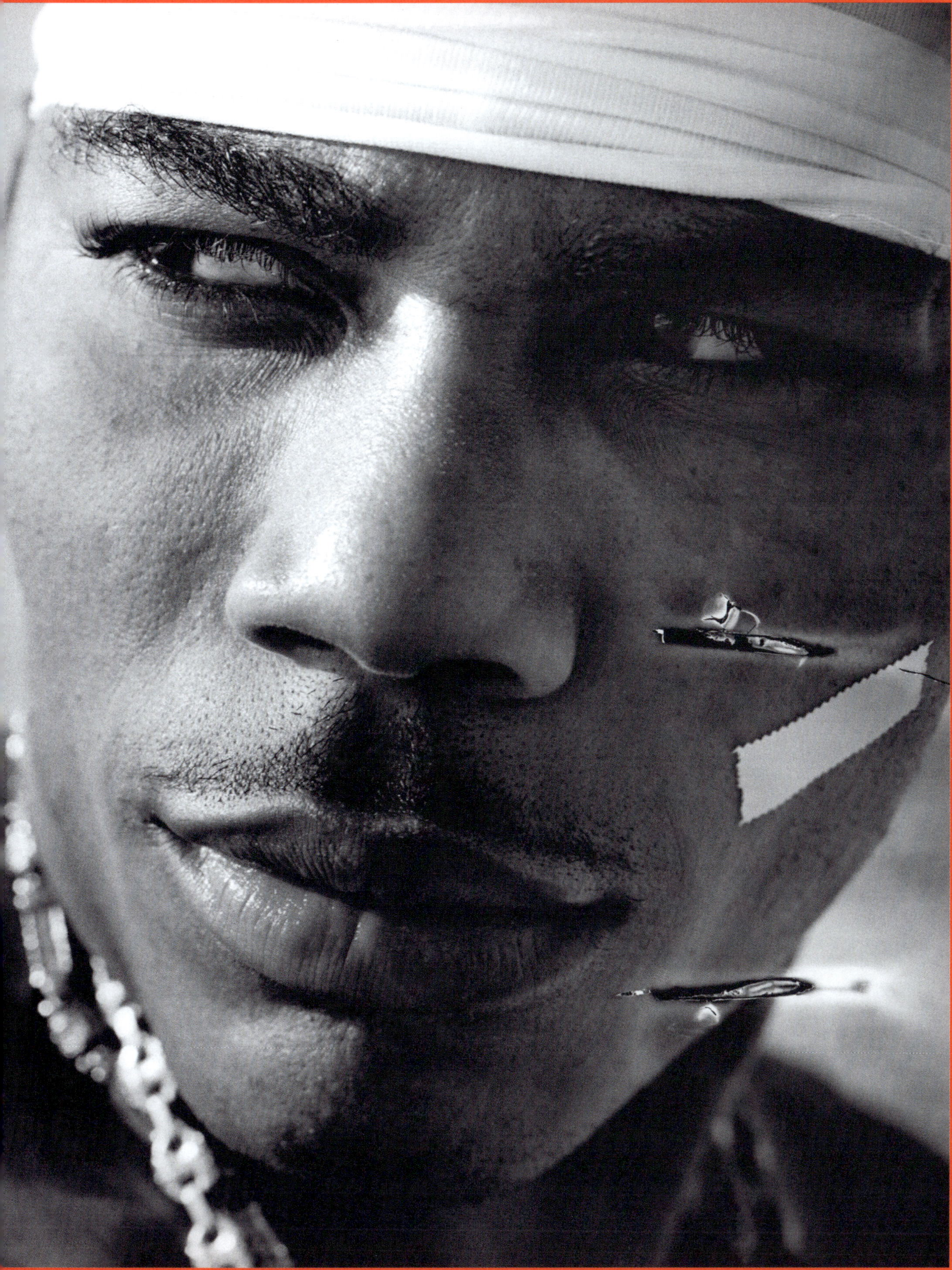

LF Is this something that you observed when you worked with Avedon. Is this a legacy that he passed on to you?

JM Yes, absolutely. I think that it's difficult to work for anybody without receiving influence from their unique style and approach to shooting. Conversely, you might work for a photographer and realize that that is totally NOT how you would do it, but this still refines your own process. I would say that Avedon was the first installment of a unique knowledge of an artists' process for me. Watching someone working on the highest level, a master of his craft, was invaluable for me. Just watching his movements, how he broke things down, how he did his job. It was Avedon's entire workflow, strategy, process, interactions, stories, meticulous nature that I got to see from start to finish. That's a very tangible gift to me. I took a lot of the approach but still had to apply it to whole new generation of hip hop, that was irreverent, loose and rugged. I didn't have all the benefits of the control that Avedon had on his set. There was a lot of spontaneous reaction at four in the morning somewhere in Brooklyn to try to make the magic happen. At that time, that was what I loved and what I was chasing. If you speak about legacy in its most pure form that's certainly the prime example of legacy to me. I got to witness a master. Avedon is one of the five greatest photographers to ever touch a camera. To me he's number one, just because I got such an intimate lesson in the creative process from him. I'm honored to have spent this time with him.

'You are only as successful as the company that you keep.'

JONATHAN MANNION

LF How would you explain your personal creative approach when you start working with an artist?

JM I have a very focused approach when taking portraits in order to get the richest performance out of somebody. It's really about breaking down their guard, building a trust, to gain access to the real person or whoever that person wants to be for the day. My sessions can be pretty intense, but it allows them to be vulnerable in a moment in a very protected and nurtured space. I am there to make them look incredible, powerful and thoughtful and achieve all ideas (even the crazy ones) in order to fulfill my set of deliverables to the label or art director. Many things come into play during these shoots. If there are artists that are more self-conscious, I tell them to put that aside for the day because I'm there to make something with them and for them. All of this is entirely about them and the images will serve to define their project forever. This psychological approach is basically to tell them that you are of service to their vision. And this is absolutely true. It's not a game.

↰ Nelly by Jonathan Mannion for *People's Magazine*, 2002.

→ Outkast by Jonathan Mannion for *The Fader*, 2000.

I would say that 80 per cent of a photo-shoot is this kind of psychology. How do you keep somebody engaged? How do you maintain your vision? How do you not stress out? How do you deal with 15 different comments and everybody's opinion about what you are doing? It's about pushing those aside and putting the sole focus on the job at hand and not get side-tracked. Then 20 per cent is the actual photography. In the process of creating, that technical knowledge should really be unconscious. A photographer must be 10 per cent present for that person. I think that I'm among the rare breed of photographers worldwide that have that extra-gear to give and the calm in pressure situations to control the outcome. It's not the loudest voice, but the most pure and truest voices that breaks through the noise.

LF What would you like your legacy to be?

JM I've always understood as photographer, that you're never just shooting for that moment, that day, that project. I'm always 5, 10, 20 years down the road. I want my legacy to be the impact that I make on the culture, how can I shape people's vision of these artists, the technical quality of my images and a mark on the individuals that I work with. This is the gift. I want to be considered a master of my craft when it's all said and done. I have dedicated myself completely to my art form and have chased it relentlessly and ceaselessly. The hard, meaningful and joyful work continues.

LF Thank you very much, Jonathan. That's a wrap.

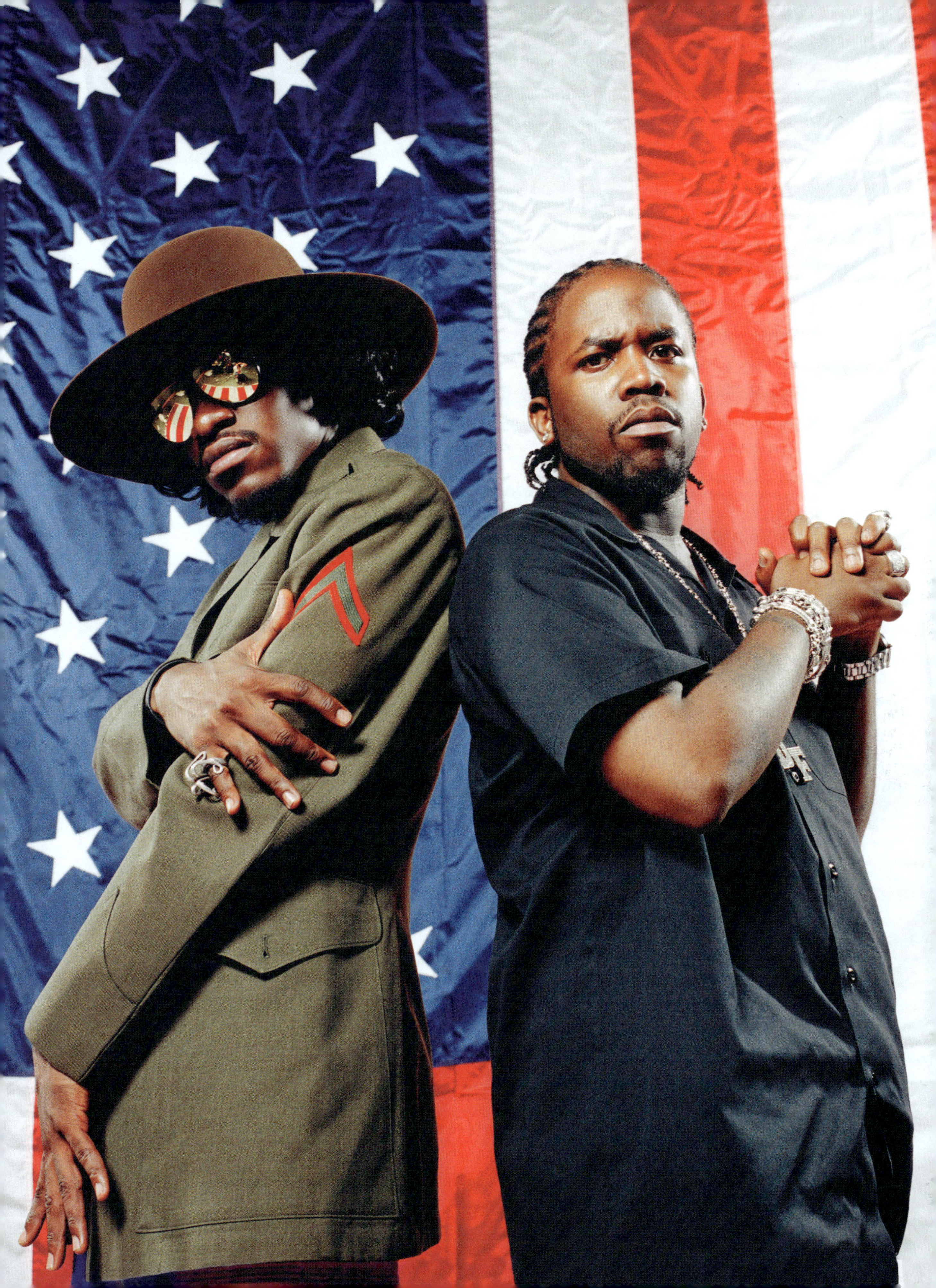

Architecture as a Collective Legacy

Gianfranco Bombaci, Matteo Costanzo and Gian Piero Frassinelli

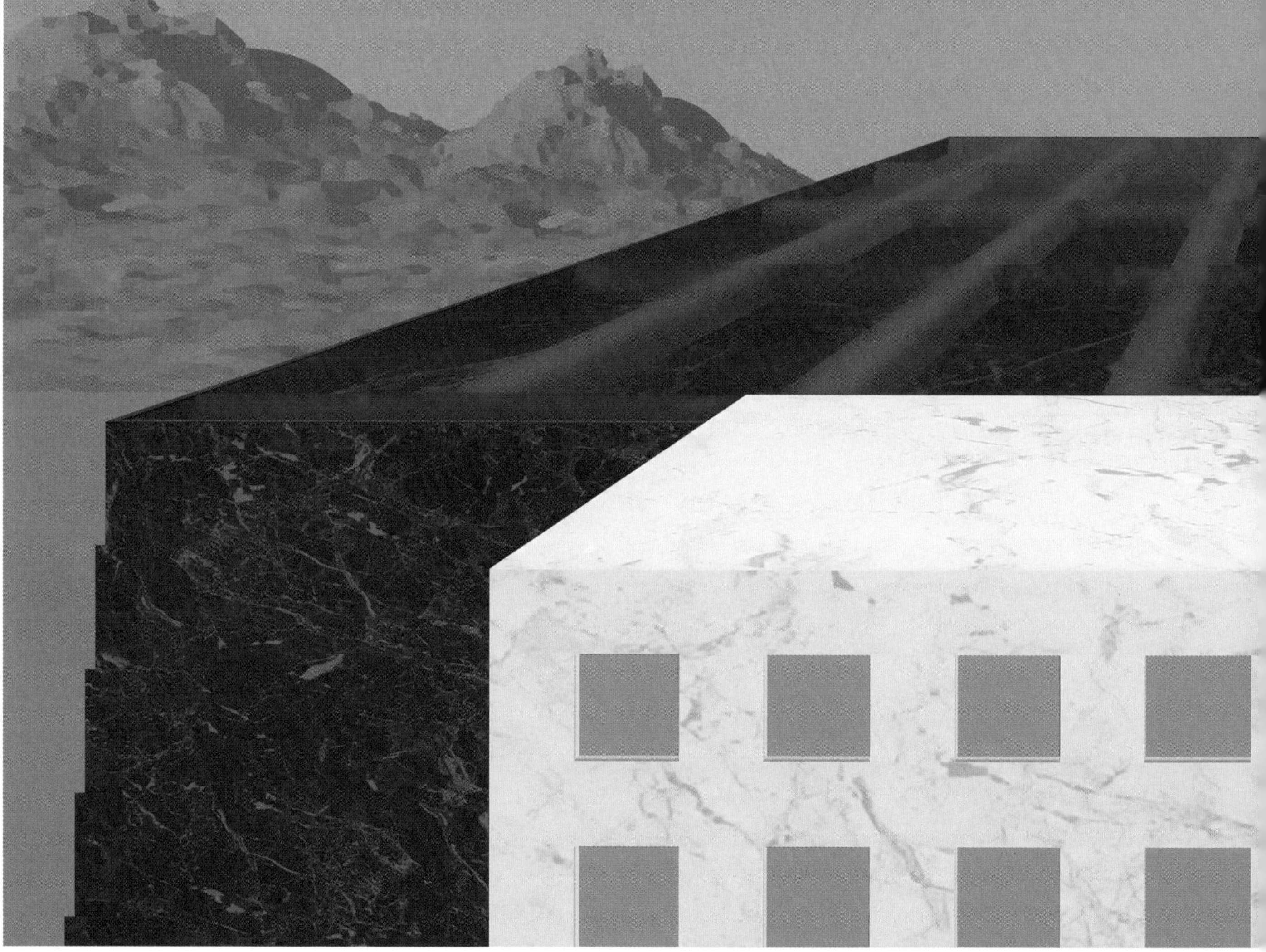

Italian architects GIANFRANCO BOMBACI and MATTEO CONSTANZO of Rome-based architecture office 2A+P/A visit GIAN PIERO FRASSINELLI, one of the five founding members of Superstudio, a forward-thinking architecture collective formed in 1966 that embraced a radical take on their practice. Together they explore architecture as a collective legacy and the intrinsic relationship between architecture and anthropology.

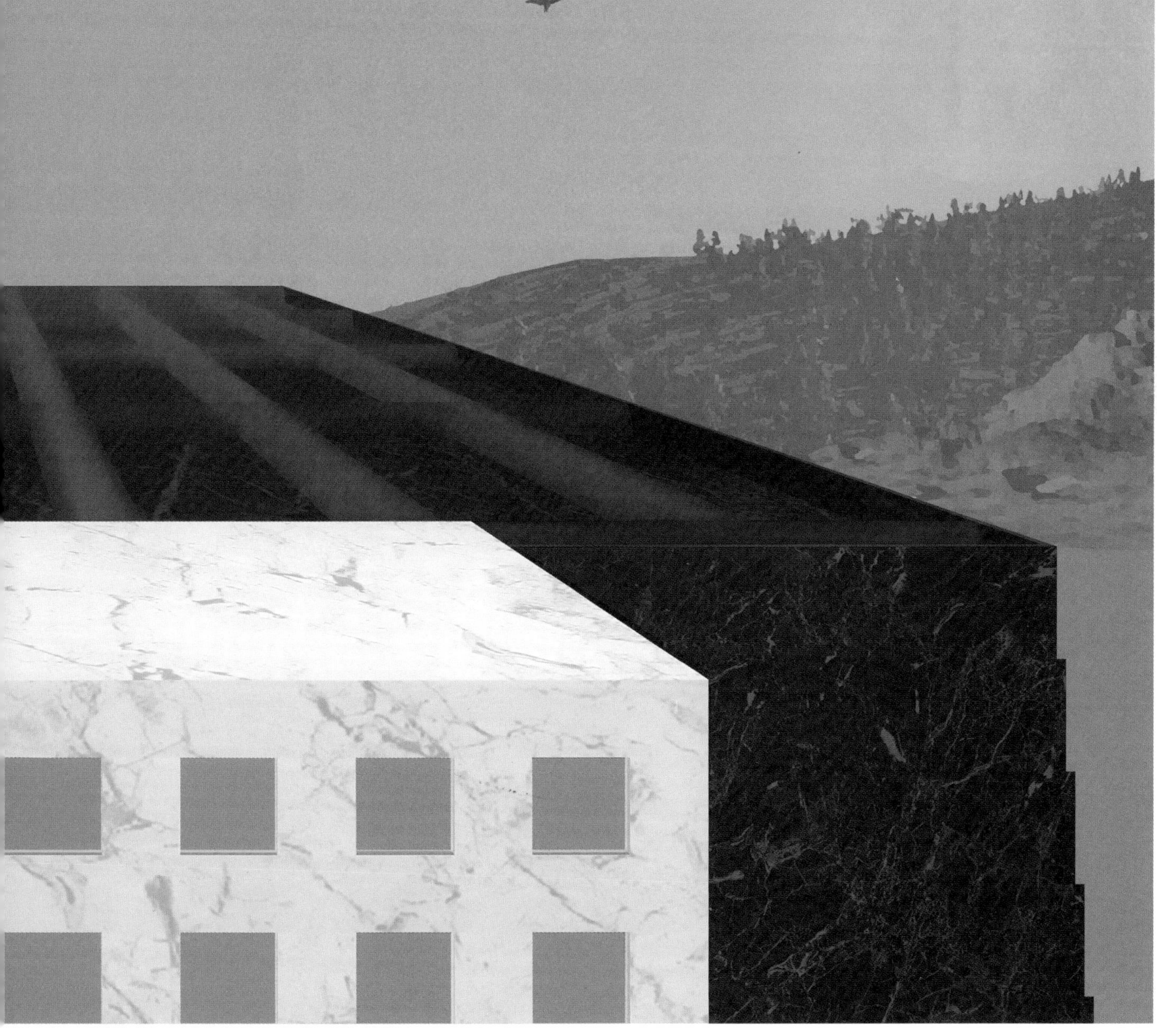

While making projects, we investigate other projects, other thoughts; we draw from the complex world that the historical and contemporary legacy constantly offers us. It is not a philological sampling work that explores the possibilities of works that have had the strength to show achievable paths and to unveil new chances.

In these terms we consider collaboration to be an instrument for survey. It's a way to build an idea of architecture: it's not simply an occasional fact to address the need for the most complete group to solve a problem.

It is always a form of sharing. Through collaboration, the architectural project implicitly abandons the idea of authorship. Throughout this process of exchange, architecture can overcome the obsession for a precise image, or even an established language. Therefore, architecture can be dedicated only to architecture.

In the last ten years we had built the chance to collaborate in several competition entries with some key figures in the history of architecture, known for their radicalism and experimental approach. We worked with Yona Friedman on the design of a square, where he pushed us to express a strong vision by overlapping one of his nests as a gigantic sculpture. We shared two competition projects for two museums with Andrea Branzi. His clear way of thinking and his straightforward ideas guided us to the development of non-figurative architectures, where humans and animals could share the same universal spaces. We designed another museum with Gian Piero Frassinelli, a former member of Superstudio: an Ethnographical Museum in Budapest where Frassinelli drove us through a stimulating attempt at linking anthropology and architecture. This has resulted in a new research project—the central archive for human cultures—based on a text written by Frassinelli. This project is at the core of the shared exhibition Savage Architecture, which has been traveling throughout Europe for a couple of years. We even collaborated with Ettore Sottsass after his death, giving life to one of his inspiring drawings—an axonometric view of a mysterious black monolith, which now is a real exhibition pavilion in Orléans.

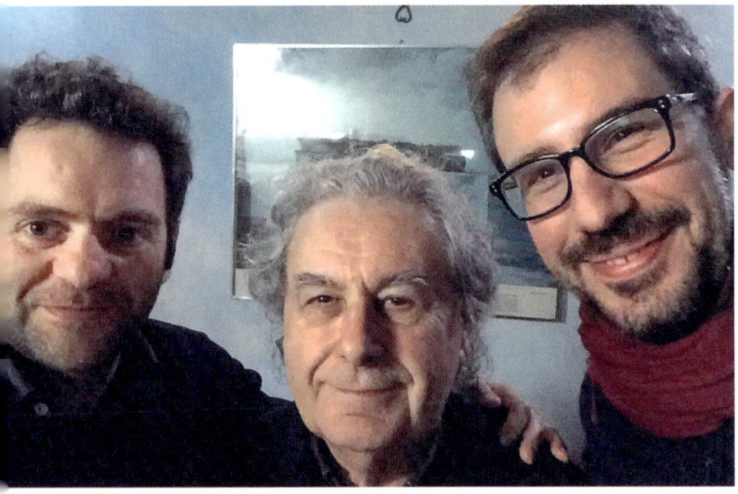

By collaborating with these architects, we profoundly experienced their approach and their way of thinking. We had the opportunity to draw together their coherence, going beyond the needs of a competition brief. We understood how the project can become a research tool, useful to investigate and criticize reality and, at the same time, able to build a new vision.

The following dialogue collects some fragments of a long discussion we had with Gian Piero Frassinelli after the first venues of the Savage Architecture exhibition. The aim of the dialogue was the comprehension of possible further developments of the research for an anthropological approach to architecture—a mostly impossible attempt at sharing a possible interpretation of his legacy.

MATTEO COSTANZO Starting from our frequent meetings over the past several years, we started to focus our interests about anthropology, coming to appreciate and study the writing of Claude Lévi-Strauss, in particular the book *The Savage Mind* (1962), which influenced the title of the exhibition we did together at the Architectural Association in London[1].

We know that, in Superstudio, you strongly supported the anthropological approach to architecture. Do you want to tell us, first of all, about the origins of this attitude and how it developed within the group?

GIAN PIERO FRASSINELLI When I first arrived at Superstudio, I continued pursuing my previous projects, which were already partly addressing this question. I was interested in architecture, but was

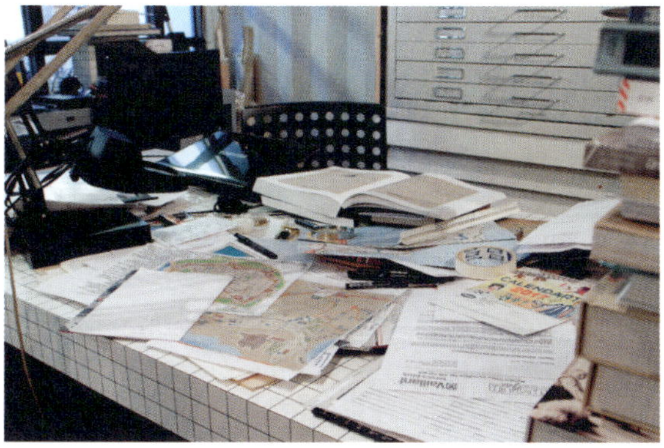

also very curious about anthropology. My interest in the topic increased during the development of my thesis project, and afterwards I tried to introduce it to the Superstudio office. When I began to talk about topics relating to anthropology, which at first were mainly concerned with what was happening inside the Continuous Monument—the partners' response was mainly resistance, at times even hilarity. They teased me when it came to these topics. No one there had seen my thesis. I had been employed as a draftsman. During the first year I executed what they assigned me. Later, I slowly began embedding anthropological themes into the work. I was not actually considered a member of Superstudio until after I wrote the *Twelve Ideal Cities* in 1972. *The Twelve Ideal Cities* became a kind of entry point: they opened an unexpected window in Superstudio.

The initial lack of interest in anthropology faded and by the *Five Fundamental Acts* (1971–1973) there was, amongst the group, a kind of awareness of the anthropological topic inside architecture.

The Five Fundamental Acts led then us to work on the *Extra-Urban Material Culture* (1974).

GIANFRANCO BOMBACI We would like to better understand the transition between your interest in anthropology and the design of architecture from this perspective. Your thesis was about an anthropology research centre and was an early attempt at establishing a direct relationship between these two fields of interest. There was an incredible shift in the work once this aim became the clear focus of the project, similar to *The Twelve Ideal Cities* (1971), where the architecture was not just the place where people studied a science, but actually the concrete translation and image of that science.

GPF For me this was an attempt: I wanted to give a physical form to the concept of anthropology in architecture. I always tried to do this in my projects.

My ideas on anthropology also played an important role for the social housing building in Barberino Val d'Elsa. The Val d'Elsa project focused on accommodating former agricultural workers who had moved to the city. I decided not to design a condominium. Farmers, accustomed to their freedom and independence, would go into crisis if forced into mandatory cohabitation. I tried to design this single building as if it were a series of individual houses. Each one had its own staircase accessible from a central courtyard where children could play, protected inside the 'U-shaped' building. The House of the Four Winds in Amsterdam, a project I developed many years later, is also a good example of this approach. It is considered one of the five houses in Amsterdam that has had the strongest social impact. In my small way, I believe I was consistent with my interests.

MC Your consistency is evident and helps advance the discussion. We are curious to understand if, apart from the theoretical assumptions, it is possible to deduce any

↰ Exterior view of *The Central Archive of Human Culture*, 2016. Design team: 2A+P/A (Gianfranco Bombaci, Matteo Costanzo) with Gian Piero Frassinelli.

← The desk of Gian Piero Frassinelli's in Firenze, Italy, 2017.

↙ Matteo Costanzo, Gian Piero Frassinelli and Gianfranco Bombaci, Firenze, Italy, 2017.

↓ Interior view of Gian Piero Frassinelli's home studio in Firenze, Italy, 2017.

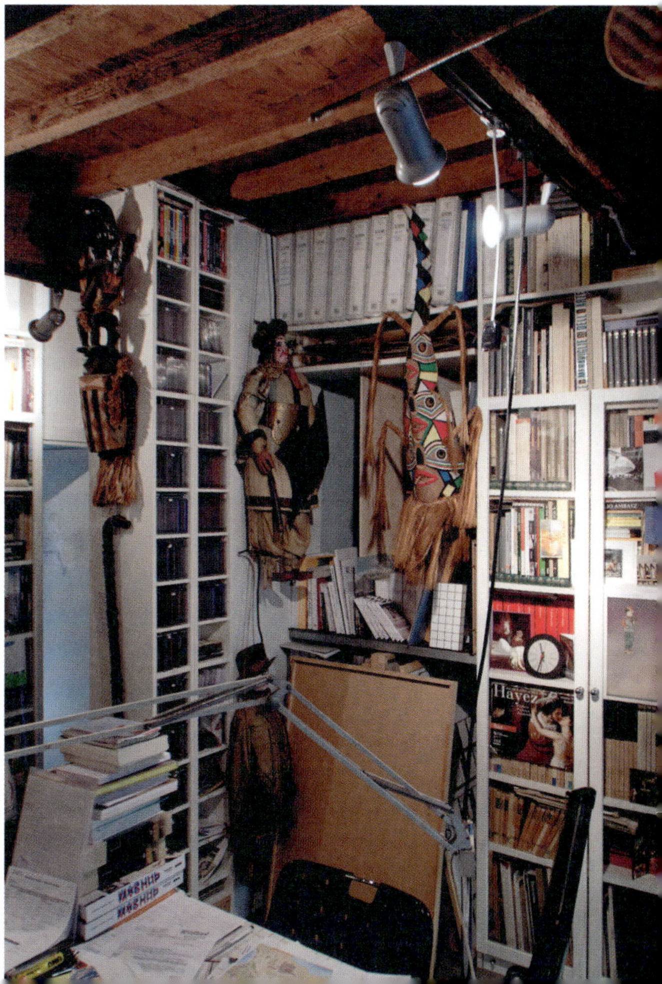

'I wanted to give a physical form to the concept of anthropology in architecture.'

GIAN PIERO FRASSINELLI

architectural tools as a means of interpreting your anthropological approach. The feeling is that this was mainly a pre-design investigation in Superstudio: a phase of research that was supposed to be developed before starting the project. How can this become a useful instrument during the development of the project?

GPF I have always focused on this, both in the few projects that I have built, as well as the many others I designed. I never started, as Adolfo Natalini used to, from facades; that is to say, from the outside. My projects always started from the interior, but not in plan. I prefer to design using sections, which are more human, because they also show the stairs, that is to say, the physical fatigue of the men going up and down. The section gives you a point of view—it shows the height of both the building and the rooms. I always hated small rooms and have tried to make apartments that differ from one another. The individual apartments, in both the House of the Four Winds and those in Barberino, are all different, which is actually a very strong approach. What is important to me is that when one enters the apartment of their neighbour, they discover a different home than their own. Houses are personal spaces; it is shocking when your neighbour has the same house as you.

GB We are often tempted to tackle the problem through a typological study, but at the same time we think that it is the wrong approach. Working through typologies seems too definite, or at least an overly simplified attempt at categorizing behaviours that are more complex. The Fundamental Acts enunciate something far from any concrete consequence. What led you to state precisely those five acts? How can we reclaim this theoretical thinking without losing any enthusiasm for architecture?

GPF Simply, Natalini proposed *The Fundamental Acts* one morning. I did not agree, because they were not consistent. They had no scientific meaning—for sure not anthropologically. *Life* was already finished for the MOMA exhibition and was essentially the logical consequence, the extreme consequence, of the Continuous Monument (which was finally liberated). Then Adolfo proposed to develop *The Fundamental Acts* hoping to make our discourse more global and inclusive. At that point, the group was convinced of the value of anthropology as a field of research. We split the five acts between us and I chose *Ceremony*, while also contributing to both *Love* and *Death*.

Over time I realized that it was my obsession for anthropology that led me to design. You have to adapt, to consider the people who are supposed to use these spaces. Spaces—not functions—because functions are defined by rationalism, which is fine. What I have always criticized about rationalism is the lack of spirituality, of psychology, of confrontation with the social, with the non-physical. Great architects compensate for this lack with their imagination, but normal architects do not have the ability to make this interpretation.

MC Developing our interests in anthropology, we searched Lévi-Strauss' books for pages that might influence architecture. We have identified some topics that we would like to discuss with you. *The Savage Mind* appears to be an instinctive part of man, able to relate naturally to their specific environment. Another aspect is that the savage mind is basically a rational mind. Therefore, an architect who goes back to this idea can still produce a rational form. It relates anyway to our modern traditions. Finally, there is the concept of bricolage, which we understand as the difference between Western men—those who are comparable to the engineer—and the figure of the bricoleur. These two figures describe two different approaches to intellectual tools and history. The engineer builds a progressive history while the bricoleur does not archive anything, because everything is reusable. We are curious to understand how the same thing can happen in architecture.

GPF Your discourse, from my perspective, seems out of focus. I think that we have two different points of view: mine is no longer an architectural perspec-

→ Photo-Montage by Superstudio for the film *Supersurface - An Alternative Model for Life on Earth*, 1972.

↘ Competiton entry for Ethnographic Museum, Budapest, Hungary, 2014. Design team: 2A+P/A (Gianfranco Bombaci, Matteo Costanzo) with Gian Piero Frassinelli.

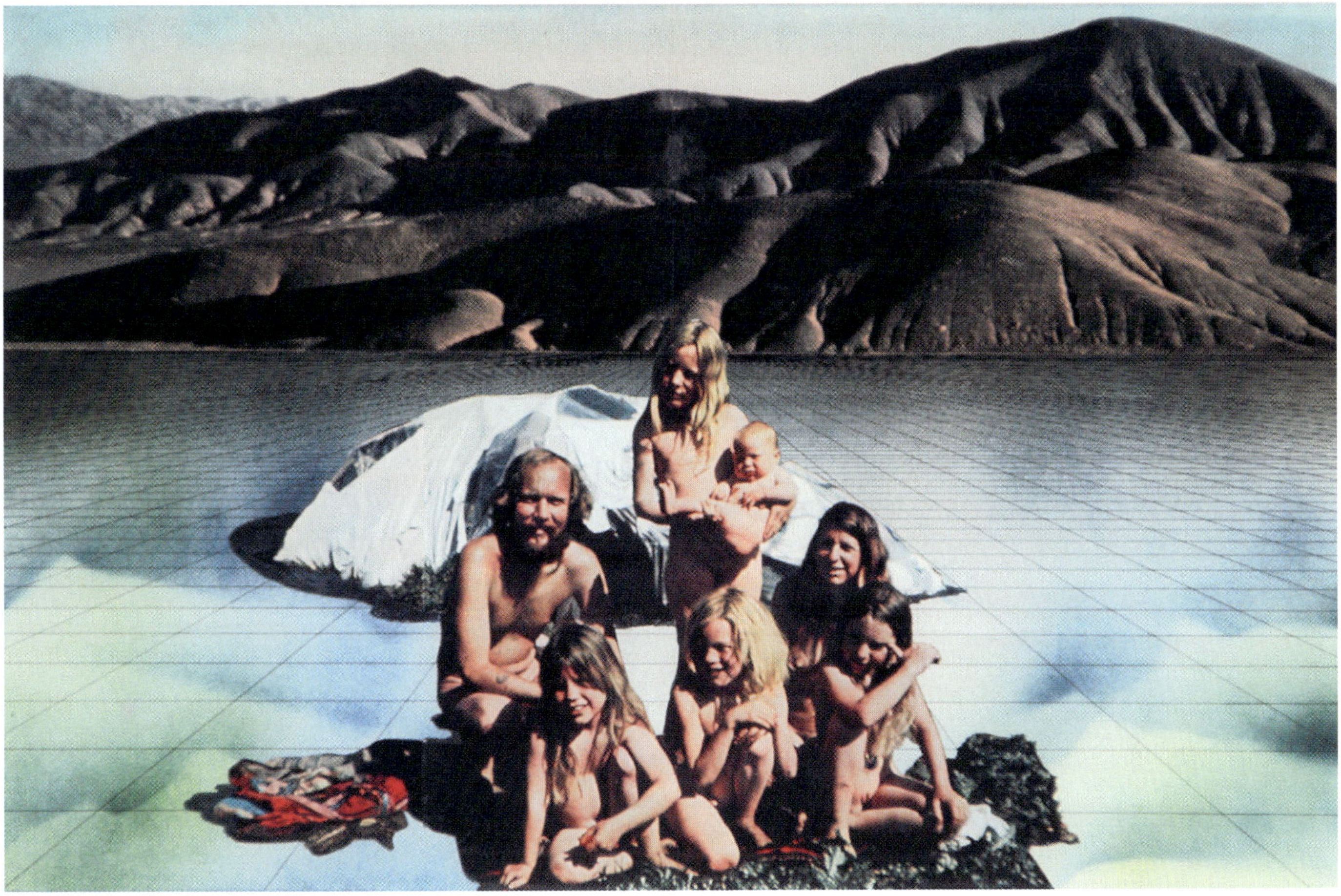

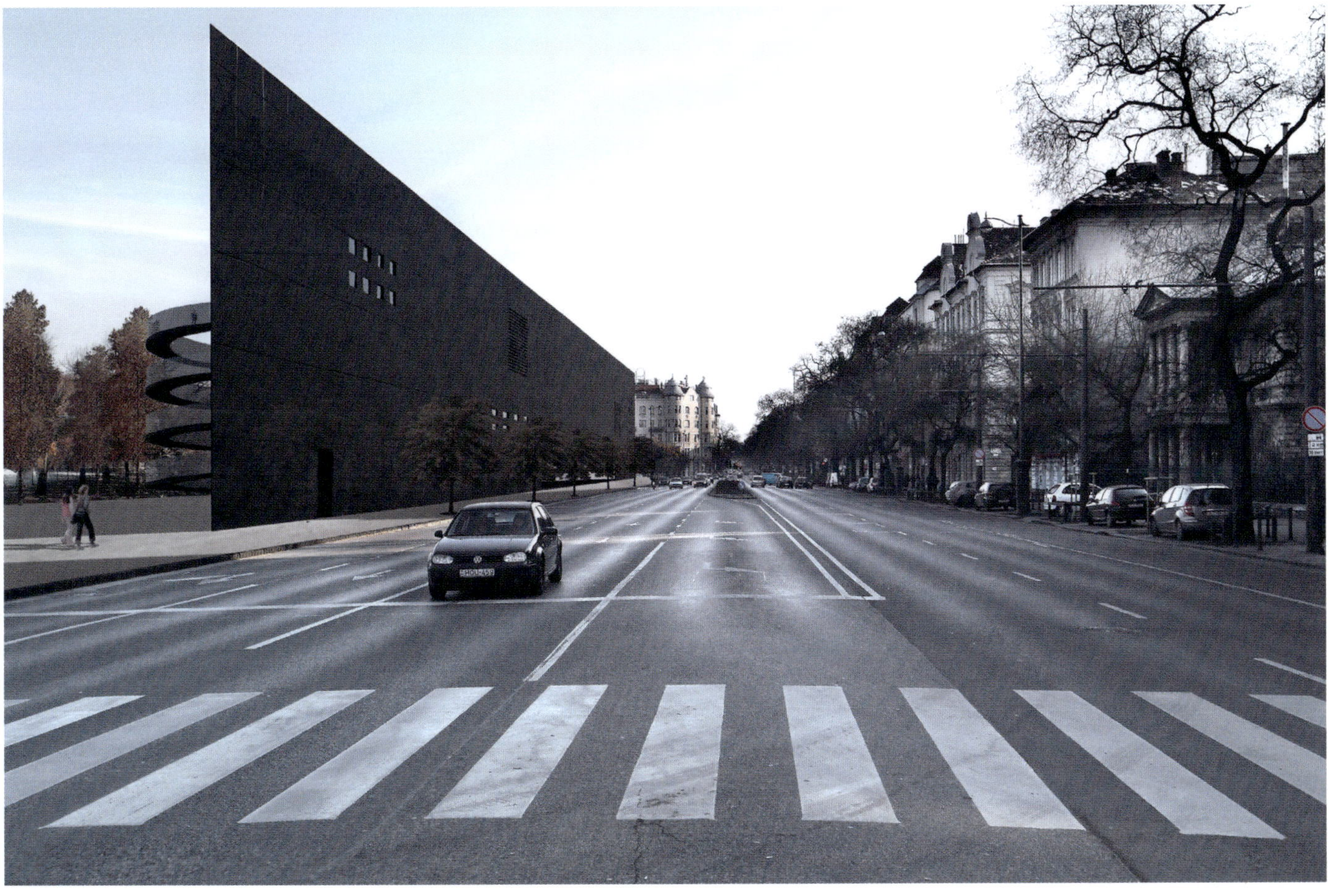

‘You have to adapt, to consider the people who are supposed to use these spaces.’

GIAN PIERO FRASSINELLI

tive, at least not in the sense popular within universities. I have always distanced myself from the profession, so far that I completely failed from the point of view of the project. On the big drawer that contains the archive of all my projects, I wrote a consoling epigraph: 'There are other worlds, other types of dreams. Dreams in which failure is conceivable, honourable and sometimes even worthy of the effort of a person.' It is a phrase taken from a book by Arundhati Roy, significantly titled, *The End of Imagination* (1998).

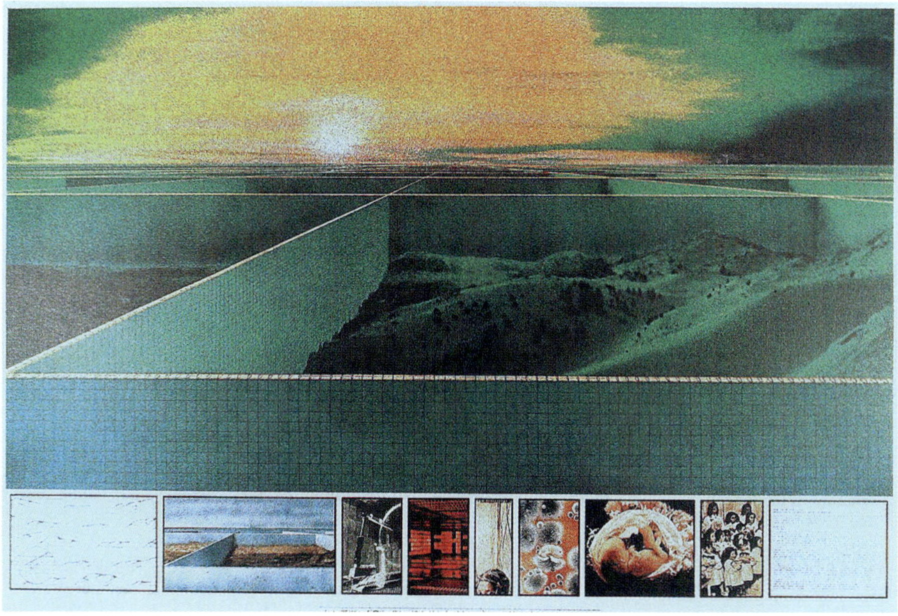

However, trying to get closer to your perspective, I would like to make you think about the fact that half of human cultures don't know the meaning of history; they have no interest in the Western concept of history. All the civilizations without books—which do not have writing as we know it—are not interested in history. They are not interested in what happened a year ago. The past is already a myth. Civilizations like these exist in another universe. The fact that they don't want a history totally changes the mentality of both the individual and social group. Relative history is a fundamental principle of anthropology. Other cultures—the ones that do not have books—have a way of seeing history related to a deity, or to a certain kind of religious tradition. Our Western way of thinking is rather absolute. An architect who wants to deal with anthropological architecture should understand these basics; he must change, even overthrow, his current mentality. Nothing is certain with cultures. It is not true that there are basic features, shared amongst all cultures. There is no common ground; everything is relative in the field of anthropology, even the concept of the human being or the 'self.'

GB In the 60s and 70s you were among the first to question the modern movement. These were the years when alternative projects were tested, bringing to light the most contradictory aspects of modernism.

After 50 years, we are still confronting a modernity that has already shown its limits and failures; we are suspended in a postmodern stall. Again, we face a moment of great crisis, but this moment also allows us to question the given postmodern scheme. Do you think there are opportunities to take a similar attitude today?

GPF Many years ago, before Sculptures in the Environment's (SITE) famous project, High Rise of Houses, I worked on a similar idea. I proposed the creation of a building conceived of as an infrastructure, which was supposed to be sold per cubic meter. Buyers purchased a volume that they would then build themselves.

When Fons Elders told me about a contest for a social housing building in Amsterdam, I suggested something similar. I designed a reinforced concrete frame with only services, stairs and elevators. The rest would be self-made by the people in Amsterdam. This system allowed people to see and join different cultures—an experience they seemed ready for. In the project I drew an Arab house or Native American, thereby building a large multi-ethnic infrastructure.

This is another important note: the freedom to design is a sort of bricolage that becomes architecture.

MC We are very interested in this aspect. We are trying to conceive of architecture as something that gives users the freedom of customization. A neutral architecture made of primordial forms of spatial organization—the minimum needed in order to allow

↑ Superstudio, *The Twelve Ideal Cities*, Photo montage, 1971.

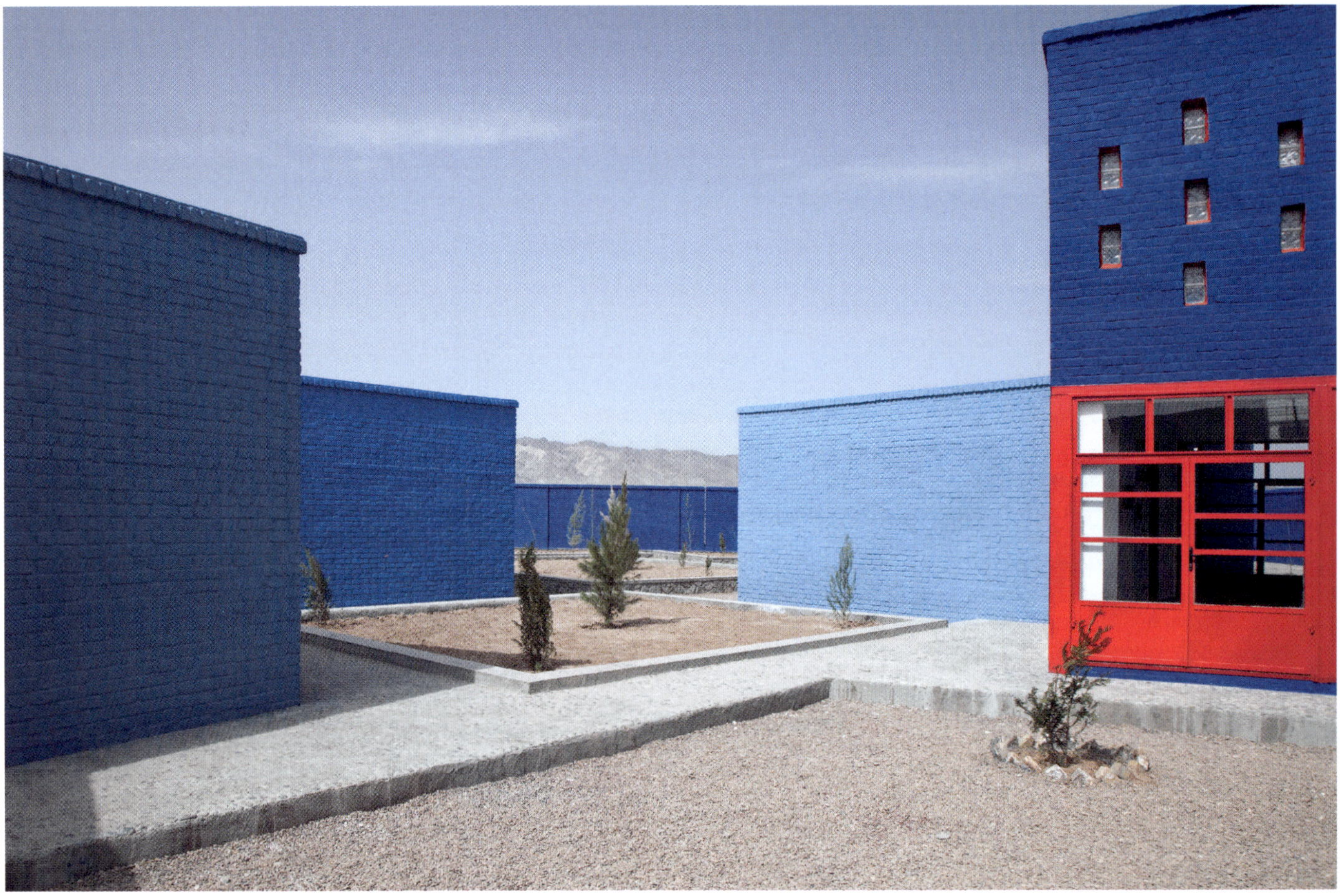

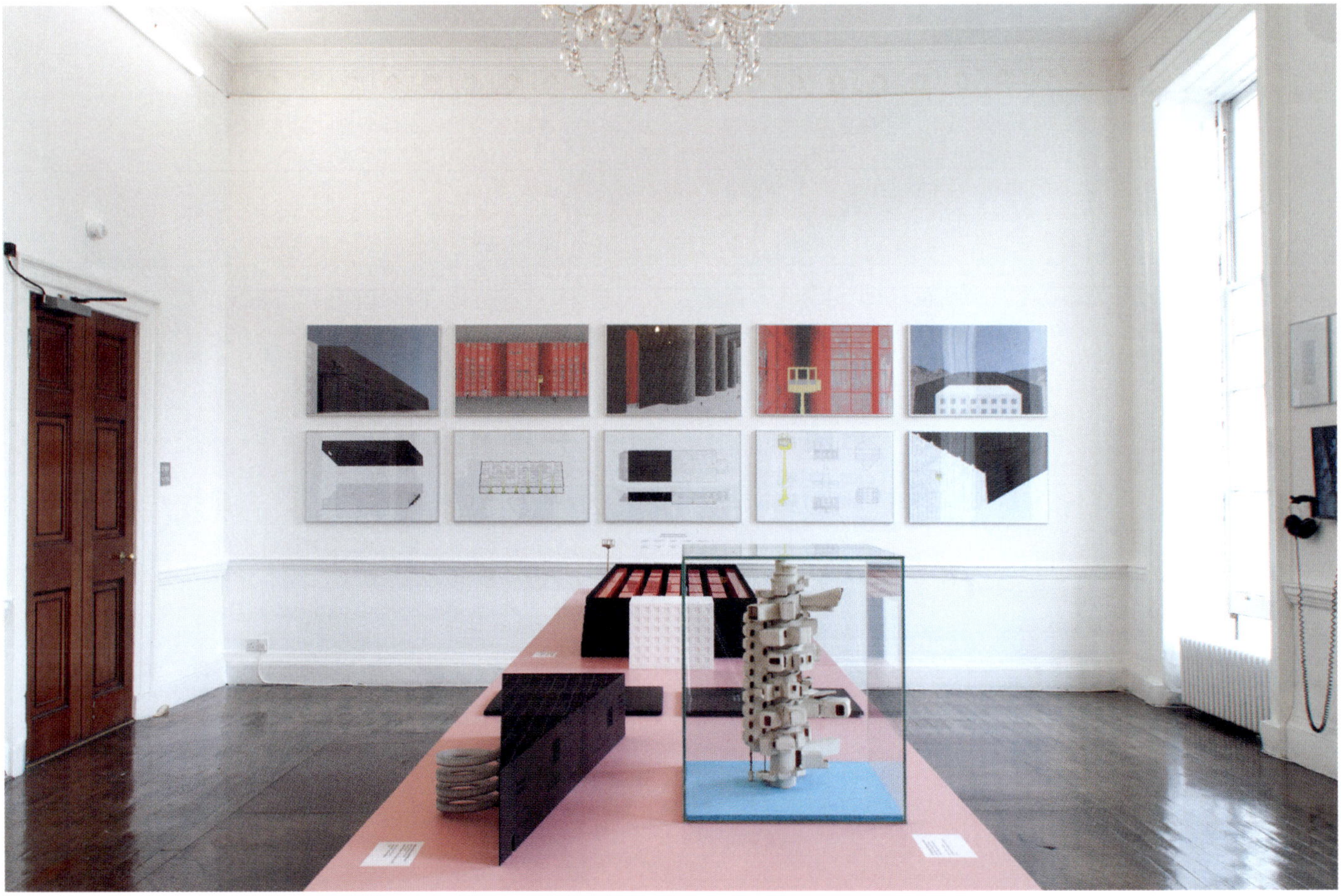

people to carry out various activities. Similar to the scenes of Giotto's Scrovegni Chapel, where in each scene the architecture in the background is the minimum device necessary to ensure the performance of a specific action.

GPF We are facing this challenge for the first time in at least two centuries. In the past, architecture was strictly connected to a specific form of power, which was represented, defended and depicted. The architect was not interested in the life of normal men, fortunately. When the 'powers' gave people the freedom to arrange their own solutions—without being harassed by wars or taxes—they sometimes produced masterpieces, but certainly people always found the best available way to survive. Even in Giotto's work, the backgrounds are manifestations of power, palaces and churches. People are in the foreground, breaking from the previous Byzantine style.

MC About functionalism, for example, in the office we often wonder about how to design the kitchen. If we consider the kitchen to be the place where the ceremony of eating takes place, then everything completely shifts after the Frankfurt kitchen, which optimized movements in order to reach the 'existenzminimum' (subsistence level). There is a limit between rationality and extreme functionalism. Today, maybe a kitchen with a large table and a fireplace is more interesting than the modern Frankfurt kitchen. We try to overcome typological modernist considerations, instead, starting from the rituals or the behaviours that we imagine may happen in the space.

GPF With globalization, masses of people are coming to us from other cultures—or on the contrary, many of us find ourselves within other cultures—there is no longer a unique way to design a kitchen or bathroom. There is no single way to develop the layout of an apartment. This is something that we must start thinking seriously about. The houses should be blank spaces where everyone can organize their own way. Unfortunately, not only for us, but also for those who come from the Middle East and Africa, people no longer have the capacity to design their own spaces. They need a specialist. Perhaps a team of designers from different cultures would be able to interpret their different needs. Unfortunately, I do not see any other possibility.

GB Another interesting consideration is that our method of living is changing. Increased mobility, social instability, job insecurity, technology, and the European education system—we live in one city but may work or study elsewhere. This has led to the failure of the European bourgeois dream. Single parents are more common than complete families. It seems clear that the urban response cannot be the same. The hypothesis of Savage Architecture seems to be a line of research that might address this situation. Where the home is the ground on which the most important game is played. We want to understand whether or not, through an anthropological reading, we can find different forms of aggregation, or spaces to live, by sharing parts of our lives. We're imagining how to introduce this strategy through a project.

Immaterial labour no longer needs a defined space or a precise schedule; this is changing the way of structuring the city. In this sense, the collective house is a collector of multiple activities, where life and work are intertwined. We are currently developing these opportunities through our experience and work with students. Again, the feeling is that an anthropological, rather than a typological gaze, is the most effective way to undermine a preconceived scheme.

GPF The bourgeois mentality is setting. The problem is that politics must deal with this situation as well, but it seems to be something they do not even think about.

The condominium unfortunately is now a place of conflict, where the individual vents their frustration. The biggest problem is the schematic thinking of the people maintaining the government's power, while at the same time this thinking has also led to the deprivation of people's individual design skills.

Your work is extremely interesting and I'd like to follow the outcomes for as long as my age will allow me.

← Maria Grazia Cutuli School, Primary School, Herat, Afghanistan, 2011. Design team: 2A+P/A (Gianfranco Bombaci, Matteo Costanzo), Mario Cutuli, IaN+, ma0/emmeazero. Photo by Giovanna Silva.

↙ Exhibition shot from *Savage Architecture* at Architectural Association, London, 2016. Design team: 2A+P/A (Gianfranco Bombaci, Matteo Costanzo) with Gian Piero Frassinelli. Curator: Davide Sacconi.

1
Savage Architecture, Gian Piero Frassinelli, Superstudio and 2A+P/A, curated by Davide Sacconi, exhibited firstly at Architectural Association in London in March 2016 and then at Kent State University in Florence, at Fondation Civa in Brussels, at Polythecnic of Milan, at Temple University in Rome, and at Studio Lo in Berlin.

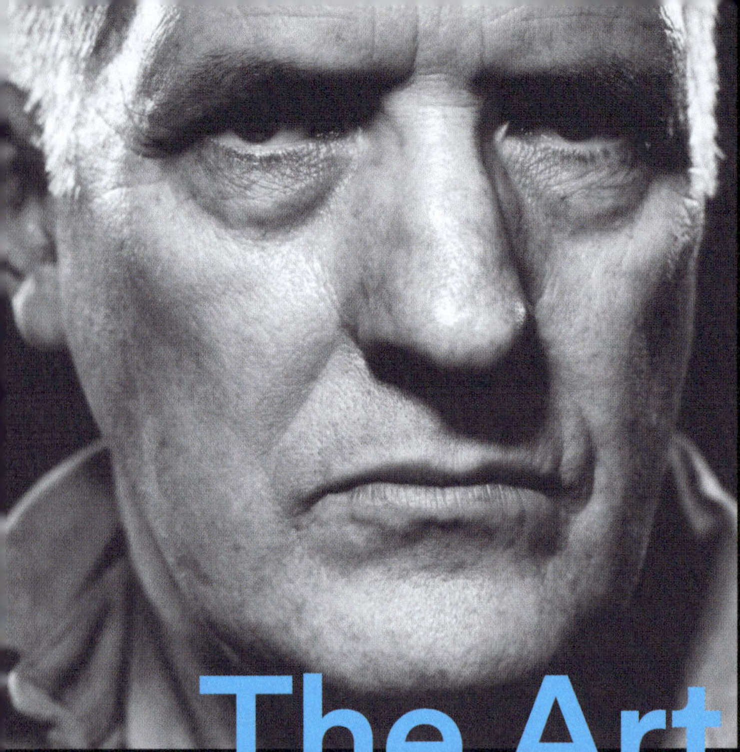

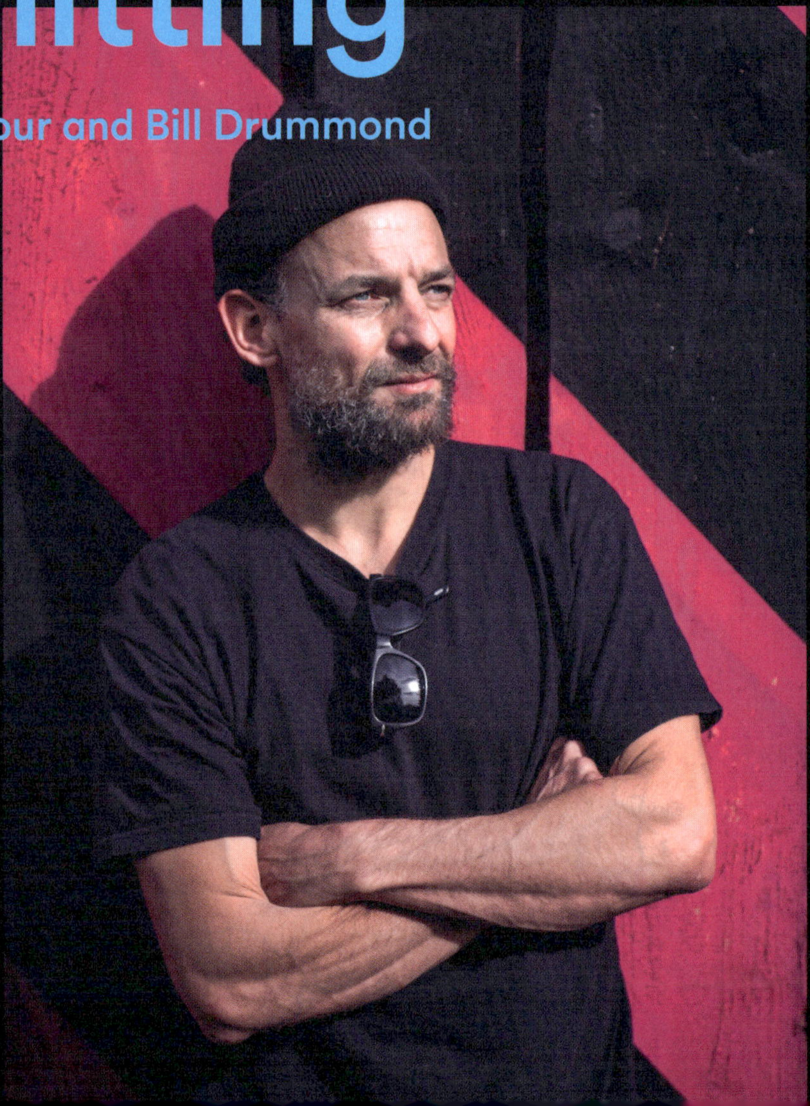

← Portrait of Bill Drummond, 2010. Photo by Thomas Ecke.

↓ Portrait of Jerszy Seymour. Photo by Milos Djuric.

The Art of Knitting

Jerszy Seymour and Bill Drummond

In this equally moving and humorous email conversation, Scottish artist, musician, writer and record producer BILL DRUMMOND, co-founder of late 1980s avant-garde pop group The KLF and its 1990s media-manipulating successor, the K Foundation, interviews British-Canadian enfant terrible of the design world JERSZY SEYMOUR.

11 MAY 2018, 11:40 AM
(BILL DRUMMOND)

Good Morning Jerszy,

I hope it is good one wherever you are.
As you may or may not know Lukas Feireiss has brought us together.
As you may or may not know, I have a strict regime when it comes to how I approach what I do.
As you may or may not know, this strict regime has a tendency to stray—even off limits at times.
One aspect of my current strict regime is that I do not answers questions.
Of course, when one of my children ask me 'What time will you be home, dad?' I attempt to answer them.
As I do when the ticket inspector on the bus asks to see my Freedom Pass.
When it comes to my 'creative' life I do all I can not to answer questions.
I consider my job is to be asking questions.
In 2014 this question-asking evolved into me doing something called Forty Minute Interviews.
Please see attached Penkiln Burn Poster 553.
Since that poster was published in 2014, the regime has now become tighter.
I now just do these Forty Minute Interviews at arms' (e-mails') length.
Except when I stray off limits and decide otherwise.
Now please read the Forty Minute Interview that I am now conducting—also attached.
As you will note, I am only part way through it.
The next question will be asked after I have hit send on this email.
One of my other current strict regimes is that when it comes to writing, I only write plays.
Please find attached the first draft of a play that I have written in this past week.
Taking all of the above into consideration, I would like to invite you to be interviewed by me via email for forty minutes.
In return I would like you to invite me to write a play on a subject matter of your choosing*
*But of course, that choosing, meaning your freedom of choice is being tampered with here, must not reference anything that might relate to The Justified Ancients of Mu Mu.

Yours,
Bill Drummond

14 MAY 2018, 08:51 AM
(JERSZY SEYMOUR)

Dear Bill

Thanks very much for your email and that is good to hear you.
I am happy to accept your proposal.
I am quite exhausted, the voyage in Greece, 'The Wandering School Part 2: Revolution or Bust!' with the Dirty Art Department that I hoped to invite you to join a moment with us has left me feeling quite bust and wondering what can be possible.
Perhaps I would ask you to write a play about what happens to a group of people who set off on a derive with the intention (I know paradox-ical as there should be no intention in a derive) in making the revolution happen (let's say in a

contemporary way without violence) to achieve a universal, emancipated and egalitarian society that accepts singular individuality and doesn't forget problems of the human soul.
What do you think?

All my best
Jerszy

16 MAY 2018, 10:04 AM (BILL DRUMMOND)

Morning Jerszy,

Thank you for your email and your willingness to engage with whatever this is.
My first question to you is:
When you were six, what did you want to be when you grew up?
The title of the play that I will write in response to your request is:
The History of Knitting.
I hope to have the set and first few pages of the play done in the next week.

Yours,
Bill Drummond

17 MAY 2018, 10:41 AM (BILL DRUMMOND)

Morning Jerszy,

A mistake has been made.
The first question that I needed to ask you was:
Why did you jump?
The knitting has begun.

Yours,
Bill Drummond

18 MAY 2018, 08:45 AM (JERSZY SEYMOUR)

Dear Bill

Good morning to you too. I am happy you have changed the question, I don't remember to seem having a clear idea of what I wanted to do at the age of six, so I can respond easier to the abstract question of what made me jump.
When I was growing up my family life was quite unstable and with the blinded political education in the UK I didn't go looking for deep questions of society or internal matters of the soul. I first studied engineering, and became involved in the London night life scene (lightly) DJing at places like the Wag club in the late 1980s which was more hedonistic than political, and even if the politics of class, culture, and race where everywhere in this period, I had no tools to deal with them. Nobody had given me a copy of the Communist Manifesto or the story of O from Georges Batailles. I then studied design at the RCA, and I think I would have just been happy to design speakers for clubs, so light was my outlook.

Jump
After graduating I moved to Italy with no particular idea, but two important things happened, first I became in touch with the work of the Italian Radical Architects of the 1980s—Sottsass, Mendini, Archizoom etc. I would meet some of them and I worked in that environment absorbing a something else; a radical idea of world building that could be both political, poetic and real (or seemingly) at the same time. This was when I was introduced to the idea that design could be a radical tool.
The second important thing is that my interest from the clubbing scene put me in touch with the Italian Centro Sociale scene, left wing or anarcho-left wing occupied buildings that ran as night clubs, concert halls, libraries and social centres—some huge, such as Leon Cavallo, and others smaller such as Pergola or Cox18. Here, I started to become familiar with the Italian movements such as Operiao Autonomo, but also I started to read, and read and read and read.
I am looking forward to the knitting

All my best
Jerszy

21 MAY 2018 02:09 PM (BILL DRUMMOND)

Dear Jerszy,

Thank you for the response to my first question. However, before you consider answering my second question:

ABANDON ALL ART NOW

AWAIT FURTHER INSTRUCTIONS. MAJOR RETHINK IN PROGRESS.

THE K. FOUNDATION, PO BOX 91, HP22 4RS THE U.K.

*** THE MILLION STITCH BLANKET**
by Tenzing Scott Brown

The Million Stitch Blanket
is a play in three acts.
Act One has only two characters.
They are:
Cindy and The Monkey on My Back.
Acts Two and Three will have
other characters, but as yet, we
do not know who they are.

ACT ONE:

Cindy is sitting at a bus stop.
It is the bus stop at Albion Parade.
From here you can catch the 73 or 476.
These two buses can take you
into the centre of London.
But for that you would have to be at the
bus stop on the other side of the road.
Cindy is sitting at the bus stop
where the buses stop to take
you further out of London.
Cindy is sitting with a pair of
knitting needles in her hand.
She is knitting very slowly.
Her wool is white.
She looks pissed off.
She may have dropped a stitch.
She then puts the knitting down
and looks on her phone.
What she is looking at is a YouTube
clip that is showing her how to knit.
She then puts the phone away.
And returns to attempt
to do the knitting.
There is no one else at the bus stop.
Then into the scene walks a man.
He to sits down on the
bench at the bus stop.
He has a small haversack.
From it he takes out some knitting.
And attempts to start to knit.
His wool is black.

CINDY:
I take it you are what he calls
The Monkey on My Back.

THE MONKEY ON MY BACK:
And I take it you are Cindy.

CINDY:
Yep.

THE MONKEY ON MY BACK:
So, you got your knitting?

CINDY:
Yep.

THE MONKEY ON MY BACK:
So, what did he tell you other than to
meet me here at 11:17 this morning?

CINDY:
Well you got an email from him.
What did he tell you?

THE MONKEY ON MY BACK:
But you have been an inner voice of his for
at least the past year. I am new to all of this.

CINDY:
Yes but, up until now I have only ever
existed while he is sitting in the Bodega
Fifty, that's if we discount the one where he
attempted to write like he was making out
that me and him were all post coital in...

Anyway, he told me that you
only existed when he was in his
room in front of his screen.

THE MONKEY ON MY BACK:
Yeah well, it seems that we have been let
loose, given a mission or something.

CINDY:
And what am I supposed to call you? I mean
I can't call you The Monkey on My Back.

THE MONKEY ON MY BACK:
Well...

The Monkey on My Back
pauses to think.

He doesn't call me anything.

CINDY:
Well I guess I will just call you Monkey.

THE MONKEY ON MY BACK:
And you?

CINDY:
Cindy is fine. I am used to it now.
I have to admit you are not
what I was expecting.

THE MONKEY ON MY BACK:
What do you mean?

CINDY:
The way you look. I was expecting
you to look more like him. Older.
More of a stoop. I mean I know you
are wearing the same clothes as he
wears, but he doesn't shave his head.

So, look Monk, you don't mind if I call you
Monk, it sounds better than Monkey?

THE MONKEY ON MY BACK:
Call me what you want.

CINDY:
Just so we both understand what it is we
are supposed to be doing. I understand
he agreed with some German or Italian or
somebody from somewhere that he was not
going to do an interview for some book,
but instead he would write a play. And he
asked this bloke – Jerszy something.

THE MONKEY ON MY BACK:
Jerszy Seymour.

CINDY:
Yeah him.
He asked this Jerszy to suggest
the subject matter of the play.

THE MONKEY ON MY BACK:
Yep. I've got it written down here.

The Monkey on My Back puts
down his knitting and pulls a
folded up piece of paper from his
top pocket. Unfolds it and reads.

"Write a play about making the revolution
happen, without using any violence, to
achieve a universal emancipated and
egalitarian society that accepts sin-
gular individuality and doesn't forget
problems of the human soul."

CINDY:
So Monk, have you got any
idea what that means?

THE MONKEY ON MY BACK:
Well I had to look up 'egalitarian'.

CINDY:
And?

The Monkey pulls out his phone.
Presses a few keys. And reads.

THE MONKEY ON MY BACK:
"Believing in the principle that all
people are equal and deserve equal
rights and opportunities."

CINDY:
And does that square with accept-
ing singular individuality?

THE MONKEY ON MY BACK:
Anyway, before we get to any of that,
according to his email to me, you were
going to explain what the knitting is about.
I mean I have taken the time to go on those
You Tube links and I have learnt to cast
on and done at least half a dozen rows.

CINDY:
It's The Million Stitch Blanket.

THE MONKEY ON MY BACK:
Yeah. And?

CINDY:
He must have told you. I mean for the
past month that is all he is ever been
doing, this knitting. Every time he
is in the Bodega Fifty he is knitting.
Something about he has got to get
200 more squares knitted before he
gets to Beijing in China next year.

THE MONKEY ON MY BACK:
Well he might be knitting while he is in
the Bodega Fifty and you are the voice in
his head while he is doing it, but when he
is in front of his screen in his room and
I am the voice in his head, his fingers are
taken up with writing these words. No
time for knitting of any sort. And he hasn't
written anything about any sort of knitting
since I have been a voice in his head.

Cindy puts down her knitting,
takes out her phone and reads.

CINDY:
The Million Stitch Blanket
Is made up of 1,000 knitted squares:
200 red squares
200 blue squares
200 yellow squares
200 black squares
200 white squares
Each square has forty rows
Each row has 25 stitches

The Million Stitch Blanket
Is being knitted
In different cities
In different countries
By different people
At different times
As part of the Twelve Year Tour

The Million Stitch Blanket
Can be knitted by you
By knitting
One stitch
One row
One square
Or more

The Million Stitch Blanket
will be completed
In the year 2026
It will then be presented as a gift
From the People of the World
To the People of Birmingham.

THE MONKEY ON MY BACK:
Birmingham?

CINDY:
Forget Birmingham that is irrelevant.
According to his email, he has been doing
Knit & Natter sessions all over the place.
Kolkata in India, Belgrade in Serbia, Lexing-
ton, North Carolina and even Birmingham.

THE MONKEY ON MY BACK:
What the sod is a "Knit & Natter session".

CINDY:
You know, where people get together and
do their knitting and talk about anything.

THE MONKEY ON MY BACK:
Anything?

CINDY:
Well how the fuck would I know,
I have never actually been on a
Knit & Natter session, and have no
sodding idea what goes on at his.

THE MONKEY ON MY BACK:
And Birmingham? Is that Bir-
mingham, Alabama?

CINDY:
No Birmingham, England. But forget
Birmingham. You need to tell me what
we are supposed to be doing today.

THE MONKEY ON MY BACK:
Or else what?

CINDY:
Or else he gets rid of us as his inner voices.
Dumps us for younger smarter models.

THE MONKEY ON MY BACK:
Well fuck him. That would be his loss.

CINDY:
Yes I know, but with all this social
networking and algorithms and
everything else, there are less and less
openings for inner voices. Nobody
bothers with them when they can just
chat to friends at anytime on line.

I've told you about the knitting
you are supposed to tell me what
he told you in his email.

THE MONKEY ON MY BACK:
That we catch whatever bus that
comes along first. Stay on the bus
until the end of the line. Get off.
Find the first homeless, rough sleeping
beggar, sit down either side of him...

CINDY:
Or her...

THE MONKEY ON MY BACK:
Or her. And we teach them to knit in ex-
change for them telling us how they think...

The Monkey stops and looks at
his phone again and reads

"the revolution can happen, without
using any violence, to achieve a universal
emancipated and egalitarian society that
accepts singular individuality and doesn't
forget problems of the human soul."

Cindy is looking elsewhere as if
she is not really listening. Then she
notices something down the road.

CINDY:
The bus is coming.

And that is the end of Act
One of this play.

↰ One of the adverts the K Foundation ran on national newspapers in July 1993, for which they paid between 5000 and 15000 GBP.

→ Jerszy Seymour Design Workshop, *Amateur Workshop #6, A Perverts Guide to Design*, Broehan Museum, Berlin, Germany, 2016.

Please find attached Act One of the play *The Million Stitch Blanket**.
However, before you read that, read the *Drummond's International Grey* play that is also attached.
Your question number two is:
If you had to move to a city in South America, which one would it be and why?

Yours,
Bill Drummond

*You will note that the title of the play has changed.

25 MAY 2018 08:39 AM (JERSZY SEYMOUR)

Dear Bill,

Thank you for your mail and the plays.
I very much appreciate the bed that supports life's inner emotional moments, birth, passion, dreams and death as the art work, and your squabbling inner voices, Cindy and the Monkey on your back in Drummonds International Grey.
I have a comment about the use of the word international, and refer to a work of mine, *The Extra National Assembly #1*, a place to discuss what a society could be beyond the concept of nations.
I think that the current concept of nations is one of our problems in the face of a globalised neoliberal capitalism. Of course, I dream about some form of universality within society.
Thank you also for the beginning of the new play, the Million Stitch Blanket, ha! I am very happy Cindy and Monk (the Monkey on your Back) meet and discuss my proposal for the play. I must admit, I feel quite naked in how my words will be discussed by these two quite brutally honest figures! Probably best that way. I certainly will not look for a fig leaf.
For your question number two, which city in South America would I move to if I had to, I must admit I have always been very curious about South America but have never visited. Of course, its alternative version to European colonialism that gave birth to some of the worst dictators but also socialist causes have always intrigued me as well as its ancient mysticisms and nature. Which city would I move to?

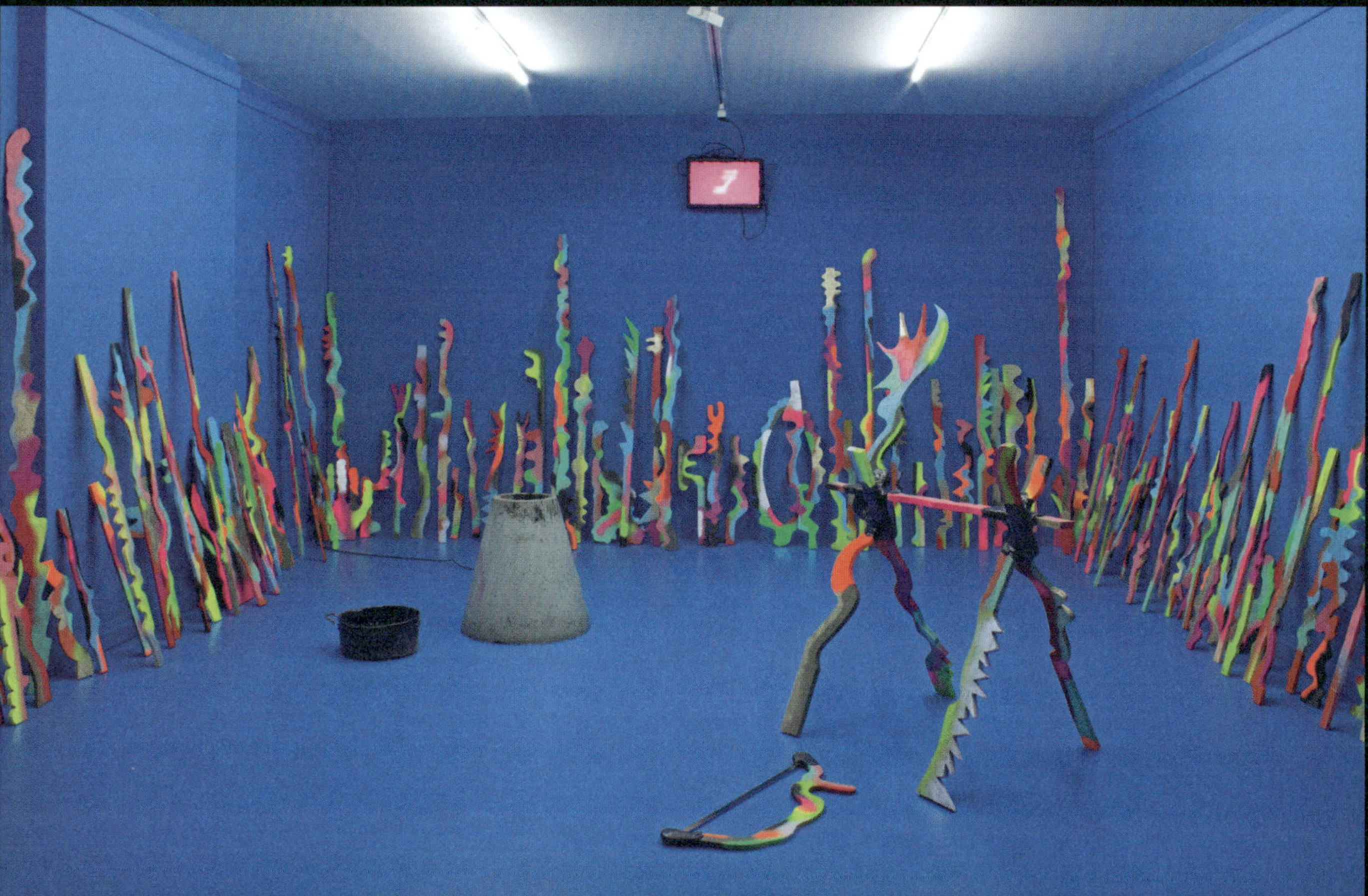

I think first I would got to visit the 'poorest president in the world' Jose Mujica in Montevideo, Uruguay. He renounced all his riches to give to the people, did not even claim his salary, and lives on a farm on the outskirts of the city. I think he could give me some advice. This would be a beginning.
I look forward to your next question.

All my best
Jerszy

NOTICE

FORTY MINUTE INTERVIEWS

You can be interviewed by Bill Drummond

You can be interviewed in private or public

You can reveal as much or as little of yourself as you choose

You can have the interview recorded or filmed

You can use the documentation in whatever way you choose

You can respond to this offer by contacting talk@penkilnburn.com

pb Poster 553 2014 www.penkilnburn.com

07 JUNE 2018, 06:48 PM (BILL DRUMMOND)

Dear Jerszy,

Attached is the play so far.
You will note that Act Two is yet to have arrived, thus we are already in the throws of Act Three.
On Monday, I worked as an assistant undertaker – this being part of a new career path I am following.
The funeral in question was for a young man (25) who had died of a drugs misadventure.
The funeral service was carried out under the spreading branches of an oak tree, at the edge of a forest—it must have been several hundred years old.
The young man was buried in a freshly dug grave deeper in the forest.
The mother of the young man was probably not yet 50.
It might be sexist to say, but no mother who has given birth to a child should then have to attend her offspring's funeral. This being something that my great grandmothers on both sides of my family had to do due to the First World War.
Up until now, I had always assumed that I would want to be cremated. Thus, no grave for my family to feel they have to tend to but—
Something about this burial in a shallow grave in a woods—there was going to be no head stone etc.
As the grave was shallow, it would not take long for his body to be eaten by worms etc. Thus, far better for the environment than being cremated.
My question for you is:
Would you like to be buried, cremated, or even buried at sea or maybe other?
I was going to ask you—at what age do you think you should die? I will leave that one just to be pondered on.

Yours,
Bill Drummond

11 JUNE 2018 10:42 AM (JERSZY SEYMOUR)

Ahh Dear Bill,

You said this would go where it will go and so it does.
Firstly, thank you for act three. I am happy to see

the questions and discussion unfold
and yes, it is probably only then, with the breakdown of national borders, that we will be able to see what such a revolution could be.
Then let's see if we print the next part. Maybe it is good for me because I have never been able to talk about it publicly.
With your story about the funeral, you hit straight to my human soul and a huge scar. You see, I had a son, Ruven, a super beautiful ray of sunshine who died at six months old. He died in my arms. I dug his grave next to a large tree deep in the forest, I buried him, and I made his grave stone. The story to his death is every bit as hard, the mother left me to be with somebody else and then at six months old either he or she shook Ruven to death.
The court couldn't prove who, so neither was convicted (although don't wish prison on anyone). It is hard to forgive myself for not being there, it is almost impossible to forgive her, although this is what I wish as much as for her as the reparation of my own soul.
Although I do not know how I want to be buried, I know it is more for the people around you, whom you love, so in the way I decide, I will think about them. The age I will leave to destiny.
This mail leaves me in tears.
They say it is good to let things out.

Yours
Jerszy

14 JUNE 2018, 12:05 PM
(BILL DRUMMOND)

Morning Jerszy,

Your email is a difficult one to respond to for obvious reasons.
I am aware from the internet that you are 50 years old, thus not in the first flush of youth, but still considerably younger than myself (65).
What you don't say is if you have had any other children. Have you?
If you have not, would you consider at this stage in life having any others?
I have been a serial father—seven in all, spread between four mothers. This has meant I have been changing nappies for nigh on 35 years. It has also had a profound influence on my working life and where I can live. As in, where I have lived for those past 35 years has been decided by my role as a father. It seems that you have chosen to live in various cities in various countries. Do you feel it has been good for you creatively to have been able to have lived in these various cities in various countries?
Then there are the time constraints.
For me, I like to think that the time constraints that I have help me make better use of the time that I have. As in today, I had to get my five-year old up and ready for school, and then get back to my flat for 8am, where my 18-year old, who had only got back from working a night shift on an event, to make sure he was alright and had breakfast. Now I am writing up the play, based on what happened yesterday. I have to get a stack of administration done. Then I have to pick up my five-year old from school at 3:30pm, take him back to his mother's flat—she is having to look after her mother—and I will be making him his dinner and probably putting him to bed. If I have time after that, I hope to get back to mine to do some work done on my 25 Paintings—they are having their annual repaint—this time from Bangla to American English.
As for the play—you will note that I have not had the second part of Act Three back from Tam Dean Burn yet, but in the meantime, I have made headway with Act Two. You will also note, that the second half of Act Two will not be done for another week. I should add that dialogue used in Act Two is almost word for word—well, as much as my memory was able to do so. The conversation happened yesterday, and I have only had the time to get it written up this morning.

Yours,
Bill

28 JUNE 2018, 10:37 AM
(JERSZY SEYMOUR)

Dear Bill,

Yes I understand, it also took me a bit to respond. I haven't had other children, I think because I was not mentally ready, but I am now and am hoping. In many ways right now, I think if I can be a good father, this will be the biggest step towards a revolution I can make.
Something I work on also right now is a model for children's education, obviously it is to them

the future, and for us to create the best condi-
tions for them to confront it. In a very simple way I see the history of children's education being between creating pillars of knowledge for the power of the state, and the counter-reaction we can see from Montessori, Steiner to the 1960s and Joseph Beuys which was all about the individual creativity.
The critique of this is apparent—we either create non-thinking automatons for a kind of fascism or self-centred 'everybody is an artist' individuals that feed the neo-liberal scheme. Whilst creativity and knowledge are fine in themselves, my simple idea on this is to create a pedagogy based on the idea of how the individual can be content with themselves and how the individual can be content with the world and society around them. This figures self-knowledge and collective approaches. Of course, always Love.
Thanks for the beginning of Act 2. I am happy Timmy Thomas's song *Why can't we Live Together* gets mentioned. Didn't Sade to a great cover of that too? Two questions, if the right word is not revolution (by the way the word in its subversive sense comes from Copernicus's *On the Revolution of Celestial Spheres* and then I think the church chopped his head off) what would you use? Re- evolution? What do you use the metaphor of knitting for?
I hope you are having a great day with all of your kids,

All my best
Jerszy

28 JUNE 2018, 07:37 PM
(BILL DRUMMOND)

Dear Jerszy,

Thank you for your email.
Why Can't We Live Together by Timmy Thomas is one of my favourite records of all time. I love the fact that it takes so long before the singing comes in and for all that time it is just the organ and the primitive drum machine.
As for your two questions—I don't know if I trust

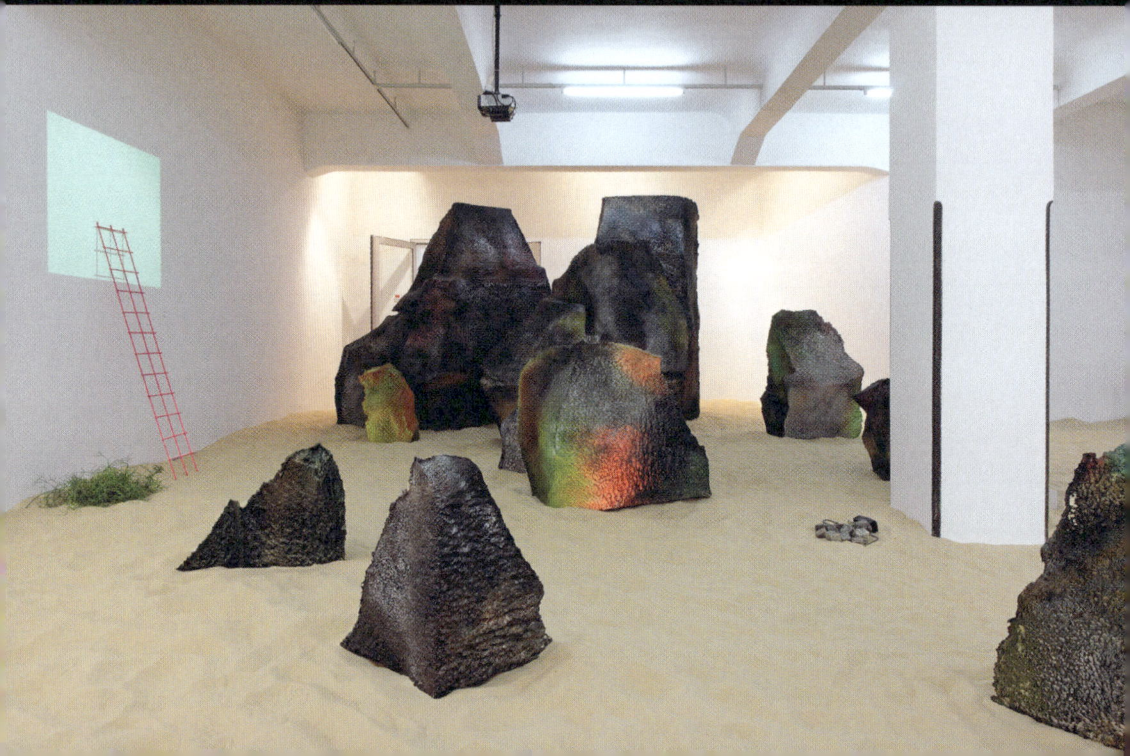

ACT THREE – PART ONE:

Cindy is back sitting on the bench at the bus shelter.
She is knitting.
Her knitting is more confident than before.
She is thinking.
She puts down her knitting.
She looks to see if her bus is coming.
It isn't.
She looks out at the audience.
She looks at her phone.
She looks back out at the audience.
She addresses the audience.

CINDY:
You know that actor that plays Drummond in these plays that Tenzing Scott Brown has been writing?
And has been playing The Monkey on My Back in this play so far?
Well that actor is called Tam Dean Burn.
Now Tam Dean Burn is an artist in his own rite.
He doesn't just exist to mouth the words of whoever is writing the play or the film or TV programme that he is in and you might be watching.
Tam Dean Burn has his own thoughts and opinions.
And he writes words.
His own words.
He is also a card-carrying member of the Communist Party of Great Britain.
He even stood as a candidate for them in Glasgow Central constituency back in the 1992 general election.
Lost his deposit of course.
But he has opinions.
So I texted him the quote.
The one that this play is supposed to be based around.
And if you have forgotten.
This is it again:

'Write a play about making the revolution happen, without using any violence, to achieve a universal emancipated and egalitarian society that accepts singular individuality and doesn't forget problems of the human soul.'

I phoned him earlier, after we got back from doing the bus ride thing and met up with the pair you met in Act Two.

I thought he might have a take on it.
And he did.
And as he was telling me all this stuff about the crisis of capitalism, I scribbled notes.
And from those notes I have decided to write Act Three of this play.
From what I understand Tenzing Scott Brown has not even got around to writing Act Two of it.
And just to make things clear to you.
If it was not clear enough already.
The actor playing The Monkey On My Back in this play so far is Tam Dean Burn.
This Tam Dean Burn is about to come back onto the stage, playing a version of himself.
I am hoping he will have changed from the costume he was wearing as The Monkey on My Back into what we might think a card-carrying member of the Communist Party of Great Britain should be wearing.
And when he comes back on stage, him and I will have a conversation.
A conversation that I have written.
Words that I have written based on the conversation that I had with the real Tam Dean Burn earlier this afternoon.
He might think I have compromised some of what he originally said.
I guess some of it will have got lost in the translation from real life conversation to the conversation as acted out on a stage in front of you.
But my main concern is that he will have learnt his lines.

Cindy stops talking to the audience and looks down at her phone again.
She has just received a text message from Tam Dean Burn to say that he will be there at the bus stop in a minute. And that he has brought his knitting.

Cindy looks up from her phone.

Tam Dean Burn enters stage right.

CINDY:
So I take it you have brought your knitting.

TAM DEAN BURN:
Right here in my bag.

Tam Dean Burn pulls his knitting out of his bag.

And I have learnt to knit.
So what was it you wanted to talk to me about while I knit this square for The Million Stitch Blanket?

CINDY:
I want to get your response to that quote I sent you about making the revolution happen…

TAM DEAN BURN:
Yeah, yeah, yeah.
You see it is not about making the revolution happen.
It is going to happen anyway.
Even if not in our life time.
And it will be brutal.

CINDY:
So do you think the rise of the popular right across Europe and other parts of the world are a fore taster of what is going to happen?

TAM DEAN BURN:
What?

CINDY:
Well the workingman that could be relied on in decades past to vote Labour or for whatever the left leaning party in whatever country, no longer feels the need or tribal loyalty to vote that way. They are drawn to voting for the popular right parties.

They no longer are motivated to vote against what they see as the fat greedy mill owners, that no longer exist.

Instead they vote against Polish bricklayers and Estonian plumbers who they think are taking their jobs.

Or in Italy they vote against the Africans attempting to get across the Mediterranean.

Or the illegal immigrant in the queue ahead of them at A & E at the local hospital.

Or…

TAM DEAN BURN:
Forget all that.
That is nothing compared to what is going to happen.
Will happen.
The Crisis in Capitalism will go way beyond all of that.
Europe needed the First World War to sort out its problems with competing empires.
Europe needed the Second World War to make Western Capitalism work.
Then Capitalism had its boom years of the 50s and the 60s.
But the workers…

CINDY:
But in the future there will be no workers only consumers.

TAM DEAN BURN:
There might be less workers now in this country. But there are far more workers in Bangladesh or wherever my trainers were made in. But that is almost beside the point. And yes in one sense you are right Capitalism might not need the workers to be working in the mill, but they will need them to be consumers. If there are no consumers there cannot be any Capitalism.

CINDY:
But do you think in the short term that the rise in the popular right will lead to Fascism as it did in the 1930s?

TAM DEAN BURN:
Fascism does not suit the needs of Capitalism.
Capitalism does not want centrally planned government.
Centrally planned Fascism will fail in the same way as any top down government would fail, be it of the far right or perceived left.
In the end all top down methods of government can only work with the use of fear and threat of violence.

CINDY:
But surely that is why the market place that is central to Capitalism works better than any of the other options including your Communism?

TAM DEAN BURN:
But the market place does not take into account the ecological forces that will undoubtably be unleashed in the coming hundred years. It will make the potato famine in Ireland of the 1840s seem like nothing compared to what is in store.
And there will be nothing the market forces will be able to do about it.
Market forces can never see further than the next set of results for the shareholders.
Our children or grandchildren will have to deal with going back to an age that is well before…
The national borders we have now will mean nothing.
Half of Africa will pour into Europe.
People will go anywhere they think they will be able to get something to eat.
It will be only then that us as a species might be able to learn from whatever is going to happen.
It will only be then that the revolution will truly happen.

CINDY:
And what about "singular individuality and doesn't forget problems of the human soul"?
Or are they just decadent aspirations of the pampering times some of us have been living through?

At this point Tam Dean Burn leaves the stage.
There is no explanation.
He is gone.
Like he was never there.

Cindy puts her knitting away.
Pulls out her phone.
She is reading an email from Tam Dean Burn.
Not the one that the audience have just seen performed in front of them.
But the Tam Dean Burn that is in Glasgow.
And that Cindy spoke to earlier on the phone.
And who said some things that Cindy then attempted to turn into the words for Act Three of this play.

Cindy had emailed him what she had written.
And now he has emailed her back.
With a completely re-written version of what she had written, and the audience have just heard performed by the actor playing Tam Dean Burn.

More later.

ACT THREE – PART TWO:

Tam Dean Burn walks back on the stage.
He is holding in his left hand the script for this play.
He looks at the audience.
He looks at Cindy.
He looks at the script for this play.
He looks back at Cindy.
He looks back at the audience.
He looks back at the script for this play

And he rips it up.
And drops the torn-up script onto the stage.

From his back pocket he pulls out his knitting.
But before he starts knitting he addresses the audience.

TAM DEAN BURN:
I learnt my lines.
It is my job as an actor to learn my lines.
To make those lines come alive when I am on stage.
And you are sitting there listening to me.
But sometimes something else has to be said.
And sometimes the Monkey on My Back is just the Monkey on the back of whoever has written the play.
I have my own words
And I have My Own Monkey
And right now, My Own Monkey is going to speak.

Tam Dean Burn turns his head to his left.
He is now My Own Monkey.

And My Own Monkey is addressing Tam Dean Burn.

MY OWN MONKEY:
So you're given that opportunity to explain and promote the beauty of revolution, something that you're supposed to have been wrapped up in all your adult life, from The Dirty Reds punk band on, and all you can do is fire off doom and gloom and half-baked notions of why capitalism is such a bad thang.

My Own Monkey then turns his head to his right.
He is now Tam Dean Burn.
And Tam Dean Burn is addressing My Own Monkey.

TAM DEAN BURN:
Get off my back, I'm getting on with my knitting.
At least that is doing me some good.
At least that offer from Bill offers a sliver of hope of me staying sane and alive.

MY OWN MONKEY:
Oh, for fuck's sake, have you really retreated into such a little corner.

My Own Monkey sings to the tune of Jesus Bids Us Shine:

"You in your bright corner
And I in mine."

You've admitted to Drummond in these exchanges that you dropped out of party membership when you dropped your first E. Now, are you saying that you've so little to offer the struggle that is all you can do is knit?

TAM DEAN BURN:
Look politics is in my blood, that's abundantly clear to me.
Why else would I have spent the time right before this scene reading in the Weekly Worker about the latest meeting of the Communist Party of Great Britain…
Okay, I had hoped it could inform my attempts to argue against the onslaught, I knew was coming from you. But it is also what interests me most and I do wish I could have made a better case for the revolution in the last scene.

MY OWN MONKEY:
Well, come on then, do it now.
Put that knitting down
And stand up for your rights.

TAM DEAN BURN:
No!
This knitting is now part of the revolution for me now.
One:
It rids me of any of the macho bullshit that has contaminated the left for so long. Just look at the Socialist Workers Party and the mire they have ended up in and…
Two:
It's another healthy, new pursuit that does hopefully increase my chances of staying alive and being around when the revolution does come.

This knitting represents the second half of that request – the one about accepting the singular individual and not forgetting the problems of the human soul.

MY OWN MONKEY:
Aye right!

↰ Bill Drummond, *Notice Forty Minute Interviews*, 2014.

← Jerszy Seymour Design Workshop, *The Universe Wants to Play*, Galerie Crone, Berlin, Germany, 2013.

ACT TWO:

Although the events in Act Two of this play happen before the event in Act Three of this play happen. Act Two of this play will be performed after Act Three of this play.

This is unless the director of a particular performance of this play decides otherwise.

Cindy and The Monkey on My Back get on the bus.
It is the 476.
They stay on the bus all the way to the end of the line.
The end of the line is Northumberland Park somewhere near White Hart Lane.
White Hart Lane is the home of the Spurs

"And if you know your history, it's enough to make your heart go whoa-oh"

Cindy and The Monkey on My Back get off the bus.
They wander about looking for:
The homeless
The downtrodden
The oppressed
The outcast
The forgotten.
But there are none to be found.
Or none that look like they could be in a play with interesting things to say.

So they get back on the bus.
And they stay on the bus
Until the bus is back at the stop they got on at.

Well not the stop they got on at
But the one across the road from it.

Cindy and The Monkey on My Back cross the road.
Sitting on one of the benches in the triangular garden behind the bus stop are two drinkers. One is a young white man, the other is a not as young mixed-race woman.
They are regulars.
They have with them their Staffordshire Bull Terriers.
But for the purposes of this play we can forget about the Staffordshire Bull Terriers.
The two drinkers are drinking a brand of strong (8.5 proof) Polish larger.
Cindy recognises the young man, as he often is begging by the cash machine by the local Tesco Metro.
The Monkey on My Back recognises the not as young mixed-race woman as she is often in front of him at the queue in the local off licence on Albion Parade.
They both recognise both of them, as they are often sitting on this very bench, with their two Staffordshire Bull Terriers, while drinking strong Polish larger.

The Staffs bark and show their teeth
Cindy bends to stroke them
The Staffs stop barking and let Cindy stroke them.
And for the sake of this play
And the rampant ageism that goes on in this world
Especially when it comes to judging woman
Especially when it comes to judging mixed race women
Especially when it comes to judging mixed race women who sit on a bench in the middle of the day drinking strong Polish larger.
We will name them just as The Man and The Woman.
Or might that be innately sexist?
Should that be just Dog Owner One and Dog Owner Two?
No!
As when this is performed as a play there will be no dogs.
Not even Staffordshire Bull Terriers who are friendly when stroked.
We will just know them as The Man and The Woman.

CINDY:
I hope you don't mind us coming up and bothering you like this.

THE MAN:
Cool.

THE WOMAN:
She just wants you to stroke her as well.

THE MAN:
She is her mother.

THE MONKEY ON MY BACK:
Do either of you knit?

THE WOMAN:
I knit.

THE MAN:
She is good at knitting.
She is also good at typing.
She can do anything.
She can...

THE WOMAN:
What are you knitting?

CINDY:
It is The Million Stitch Blanket.

THE MAN:
The what?

THE MONKEY ON MY BACK:
It is something called The Million Stitch Blanket.
We are sort of helping a friend out.
He is supposed to be knitting this blanket that is made up of one thousand squares. And each square has one thousand stitches in it.
And he is knitting all over the world.
And everywhere he knits it, he knits it with other people
And chats to them.
He calls it Knit & Natter.

CINDY:
We are sort of doing him a favour.
Although to be honest I don't think he deserves us doing him a favour.

THE MONKEY ON MY BACK:
He wanted us to go out and find somebody,
Somebody who is just sitting and taking it easy.

The Man & The Woman answer in unison.

THE MAN & THE WOMAN:
And that is us?

Cindy & The Monkey on My Back answer in unison.

CINDY & THE MONKEY ON MY BACK:
I guess so.

THE WOMAN:
So you are knitting squares for this blanket.

THE MONKEY ON MY BACK:
Yes.

THE WOMAN:
You want me to knit some?

CINDY:
If you are okay with that?

THE WOMAN:
Yeah, I like to knit.

The Monkey on My Back hands The Woman the knitting he is holding in his right hand.
The Woman starts to knit.
She is good.

How much do you want me to knit?

CINDY:
Just a row will do.

THE MONKEY ON MY BACK:
But knit more if you want.

The Woman keeps knitting.

THE MAN:
So what's the deal?

CINDY:
Well...

THE MAN:
You haven't just come over here to talk about knitting?

CINDY:
Well, it's kinda complicated...

THE WOMAN:
You are not undercover cops or something?

THE MONKEY ON MY BACK:
Not undercover cops, but I like the idea that we are undercover something.
But I am not too sure what that is.

CINDY:
Anyway, we have been asked to do some research into the revolution.

THE MAN:
The what?

CINDY:
You know, the revolution.

THE WOMAN:
What revolution?

THE MONKEY ON MY BACK:
Well when I was young back in the late 60s or early 70s, we used to talk about when the revolution would come and...

THE MAN:
But that was back then. There isn't going to be any revolution. For a revolution to happen you need to have young people willing to make it happen. Young people today don't give a shit about anything, let alone a revolution.

THE WOMAN:
He's right. I got kids. They would do nothing to make a revolution happen.
They just want spend their time smoking weed and playing on...

THE MAN:
If today was 1944, you would never get young men willing to land on the beach at Omah. Hitler would have won the war.

THE WOMAN:
Since the collapse of the Soviet Union and then Chavez and look at North Korea, no young people are interested in revolution.
Unless it is in a computer game or a film.

Revolution is history.

THE MAN:
It's like music today.
It is all shit.
Even hip-hop.
People used to make music that would inspire people to want to... Well if not start a revolution, at least try and make the world a better place.

You see, she can not only knit and type, she is a singer / songwriter. She was great at it. But then nobody wanted her songs. Or the record companies didn't. They just wanted the shit.

THE WOMAN:
So what is the point?
The revolution is not going to happen if the young people don't want it to happen.

CINDY:
Okay, I got an idea.
You write a song that you think can inspire people to make the world a better place.

THE MONKEY ON MY BACK:
Not just 'Why can't we all just live together?' type song. But one that almost demands change.

THE WOMAN:
But no one will want to hear it.

CINDY:
That is not the point.
You write the song.
We will come back in a week and you can sing us what you have written.
If you need a guitar he can bring one.

THE MAN:
And what does she get?

THE MONKEY ON MY BACK:
Well right now, I will get you a couple of cans of whatever you are drinking.

CINDY:
And next week, if you have written the song.
A song you can be proud of.
We will give you one hundred pounds.

THE WOMAN:
And can I knit a whole square for the Million Stitch Blanket?

THE MONKEY ON MY BACK:
Deal!

THE WOMAN:
Yeah but, before we shake hands on the deal, I want you to agree to show me how much of the blanket has been done. I will bring you my song, if you bring me your blanket.

CINDY:
Deal!

All four shake hands of it.

The End of part one of Act Two

ACT TWO – PART TWO:

Yet to be written.

revolution. The idea of them is usually sexy in hindsight. Also, with hindsight they never seem to deliver the goods they promised. I guess I never give up hope. With the Arab Spring, I truly believed it was going to work, and of course the countries in questions ended up in a worse place than they were before. I guess it has to be 're-evolution'.
I guess John Lennon summed it up in his *Revolution* song back in 1968.
As for the knitting, I don't think of it as a metaphor. Knitting is something that I learnt to do in my first year at school. I like the fact that any time I start knitting somewhere people will stop and start talking to me. It was from that the idea of the *Million Stitch Blanket* grew. It seemed as natural as part of my twelve-year world tour. If I do get pretentious about it, it is because I like to think that all of those conversations from around the world will be knitted up in the blanket.
As for 'all of your kids', bar one, they are all basically grown up. They have been sent to challenge me in all sorts of ways. They do that very well. Hope to have the last bit of the play and the song from The Woman across the road with you within the next 48 hours, and I guess that will be it.

Yours,
Bill Drummond

29 JUNE 2018, 09:30 AM
(JERSZY SEYMOUR)

Dear Bill
I just listened to Timmy Thomas again—yes truly great.
I look forward to the song from the woman across the road,

all my best
Jerszy

10 JULY 2018, 12:44 PM
(BILL DRUMMOND)

Morning Jerszy,

Everyday over this past week, I have been hoping for the woman on the bench across the road to turn up on the bench across the road, so that I could sit down with her and transcribe her song that was going to save the world—or something; but she hasn't turned up. And—
Everyday over this past week, I have been hoping for Tam Dean Burn to e-mail me his last contribution to the play, but stuff has been happening in his life, that has meant he has not got it done. Thus, I think that is it.
Rather—it is it for the time being and for the deadline for copy for this book.
Maybe further down the line the play will get completed and the song that will save the world will get written, but for the time being, I have to order some more blue wool for the *Million Stitch Blanket* and go and watch the rough cut of a film called *Best Before Death*.
For the time being, I guess we have to leave it with the sound of Timmy Thomas singing *Why Can't We Live Together* hanging in the air.

See you at the barricades, babe
See you when the lights go low, Joe
Hear you when the wheels turn 'round
Someday when the sky turns black

Yours,
Bill Drummond

Beside the Point. The Architectures of Denise Scott Brown

Andres Ramirez

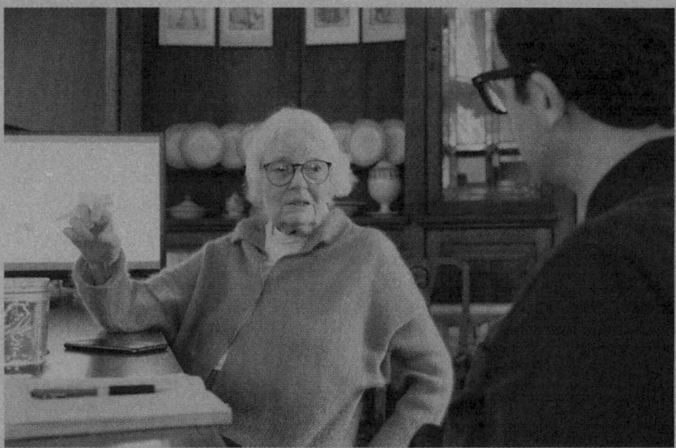

DENISE SCOTT BROWN and her husband Robert Venturi are among the most influential architects of the 20th century, both in theory and practice. Based on numerous personal encounters and an evolving transgenerational friendship, Colombian writer and curator ANDRES RAMIREZ reflects upon Denise's legacy as architect and thinker.

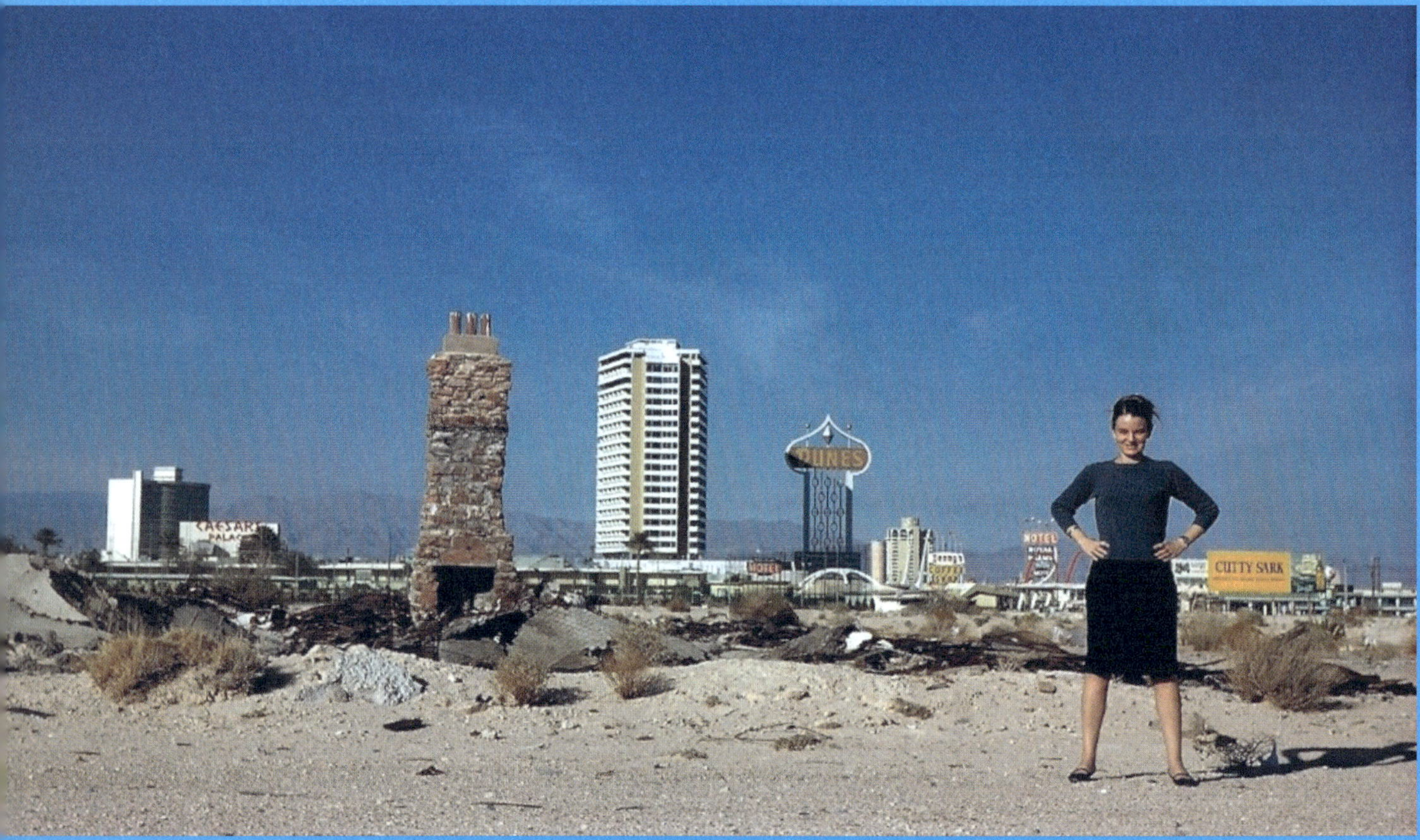

At the time of our first meeting, Denise was 85 and I was 30. Denise showed me pictures she had taken on her iPhone while traveling by train from Philadelphia to New York, capturing the vestiges of industry along the way. Long before Las Vegas she learned how to use a camera, not merely to document building forms, but to explore and express ideas about architecture. Photography helped her understand the radically different environments she stepped into as a young architect. 'I was passionately taking photographs of things I liked that had to do with ideas,' she tells me. It soon occurred to me that photography—not architecture—was the genesis of ideas that made her one of the most influential architects of the last century.

It's fascinating to look at the photographs Denise took in the 1950s and 1960s in South Africa, Venice and Philadelphia—a time when architects rarely travelled or used cameras. Most of these images preceded her time spent collaborating with Robert Venturi, and exposed her intuitive fascination with popular culture, vernacular forms, and the communication of architectural information. Denise explained to me, as she has done to hundreds of students before me, how photography allowed her to develop ideas, illustrate research findings, and redirect them back towards design.

Coming to architecture from the social sciences, I've never cared for the buildings themselves as much as for architecture's symbolic functions. My work excludes design and construction, and instead investigates architecture and urban practices as a source of contemporary culture. Although we are from different margins of the profession, Denise and I share the conviction that architecture can be a cultural asset and a public good. Her life's work is testament to the fact that architecture need not materialize into three-dimensional spaces to exert influence. Few virtues can be attributed to bricks and mortar alone, which is why architects should aspire to affect more than the built environment alone.

In order to serve, architecture should venture beyond its traditional domains, accessing other fields of knowledge and helping shape the social, cultural and political dimensions of everyday life. Successful architecture is powered by ideas that effectively cross-pollinate other disciplines and inspire collective action. To endure the test of time, architects need to be ready to produce more than just buildings. This leap of faith takes curiosity, wit, and more importantly, it demands a special kind of courage for a lifetime's worth of perseverance.

'I have always mixed writing, drawing, architecture and speculation'.

According to Denise, the first function of a building should not be the only program that concerns architects. Therefore, if architecture can have

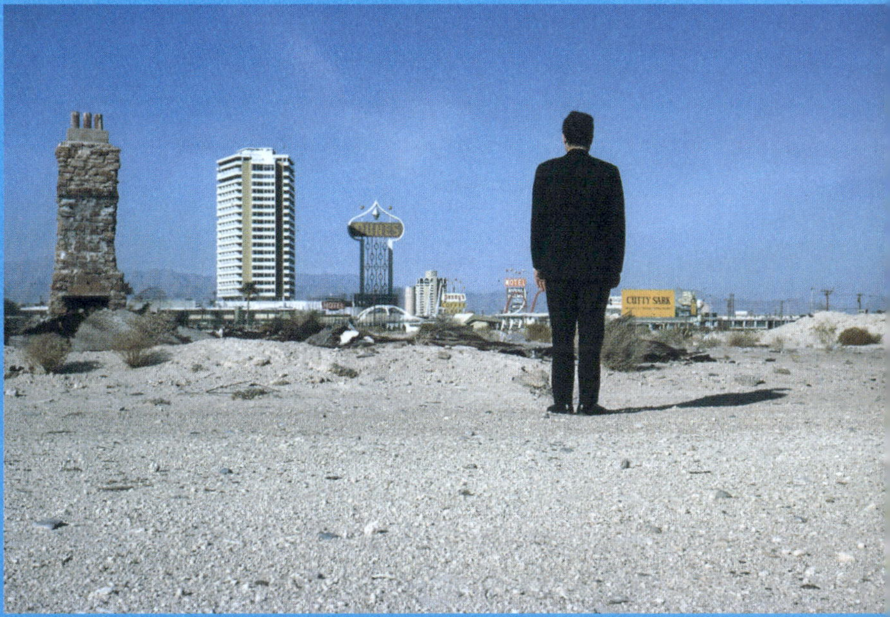

more than one function beyond the material world, shouldn't architects do more than design? Denise encourages architects, planners and scholar to open a wider window onto the world, to learn from practitioners in different contexts. It's not enough to just look to oneself—multi-disciplinary processes result in better design because they are more responsive. Denise was never afraid to branch out and learn about complementary subject matters. She delved deep into social planning and regional economics, which allowed her to understand economic behaviour and social payoffs, such as self-respect and creativity. These are skills no architect should shy away from, and she maintains their continuity. 'In my work,' she says, 'it all goes together. I couldn't do the one without the other.

↰ Andres Ramirez in conversation with Denise Scott Brown, 2017. Courtesy of Plane-Site..

↑ *Bob a la Magritte*, Las Vegas, 1966. Photo from the archives of Robert Venturi and Denise Scott Brown.

← *Denise Scott Brown in front of the Las Vegas Strip, 1966.* Photo from the Archives of Robert Venturi and Denise Scott Brown.

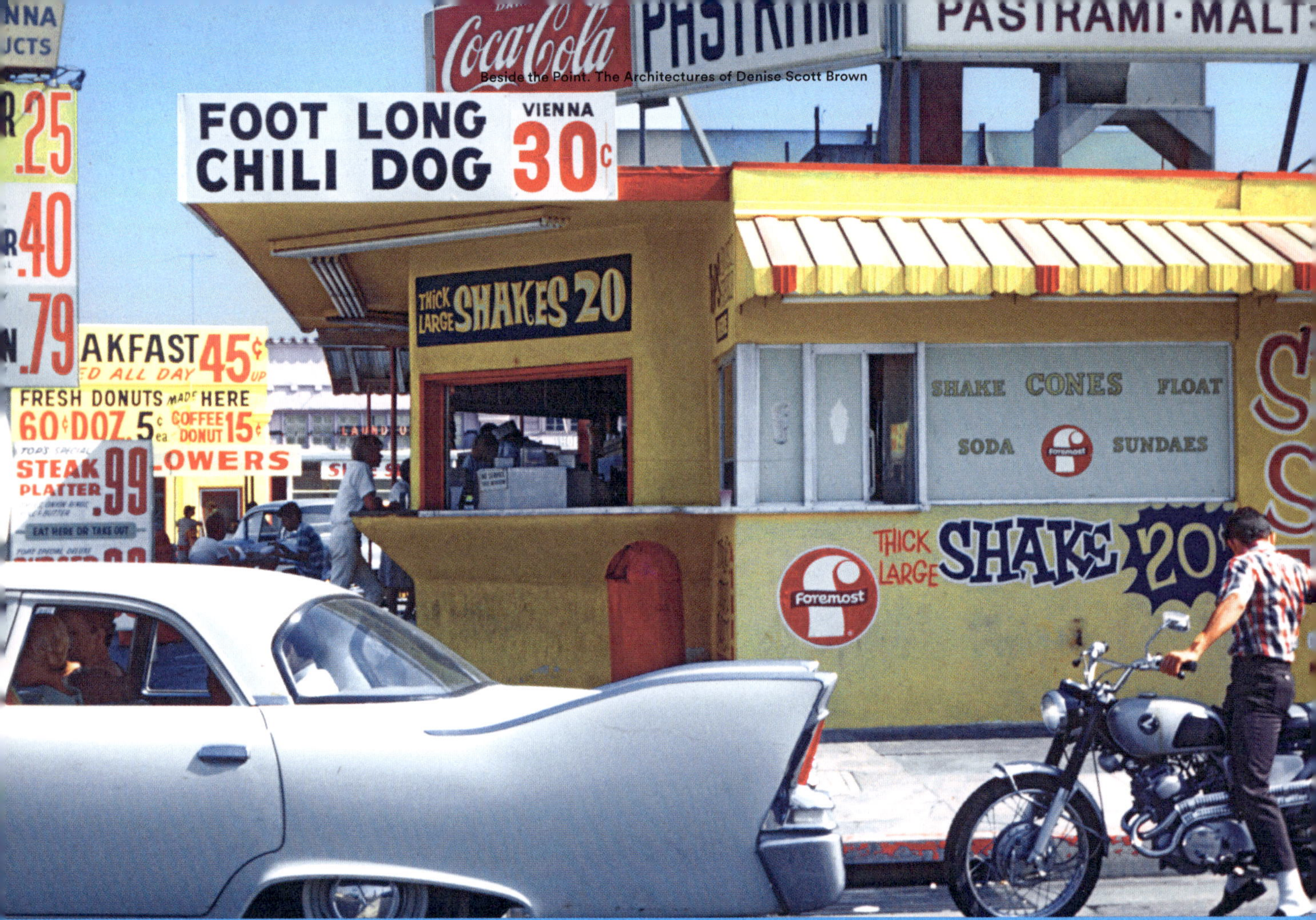

I'm just like that.' Denise has paid the price for her interdisciplinary approach to architecture and some architects don't consider her as one of their own. Her varied interests, including planning, business management, interior design or preservation have been used to unflatteringly characterize her. She is described by some as a great teacher or as having a way with words. She feels an architect at heart, but her unusual skillset makes her an easy target for those worried by the thought that design can originate in two heads, as opposed to just one.

Denise's early photography offers a template for research, theory and design, a refreshing approach in a time of digital media overload. They are testament to the idea that communication will always be an essential function of architecture. Photography, however, is only one of many conduits for this practice. She's also a passionate writer, using her words to speak her mind and raise awareness about critical issues across various professional circles. 'I am a person who uses words in architecture.' she says, 'As a small child I was very proud of my early language skills.' The spectrum of these words includes books, lectures and speeches, research manuscripts and planning guidelines, exhibitions and the much-celebrated cartoon drawings of buildings with speech bubbles.

Learning from Las Vegas, which Denise co-authored, remains a refreshing and influential book across a number of disciplines. Using her photog raphy 'to express an idea,' as she put it, the book pulled together vernacular architecture of all types—from neon casino signage to duck-shaped, decorated sheds; this varied vernacular initiated a broader cultural discussion that continues in universities around the world. Today, it is integral to architectural theory, and 46 years after it was originally published, the visual manifesto has been translated into 18 languages and is still in print.

Her bibliography spans six decades and exceeds her husband's—not that anyone is counting. A pill-sized version of her life's writing can be found in *Having Words*, a selection of Denise's most powerful essays. Printed by her Alma Mater, the

Architectural Association London, the eclectic collection of texts uses architecture as a springboard to discuss art, urban design, planning, pedagogy, sexism, as well as the 'star system' that rules the profession. The book is evidence that, in fact, words, too, are building materials. At 12 GBP, the bright yellow, pocket-sized paperback is nothing short of a standalone curriculum. Denise's influence on today's architectural discourse is validated by the book's popularity on Amazon.

Half a century after Las Vegas, photography has since established itself as a sub-discipline of architecture—a development that Denise can be partially credited with. Visual communication in architecture may result in building better buildings, but thankfully, it is not its sole purpose. Through photography, a growing number of doers and thinkers can also contribute to architectural practice, without having to lay down a single brick. Based on the interdisciplinary understanding that architecture is not limited to buildings per se, curators, critics, historians and writers are free to revel in the contemporary.

Another way I understand Denise is through the creative relationships she has had throughout her life. Speaking openly about influence (which, for her, is a two-way street), Denise prides herself on a lifetime of intellectual teamwork. Aside from her most far-reaching and frequently discussed collaboration with Bob Venturi, she also celebrates others, including her first husband Robert Scott Brown. Among them are also architect and planner David A. Crane, planner and educator Paul Davidoff, regional economist Walter Isard, ethnomusicologist Charles Seeger, and (my personal favourite) sociologist Herbert J Gans—all of whom influenced Denise and vice-versa. Unfortunately, most are unknown to the average architect. The challenge for architects is to absorb knowledge from various fields and apply it to architecture, but not only to the design part.
The terminology we use to distinguish architecture from planning, communication and even political activism is extremely narrow and out-dated. If architecture is to be an umbrella discipline, it needs to broaden its reach and disciplinary boundaries to include the extraordinary knowledge produced by unconventional thinkers. Denise held all the roles she ever hoped to hold. Looking back at a lifetime of achievements—not without setbacks and frustrations—she still questions what it means to have a career in architecture today. Since obtaining her degree in 1955, the job description for architects has changed enormously. Each generation inevitably brings new perspectives to the field, but the commitment to discovery and critical inquiry should remain central to architecture.

Denise says she is addicted to practice—by which she means making buildings—over everything else she's ever done. Over their career, she and Bob Venturi designed over 180 buildings. Regardless of the size or program, she fought to make buildings 'useful and beautiful, in that order'. Successful design brings space to life, not necessarily because it is beautiful, but because it is functional. For Denise, true beauty in architecture exists when buildings confront local problems and employ a broad set of tools. Anything else is a farce. Denise and Bob carefully studied questions of scale (they had much to say about the inhumanity of the human scale in modern architecture) and designed with the community in mind. If architects observed their environment using various and varying skill sets,

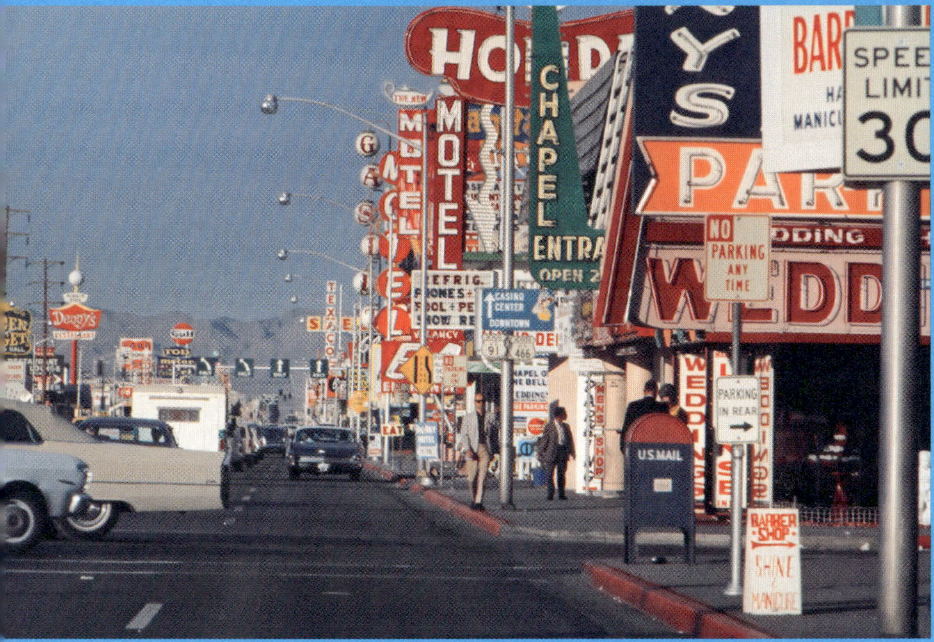

← *Los Angeles, 1968*. Photo by Denise Scott Brown.

↙ *Architettura Minore on the Las Vegas Strip*, Las Vegas, 1966. Photo by Denise Scott Brown.

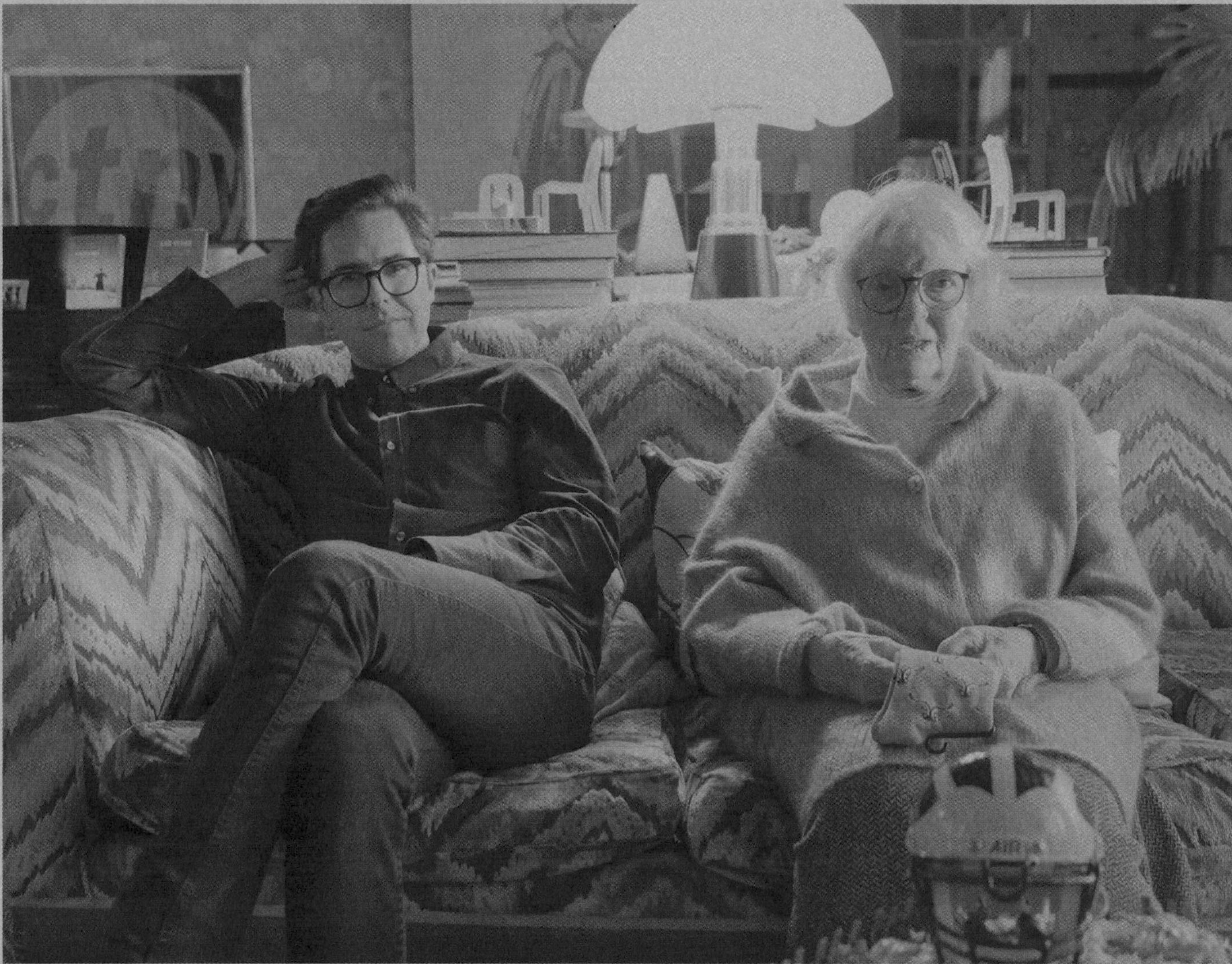

‘I love monumental buildings that laugh at themselves a little.’

DENISE SCOTT BROWN

they might better understand the patterns around their projects and apply them to their architecture. You really can't afford to ignore the everyday environment.

Few of Venturi, Scott Brown and Associates' (VSBA) buildings received as much attention as the Vanna Venturi House or the Guild House. The projects that followed these icons of early postmodernism are underrated, if not entirely misunderstood. Her fascination with popular culture was not shared by her generation; they may have found Las Vegas exciting, but didn't necessarily trust her aesthetics. While a younger generation widely acknowledges the importance of popular taste, some are still not convinced by the buildings that resulted from it. For better or worse, it seems to me that the reach and resonance of Denise Scott Brown's argument lies in her radical ideas and not in her building portfolio.

Denise's work has been unusual and even scandalous at times. Some dislike VSBA buildings on the grounds that they are slightly weird, even shocking. Behind the style and aesthetics, however, is a great deal of integrity, independent thinking and a certain idiosyncratic, human quality.

The power of Denise Scott Brown lies in her convictions—as an architect and as a person. She has fought countless battles to introduce new ideas and values, against professional chauvinism, and to claim rightful authorship for her work. It was not easy to speak out and jeopardize her professional career. *Room at the Top: Sexism and the Star System in Architecture* was published in 1989, 10 years after it was written. The piece is still eye opening and alarming, especially to those of us who were not around when she wrote it. Despite her fight against gender discrimination, and her position as an outsider, Denise thinks of herself more as an architect than a feminist activist—not that the two are mutually exclusive. The profession has come a long way since the essay was first published, but not quite far enough. Things remain as male-dominated at the top as they always were.

Although her battles remain as relevant as ever, Denise has also undeniably changed the shape of architecture. She led the way for an architecture rooted in experimental research, interdisciplinary design, and activism. True influence in architecture defies the banality of form and the temporality of function. Ideas can be so much more powerful than any building. That's why we don't measure success in square meters or style. Legacy does not need to be built; it requires no space at all. Architectural legacy lies within the resonance of brave messages that effectively change our society and survive from generation to generation.

↖ Andres Ramirez and Denise Scott Brown in her living room, 2017. Photo by Plane–Site.

Like many of my peers, Denise Scott Brown finds it difficult to define what she does. Her work is broad and deep, and never confined by the conventions of her practice or time. Denise continually redraws disciplinary boundaries to show us that architecture can also function as a lens through which we understand our own culture and ourselves. Denise's influence goes both through and beyond the buildings she built, and spills across disciplines and generations. The magnitude of her contribution to the field of architecture is only just beginning to surface. Denise Scott Brown is a role model and grandmother to a lot more people than just architects. Then again, architecture is not only for architects.

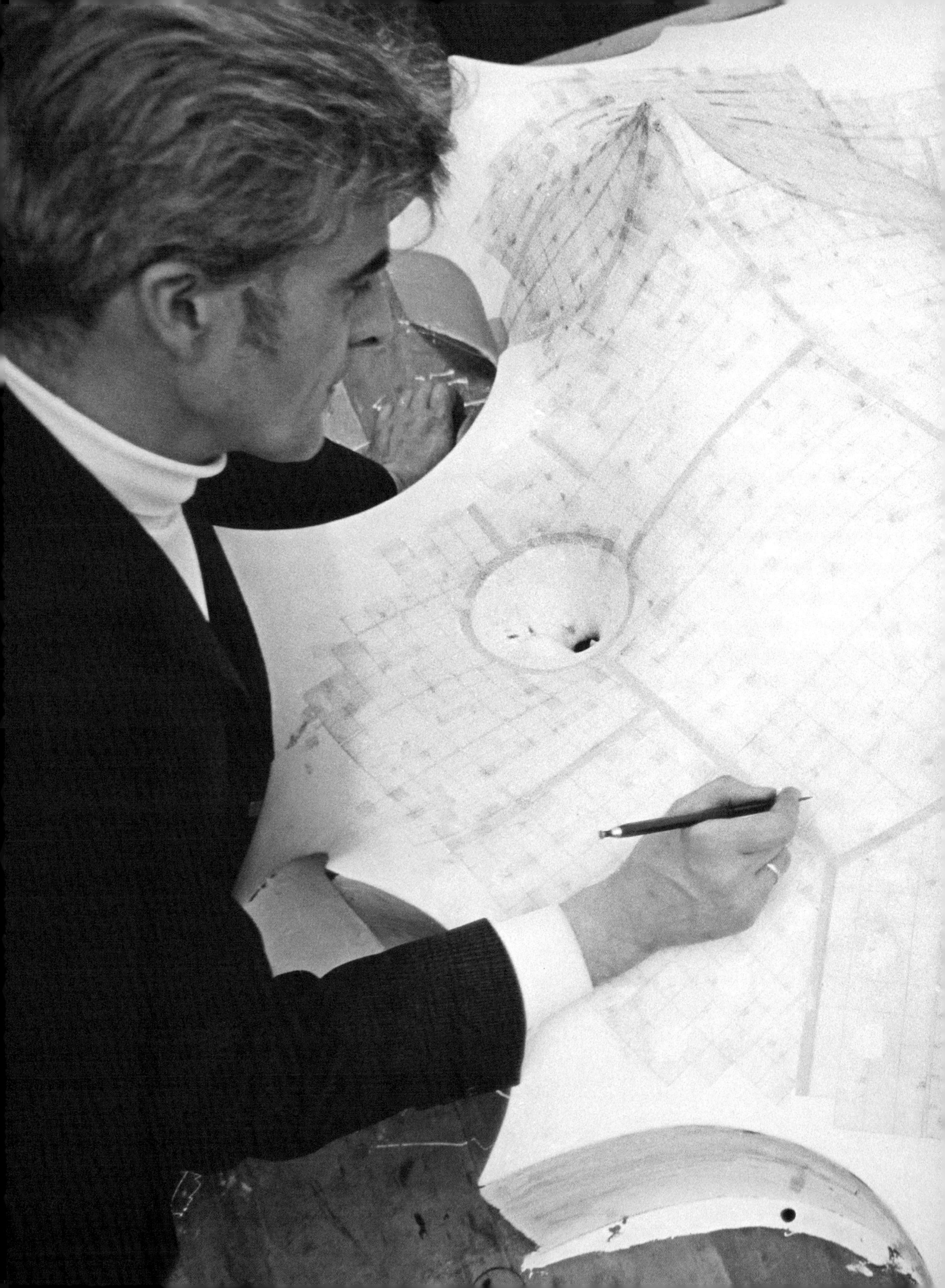

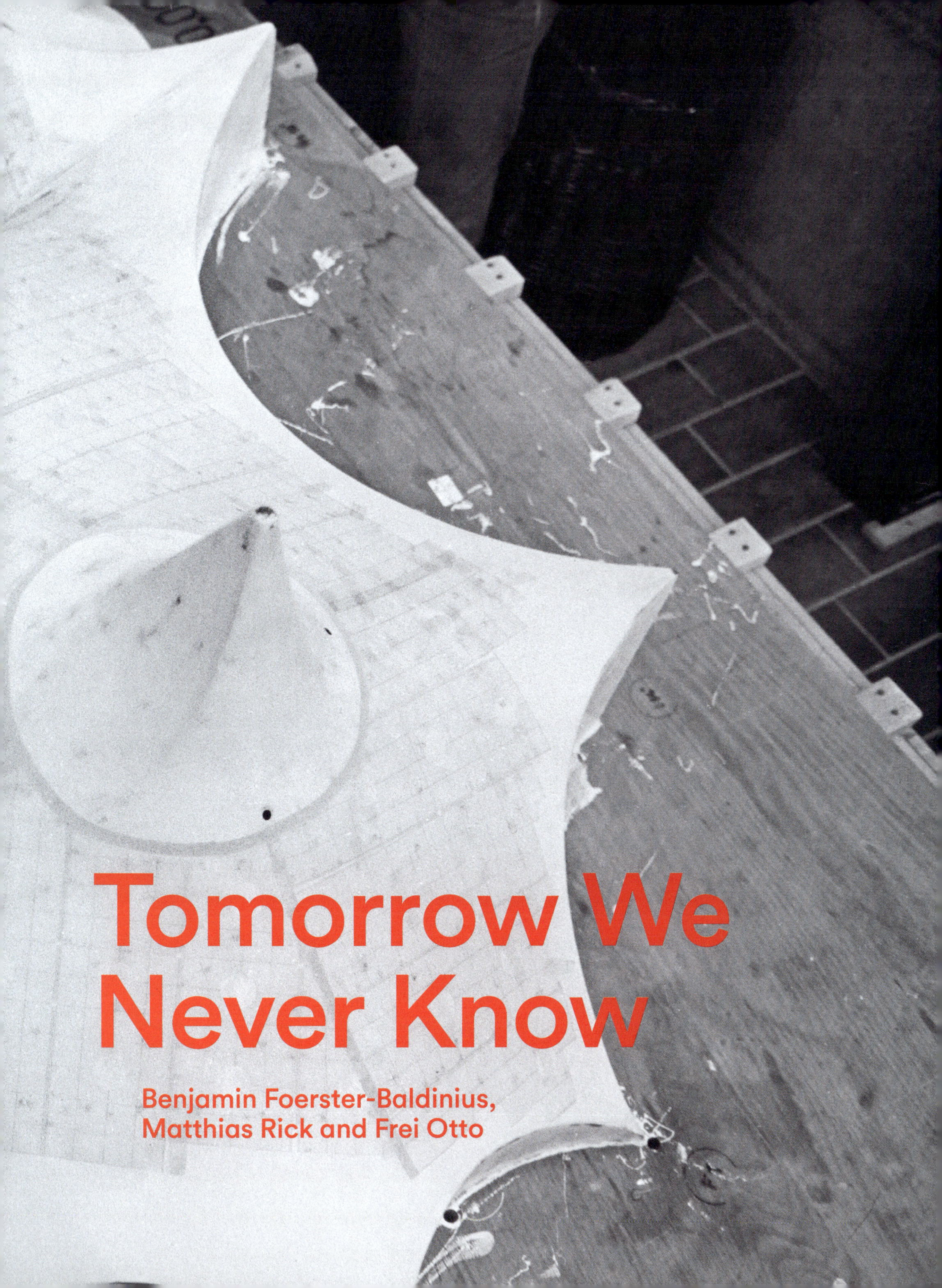

Tomorrow We Never Know

Benjamin Foerster-Baldinius, Matthias Rick and Frei Otto

The late FREI OTTO is regarded as genius and visionary spirit in the world of architecture and engineering. For this interview BENJAMIN FOERSTER-BALDINIUS and the late MATTHIAS RICK of the architecture collective RAUMLABOR BERLIN meet him in his home in the South of Germany to talk about his upbringing in architecture and the future of the profession.

RAUMLABOR BERLIN How did you get into architecture?

FREI OTTO My dad was a sculptor, and I have a taste for sculpting. I would also have liked to have become a sculptor, but studying fine arts was, as still is, the first step on the path towards financial struggle. It's very difficult to earn a living from it. With architecture on the other hand, if you manage to win a project you can just about eke out an existence.

I was always—and still am—inspired by the relationship between man and sculpture. The fact that I actually ended up in architecture was perhaps more of a coincidence than anything else. I've always been interested in the processes, the forms and origins, and what they could reveal. That has become a big part of my life, rather than the act of designing, and by 'that' I mean consciously creating a form for form's sake.

RB Much like the work of a sculptor, would you agree that your work focuses on the discovery of forms and their potential?

FO Yes, without a doubt; but my work also incorporates many other concepts, such as the objects' relationship to people. This relationship is also alluded to in sculpting, of course; the relationship to people or to the human body is at the very heart of a sculptor's work. The same is true for architecture, the starting point for which is the creation of dwellings for people. This is predominantly a functional task that has nothing to do with purely aesthetic forms.

RB Returning to our initial question, could you tell us how is it that you got into architecture?

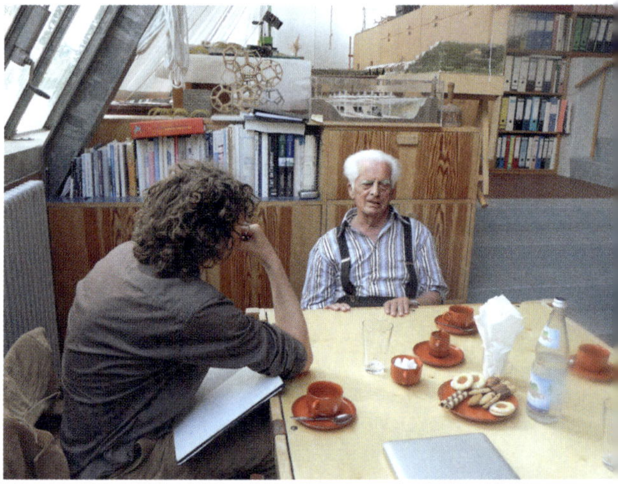

FO I had quite an unusual introduction to the world of architecture. I got my first taste of the profession while I was interned in a prisoner of war camp in Chartes, the birthplace of early Gothic architecture, which uniquely combined lightweight structures and stone. The town's cathedral was only a few kilometres away from our camp, we could see it all the time.

In 1945, while I was still being held as a prisoner of war in Chartes, an architecture competition was held to come up with better good ways of burying our dead. I took part in the competition, sketching my design on a small piece of paper. I was then called up to join the group that was charged with the task of constructing three cemeteries. The chief architect was a fan of modern architecture, Dr Leopold

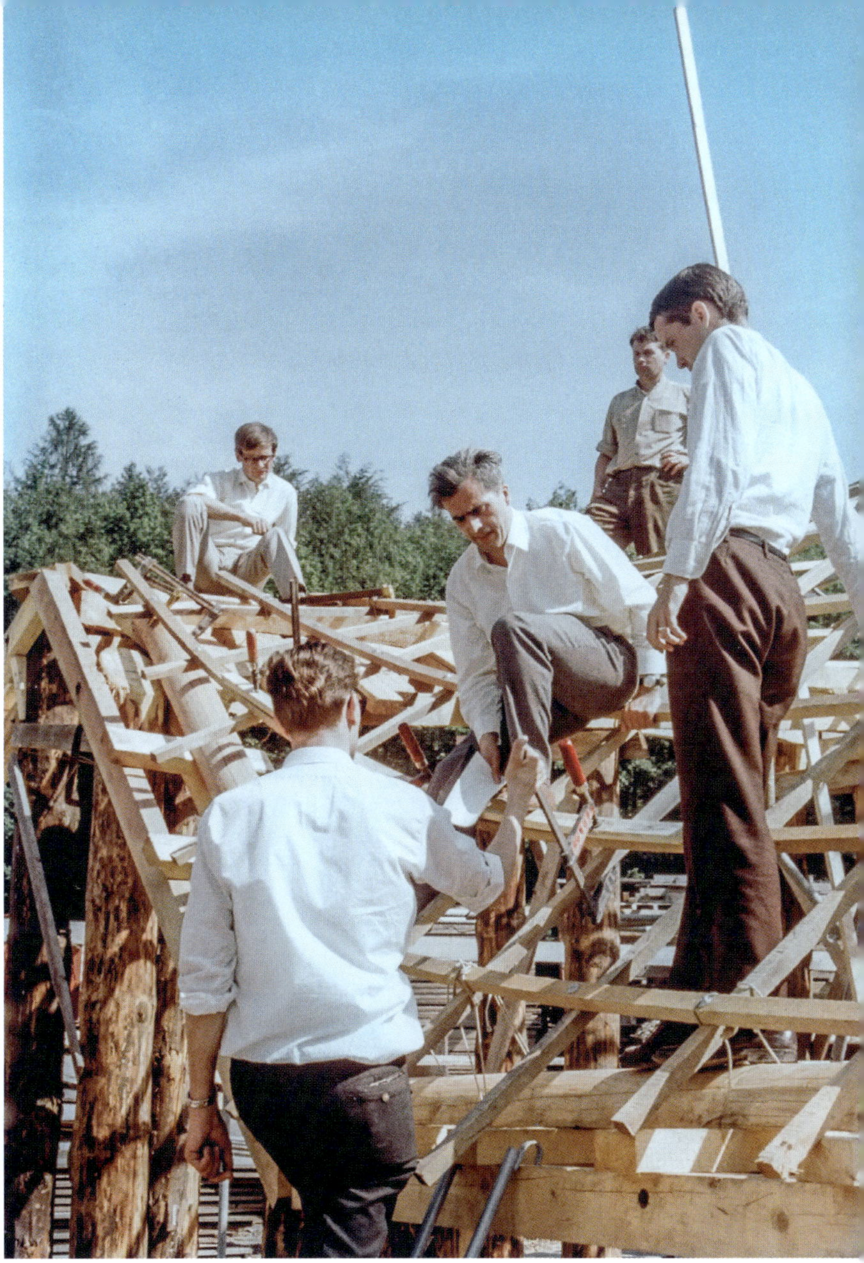

Kohlmann from Berlin-Dahlem. At some point he was allowed to return home due to his age, after which I took on the role of camp architect and had to stay on longer. There were actually a lot of architects who were prisoners at the camp and they taught me a lot—it was almost like having private tuition, in a way.

We organised ourselves into a construction group so that we could also do a bit of construction and structural work for the French as well, both in the city and for the military. We also had to do some interesting odd jobs for the officers, who used prisoners so that they could continue pursuing their own hobbies. We tried to barter for materials like natural stone for the cemeteries or cement for other construction projects, which usually worked quite well. We also made all our own tools. That was really interesting. When we needed steel, we usually repurposed the springs from tanks that were left stranded in the area, and all kinds of things like that.

I was one of the last ones to return home. I went back to Berlin and enrolled in the Architecture programme at the Technical University of Berlin (then the University of Technology in Berlin-Charlottenburg). There were several thousand applicants for only twelve places. One of them dropped out, and I—13th on the list—was able to start studying in 1948.

RB Who were your main role models at that time?

FO A question like that isn't as simple as you might think. I did look, of course. Without a doubt, the first architectural work to inspire me was the cathedral in Chartres, and as the son of a sculptor and stonemason, my father was also an important role model for me. My father was a member of the German Association of Craftsmen, whose best-known chairmen were Mies van der Rohe and Walter Gropius. However, I only really came across modern architecture during my studies in Berlin. My friendships with Mies van der Rohe and Walter Gropius until the end of their lives also had a huge influence. Both visited me in Berlin before I moved to Stuttgart. Walter Gropius was the most attentive listener I have ever met. He asked the most precise questions and always wanted to see everything we were working on at my modest studio in Zehlendorf. Funnily enough, I helped Mies van der Rohe with the National Library. As often happens with architects, we bumped into each other unexpectedly many years later on a construction site. That's where decisions are made. There's no talk of aesthetics and all that nonsense, just hard facts: will the building be strong and stable enough for the intended function?

RB Who or what inspired you to get involved with flying roofs?

FO That would be lightweight construction. Well, actually, flying—among other things—got me into flying roofs. I was already flying gliders by the age of 14. School at that time was very technical, and glid-

↰ Frei Otto working on the model of the swimming pool canopy of the Olympic Parc, Munich, 1970. © saai | Südwestdeutsches Archiv für Architektur und Ingenieurbau, Karlsruher Insitut für Technologie, Werkarchiv Frei Otto.

← Frei Otto in his home studio with Benjamin Foerster-Baldinius, Warmbronn, Germany, 2010 © raumlaborberlin

↗ Frei Otto and colleagues during test constructions © saai | Südwestdeutsches Archiv für Architektur und Ingenieurbau, Karlsruher Insitut für Technologie, Werkarchiv Frei Otto

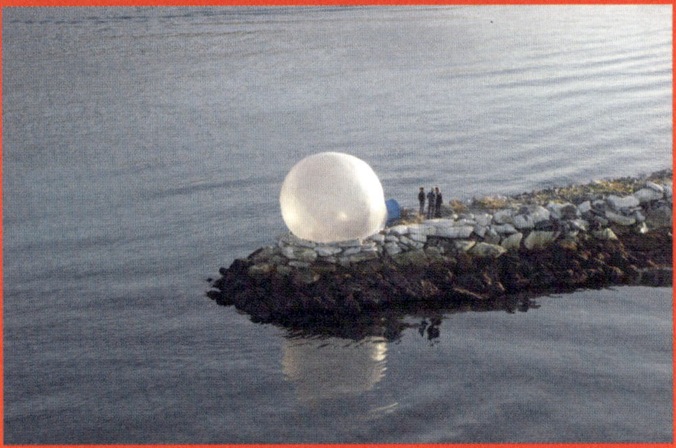
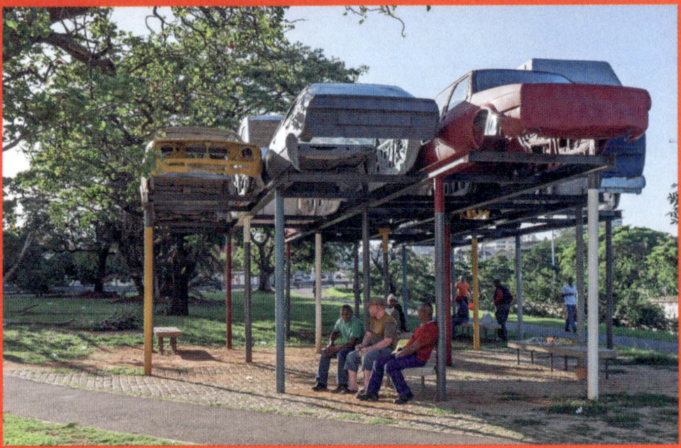
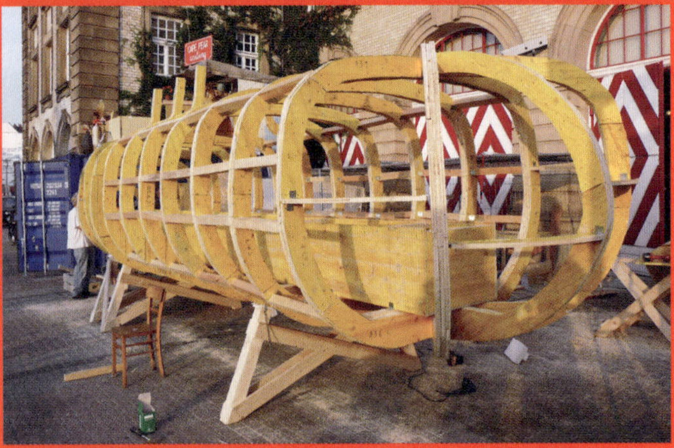
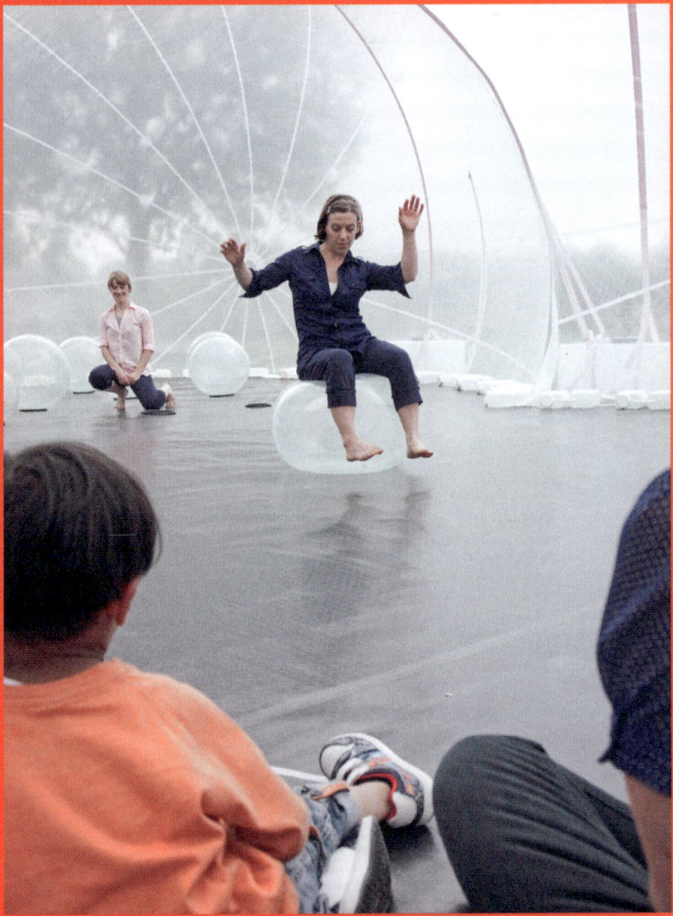
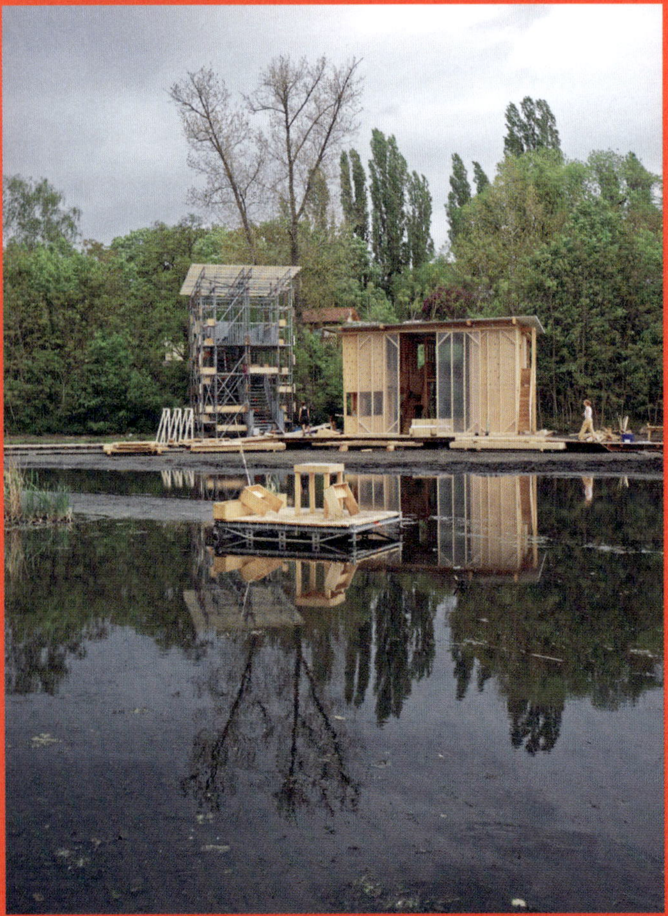
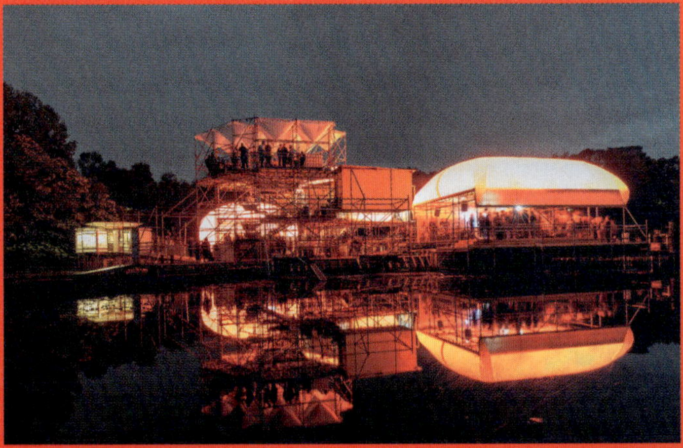

> 'People are so incredibly adaptable and can adapt to anything that happens or that they stumble across.'
>
> FREI OTTO

ing was a great sport. After I'd finished secondary school I was immediately drafted into military service as a fighter pilot and completed the pilot training programme. I was part of a fighter squadron and it was our duty to protect southern German airspace, although I never actually flew an armed plane. My main task was to get to know and to fly all kinds of modern aircraft, both during the day and at night.

RB Would you say that the flying roofs were actually a combination of your hobby and your passion?

FO In a way, yes. In both flying and architecture you need to master the laws of physics. People always talk about architecture as being a form of art, but for me architecture is all about applied physics.

My time as a prisoner of war and the post-war years taught me how to construct things using as little material as possible, because the major cities were in ruins. I saw with my own eyes the air raids on the cities of Munich, Augsburg and Ulm from the air. Now that's quite an unusual way to get into architecture, watching a city being destroyed from a bird's eye view. My interest in minimal structures and lightweight construction definitely started during that period.

RB That's one aspect of your work as an architect, but you are also interested in people. You also studied sociology, is that correct?

FO Just a bit.

RB That's also an essential part of our work; we are interested in the potential and possibilities of architecture, in terms of both participation and appropriation.

← Raumlabor Berlin projects. Top to bottom, left to right: KA No - What now, Tromsö, Norway, 2017 © Roger Jardine; Rush Hour Rest Stop: Acknowledging everyday practices, Durban, South Africa, 2014 © Roger Jardine; Cape Fear, Mannheim, Germany, 2008 © raumlaborberlin; Kitchen Monument, Germany © raumlaborberlin; Floating University Berlin, Germany, 2018 © raumlaborberlin; Floating University Berlin, Germany, 2018 © Victoria Tomaschko, raumlaborberlin

FO I'm a little confused by the word 'appropriation'. I'm not sure what you mean by that here. I think you have to explain what you mean. What is appropriation?

RB I would say it's the self-ownership of spaces that already exist or are newly created. For example: I move into a new flat, which already exists, and I make it my own. This processes of making an existing flat my own, by adding my own carpet and pictures, is an example of me appropriating that space.

FO I see, yes.

RB The same concept can be applied to the city as a whole, when citizens make public spaces their own; they live there, they use it, they have ideas about what to do with it, about what they are actually allowed to do with it.

FO People appropriate anything and everything. That means that architects could actually build anything they want, regardless of whether or not it's functional. People are so incredibly adaptable and can adapt to anything that happens or that they stumble across. I've done a lot of work on adaptive architecture, and written a lot about it, too. I think that's what you mean, but you call it appropriation. We called it adaption, but I think it's actually a similar concept. For me, adaptive construction wasn't and isn't about adapting the form, but rather adapting to changing tasks and perspectives. My good old friend **Yona Friedman** **(page → 224)** is an example of this. With his *Mobile Architecture* (1956), which to some extent contradicted modern architecture, he called for and promoted mobile architecture as a way of adapting the city. In the 1960s and early 1970s he collaborated with a colleague of mine, Eda Schaumann, in India, which turned out to be a great success.

RB Since you mentioned Friedman: at the time you also co-edited *Architecture Mobile* in German. How did you get involved with that? Why did you think it was important?

FO I supported and helped him where I could. As a friend, it's as simple as that. I also see a parallel between his work and mine. One thing didn't influence the other, it happened at the same time.

RB Now let's move from the past and into the present. You once said that you work at the boundaries of architecture. Where are these taking you and your work today?

FO Are there even any boundaries?

RB We're always labelled as being 'on the edge' due to the things we create. Labelling your work as 'classical architecture' isn't really appropriate, because other interests such as sociology and theatre also come into play.

FO Besides physics, I was also interested in biology. When I was at school in Berlin I had some remarkable teachers for philosophy, religious studies, German literature, music and history; they were well-read in both ancient and recent topics. One of my teachers was the biologist Gerhard Helmke, one of the directors of the Max Planck Society in Berlin. His specialist area was teeth development but he was also interested in lightweight construction, particularly large and small and very small structures that emerge in all fields of biology. While I was working as Peter Pölzig's assistant, the son of Hans Pölzig, I set up the Biology and Construction research group in Berlin. Then when I got the call from Stuttgart to set up an institute here, I took the group with me because there was nobody in Berlin to lead them.

'I was always—and still am—inspired by the relationship between man and sculpture.'

FREI OTTO

RB How did you try to convey your views on architecture and construction to your students?

FO Not unlike Walter Gropius, I also believe that the final design of a building depends on how that building evolved. If you approach the development of an object with an open mind, you're more likely to create something new and unknown. Strangely enough, my creations that have had long-term success are those where I was trying to solve previously unknown technical and human challenges. One thing is absolutely vital, which most academies still don't particularly value; you shouldn't start with a preconceived form, your starting point shouldn't be: I absolutely want to do that, I absolutely want to create this and that form, or whatever you call it. The form should still be unknown. It's about how you approach the unknown. In some ways, I don't start by designing a form; I search, I look. Form isn't necessarily designed, it has to be found. I suppose my teachings, if I even had such a thing, can be summarised as a fundamental scepticism about words and sentences and a belief in a finished, functioning object that was created to fulfil peoples' tasks. In other words, the form emerges right at the very end, as a technical-scientific and economic result of the age in which it was created.

→ View from the upper tier of the stadium looking toward the spectator stand during the 1972 Olympic Games in Munich, Germany. © saai I Südwestdeutsches Archiv für Architektur und Ingenieurbau, Karlsruher Insitut für Technologie, Werkarchiv Frei Otto; Werkarchiv Günter Behnisch & Partner.

RB If we could ask just one final question; what do you think will be the main challenges facing architecture and architects in the future?

FO I don't know what the future will bring, nobody knows. Will Central Europe be struck by another deluge? We have no idea what's going to happen. There's some evidence to suggest that it will. For a start, the Netherlands could end up under water. I have no idea. If you're an optimist, you'll see things differently than if you're a pessimist. For me, one thing is certain; we simply have to do everything we can to survive man-made and humanitarian disasters. I really mean that. I've seen a lot in my life. My message to tomorrow's architects would be this: put creative discussions on the backburner for a while and focus on understanding and disturbing the destructive forces of major natural phenomena and catastrophes. When will the next asteroid or comet hit the Earth? Around 10,000 years ago, not too far away from where we are now, a celestial body crashed into the Earth and wreaked all kinds of havoc across the planet. That wasn't really all that long ago. Today, there are many more people on the planet than there were then. The losses would be catastrophic. Who will want to talk about architectural styles and forms then? It would be immaterial. However, it'd be interesting to see how people created a modern Noah's ark, so new ways of saving people. Well, you might not have heard what you wanted to here. I don't have any magic formulas, I'm afraid.

RB We came with an open mind.

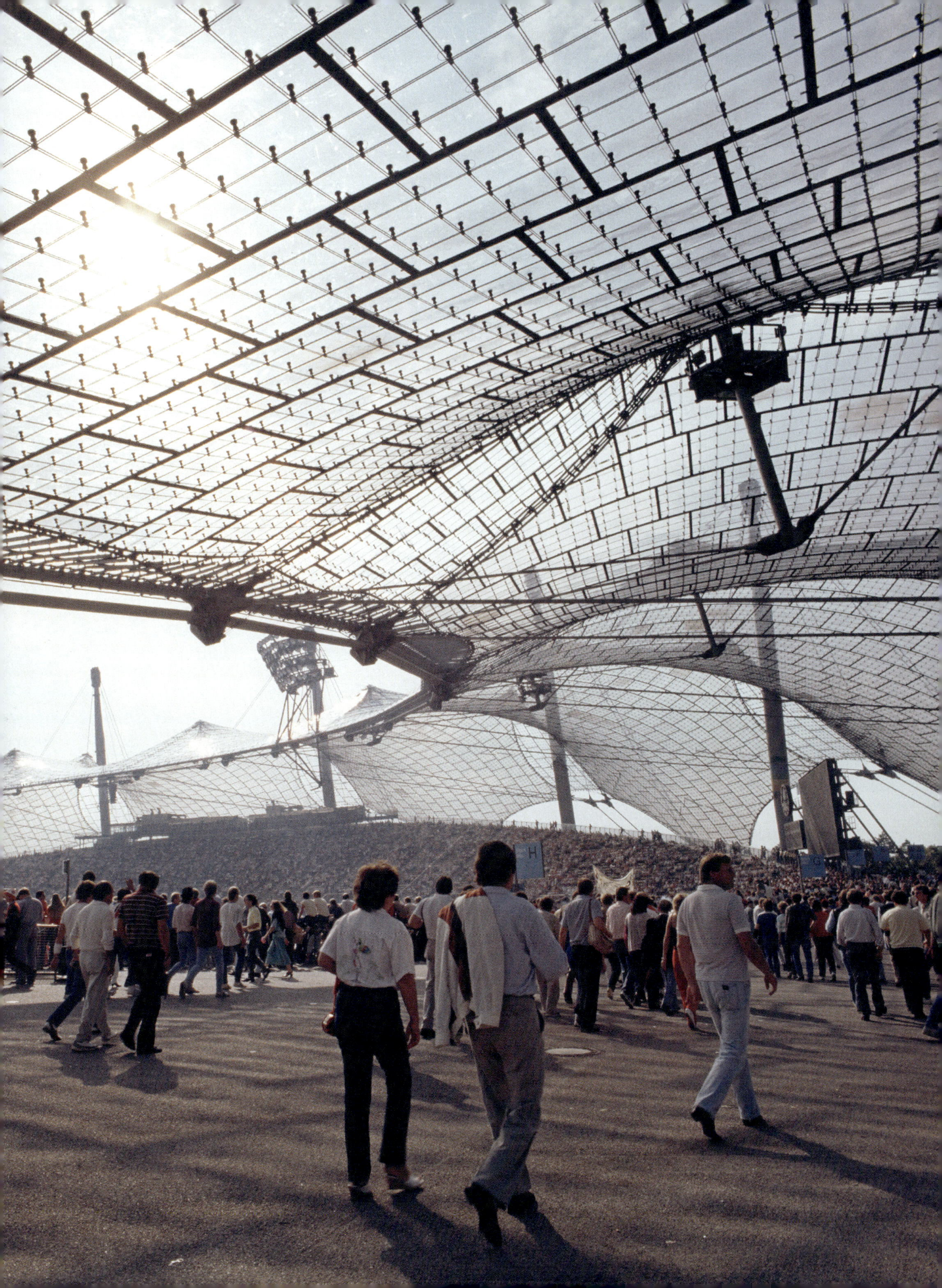
H

Activism and Architecture

Carson Chan and Phyllis Lambert

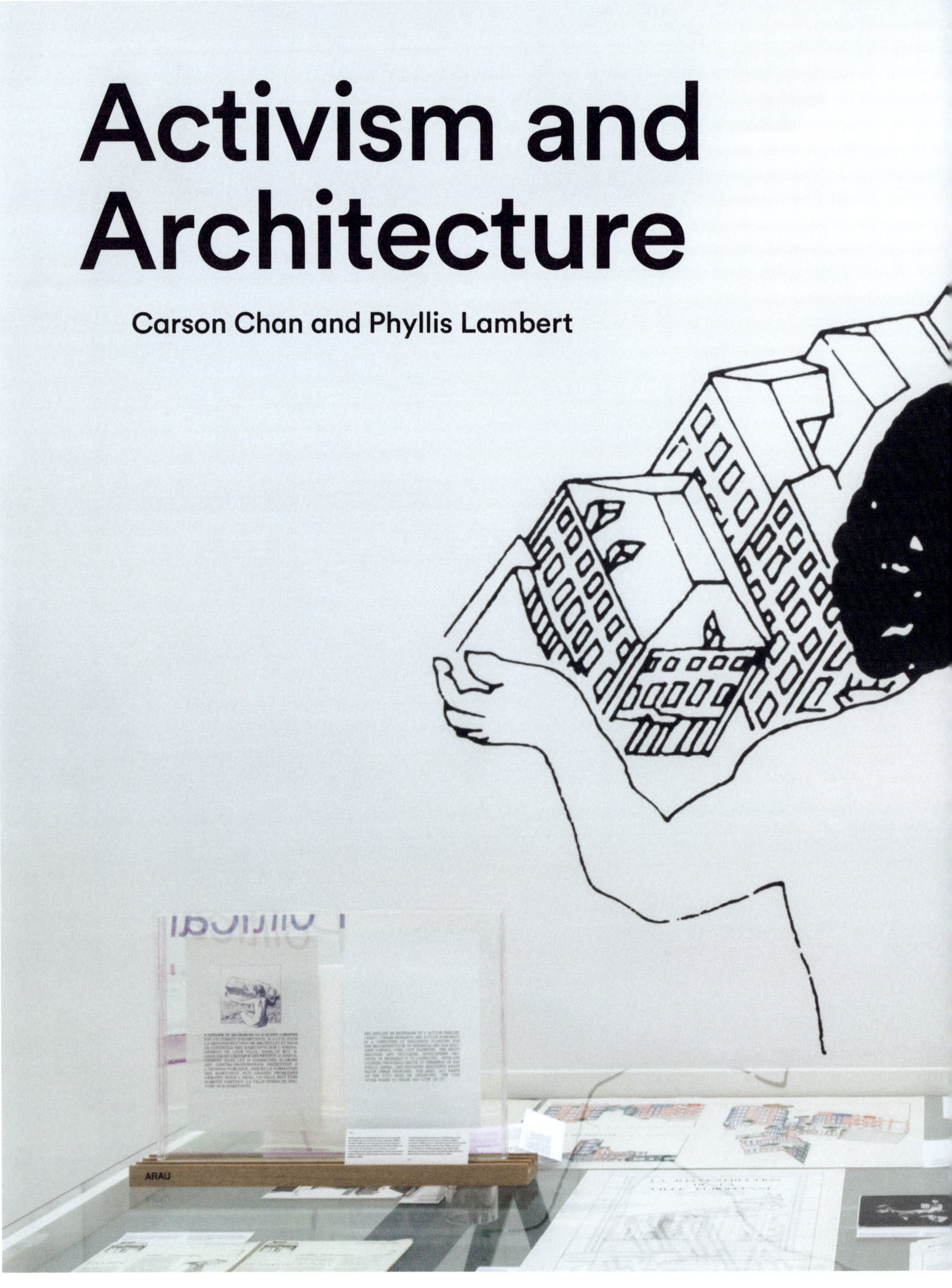

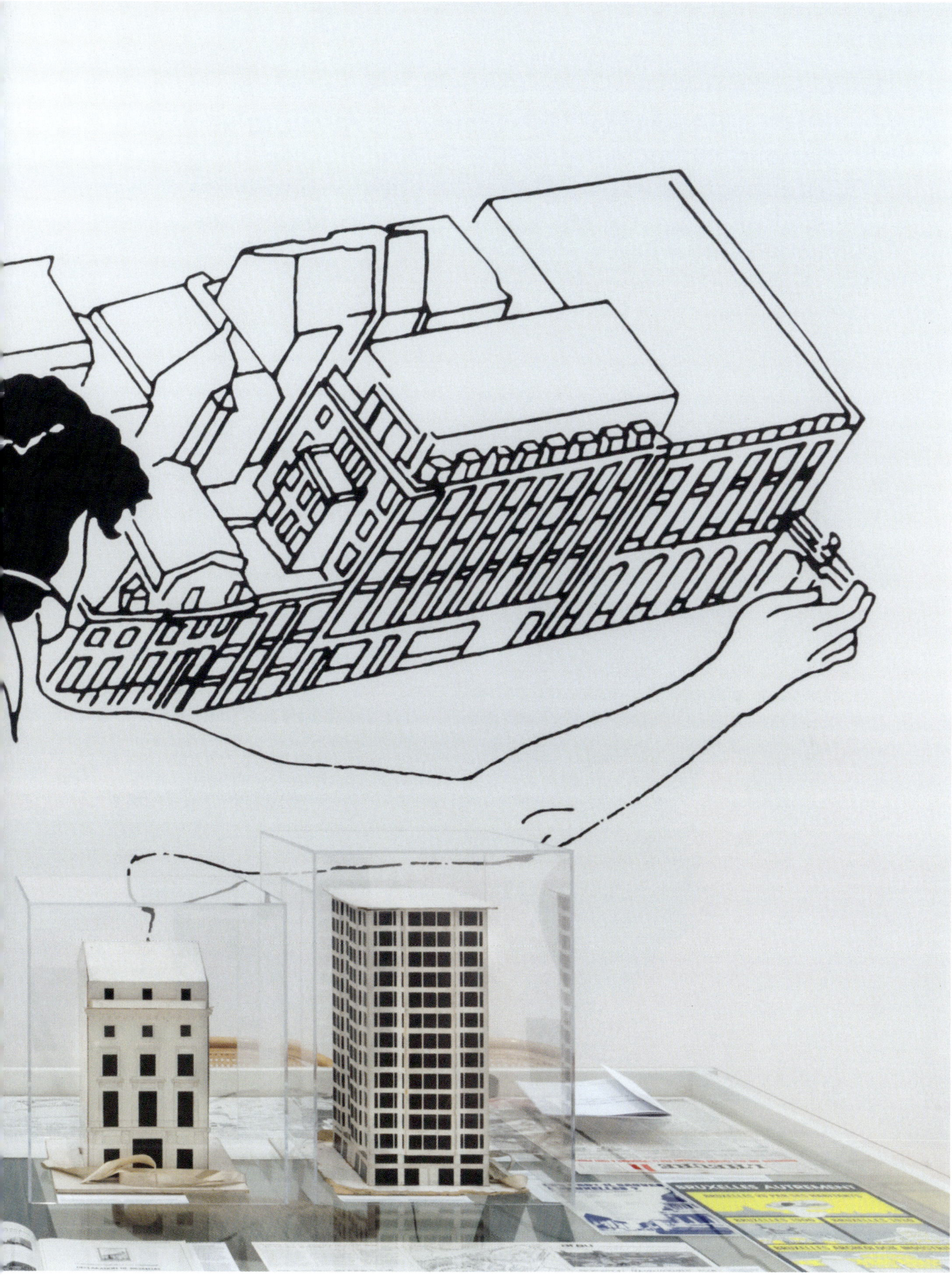
BRUXELLES AUTREMENT

PHYLLIS LAMBERT is widely considered to be among the most influential female figures in architecture. Here, Canadian curator and writer CARSON CHAN talks to the enigmatic founder of the Canadian Centre of Architecture (CCA) shortly after her 90th birthday about her view on legacy and preservation and what's next.

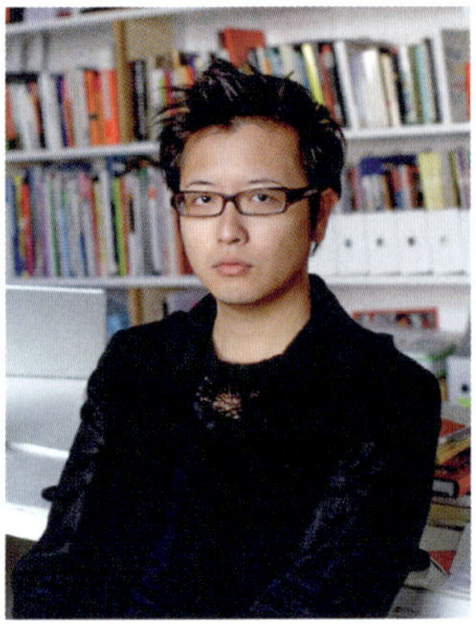

CARSON CHAN As a child you had wanted to be an artist, a sculptor. Today, you are a leader in architectural preservation and restoration. Is this how you see your legacy?

PHYLLIS LAMBERT Yes, I was an artist when I was younger, but I don't think that I'm a leader in conservation and preservation: I'm an architect. My concern is architecture, while conservation and preservation are a means to an end, not an end in itself. After the Second World War, many European cities were so heavily destroyed that they had to be torn down. I guess Americans thought they had to do the same thing. It was terrible. Working in conservation and preservation helps create a decent city. It's working against the idea that people and the places they live in are expendable.

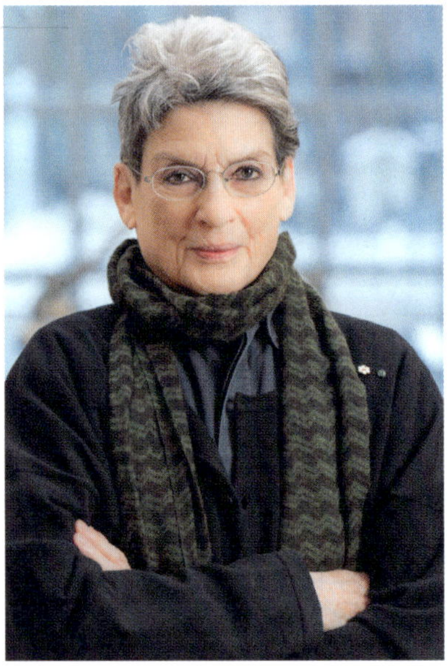

CC The opposite of expendable is essential. When did you discover the constitutive relationship between people and place?

PL I was at the Illinois Institute of Technology (IIT) in Chicago learning to be an architect from 1960-63. Well, I was first learning to be an architect from building the Seagram Building (1958) with Mies van der Rohe and Philip Johnson, and then I became a student at the IIT. At the time, perfectly good buildings in downtowns were being torn down for no reason. There was a terrible destructive, self-serving sense in people. Thomas Edison said that babies in America are born looking at their cradles and twisting their heads around to see how they can make a better one. I really cannot be called a conservation and preservation architect. I'm an architect: I'm concerned with the city and how the city grows and what is needed to make that grow. What's needed is input from the citizens, there's no reason why a couple of bureaucrats should decide on how an area should be developed. People who live there know a lot more. Expertise, knowledge, and the city, these should all be brought together to form the architecture of the city.

CC You've picketed at protests to save historical buildings. If you're not a preservationist or a conservationist, can we call your work through groups like Heritage Montreal and Save Montreal activism? You mentioned the tearing down of America's downtown fabric to make way for high-rises, many of which didn't materialize because of the oil crisis. Is this the fate you wanted to save your hometown Montreal from?

↰ Installation view of The Other Architect, Canadian Centre for Architecture, Montréal, Québec, Canada, 2015. © CCA

→ Mies van der Rohe, Phyllis Lambert, and the model of the Seagram Building from "The Seagram Spotlight", October 1955 published by Joseph E. Seagram and Sons, Inc. Phyllis Lambert fonds, Canadian Centre for Architecture.

↙↙ Phyllis Lambert, architect and CCA Founding Director Emeritus © CCA.

↙ Portrait of Carson Chan. Photo by Martin Thacker.

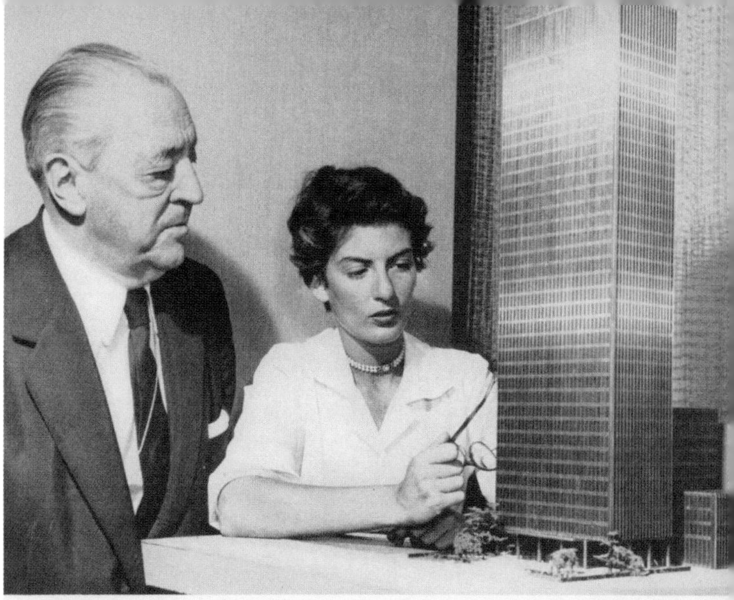
ARCHITECT Mies van der Rohe and Mrs. Phyllis Lambert discuss some of the problems involved in the construction program, as they study a model of The House of Seagram. The interesting lines of the structure and the plaza and park areas are indicated in the model.

THE BIRTH OF A BUILDING

A vast amount of planning takes place before the derricks punch holes in the ground, the cement mixers pour their brew into the base and the steel skeleton rises majestically into the air

26 • *Seagram Spotlight*

PL I am an activist, but that's part of being an architect. There are times when you have to do different things in different ways. Firstly, I must say that we began building the Seagram in New York, a major building, by tearing many others down. Architecturally, the Seagram Building was absolutely necessary at the time. There was Skidmore Owings Merrill's Lever House (1952), and of course the United Nations Headquarters that Le Corbusier had sort of conceived (1952). At the time, to build was to make something new and modern to the very best of one's ability. But then I went to architecture school in Chicago and saw the wanton destruction there, in American, Canada and the rest of the world. This was the moment when I knew that we had to stop this kind of architectural destruction.

CC You saved many of Montreal's iconic greystone buildings. The city has retained much of its late 19th and early 20th century architecture in no small part due to your efforts. What do you make of the fact that your personal objective has such a defining presence in Montreal today?

PL Well, neighborhoods of greystone buildings correspond to the history of Montreal. Again, it was about stopping the reckless demolition of the city's past. I was photographing the greystone building's when I realized this. If you want to build a new building, it has to be in an appropriate place. Part of the Canadian Center for Architecture, which I founded in 1979, is in the historic Shaughnessy House, so you can say that the CCA was part of an act to stop this kind of thoughtless destruction.

CC The CCA both a lesson in the value of historical preservation, and, as an archive and exhibition space, a place where architectural knowledge is stored and produced.

PL Through the wanton destruction, it became clear to me that the public needed to know more about architecture. They know something about sculpture, music, painting, but they don't know a thing about architecture. To most, it is a commercial venture. In fact, it is a medium that creates the cities and environments we live in. It effects how we think – and that's important. Founding the CCA was my way of taking an active stance in what I see happening around me. Does that make me an activist? I'm a historian. I'm an architect.

CC Traditionally, we think of architects as authors of building-sized objects. You've been talking about cities and environments. When you walk around Montreal do feel a sense of authorship in areas you saved from demolition?

PL What difference does it make? I did what I did because I thought it was important. Now when I visit these places and see it thriving, I think it's wonderful. I guess, being an author is part of the whole process.

CC The question of authorship is interesting to me particularly in the context of the Ben-Ezra Synagogue in Cairo, the fifteen-year restoration of which you completed in 1995. It's a building that has stood in the same location in various forms for about a thousand years. How did you decide which historical moment to restore the building to? I also see you as a historian. For me, there's a strong authorial voice in determining how history should be read.

PL You don't restore to any point at all. The building that was there was built in the 1890s. We found eleventh century foundations; There's a great history of this building that can be found in Hebrew, biblical, and travel literature, and caliphate documents. Sharia law maintained the building as it was originally. If a building is to be rebuilt or restored it cannot be bigger, or taller, or more richly decorated than what was documented. The way I see it, we weren't restoring the building to a particular historical moment, we were just making it healthy again.

CC What drew you to this project?

PL I saw the building as evidence of the interfaith connection between Jews, Christians, and Muslims through a thousand years of architecture. This was a building that was once enclosed within fourth century Roman walls. The original synagogue was there since the middle of the ninth century. It was pretty much in continuous use until the 1967 war, when it was abandoned and proceeded to deteriorate. The most important work we did was to document and publish it (*Fortification and the Synagogue*, 1994) so that this interfaith connection is known to everyone, not just locally. To me, all this work is being an architect.

CC I ask because in Germany, where I live, restoration is contentious work. Since the Second World War, buildings built or used by both the Nazi and the East Germans have been "restored" to their pre-twentieth century conditions, effectively erasing the more recent and difficult histories.

PL You might find this interesting: The Shaughnessy house was added to after it was built in 1875 and the additions were absolutely horrible. My view of restoration is to basically take what's in front of you and don't change it. However, the additions made to this house were done in such a thoughtless way, it was impossible to connect it to a new building. The house was so beautifully planned and put together to begin with. We took down the additions; It really depends on what you're dealing with.

CC In the mid-1970s you were also involved in the restoration of the Biltmore Hotel in Los Angeles. It was a very important building in early Hollywood. How did you become involved in this project? How did this become your cause?

PL As you know, my family had a developing company. I wanted to prove that a building could respond to its context socially, be architecturally distinguished and be financially successful at the same time. I had formed an architectural development company with Gene Summers, who had worked closely with Mies. The plan was to make money. If I was going to hit the same terms as my family I was going to have to make money. I set out to prove this with the Biltmore, and it was marvelous. We bought it for ten million dollars, otherwise it was probably going to be torn down, or turned into an old person's home. My concern was never to preserve Hollywood history. My concerns are the architecture of the city and the people who live there. I want to make the city as wonderful as I can for the enjoyment of people. Buildings shouldn't be kicking people around. When I returned to Montreal, which is not a big city, my mission became clear. I realized how very important it was to have public consultation in city planning. I worked very hard to democratize the process.

CC What you're talking about is perhaps the hardest part of being an architect: To figure out how people will react to a building, how people will use a building, and how that building will contribute to its context. Can architects really design how a building is used? It is futile to plan a programmatic legacy?

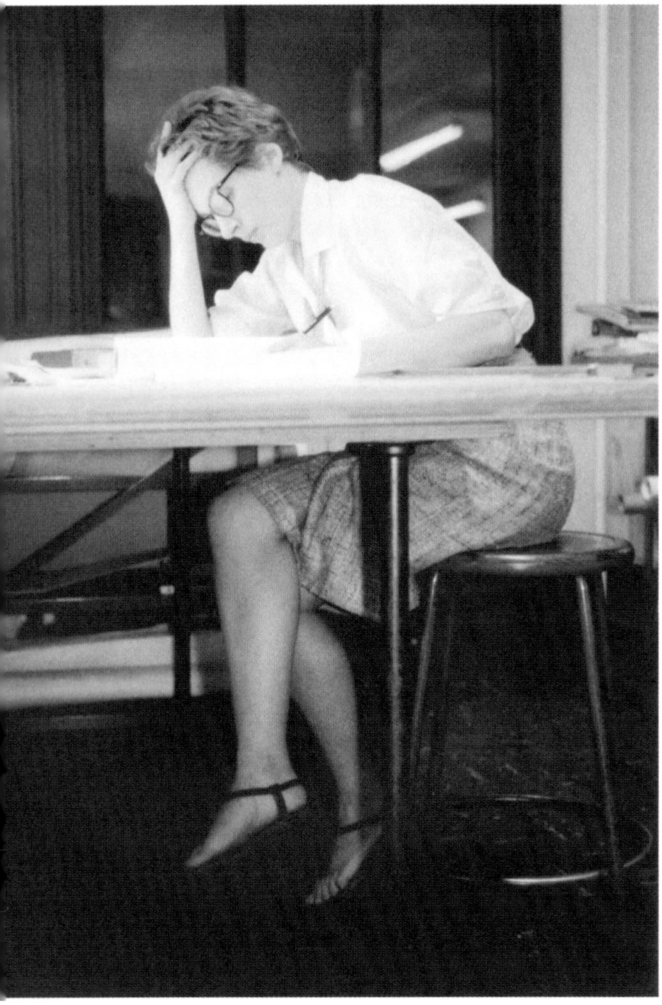

↙ Edward Duckett, photographer Phyllis Lambert working at a drafting table in the office of Mies van der Rohe, 1959, polaroid print, 13 x 8.5 cm, ARCH277553.001, Phyllis Lambert fonds, Canadian Centre for Architecture, © Edward Duckett.

→ View of the Canadian Centre for Architecture (CCA), Montreal, Québec, Canada © CCA

↘ Researcher in the CCA's study room. © CCA.

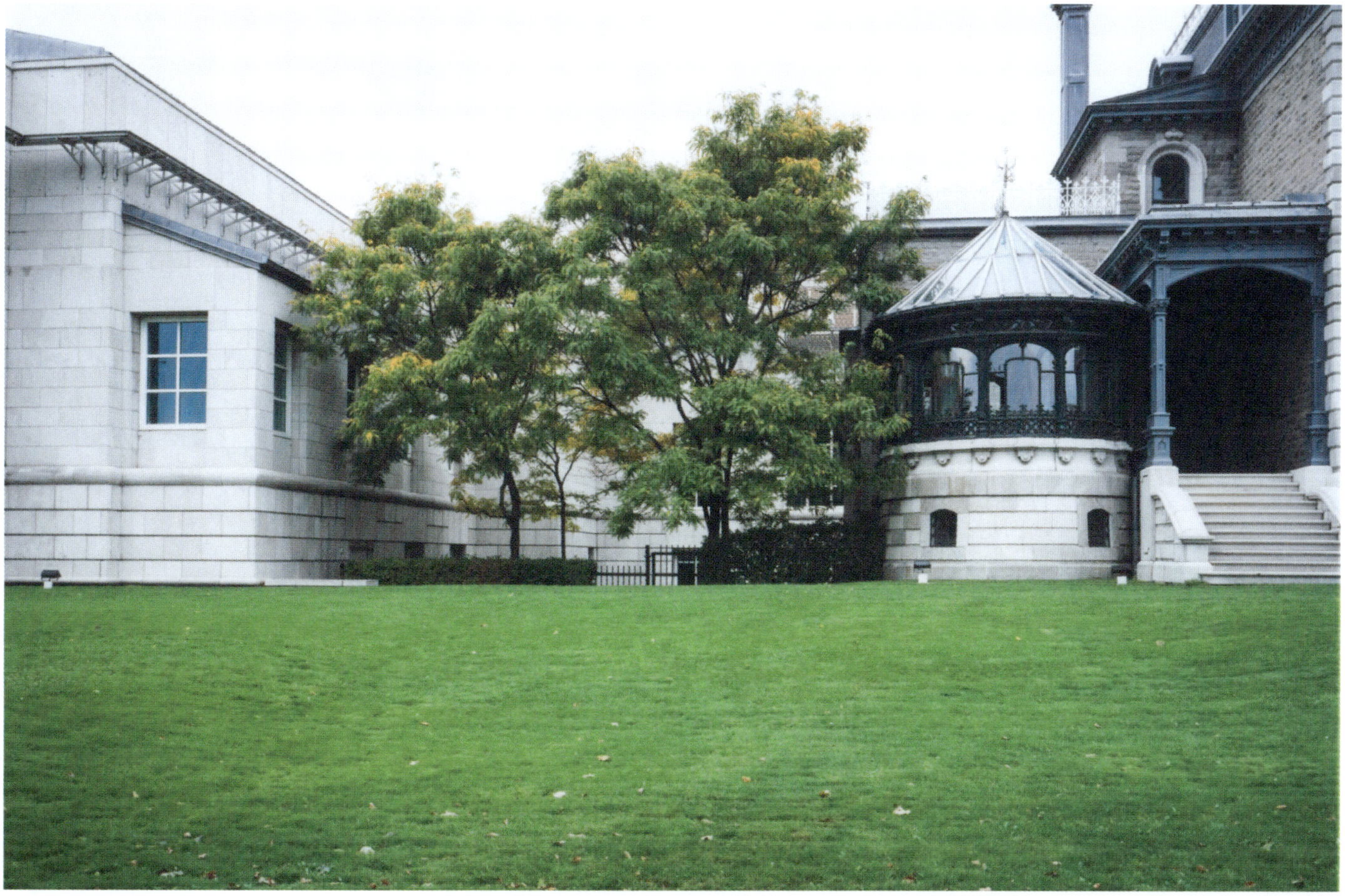

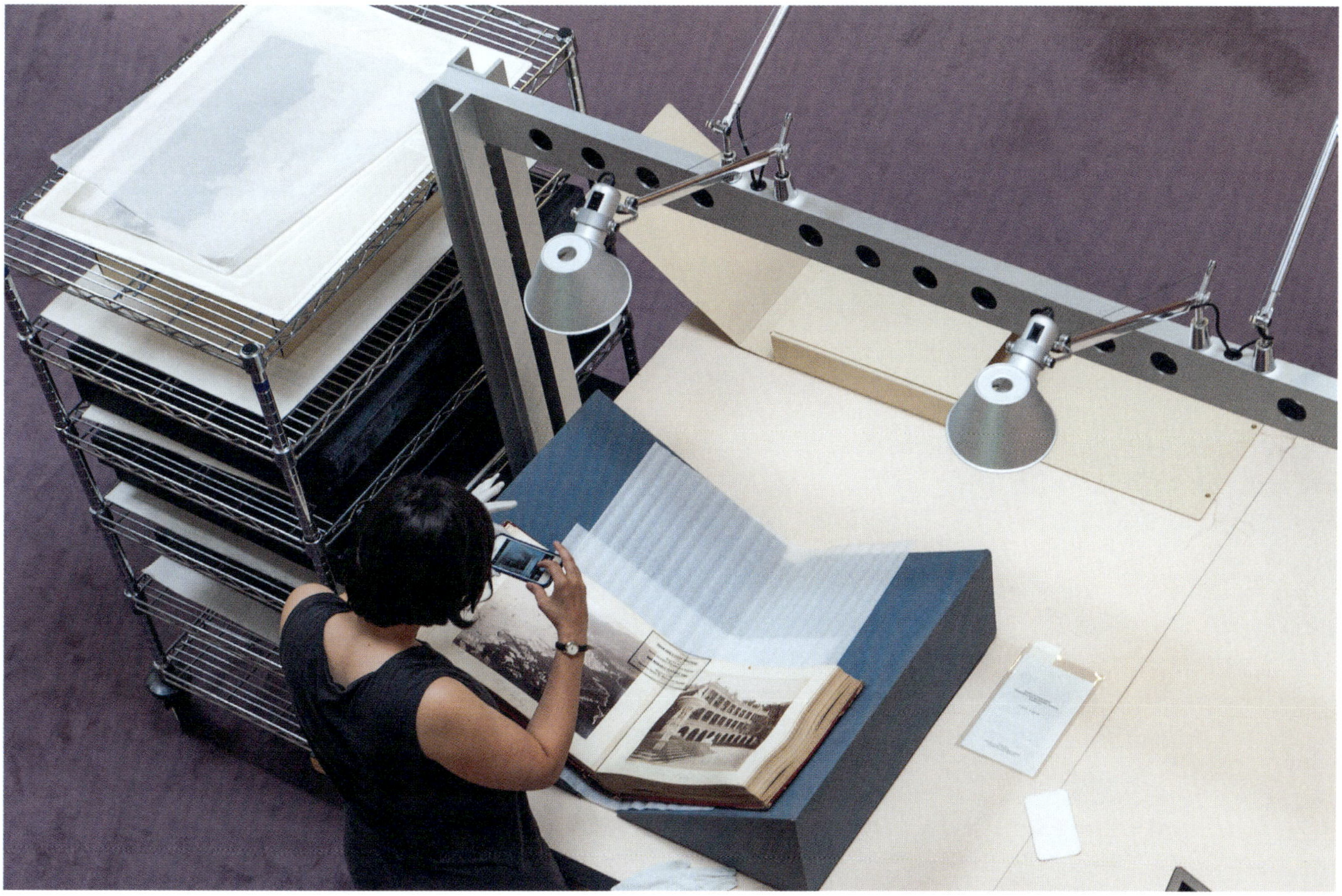

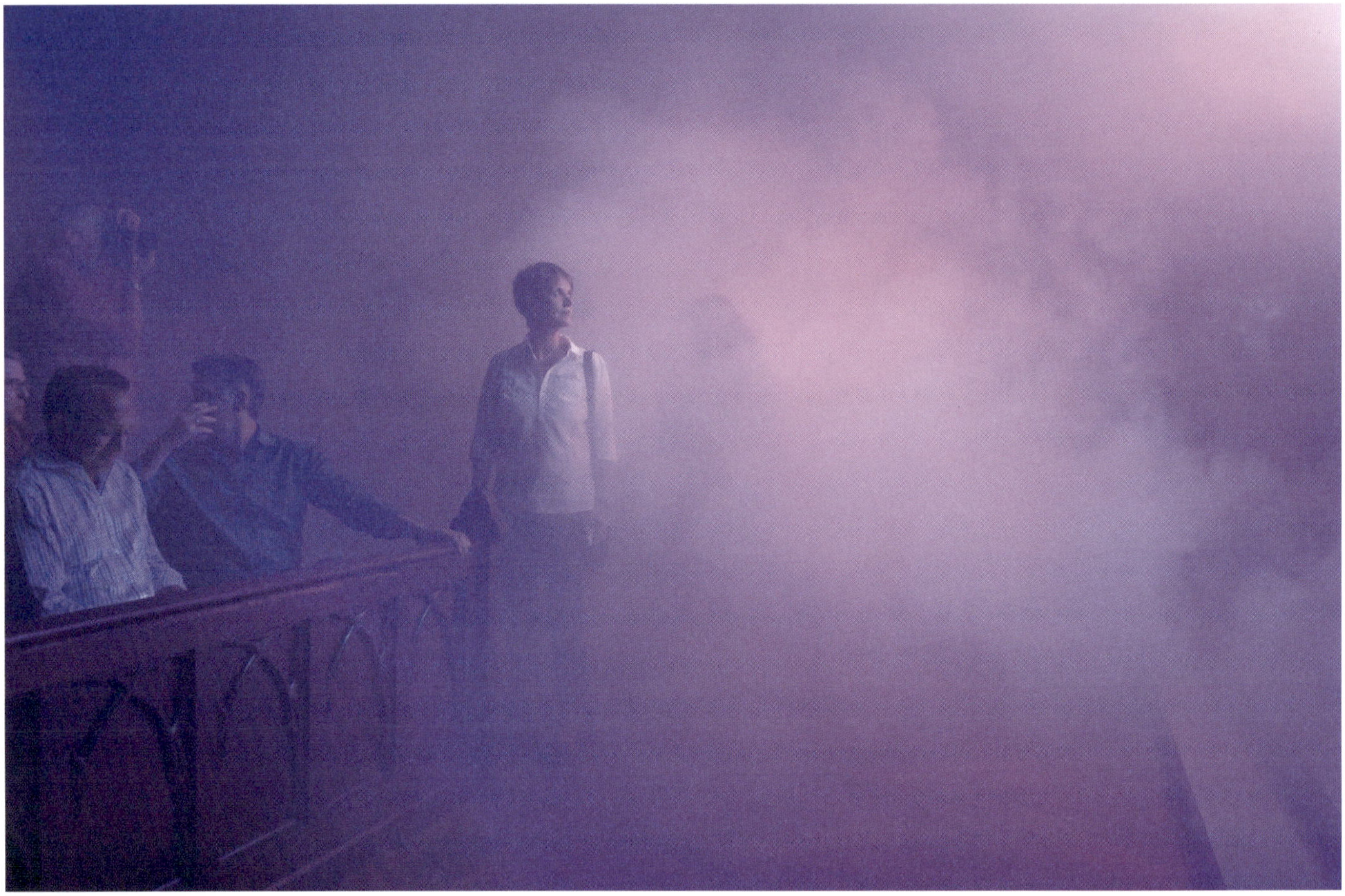

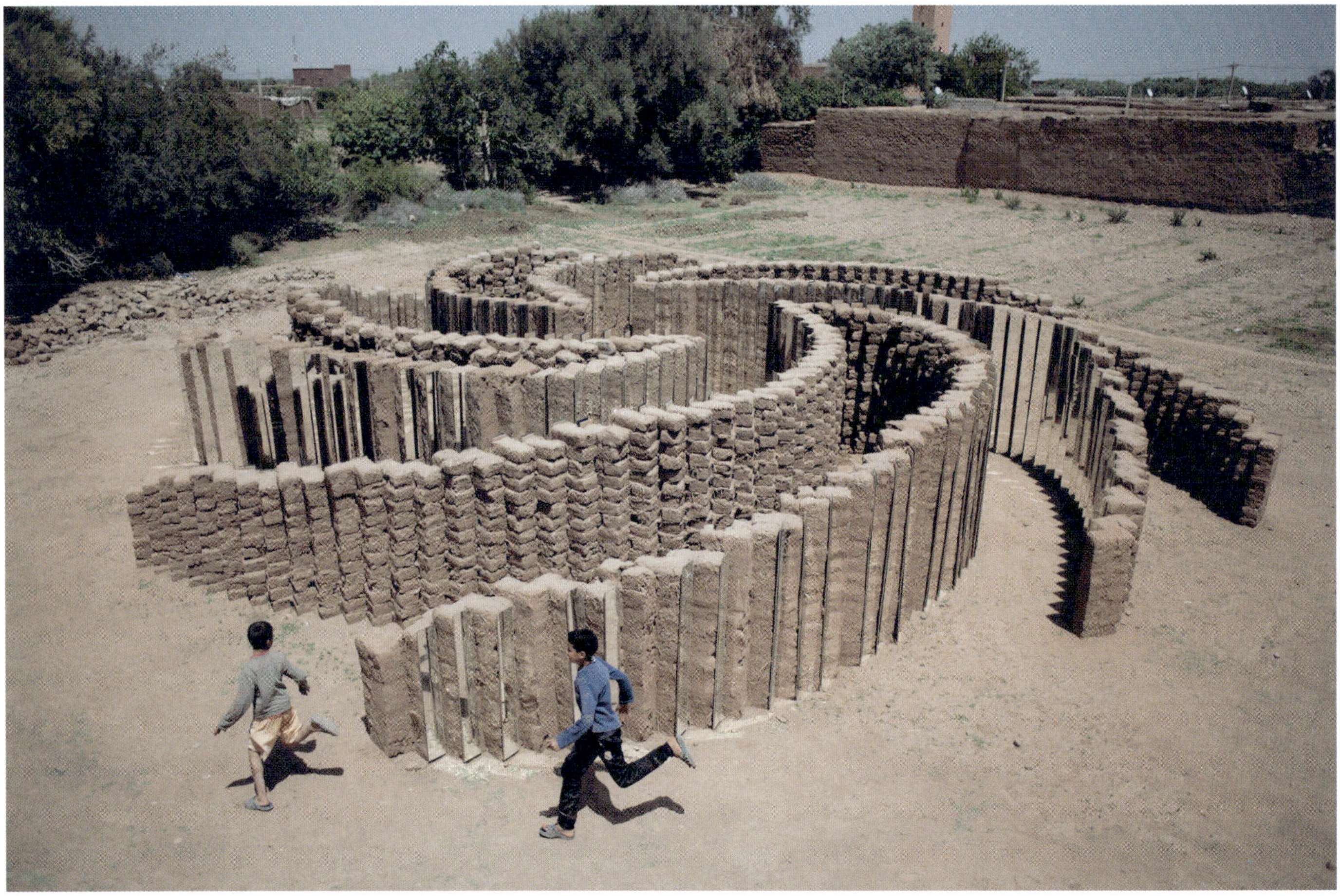

← James Clar, *Pixelated Serenity*, 2015, Dallas Aurora, 2015. Guest Curator Carson Chan.

↙ Elín Hansdóttir, *Mud Brick Spiral*, 2012, 4th Marrakech Biennale, Curators: Carson Chan and Nadim Samman.

PL It's not a futile thing at all, it's a logical thing! It's absolutely logical. I was part of the fight to keep Milton Park, the six blocks of greystone houses in the center of Montreal east of McGill University, from being demolished and redeveloped. By 1979, through Heritage Montreal, which I headed, the Canadian Mortgage and Housing Corporation (CMHC) bought the properties that had not been demolished, and with the resident community we transformed the houses into non-profit co-operative housing. There were lots of fights with the CMHC, and I mean a lot of fights. They had already built some ghastly thin-walled high-rise buildings with small units on the part that had been demolished. I've been in them and they are low quality. What kind of a society do you have where you have nothing but one or two room homes? You want people who want families in the downtown. This is exactly what we provided for at Milton Park, and we did it without any evictions while guarding it against gentrification. Students, architects, and urbanists come from around the world to see what could be achieved.

CC The architect's work is to create a sense of belonging in the lived environment and as you've shown, this doesn't always require building new buildings. Most architects today are what I would call a designer – they merely design buildings. They've relinquished the responsibility of building communities, discovering what a community needs, and maintaining those needs through architecture.

PL Yes, that's a problem. It's absolutely wrong.

CC Mere form-making is faster. For most architects, the work of actually going to communities and talking to people takes up too much time and energy.

PL Of course. If you want to do something, everything you do takes a lot of time and energy. I mean, look at **Rem Koolhaas'** work **(page → 18)**. He has brilliant forms but he also creates buildings that work marvelously. Look at his Seattle Public Library. He manages to make something beyond the dreams of what people thought a library could be. It's something that has become so very popular with the public. It's marvelous. If you can make form and place, that's wonderful. But you have to do first things first. You have to make it at a place where you're adding to the quality of the city, to the quality of the lives of people. It has to be a place they can identify with.

CC Absolutely. Ricardo Scofidio has said that when he saw the Seagram Building, he understood how important that building was for New York City's identity. What does the Seagram Building mean for you today when you see? Do you see your identity tied to Manhattan's urbanism?

PL I see it as a marvelous, wonderful building. I see something that has such a sense of place and is so gentle, yet so strong, and I wonder why other people can't do something like that. That's what I think. Look at all the junk that's built around it.

CC There have been so many copy-cats.

PL Mies was always curious. He was constantly wondering what the world was about, what kind of world it was, what made it matter. He concluded that the mid-twentieth century world was one of economics and technology. He was always trying to answer questions. Then take the architects who built the buildings to the north and south of the Seagram. They just took some marble here, and some of that there. Those are just products, not architecture.

CC But could we say that the Seagram Building promoted facile copy-cats by being so singular and iconic? The monolithic form, the I-beam details, the plaza. Its legacy is its indelible image, no?

PL It would be wonderful if they actually copied it! Mies said "I want to make an architecture that everybody could do." Unfortunately they only copied how he articulated the skin, making it in aluminum or in some other way. The Seagram Building is a beautiful bronze tower with a plaza that sets it back from the street. You cannot forget about the plaza. Where else in New York City other than Rockefeller Center does a building offer people a place to sit down, breathe, enjoy where you are, and watch other people. If you don't copy the plaza, you're missing the point.

CC Well the plaza is certainly your legacy. You pushed the city to allow the plaza to be there.

PL The Seagram building pushed New York City to change its zoning laws to allow for plazas. 1916 zoning laws required towers to step up to the highest point. Twenty-five percent of the lot could be built as tall as one wanted, so we built a tower on just that twenty-five percent. Subsequently, to encourage plazas the city gave developers ten square feet of added volume for every square foot of open space. Everyone did so.

CC You've said that it's easier to fight for someone else, than it is for yourself.

PL Oh yeah, that's absolutely true. I don't go out selling myself. "This is my and I want you to build it."

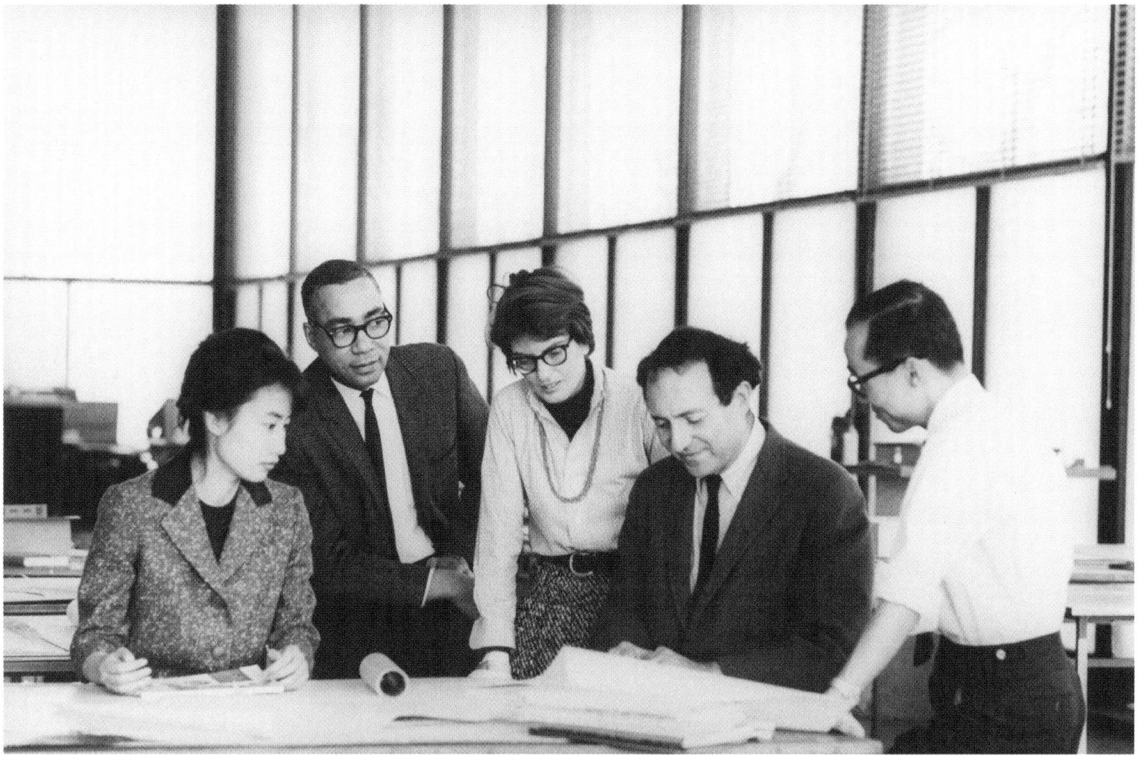

I'm not good at that. But, if you have a building that's very important, or you have a project that's very important, I'll go fight for it if I can see the thought and logic in project.

CC You were both the director of planning and the client for the Seagram Building. Your office was right next to Mies' and Philip Johnson's. How did you manage being a zealous advocate for both your father, who was the president of Seagram, and the architects' interests? Was it ever a conflict?

PL It was perfectly simple. I was the one who told my father that he couldn't build the building that was first proposed by another architect. Once I chose Mies I realized that if I wasn't going to stick around and make sure that he could build the building that he wanted, then it would never get built. Nobody, including the building committee, had ever heard of Mies. The associate architects, Kahn & Jacobs, tried to add a bay to Mies's three by five bay building. So I went down to their offices and I said, "Look here, Mies is the architect of this building. You're here to carry out his projects and specifications with him, but not to design the building." They said, "We didn't change the building." What do you do with people like that? We then had a huge meeting with everyone. There's a wonderful photo of me with a thousand pair of ears around me. You know, nothing ever happens easily.

CC Did you always fight for the architect's side?

PL Oh no, but my job was to see that Mies built a building he was quite proud of. What was the point otherwise? I was young; compromise wasn't a word I had ever heard of.

CC Thinking about legacy and architecture evokes temporalities that are longer than one person's lifetime. For my generation, climate change and anthropogenic environmental degradation are the key legacies of our world. When you graduated from the Illinois Institute of Technology (IIT) in 1963, Rachel Carson's book Silent Spring (which started the environmental movement in the United States) had just come out a year before. James Marston Fitch, who taught at Columbia University then was one of the country's foremost advocate of environmental thinking. Do you remember the moment when environmentalism entered architectural discourse?

PL I certainly do. I took a course at the IIT on the environmental impact of planning. I later taught a course at Malcolm X College on the same topic. I had sensed this conversation about the environment coming but Rachel Carson's book certainly brought it all together in a very clear way. Who are the leaders in architecture trying to clarify this question? I don't know. There is a high level of consciousness about environmental protection in the general public, but it doesn't seem to be the topic it needs to be in architecture. I can't stand this LEED certification stuff because it's so superficial. You put in the right material and then you get a gold medal. I see conservation and restoration as tools. Now we have a very powerful tool in the computer. It hastens our ability to work on environmental issues because of the depth of analysis it provides. It makes data out of our surroundings.

CC As tools, conservation and restoration come in handy for architects in our age of environmental concerns.

PL Yes, and because I see them as tools, I avoid them as titles. As an architect I use a lot of tools, many bodies of knowledge. I read a lot and make sure I'm aware of what's happening. Many big firms think that they have to make a lot of money, but that's not the way to be an architect. To be an architect is to look and listen. You have to look at the broadest level of design, art, theatre, film, everything. Peter Eisenman's contribution to the field is the idea that architecture is an art form to think with. A really good architect sets the field. I can't think of anybody working seriously on the environment right now.

CC I see offices re-branding themselves through environmental concerns—greenwashing their work retroactively. As you pointed out, people are so mired in the bean-counting of LEED's point system, that they lose sight of why understanding climates and the environment is fundamental to architecture.

PL Most architects can't think for themselves.

CC Thoughts and ideas last longer than buildings. The CCA's work, through exhibitions, collecting, grants, research, is to foster new ideas. As an architecture project, as an institution that produces knowledge, its legacy will outlast everything.

PL I certainly hope so. It's a struggle to ensure this. The CCA's collections are great, it has marvelous facilities, it has a marvelous director, but what happens when I'm not around and the director's not around? Look at architecture schools, which also produce architectural knowledge. Some were great twenty years ago, and not so great now. You have to expect that things change. Maybe an institution is not unlike buildings. They go in and out of favor, for this and that reason. So you just hope. You draw it and set it up so that its traditions will hold. We have one of the world's great architecture collections, and just the very aura of it poses strong questions above and beyond asking "what is architecture," or "what can we do with architecture." The CCA has evolved over the years, and that will continue to happen. If it doesn't change, then it's dead, no?

CC You just turned 90, what would you like to do now?

PL I have lots of other things I'd like to do. I would like to be always at the edge of thinking about architecture.

← Unknown photographer, Unidentified student, David Sharp, Phyllis Lambert, Myron Goldsmith and Jin Hwan Kim in a Master's class studio, School of Architecture, Crown Hall, Illinois Institute of Technology (IIT), ca. 1961, gelatin silver print, 20.5 × 25.5 cm, ARCON1993:0030:001, Phyllis Lambert fonds, Canadian Centre for Architecture.

↓ Cedric Price, *The Village Brain* for Olympia, 1971, red coloured pencil over positive photostat, print on emulsion coated paper, 30.1 × 21.1 cm, DR1995:0253:005:004, Cedric Price fonds, Canadian Centre for Architecture, © CCA.

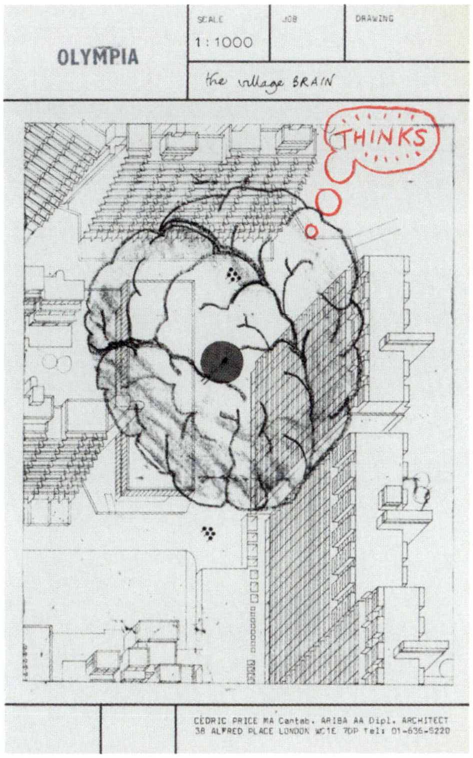

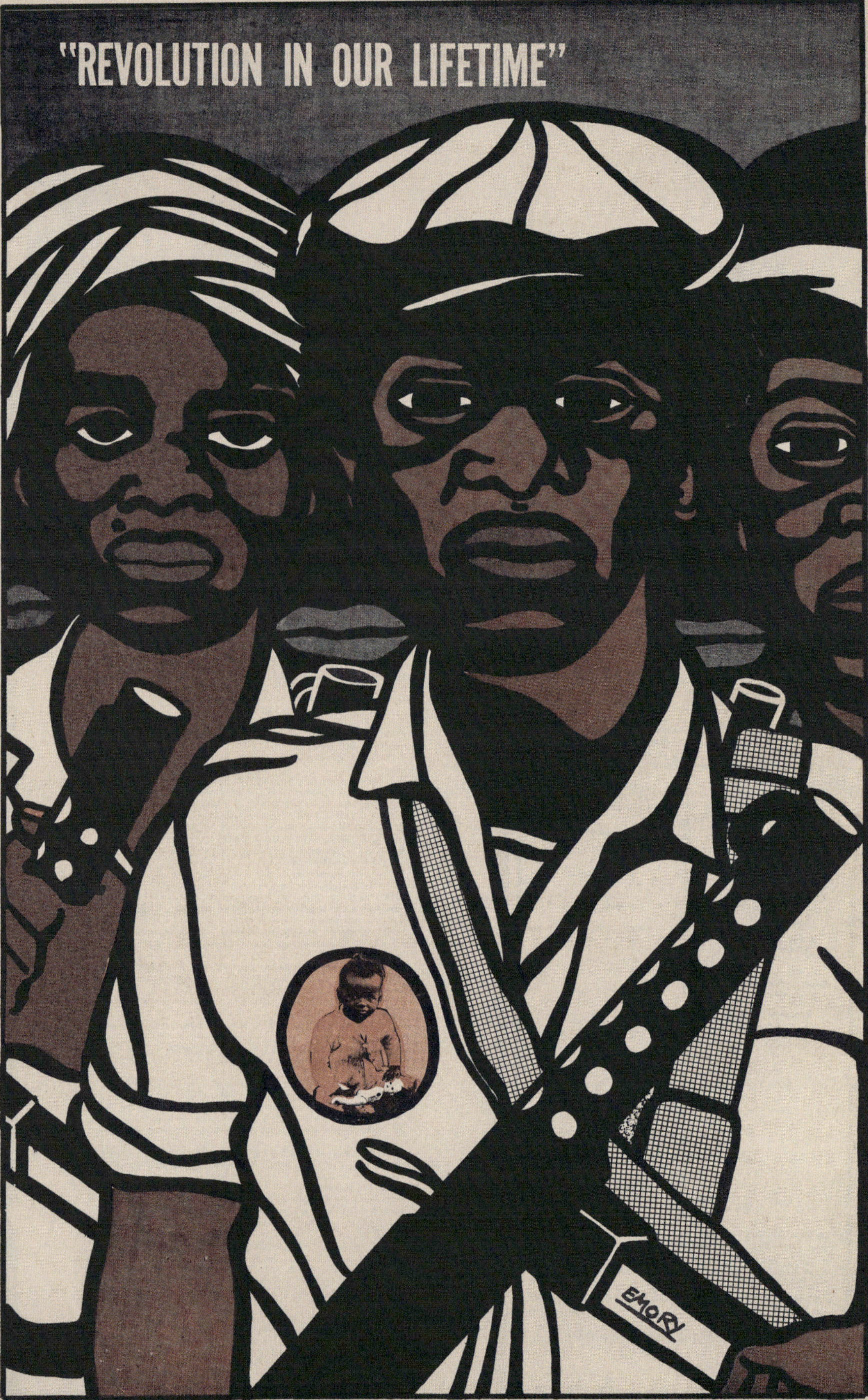
"REVOLUTION IN OUR LIFETIME"
EMORY

Power to the People

Erik de Hart with Farida Sedoc and Emory Douglas

← Emory Douglas, *Revolution in our Lifetime*, 1966. Photo courtesy of Emory Douglas / Art Resource NY c/o Pictoright Amsterdam 2018.

→ Farida Sedoc, *Radical Cut-Up series*, collage on paper, 2017.

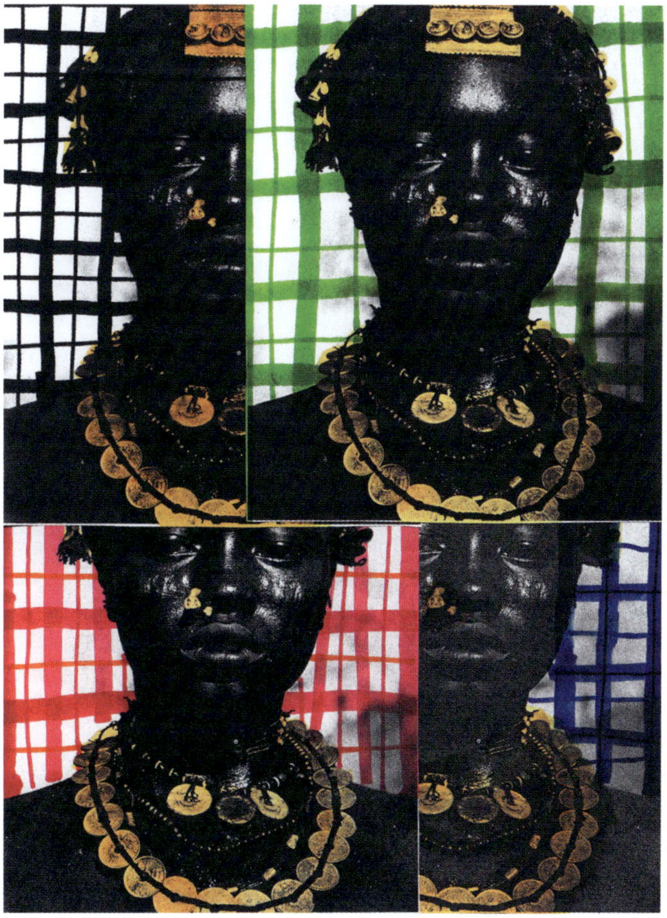

American artist and illustrator EMORY DOUGLAS was an integral part of the Black Panther Party, joining as Minister of Culture for the party in 1967 and designing artwork that became potent symbols of the movement. Together with Amsterdam-based artists ERIK DE HART and FARIDA SEDOC a conversation unfolds about their upbringing and education, the revolutionary times of the 1960s and the link between art and activism.

↙ Portrait of Emory Douglas. Photo by Jos Wheeler.

↗ Emory Douglas, Revolutionary Posters, 1977. Photo courtesy of Emory Douglas / Art Resource NY c/o Pictoright Amsterdam 2018.

↓ Farida Sedoc, 2018. Photo by Erik de Hart.

ERIK DE HART Hi Emory and Farida. Just to start, and an idea from where you came from—could you tell me something about your parents?

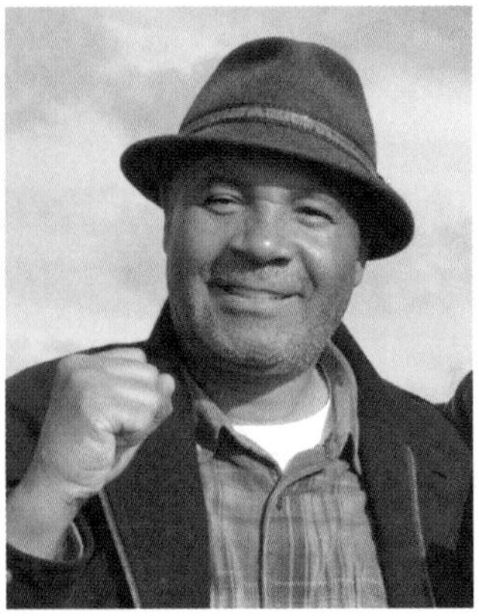

EMORY DOUGLAS I was born in Grand Rapids, Michigan in 1943. Actually, my mother was born on a boat on a river. Those were the times back then. She was a legally blind woman and eventually she got to work at a State-ran concession stand at a youth detention centre. She was a sweet, caring woman and sold candy, sandwiches and cigarettes. Sometimes, she would slip some sandwiches to young black men who came to hang out because they liked to hang out with her at the stand. I also used to hang around there with my mother after school sometimes.

I had asthma as a child, and due to the humid continental climate of Grand Rapids my mother sent me to the warm-summer Mediterranean climate of the San Francisco Bay Area where she had a sister where I would stay when I was about seven years old.

My father and mother were separated when I was three or four years old. I met him once. It's a funny story, it was 1969 and I was sent to Detroit for a conference where Robert Franklin Williams, president of the Monroe chapter of the The National Association for the Advancement of Colored People (NAACP), was about to speak. He was quite radical and promoted armed black self-defence and eventually got exiled. He went to Cuba, Tanzania, and China where he eventually got on the front page of the Peking Review newspaper. This made the Chinese identify with the struggle, the revolution. When he came back to the US he went to Detroit; they refused him in North Carolina because he was still in exile. Huey couldn't go so they sent me to deliver him a message at the conference. During this visit I got an address to connect with my dad who lived in Detroit. While we were riding around in a car looking for the address we saw a man on the street and asked him if he knew Henry Douglas. The guy said; 'I'm Henry Douglas!' (Laughs) That's how I met my father! We kept in touch ever since. Although I haven't seen my biological dad much in my life I always had a sense of extended family. It might not have always been blood family but befriended, extended family.

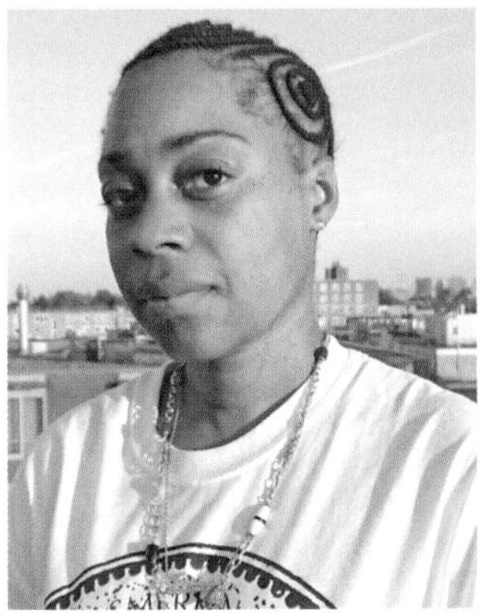

FARIDA SEDOC The funny thing is that my dad is also blind. He wasn't born like that. According to my uncles and his friends my father was a great football player before he became blind. Unfortunately, he became blind because of a

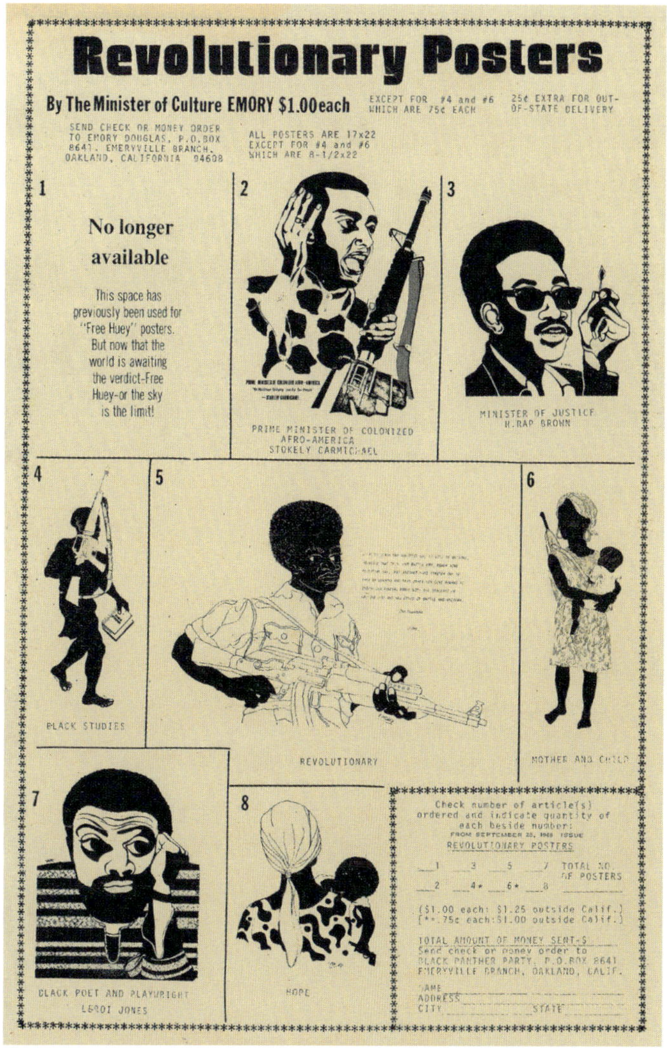

serious accident at his job. The company he worked for in Surinam made sure he immediately could go to a hospital in Rotterdam, the Netherlands, because they could treat him better. He had an extensive period of healing in a revalidation centre.

My mum and dad lived in Ermelo for this period. Where he eventually recovered and learned how to work being visibly challenged. I was born here in 1980. My parents met in Suriname but connected in The Netherlands.

We moved to Amsterdam when I was two years old, to the north part of the city. My mum is a therapist. I remember her working as a teacher, social worker and studying a lot while my dad and I spent a lot of time at home. We talked a lot about football, tennis and listened to music.

> **EDH** What did you see? I remember watching heaps of great cartoons as a kid back then, like Transformers, G I Joe and such, MTV but also Reagan and Gorbachev were on news on the daily.

FS Yes! Reagan, Gorbachev and the Iron Lady. I must say the local and international politics were on fire that period of time. Apartheid, the squatter riots and just seeing people revolt against all the rules and regulation and decisions politicians planned for the people. The message I got from this is that you don't have to accept it, get up stand up and do something. I also remember great music. I sat in front of the TV for hours and hours. From watching Michael (Jackson) do the moonwalk on the 25th Motown anniversary, to Yo! MTV Raps to my dad playing a lot of his records—Marvin Gaye, Fela Kuti, Burning Spear. My mum was working and studying and dropping me off at sports (gymnastics and track and field) and any of my cousins' houses whenever I felt like being with people of my own age.

My mum's work ethic was evident. She was—and still is—constantly helping people through the work she does. She continues evolving in what she does by studying and bettering herself as a teacher and therapist. My dad's character is what really stayed with me, I think: his happy-go-lucky nature, thus strong and resilient and optimistic during the physical challenges he faces every day.

> **EDH** I can imagine that the things you saw on TV and the way your parents were had an impact on your practice as an artist Farida. Emory, can you tell us about some of the events which were influential on your art?

ED Around the age of eight, this was my first conscious awareness experiencing racism. I was traveling with my aunt by bus to Oklahoma—we were heading to Tulsa. We stopped at a bus station to catch another bus. Once we stepped into the next bus I remember seeing 'coloured only' signs, and my aunt holding my hand and telling me that I could sit here and not there; use this bathroom but not that one.

Thinking back now, once in a while during their patrols, the police came to stop at the concession stand where my mum worked. It was one of the first times I would witness a form of police harassment and ethnic profiling. The young black men at the stand, known to the police as gangbangers, were either charged or arrested and imprisoned just for hanging out at my mum's stand.

At home, my family often spoke about their encounters with racism amongst each other. I remember Nat King Cole had a 15-minute television show which was very popular. I remember being intrigued by the discussions of two black gentlemen on TV at ten or eleven o'clock in the evening. Now I know that they were Paul Roberson and W E B

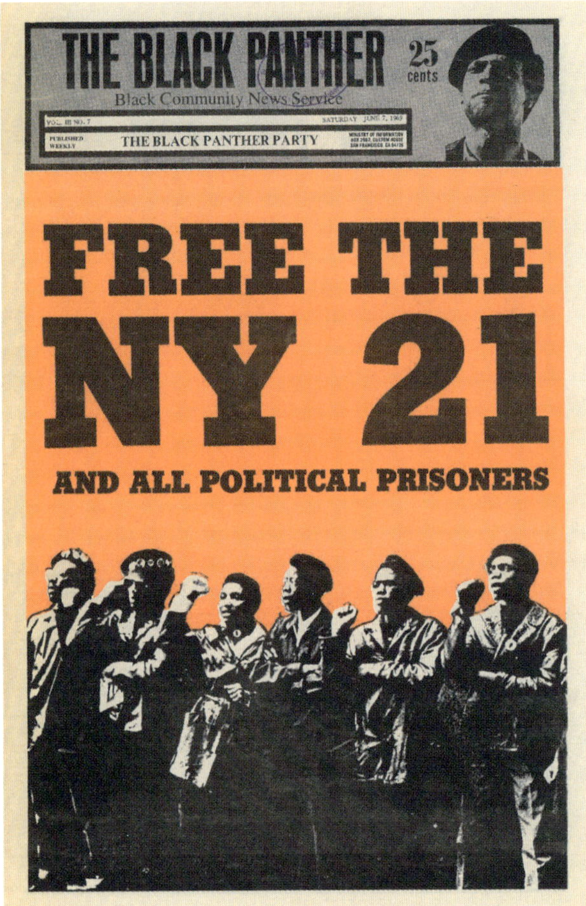

↑ Emory Douglas, *Free the New York 21*, 1969. Photo courtesy of Emory Douglas / Art Resource NY c/o Pictoright Amsterdam 2018.

→ Farida Sedoc, *Move On Over Or We'll Move On Over You*, custom digital print, 2018.

Dubois. Dubois had a socialist organisation, whose office was firebombed—about three or four blocks away from where I stayed.

I saw the action at the front of the Civil Rights Movement down South, the marches, reports of lynching, and even the protests in South Africa. As a child I also watched the Cuban revolution unfold, but that I only realised that years later when I got involved with the movement.

EDH Did you ever meet Malcolm X? How did you get involved with the Black Panthers?

ED I saw Malcolm X on TV when he was still at the Nation of Islam. He was on the East Coast, in New York; I was on the West Coast in San Francisco, you see. He came to visit San Francisco for a street talk once in the now gentrified Philmore District. I was there with some college activists. That's where the start of the Black Panther party was, the Black Arts movement. Black consciousness, Black awareness, Black revolutionary types. I got involved with the Black Arts Movement when I studied at San Francisco City College.

The first or second black student union was in San Francisco. I was at City College all the time to hang out with them. They invited Amiri Baraka, (back then still known as Leroi Jones) to do a theatre show. While I was with them, they would do street theatre and we became tight and he asked me to make the props for his theatre plays. They knew my art by then, in the Black Arts Movement. After Malcolm X died I was asked to make a poster for the activists I was involved with because they invited Betty Shabazz, to honour her. I went to the meeting for the event, and nobody knew about the Black Panther Party back then, they said there was some brothers coming over for the security for the event. They happened to be Huey Newton and Bobby Seale. After this I asked them how I could join. I gave my number and connected with Huey, who gave me a tour and later that day we met up with Bobby.

You see, dealing with self-defence, police murders and all that, people wanted to do something. It was very intense during this period. Looking for something to get involved in, the Black Panther Party appealed to me. There were around 300 rebellions all across the country.

EDH Was there a mandatory literature list or did people need to know certain things to become members of the Party?

ED No, everybody who wanted to contribute was welcome. We weren't all intellectual scholars. People wanted to confront racism and change it. Street people came in, intellectuals, politically conscious people. Everybody went to lectures to educate themselves for the cause. There were different phases and levels. Political consciousness was on different levels. Huey worked at a law firm so that's why he could apply this knowledge to develop the organisation. The Ten Step Platform was also based on other platforms of other political organisations as the one of Marcus Garvey or the Nation of Islam and such, but to our own interpretation and needs.

EDH Knowing that you were involved in Hip Hop, how did you see that on the Hip Hop scene in Amsterdam? Was everybody welcome?

FS It was pretty organic. Back then Hip Hop was not as mainstream and popular as it is today. It's something you had to discover, it was very underground and quite niche, even elitist, although it rose from the streets. You either loved it or not, and if you did, you'd meet like-minded people to share it with. You knew everything about it, and dressed the part, too. For me, it was the beginning of a sense of style. In clothing, in the way I looked, walked and talked and just carried myself as a young person. In my time, conscious Hip Hop was the cool thing. Knowledge of the self, empowerment, emancipation, the union of the collective but still being unique and fly was very much a thing. It was like an unforced study in self-expression, research and how to be original in everything you do. We all flocked together as soon as you knew that someone also loved it and formed a little crew.

EDH The early 1990s A Tribe Called Quest, De La Soul, Gang Starr, Wu-Tang Clan, Nas—it a great time in Hip Hop. Actually, Digable Planets' *Blowout Comb* sleeve artwork made me aware of the Black Panther movement and the revolutionary art of Emory in the first place. Talking about legacy, Hip Hop is a sampling sport. If it wasn't for Hip Hop I wouldn't know about a lot of jazz, soul and funk musicians. Emory, did music play a big role? What music did you listen to?

ED Acts like W A R, Curtis Mayfield, Marvin Gaye, Aretha Franklin, The Impressions, in the 1960s, a lot of them were inspired by the Civil Rights Movement, the context was their music. The Black Panthers also used to have a singing group called The Lumpen.

EDH Do you see a link between activism and Hip Hop?

ED Tupac's mum was a Panther and he was a member of Digital Underground. Public Enemy was a continuation of the movement. They informed and shared our message in their own words and style to the new generation.

EDH I see Digital Underground was also inspired by the freedom in the Funk and the psychedelic artwork of Pedro Bell. Farida, you used to listen to a lot of music with your father, too, right? Was he a big influence on your musical taste?

FS Yeah, very much. He and my mum had a big record collection. Our sound system at home was no joke—real thick sounds. I think this early influence into mainly soul, funk and reggae drew me to Hip Hop. I felt like I recognized the samples while not being aware I had heard them before as originals at the time moment, but I was just feeling the beats. Later, I realized these were samples from the sounds my parents use to play at home.

EDH And Emory, how did you two get into art?

ED I was basically self-taught. Although I had a basic foundation of professional skills because I had some training from 1964 -1967 at City College where I took up advertising art. This made me prepared me for the production aspect of designing. I followed design, print press and animation classes as a junior. At college the teachers compared the quality of the work on a professional level. There, I learned to critique and evaluate my work. At one time someone from the Science department needed technical illustrations of chromosomes. I took the job and got paid for it. I also did lettering to a point—I did a lot of posters. There was an open position at the silkscreen factory, and teachers connected qualified students to work there. I learned the principles of silk screening the old school way. He sent me to department stores and had me work in the production department. I worked there designing their newspaper advertisements. I learned a lot here and through this experience. While at school you learn the theory and my jobs got me to experience production, therefore I could take on the BP newspaper. At the height we had a 400,000 readership. In the beginning there were a lot of errors. It took time to refine the paper, until it developed into a quality issue. Each issue informed me for the next one. I was in charge of the production aspect of the newspaper: typesetting, layout, cut and pasting, artwork.

EDH Farida could you tell me more about your work process?

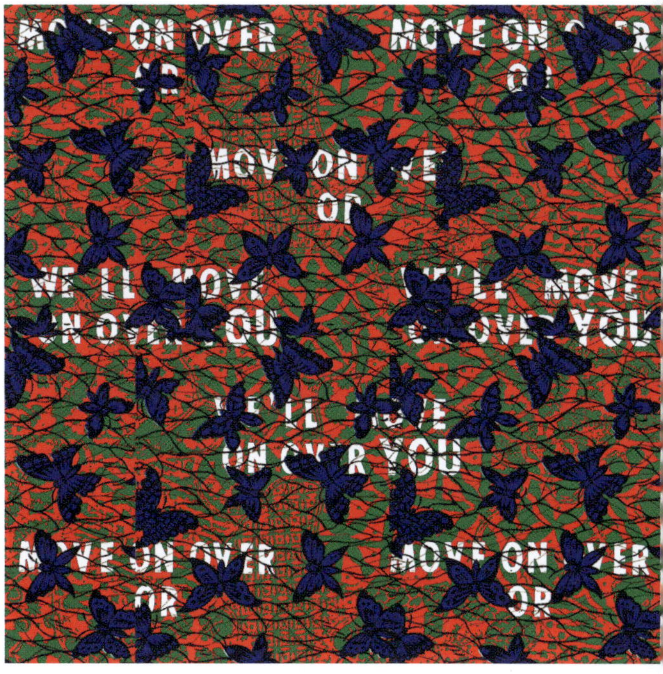

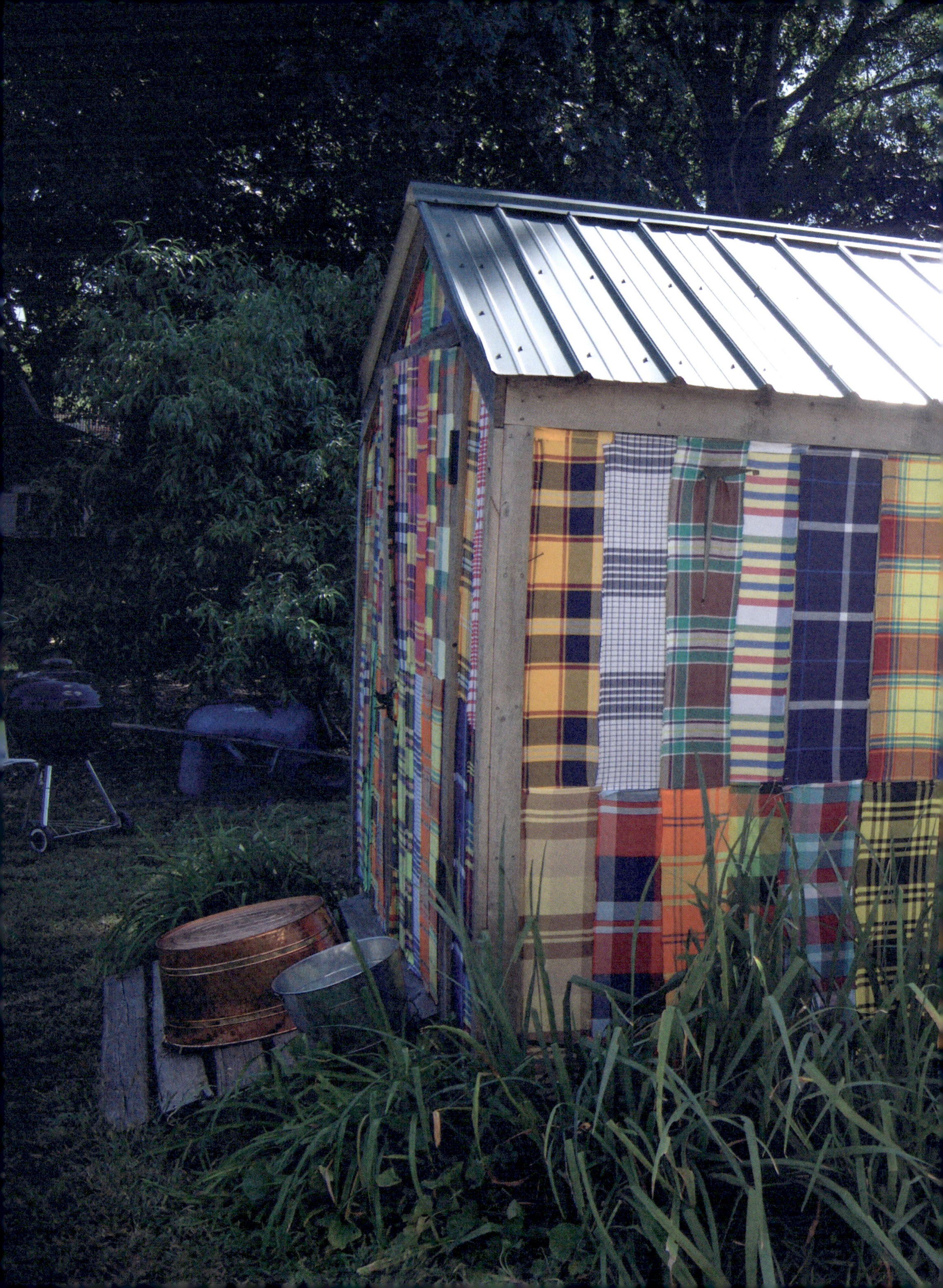

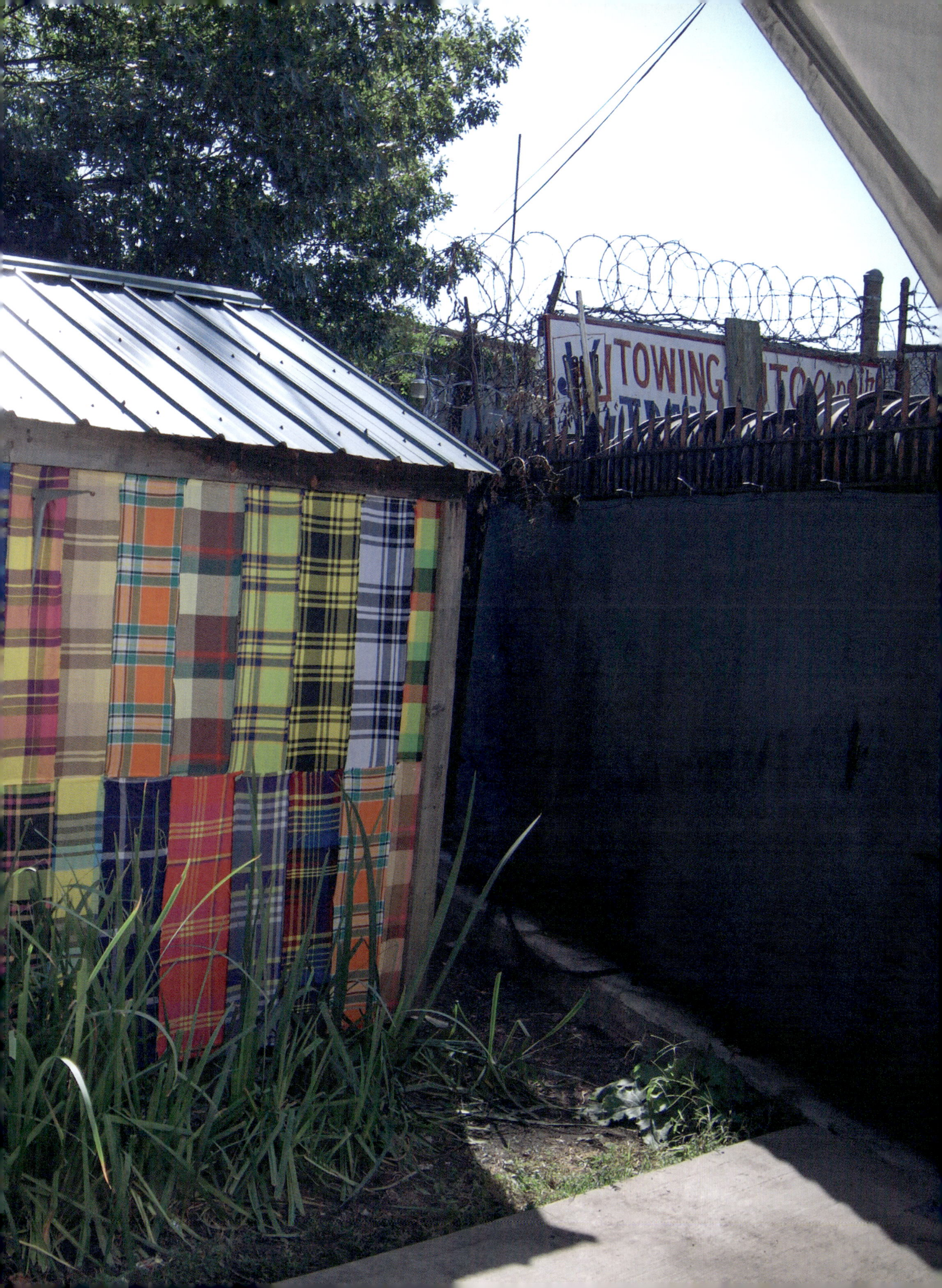
TOWING

↰ Farida Sedoc, *The Shed*, installation at Wyckoff House Museum, Brooklyn, NYC, 2016.

FS I also consider myself an autodidact. Having spent only a few years in art school, I discovered my passion for silk screening. The story was always more important to me than the shape, seeing as I was in the fashion department. The mood, the story, the feeling, the idea, the concept is where I start. In school I learned to create a mood-board to express my ideas, and from this experiment with graphic texts and shapes. I like to cut and paste and mess around in photoshop with it. From the start my work was political. Not intentionally, but just because I was on the streets so much, hanging around with friends— that's where everything happened, those were my experiences I expressed in the work. Let's say the positive side is that you can see in the use of colours and the critical message often in the graphics. 20 years ago, I started to design T-shirts. Till this day it's something I love to do. Being part of exhibitions by the Stedelijk Museum in Amsterdam or the Van Abbemuseum in Eindhoven, I always stress the importance for me to create a T-shirt to communicate the message, so people can grasp in a split second the context of the exhibition and the artists. My more abstract work is developing as we speak.

EDH Are there any specific contemporary figures who really inspired you to make art or inspire your work today?

FS I was heavily influenced by fashion, and in particular streetwear, the styles of certain individuals in the streets of Amsterdam challenged me to dress better and evolve in style and to have thoughts on this. It was possibly the first encounter with conceptual thinking for me. Also, the MTV video clips in the 1990s shaped my aesthetics in terms of the use of colour and the ability of conveying a message through graphics. In terms of contemporary artists who influenced me: Richard Bell, and of course Emory Douglas.

EDH Emory, were there any specific contemporary figures in your time who really inspired you to make art?

ED While I lived in public housing in San Francisco with my aunt, we'd receive an annual calendar featuring black art. I was intrigued by the art, by Charles White who was married at one point to Elizabeth Catlett. They were well known black artists. (Charles White also became a teacher of **Kerry James Marshall** **(page → 96)** and David Hammons). Another artist, Charles Bible inspired me too. He used to live downstairs from me and was making a portrait of Malcolm X. I asked him about his process and was very inspired by what he told me.

Any artists I may have been inspired by or what I have seen—I never tried to duplicate. I try to develop the work itself in the spirit of a context. Once I was part of the Black Arts Movement I began to understand the connections. All the struggles worldwide, the political posters from Cuba, socialist posters, I was very much inspired by Organization of Solidarity with the People of Asia, Africa and Latin America (OSPAAAL). The Vietnamese struggle—a lot of resistance—the Palestinian struggle, the Chinese struggle, solidarity with the African-American struggle. All those posters were very inspirational. I never duplicated them, but was inspired by them. I observed the Asian art—the lines—I think the combination of all this is the foundation of my work. The Cuban artists used to duplicate, remix my work. That wasn't a problem for me. We all were sharing ideals. This was about a movement that transcended borders.

EDH After the Black Panther Party (BPP) was dismantled by the US Government, the FBI and COINTELPRO, how did you deal with that in the 1980s?

ED After the BPP, there was a lot of tension during that time. I was so stressed that my hands could not stretch fully. I began to look into healing and yoga meditation and I started to focus a bit more on my family and craft. I was 36. The newspaper Sun Reporter was black owned since the 1930s it was a radical and modern newspaper and I was already intrigued by the papers artwork as a kid. The newspaper was owned by Dr Goodman, he was a civil rights activist and a Black Panther supporter. The black press paper was not like the other papers which were controlled by advertisers. Actually, we bought our printing equipment from them when they upgraded. Dr Goodman also interview Malcolm X once, six months before the party was over. Everybody knew what it was. We weren't going to go further. Dr Goodman knew my art skills from the beginning, so he asked me to work for the black press production work. I did this from 1984-2005. I also focussed on my mum and her health—I took care of her for about 14 years. I kept practising and made my garage to my work area. I did a lot of community graphics in the 1990s and 2000s. It was a conscious development. I had learned from my work in city college and at the party. I had to critique and evaluate my work all the time, I had to be constructive and find ways to move forward and be more efficient. Never to get frustrated. The BPP taught me to work anywhere at any time. We had a mobile studio. Sometimes we didn't even have tables! We used doors to work on, and even after the BPP it was about finding practical solutions to get the job done.

I read a lot about yoga and practised this discipline, it helped me not to trip out. I smoked as a youngster—I kept quitting and starting again. After I turned 22, I realize what it was, and I got it under control. In 1980, before I left the BPP, I wasn't eating pork. There were vegetarians in the BP and I admired the aura about them. I got this cookbook from this hippy community—you can make anything from soy beans! I had a daughter and a son and cooked everything in the book. I have two kids, a son and daughter and five granddaughters.

EDH Sometimes, I am a bit concerned that the emergence of certain technological devices and the internet made it more difficult for people to focus and to unite under a common cause. People in the server Civil Rights Movement during the 1960s were conscious and concerned about US imperialist agenda, nowadays, people unknowingly or willingly sign up to agitator indexes without questioning the status quo. What do you think about revolution now and how can we walk united toward a future world of co-operational humanism in this digital age?

ED There has been a break in the context of the historical relevance of the 1960s to what's happening today. Today results in negative empowerment. The individualistic thing instead of working for the collective spirit of overcoming and confronting the challenges that exist today. If you've got eyes, you have to look all the way through life. This is an extremely different context than the 1960s. The desperation is still the same today. There are challenges. Not the same model. Pyramid models? Circular models? Top-down is not what's needed today. The spontaneity of movements today—you have to deal with what is. You can look at the blueprint to be inspiring but not duplicate it.

Movement art—it's about the interconnection between why we were making the art and the art itself. Everything has a beginning, a middle, and an ending. We came out of the context of the times. The repression was an attempt to dissolve us by any means possible. A lot of people see that now—the struggle. Organisations had to shift and change from what was to what is now.

In the party was savvy enough to be able to take care of everyone in the party. As an individual you go into the job market—you have to figure it out. For me, they are looking to what I'm doing. I automatically have a following because of the social, political, and social justice. It's not like you're going to be a millionaire and make sure that it's beneficial to you.

I work with the artists' rights society—they work out the legal stuff when people want to do something community based. When it comes to museums, institutions, Universities—they have to pay for this. I design a lot of exhibition posters. I always request that they send me a shipping address and take care of it. They want the work—no problem—they paid for using it in the exhibition.

EDH What about your work today?

ED I'm retired! No deadlines but my own. When something is on my mind, I work on it in my own time and can get back to it 6 months later. Collective work or exhibitions—I'll do that. In May I'll be 75, so no stress. 50 years of work, at this age you can't deal with that stress. At my house, I have my printer on which I do a lot of prints, when I travel and locally. For now, I kick back and relax to do whatever I choose to do. I still get out there from time to time. Like how Farida and I worked together on the Frontier Imaginaries exhibition for the Stedelijk Museum in Amsterdam. I have a print exhibit in Ohio coming up, where I will meet my friend Richard Bell in Australia and after that New Zealand, then Detroit. I keep busy.

EDH Farida, how do you work today?

FS I'm not retired yet! My daily practice consists of working with kindred spirits, art foundations, institutions and museums, being part of exhibitions, or commissioned assignments. If not, I seize the time.

Digital design pioneer GREG LYNN examines together with internationally acclaimed Los Angeles-based architect FRANK GEHRY the foundations of digital architecture and the power of computer rationalization in this interview which was conducted as part of the exhibition Archaeology of the Digital, curated by Lynn at the Canadian Centre for Architecture.

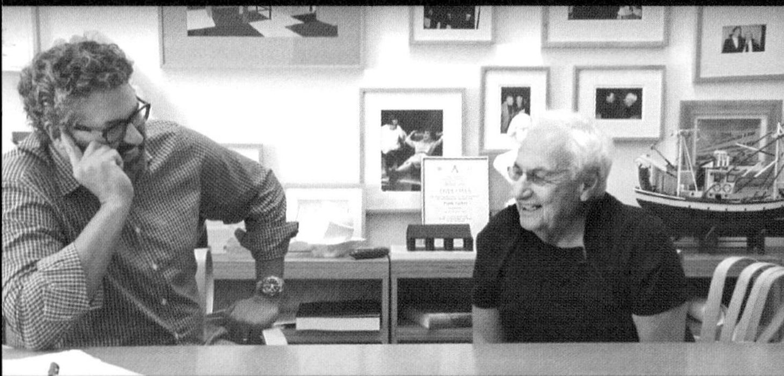

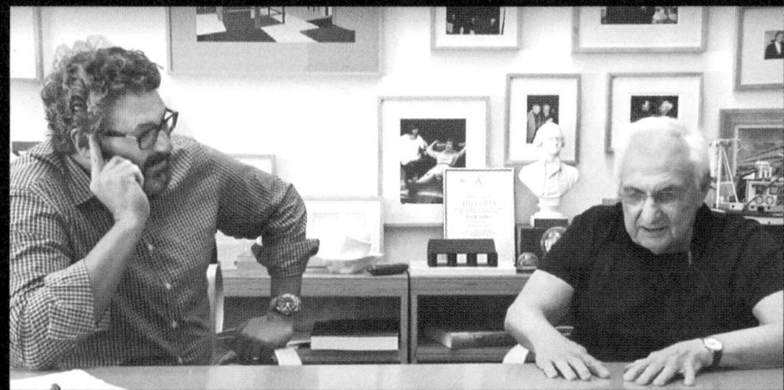

GREG LYNN When did you start using computers in the office?

FRANK GEHRY It was right after we built the Vitra Design Museum. As you probably remember, there's a stairway in the shape of a caracol (snail) that is expressed on the façade as it spirals up, and there is a zinc roof on it. Toward the top there's a kink. The roof goes up, kinks, and then continues. At the time, to define it for the builder, we drew it using what I'd learned in school: descriptive geometry. The builder used those drawings, and he ended up with the kink! He started simultaneously at the bottom and at the top, and—kink—it didn't work. I said to the people in the office then—Jim Glymph had just started working there—'You know, I want to use shapes like that. How do I draw them so I don't get a kink and so that it's clear how to build it?' Jim called IBM, who put him in touch with Dassault Systèmes. That's when Rick Smith came into the picture. Once we started, there was no turning back.

The first thing we did was the Fish in Barcelona. We were working with Massimo Colomban, who was the head of Permasteelisa at the time. Massimo's company was building the steel tower for Bruce Graham's Hotel Arts in the Olympic Village, and they asked me to design a fish sculpture. My initial design was a wave, and then, pretty soon it became a fish. We were working with Skidmore, Owings & Merrill (SOM) and they were using AutoCAD at the time, while we were already starting to use CATIA (software suite for computer-aided design). SOM insisted they could do it using CAD, but Colomban came in to the office to say, 'Look, I can't build from this.' We showed him the CATIA files we had produced, and he went back to Italy. Two weeks later he called me up and said: 'Perfetto!'

After that was Bilbao. I remember we sent a team over for the bidding on the steel structure. There were six bidders, and we taught them each how to look at CATIA files and take the numbers from them. We got six bids, 1 per cent spread, 18 per cent under budget. That's when I realized it was a magic trick. It all came together, except at the last minute they couldn't close the structure, so there was an extra cost of $2 million, but that was nothing compared to 18 per cent under budget. After that there was no turning back, because the clarity you got from using CATIA was so strong.

GL When I first saw the Lewis House project, I thought that it was native computer; but when I met you, you made a point of saying that I was a native computer person and you were not, which I still don't understand. I thought the language was coming from the computer, but you always insist that it's not. I still think you have an intuition for digital surfaces that most other people don't have. Tell me why I'm wrong.

FG I use a pencil to draw and I make three-dimensional models. I don't have the capacity to design directly on the computer.

GL That is true, but you've still got an eye for the computer.

FG Well, the one experience of computer design I had was, actually, when we were working on the Lewis House. We had one of my people working on the entrance to the house on screen while we were folding fabric for the model and spraying it with wax so it would harden—it looked really weird. The guy got it scanned and put into the computer.

There we were, in front of the computer, trying to design this shape, but trying to follow him was excruciating! It was like I was in a vice of pain, as if somebody were tightening screws into me. That's what it felt like. I'd ask if we could do this or that and the computer guy would do it. Finally, we got the shape that we called the 'horse's head' which is simi-

✓ Frank Gehry in conversation with Greg Lynn, 2013. Source: CCA www.cca.qc.ca

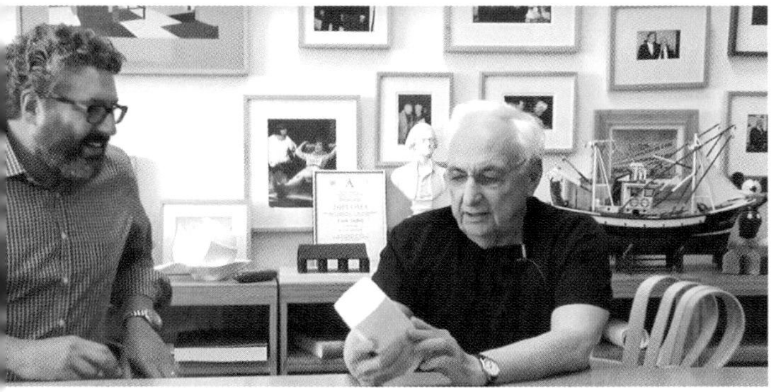

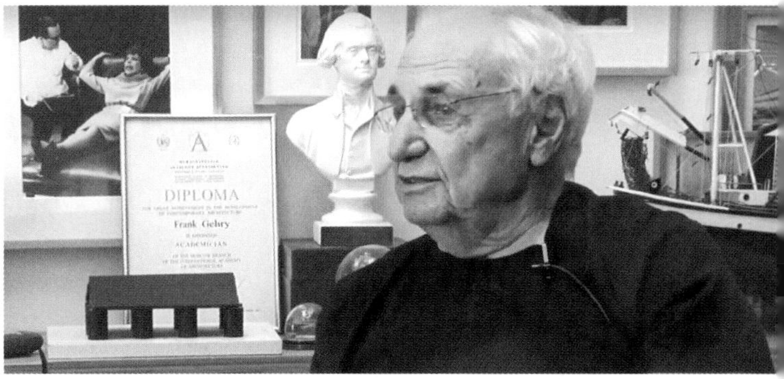

> 'The personal intervention, the brain that transforms it into art, is needed to get beyond the recognizable language of the computer program.'
>
> FRANK GEHRY

lar to the one built as the conference room of the DZ Bank in Berlin. To answer to your question, that's what I mean; that I'm not hand-to-eye coordinated with the machine. You are, because you manipulate it personally—you don't have a surrogate. You spend endless hours refining it—it's your métier (occupation). You know how to do it and I don't. I've tried several times since to design on the computer, and I just can't. I don't have the patience.

For me, the problem with designing buildings on the computer is that some of the resulting work retains the fingerprints of the software system. You can recognize a RHINO building—that's not a building by an artist, it's a RHINO building. Somebody has to overcome that; I think that's what you're doing. I hope you're doing it!

GL Well, now the big commercial offices are so onto this stuff that they do these whimsical moves, which the computer lets them execute efficiently and economically, but they come out really sterile, at least in my opinion. I never thought I'd see that.

FG There's no artistry to the way it's done. The computer has become an opportunistic gadget for most of the profession. It's not taken seriously as a métier for design, for really coming up with a language that is unique and personal. The personal intervention, the brain that transforms it into art, is needed to get beyond the recognizable language of the computer program. That's what I think—that's my manifesto.

GL I'm curious to know how the computer surrogates entered your life for the Lewis House and where they are now—how they turned into Gehry Technologies (GT). I also wanted to ask about how you collaborated with artists and other architects on Lewis House, and if the computer played any role in that.

FG The computer played little role in the project. I did one form—that was it. Bill Mitchell from MIT tried to get us on the computer earlier. He did two projects for us to show me how. He did the American Centre in Paris and the Fish sculpture for Barcelona that I mentioned earlier. The images he created for the American Centre were just horrible and I said, 'Bill, these are just like renderings. There's no soul, no heart, no nothin'!' The Fish sculpture got better; the rendering was quite beautiful. I didn't turn the idea of using computers off entirely, because that project made me think that there was hope somewhere.

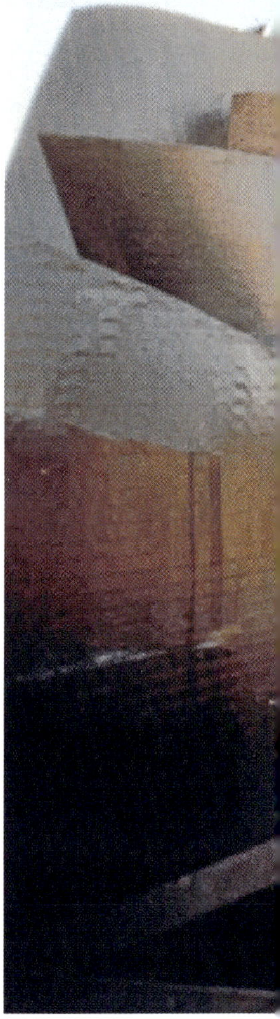

Now, how did I get to GT? We started using CATIA on everything, which was really too complicated and too expensive for the construction industry, so we developed an add-on for ourselves called Digital Project, and Dassault urged us to commercialize it. I remember Jim and the guys hired some salespeople to sell Digital Project, but we failed. It was just not our thing; we didn't know how to do it. It was still too complicated and expensive for our industry. The work stations were $15,000 each. No small office could afford it; no consultants could afford it.

As a result, we shut down the sales thing. It cost us a lot of time and effort. Dassault helped us

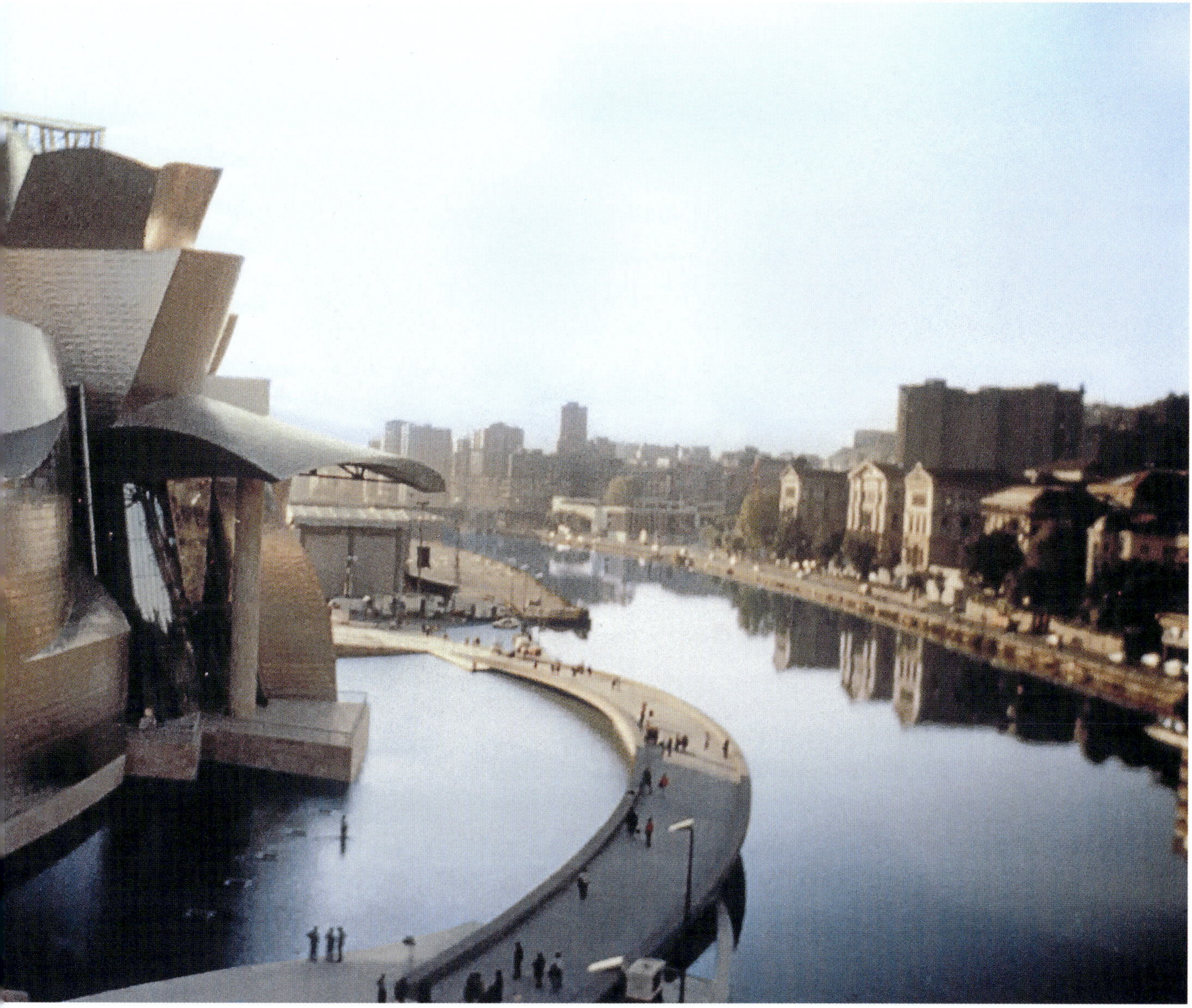

out financially for a while, so that's how they ended up owning ten to eleven per cent of GT. They had urged us to start a company, thinking that we would sell software, and that we would bring them into the construction industry.

Slowly, that small company started to get work. The first big job was for Swire in Hong Kong, for the building they now call Opus. It was an 80-storey building, then named One Island East, that they were working on with a Chinese architect. They hired our tech team, and I think we had 15 people on the job for a couple of years. They had an office about the size of this room, and they brought in all the consultants and representatives to the same room, where they did all the drawings for One Island East. They saved 12 per cent on construction costs. The Swire construction guy said 'This is great. We're going to use it on everything. And we should work out a way for GT to get a piece of the savings.' It was his suggestion. Trouble is, the newer guys who have replaced him—they're not into it.

↑ Gehry Partners, LLP, Guggenheim Museum Bilbao, Bilbao, Spain, 1991-1997. © Sydney Pollack.

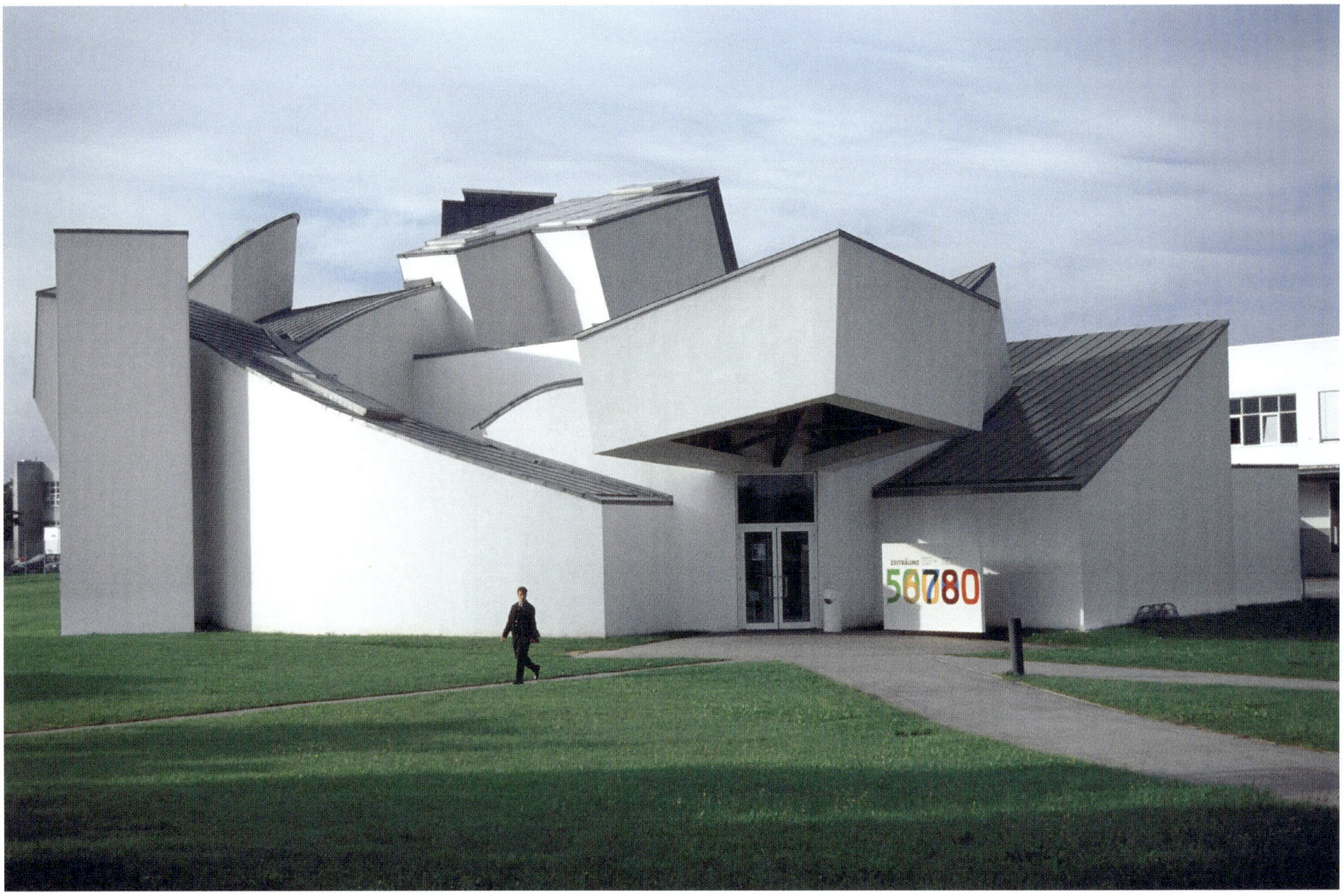
ZEITRÄUME

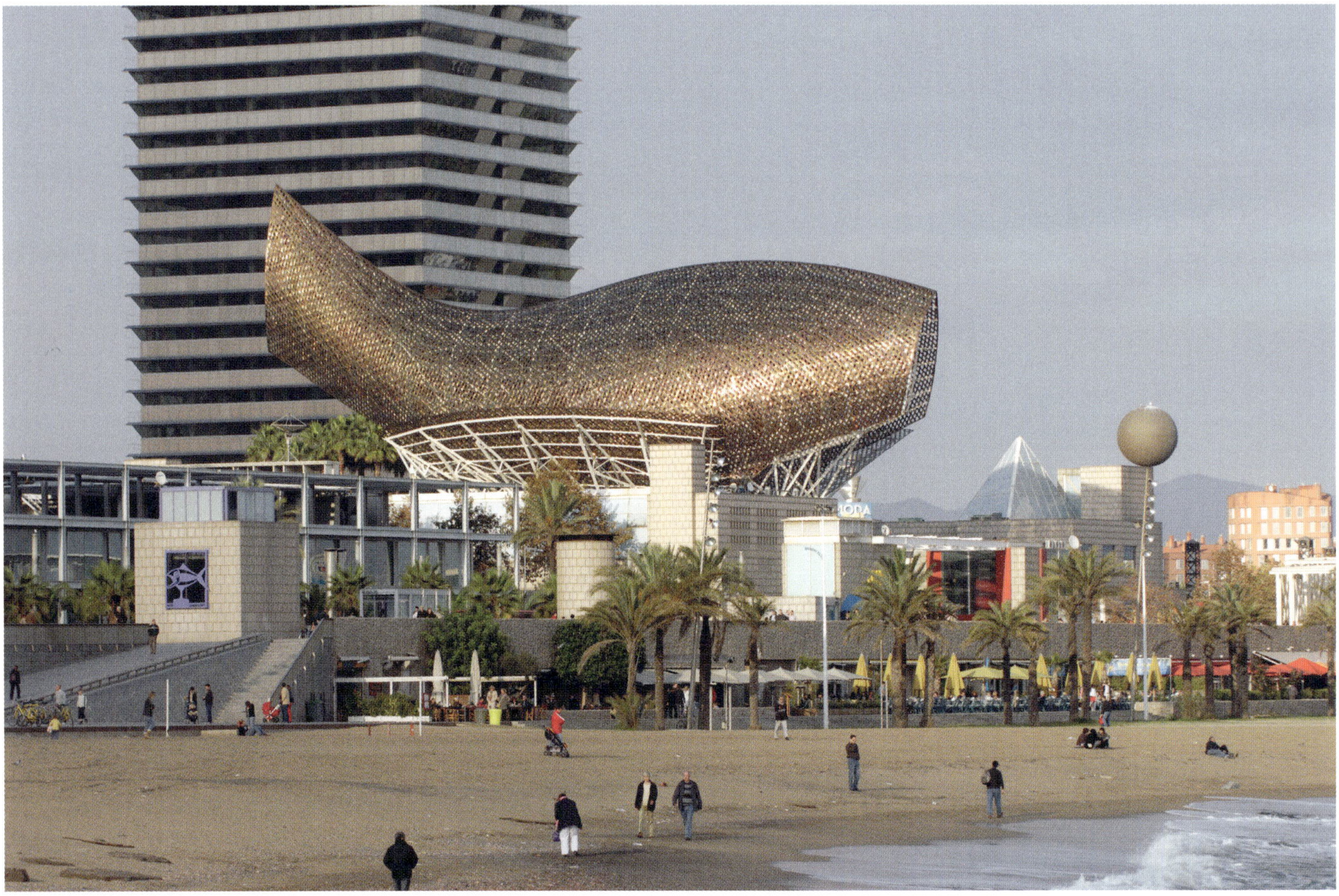

GL You know, any PhD student who wants to do some research on the use of digital technology in architecture has to look at these things, but often can't, because the files are gone. I think the fact that you have original files dating back to the 1980s and 1990s is because it was a critical part of your design process.

FG Mm-hm.

GL I'm going to ask one thing about Richard Serra, Lewis House and the computer. Didn't that all happen together? I ask, because Tensho Takemori told me it was Rick Smith who first showed Richard the computer. And Richard said, 'This is something that I need for my art.' Now everybody—**Olafur Eliasson** **(page → 30)**, Jeff Koons—is working just like us. They're all using things like CATIA. They couldn't do their artwork without digital technology now, and I'm just curious, you know—

FG Okay, so here's how it happened. We were designing a building, the Gehry Tower in Hanover, and the model was here when Richard came by. He used to come by often. He's a good friend, respected colleague and artist, etc. He said, 'How do you do that? How are you going to build that?' And I said, 'Well, we've got this computer guy, Rick Smith. He's over there. He does the drawings.' Then Rick donated his services to Richard for a while. He was doing the Torqued Ellipses (1996–99); or he started to right after this. He made a few pieces like this that were vertical, where he torqued the metal. You know, talking about it in this way sounds like I'm saying he stole the idea from me, but twisting a piece of metal is not proprietary.

GL Yeah, yeah.

FG That's just what we do. We all share information with each other; I felt it was like that. Richard called me from the mill. They had these 11-foot tall sheets of steel going through the rollers, because first, you send the sheet through so that it torques in the different ways you want it to. The software program was running the machine and he called me up, he was so excited, he said, 'I can't believe it! Half-inch tolerance!' He was very happy.

GL You said to me before that you're amazed at how artists now work like architects in the city. But I also think, technologically and digitally, their medium has shifted a lot like ours—for some, anyway.

FG Well, there are different things going on. I don't remember exactly but in the 1970s, or maybe early 1980s, there was a conference at the University of California, Los Angeles (UCLA) about art and architecture. I think Siah Armajani was actually there, and Richard was there, and I was there. The moaning on the artists' part was that they were just the plop in the plaza; they were being marginalized. The architecture was bigger than them; it trivialized and overpowered them—whereas we architects had it all. There was a lot of envy at that conference, and there was nothing you could say. I do, however, remember Richard was tough on everybody, and Siah was king at that point because he had built a bridge in Minneapolis that was as big as architecture. That was the road forward.

It was after that, or just about the same time, when I was working on the Chiat/Day building and saw the chance to give Claes Oldenburg a front piece. So, to say, 'Okay we can collaborate, and you, the artist, can have front and centre. We're open to collaboration and to playing with you.' That's what it was about.

← Gehry Partners, LLP, Vitra International Furniture Manufacturing Facility and Design Museum, Weil am Rhein, Germany, 1987-1989. View from Charles Eames Strasse. © ThomasMayer-Archive.com.

↙ Gehry Partners, LLP, Fish Sculpture, Barcelona, Spain, 1992. © Thomas-MayerArchive.com.

GL Were the binoculars done in CATIA or were those drawn? I was curious to know who drew (and who draws) that stuff.

FG I think they were done in CATIA. They must have been.

GL I remember in the late 1980s and early 1990s Frank Stella, all of a sudden, wanted to be an architect because he had a computer. It was pretty straight up: I now have a computer so I'm going to do architecture. Do you remember all that?

FG Yeah, he talked to me about it. And he did the little house for Philip Johnson in New Canaan.

GL The Monster?

FG The Monster. Philip—I'll never forget this!—Philip called me up and asked, 'The world's greatest living architect just surfaced,' and I asked, 'Who's that?' He said, 'Frank Stella.' He sent me these images for the Monster, which I guess came out of a combination of something I was doing and something Richard was doing—or something. There was a mélange of influences going on. Frank's early representations of the Monster were very seductive—more seductive than the building when it was built. He didn't quite know how to connect the dots... that's what I've been talking about. He couldn't get his artistic sensibility through the computer to the finished building. That's what's missing; the missing link that I always felt.

GL Would it be fair to say that the gesture, or the image, for the Lewis House was tan-

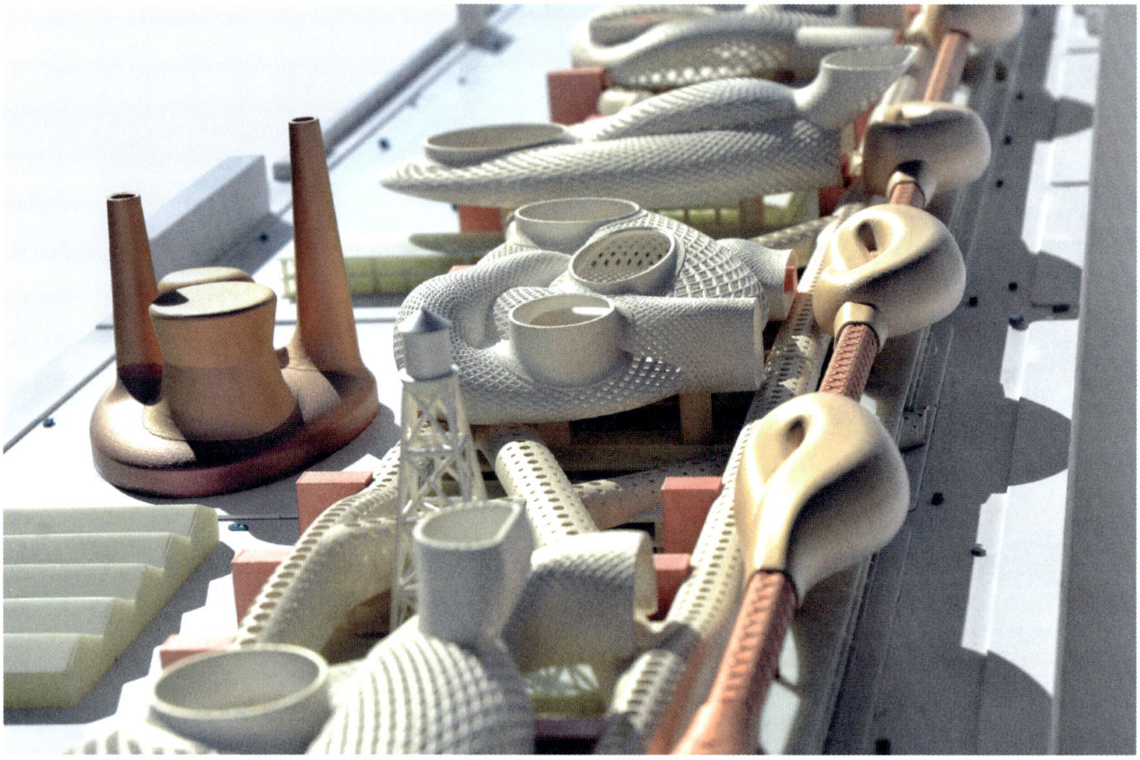

gled up with the computer in a different way than the Barcelona Fish or the Gehry Tower in Hanover or a lot of those other projects? I mean, when you look at the archive, you see a lot of exploration and creativity, but the computer is in the mix in a very undecided way. Whereas in other projects it's clear the computer is.

FG Well, if you're talking about me and the computer, I designed pretty much without it up until about three months ago, when you caught me—

GL I was going to say! I wasn't planning to bring it up because I wasn't sure you wanted it on record.

FG No, no. It's fine, I think.

GL It's the first actually native one.

FG Yeah. It is. I'm a virgin! Up until that point, I wouldn't do it. I would take the drawings and stuff to the edge of the precipice, and then turn it all over to GT for production, management, construction—all of those things, but no sooner in the design process. Up until the competition for the National Art Museum of China (NAMoC) in Beijing, that is. I did it sort of seamlessly without realizing it, and you caught me. (Laughs) You said, 'Great—I'm so excited you finally crossed the line!' We crossed the Rubicon, that's right. I decided I was just going to work on it myself. I didn't want to bother anybody. I got the site plan—I didn't even realise I did this. I got the plan and I taped it down, then laid a piece of tracing paper over it and started sketching. And then I wanted to hard-line it, so I said to my assistant, 'Where's my T-square?' She said, 'What do you mean?'

GL (Laughs) What's a T-square? Is that a trick?

FG So, I said, 'Well, just go out and buy one, and get me some triangles too.' (Laughs). So they bought it all and I mean, everybody was laughing at me. I couldn't do it! Even, up to that point, I had my slide rule on my desk.

↑ Greg Lynn, Center of Fulfilment, Knowledge and Innovation, Venice Biennale 2016. Courtesy of Greg Lynn FORM.

↗ Gehry Partners, LLP, Lewis Residence, Lyndhurst, Ohio, 1985-1995 (unbuilt). Final Model, wood balsa, cardboard, and Plexiglas, 51×292×153 cm, ca. 1995. Images provided by Gehry Partners, LLP.

Originally published in Greg Lynn (Ed.) Archeology of the Digital, Sternberg Press, 2013.

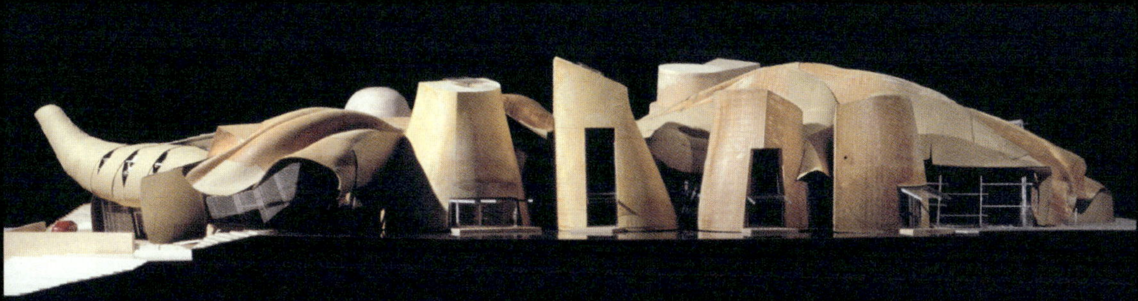

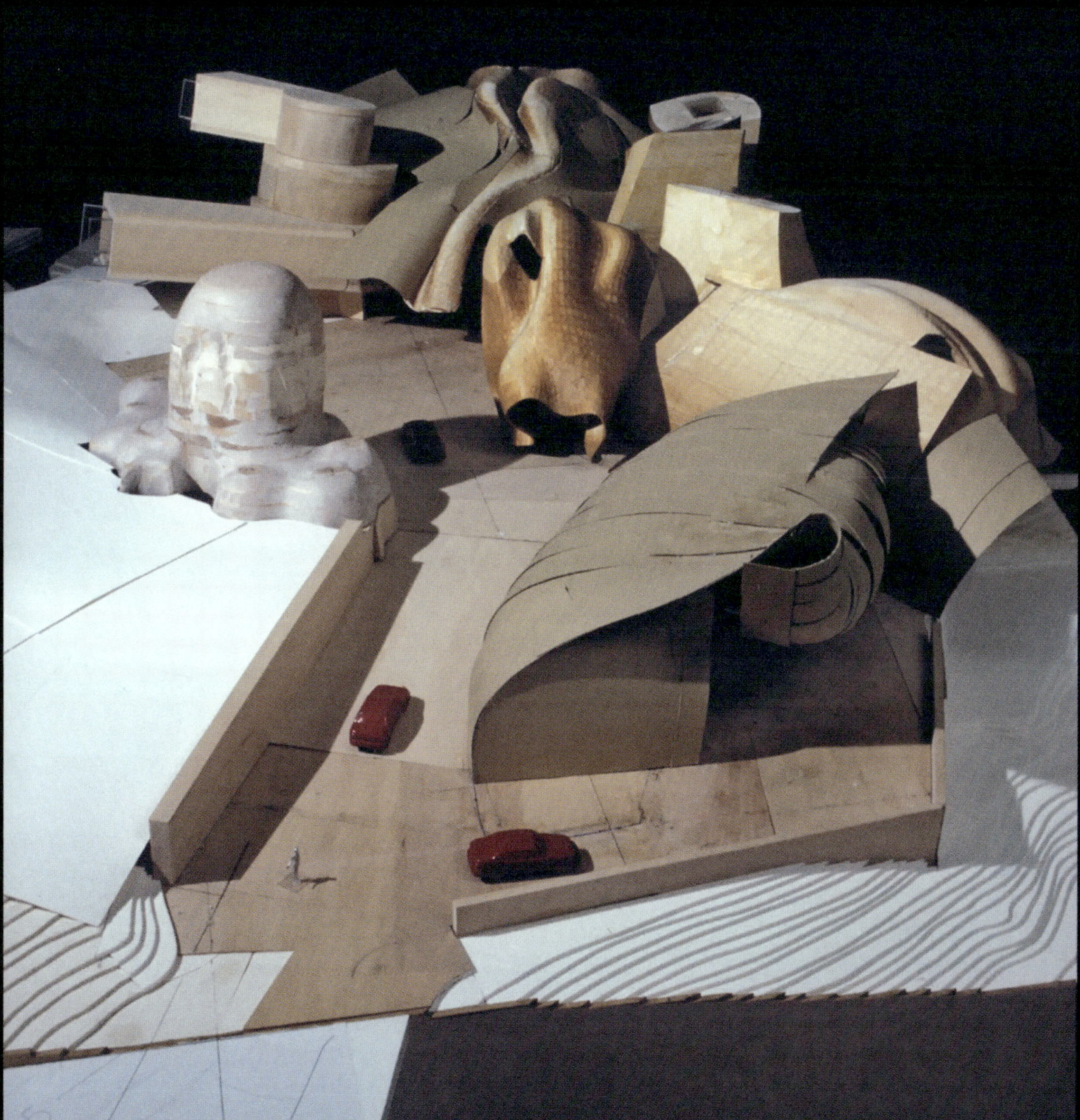

A Field Full of Responsibility

Sophie Lovell and Dieter Rams

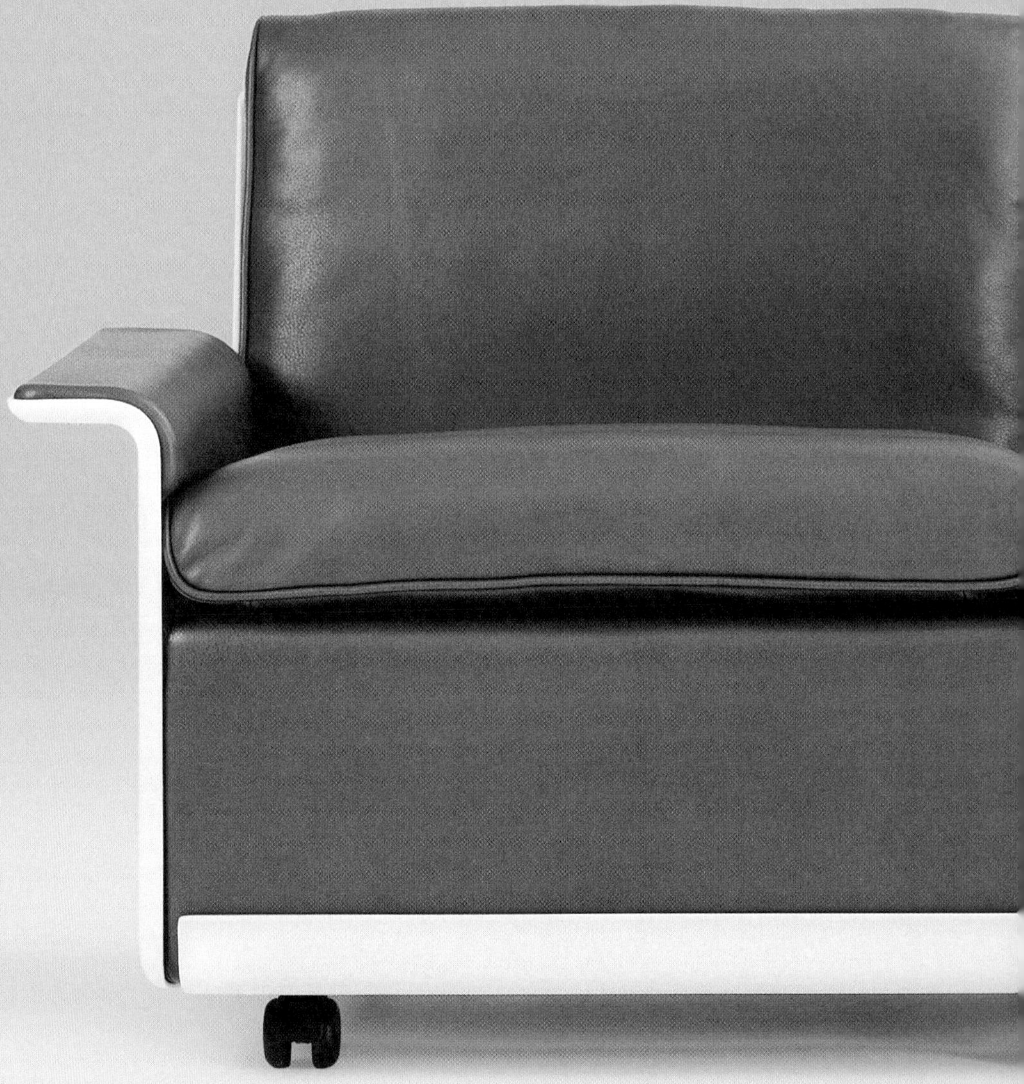

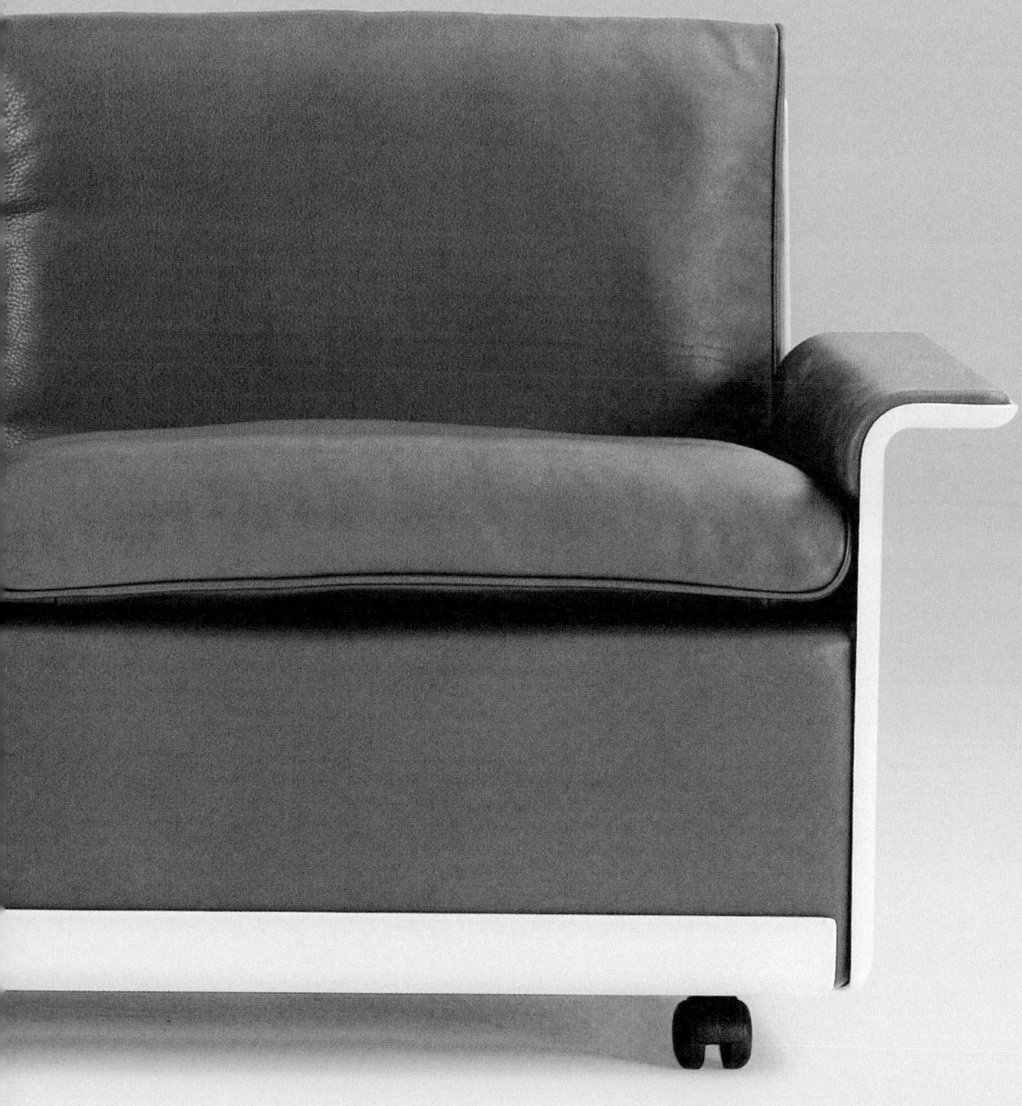

The design and architecture writer and editor SOPHIE LOVELL is the author of the biography DIETER RAMS: *As Little Design as Possible* (2011). She has spent many hours talking to and interviewing German industrial designer Dieter Rams and shares here for the first time a transcription of one of their conversations about German design, design and politics, Buckminster Fuller, pollution, the environment and our obsession with 'things'.

Dieter Rams is probably Germany's most famous living designer. He was born in Wiesbaden in 1932 and worked first as an architect before moving to the German consumer products company Braun in 1955. In 1961 he became head of design there and remained in the post until 1995. During that time, he and his team designed some of the most well-known domestic electrical products of the 20th century, including radios, cameras, stereos, kitchen appliances, lighters and shavers. Parallel to this, he also designed furniture for a small company called Vitsœ + Zapf (now Vitsœ), some of which is still in production to this day. Rams is best known for his Ten Principles of Good Design: 1) Good design is innovative; 2) Good design makes a product useful; 3) Good design is aesthetic; 4) Good design makes a product understandable; 5) Good design is honest; 6) Good design is unobtrusive; 7) Good design is long-lasting; 8) Good design is thorough down to the last detail; 9) Good design is environmentally friendly; 10) Good design is as little design as possible. Although they were first conceived in the 1970s, and despite dramatic advances in technology, these rules still hold true for design and designers today.

↰ Chair Programme by Dieter Rams for Vitsoe (ID595). © Vitsoe.

→ Sophie Lovell in conversation with Dieter Rams, 2018. Photo by Gary Hustwit.

SOPHIE LOVELL Design is a relatively young discipline. How much understanding of 'design' in industry was there when you started your career?

DIETER RAMS There were very few firms, in my opinion, who really took design seriously. When I started at Braun in 1955, the most notable firms were Herman Miller, Knoll, Wohnbedarf in Zürich and Olivetti. Back then in Germany, Braun was making design history more than any others, more than Siemens, more than Rosenthal.

SL Industrial design was already an established entity by the 1950s, the Bauhaus, the Deutscher Werkbund, for example.

DR Yes, and naturally they were points of orientation. Despite their internal quarrelling, the Werkbund did have an influence, but in my opinion, it was far more the Ulm School of Design that became the successor to the Bauhaus. Max Bill was the first director there and he studied at the Bauhaus under Kandinsky, Klee and Schlemmer—so he was closer to it than the others who came later.

SL The school didn't last long though, did it? Only 15 years or so, from 1953-1968.

DR That's a whole story in itself. The school only existed until the mid-1960s. It got so involved in theory that it pretty much lost the connection to practice. Then there was student unrest in the 1960s, and the local government was not too keen on the whole thing so it stopped the funding. There were lots of reasons why it did not continue. The only really lasting things they achieved were the projects they were able to realise with industry, such as Otl Aicher's (co-founder of the Ulm School) work with Lufthansa and Braun. Hans Gugelot, who designed for Braun, also designed a carousel slide projector for Kodak, and so on.

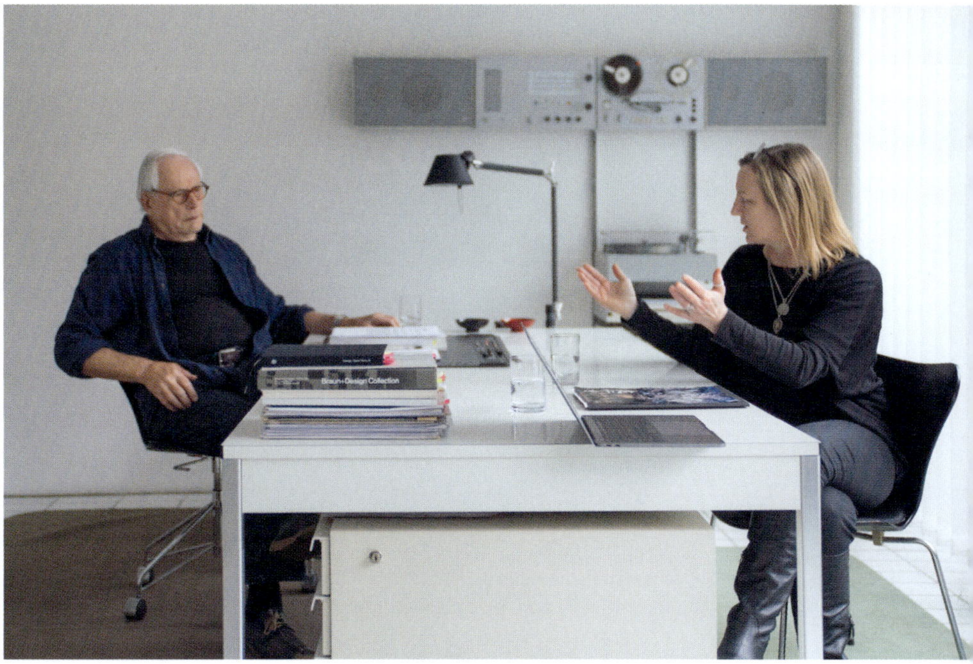

SL Nevertheless, Ulm design gave a decisive impulse to Braun.

DR Absolutely, Ulm was significantly important for the company. I was already on the same wavelength. My credo back then was to realise things as simply as possible—it's something I had already learned that when I was doing architecture. For me personally, Ulm was just a continuation of that. It was very important for the Braun brothers (Erwin and Artur, who took over as heads of the company after their father's death in 1951), who had decided to approach things differently.

SL In the second half of the twentieth century, the term 'German Design' came to represent good quality, practicality and functionality. All things that Braun products typified during your time there.

DR You mustn't forget that German design development was interrupted. It began at the beginning of the twentieth century with Peter Behrens and the founding of the Werkbund. It was then interrupted by World War I, slowly came back in the 1920s with Bauhaus etc., and was then interrupted again in 1933 because the National Socialists didn't like it. Then again there was another difficult beginning, reimported via Gropius and Mies from the US. The thread that has held through all this, from the Bauhaus in particular, is the social component. German design has always had a social aspect.

SL Was this was also true of German architecture?

DR Yes. A number of architects went to Russia after the war, they believed in the social aspect, in the promise of communism. Many of the designers around at the time were left wing too.

SL Braun was also very connected to architecture, wasn't it? Braun objects were exhibited in modern apartments of the 1950s' International Building Exhibition (Interbau) in Berlin as part of an effort to show people how to live in a new, modern, 'democratic' way that was so very different from what had been before.

DR Yes of course! It was 1957! I remember going there. It was my first flight in an airplane. We flew over Berlin and it still lay half in ruins. Then suddenly, in the middle of it all, was the Interbau. It was incredible. There were the first patio houses, buildings by Le Corbusier, Jacobsen, Niemeyer and all the others. Large windows, fitted kitchens, underfloor heating. And the new interiors were restrained, they were not encrusted and overloaded like before, and the way they were furnished put the life of the inhabitants more in the foreground.

SL Another German designer, a contemporary of yours, Gunter Kupetz quoted Charles Eames

'Designers, architects and all those working in the applied arts do not work in a vacuum.'

DIETER RAMS

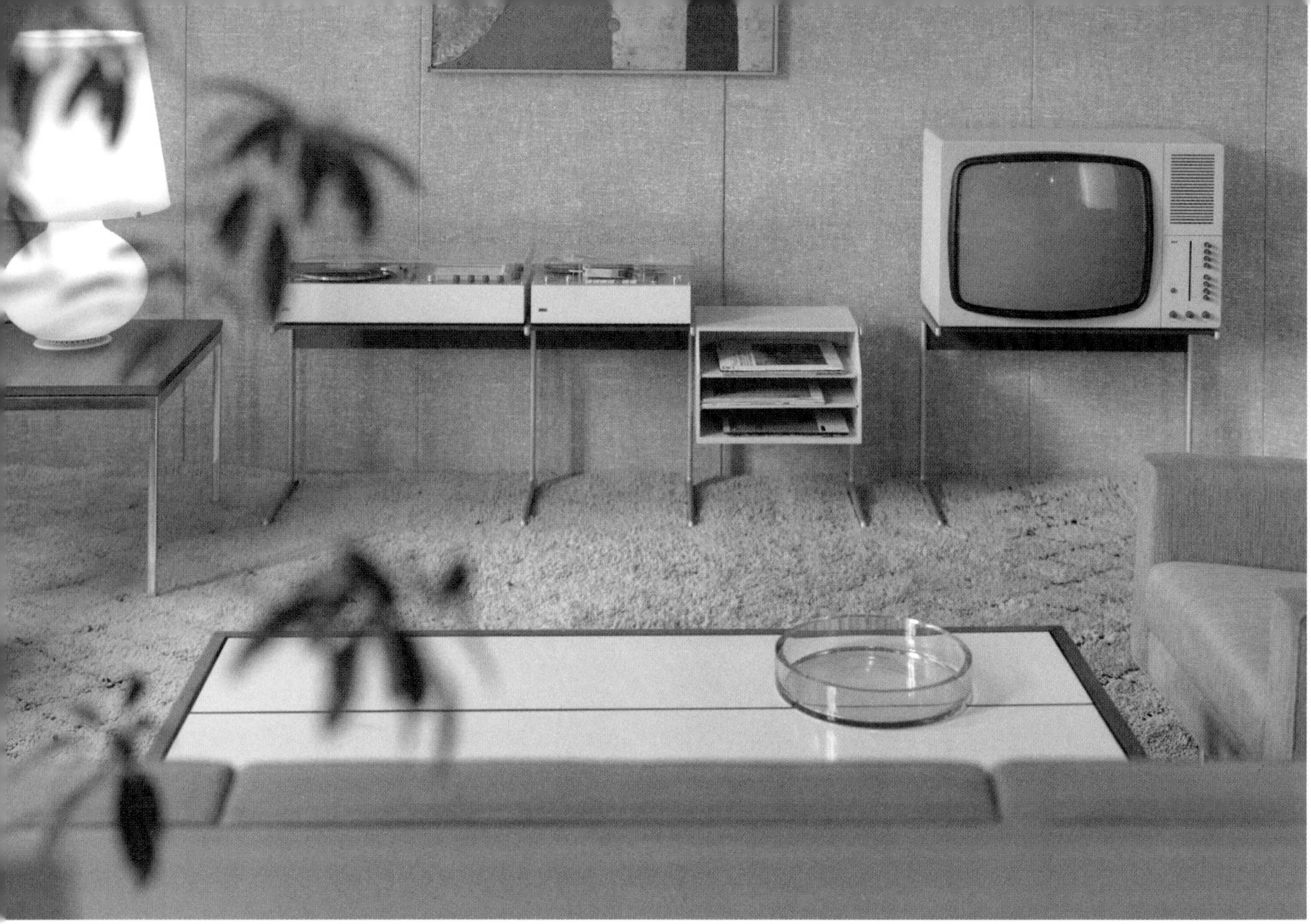

↖ Compact music system audio 2 (1964), tape recorder TG 60 (1965), TV FS 600 (1966) on stand system (1967), design by Dieter Rams.

↘ Compact music system with record player audio 2 (1964) and loudspeaker L 450 (1965), design Dieter Rams, 1964.

to me once, who said: 'Design should bring the most of the best to the greatest number of people for the least'. Would you agree?

DR I greatly admire Charles Eames, he was one of the best designers ever—but I imagine that he was more influenced by the material side, than the social. The situation was very different in the US to here back then. They also had more money available—for moulds and experimenting, for example. Interestingly, Eames came to new ways of shaping plywood through the design of medical leg splints for the military in World War II.

SL Who do you believe is responsible for the quality of the products that are available to buy in the shops? Just the manufacturer, or the designer as well?

DR Always both—together. Designers, architects and all those working in the applied arts do not work in a vacuum. We are dependent either upon the client or the company when it comes to realising our designs, and there are also certain limits: we can only do what the respective company is able to do. There is constant discussion and interpolation.

SL You have been concerned with sustainability and the environment, with respect to design for quite some time, haven't you?

DR Yes, always really. I haven't really moved from my original position—of reducing things to the essentials—so in that respect, the ecological aspect was always included. It has increasingly preoccupied me since leaving Braun. The situation has become more pressing, so I have concerned myself with it more intensely.

SL You once proposed the idea, quite some time ago, that products should remain the property, or responsibility, of the manufacturer and that when they break, or their usefulness is over, the manufacturers should take them back and either mend or recycle them.

DR Yes, but that never happened, it was just an idea.

SL In general though, this principle of yours, that 'good design should be long-lasting' and easy to repair actually goes against the interests of your employer—the manufacturer—doesn't it? How did you balance that with the company's goals?

DR Of course it does, but I was really fortunate in that I was able to inspire people, either from the company side or the technical side, and they inspired

'We have to be much better at learning from our mistakes, not just making the same ones over and over again.'

DIETER RAMS

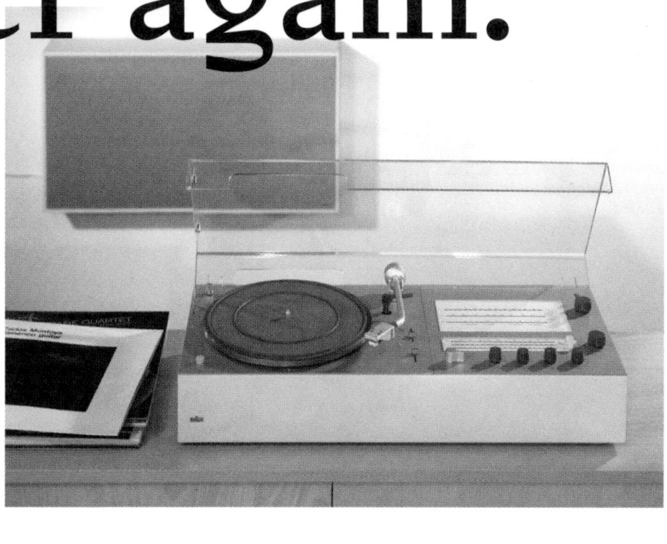

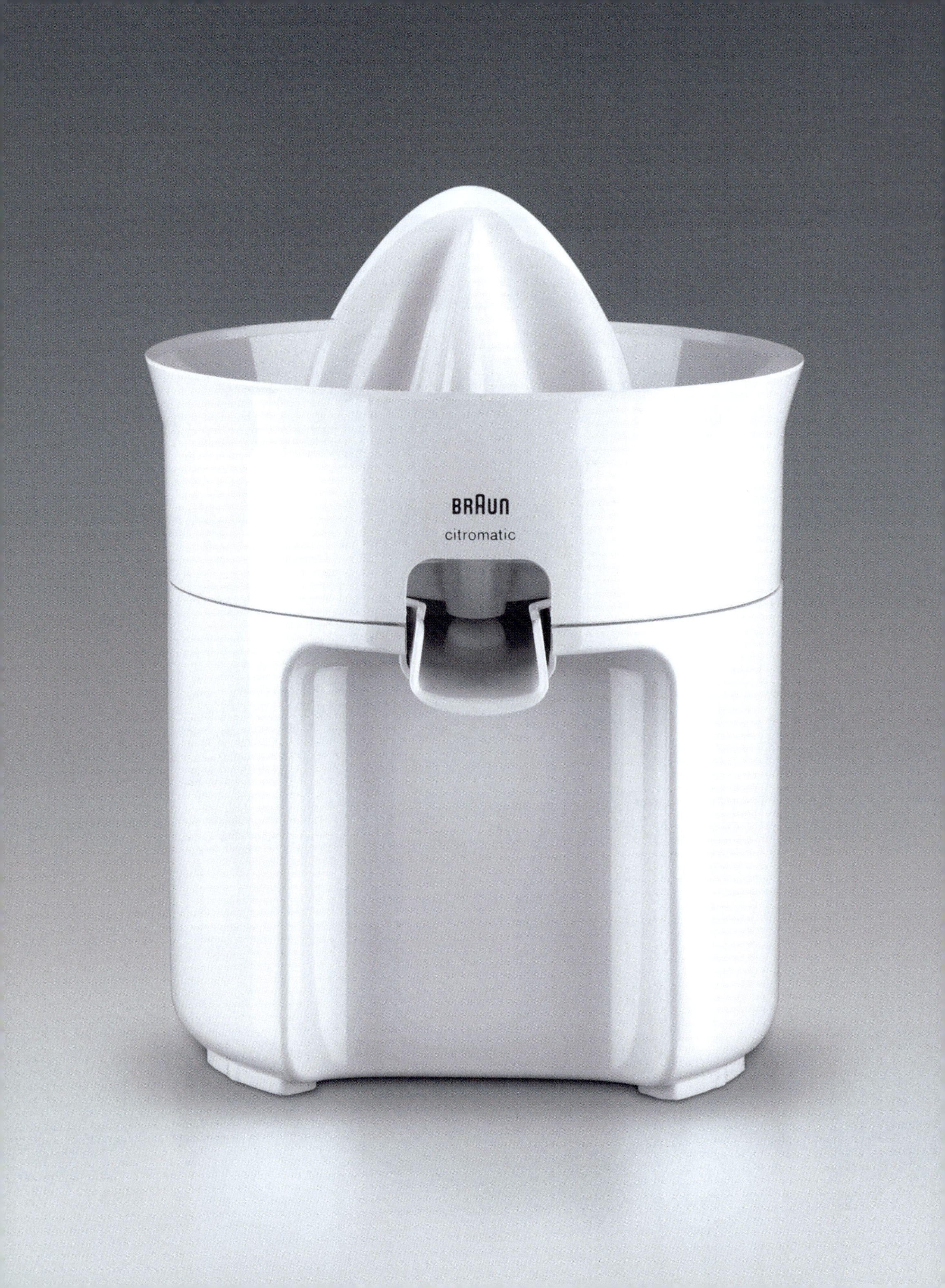
BRAUN
citromatic

me in return. That is also something fundamental. That wasn't your question was it?

SL I mean this tendency towards built-in obsolescence in manufacturing, of actively making products with a limited lifespan as a strategy in order to make customers buy more and more often.

DR It was an issue, but it was an idea that horrified, not just me, but Erwin and Artur Braun in their time as well. Take so-called 'American styling', which was well-known at the time, automobiles with chrome grilles and tailfins and so on. The intention there was clear: stimulating a desire to buy through superficial attraction. This was something we didn't want at Braun. Of course we wanted to sell our products, but we believed there was a different way.

SL Longevity through good design? You believed that would sell products?

DR Good design should be useful. The Braun 'Citromatic' MPZ electric citrus juicer, for example (designed together with Jürgen Greubel), was first developed in 1972 and produced in a Braun factory in Barcelona for the Spanish market. At the time there were importing restrictions in Spain and I was there quite often. A while later, I realised that almost every tapas bar in Barcelona had one on the counter. This was because you could press the juice directly into a glass, which was an innovation of ours, the juicer did not drip and was easy to clean. The citrus press remained in production for years. They were still making it when I left the design department in 1995. It was an unbelievably long-lived product.

SL Do you think retrospectively that your collective attitude at Braun was one that helped both save and make the reputation of German design? And is this why 'Made in Germany' came to be a catchphrase for quality and long-lasting products? Back in the late-19th century, when the term was coined by the British government it meant exactly the opposite.

DR Yes of course. I think, too, that the future of the German economy depends on it. I refer here to Germany as a brand. You can compare the individual states to big companies and, in this respect, I regret a great deal that politics does not concern itself more with design. Politicians are essentially businessmen in a global sense. It is a competition and the best are those who profit the most. You can't just follow a single line anymore. It only works together. With new technical ideas, for example, but always in combination with design—design in the sense that it has this social aspect and a cultural part as well.

We must not take the path towards superficiality; towards everything and nothing. People try and excuse this with zeitgeist; I think we have to keep things a lot longer. It's all about usefulness and durability. In the end, we are all responsible for our work and responsible for our environment.

SL Let's talk about aesthetics.

DR For me the aesthetic quality of a product is an aspect of its usability. It is about relieving the object from ballast and making the chaos in which we are forced to live somewhat more bearable—through simplicity.

SL Would you say that aesthetics and simplicity belong together for you?

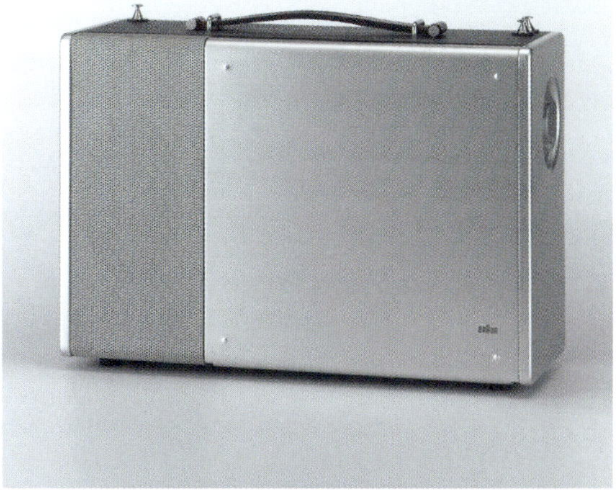

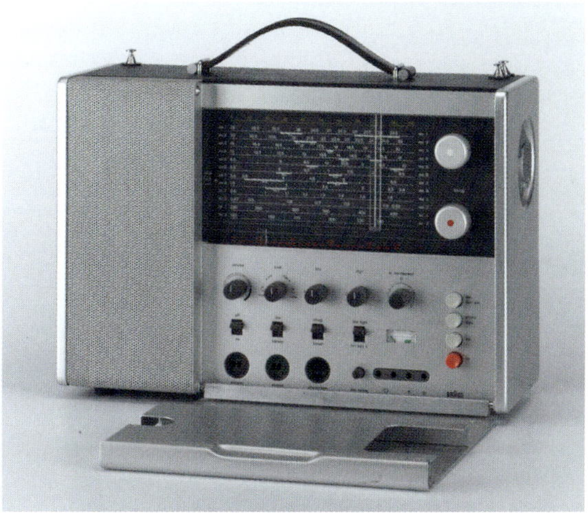

↗ Multi-band radio T 1000 CD, design by Dieter Rams, 1967.

← Juicer MPZ 22 citromatic, design Dieter Rams and Jürgen Greubel, 1972/1994.

DR Absolutely. Aesthetics is not about adding some ornamental bits and pieces that had some kind of historical role once upon a time—like with postmodernism. That is a false understanding of aesthetics. Simplicity, in my opinion, can exert a fascination. Take the Apple iPod, for example, it signalises simplicity through form, and that happens far too rarely. The combination of designer and businessman with Steve Jobs and Jony Ive was amazing, they must have both sought and found one another. There was nothing like them for miles around.

SL What is it about you, do you think, that has given you this consistency of vision in your career—your stubbornness?

DR The career of an architect is not a normal one, it is more a calling. You become so convinced of something that you also try to see through what you think is right. The same was true of my time at Braun. In the first three months I was only occupied with my role as an architect there. There too I had to prove myself, to assert myself, because that was my livelihood. Then when I moved to industrial design, I had to prove myself again because I had never worked in that field before. I was used to hard work from my previous job with Otto Appel architects. When we had a competition project running, we worked really hard—through the night if necessary. When I started at Braun I thought: 'What are they doing here? They don't work, they just mess around and are always having parties just because they need to promote themselves'. I had to assert myself there as well.

SL Fame reached you very early in your career with Braun. How did you deal with it? Were you aware that you were becoming so well-known?

DR I didn't really think about it to be honest. That's not what it felt like. Back then we were named as the designers in the catalogues, me along with the others. I was named as the designer of the SK-4 phonograph (which had a revolutionary Perspex lid) along with Hans Gugelot from the Ulm School. Then I was automatically named on projects as Braun began to win prizes for its design and when its products were added to the collection of the Museum of Modern Art (MoMA) in New York, for example. When I became head of the Braun design department in 1961, I was named even more often and so I became 'successful'. I wasn't really aware of it except when my colleagues pointed out that I kept being mentioned everywhere.

↗ Table by Dieter Rams for Vitsoe (ID233).© Vitsoe.

→ Universal Shelving System by Dieter Rams for Vitsoe (ID5843). © Vitsoe.

SL Were there other famous designers you met back then who had left a particular impression on you?

DR Buckminster Fuller, I was really excited by him. I will never forget hearing him for the first time at the International Design Conference in Aspen around 1967 or 1968. A large number of American designers, along with lots of young European ones, came to hear him speak. Fuller talked for four hours straight and you could have heard a pin drop in the room, the whole time. It was a fantastic experience.

SL He was one of the first who really began to express concerns about the planet then, wasn't he?

DR Yes, the whole conference was strongly influenced by what was later to become a big issue. Back then it was only the very beginning of the protests against pollution. The beginning of this call to look at what we were doing to our landscape was there and there were amazing people discussing it.

SL I have the feeling that there was not a great deal of concern in the West towards the end of the 1950s and beginning of the 1960s about pollution, or that we might run out of anything. There was plenty of oil, plenty of water.

DR Not really, the problems were apparent back then—that's why there was this conference. We were also already talking about recycling. We already knew that an industry that was capable of production was also capable of taking things back, the question was: how? How to create the loop. Even today we are not really on the right path with this. Perhaps if they had worked it out together with designers more and not just politicians we would have less pollution now. In the meantime we know more forms of waste treatment are possible, but the problem is still acute and better design solutions are still possible.

SL Do you still believe that good design can make a good society?

DR Yes, but we need much more. We have to be much better at learning from our mistakes, not just making the same ones over and over again. I suppose one would have to be a politician in order to enforce change, but I still believe that there must be a way that involves better and more intensive collaboration between industry, politics and design. Design cannot do it alone. There is still a lot to do and there are also many ways to do it—to change society as well. The Bauhaus tried to do this; the Ulm School too, as representatives of the Bauhaus and with the help of a masterplan and money they had a mandate—and they understood it as a mandate—to change our society. It absolutely worked at the beginning, but unfortunately tore itself to pieces, if I can put it like that.

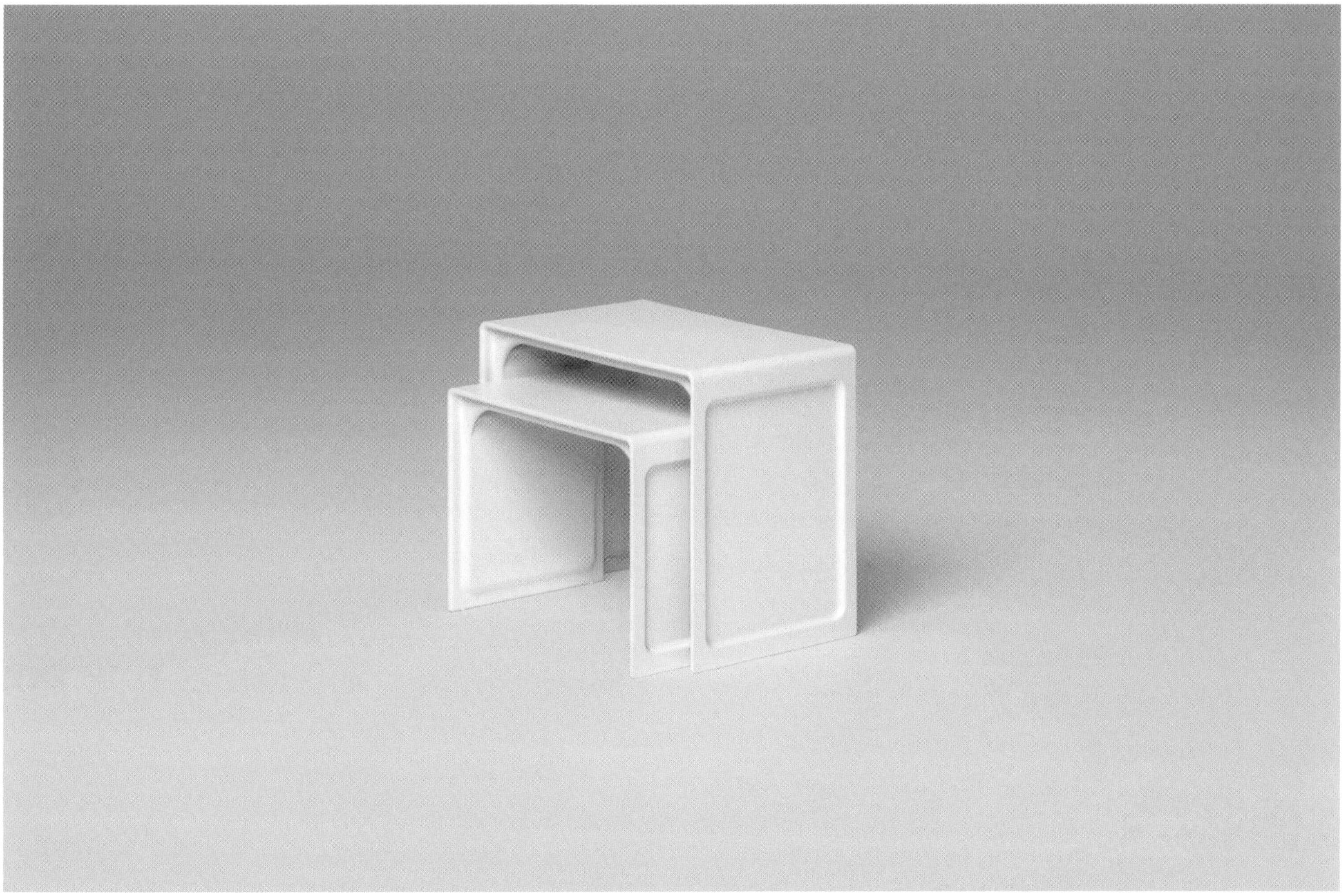

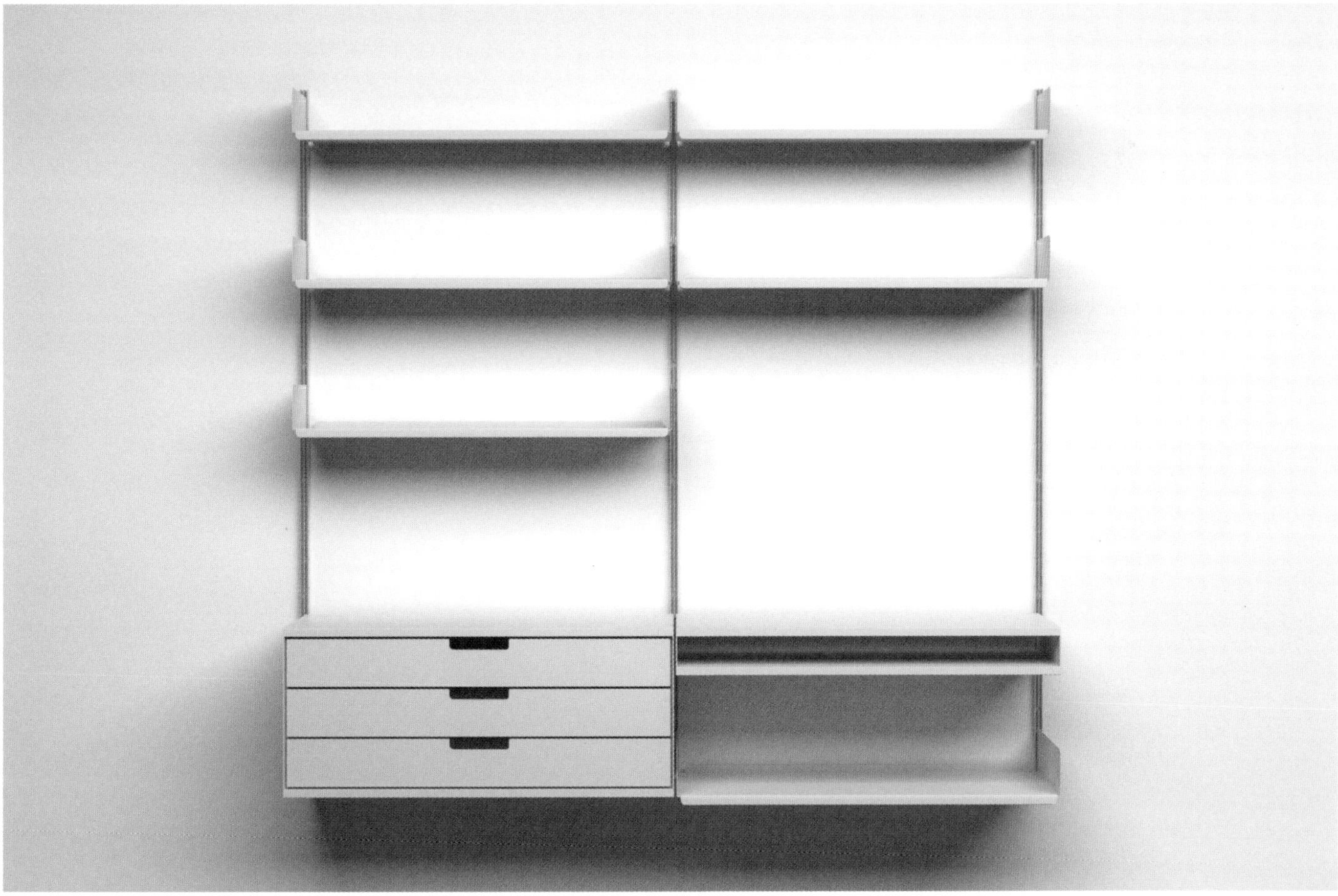

> 'Design is a field full of responsibility and this responsibility will become greater in the future.
>
> DIETER RAMS

SL How do you feel about being called the incarnation of German Design?

DR This statement is wildly exaggerated. I mean, I really don't see it that way in connection with myself. I am only a co-representative. Of course I am happy to be called, as you once wrote so nicely, 'the designer's designer'. I see that there are some who think in a similar way or in similar directions such as Jasper Morrison or Naoto Fukasawa, but above all Jonathan Ive. It is of course the best thing that can happen for a designer, to get a letter from someone like him that says that things that I have written have influenced him. For me that is a great compliment.

SL Someone once said that you make 'furniture machines' rather than furniture. What would you say to that?

DR Yes, that is where the problem begins: 'cold like machines'. People have said that my furniture is for hospitals, offices etc. It is a prejudice that you can only disperse by example, not with words or pictures.

SL Does one have to buy into the 'lifestyle' when one decides to buy and live with your furniture?

DR For heaven's sake no! I hate this word 'lifestyle'. Good things always go together. They just have to all be good. You notice at once if something isn't if you have even a modicum of sensitivity. A lot depends on the quality of details, but also on education—the qualities and differences between materials has to be learned. The difference between what is real and what is a copy has to be taught.

SL Where does personal style come into it for the user?

DR I have nothing against personality, but that has nothing to do with style.

SL You hate it when your style of design is described as functional though, don't you?

DR I have always been against all kinds of '-isms', I have always rejected the idea of a so-called 'Braun style', and I have always rejected the use of the term 'functionalism' as if functionality were a style. There will always be functionality, but functionalism is not a style. I don't like the term 'style' either; or this whole thing about 'trends'. All these new styles that keep coming up—to hell with all these trends!

SL Do you mean that functionality, as in technical considerations, should dictate the design than the ego of the designer?

DR Exactly. One forgets so easily that a good redesign, for example, can be so much better than designing something completely new. That's not because the new can sometimes repel us, but because it tries to be ahead of its time, but often isn't. Good redesign is urgently necessary for many things, but sadly not spectacular enough for the media. I am, in this respect, very conservative. Products can be revolting, like people, but they are not even people or even artworks—although some people would like to make them so. Design should allocate products to the right places in our lives. These products should be as neutral and modest as possible and allow the user space in which to express themselves—they should be something natural and that is where they should stay.

SL Design is still such a very young discipline in so many ways; barely a century old. In fact, much of the evolution of what we understand to be design has occurred in your lifetime. What do you think has been learned and will need to be remembered in the future?

DR I hope it has become clear that design is a field full of responsibility and that this responsibility will become greater in the future. For the value and legitimacy of design will be measured in the future by the contribution it has made to our continued survival on this planet.

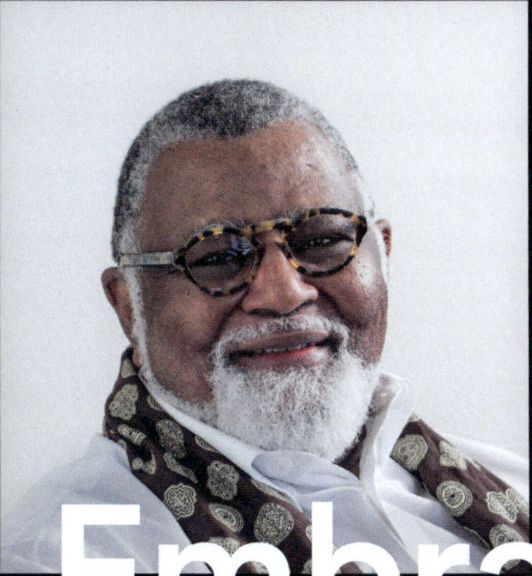

Embracing the Awareness of the World's Many Cultural Avenues

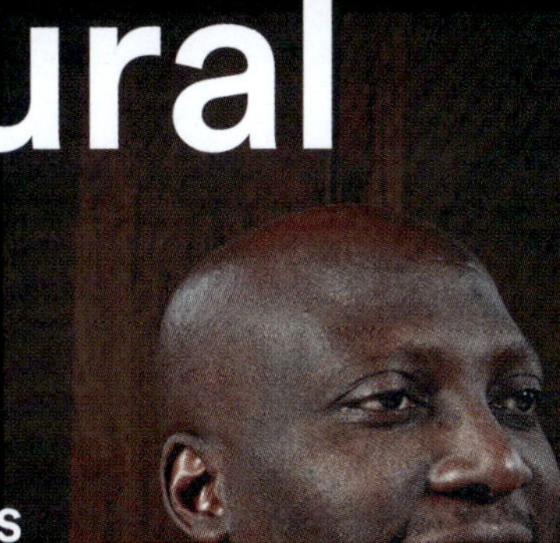

Kunlé Adeyemi and Alexander Smalls

Nigerian architect, designer and urban researcher KUNLÉ ADEYEMI talks to Harlem-based restaurateur, opera singer and author ALEXANDER SMALLS about the role of music and food, the food ways of the African diaspora and the legacy of Harlem in past, present and future.

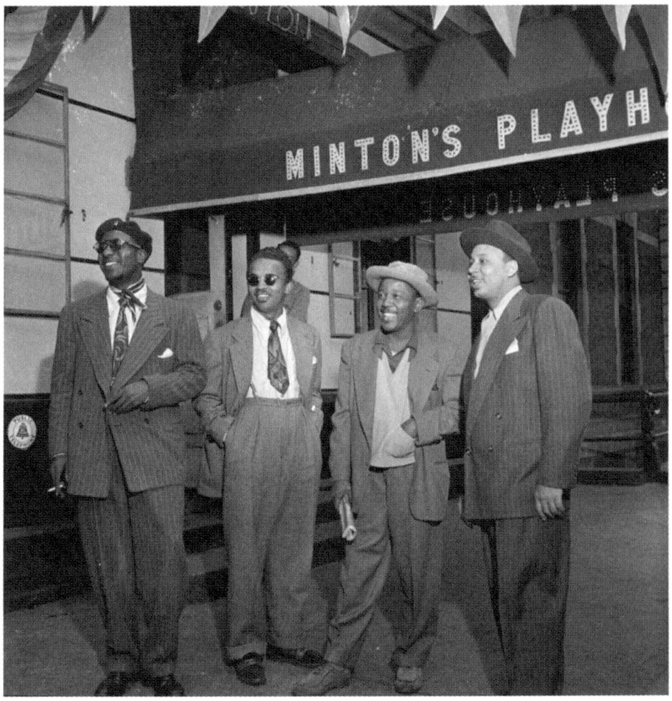

KUNLÉ ADEYEMI A Where do we start? There are so many questions I would like to explore with you regarding the topic of legacy. Your background is both in music and cooking. You are a world-renowned opera singer and the winner of both a Grammy Award and a Tony Award for the cast recording of *Porgy and Bess* by George Gershwin with the Houston Grand Opera. You were also the visionary of the award-winning restaurant The Cecil and its sister restaurant Minton's in New York, serving as its co-owner and Executive Chef.

Tell me more about your upbringing—where you grew up and the role music and food played in your childhood?

ALEXANDER SMALLS I grew up in a loving family—three sisters, my parents and a host of intruding extended family. We lived in an average-size town in the North-Western part of the state of South Carolina. It was a modest home in what was the first somewhat affluent community of Black professionals. They were middle class families with manicured lawns, gardens and new cars in every driveway. My grandfather, who was a farmer, had moved the family to Spartanburg from Charleston, South Carolina before I was born, in search of a new life and opportunities. The first thing I noticed as a boy growing up was that my family ate differently from my friends and neighbours. It was not only the kinds of foods we ate that were different, but the importance we placed upon meals, fellowship and family around mealtime was also different. Understanding the geographic and cultural differences between what we called Low Country (Charleston, Beaufort and The Gullah Islands), verses Up Country (northern party of the state), Spartanburg, Greenville area, lead me to realize the power of ones' cultural region and traditions over an adopted location.

Once our health and wellbeing were addressed, individually and as a family, food was the most important subject we dealt with daily. It seemed we got up from one meal while planning the next. It was not just what to eat but how—where should it come from? The supermarket or grandpa's garden or independent markets? Often, we shopped at butchers where you always found farmers and lots of people telling stories—they were just sitting around signifying and calling neighbours out for various things they'd heard or claimed to have seen them do. These people seemed to know everything about everybody. They also knew how to cook whatever you were buying and owned a recipe like it was a badge of excellence. I was fascinated with food and with those who cooked it. It didn't take much to understand that the person who cooked had all the power—this is what I wanted for myself. I started my culinary interest by helping my mum cook, and helping anybody else who would allow me. I loved turning on that gas stove and directing the flame to the metal pot full of goodness. My mother had a rule: if you liked something and wanted it too often, you had to learn to make it yourself. In my case, this rule served her well. Food was like gold—the fuller the larder the richer we were. I saw food as currency and I loved spending it—yes!

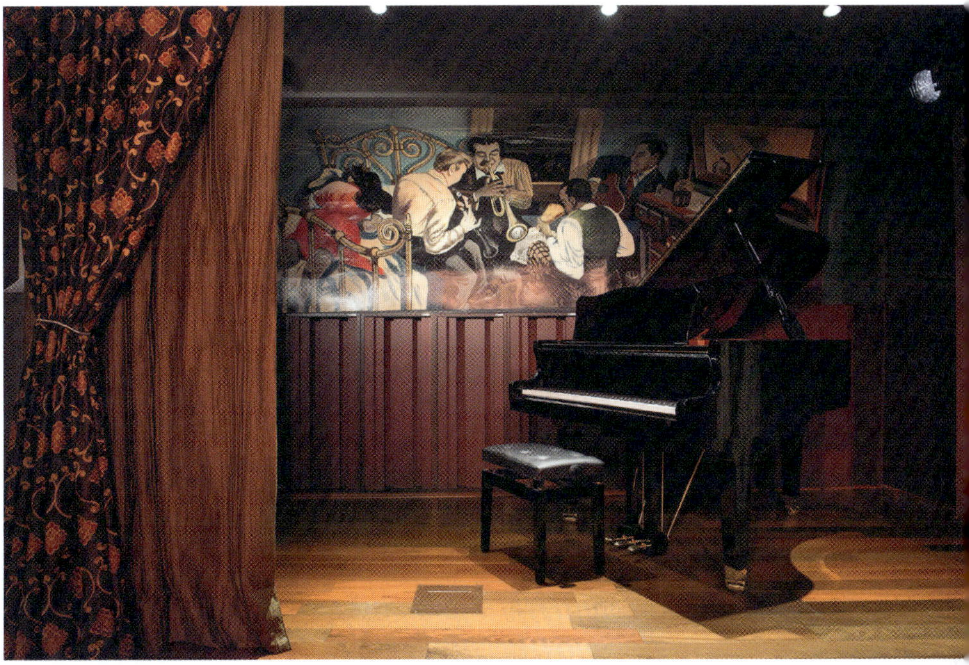

At around age seven I had exhausted my toy trunk and for my birthday I got my first piano—this became my life line. I loved music from birth and nothing had a stronger effect on me than music. Seeing a professional artist of any kind performing on television or the occasional live performance was intriguing and captivating. I would imitate them as if I were in a trance, caught up in the dynamic of their creative energy, imagining myself as the object of their musical expression. I wanted to own and feel the power and command of performance. I knew I was an artist in training.

Music changed my life. It not only fed my soul and spirit, but for a long time it also gave me my identity. Studying classical music, and later opera, made me bigger than life to everyone around me. There weren't many little black boys of colour running around my town singing in foreign languages at three times louder than most people argued. Music was my refuge, my safe place and it rewarded me and gave my uniqueness a safe space.

KA You have spent decades traveling the world and studying the cooking techniques, cultures and 'food-ways' of the African diaspora. Through the course of your travels, you developed a unique insight and passion for the influence of the migrating people of Africa and how, through their culinary efforts, they changed the palette of our global expression. Could you elaborate on the cultural and culinary legacy of the African diaspora? Did West Africa and its cuisines have any particular influences on you?

AS Through my travels I first observed the African communities in Europe, particularly in France, England and Italy where many African and Caribbean immigrants lived and celebrated their cultures almost definitely. There I was, introduced to the ways, the foods, art and lifestyle of the African people—mostly West African. Living in Paris as a young opera singer I befriended a West Indian friend from Martinique who exposed me to a smart, talented, well-educated group of West Indian and African professionals. They were all world travellers who spoke several languages and embraced their awareness of the world's many cultural avenues and countries with ease, dignity and grace. The differ-

↰ Portrait of Alexander Smalls. Photo by Beatriz da Costa.

↰ Portrait of Kunlé Adeyemi. Photo by Mark Horn.

↖ Thelonious Monk, Howard McGhee, Roy Eldridge, and Teddy Hill, Minton's Playhouse, New York, USA,1947. Photo by William P. Gottlieb. Source: United States Library of Congress's Music Division.

↗ Piano and mural at Minton's Jazz and Supper Club. Photo by Evan Sung.

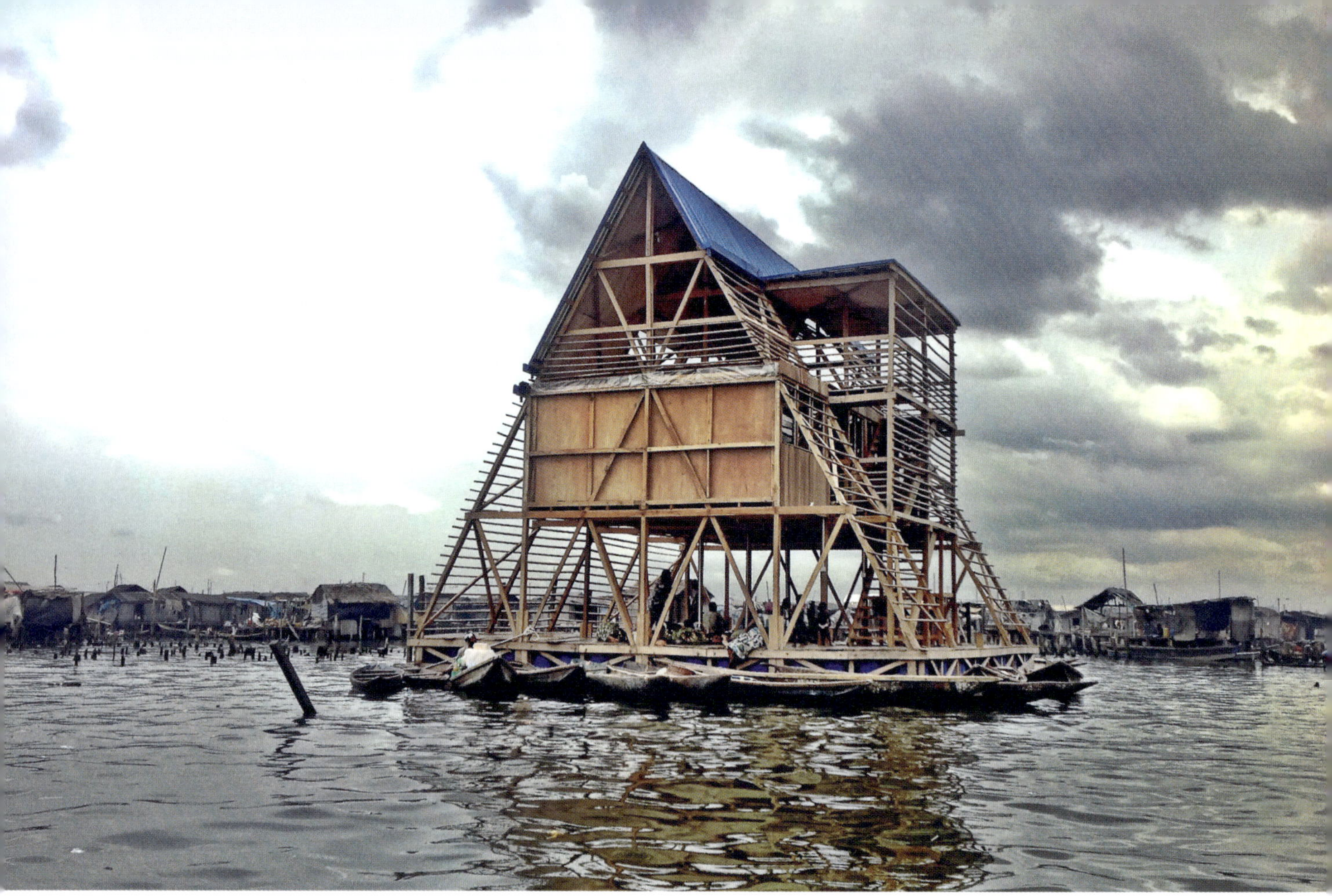

ence between them and me is that I only considered myself American, while they were globetrotters, citizens of the world and they owned that distinction. It was a feeling, a mindset and an awareness of life I wanted, too. I also began to recognize the culinary practices of my new friends, and ways of cooking that were much like those of my family. It was similar to the way my father's parents from Charleston, South Carolina cooked. It occurred to me that through food I could trace the steps of my culinary heritage, mirroring who I was culturally through the great link I shared with other people of African descent. In the most innocent way, in search of my global identity I began to search for myself in the the foodways of the African Diaspora. With every African country, which led to Asia, South and North America, every bite I took became my journey. Though I would first travel to North Africa, then South Africa, and eventually West Africa would be the cradle by which I found the heart of myself and the foods of my heritage.

KA Your latest book *Between Harlem and Heaven* follows that thought and is basically a culinary journey through space and time that started more than 400 years ago. It's a testimony to the fact that food transcends borders. Can you tell me about the making of this book?

AS The book is a testimonial to the foodways of the forced migration of enslaved African people and their contribution to the culinary arts—it's a history through food. It is my interpretation of their influences on global culinary, how—through slavery—they created and transformed world cuisine. I think of it as the silver lining—the one true expression, the heart, soul and spirit of amazing people who endured so much. I see their humanity living in these pots and pans, their culinary offerings of love and nurturing, how they continue to feed the world. If there could be a new culinary language, a discipline that captures the essence of their best, it would be captured in these recipes is my hope.

KA As reputably the first Afro-Asian-American brasserie in the world, could you elaborate in how far these lessons also informed the foundation of your Harlem based restaurant? What was it like in the beginning and how has it change since then?

AS I spent a lot of time thinking of what Afro Asian American cooking meant, what it entailed as an

← NLÉ, Makoko Floating School, Lagos, Nigeria, 2012. The Makoko Floating School is a prototype floating structure, built for the historic water community of Makoko, located on the lagoon heart of Nigeria's largest city, Lagos. © NLÉ.

↘ Longshot of Alexander Smalls' award-winning restaurant The Cecil. Photo by Lucy Schaeffer.

idea. Looking at the slave routes and the far range of African influence on five continents, I needed an expression that didn't tax or overwhelm people but was also accurate in its description and appeal. Afro Asian American encompassed the weight of what was needed to express and experience the intent while being relatable and all-inclusive. The Cecil Restaurant, located in and named for the famed and legendary Cecil Hotel, which houses Minton's Playhouse, is the birthplace of Bebop and where all the African American great jazz and performing artist used to stay. It is also a national treasure in the heart of Harlem. Harlem is considered the global epicentre of Black culture and an important historical hub for people of the African Diaspora and legendary advances for People of Colour. Creating this restaurant in the centre of this cultural community was a no-brainier. Harlem has earned its status and importance in the annuals of Black history in the world.

KA The choice of Harlem for your restaurants is significant. In 2014 you were even awarded with the Legacy Award by *The Amsterdam News*, one of the oldest African American newspapers in the US, for regenerating the Harlem Renaissance constantly through your work. Could you explain what you see as the legacy of Harlem in past, present and future?

AS That is a huge question that really deserves its own chapter. Hopefully I address parts of this question in other questions as well. Let me first say also in 2014 The Cecil was awarded by *Esquire Magazine*, The best new restaurant in America. This award highlighted The Cecil's uniqueness, great food and its innovated style of food preparation and passionate culinary revolution. Harlem's legacy is having been a rich and important container for Black life and evolution from slavery until now. It was the largest slave market, rivalled only by Charleston, South Carolina—both very important life canvases for me. Harlem was truly the most important international community for the evolution of Black life in America and the world

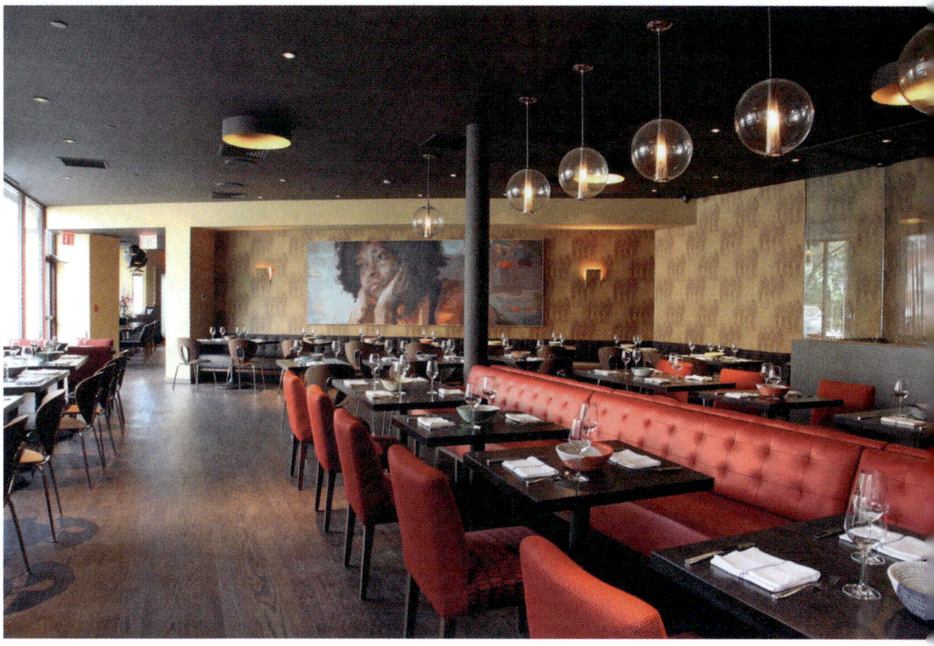

Harlem has always been one of the best barometers and stages for Black life seen through the lens of education, artistic expression, human rights and food arts. From the Harlem Renaissance to the civil rights movement and financial power and advancement. There is no more perfect place from which to advance the cause and regard, in this case of food, than my beloved Harlem.

KA Can you tell me about your work as board member and Artistic Director of Opus 118 at the Harlem School of Music?

AS I was asked to join the board and I did so rather reluctantly. Not because I didn't believe in the work they did but I have always had issues with belonging to organized groups or initiatives that required maintenance and constant attention. Despite my reservations after meeting the president of the board, I agreed, and after a year of service she decided to retire and named me her successor. Reeling from shock, I proceeded like someone with something to prove. The students were Black and Brown kids from the humble communities of Harlem, for the most part. I was on hiatus from opening and running restaurants and the organization I inherited was mostly run by a White board of perfectly nice people, but I felt that I needed to reengage and build a board that reflected the kids we served. I felt it would better address their needs.

I was dedicated and felt an enormous fulfilment campaigning and providing leadership that

> **'Harlem has earned its status and importance in the annuals of Black history in the world.'**
>
> ALEXANDER SMALLS

I was determined would make a difference. Then the unthinkable happened—as chairman of the board I had to fire the head of the school, and since we had no money I found myself being the new director, running the entire operation. I was successful in maintaining the financial aid already in place as well as raising a lot more money from various foundations and private donors, serving the needs of the school, creating performance possibilities for the kids was a constant desire. I was proud of my work at the school. Inspiring talented young people who, through the arts, were getting an opportunity to learn artistic skills that would define so much of their lives, and because of the kids, their families were being lifted. They were engaged and educated about a new consciousness. We were changing the lives of families, providing hope and allowing them to discover the excitement of feeding dreams that matter. It was a special time in my life I will always treasure.

KA You have an incredible network or great people. What or who has been the greatest inspiration for what you are doing?

AS The list is long for a myriad of reasoning. I have been fortunate throughout my career to have met and known some of the most interesting and extraordinary, talented, intelligent and mindful people I could have hoped for. People whom I truly value and sincerely treasure—truly far too many to name, so I won't. I can tell you that there have been a few mentors, great family examples and champions, close friends who've held me up and supported me through the best of times and the alternative. I have been blessed with the gift of long term enablers, companions that encourage me and root and cheer me on in life. I can certainly say, aside from my parents, my uncle Joe, who was a chef in NYC for many years and his wife aunt Laura, who upon my birth, hearing that a son had finally been born, left New York and moved back home to South Carolina, to help shape the new lion in the family—me. They were my cultural and artistic mentors and teachers. Aunt Laura taught me piano and music expression while uncle Joe taught me how to cook and to dream with no limits. My most important years were shaped so much by this very important relationship. As a young child, well into my formative years I was intensely close to them and was influenced by their love for the arts, literature, food and cooking. I know without a doubt had they not given so much of themselves to me, my life would have been very different to say the least. They totally shaped me and prepared me to be the person that I am today.

KA What are your most memorable moments and encounters throughout your career?

AS Firstly, discovering the miracle and complete satisfaction of my own personal power, that I had the ability to create value, command interest, attention and deliver what people wanted more of—that was very satisfying to me; being chosen to give the commencement speech from elementary school

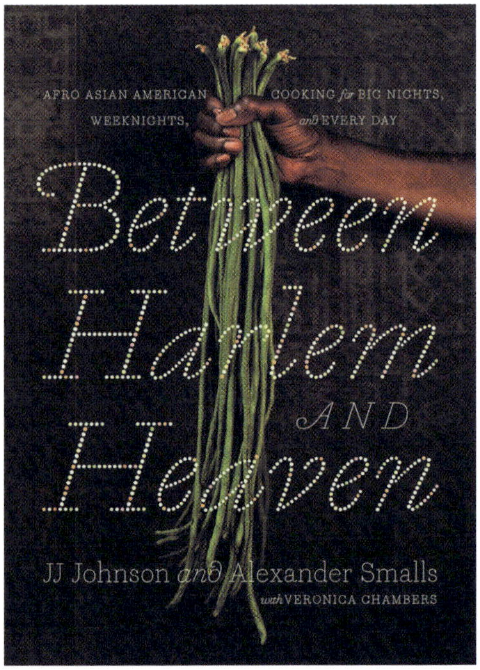

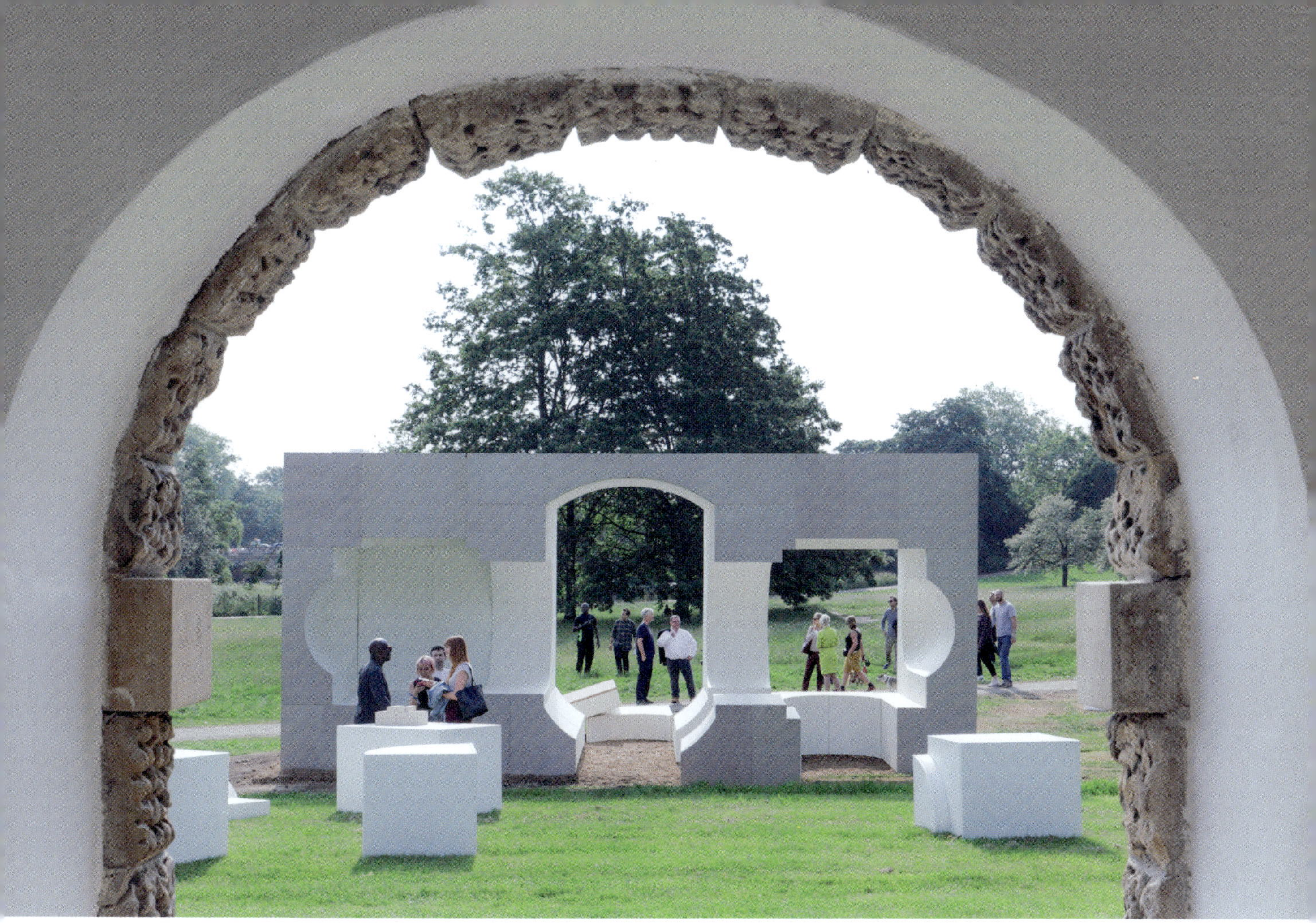

↑ NLÉ, Serpentine Summer House, London, 2016. A space for shelter and relaxation. The design is based on projecting an inverse replica of the historic Queen Carline's Temple. © NLÉ and Iwan Baan.

↙ Alexander Smalls and JJ Johnson, *Between Harlem and Heaven: Afro-Asian-American Cooking for Big Nights, Weeknights, and Every Day*, Flatiron Books, 2018.

was probably the first major moment. In junior high, I was selected to sing for the high school chorus and given solos at 14, beating out upper-class men much older than me. While in graduate school, being selected and given a principal role in The Houston Grand Opera production of Porgy and Bess on Broadway resulting in a Grammy and a Tony award for the first recording of the complete opera. Years later I would celebrate the opening of my first restaurant, Café Beulah and my first book, *Grace the Table*. I would open four more restaurants, the fourth being The Cecil which was voted best new restaurant in America by Esquire Magazine in 2014. I wrote another book: *Between Harlem and Heaven,* in 2018 and yet another book in 2019, *The Essential African American Cookbook*. Still, there is so much more to do.

KA What has been the best advice you've ever been given?

AS 'If you love what you do, you will never have a job in your life." My Grandfather—Ed Smalls

KA What do you want your legacy to be?

AS That I was here. That I cared and that life mattered. That I gave my best, my all and that I was present, here to make a difference and that I contributed to the human condition. That I celebrated the amazing heritage I inherited, the legacy of my ancestors, telling their story through foodways; and that I loved deeply with my heart and power.

Extra-Architectural Aspects

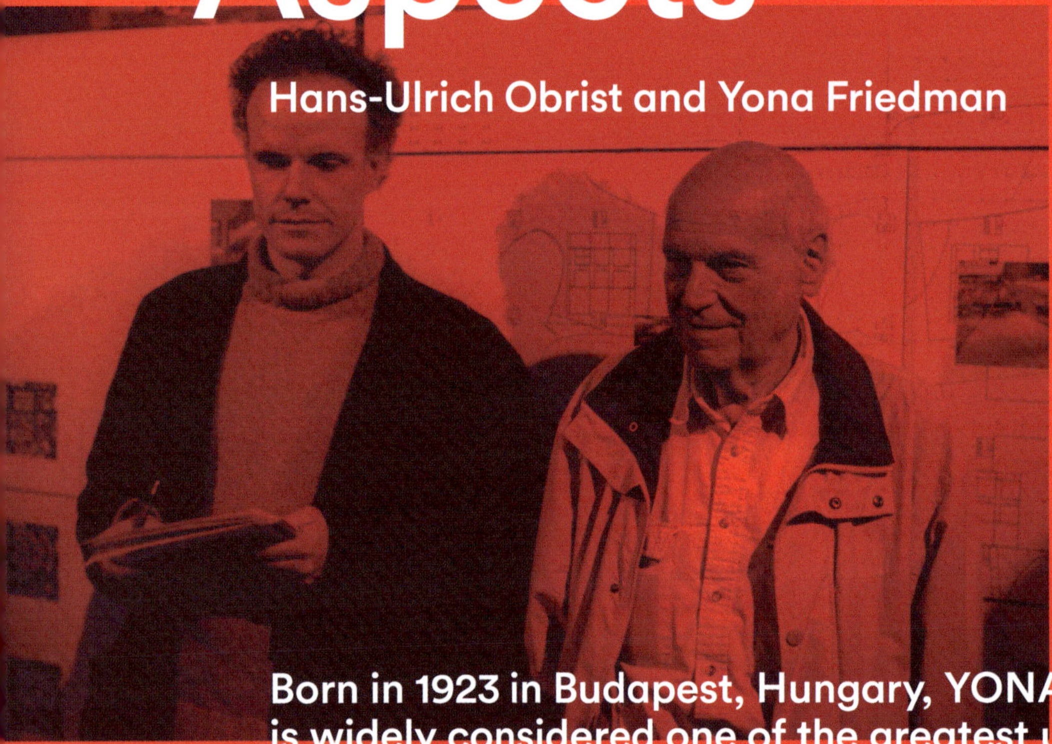

Hans-Ulrich Obrist and Yona Friedman

Born in 1923 in Budapest, Hungary, YONA FRIEDMAN is widely considered one of the greatest utopian visionary architects of the 20th century. Currently based in Paris, he is just as much a sociologist as a designer of buildings. In this illuminating talk with The Conversation Series editor HANS ULRICH OBRIST, he touches on the needs of the individual in heterogeneous urban societies, past and future projects, utopia, influences and metaphysics, revealing a wise and deeply animated humanistic intellect.

HANS ULRICH OBRIST Let's begin at the beginning. You mentioned that you grew up in a very positivist environment and developed a positivist attitude towards science and faith in science. I quote: 'As a child, I discovered that not every prediction in that positivist environment came true, and at that point I realized there was absolutely no way I could predict the action of others.' This, one could say, is the idea you've always addressed in your architectural work. I was wondering if any decisive encounters with scientists led you to make this statement. Did you meet Ilya Prigogine, for instance?

YONA FRIEDMAN I met Ilya Prigogine back in 1977. Long before that I had met Werner Heisenberg. I went to his seminars in 1941.

HUO Was Heisenberg a teacher of yours?

YF Heisenberg was in Budapest in 1941 as a guest lecturer at a seminar. I was still in secondary school, but the seminar was open to the general public. I was obviously very impressed.

HUO Afterwards, what role did science play in your career? You studied architecture and other multidisciplinary fields.

YF Like you said, my career in architecture, which was formed by my approach to science, is based on the fundamental importance of individual behaviours and actions and the unpredictability of such actions. An individual's actions are completely unpredictable even for him or herself. This doesn't, however, mean that these unpredictable acts aren't decisive. As far as the field of architecture is concerned, plans are no more than statistical fictions. No individual, whether in particle physics or sociology, behaves according to abstract laws; call it the 'principle of individuality.' This principle postulates that one individual cannot be substituted for another, and that two facts that are considered to be identical are not. This is a law, of course, so you could say I'm living a contradiction; but the difference is that the principle of individuality, in contrast to other laws, can't explain what will arise as a result.

HUO Is that due to complexity?

YF That observation goes well beyond the concept of complexity. I prefer to call it 'complicated,' because the maximum complexity of a set is limited by a number of possible relationships between the terms of that set. As far as 'maximum complication' is concerned, it may be infinite. That which is 'complicated' can be achieved by applying an indeterminate number of arbitrary rules. To visualize this, just take a line. Its complexity is minimal. However, I can twist it as much as I want and, by doing so, I increase its com- plication, but not its complexity.

← Yona Friedman and Hans-Ulrich Obrist, 2004. Photo by Aedes Architecture Forum.

HUO After you left Budapest for Israel, you started out as a construction worker, but at the same time you developed your theories in a very interdisciplinary way, by digging up elements in all kinds of fields: in engineering, sociology and science, in particular—which led to your ideas of mobile and participatory architecture. You presented these ideas at the CIAM [Congrès International d'Architecture Moderne] in Dubrovnik in 1956. Could you tell me how you honed this interdisciplinary theory of architecture?

YF Perhaps I'm not very disciplined, but essentially I don't believe that a discipline provokes anything other than an unjustified monopoly. I'm simply a normal human being who projects an image of the world for himself, without creating barriers between the elements of this image. I have the value of externalizing, of expressing my image of the world. I dare to talk about science without having a diploma in science; I talk about architecture as sociology and about sociology as communication.

I've tried to build theories based on the same logic in science and sociology; the 'principle of individuality,' 'mobile architecture,' 'urban mechanism,' the 'groupe critique' can all be observed as expressions of the same logic.

Some 20 years ago, I wrote an article entitled *The Right to Understand*, in which I asserted that all human experience could be expressed in comprehensible language. Then, I showed that academic people attempt to interfere with language. They do it for different reasons—in some cases to maintain a monopoly, or to maintain a class system. We live in a class system of formulated concepts. We have a tacit idea of the world that is. I don't want to use the term 'interdisciplinary,' I prefer to say 'global,' because the first of the two means that I accept disciplines, and the word 'global' is like any person in an African tribe or the natives in the Brazilian forests who are architects, scientists, hunters or cooks at the same time.

HUO They have generalist knowledge.

YF Yes, and I am a cook, too, and I like it. I decorate my apartment because I like it. I don't sing because I don't like my voice, but I wouldn't have minded had I been able to do so.

HUO So instead of using notions such as 'interdisciplinary,' 'multi-disciplinary,' and 'trans- disciplinary,' you'd rather use the term 'global'?

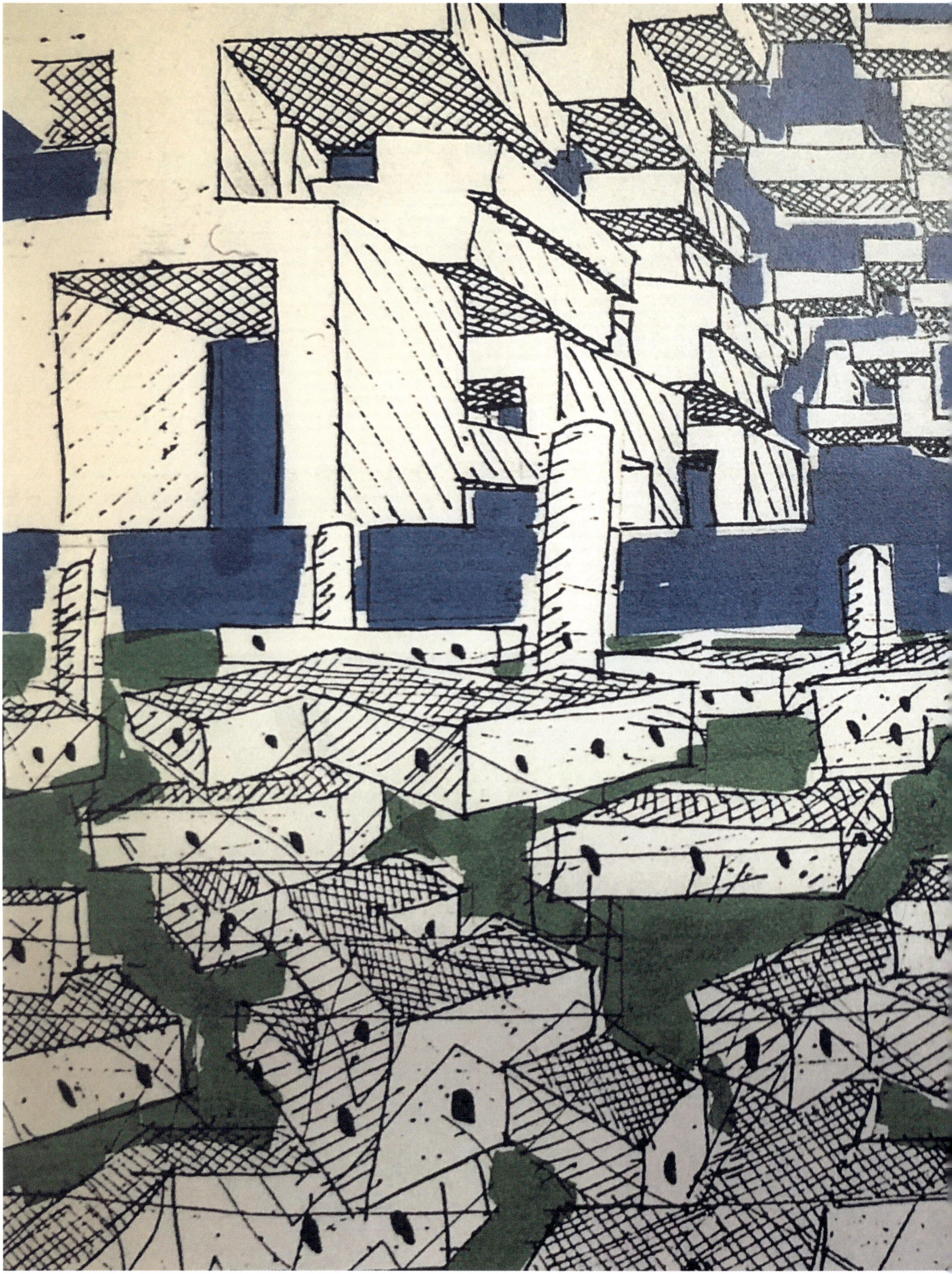

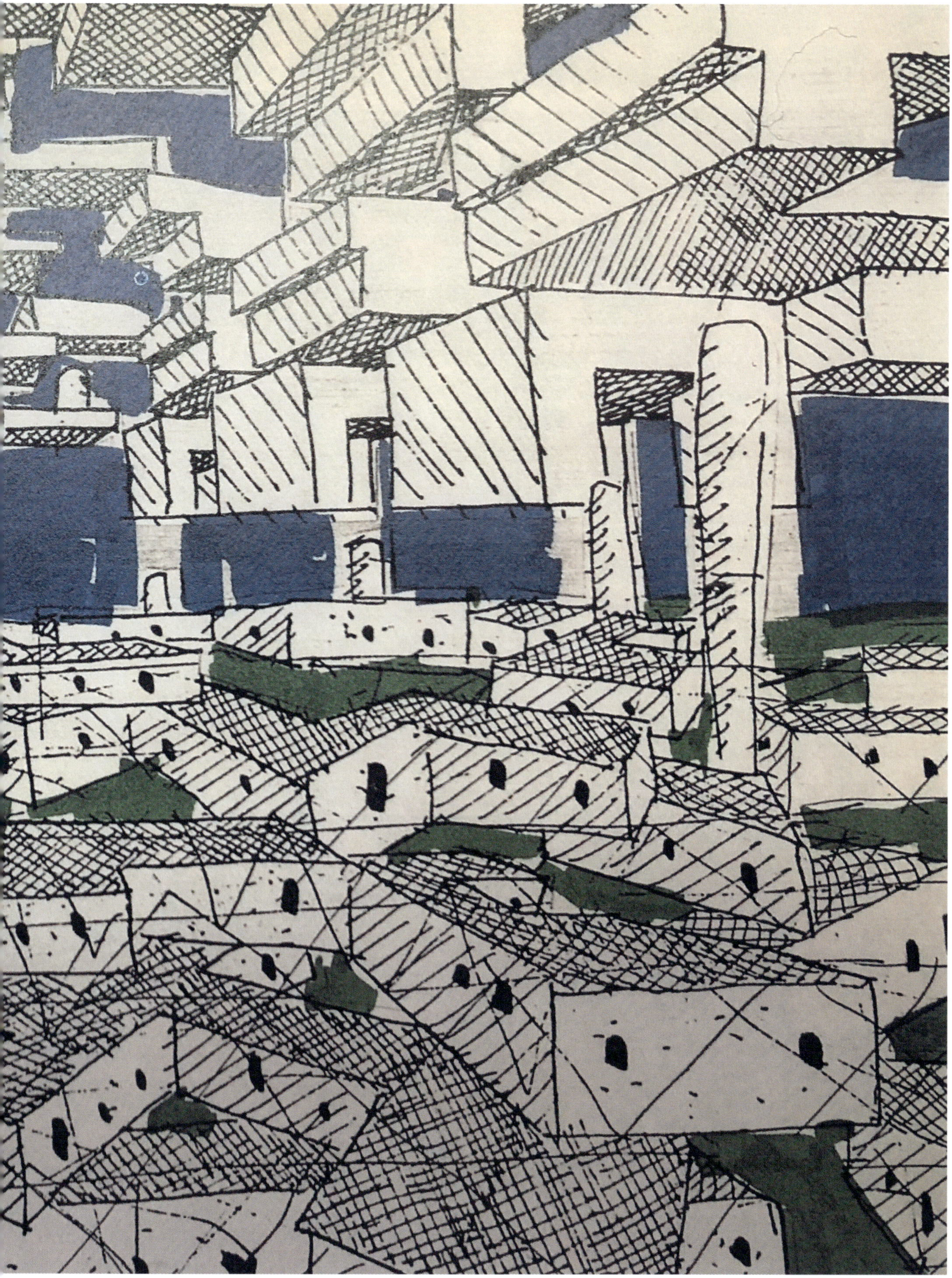

YF I accept 'global' and the globe because I can't get round it for the moment. It's a closed system, but the broadest closed system possible. By the way, you know I learn a lot from my dog—I say that very seriously. You see, my dog's behaviour shows me a global panorama with no discipline. He knows how to behave when faced with isolated and often irrational phenomena. There's no way to express this rationality I call 'surrationalism.' Like realism and surrealism, there is rationalism and surrationalism. It's a global rationalism, which is totally closed and cannot be communicated in words. We're talking about human intelligence. My dog understands me, but I don't understand him. Who is more stupid?

HUO In his book called *Seven Experiments That Could Change the World: A Do-It-Yourself Guide to Revolutionary Science*[1], Rupert Sheldrake speaks about experiments with dogs, too, and he mentions that a dog knows when his owner is going to leave at least 10 minutes prior to the event.

YF It's true. I've tried to work based on this idea, and to say that my dog lives in a time framework that's different from mine.

HUO In rather odd ways, it leads us to the problem of the city and of town planning. Frequently the way cities are organized rules out the possibility of dialogue, and of communication. In 1957, you established the Group d'Etudes d'Architecture Mobile—[GEAM] and got in touch with **Frei Otto** **(page → 170)** who later published your manifesto *L'Architecture Mobile*[2]. At the time, you stated that urban planning had failed completely —the traffic congestion, the poor-quality accommodations, and the exodus from the city on the weekends—and you developed new models with new ideas concerning the pattern of movements in the cities. How have your views on city planning evolved over the years?

YF Some 10 days ago I gave a conference at Columbia University where I touched upon these subjects. For me it's very important to distinguish between the 'hardware' and the 'software' of a city, the latter of which is an unknown quantity. We talk about urban mechanisms that explain things to some extent, but a city is not used in the same way. All it takes is for people to get together, to change their routes, to walk some other way for the city to change. If, for any reason, people decide not to walk down a given street, then it's not the same city anymore. A city can be different by day and by night; there are night cities and daytime cities, summer cities and winter cities, etc. It's the same 'hardware,' but the city is completely unpredictable. And this leads to the idea that all predications regarding the city are statistics and are false. This is something that has never really been seriously considered. Like I said at the beginning, people's behaviour is as unpredictable as the behaviour of a group of individuals. Up until now, we haven't attached any importance to the fact. For example, I can't predict how people are going to sit when they go into a cinema or a conference. You have commercial centres people don't go to, piazzas that people avoid, and small cafes that people just love and would wait in line to get inside.
The way time and space will be occupied is unpredictable. For that reason, we are in a society where the centre is shifting all the time. I've formulated a hypothesis called 'weak communication' – one

> 'There's no intelligence that can understand everything. This means that there's no rule that can predict what a city will be like or how the citizens will use that city. There are only general guidelines that can change at any given time.'
>
> YONA FRIEDMAN

↰ Photo montage of a Ville Spatial, 1959-1970. © Yona Friedman.

↗ Yona Friedman in his apartment in Paris. Photo by Hans-Jürgen Commerell.

network connects everybody, but each person is the centre of a small group; his neighbour is that of another group. Everybody has his own 'private city.' The people I communicate with in the city belong to my private city. The people I connect with on the Internet belong to my private city. There are no two private cities that coincide. This means each of us is a mini-centre within an immense system of behaviours.

HUO What about your mobile structures that echo the visions of contemporaries like Constant [Nieuwenhuys], Cedric Price, Peter Cook and [the avant-garde architectural group] Archigram? What about the notions of the ephemeral and non-linear, when they're applied to city models?

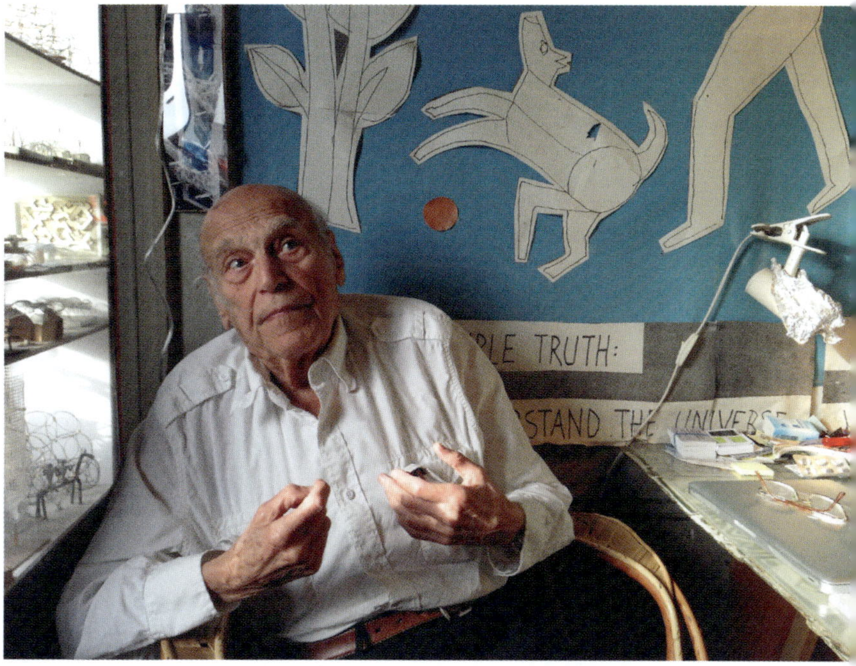

YF Since the early 20th century, writers, or rather, narrators, have debated about linear narratives. Marcel Proust's entire effort was to escape linear narration, but this is impossible: narration is necessarily linear. You can make a narrative structure complicated. Now, if you observe the behaviour of a person in the city, we can only observe their itineraries. That's a necessarily linear perspective. It's impossible to imagine an itinerary that isn't linear. These itineraries are highly complicated if you observe them and know them all, but nobody knows the reasons for their complexity. Sometimes I watch the news on television, and in the background of the image there's a man who crosses the street without looking at anybody. I see what he's doing, but I don't know why he's doing it. No theory can give me the answer. If we go further, we can postulate that the man himself doesn't know why he does it. What I mean is that there are individual acts that can't be explained theoretically, contrary to what was believed in the 19th or even in the 20th century. For me, there's no intelligence that can understand everything. This means that there's no rule that can predict what a city will be like or how the citizens will use that city; there are only general guidelines that can change at any given time. And this leads to the idea that we should make the 'hardware' as soft as possible. That was my theory of mobile architecture. Hardware should be adaptable. In all the models and drawings I've made over the past fifty years, I've tried to concentrate on allowing them to serve or visualise the irregularity that comes from each inhabitant shaping his niche in his or her particular and unpredictable way. Twice in my lifetime, I've had the opportunity to test this case in real life, to let real people conceive their own ideas about their workplace, and fit themselves more ideally into a collective plan, in their own way, without me counselling or persuading them. The object they conceived was materialized twenty years ago, and it has been continuously changing with every new generation that has worked there since.

HUO We've hardly touched upon your realized works, such as the Museum of Simple Technology (Madras, India, 1982–1986), which was designed as a cluster of hut-like units demonstrating building techniques that could be appropriated by the poor to improve their own dwellings. You've said that we could all learn a lot about town planning from India.

YF The interesting thing about marginal areas or the Third World in towns is that the systems of property, as well as the whole social organization, is much more elastic. In the Turkish Empire, you planted a tree and the land in its shade was yours, which means land could be acquired without payment. This is what happens in the marginal areas of Istanbul. People plant trees. You can determine how long the neighbourhood has existed by looking at how high

‘I have the value of externalizing, of expressing my image of the world.’

YONA FRIEDMAN

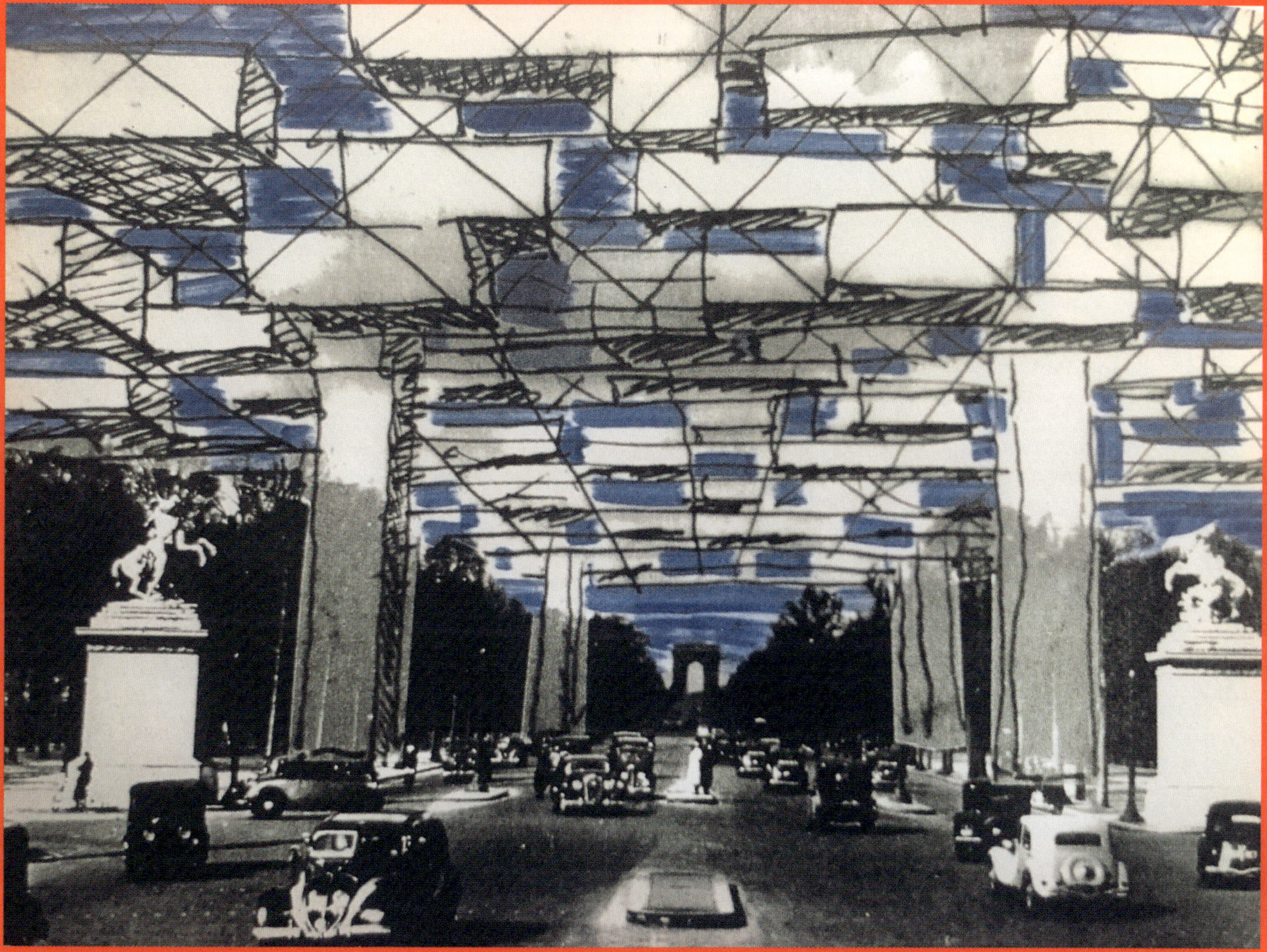

'An individual's actions are completely unpredictable, even for him or herself.'

YONA FRIEDMAN

the trees are. The rules of property are different in these places. They're not pre-planned or abstract. Property in our system is abstract. There's a piece of paper with a drawing on it; this paper with the property explains everything. In the Third World, property is much more tangible and material.

HUO That calls to mind Kowloon, or the walled city in Hong Kong.

YF Hong Kong was highly planned. Many skyscrapers have 'savage' facades. However, we'd have to consider just how many rules actually exist in the city of reeds on the sea and whether they're respected. The rules of property are different, but they're not abstract. In reality, I've tried to put abstraction in its place: the importance of the individual as opposed to statistics is the importance of reality as opposed to abstraction.

Abstraction is necessary, but not to the point of saturation. Abandon abstraction. We need a new balance.

HUO Could you tell me more about your Museum of Simple Technology?

YF I called it a museum because it was more a vehicle of communication, a kind of soft museum. I used a system of communication involving posters with very simple drawings and very simple texts— similar to comic books. Even the most complicated and abstract things can be explained using comic books. The posters were for people with no formal schooling on specific subjects such as health or food. Most importantly, they were an incitation to invent. I was

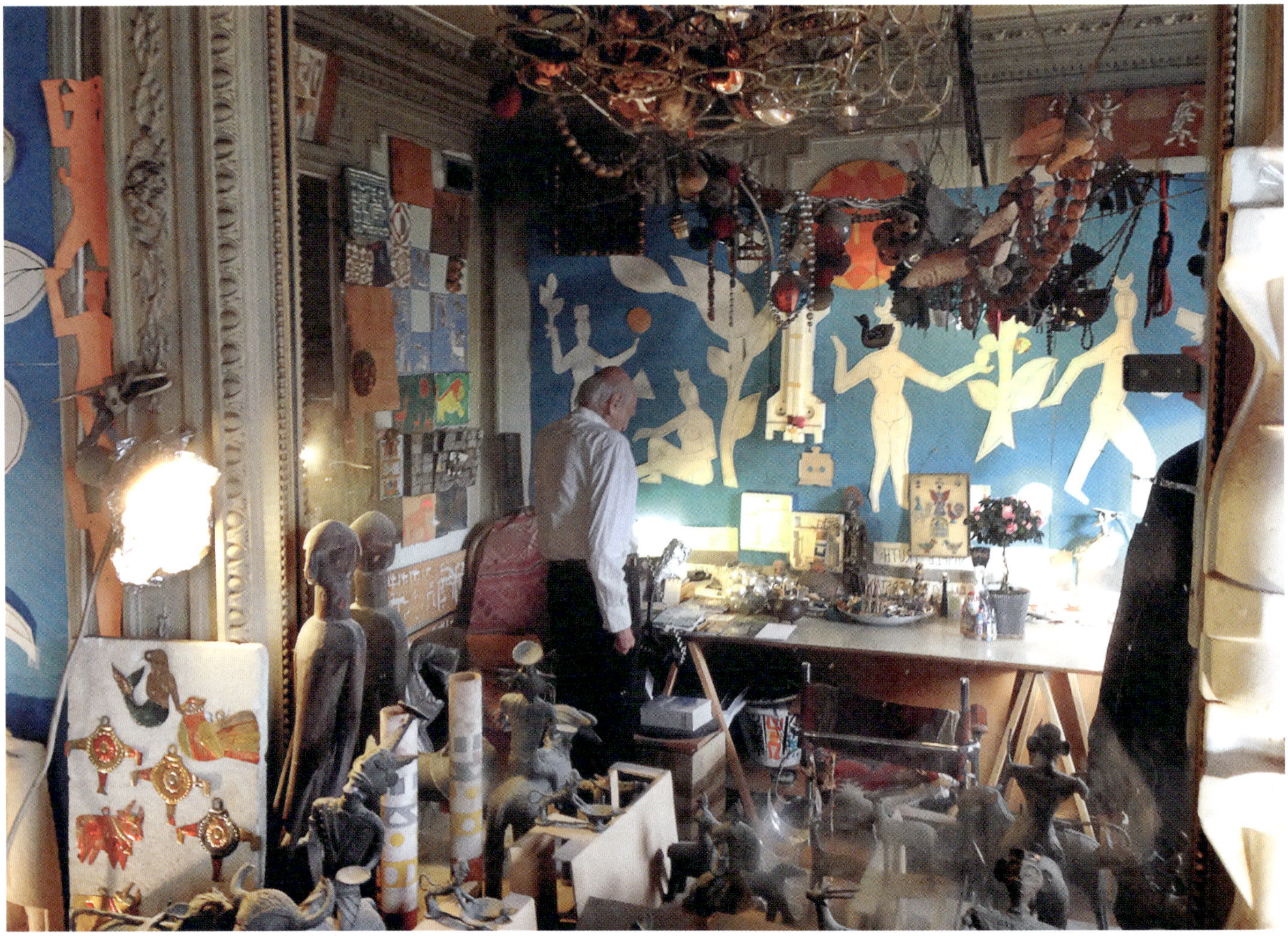

not telling people, 'You should do this and that,' but rather, 'You are able to invent ways to improve this and that.' The posters were vehicles of communication that led to consensus. They were widely distributed in India, maybe to 10 million people. With the Museum of Simple Technology, the idea was that the things explained in the manuals are to be seen in the objects on display. The museum presents the manuals as if they were mural newspapers. They were also distributed by the local press. It's a didactic museum, not a museum for preservation. The building was made to exhibit these simple and economical techniques.

HUO You developed these do-it-yourself manuals for almost a decade. How many are there?

YF Several hundred. The United Nations wanted to develop this project further, so we worked on the Communication Center of Scientific Knowledge for Self-Reliance in Paris, which I directed; but at one point, they cut the budget. At least I was able to show that this sort of thing is possible.

HUO In 1970, for your entry for the Centre Beaubourg competition in Paris, you proposed transforming the site into one large, covered public square. In line with the principles of mobile architecture, nothing was predetermined in terms of use; it was just about volumes—movable and transformable volumes.

YF Yes, because for me, museums are defined, above all, by their audience. For example with the manuals, I tried to show the global nature of the problems faced by an audience without any formal schooling, and focused on what even the poorest people need to survive: health, water, social organization. That's what's important for the audience. The Centre Pompidou is a mixture: you have the conservation of artworks with the Musée National d'Art Moderne, you have the library, etc. What I proposed to Pompidou in 1970 was a skeleton, an outline, a physical and—why not—spiritual framework within which to work. I made the same proposal to the Museum of Modern Art in New York. The way the volumes are organized can be changed. With each new generation, a museum should change.

HUO Can we talk about mutating buildings?

YF I prefer the term 'constantly changing buildings' because the city is constantly changing. There are no rules in nature. A museum is also an image of the world.

HUO My last question is about your un-built roads. I was wondering whether you could tell me about one of your unrealized projects, one that was too big, or too small to happen, or a forgotten project you'd like to mention.

YF There's a project I published in 1960 or 1961. It is a map of Europe showing the main railway lines. I made the statement that Europe was the 120-odd cities on this network. 35 or 40 years later, during a conference related to German reunification, I spoke about Europe as a 'continent city,' with the railway network becoming a commuter network linking the existing cities. All French cities today are connected by the [high-speed] TGV [train] network, which makes distances smaller. Today it only takes three hours to travel from Marseille to Paris; in 1960 it took eight. It's this continental fabric that's become the 'new city.' All my ideas of self-planning—the continent city, urban agriculture, and mobile architecture—are interrelated. They're not separate projects. I really don't consider myself entirely an architect, because the extra-architectural aspects interest me more. The purely professional side seems banal to me.

First published in Hans Ulrich Obrist, Interviews. Volume I, ed. Thomas Boutoux (Milan: Charta, 2003).

↰ Photo montage of a Ville Spatial over the Champs Élysées with a view of the Arc de Triumph in the city centre of Paris, 1959-1970. © Yona Friedman. Courtesy of Marianne Homiridis.

↙ Yona Friedman in his apartment in Paris. Photo by Hans-Jürgen Commerell.

1
Rupert Sheldrake, *Seven experiments that could change the world: a do-it-yourself guide to revolutionary science* (London: Fourth Estate, 1994).

2
Yona Friedman, 'L'Architecture Mobile' *The Institute* (Berlin: Institute for the Development of Light Weight Building, Berlin, 1959), pp. 34–42. Cf. Yona Friedman, *L'Architecture mobile, vers une cité conçue par ses habitans* (Paris, Tournai: Casterman, 1970).

Methods of Indirection: Talking to Walter Benjamin Through the Arcades Project

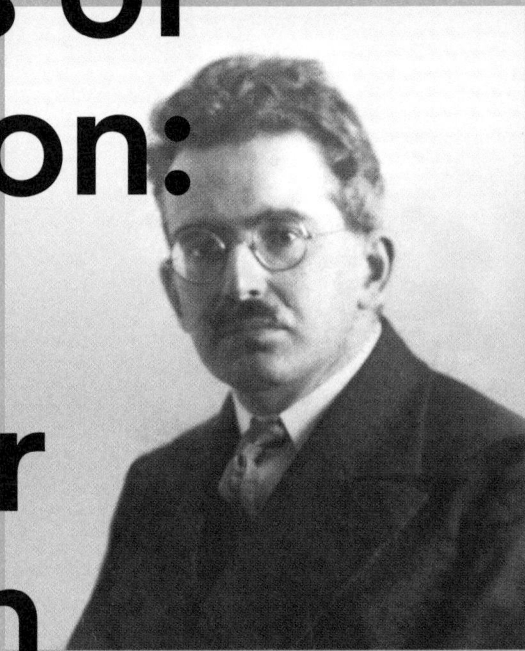

Luis-Berríos-Negrón and Howard Eiland

Puerto-Rican artist LUIS BERRÍOS-NEGRÓN talks to American writer and Walter Benjamin scholar and expert HOWARD EILAND about the German Jewish philosopher, cultural critic and essayist explores the notion of legacy by questioning the translatability of a work of art and its potential for renewal.

'With an implicit glance at the Greek etymology, (Walter Benjamin) defines his method as one of indirection, detour, the roundabout way, even while and ruse: 'Methode ist Umweg.'

HOWARD EILAND

I've wanted to talk to Walter Benjamin ever since encountering his *Arcades Project* (1982). As much as that desire may be attuned with Benjamin's own commitment to bringing the past forth into the present—I can't. I therefore turn to *Arcades* translator and Benjamin scholar, Howard Eiland.

Now, translators are not protagonists. Just like speechwriters, a translator hovers in the background. When that heavy-hyped slab of paper was first slammed before me (first edition of Harvard Press 1999), I surely overlooked the name Howard Eiland. Instead, I jumped at the obvious. I was quick to sense that this thing was not really a 'book', but a hand-held archive of loosely associated, and even deliberately dissociated, materials. It immediately registered as ambitious and genuine—not just in volume but in magnitude. Benjamin seemed to collapse his entire scope of research into the Parisian arcade as a vast object of historical and technological analysis. It became his *Passagen-Werk*—something he and Franz Hessel originally conceived in 1927, and which he himself bravely carried out over the succeeding decade before being interrupted in 1940, when his lonely and sometimes desperate seven-year exile came to an end with his suicide on the Spanish border (an end still disputed by some). In a letter written in 1930, Benjamin deemed the *Arcades* 'the theatre of all my struggles and all my ideas.' It had become for him—as it now perhaps becomes for us—a literary laboratory for testing his ideas.

Truth be told—the first time around, after one pass, I was exhausted, and the book was retired to my shelf. It absolutely lingered there; breathing. How do I return to the *Arcades*? For the past decade or so, I have been largely processing my own work through the manifold of 'greenhouse'—as technology, archive, display; as gas, effect, superstructure; as environmental form, and as messianic technic. It was inevitable that I had to return to the *Arcades*. Not just because Benjamin meticulously objectified the glass and iron arcades as method and catalyst of research, but because, to me, 'greenhouse' both precedes and succeeds the arcades themselves as display and index of what was—and is yet to become—'natural history.'

← Portrait of Walter Benjamin, 1928. Source: Akademie der Künste, Berlin - Walter Benjamin Archiv.

Such a claim entails long engagement, one that, in my case, will endure for the rest of my life. And, that's just fine. It is in the awareness of such engagement and of the impossibility of seeking Benjamin's own guidance that I turn to Eiland. There are, of course, many living scholars whose interpretations are indispensable to the study of Walter Benjamin, including Susan Buck-Morss and Giorgio Agamben. Benjamin himself argued that 'translatability' is what gives life—or rather an afterlife—to a worthy work of art — where art occupies the most privileged place in the idea of 'progress'. After musing on these two vertiginous parameters, it seemed advisable to speak to a translator, namely Howard, in order to get closer to the mind of Benjamin. It has proven to be a privilege.

The following are excerpts of an interview that started at the Harvard Co-op in 2016; a conversation that continues to this day, by way of intermittent emails and other correspondence.

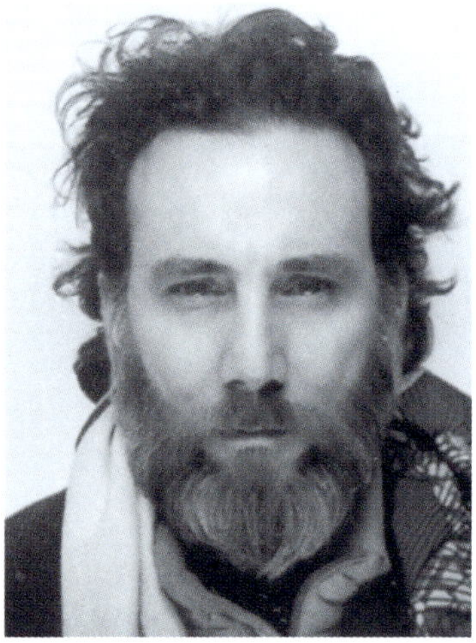

← Luis Berríos-Negrón, 2014.

→ Luis Berríos-Negrón, 'Farm' section of 'Earthscore Specularium'. Materials: polycarbonat, pine wood, aluminium, PVC, steel, plants, fish, ducks, chickens, people. Färgfabriken, Stockholm 2015. Installation photo by David Fischer.

↓ Howard Eiland, 2018. Photo by Julia Brown.

LUIS BERRÍOS-NEGRÓN Could you go back and situate yourself, as you prepared to make the first comprehensive translation of *Passagen-Werk*, as you branched out to inform yourself about Benjamin, in general, and for the *Arcades*?

HOWARD EILAND I had done no published translation work at all when I was commissioned to translate the *Passagen-Werk*. I had submitted a manuscript on Heidegger to Harvard Press, and, though the manuscript was never published, the readers for the press had praised my translation of passages from Heidegger's notoriously difficult texts; as a result, they took the chance and hired me, despite my complete lack of professional experience, to translate Benjamin's no less difficult 'magnum opus' (masterpiece), this strange and ungainly composite—the publication of which made a bigger splash than was expected.

I might add here that, as different as Benjamin's writing is from Heidegger's in subject matter and tone (not to mention their politics), one finds striking similarities between their vocabularies. I would suppose that this has something to do with their having in common an education in the tradition of Southwest Neo-Kantianism. They both studied with Heinrich Rickert (both were in Rickert's Henri Bergson seminar in Freiburg in the summer of 1913), and Benjamin read widely in phenomenology as well. My experience with Heidegger came in handy when I encountered Walter Benjamin.

The eight or nine years of labour spent in translating the *Passagen-Werk* (the responsibility for which I shared with Kevin McLaughlin, who took on a large portion of the French), was an extraordinary education in itself. Not only did this entail a great deal of library work—these were still pre-internet times—in researching Benjamin's several hundred cited sources, in learning about the authors he so carefully quoted and the historical contexts he drew on, and in searching for published English translations of the cited texts. There was also, of course, much reading to be done in order to be able to properly 'hear' what Benjamin was saying in this polyphonic monster machine of a text.

LBN Would you comment on how the term 'interlinear' (appearing in Benjamin's essay *The Task of the Translator*, in *Illuminations*, 1969) have relevance to legacy?

HE Benjamin is talking here about 'translatability' as a quality distinguishing literary texts: the 'higher the level of the work,' the more translatable—that is, the more amenable to 'einer formvollen Übersetzung' (flawless translation), one formally or literally distinguished. Newspaper stories, bare statements of content, are not suitable for the art of translation. A work must have within itself, within its form and content, the potential for renewal in order to be truly translatable; a translation, Benjamin says, constitutes an afterlife or legacy of the work itself, which is to say, the work's rebirth and transformation in a new historical context. Thus the concluding sentences of the 'translation' essay: 'all great texts contain their potential (virtual!) translation between the lines....' (What exactly does 'between the lines' mean here?)

LBN How about what you indicate are his observations about the 'interlinear versions' of 'sacred writings', as the 'Urbild' or ideal of all translation?

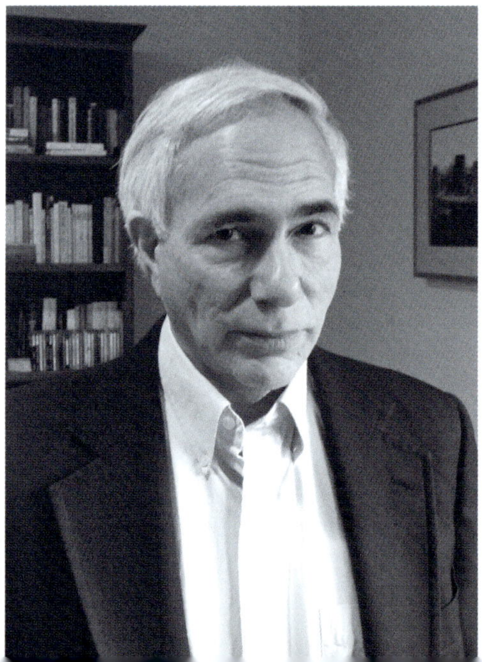

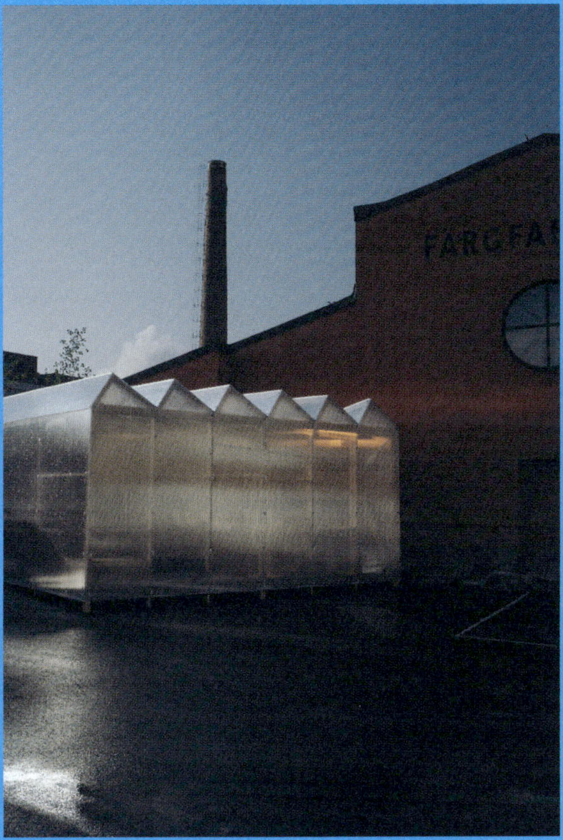
FARGFA

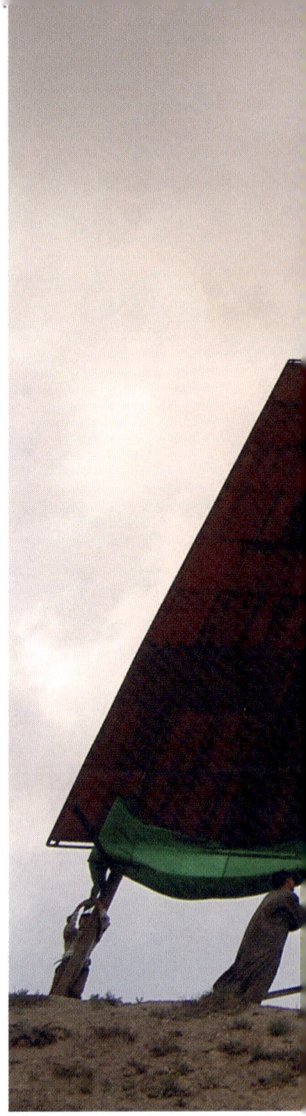

> 'A work must have within itself, within its form and content, the potential for renewal in order to be truly translatable.'
>
> HOWARD EILAND

HE This observation would go together, I think, with the emphasis on 'words rather than sentences (as) the primary element of the translator,' since the interlinear version usually follows the word-order of the original rather than the syntactic logic of the translator's language. In our (initial) conversation at the Harvard Coop, I was stressing something similar regarding my own translation practice: the attempt to 'mime', to stay as close as possible to the syntax and diction of the original while remaining at all times attuned to English idiom. The hope was that by these means it would expand the resources of my own language in something of the way Benjamin describes in his essay. One doesn't want the result to sound like a translation, but it should nevertheless reflect something of the character, the flavour, the feel, of the foreign language that is its source. What Benjamin invokes as 'formvolle' (form-full) translation depends, I believe, on this rigorous free-play with idiom, on this ear for idiomaticity and the possibilities of transformation within the boundaries and rhythms of the idiomatic, boundaries no doubt fluid in some indeterminate degree.

LBN You pointed earlier to the 'afterlife' of the text, specifically as a 'potential for renewal'. What do you mean?

HE I would say that, in the highly paradoxical Benjaminian logic, there is ultimately a sort of complementarity between objectivity and metaphoricity. Due to the express priority of language, metaphoricity is infinitely extended, as in Nietzsche and Derrida; all concept is infected by metaphor, beginning with the concept of concept (what is 'grasped together'). To the common sense that distinguishes language as an instrument from things as objects, it is merely a metaphor to say that a work of art has a life and an afterlife. Benjamin means it literally. The work has an objective life and an afterlife that both develop through history in the form of translation, criticism, and other art: the form of tradition. The commonsensical dualism that undergirds both the conventional understanding of metaphor and the conventional understanding of object has ostensibly been transcended in his extension of the meaning of 'life,' in his oceanic art and philosophy.

LBN With that in mind, what do you think were the reasons for Benjamin's choosing the arcades as a historiographical object, even as an apparatus for 'translation'?

HE The image of the arcade, for Benjamin, comprehends a century-long historical process, what he thinks of as reflecting the decline of the bourgeois class. In its seedy, phantasmagorical obsolescence, at the end of the 19th century, as you know, the Paris arcade is characteristically home to fortune-tellers, streetwalkers, detective agencies, and the like, as opposed to the ultra-luxurious shops of the beginning of the century.

The image of the arcade, is an image of spatio-temporal passage. Passage and threshold. Transparency and partition. The arcade is a medium of reflection: per skylight, vitrines, marble walls and floors, 'mirror-walls,' and, above all, shop windows. At every turn, the pedestrian is drawn into some historical theatre of reflections—a world of superimpositions, threshold upon threshold. In other words, the historian's present moment opens up and becomes transparent to a series of past moments—a kind of historical palimpsest; as Adorno would write in 1955 '(Benjamin) immersed himself in reality as in a palimpsest.'

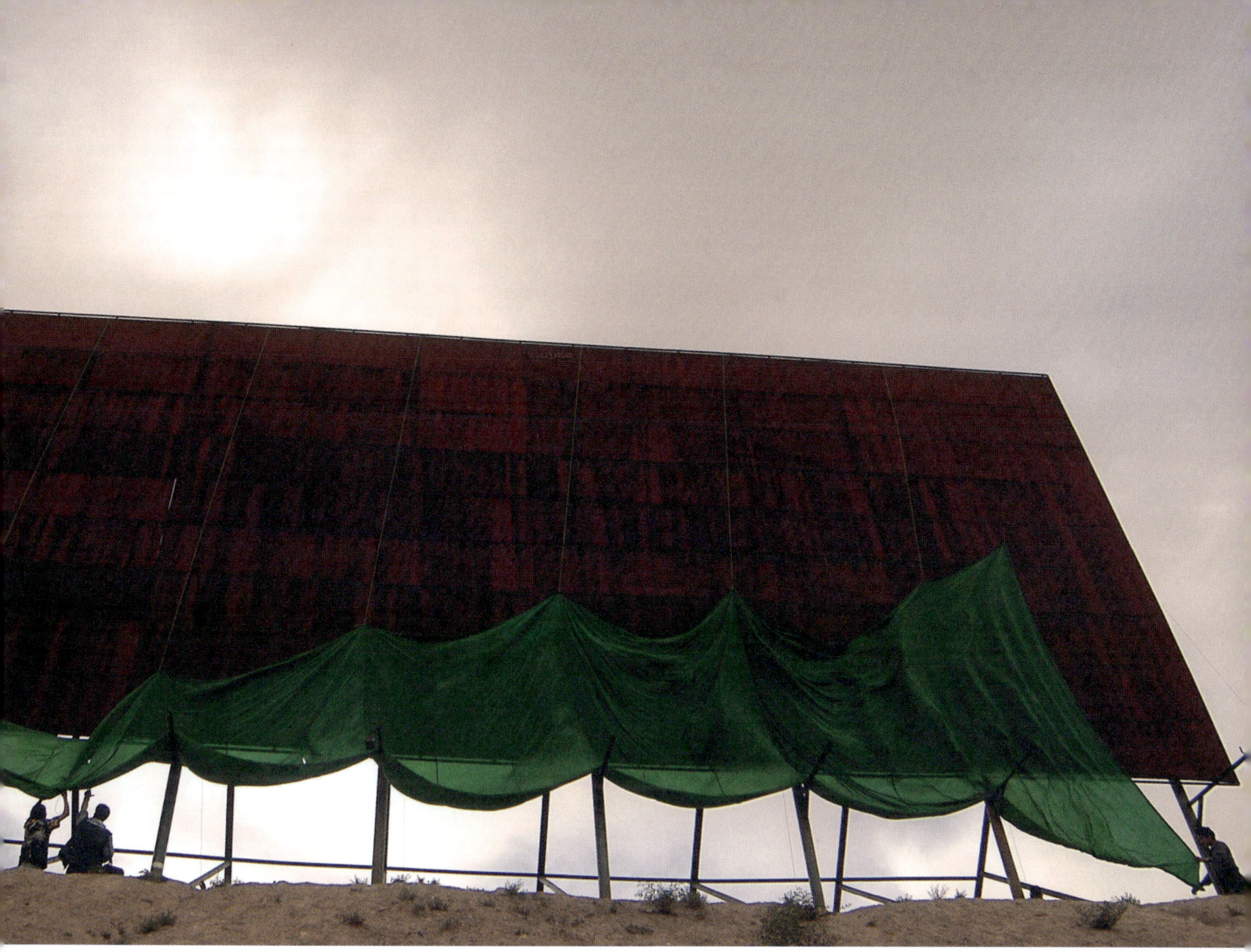

LBN An unfinished palimpsest on top of that. Is there any worthwhile reason to add convolutes to the *Arcades*?

HE By conventional or commonsensical standards of judgment on the matter, the *Arcades Project* is clearly unfinished. Indeed, at one point in the text, Benjamin refers to the 'fundamentally unfinishable collection of things worth knowing' as having its prototype in 'study'—no doubt a kind of oblique reflection on his own grand collection and endlessly sprawling study that is the *Arcades Project* itself. But I would also adduce here the argument Agamben has made in introducing his new edition of Benjamin's Baudelaire[1] book, which is itself an offshoot of the *Arcades*. The familiar editorial distinction between completed work and incomplete work becomes problematic in Benjamin's case; Agamben argues—especially where a posthumously published work like the *Arcades Project* is concerned—a work in which we find an 'intimate interpenetration of documentation and construction,' resulting in a kind of 'hybrid of material and form, research and draft (Forschung and Darstellung), reading and writing'.

LBN It is truly one of the great unfinished works, which in its incompleteness seems to call for multiple, imaginary completions.

HE The hybrid form in itself—in this case, citation plus commentary and Reflection—might well serve as a model for other critical-creative projects. There is certainly much evident opportunity for following up on Benjamin's research in the *Arcades*, for exploring and further contextualizing the materials he cites and tracing the manifold connections.

↑ Luis Berríos-Negrón, installing of ,*Verde que te quiero verde (Dest ba dest)*' as end-project installation for a public art workshop with art and architecture students, Dimensions variable. Materials: polyethylene fabric, rope, stones. CCAA, Kabul 2006. Process photo by Massoud Hosseini.

1
On Benjamin's *Baudelaire, in Walter Benjamin and Theology*, ed. Colby Dickinson and Stéphane Symons (Fordham Univ. Press, 2016), pp. 217-30).

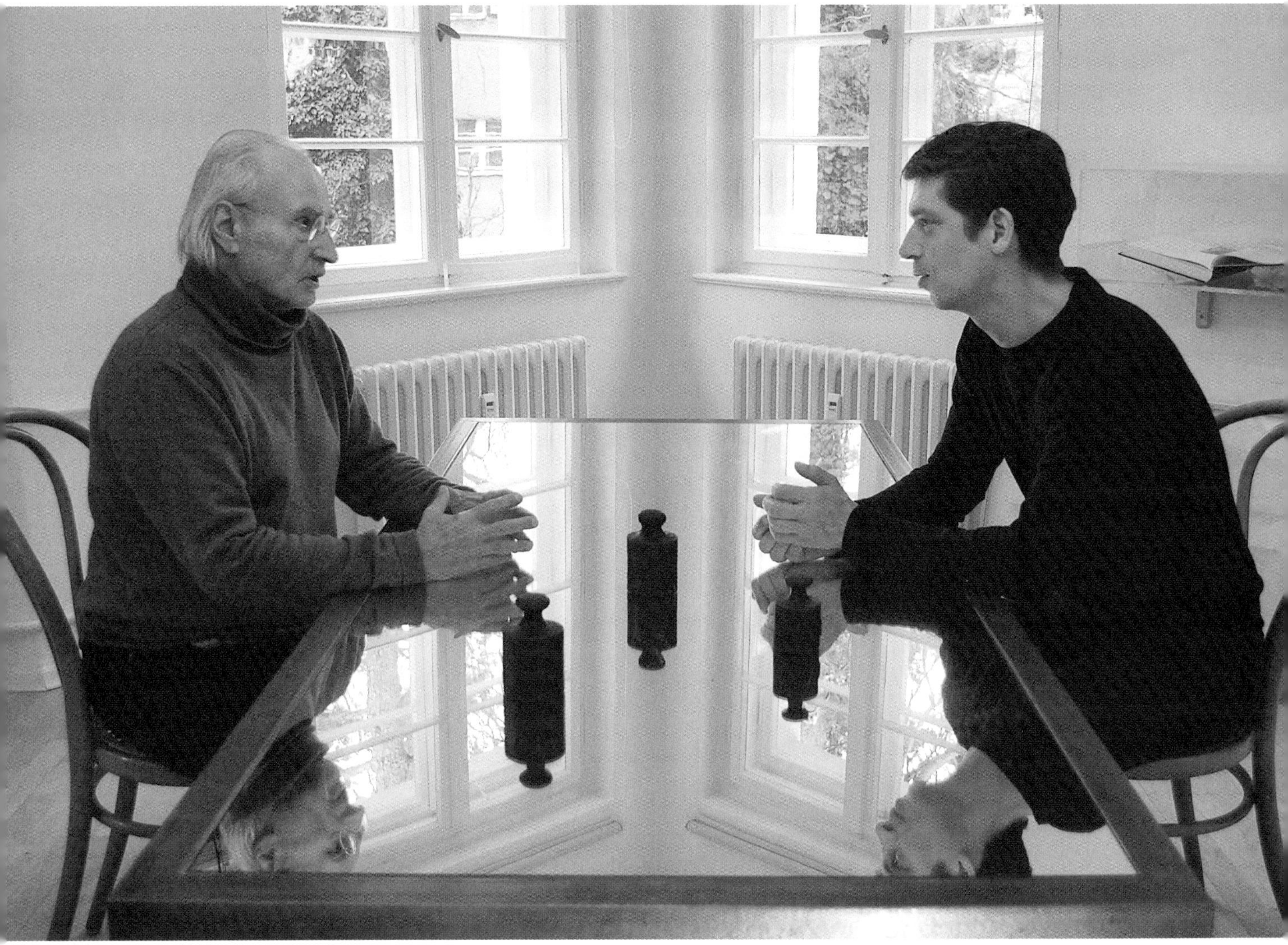

It's the Message That Counts

Ludwig Engel and Zamp Kelp

German futurist and urbanist LUDWIG ENGEL sits down with architect ZAMP KELP, co-founder of Haus-Rucker-Co in 1967, an architecture group with a notorious reputation for their wildly spectacular interventions and installations. They engage in an equally personal and theoretical discourse about the 1960s, architecture as narrative structure and the construction of utopias.

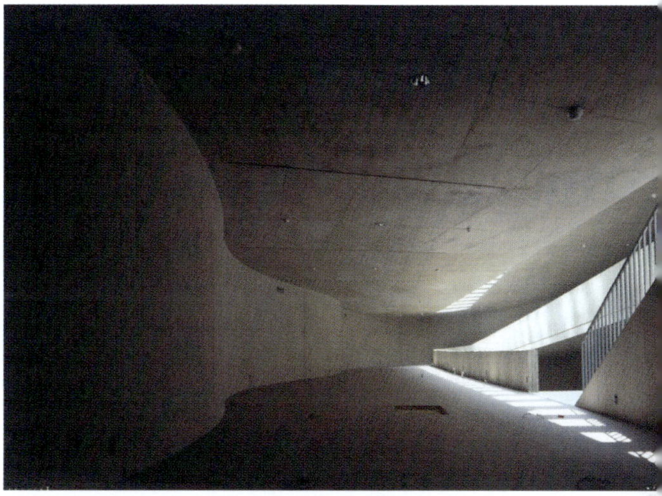

LUDWIG ENGEL I was recently researching the year 1967, which is often described as a turning point: the hippie movement peaked that year in the 'Summer of Love' in the USA while it turned dark and brutal in Europe with students protesting everything, everywhere. Maybe we can start with that? You were a young man back then. Did you experience that sort of shift in Vienna?

ZAMP KELP Well, I can't offer you any revolutionary tale that would really prove your point. There was a noticeable hunger for change—even in Vienna. For me personally, 1967 is of course important because Laurids Ortner, Klaus Pinter and I founded Haus-Rucker-Co—a magical constellation with great momentum, with Manfred Ortner joining in 1971. Superstudio and Archizoom in Italy and Utopie in France were already around, closely aspired to work in the same direction. Vienna was less political than Florence, Paris or Berlin. The younger generation was more interested in the creative and artistic aspects of life. The protests in Vienna culminated in a demonstration in the university's auditorium, introduced by the 'Wiener Aktionisten', which produced a scandalizing reaction in the Viennese public in those days. That was about it, if I recall correctly. Around the same time, we presented *Yellow Heart* (1968) in the excavation pit for the new police headquarters on Ringstrasse. In *Time and Narrative* (1983) Paul Ricoer says something along the lines of 'time is nothing, if we don't tell it'. That was our ambition: to create an update for architecture as the great narrator of human history. We had the feeling that architecture as it was practiced back then canonized an outdated idea of time, monument and landscape. It felt like architecture had lost its ability to give orientation, to create identity. Instead, it left us with a very diffuse feeling for heritage and homeland. Did we succeed in, at least, addressing that issue?

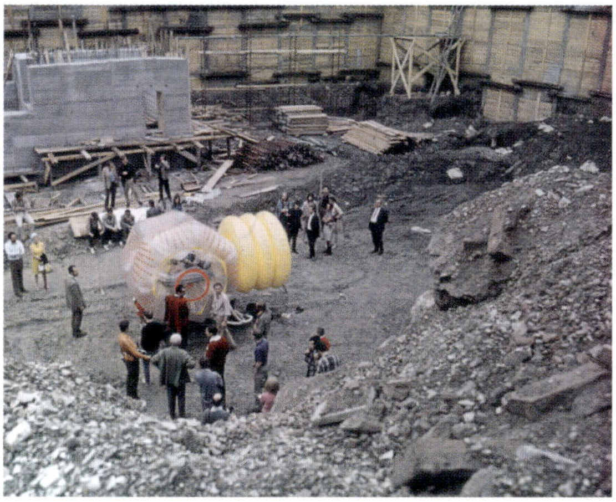

↖ Zamp Kelp and Ludwig Engel in discussion at Zamp's Zero Gravity Table, Berlin, Germany, 2018.

↑ *Neanderthal Museum*, inside view, 1996. Blueprint planning: Günter Zamp Kelp and Julius Krauss/Arno Brandlhuber. Detailed planning: Büro Zamp Kelp, Dusseldorf, Germany. (1993 -1996). Photo by M. Reisch.

← Haus-Rucker-Co, *Yellow Heart*, Vienna 1968. With Yellow Heart Haus-Rucker-Co pushed the experiment of spatially expanding consciousness to its very limit. Here, the mechanized pneumatic construction is turned into a breathing, metabolizing being that absorbs its temporary inhabitants and takes them in with the meditative rhythm of an interior space contracting and expanding.

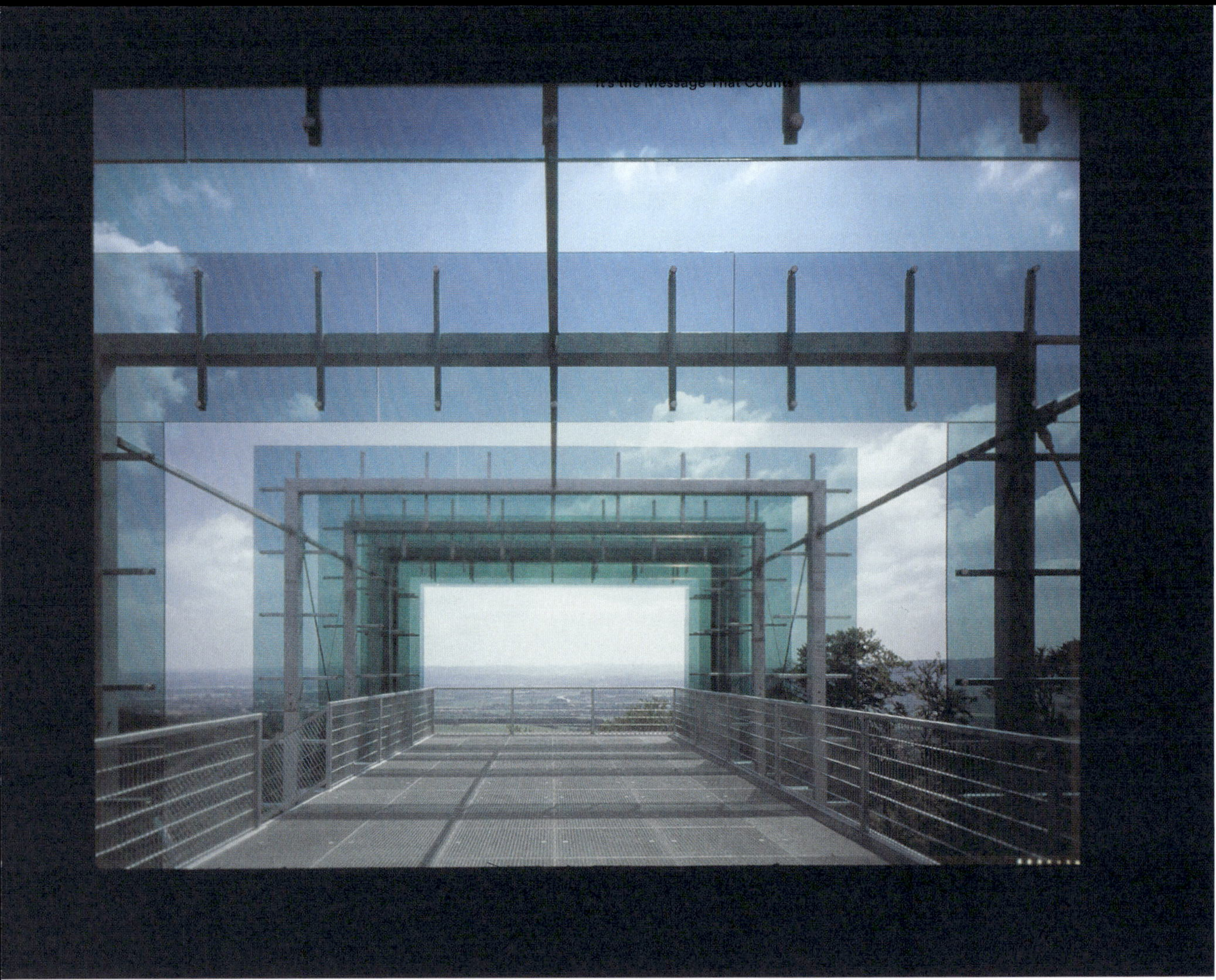

LE Definitely. I think narrative structures—that also includes architecture as a representative of a specific epoch—have always shaped our understanding of time and space. Thus, architecture represents what we can see as heritage and what we can consider to be home, to a large extent. Crucially, you introduced three new dimensions: improvisation, temporality and virtuality (philosophy). These dimensions shape contemporary space much more than they did back then when *Yellow Heart* was pulsating in the pit. Not only has the feeling that time is running faster increased, but global processes have also accelerated. Buffering for example—the short latencies, while a website or a video loads—today are incredibly short intervals, yet they seem excruciatingly slow to us. These accelerated processes within a given time frame—that's how the acceleration of time would be described correctly—leads to an immense fragmentation among the people who operate in parallel within the same time frame. To rethink the relationship between time and society, we need to stop fighting acceleration and instead accept acceleration as the fundamental basis of our time. I think you did exactly that with your interventions. Later, you substituted plastics and inflatables with stone, steel and glass—it became less improvised, more monumental. Would you agree? I see less of your interventionist pragmatism in your later projects like *Neanderthal Museum* (1996) and *Millennium View* (2000).

ZK *Neanderthal Museum* and *Millennium View* are works that carry all attributes of completed architectural building processes. In that sense, you're right. They still breathe what you just coined 'interventionist pragmatism'. At least in the message they carry: *Neanderthal Museum* is a spiral of time and thus questions the cyclical model of societal development with its galleries that submerge from the ground to the tangential high point. The spiral points into the open and the museum therefore is a synonym for society's uncertainty that we are confronted by in the digital age. *Millennium View* is a mark in a landscape in flux and symbolizes the transition between the 20th and the 21st century. It developed the theme of the staircase we addressed with Haus-Rucker-Co—our unrealized project Big Piano without the artificial cloud at the top. *Millennium View*, with its observation deck is also a metaphor for the fragmentation of our visual perception and can also be linked to Frame Building—a speculative instrument for field research we realized in the context of documenta 6. Both projects carry a critique of our perception of time and can therefore be again linked to our earlier works.

LE For example, the *Environment Transformers* (1968). Their purpose was to fragment, to defamiliarize our visual perception in order to reinforce the users' awareness for the lived-in environment—an analogue augmented reality. Today's digital communication technology has indeed created an equivalent of your kaleidoscopic apparatuses: we're currently at a point where we don't know how this new perspective on the present will shape our understanding of it. Your transformers were—like many of your small-scale interventions—extremely visionary. Funnily enough, pictures of your transformers are still used widely today to illustrate the invisible aspects of digital processes. There is no turning back now—the fragmentation of the perception of the world, as anticipated by you, is today's basic condition. LSD doesn't help us anymore. We need to accept that we are already deeply rooted in the digital infrastructure of our planet. Only then we will be able to cooperate on societal resonances, repair today's hyperfragmentation and can continue our collective work on the Social Sculpture.

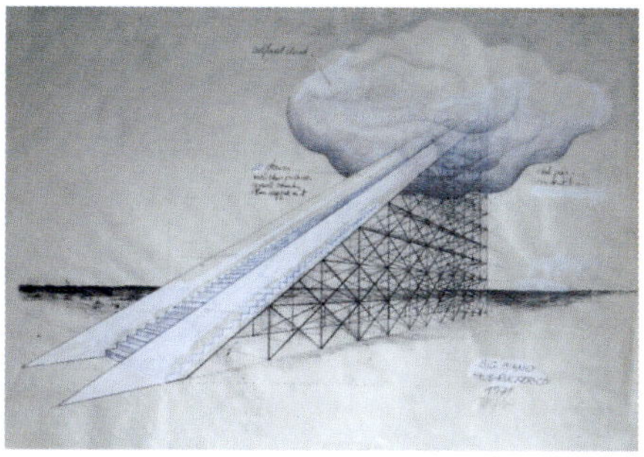

ZK That's Beuys, no? Also, a bit of Niklas Luhmann, I reckon? In his systems theory he says, 'society doesn't exist as the entirety of people anymore but as communication'. Peter Sloterdijk on the other hand, has described the current state of Western society as an amalgam of egocentric individuals with limited

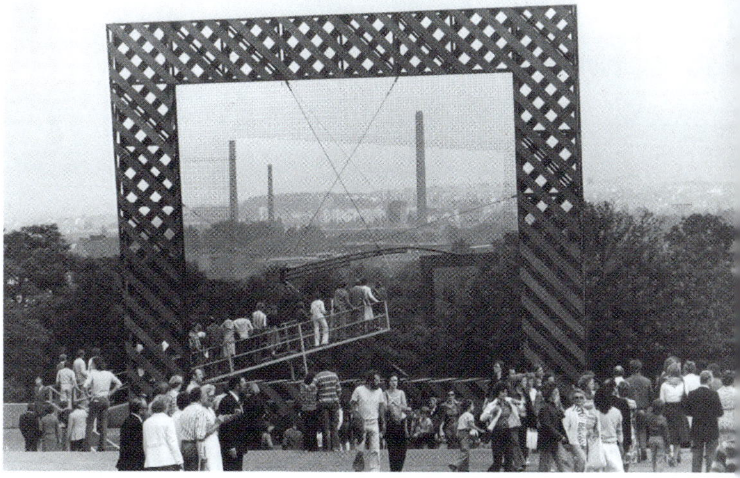

bonding capacities, which brings him to the modern apartment as an atomic and egospheric form of living that can only be described as individualistic foam. Do you see any way to bridge that divide? To rewire society and individual?

LE For me, Luhmann is relevant through his theory of societal resonances, which is quite central to my understanding of futurology, as the new that can only be recognized as something new when it reverberates within society. The possibility to think society as a project of transformation is premised on the systemic belief that the message can already trigger change. Sloterdijk's claim in his book *Foams: Spheres — Plural Spherology* (2016) resembles a sort of communication breakdown that he frames as the singularisation and fragmentation of the individual in its own filter bubble. In both cases, human interaction is seen as the lubricant for building a society. Which brings me to the current condition of our cities' public spaces as places for debate. They appear to be in danger from two sides at the moment; increasingly fewer public places are really public. Instead, they are controlled by particular house rules and guarded accordingly. In the pub-

↖ Zamp Kelp, *Millenium View*, Steinbergen, 1997-2000. Photo by M. Reisch.

↑ Haus-Rucker-Co, *Big Piano*, New York 1971. In Big Piano a built environment blends in with the natural surroundings, becoming a lived-in environment. Surroundings turn into a lived-in environment: sound stairs lead into a cloud. Every step is a note. Gladly, we would like to listen to the cacophony triggered by the users as they hasten up and down this Stairway to Heaven (Led Zeppelin) turned piece of architecture.

← Haus-Rucker-Co, *Frame Building*, documenta 6, Kassel 1977. On a jagged path the visitor ambles between notch and bead sights, perceiving himself as a projectile moving towards the city below. Particularly as an unconscious end to temporality: realized for documenta 6, Frame Building thrones atop the city valley of Kassel to this day.

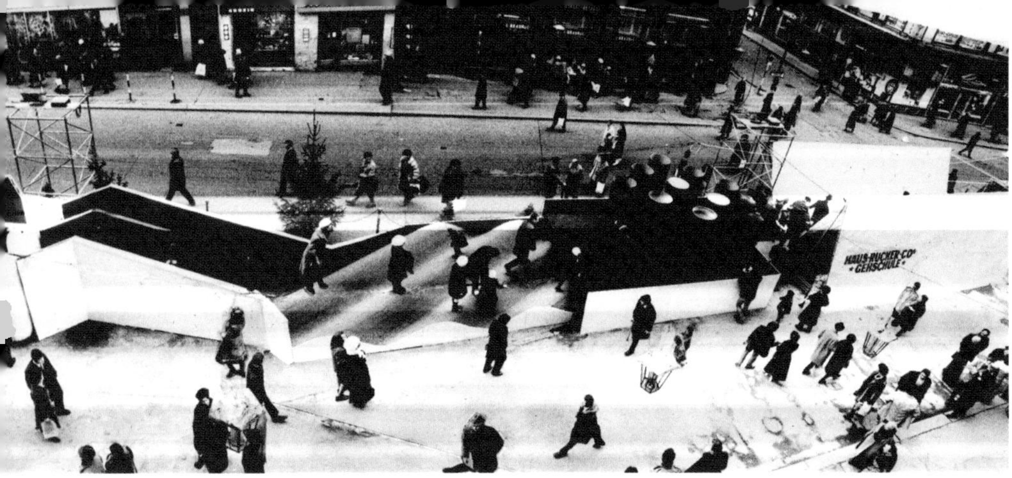

Interpersonal relationships are brokered by a dating app. Communication options presented to us from the outside, organize people's lives today. Well, when I talk like that I always ask myself how much of my ideas of the future are based on the past and not the present. I read this interesting sentence in Robert Menasse's *Die Hauptstadt* (*The Capital*, 2017)—in English, not translated in the German original text: 'The past forms the future, without regard to life.' What do you think?

lic spaces that are still available, technology leads to a quite passive coexistence. The only public interaction between strangers we see today are articulations of aggression after a supposed act of transgression. I actually hope in reality it's not as bad as I put it, but what do you think? Maybe that's nothing new at all. For example, your *Walking School* (1965), intended as a tool to rethink the way we walk through public spaces, was instantly vandalized, wasn't it?

ZK I think there is a big difference between an artwork that intends a negative emotion and an artwork that provokes vandalism, though rejection might also lead to an initial positive effect on communicative interaction. In fact, it is important to acknowledge the way that fear can stimulate the need for interpersonal relationships. Haus-Rucker-Co's first intervention in the public sphere was the installation *Balloon for Two* (1969). Two people floated in a transparent bubble about ten meters above ground on Viennas Apollogasse and bonded during this collective yet risky experience. The *Walking School*, on the other hand, may have been too didactic—not just in the set-up but also in the title. It somehow rubbed the promenaders of Vienna's inner city the wrong way. I don't really know why, but it triggered the most destructive instincts. The *Walking School* was vandalized in one of the first nights of its existence and later removed by some official entity. *Oasis No.7* (1972), which we produced for documenta 5, was also damaged with a nail on a long latch in the night before the opening. Anyway, I guess that's at least proof of some physical communicative interaction, as you have noted. Today we experience a shift in communication which becomes ever more closely tied to long distances, not least thanks to our smart phones. Physical togetherness in public spaces is almost exclusively limited to soccer matches, music festivals and other staged events.

↑ Haus-Rucker-Co, *Walking School*, Vienna, Austria, 1972.

→ Haus-Rucker-Co, *Environment Transformers*, Vienna 1968. Photo by Zugmann. Haus-Rucker-Co's iconic Environment Transformers, technoid helmets that expand horizons optically, abduct their wearers to a visual course of new perspectives on the urban surroundings.

LE I'm not really sure what Menasse means with 'without regard to life'. Does it imply ones powerlessness as time mercilessly moves forward without regard for the individual? I can't really agree to that, it's too fatalistic for my taste. I agree that the future cannot be known, nor directly influenced, but it sounds like an excuse for remaining passive to me. Do not produce the future in the future. What if one would say: 'With regard to life, the past informs the future.' With that the human being is the actor who deals with what is coming. By combining his experiences with his hopes for a vision of a future, he is motivated to navigate these unknowable waters. I think I like it better, because I don't believe in 'the future' as something apart from human's capacity to define time.

ZK I honestly would not have imagined that I'd feel this contemporary digital revolution as intensively as I do—despite the often visionary projects we did, to quote you there. The apparatuses we designed for our *Mind-Expanding Program* (2015) had the intention to spark communication and the ambition to transcend awareness. 50 years later, we are at the verge of a superintelligence developing with an artificial dynamic, that will open up possibilities for our cognitive and sensory functions that will surely surpass the imaginable. Architecture and design will be essential to shape the processes that inform this superintelligence. I don't get the sense that people as society really partake. Take our dystopian scenario for *Cover—Survival in a Polluted Environment* (1971) in Krefeld for example, where we covered the Mies van der Rohe villa with an air-inflated tent to create a synthetic reserve. It seems more relevant than ever when we look at the metropolises

'I honestly would not have imagined that I'd feel this contemporary digital revolution as intensively as I do—despite the often-visionary projects we did.'

ZAMP KELP

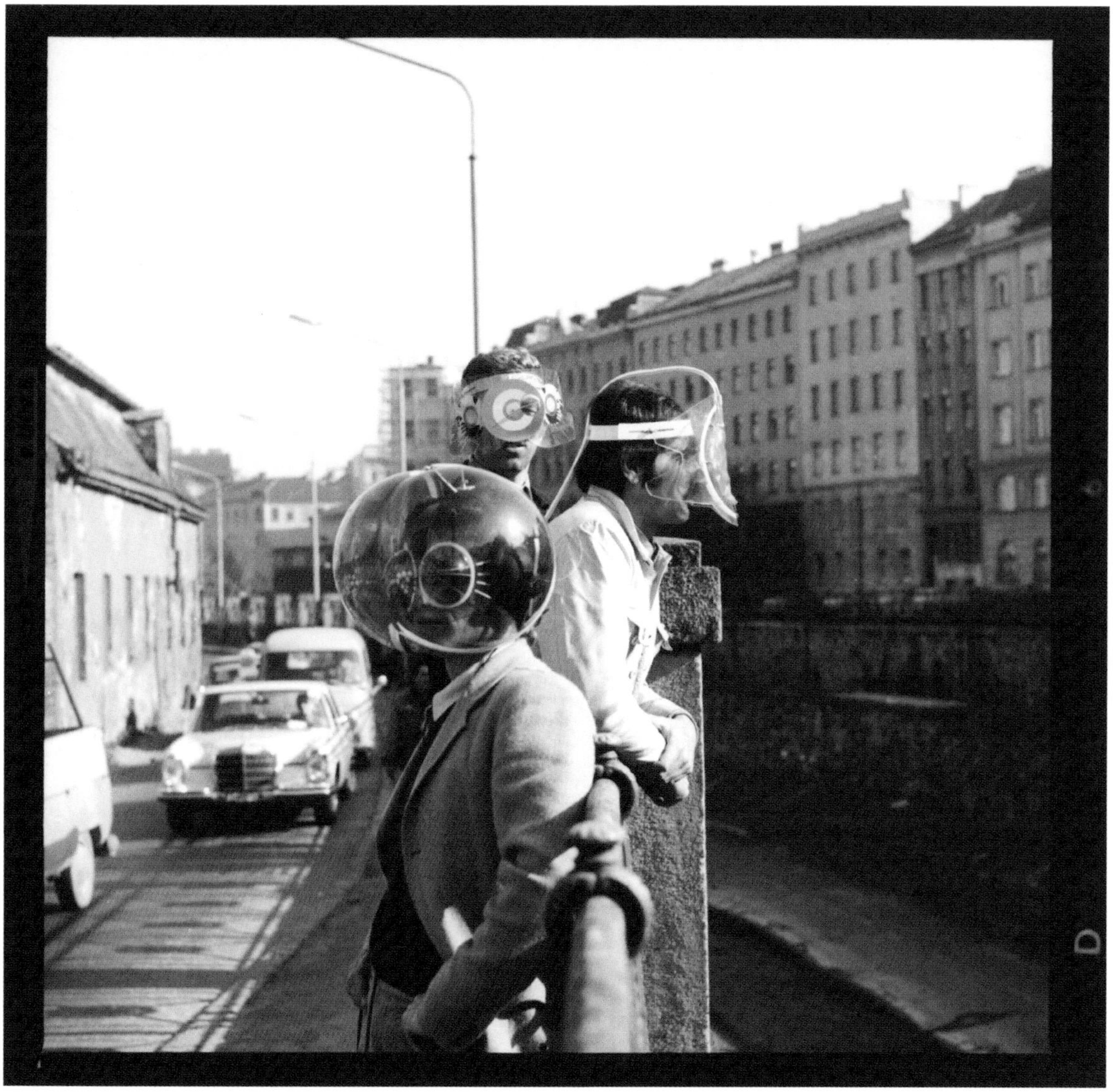

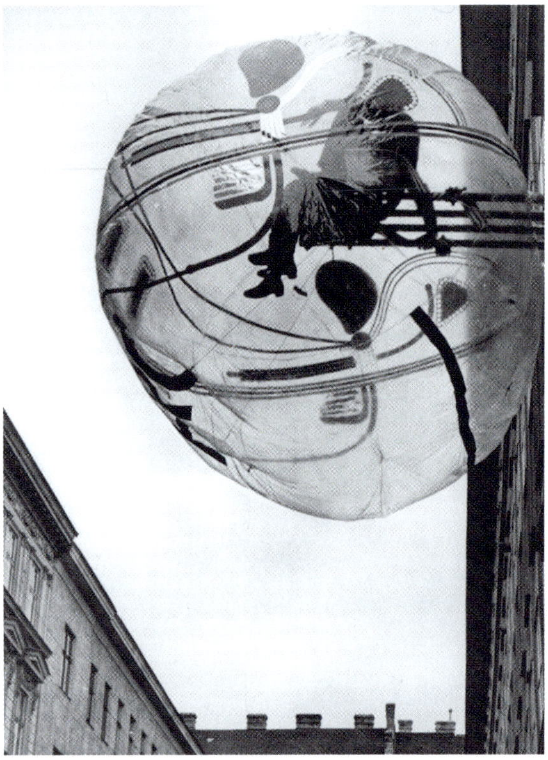

← Haus-Rucker-Co, *Balloon for 2*, Vienna, Austria, 1967. This is a 1:1 prototype installation in the experimental field of the spatial expansion of consciousness, was the first project Haus-Rucker-Co undertook as a team. The quest for expanding consciousness "by new, unprecedented spaces, objects and everyday utilities" shaped the works by Haus-Rucker-Co during their initial phase.

in China or even the air pollution problems we face here in Germany. Again, external effects of a man-made future!

LE It's interesting to talk about the effects of future-oriented acting that no longer can be controlled like climate change or artificial intelligence. The uncontrollable consequences of human acts are based on well-intended visions in the past, no? What's still left of the utopias that have inspired you? Or to put it differently: do you still think that utopian thought can productively engage with world affairs?

ZK Definitely! Tatlin's Monument for the 3rd International with its geometric parts rotating at different speeds, and Lissitzky's weightless constructions floating in nothingness are still relevant examples of the historical discussion about object and space and until today shape my conscious. Visionary construction was always an integral part of my projects. The construction of utopias is part of an aggressive world view that refreshes our actions with speculative moments, foils our realities.

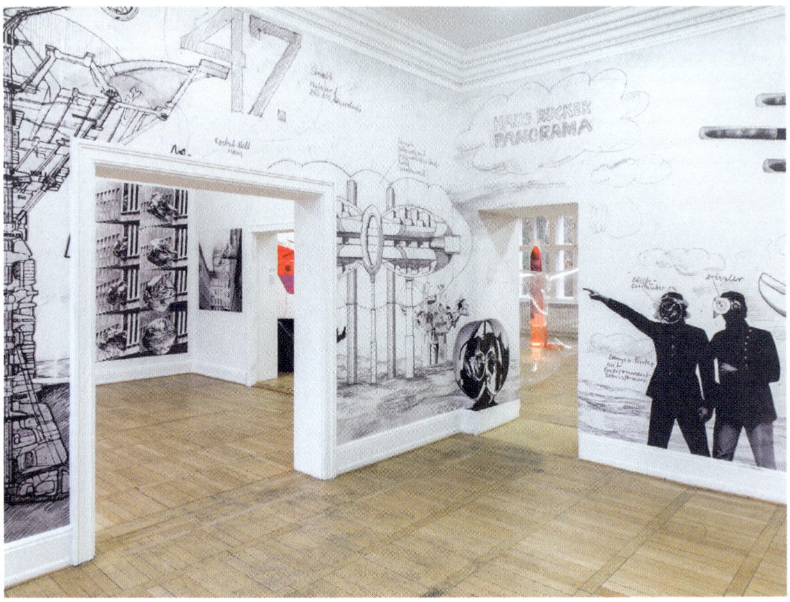

↓ Installation view of *Haus-Rucker-Co: Architectural Utopia Reloaded* curated by Ludwig Engel, Haus am Waldsee, Berlin, Germany, 2014. © Roman März.

LE How does it feel to leave so many of your ideas unrealized? Was your job rather to refresh our action with speculative moments than to build stuff?

ZK The idea or message that is attached to a building or a design was always the most important part to me. When ideas are being realized, they are being steadied, they reach the final point of their becoming. Take my *Neanderthal Museum* for example: It is built time, or the attempt to make time visible at least. If ideas continue to live on as ideas, they remain open windows through time. Many ideas open many windows, they are life's oxygen. I love ideas.

Ludwig Engel is a futurist and urbanist. Together with Zamp Kelp, he curated the exhibition 'Haus-Rucker-Co: Architectural Utopia Reloaded' at Berlin's Haus am Waldsee in 2014.

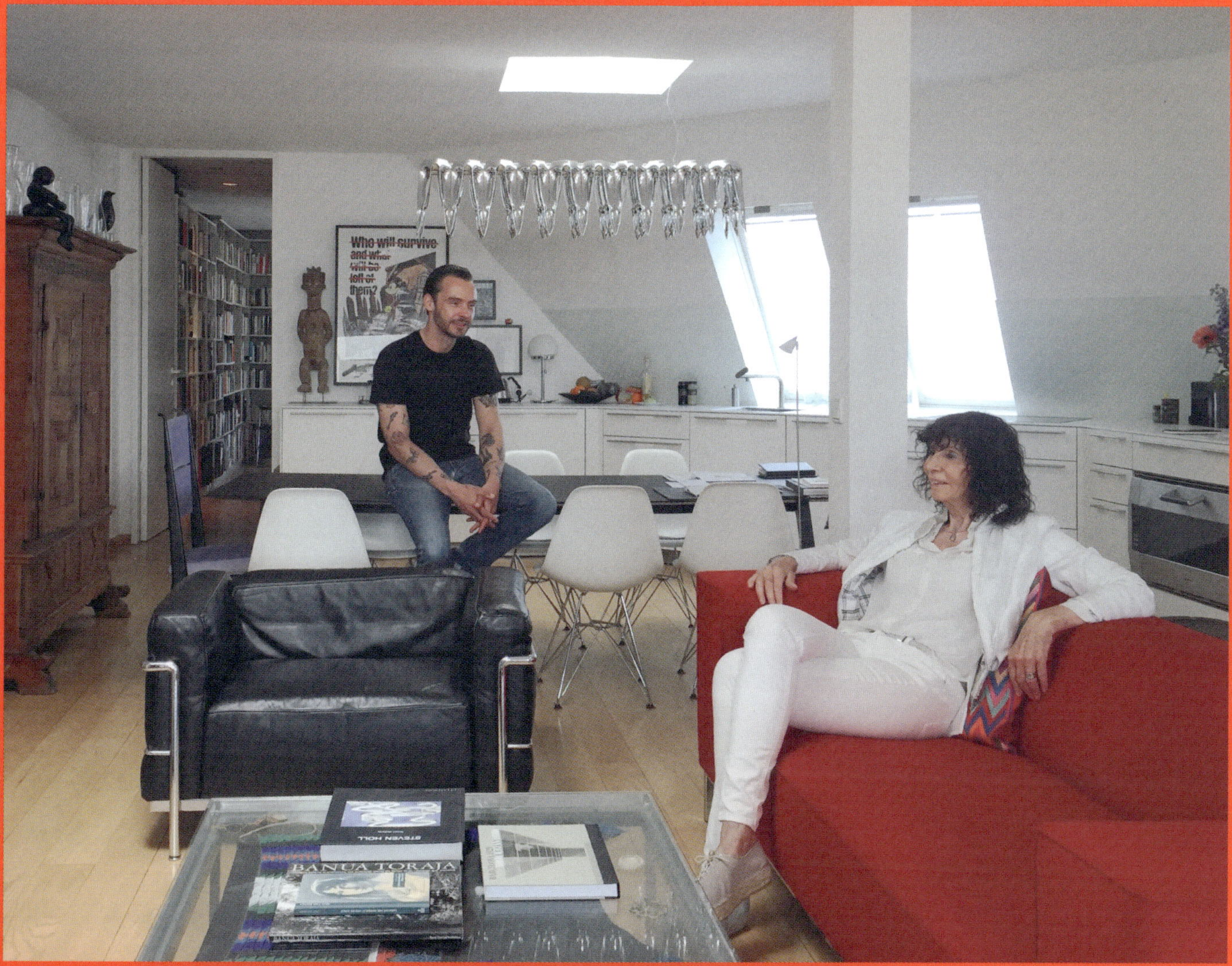

Curiosity as a Way of Life

Lukas Feireiss and Kristin Feireiss

In a conversation between mother and son, LUKAS FEIREISS explores with the German gallerist, architecture curator and writer KRISTIN FEIREISS their personal family legacies, growing up in a creative environment and various mentorship relationships throughout life.

LUKAS FEIREISS I'm trying to explore the personal, creative and intellectual legacy of an older generation and its effect on a younger generation in this book. In some case, literally between parent and children, in many cases between mentor and students, or just friends. To begin with, what's your understanding of legacy?

KRISTIN FEIREISS There are many ways to understand the term 'legacy', but if we concentrate in our conversation on legacy as something that is part of our history or some sort of spiritual and intellectual family heritage from an earlier time, it has followed me throughout my entire life due to the early passing of my parents and my brother. To me, legacy means to find out what my parents have passed on to me through their personalities as well as their lives and their way of living and treasure it. Only later did I realize how much my thinking and acting was also marked by my generous, brave and unconventional grandmother, with whom I spent a very happy childhood after my parents passed away. Sometimes I think that her legacy also lives on in you. Independent of these family ties however, there are also many other people whose legacy I've absorbed throughout my life.

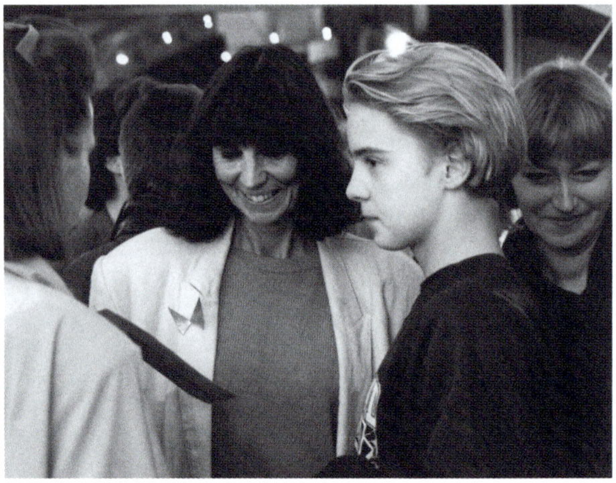

LF Now at the age of almost 76 years, looking back and looking ahead, what do you think is your legacy or what would you like your legacy to be?

KF The first time that I thought about my legacy was actually not so long ago, when some important people at various public events started talking about what they considered to be my outstanding life achievements. The many honours I've received over the years for my special achievement in the cultural field—ranging from the Cross of the Order of Merit of the Federal Republic of Germany, the Knight in the Order of the Netherlands Lion to the Honorary Fellow of the Royal Institute of British Architects and or the Austrian Honorary Cross for Science and Culture—I've always regarded from a rather pragmatic point of view as a helpful asset in finding potential sponsors for future project of our gallery and architecture forum. Obviously I was also very proud of all this positive feedback.

However, only in recent years I've come to understand that I am also some sort of a role model for a few people. At various events such as openings at our Aedes Architecture Forum or our Aedes Network Campus, which my partner Hans-Jürgen Com-

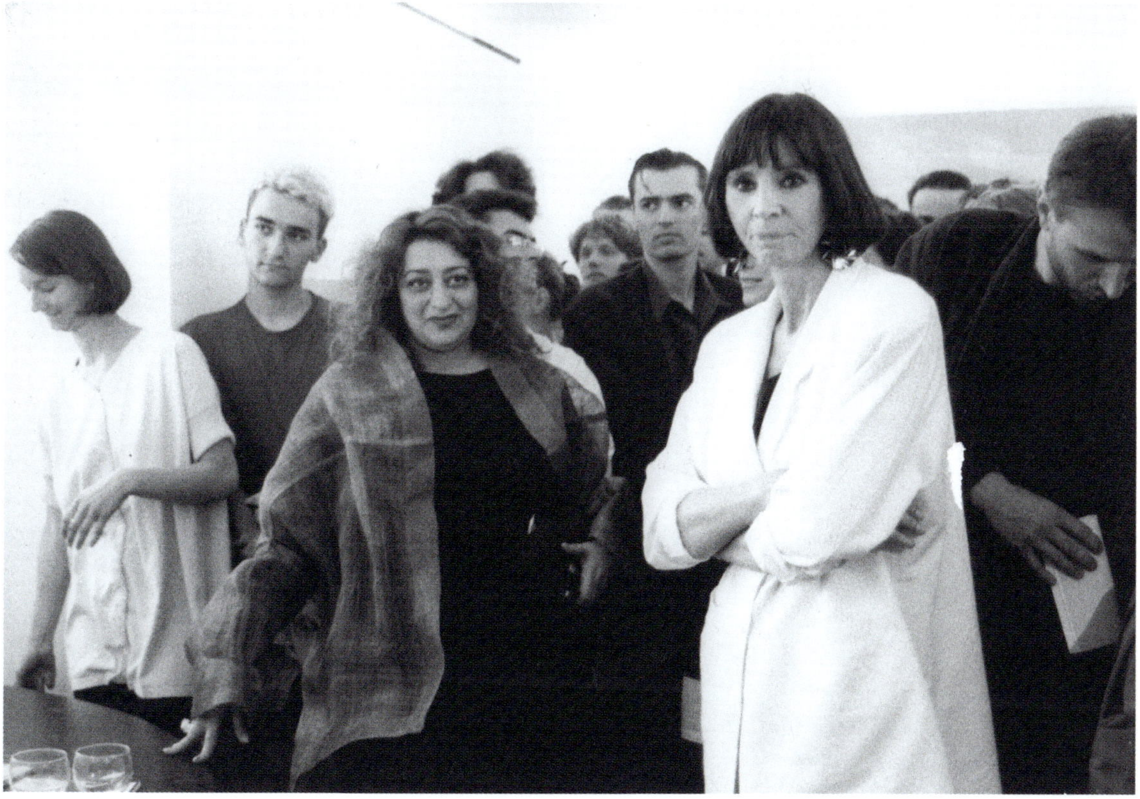

merell started in 2009, at lectures, panel discussions or jury sessions, different people, often young women, come to me and tell me how I've influenced their life through a conversation we've had, or a piece of advice I've given them. To encourage others to strive and go their own way without having been even aware of it at the time all is something wonderful. To answer your question, I would be happy with that type of legacy for myself.

LF Despite, or maybe because you've been married four times, family has always been a main driving force for you. Yet your own parents you only know of from stories, as they tragically died in car accident when you were a little girl, and too young to remember. You dedicated an entire book *Wie ein Haus aus Karten* (2012) to the personal exploration of your family's past. What have you learned about yourself and our family's legacy during this process?

KF I was only five years old when my parents and my brother died. Many decades later, I realized that my entire childhood memory—until I was about eight or nine years old—had been completely erased by that traumatic incident. Without memory there's no legacy. Therefore, the quest to find my roots, and learn about my parents, their characteristics, their talents, their doubts etc held a strong grip on me. Having worked as a journalist and having learned to research and express myself in written form, along with my natural curiosity helped me a lot in writing this book. A process which became literally an existential endeavour.

What did I learn? It's hard to say in a few words. I think that my parents and my grandmother's legacy is partially responsible for my drive. They were all very stubborn and free-spirited with big hearts and a remarkable intellect. They loved the arts and they were all in their own way out of the ordinary. They are my role models, my roots, my legacy. Whilst writing my book I read my mother's old diaries and even found my parent's last will. It was meant as a legacy, that would support their children beyond their own graves. In it they encourage

↰ Lukas Feireiss and Kristin Feireiss in her Berlin appartment, 2018. Photo by Hans-Jürgen Commerell.

↑ Kristin Feireiss, Zaha Hadid and in the back Patrick Schumacher at the opening of Hadid's exhibition *Vitra Firestation* at Aedes Architecture Forum, 1992. Photo by Regina Schubert.

← Kristin Feireiss und Lukas Feireiss at an opening at Aedes Architecture Forum, 1992. Photo by Regina Schubert.

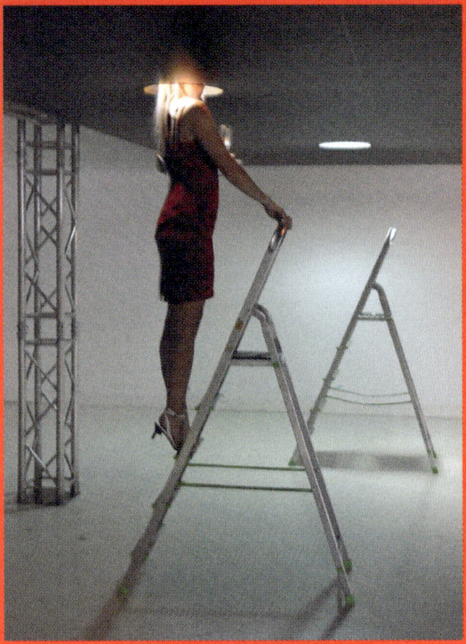

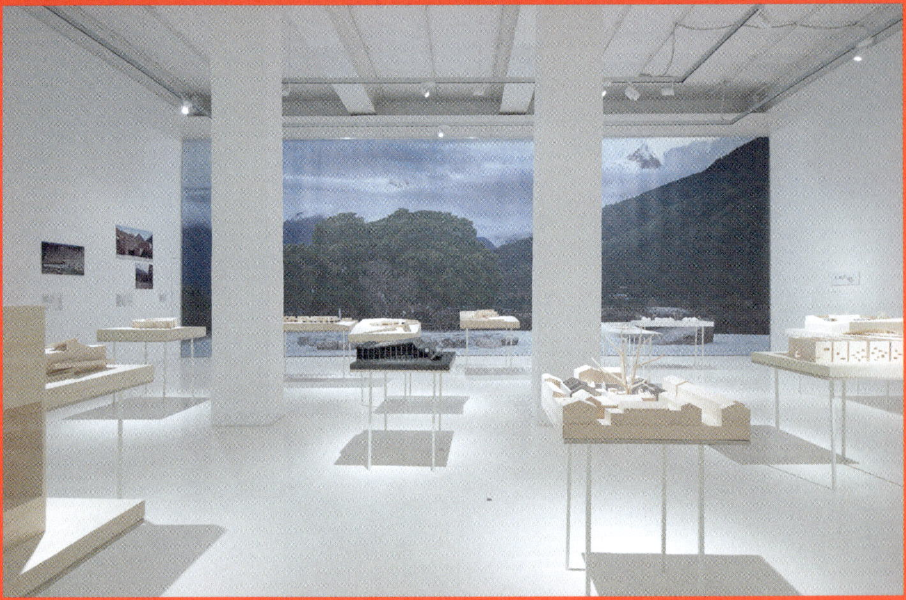

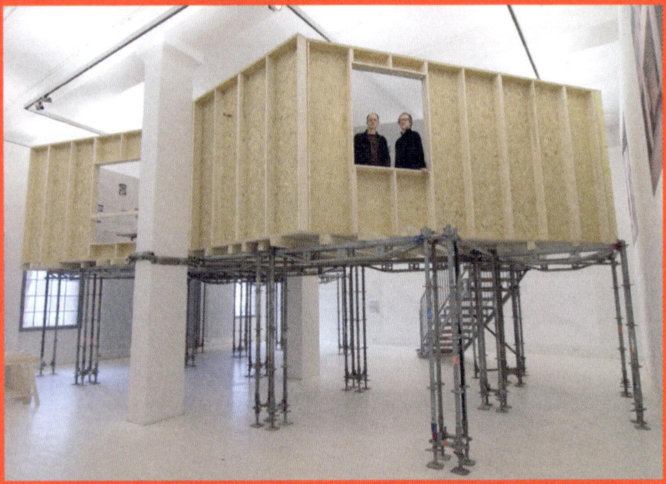

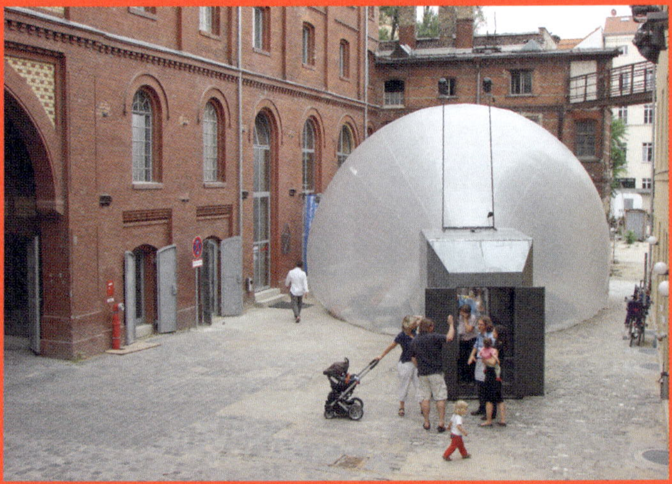

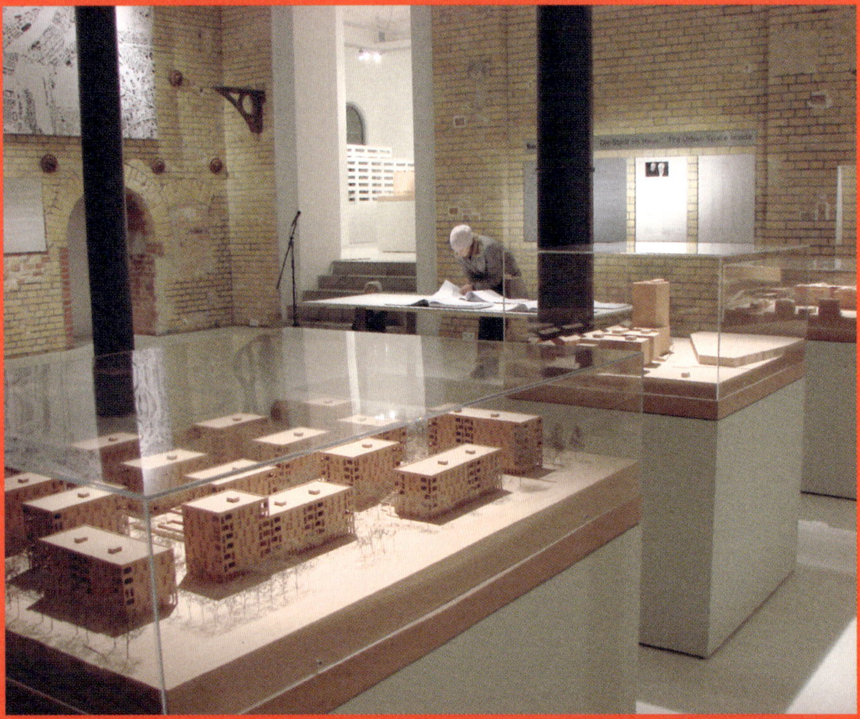

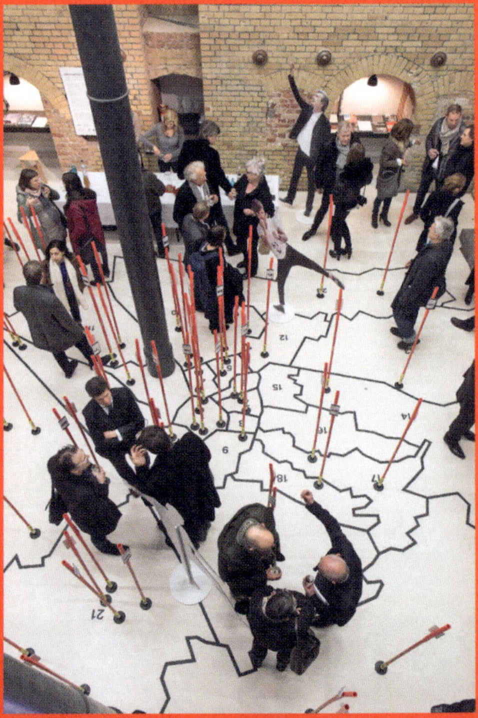

> 'There's something contagious about conviction, and I think that's only possible if you stay true to yourself.'
>
> KRISTIN FEIREISS

us to become free and independent human beings, stay true to ourselves, self-confidently go our way and to have the strength and courage not to follow the mainstream. It's an extraordinary piece of advice that helped me through many difficult periods. In principle, it's also my legacy to my children and grandchildren. I remember you telling me after the book was published: 'You've done a lot of amazing things, but this is by far the best.' Are you aware that you also contributed to the making of the book when you interviewed an old friend of your grandparents to learn more about them? I still have the three audio-cassettes. I think you were only 18 years old. What made you do it back then?

LF I think, due to the early passing of your parents, your stories of my grand-parents and our ancestors, in general, were really of epic dimension. Your parents, and in particular your father, became this mythical figure for me, a ladies man, but a die-hard Catholic, that allegedly spoke seven languages, opposed the Nazis, established overseas business connections to South America (thereby picking up an old family lineage that traces back to 18th century Mexico), became the king of the black market in Frankfurt after World War II, and then died mysteriously with his wife and oldest son in a car crash shortly thereafter. As I found out, things were actually even more complex and ambiguous than that. History knows of many diverging tales. At the time, I think I just graduated from high-school, I was simply curious.

Let's look outside of our family. You connected deeply with many different people in your life. Who were your mentors and what did you learn from them?

KF The often-deep connections that I have to many very different people is due to my privileged life situation, in as far as I've been created a life's work for me in which I've always been in touch with wonderful, complex and not easy-going, but always special personalities. Driven by a common interest, we worked together on various projects, most often exhibitions, catalogues and books. This doesn't work without mutual appreciation and trust. Almost always life-long friendships resulted from these collaborations. The separation between professional life and personal life never really existed for me. Your father—a doctor—had a very clear distinction between these lives. How do you in retrospect see the blending of my working and private life?

← Installation shots of various exhibitions at Aedes Architecture Forum. Top to bottom, left to right: A69 Architects, Prague, Czech Republic; von Ballmoos Krucker Architekten, Zurich, Switzerland; Baumschlager Eberle Architekten, Lustenau, Austria; Standard Architecture, Beijing, China; Raumlabor, Berlin, Germany; Viennies Architects, Vienna, Austria. All Photos by Aedes.

LF Well, it obviously affected me deeply since I can't really separate my personal and professional interests either. Having made my passion my profession, it's all one to me. Sometimes I just take that for granted. I feel very lucky and blessed. Let's return to your mentors.

KF Yes, there have been so many in my life but let me limit it to three here. The first being Julius Posener, an extremely witty, brilliant mind, pugnacious spirit and architecture historian, that opened up the world of architecture to me like no other. He was such a resourceful wordsmith and friend of men and lizards, that lived in peaceful coexistence with him and his family in his enchanted house in Berlin-Wannsee. He was a legend in his own right, but for me he was like a caring grandfather and mentor. I had the honour of helping him with his biography of German architect Hans Poelzig.

LF I remember you taking me to his house as a young child. He had a gentle smile and a steady stride. I was also absolutely mesmerized by the huge lizards that were just sitting in the sun on the windowsill. Creatures from a long-forgotten time.

KF I realize that the older I get, the more of my mentors only live on in my heart. Just like John Hejduk, the architect, philosopher, poet and imaginative artist who served as Dean of Cooper Union in New York for close to three decades. We developed a very special friendship during which he taught me that there is more than architecture between heaven and earth: an all-encompassing philanthropy and human ethic embedded in deep mysticism.

LF I will never forget when we took our first

trip to the United States. I must have been about ten years old and we stayed with him and his wife in their beautiful home in Riverdale. I still have the book on American carousel art called *Painted Ponies* (1927) he gave to me. In it he wrote 'To Lukas, to keep one's dreams throughout life.' Another special memory I have of Hejduk is him reciting a poem by German poet Rainer Maria Rilke while we planted a rose tree that you got for him in his small garden.

KF Yes, that's true. Another mentor of mine was the late Zaha Hadid. She was not only a genius architect but also one of the most generous and loyal human beings I've ever met. Maybe she was actually more of a friend then a mentor, but I admired her for how confidently and clearly she walked on her own path, and how little she cared about the opinions of others. She had no problem with being classified as a capricious diva, that's what she wanted, and most of the time I think she even enjoyed it.

LF I will never forget, driving Zaha after your 60th birthday party in Tuscany to the Airport in Pisa. Already short on time, I sped down endlessly winding country roads in the summer heat when, suddenly, the piece of paper with the directions flew out of the open car window, and the look on her face froze. Luckily we made it on time. I almost crash-parked the car in front of her gate of the airport, broke every imaginable airport security rule and even personally checked her in. It was madness, but also a lot of fun.

KF Yes, I actually remember her calling me every five minutes in panic but when you finally arrived at the airport, my phone rang again, and she just said in her deep voice: 'He made it.'

LF At your birthday party last year, the 75th, many friends and guests from completely different generational backgrounds approached me and told me how much you have influenced their life, sometimes even literally changed their lives. You mentioned that earlier yourself. I was very touched by that and very proud of you. Your commitment to those you love—whether it is your family or your friends—and for what you do —our work, your life is one of a kind. You've become a mentor yourself. What have been the most important advices you have given?

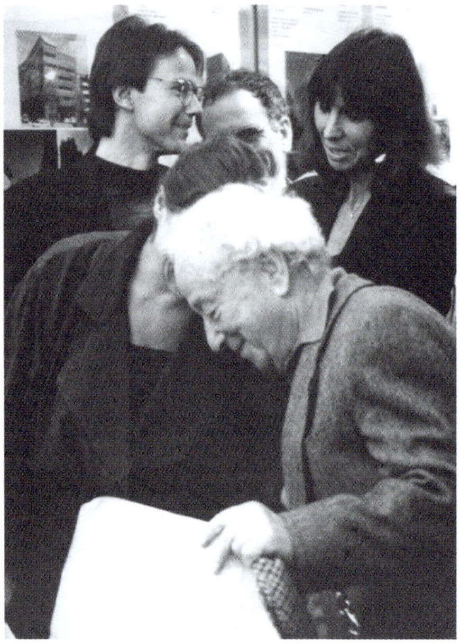

KF It's rather common-place advice really, but to simply enjoy what you are doing. Try to find a task that motivates you and for which you can also motivate others. There's something contagious about conviction, and I think that's only possible if you stay true to yourself. It's actually often more difficult to stay true to yourself than to others. Other than that, I think the contact with other people has always been most rewarding for me. To approach people unbiased and open with sincere interest in their lives and their stories. I think that's already motivation enough. By the way, since you just mentioned my last birthday party, as a young boy you once asked me tauntingly: 'Why do you always have to celebrate?' I'm not sure if I ever came you a plausible answer. Since I haven't, I'll do it now: It's because one should use any reason to bring family and friends together for a celebration. Wonderful communities develop, and new friendships are made.

LF That's true. There's always enough reason to celebrate being with family and friends. I very much love the spirit, but I have to admit that at times I rather prefer the quiet and private celebration. Your parties are more like festivals. (Laughs) When I was three years old—in 1980—you opened the world's first private architecture gallery Aedes in Berlin. Since then I've been continuously surrounded by architects and the gallery space became almost my natural habitat. Many of these architects and their children became life-long friends to me. What lead you to opening Aedes and how did you get into architecture in the first place?

KF I have always been an autodidact, by now a professional one. Neither my upbringing nor my studies of art history introduced me to

↙ Kristin Feireiss and Julius Posner, at the celebration of his 80th birthday at Aedes Architecture Forum, 1994. Photo by Regina Schubert.

↘ Frank Gehry and Lukas Feireiss at the opening of Gehry's Design Museum exhibition at Aedes Architecture Forum, 1989. Photo by Regina Schubert.

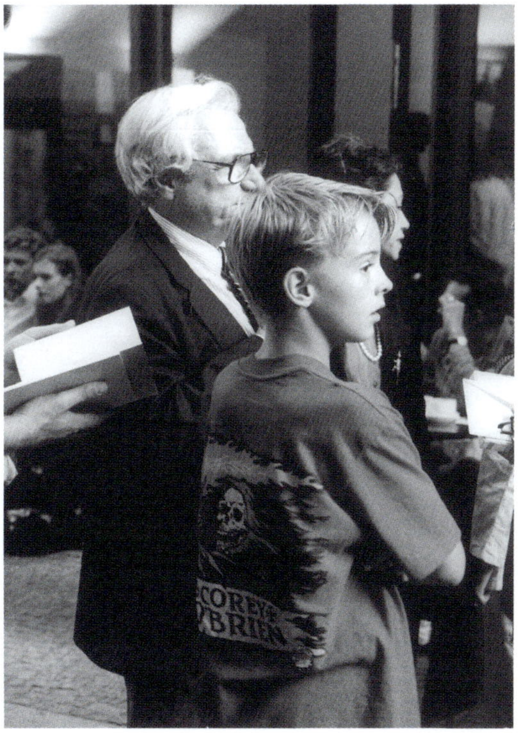

architecture. Whilst working as a journalist for newspaper and radio at the time, however, it just struck me that architecture simply didn't exist in the public awareness at all. I mean, there was the Internationale Bauausstellung (IBA) in Berlin at the time, but it only served a certain interest group. A platform where projects were publicly exhibited and independently debated simply didn't exist. Together with my partner Helga Retzer, who tragically died in an accident shortly after, we spontaneously decided to start an architecture gallery. We couldn't find any predecessors to learn from back then, but we had no idea that we were actually the world's first private architecture gallery. We found out only later. The first gallery was a small shop space of not even 40 square meters. We both had to continue working in our day jobs, however. Our basic idea for the gallery was as simple as actively creating an awareness for architecture for a general public, and beyond the expertise of only professionals. The design of our built environment is something that concerns all of us. How we live, where our children go to school, what our work situation looks like, how public spaces are designed and so forth.

LF In two years you will be celebrating the 40th anniversary of your gallery. What were the first years like, though?

KF Well, our initial idea not only to show but also to sell architectural drawings didn't really work, a few exceptions aside. However, when the Kongresshalle Berlin, an iconic symbol of the German-American friendship collapsed in 1980, we started an open call to architects around the world entitled 'In Memoriam Kongresshalle Berlin. Realistic Fantasies for a Collapsed Symbol'. Almost nobody knew us back then, but the interest in the topic was overwhelming. Architects such as Peter Eisenmann, Raimund Abraham, Peer Cook, Ron Herron, Cedric Price, Friedensreich Hundertwasser and many more send us drawings and texts. We made an exhibition with all the material, but since we didn't have any money for a catalogue we just put out an a pre-order list during the opening and with that money we were soon able to print the catalogue. That was the first catalogue of now almost 500 catalogues we published in the last 38 years. They are all in the same square format ever since.

Let me ask you something as well. In how far do you think has your upbringing in this environment influenced your own professional path and career?

LF I guess we're all a combination of nature and nurture. Both you and my father surely had a huge influence on me. Growing up in an environment surrounded by books, records, art and architecture leaves a mark. In my recollection, for example, my father almost always has a book in his hand. Despite being a medical doctor, he was one of the most well-read persons ever, and knew everything about history, literature and theatre. A very calm and collected personality. In many ways, you were the opposite. You brought in the passion and dedication to everything you were doing. Very driven. Sometimes a bit over-the-top, actually. (Laughs) Your seemingly unlimited engagement and interest in everything I did, made me feel taken very serious at an early age. It's a beautiful feeling. I believe that my roots grew rather strong because of that. For my 18th birthday you even created an exhibition in your gallery with photographs of each year of my life. That was amazing.

I've also been thinking that all of these architects that you worked with and that were staying at our house all the time were rather uncompromising characters that surpassed the bounds of a traditional understanding of architecture, freely connecting to many other artistic disciplines. More artists then architects in a way. All pretty extreme and inspiring characters, that really believed in what they were doing. Speaking of, what are your most memorable moments and personal encounters and anecdotes during almost four decades of running Aedes Gallery and being deeply involved in the architectural world?

KF There are so many unforgettable moments. Actually, one of the first involves you. I had just spread all of Alvaro Siza's Berlin sketches on our living room floor for an upcoming exhibition, when you—maybe 5 years old—came running into the room to tell me something and trampled all over the sketches. The shock on your face and your outcry I will never forget: 'I hope it wasn't an original!' (Laughs) Another one of these moments was the horror story with the drawings of Peter Eisenman. I carried all of his drawings in my luggage from New York to Berlin but when picking up my bag at the airport, I just saw my bag open on the luggage belt and all of the original drawings flying around. I almost had a heart attack, but I was luckily able to collect them all and save them from being crushed by the other bags. Miraculously, none of the drawings were damaged. Surely memorable was also the moment when I got a call from the Dutch ministry asking me whether I would be interested to become the director of the Netherlands Architecture Institute (NAi) in Rotterdam. Going from two employees at Aedes to a 100 in the world's biggest architecture museum was a quantum jump for me. When my husband Hans-Jürgen agreed to take over Aedes during my absence, I went to Rotterdam. It was very big challenge, but we succeeded. Truly unforgettable was also meeting with Nelson Mandela at a state banquet by Queen Beatrix of the Netherlands. I had just initiated the first comprehensive exhibition at the NAI called South Africa. Architecture, Apartheid and After. The brief encounter with Mandela moved me deeply. After all the injustice this man endured, he was not bitter but appeared loving, wise and benevolence. A shining role model for many, also for me.

> ## 'History knows of many diverging tales.'
>
> LUKAS FEIREISS

LF Around the time of the aforementioned exhibition about South Africa, your interest in African sculptures started, if I remember correctly. Now they are all over your apartment. What's the story behind this?

KF Yes, indeed. I am immensely intrigued by African sculpture. From the very first sculpture I keep a little notebook in which I draw a small sketch of each sculpture, and log all the available information: measurements, materiality, country, region, tribe and special characteristics. Since my childhood I've been fascinated by African culture, tradition and rituals and later my travels in South Africa, Togo, Ghana and Mali only fostered my interest in African sculpture. In the beginning I collected rather spontaneously, then I eventually started researching in books and on the internet. I still do. As you said, now these figures and masks populate our entire apartment.

LF I sometimes wonder what their legacy is! Back to your legacy now—I have learned many fundamental things from you which are very much in line with your parent's last-will and advice to their kids. We spoke about it earlier. Another thing you've taught me is to always prepare well but also not to stress if it doesn't work out the way I wanted it. All we can do is prepare, you used to say. That's what I tell my son today as well, by the way. Most importantly, I've learned to follow my passion. I wonder, if there has been some sort of secret formula to your success?

KF Success is always a question of perspective. In my lifetime, my understanding of success has changed a lot. My youth was very much dominated by my foster-parents and their family in which everybody wanted to be a winner. My foster-father's motto was: 'Defeat starts with second place.' This is also how he lived. I suppose that this attitude was—sadly enough—initially my motivation as well. I wanted to show them that even I, the black sheep of the family, am also a winner. Your father, Lukas, however could never relate to this ambition of mine at all. Once I finally found my own way professionally however, it was really

→ Various projects by Lukas Feireiss. Top to bottom, left to right: Studio Spass for *Street - Live Issue* (Wereld van Witte de With Festival) curated by Lukas Feireiss, Rotterdam, 2012; Studio Lukas Feireiss, Tattoos for Architects, 2015; Exhibition view of *Testify! The Consequences of Architecture* curated by Lukas Feireiss at Deutsches Architektur Zentrum, Berlin, 2011. Photo by Till Budde. Book cover of *Imagine Architecture. Artistic Visions of the Urban Realm* by Lukas Feireiss, Gestalten, 2016. Cover shot and spread from the book *Memories of the Moon Age* (Spector Books, Leipzig) by Lukas Feireiss, 2016; page view of *Planetary Echoes. Exploring the Implication of Human Settlement in Outer space* (Spector Books, Leipzig) edited by Lukas Feireiss and Michael Najjar, 2018.

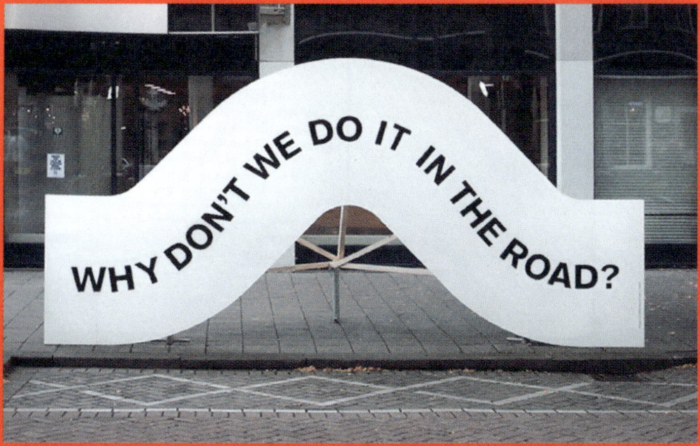
WHY DON'T WE DO IT IN THE ROAD?

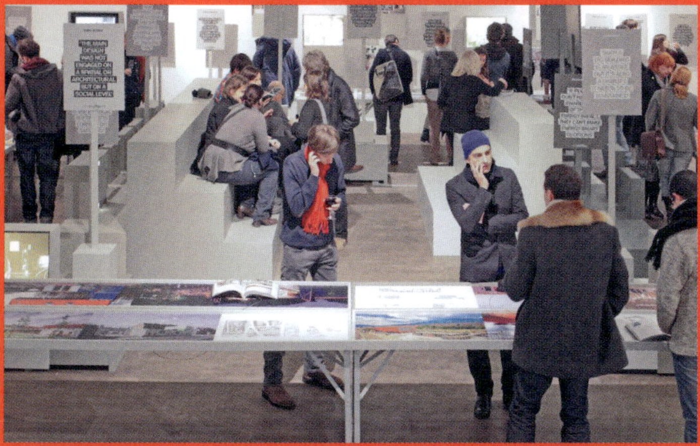

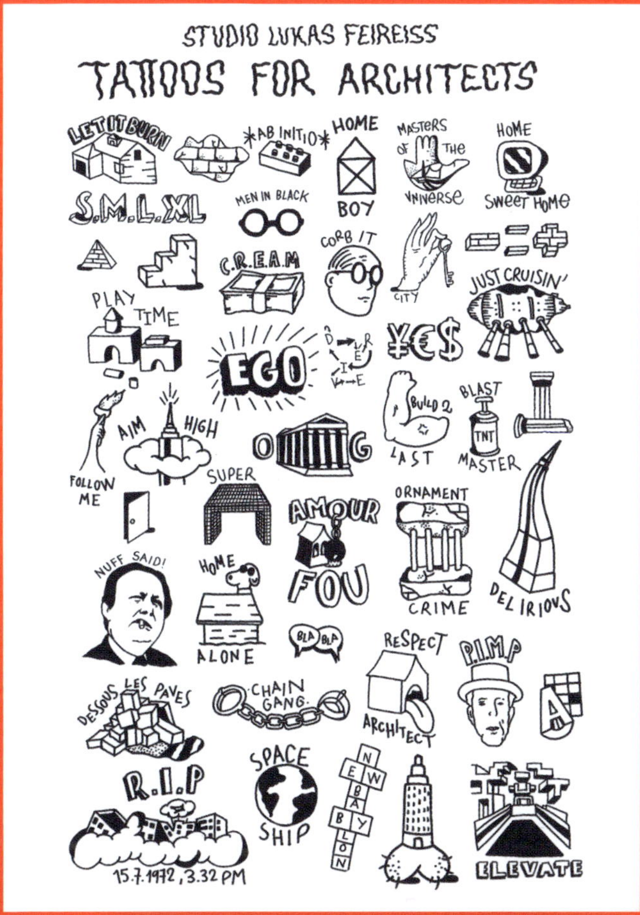
STUDIO LUKAS FEIREISS
TATTOOS FOR ARCHITECTS
LET IT BURN
AB INITIO
HOME BOY
MASTERS OF THE UNIVERSE
HOME SWEET HOME
S,M,L,XL
MEN IN BLACK
C.R.E.A.M
CORB IT
CITY
JUST CRUISIN'
PLAY TIME
EGO
¥€$
AIM HIGH
BUILD 2 LAST
BLAST MASTER
TNT
FOLLOW ME
SUPER
AMOUR FOU
ORNAMENT CRIME
DELIRIOUS
NUFF SAID!
HOME ALONE
BLA BLA
RESPECT ARCHITECT
PIMP
DESSOUS LES PAVES
CHAIN GANG
R.I.P
SPACE SHIP
NEW BABYLON
15.7.1972, 3.32 PM
ELEVATE

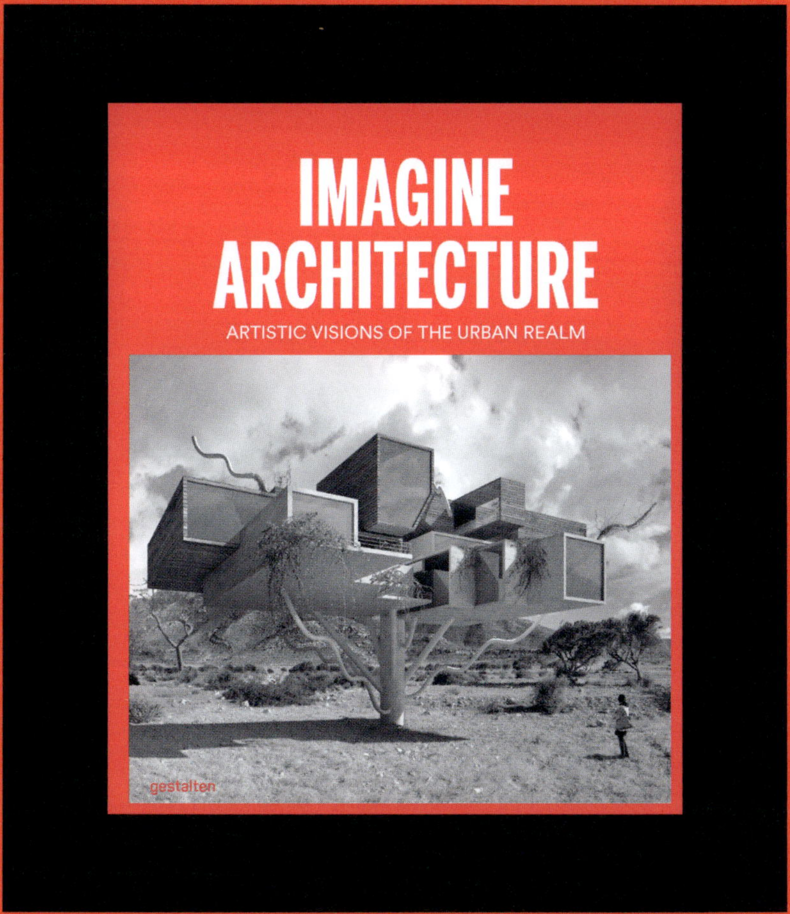
IMAGINE ARCHITECTURE
ARTISTIC VISIONS OF THE URBAN REALM
gestalten

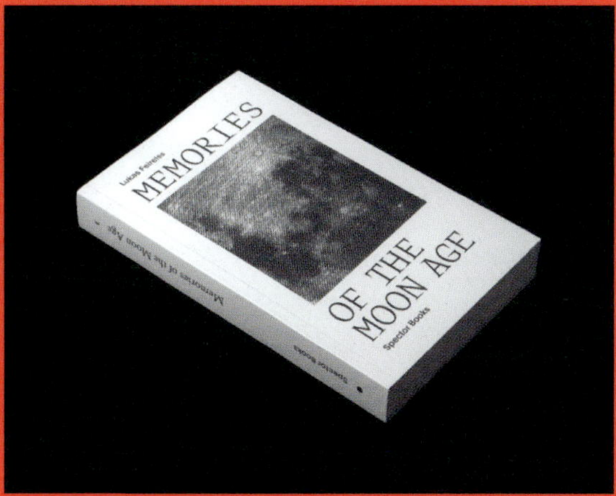
MEMORIES OF THE MOON AGE
Spector Books

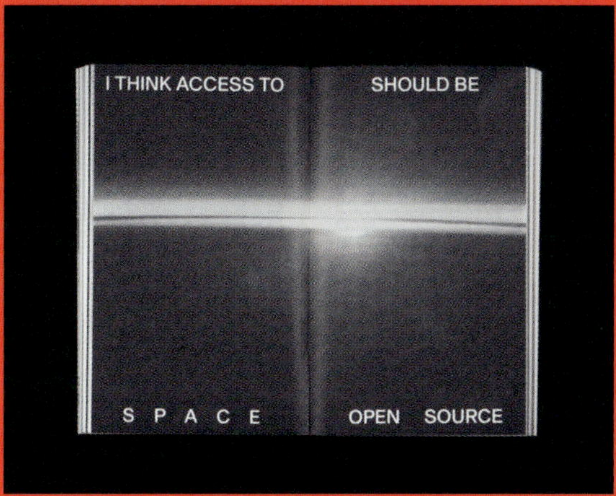
I THINK ACCESS TO
SHOULD BE
S P A C E
OPEN SOURCE

only about the joy and the excitement to do something that I really wanted with people whom I really wanted to work with. Having success with what you're passionate about—despite quiet a number of deep hits—encouraged me to carry on. Apart from that, honours and recognition are very beautiful, in particular, when you don't need them for your self-affirmation anymore. The biggest success for me, however, is the fortune of having a family, and in my case, a patchwork family that shares wonderful moments together and that has to work hard for it at times but always sticks together through thick and thin. A famous architecture photographer once asked me: 'How do you manage all of this with a family?' My answer to her was: 'How do you manage all of this without a family?'

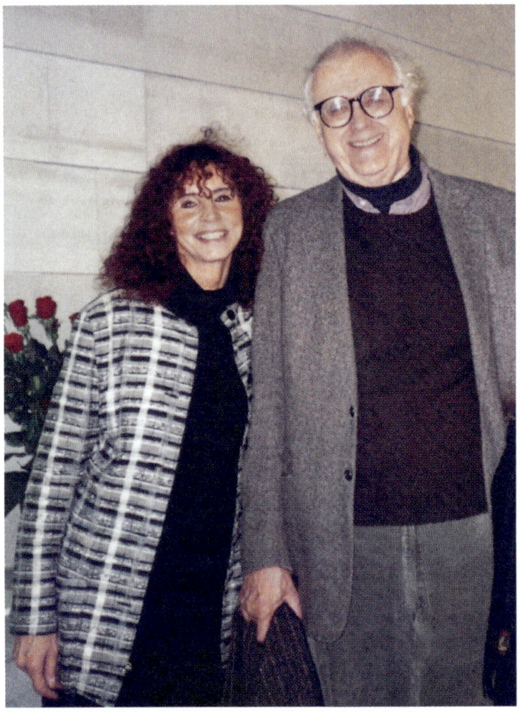

LF After four decades of intense discourse as mother son, is there anything that you have learned from me?

KF Where do I start here? Indeed, there are many things I learned from you and I am, surprisingly enough, still learning. I'm learning things that have a real impact on my life. One being, for example, your holistic view of the world and your ability to bring seemingly different fields of knowledge and expertise like philosophy, science, architecture, art, dance and music harmoniously together in your work as a curator, author, editor and educator. Beyond these intellectual achievements, I have also learned on a more general level from your deeply humane attitude. I've never been a weakling, but today your strength in mastering extreme situations in life is a real example for me. Most importantly, you've altered and expanded my view of the world simply by sharing your world with me. I think this goes both ways, actually. Obviously, there have also always been arguments between the two of us. We are both very stubborn and spontaneous. Even though I'm a little less stubborn now with age, I think. However, being of the same opinion all the time would be boring anyway. I remember very well when you said in your speech at my 65th birthday party, that we've had some friction at times, but that this friction ultimately generates heat. I believe that's true.

There's also your deep-rooted sense of independence and your determination to go your own way—that's something I admire and that I can relate to. That became obvious when you started studying comparative religious studies, philosophy and ethnology. Never for a moment did you even think about what you would do with that after your studies, I believe. Why did you choose this rather particular field of study?

LF I think I somehow always had a sincere interest in philosophical and spiritual questions, but the choice of these studies was rather coincidental. I remember reading a book on symbolism—a topic that continues to fascinate me to this day—and then noticed on the back cover that one of the authors studied comparative religious studies. This was the first time I ever heard about this field of academic study. A couple of years later, whilst waiting to apply for art school, I enlisted at Free University Berlin to bridge the time. Coincidently, I found out that Berlin was one of a few universities that offered a full programme in comparative religious studies, so I signed up for it, along with philosophy and ethnology. My original idea was to work on my portfolio for the art school for half a year whilst listening to a couple of lectures and following a few seminars. When it was time to apply for art school, I realized that I already found what I was looking for and stayed with the programme. I'm extremely grateful for these years. It's a great foundation to work from. Some-

↖ Kristin Feireiss and John Hejduk at Aedes Architecture Forum in Berlin, Germany, 1997. Photo by Hans-Jürgen Commerell.

→ Interior view of the apartment of Kristin Feireiss and Hans-Jürgen Commerell, Berlin, Germany, 2018. Photo by Hans-Jürgen Commerell.

time towards the end of my studies, I got into architectural theory. It was only then that I gradually realized what an ubiquitous and universal aspect architecture represents in man's existential nature. Hence, I specialized more and more in the dynamic relationship between architecture and other fields of knowledge. Here we are full-circle now.

KF Speaking of architecture, as much as I admired your independence, I was also pretty annoyed by it sometimes. We would have been so happy if you would have really gotten involved in Aedes, but you always declined. By now I somehow understand and respect it. At least we're working on some projects together.

LF Yes, I'm sure there will be many more future projects for us to come, like this interview for example. I very much enjoy collaborating with you and admire your professionalism. That's also something I learned from you: the admiration of true professionalism. Excellence at whatever it is someone is doing, is something I truly value very highly. However, to actually join your gallery, was indeed never really an option for me. That's, literally speaking, too close to home. You are already responsible for the architecture or space virus that got hold of me. Rest assured, I will carry on your legacy in other ways. (Laughs)

KF Whilst talking to you about what legacy means to me, I come to realize that the greatest fulfilment is maybe if something of yourself is being carried on, transformed and translated by the next generation to create something new. The best compliment I ever got was after a lecture I gave at the University of Applied Arts in Vienna on invitation by Wolf D Prix. A friend and known architect approached me and approvingly said: 'You were really amazing, but your son is better.' To me that's lived legacy.

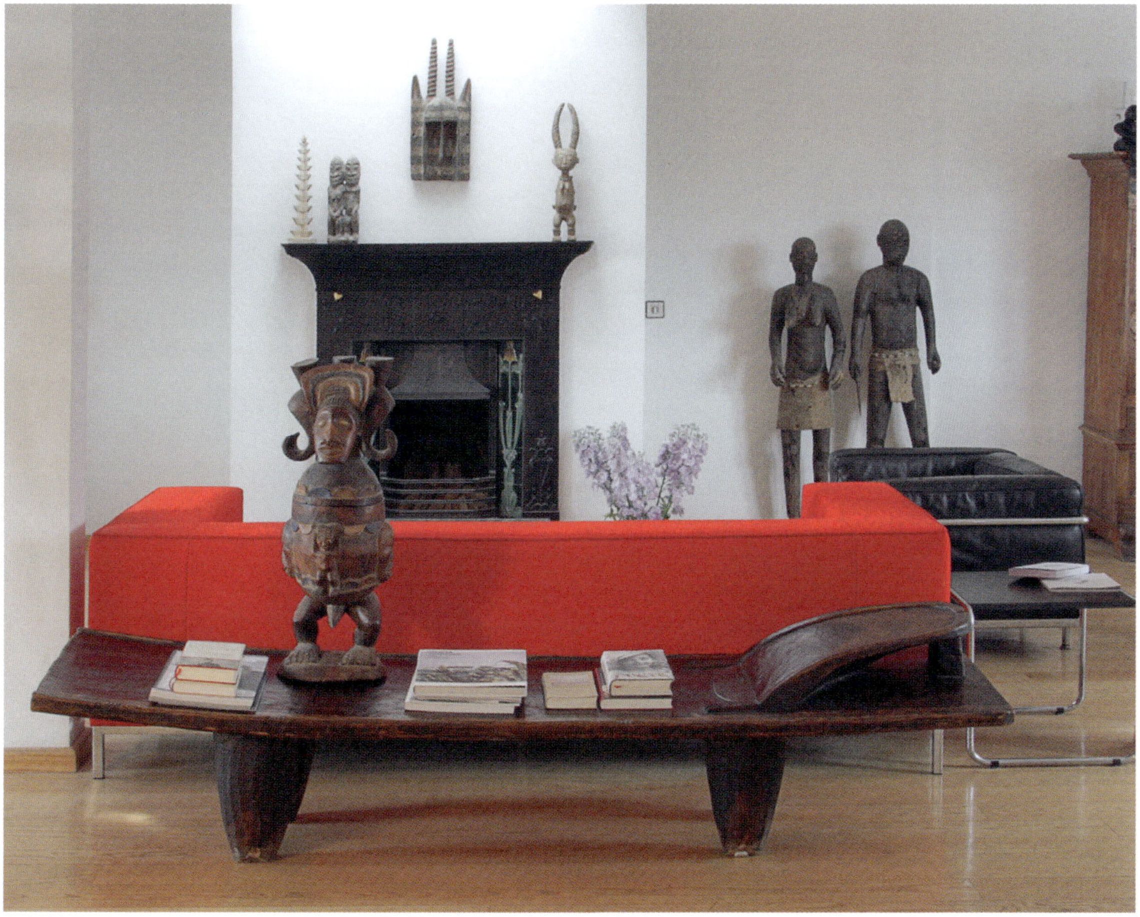

I Want to Be Remembered as a Failure

Lukas Feireiss and Ai Weiwei

LUKAS FEIREISS sits down with world famous Chinese artist and activist AI WEIWEI in the barrel-vaulted caverns of his underground studio in a former brewery in Berlin to speak about cultural heritage, retracing family legacies and living in exile.

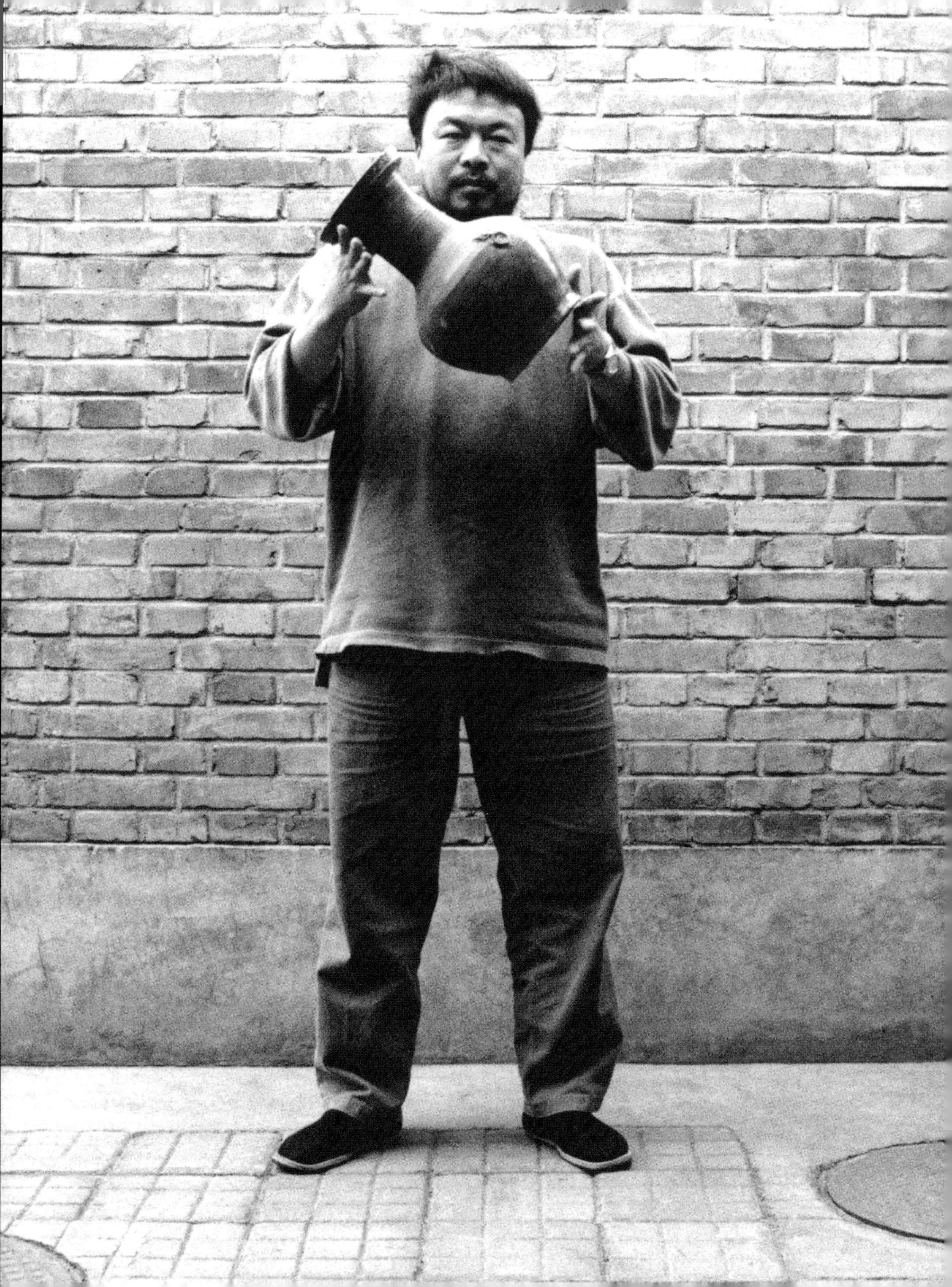

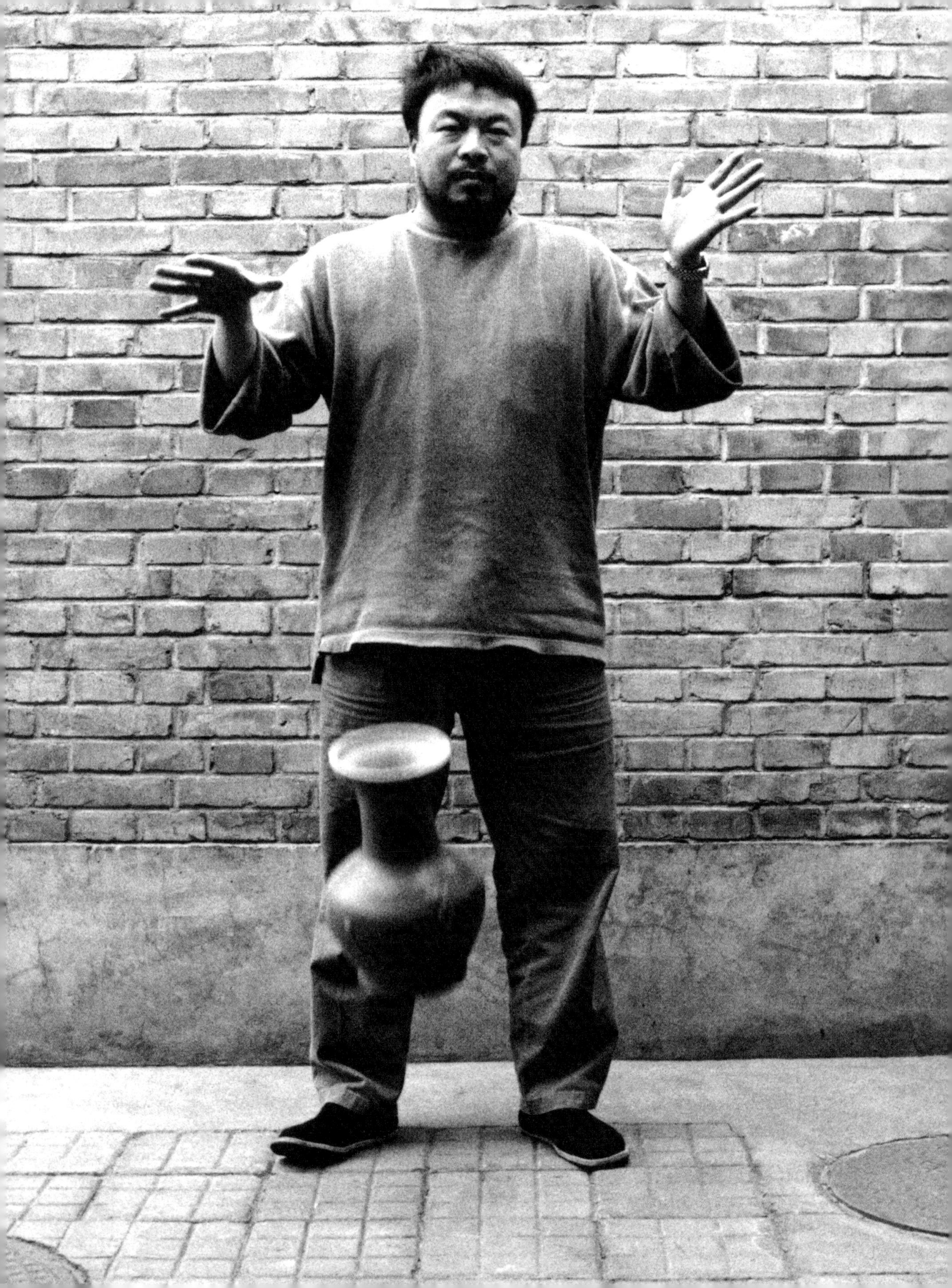

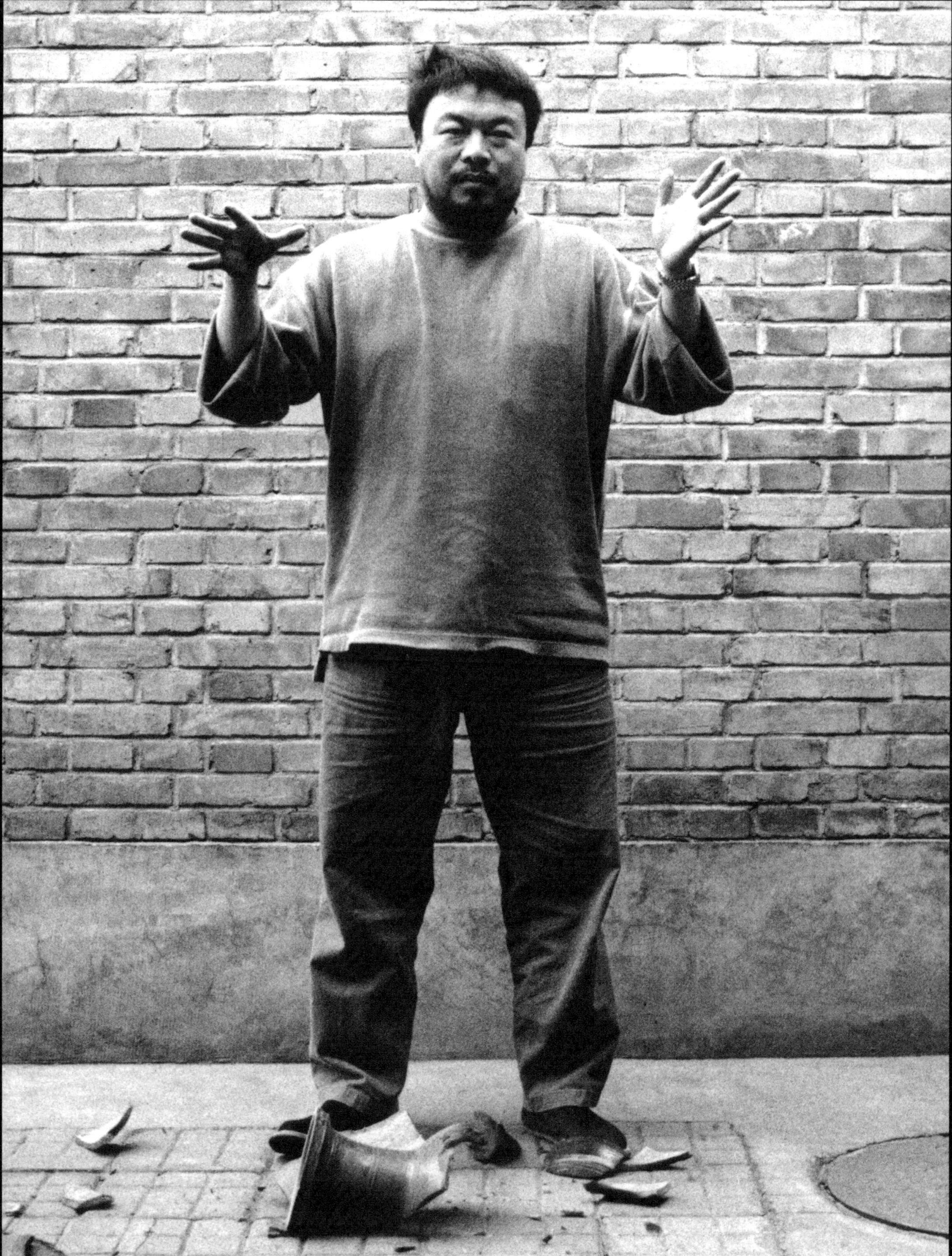

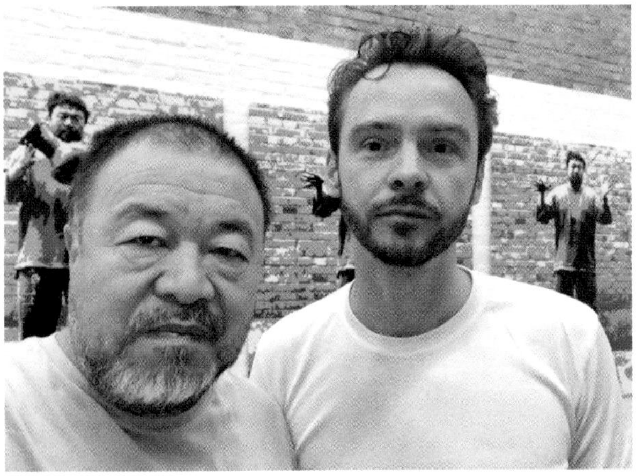

↰ Ai Weiwei, *Dropping a Han Dynasty Urn*, 1995.

← Lukas Feireiss and Ai Weiwei in his Berlin studio, 2018.

↓ Ai Weiwei and his father Ai Qing, ca. 1958.

→ Ai Weiwei with Allen Ginsberg, Lower East Side, New York, USA, 1988.

LUKAS FEIREISS I would like to start by addressing an earlier work of yours that, to me, represents a very provocative stance towards the subject of legacy, in particular cultural legacy. With *Dropping a Han Dynasty Urn* (1995), you smashed a 2000-year old ceremonial urn. The Han dynasty is considered a defining moment in Chinese civilization. This is an act of high symbolic power. In its literal iconoclasm, this smashed vase to me, seems to question the very notion of cultural legacy and memory.

AI WEIWEI My intention here was humorous, even though it obviously has a provocative nature—but provocative towards what? During the cultural revolution in China a lot of history and meaning was destroyed with clear political intent. Antiquities destroyed, temples burned, Buddha sculptures demolished. Throughout China's history you can observe the tendency of trying to get rid of what has been in the past. When I was confronted with the outcry from many antique dealers at the time, I told them that General Mao used to tell us that we can only build a new world if we destroy the old one. My act is simple, silly and has no profound meaning. From the outside, however, every act of mine is interpreted differently. Sometimes it's really surprising. I just do whatever I do. I don't think about it too much.

LF Let's talk about your personal legacy.

AW There is no legacy. The actions are all consequences of consequences of different kinds of actions or situations to which I respond to in my own way.

LF Ok, but your father Ai Qing is renowned as one of China's finest and most renowned poets. Shortly after you were born however, communist officials accused your father of being a rightist, and your family was exiled to labour camps in remote areas. As a result, you grew up in exile. To what extent has your family's legacy—and being the son of a famous father—influenced and inspired your personal trajectory?

AW Well, when I grew up his reputation manifested itself in another way. He was a famous enemy of the

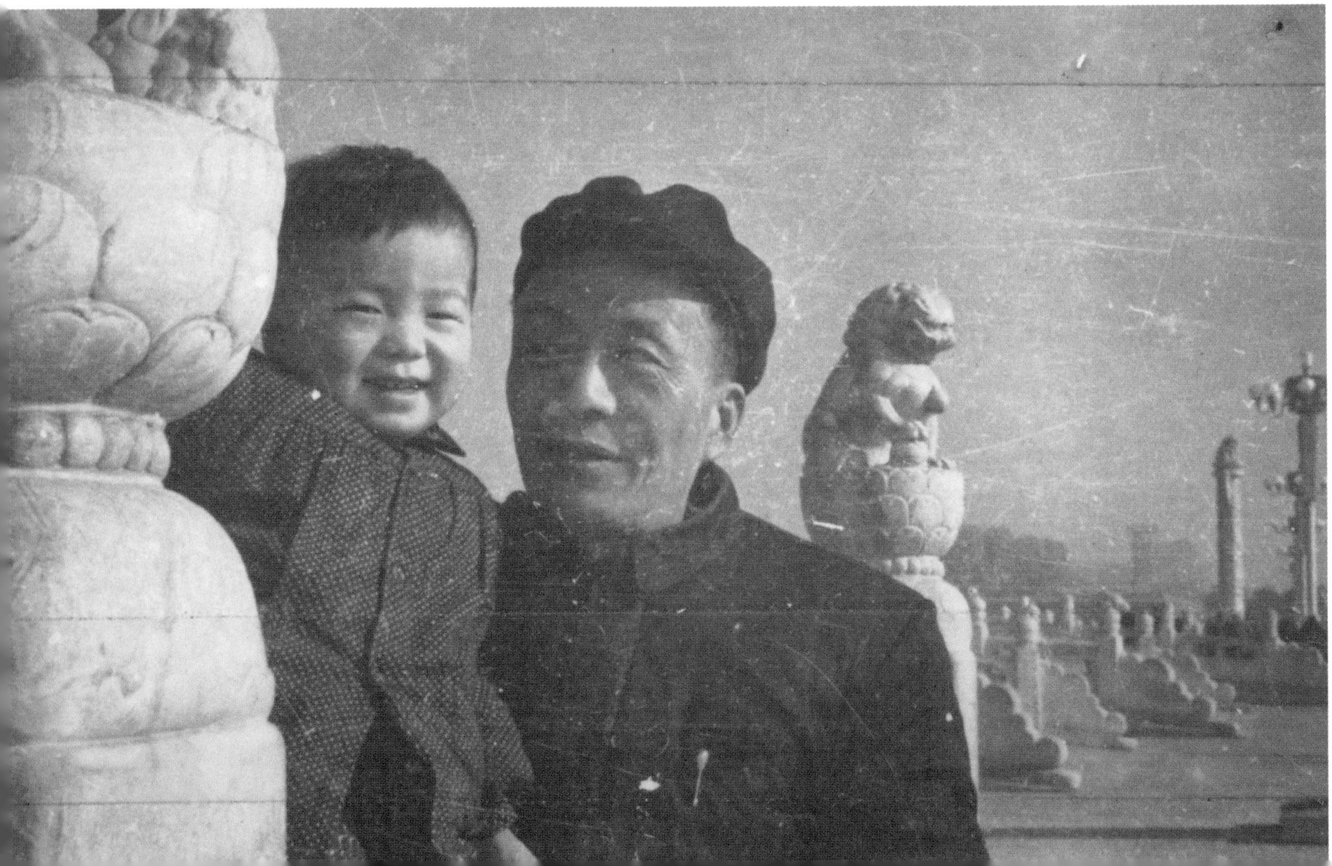

state, which meant that we were treated like criminals. At the time his notoriety was nothing we could build on or be proud of.

LF In the recently opened exhibition at the Musée des civilizations de l'Europe et de la Méditerranée you retrace your father's steps to Marseille in 1929. The show includes 50 works of yours alongside objects from the museum's collections. What has been your motivation behind this show?

AW I just needed a reason to open a show in Marseille. The only connection to Marseille is my father. He ported there about 90 years ago, when he went abroad to study in Paris between 1929 and 1932. That gave me a good reason to learn more about what Marseille is like. My father even wrote poems about the city. I also tried to imagine how Chinese people were treated at the time in Europe. Usually, they have been treated badly by Western nations. In an international military coalition an eight-nation alliance composed of Japan, Britain, France, the United States, Germany, Italy and Austria-Hungary invaded China in 1900 in order to divide it into colonial outposts for economic exploitation. In this way, the Chinese were always exploited as labour. Between 1917 and 1921 Chinese Labour Corps even served in France and were housed in camps in Calais, where today some of the biggest refugee and migrant encampments are also located. These are some of the things I explore in the exhibition. I'm trying to find out to what degree past and present have similarities and differences.

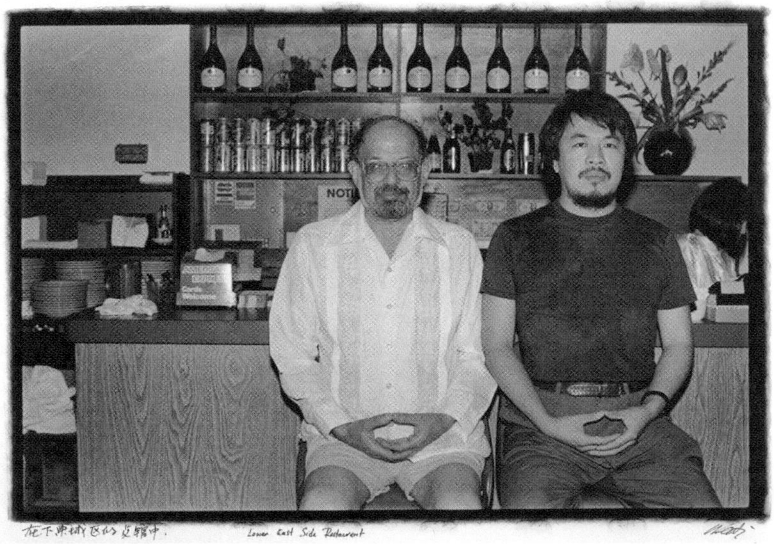

LF Talking about similarities and difference in past and present, when your father arrived in Marseille in 1929, he was roughly the same age you were when you moved to the United States in the early 1980s. You lived in New York for a decade between 1983 and 1993. Let's talk about this period, during which you documented over 10,000 photographs. A selection of about 200 photographs eventually became your 2009 show at the Three Shadows Photography Arts Center *Ai Weiwei: New York Photographs 1983-1993*. Can you elaborate on this period of your life?

AW It was actually a period of extreme difficulties; culture-wise, language-wise, and also economically speaking. To make it as someone from China in a society that cannot offer anything to support one's survival, is an extremely difficult situation. As an artist, I learned a lot though. I experienced what contemporary art is and how it is practiced. I'm also quite lucky, I think, to have spent my 20s outside of China and in New York.

LF One of the persons who, to my surprise, appears in these pictures alongside you is the famed American counterculture poet, writer and leading figure of the Beat Generation: Alan Ginsberg. I understand that Ginsberg had come to know your father on a trip to Beijing. How did you begin spending time with Ginsberg and eventually become his neighbour in New York?

AW He was just a person I met at a poetry reading at St. Mark's Church. I knew very little about him. I just noticed that everyone payed a lot of attention to this older man when he walked into the room. It turned out that he just came back from China. He read a poem about his trip in which he spoke about meeting my father. When he came down from the stage, I approached him and told him that the person he met was my father. He was very surprised. This is how we became friends.

LF Another iconic figure that you must have crossed paths with in New York at the time—one way or another—is Andy Warhol, patron saint of the Pop Art Movement.

AW I remember going to a gallery opening and hearing people say: 'Andy is here, Andy is here,' and suddenly I saw him through the crowd. It was incredible to be in the same room, but I was a nobody.

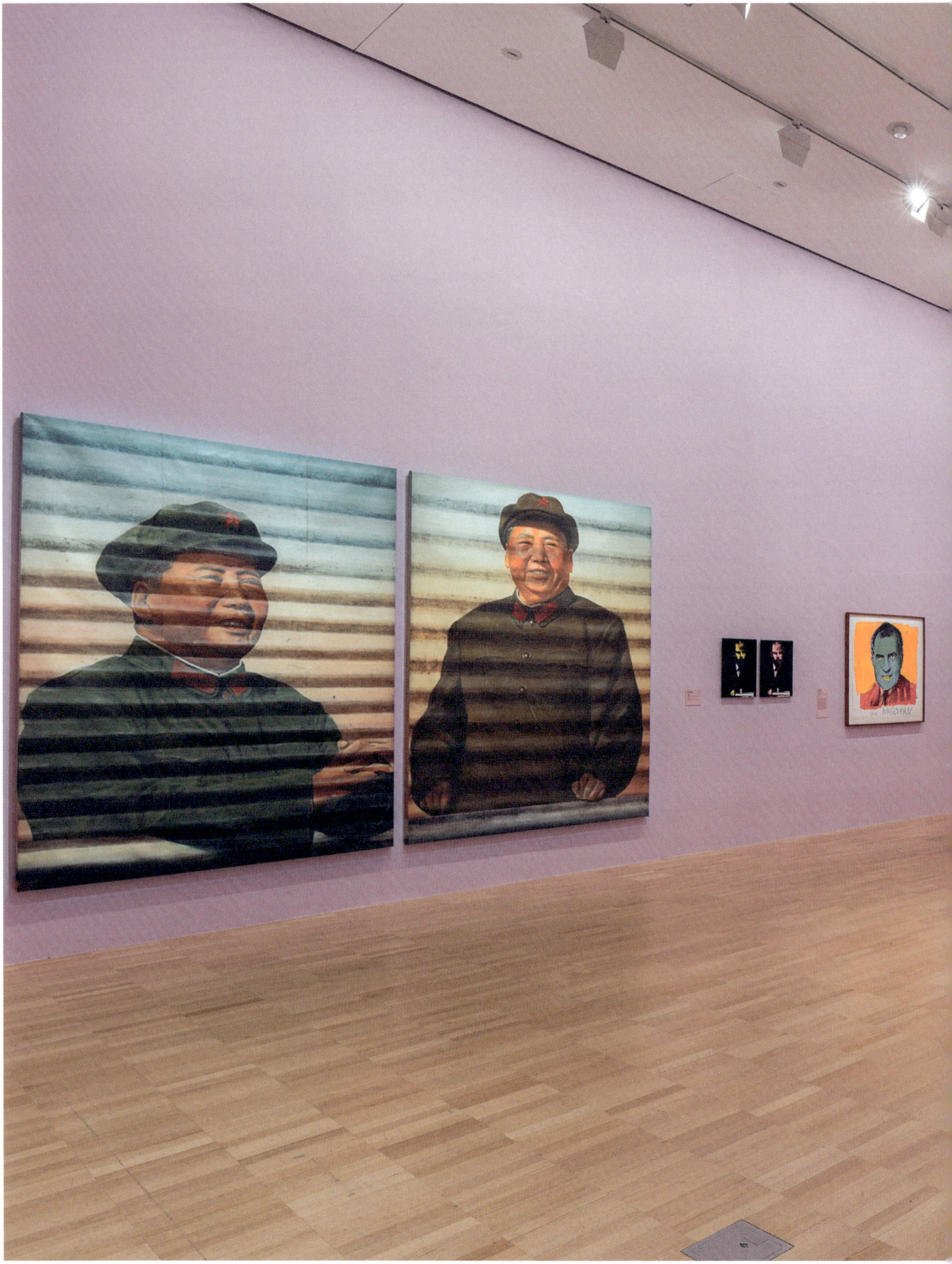

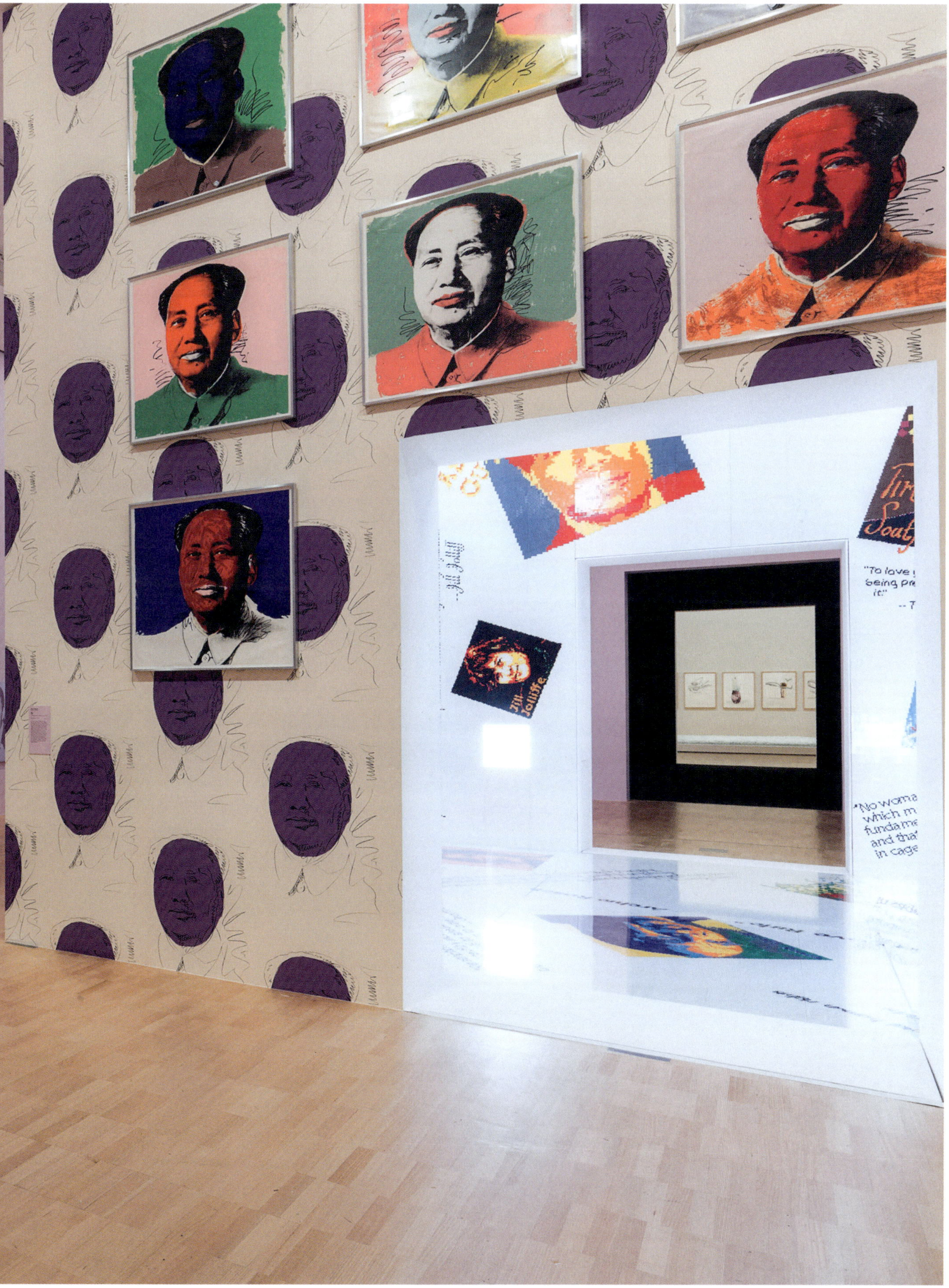

↰ Exhibition shot from the *Andy Warhol / Ai Weiwei* show at Gallery of Victoria, Melbourne, Australia, 2015.

✓ Ai Weiwei and his father Ai Qing, ca. 1993.

→ Ai Weiwei, *Han Jar Overpainted with Coca-Cola Logo*, 1995.

LF In 2016 the Andy Warhol Museum in Pittsburgh curated a fascinating dialogue exhibition entitled *Andy Warhol / Ai Weiwei* that explored the parallels, intersections and points of difference between the two of you. There are some very strong curatorial juxtapositions in the exhibition, like Warhol's Mao Zedong next to your own portraits of the Great Helmsman, or Warhol's Coca-Cola paintings alongside your centuries-old Chinese vase on which you inscribed the Coke trademark logo. How would you describe Warhol's legacy for you, personally?

AW Warhol is the most important American artist of the 20th century to me. I think he reflects more American cultural values than anybody else. I like his attitude, and I believe that he's never been really, fully understood—to this day.

LF It seems both of you compulsively record your lives and surroundings. Warhol had his tape recorder. You always have your iPhone, posting incessantly on Instagram and Twitter. What's this all about?

AW First of all, I have a bad memory. I don't trust my memory. Secondly, I'm often very bored. Even while doing an interview. I have to keep my mind fully occupied at all times. It's really just a habit. No profound meaning here. It's more like how artists used to make sketches in the old times.

LF In 1993 you returned to China when your father became ill. Around that time, you published a handmade underground publication that confronted the work of divergent artists from East and West. Amongst the notable Western artists are Duchamp, Warhol, Jeff Koons and Christo.

AW There's no such thing as a confrontation between the East and West. That's all made up cultural vocabularies. I don't care about confrontations between East and West. I do think, however, that contemporary art is a vocabulary from the West. It can only be understood against the backdrop of Western philosophical discourse—the industrial revolution and all the social changes that came along with it. Contemporary art is somehow imported to different locations around the world that also face similar kinds of societal developments. I made this publication back then, because I thought it was a good idea to introduce what has already been happening. It's not about saying it's good or it's bad, but to say that certain ideas or experiences have been established. Ultimately, the book is focused on what was happening in China during that period of time.

LF The last couple of times we've seen each other, your nine-year-old son has always been with you, playing on the side, listening attentively or doodling away. Now almost 60 years later, you are a famous father yourself, and you are also living in exile far from your home country. Do you ever think about what you want to pass along to your son? How do you regard your legacy regarding your son?

AW I don't have a personal legacy, and I don't believe in history repeating. With so many changes occurring daily in our lives, it's almost impossible to imagine what will happen in the next 20 or 30 years. My son is around because he's my son. I want to spend as much time with him as possible, because I'm working and traveling a lot. Otherwise I couldn't be a good father. I don't care about the rest.

LF You once said: 'I want to be remembered as a failure,' and further explained 'That means, that guy made an endless effort but failed.' What do you want to try and fail at doing?

AW I made a strong attempt to express my ideas in China. Of course, I think that those ideas could help China change to become a more reasonable society and a better environment for individuals. It would especially benefit young people, and encourage them to be more creative. China needs more imagination. As a result of my attempts, I ended up being detained, beaten up, and substantially fined. I've had endless confrontations in my efforts in trying to make my point clear. Still, at the end, I was being forced out of the country. I cannot even have my social media and internet activities in China. I'm totally shut off. There have even been threats to me and my family. That's what I'd call a total failure.

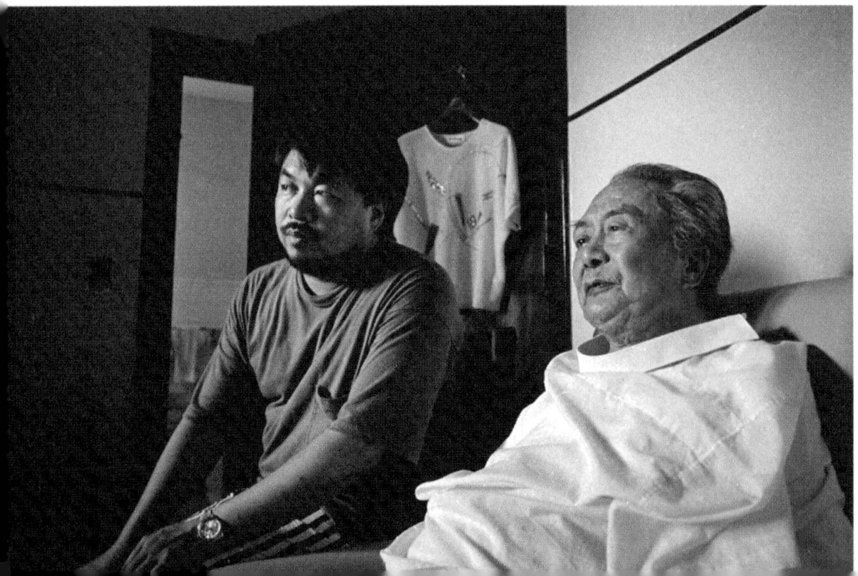

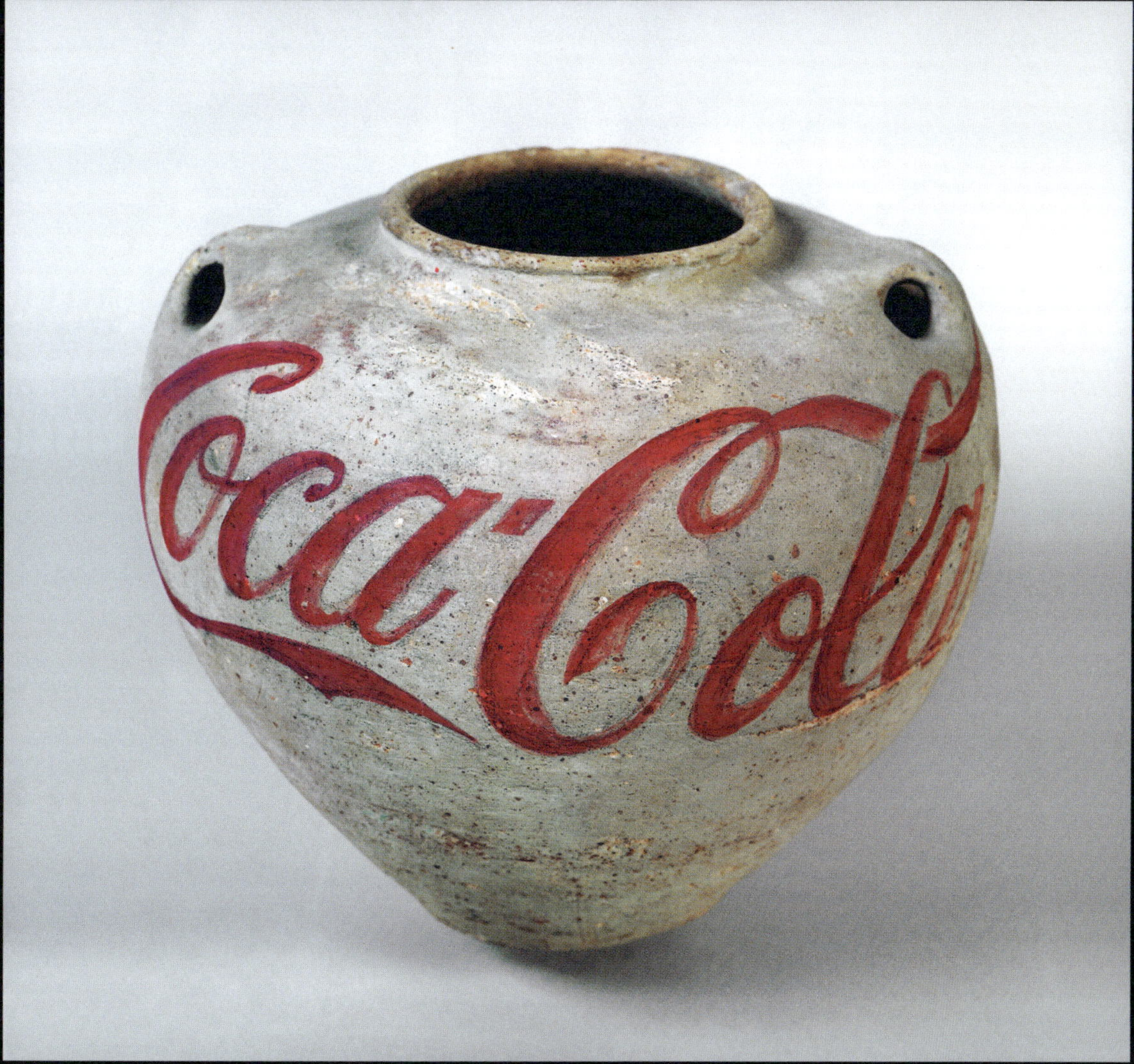

‘There is no legacy. The actions are all consequences of consequences of different kinds of actions or situations to which I respond in my own way.’

AI WEIWEI

Biographies

SIR KEN ADAM (1921-2016) was one of the most outstanding production designers of the 20th century. Adam, whose family had to leave Berlin in 1934 and emigrated to London, enrolled first at the Bartlett School of Architecture. During the war he served as a fighter pilot for the Royal Air Force (RAF). By coincidence he was engaged to do designs for a film after the war. As a result, he collaborated with outstanding designers, like Oliver Messel, and well-known directors, such as Stanley Kubrick, Robert Aldrich, Jacques Tourneur and István Szabó. Adam's name is primarily associated with the design of the James Bond films, whose sets bore his handwriting from the beginning. He was responsible for the design of a total of seven Bond films. Ken Adam worked on nearly 100 film projects, two opera productions, a multimedia project and diverse exhibitions over the course of more than 50 years.

KUNLÉ ADEYEMI (1976) is an architect, designer and urban researcher. He is the founder/principal of NLÉ and 2017 Aga Khan Design Critic in Architecture at Harvard University Graduate School of Design. His notable works include Makoko Floating School, an innovative prototype floating structure located on the lagoon heart of Lagos, Nigeria. This acclaimed project is part of an extensive research project—African Water Cities—being developed by NLÉ an architecture, design and urbanism practice founded by Adeyemi in 2010, focusing on developing cities and communities. Other projects include Chicoco Radio Media Center—an amphibious community building in Port Harcourt, Nigeria, ROCK—Lakefront Kiosk in Chicago, USA, CDL Head Office in Lagos, Nigeria and Serpentine Summer House at the Royal Kensington Gardens in London, UK.

FABIOLA ALONDRA (1984) born and raised in Mexico City is currently based in New York City and has lived in London and Milan. She is the owner of Fortnight Institute in New York with Jane Harmon and art director of 303 Gallery's publishing wing—303inPrint. Previously, she was the director of Fulton Ryder, Richard Prince's private bookshop, gallery and publisher in New York City.

Originally from Istanbul, **DEFNE AYAS** (1976) has worked as a curator, producer, publisher, teacher, advisor, and board member in the field of contemporary art and its institutions across the world. Ayas was Director of the Witte de With, Rotterdam from 2012 to 2017. Prior to her executive tenure, she co-founded many independent initiatives including Arthub Asia, a research and production initiative across Asia. Ayas was the curator of the Pavilion of Turkey in the 56th Venice Biennale, co-curator the 6th Moscow Biennale and co-curator of the 11th Baltic Triennale. In New York, she was a curator of PERFORMA, and a public programs coordinator at New Museum, where she produced live performances, critical debates and print projects with visual artists, architects, and writers.

SHUMON BASAR (1974) is a writer, thinker and cultural critic. He is co-author of *The Age of Earthquakes: A Guide to the Extreme Present* with Douglas Coupland and Hans Ulrich Obrist. His edited books include *Translated By, Cities from Zero and Hans Ulrich Obrist Interviews Volume 2.* He is Commissioner of the Global Art Forum in Dubai, Editor-at-large of Tank magazine and Contributing Editor at Bidoun magazine, Director of the Format program at the AA School, a member of Fondazione Prada's Thought Council and Art Jameel's Curatorial Council.

LUIS BERRÍOS-NEGRÓN (1971) is a Puerto Rican artist. Recent exhibitions include Impasse Finesse Neverness at the Museum of Archeology of Bahia Brazil (2017), Collapsed Greenhouse District Berlin (2016), and Earthscore Specularium Färgfabriken Stockholm (2015). In 2012, he was core collaborator in Paul Ryan's Threeing at Documenta13, and in Ute Meta Bauer's Future Archive at Neuer Berliner Kunstverein. In 2013 he represented Germany with curator Matthias Böttger in the São Paulo Biennial for Architecture, and in 2014 he was commissioned artist for the 3rd Biennial of Art of Bahia. He holds degrees from Parsons New School and the Massachusetts Institute of Technology. Berríos-Negrón currently lives and works between Stockholm, Copenhagen, and Berlin.

GIANFRANCO BOMBACI (1975) is a Rome-based architect. Together with Matteo Costanzo he founded the architectural office 2A+P/A. The office works on architectural, urban and landscape design with a particular interest in the nature and condition of the contemporary city. It engages in a broad range of activities including public and private buildings, housing complexes, urban spaces, event pavilions, temporary installations and interior design.

TÛBA ÇANDAR (1948) is a Turkish writer, editor, and author of biographies of three leading Turkish intellectuals. Her first book about the life of one of Turkey's first female architects Mualla Eyüboğlu Anhegger, *Hitit Güneşi (Hitite Sun)* was published in 2003. She released *Murat Belge Bir Hayat (Murat Belge A Life)* on the outspoken leftist Turkish intellectual and literary critic Murat Belge in 2007. Her 700-page biography of the murdered Armenian journalist Hrant Dink's life Hrant (2010) is a bestseller in Turkey. It has been published in the US under the title Hrant The Armenian Voice of the Voiceless in Turkey.

CARSON CHAN (1980) is a curator and writer currently pursuing a PhD at Princeton University School of Architecture. His current research tracks the rise of environmentalism and aquarium architecture in postwar United States. In 2006, he founded and directed PROGRAM—a non-profit initiative for art and architecture collaborations in Berlin—together with Fotini Lazaridou-Hatzigoga. He has variously organized more than 50 exhibitions internationally, including the 4th Marrakech Biennale, which he curated with Nadim Samman in 2012, the Biennial of the Americas in Denver, for which he served as the Executive Curator in 2013, and Dallas Aurora 2015, where he was Guest Curator. Carson's writing on architecture, art, and contemporary culture appears regularly in books and publications such as *Art Papers, Avery Review, Frieze, Log, PIN-UP, Texte zur Kunst*, as well as *Kaleidoscope* (Milan), where he is Contributing Editor, and *032* (Berlin), where he served as Editor-at-Large.

ARIC CHEN (1974) is Lead Curator for Design and Architecture at M+, the new museum for visual culture under construction in Hong Kong's West Kowloon Cultural District. He previously served as the first Creative Director of Beijing Design Week, and has been a frequent contributor to publications including *The New York Times, Architectural Record, PIN-UP* and others. Chen has curated award-winning exhibitions and projects, and serves on numerous juries and advisory boards, internationally. He is the author of *Brazil Modern* (2016, Monacelli), and was recipient of the inaugural Design Prize for best curator in 2017.

With a background in photography **CATHERINE CHERMAYEFF** (1957) served as special projects director of Magnum Photos, the photo agency founded by Henri Cartier-Bresson, whose foundation she is involved with until this day.

IVAN CHERMAYEFF (1932-2017) was a graphic designer who forged some of the most recognizable corporate logos of the second half of the 20th century—including those of the cable channel Showtime, the publisher HarperCollins and the Smithsonian Institution

MARO CHERMAYEFF (1962) is an award-winning filmmaker, producer, director, author and former television executive at A&E/AETN. She is Founder and Chair of the MFA program in Social Documentary at the School of Visual Arts in New York City and partner in the production company Show of Force.

PETER CHERMAYEFF (1936) is an architect and designer who specializes in aquarium architecture and exhibit design, from conceptual planning to the details of final realization. He was one of the founding members of the Cambridge Seven Associates together with his brother Ivan Chermayeff.

SAM CHERMAYEFF (1981) is an architect and cofounder of the office June14 Meyer-Grohbrügge & Chermayeff. Sam worked for SANAA in Tokyo for five years, leading projects such as the Serpentine Pavilion and curation of the Venice Biennale. He has taught at the Dessau institute of Architecture and at Columbia University, is recipient of a Graham Foundation grant and has lectured and exhibited internationally.

SERGE IVAN CHERMAYEFF (1900-1996) was a Russian-born British architect, industrial designer, writer, and co-founder of several architectural societies, including the American Society of Planners and Architects.

GEORGE EDWARD CLINTON (1941) is an American singer, songwriter, bandleader, and record producer. His Parliament-Funkadelic collective (which primarily recorded under the distinct band names Parliament and Funkadelic) developed an influential and eclectic form of funk music during the 1970s that drew on science fiction, outlandish fashion, psychedelic culture, and surreal humour. He launched a solo career in 1981, and would go on to influence 1990s hip-hop and G-funk. He is regarded, along with James Brown and Sly Stone, as one of the foremost innovators of funk music.

MATTEO COSTANZO (1973) is a Rome-based architect. Together with Gianfranco Bombaci he founded the architectural office 2A+P/A. The office works on architectural, urban and landscape design with a particular interest in the nature and condition of the contemporary city. It engages in a broad range of activities including public and private buildings, housing complexes, urban spaces, event pavilions, temporary installations and interior design.

EMORY DOUGLAS (1943) worked as the Minister of Culture for the Black Panther Party from 1967 until the Party disbanded in the 1980s. His graphic art was featured in most issues of the newspaper *The Black Panther* (which had a peak circulation of 139,000 per week in 1970). As the art director, designer, and main illustrator for *The Black Panther* newspaper, Douglas created images that became icons, representing black American struggles during the 1960s and 1970s.

WILLIAM ERNEST DRUMMOND (1953) is a Scottish artist, musician, writer, and record producer. He was the co-founder of late 1980s avant-garde pop group The KLF and its 1990s media-manipulating successor, the K Foundation, with which he famously burned £1 million in 1994. More recent art activities, carried out under Drummond's chosen banner of the Penkiln Burn, include making and distributing cakes, soup, flowers, beds and shoe-shine kits. More recent music projects include No Music Day, and the international tour of a choir called The17. Drummond is the author of several books about art and music.

BOB DYLAN (1941) is an American singer-songwriter, author, and painter who has been an influential figure in popular music and culture for more than five decades. Much of his most celebrated work dates from the 1960s, when he became a reluctant 'voice of a generation' with songs such as *Blowin in the Wind* and *The Times Are a-Changin'* that became anthems for the Civil Rights Movement and anti-war movement.

HOWARD EILAND (1948) is an American writer. He is Lecturer at the Department of Literature of the Massachusetts Institute of Technology. He received the 2011 James A. and Ruth Levitan Prize for Excellence in Teaching. He is the co-author, with Michael W. Jennings, of the first English-language biography of Walter Benjamin, *A Critical Life*. He co-edited three volumes of Benjamin's *Selected Writings*, and translated Benjamin's *Arcades Project, Berlin Childhood around 1900, On Hashish*, and his *Early Writings: 1910-1917*. He is slated to release a revised translation of Benjamin's rejected post-doctoral thesis of 1925 Trauerspiel, and continues to research on 20th century literature and philosophy, critical theory, film, and jazz.

OLAFUR ELIASSON (1967) is an Icelandic-Danish artist. His art is driven by his interests in perception, movement, embodied experience, and feelings of self. Eliasson strives to make the concerns of art relevant to society at large. Art, for him, is a crucial means for turning thinking into doing in the world. Eliasson's diverse works—in sculpture, painting, photography, film, and installations—have been exhibited widely throughout the world. Not limited to the confines of the museum and gallery, his practice engages the broader public sphere through architectural projects and interventions in civic space.

LUDWIG ENGEL (1982) works as a futurist and urbanist, exploring questions dealing with long-term strategy, the future city and urban utopias. He studied economics, communication sciences, and cultural history in Berlin, Frankfurt/Oder and Shanghai. After various teaching assignments in the fields of strategic foresight, futurology, urban planning and urban futures, he currently teaches Applied Futurology at University of Fine Arts Berlin and an Architecture Design Innovation Program at the Technical University in Berlin. Together with Zamp Kelp, he curated the exhibition Haus-Rucker-Co: Architectural Utopia Reloaded at Berlin's Haus am Waldsee Museum for Contemporary Art.

KRISTIN FEIREISS (1942) of Berlin, Germany, is an architecture curator, writer, and editor and founder of the independent Aedes Architecture Forum in Berlin in 1980. Since 1994 she has led this international platform in partnership with Hans-Jürgen Commerell and presented close to 500 exhibitions and accompanying catalogues. Together with Commerell she also initiated the Aedes Network Campus Berlin (ANCB) and The Metropolitan Laboratory in 2009. She served as director of the Netherlands Architecture Institute (NAi) from 1996 to 2001, and was commissioner of the Dutch Pavilion at the Architecture Biennale in Venice in 1996 and 2000; and a 2012 member of the International Jury for the Architecture Biennale in Venice. Between 2013 and 2017 she has been a member of the jury of the Pritzker Architecture Prize.

LUKAS FEIREISS (1977) works as curator, writer, art director and educator in the international mediation of contemporary cultural reflexivity beyond disciplinary boundaries. He attained his graduate education in Comparative Religious Studies, Philosophy and Ethnology. His Berlin-based creative practice Studio Lukas Feireiss aims at the critical cut-up and playful re-evaluation of creative and intellectual production modes and their diverse socio-cultural and medial conditions. Lukas Feireiss is author and editor of numerous books, and curator of manifold exhibitions. He has lectured and taught at various universities worldwide, and is Director of the Master's programme Radical Cut-Up at Sandberg Institute, Amsterdam.

GIAN PIERO FRASSINELLI (1939) is an Italian architect and one of the five founding member of Superstudio. Formed in 1966, Superstudio was a forward-thinking radical architecture collective that embraced a radical take on their practice. They created numerous utopian landscapes and iconic collages that influenced many generations of architects to come.

YONA FRIEDMAN (1923) is a Hungarian-born French architect, urban planner and designer. He was influential in the late 1950s and early 1960s, best known for his theory of mobile architecture.

BENJAMIN FOERSTER-BALDENIUS (1968) is an architect based in Berlin. In 1997 he founded the Institut für Angewandte Baukunst (Institute of Applied Building Arts). He is one of the members of Raumlabor, the collective of architects working at the intersection of architecture, research, urban planning and art since 1999, contributing to various Architecture Biennales in Venice. He develops and coproduces artistic projects in public space around the world and likes to talk about it. He teaches at various universities.

FRANCESCA GAVIN (1975) is a curator and writer based in London. She is the Art Editor of *Twin*, editor at large at *Kaleidoscope* and contributing editor at *Good Trouble, Sleek* and *Semaine.com.* She was the co-curator of the Historical Exhibition of Manifestall and has curated exhibitions internationally including The Dark Cube (Palais de Tokyo), E-Vapor-8 (Site Sheffield), and The New Psychedelia (Mu). She was the curator of the Soho House group for seven years, amassing a collection of 3,000 artworks. Gavin has written six books including this year's *Watch This Space, The Book of Hearts, 100 New Artists* and *Hell Bound: New Gothic Art*, and contributed to numerous publications including *The Financial Times, Dazed, Wallpaper*, Mousse, Another* and *Newsweek*. She has a monthly radio show Rough Version on NTS Radio.

FRANK GEHRY (1929) is a Canadian-born American architect, residing in Los Angeles. A number of his buildings, including his private residence, have become world-renowned attractions. His works are cited as being among the most important works of contemporary architecture in the 2010 World Architecture Survey, which led *Vanity Fair* to label him as 'The most important architect of our age'. Gehry's best-known works include the titanium-clad Guggenheim Museum in Bilbao, Spain; Walt Disney Concert Hall in downtown Los Angeles; Louis Vuitton Foundation in Paris, France; MIT Ray and Maria State Centre in Cambridge, Massachusetts, the Vitra Design Museum in Germany amongst many others.

ERIK DE HART (1982) is a multidisciplinary artist working across painting, drawing, writing and collage. He works as a graphic designer and record seller at renowned record label and store Rush Hour. As a hip hop aficionado and big fan of dense wordplay and intricate drum programming he DJs at cultural staples in the city. Music gives soul to his universe and makes him appreciate the creative imagination of humankind. Erik lives and works in Amsterdam, The Netherlands.

ARATA ISOZAKI (1931) is a Japanese architect. In 1954 graduated from the Department of Architecture in the Faculty of Engineering at the University of Tokyo. In 1963 established Arata Isozaki & Associates, the base from which he has continued to work ever since. From his 1960s work such as Oita Prefectural Library, to his 1990s work in locations as far as Barcelona, Orlando, Kraków, Nagi in Okayama Perfecture, Kyoto, Nara La Coruna, Akiyoshidai in Yamaguchi Prefecxture and Berlin, to his 21st century work in the Middle East, China, Central Asia, and elsewhere, Isozaki has created an architect so personal in its ideas and spaces that it defies characterization in any school of thought. His activities, spanning over half a century, have gone beyond thought, art, design, music, film, theatre, and of course architecture, and they have raised questions spanning multiple ages and multiple disciplines.

GÜNTER ZAMP KELP (1941) has maintained an independent architectural practice since 1987 consisting of public art commissions and architectural designs. He was a professor of architecture and design at the University of Arts, Berlin, for nearly 20 years. He lives in Berlin. In 1967 he co-founded Haus-Rucker-Co with Klaus Pinter, and Laurids Ortner. The group had a notorious reputation for their wildly spectacular interventions and installations and maintained a prolific production on both sides of the Atlantic with numerous solo exhibitions in private galleries and public institutions, along with their participation in three instalments of Documenta (5, 6, and 8). They officially dissolved on the occasion of the Haus-Rucker-Co exhibition at Kunsthalle Wien in 1992.

Dutch artist, writer and professional photographer CHARLIE KOOLHAAS (1977) grew up in London, UK and currently operates a studio out of Rotterdam, Netherlands where she lives. With a graduate background in both Sociology and Interactive Media, she is interested in documenting the process through which multiculturalism spurns new cultural hybrids, to examine the meaning of 'identity' at a time when identities are constantly dissolved and re-made.

REM KOOLHAAS (1944) founded OMA in 1975 together with Elia and Zoe Zenghelis and Madelon Vriesendorp. He graduated from the Architectural Association in London and in 1978 published *Delirious New York: A Retroactive Manifesto for Manhattan*. In 1995, his book *S, M, L, XL* summarized the work of OMA in 'a novel about architecture'. He heads the work of both OMA and AMO, the research branch of OMA, operating in areas beyond the realm of architecture. His built work includes the Garage Museum of Contemporary Art in Moscow (2015), Fondazione Prada in Milan (2015), the headquarters for China Central Television (CCTV) in Beijing (2012), Casa da Musica in Porto (2005), Seattle Central Library (2004), and the Netherlands Embassy in Berlin (2003). Current projects include the Qatar Foundation headquarters, Qatar National Library, Taipei Performing Arts Centre, a new building for Axel Springer in Berlin, and Factory in Manchester. Koolhaas is a professor at Harvard University and in 2014 was the director of the 14th International Architecture Exhibition of the Venice Biennale, entitled Fundamentals.

PHYLLIS LAMBERT (1927) is widely considered to be among the most influential figures in architecture. She founded the Canadian Centre of Architecture (CCA) in her hometown of Montrèal in 1979, and also acted as Director of Planning for the world-renowned Seagram Building in Manhattan (a tower commissioned by her family). The project is often cited as one of Mies van der Rohe's most important built works. As a practising architect, Lambert designed the Saidye Bronfman Centre (1967)—a performing arts centre named after her mother. Lambert was awarded the 2014 Venice Biennale Golden Lion in recognition of a lifetime of work pushing the boundaries of architectural innovation.

JONATHAN LETHEM (1964) is an American novelist, essayist, and short story writer. His first novel, *Gun, with Occasional Music*, a genre work that mixed elements of science fiction and detective fiction, was published in 1994. This piece was followed by three more science fiction novels. In 1999, Lethem published *Motherless*, a National Book Critics Circle Award-winning novel that achieved mainstream success. In 2003, he published *The Fortress of Solitude*, which became a New York Times Best Seller. In 2005, he received a MacArthur Fellowship. His other publications include *Chronic City, Dissident Gardens*, and *A Gambler's Anatomy.*

DANIEL LIBESKIND (1946) is an international figure in architecture and urban design. He is renowned for his ability to evoke cultural memory in buildings. Informed by a deep commitment to music, philosophy, literature, and poetry, Libeskind aims to create architecture that is resonant, unique and sustainable. As Principal Design Architect for Studio Libeskind, he speaks widely on the art of architecture in universities and professional summits. His architecture and ideas have been the subject of many articles and exhibitions, influencing the field of architecture and the development of cities and culture. Libeskind lives in New York with his wife and business partner, Nina Libeskind.

RACHEL LIBESKIND (1989) is a New York-based artist. She holds a B.A. from Harvard University. Libeskind has shown her work in exhibitions in Paris, London, Milan, Rome, Warsaw, Vilnius, Miami and New York among other cities internationally. She is a multi-disciplinary artist, often merging her installation and performance with her studio practice. Libeskind's work is characterized by a unique combination of historicist appropriation and improvisational arranging. Her work deals with issues of identity, the transmutations of past histories and the collection and curation of images and objects.

DIANA IBÁÑEZ LÓPEZ (1985) is a Spanish architect. She studied Architecture at Cambridge University and later worked as a designer at MVRDV in Rotterdam before going on to do a range of things in Cairo, London, Cologne and San Francisco. She teaches architecture at the Royal College of Art, product design at Karlsruhe University, has taught at The Why Factory in Delft and the Bartlett School of Planning at UCL and is a visiting critic at universities and art schools internationally.

British-born **SOPHIE LOVELL** (1964) is based in Berlin and is an established author, editor and art director in the fields of architecture and design. She has written a number of books, including the authoritative monograph *Dieter Rams: As Little Design as Possible* (Phaidon). She has been involved in the founding, design and editing of a number of magazines and was editor-in-chief of the ground breaking digital magazine for architecture and beyond, *uncube*. She is the Germany Editor of *Wallpaper** magazine and is also a co-founder of the &beyond collective and lovell studio, both specialising in next-level publishing. She is currently working on an innovative digital, analogue and print-on-demand book series *Archifutures for the Future Architecture* platform with dpr-barcelona.

GREG LYNN (1964) has been an innovator in redefining the medium of design with digital technology as well as pioneering the fabrication and manufacture of complex functional and ergonomic forms using CNC (Computer Numerically Controlled) machinery. The buildings, projects, publications, teachings and writings associated with his office have been influential in the acceptance and use of advanced materials and technologies for design and fabrication. As design opportunities today extend across multiple scales and media, his studio Greg Lynn FORM continues to define the cutting edge of design in a variety of fields. Because of his early studies in philosophy and architecture he has been involved in combining the realities of design and construction with the speculative, theoretical and experimental potentials of writing and teaching.

JONATHAN MANNION (1970) is a noted New York based photographer and film director. Mannion has shot over 300 album covers working with hip hop and R&B performers including Jay Z, Dr. Dre, Aaliyah, Outkast, Nas, Nicki Minaj, Brandy and Kendrick Lamar. He was also the photographer behind the Beats by Dre 'Straight Outta' campaign.

KERRY JAMES MARSHALL (1955) uses painting, sculptural installations, collage, video, and photography to comment on the history of black identity both in the United States and in Western art. He is well known for paintings that focus on black subjects historically excluded from the artistic canon, and has explored issues of race and history through imagery ranging from abstraction to comics. Marshall has work in numerous public collections including the Museum of Modern Art, New York; the Whitney Museum of American Art, New York; The Studio Museum in Harlem, New York; the Metropolitan Museum of Art, New York; the Walker Art Centre, Minneapolis; the National Gallery of Art, Washington, DC; Los Angeles County Museum of Art; Birmingham Museum of Art; San Francisco Museum of Modern Art; Art Institute of Chicago; Museum of Contemporary Art Chicago; and the Museum of Fine Arts, Boston.

HANS ULRICH OBRIST (1968) is an art curator, critic and historian of art. He is artistic director at the Serpentine Galleries, London. Obrist is the author of *The Interview Project*, an extensive on-going project of interviews. He is also co-editor of the *Cahiers d'art revue*. While maintaining official curatorial positions, he is also the co-founder of the Brutally Early Club, a discussion group open to all that meets at Starbucks in London, Berlin, New York and Paris at 6:30 a.m., and is a contributing editor of *032c* magazine, *Artforum* and *Paradis Magazine*, among others. Hans Ulrich Obrist has lectured internationally at academic and art institutions alike. He lives and works in London.

FREI PAUL OTTO (1925 -2015) was a German architect and structural engineer noted for his use of lightweight structures, in particular tensile and membrane structures, including the roof of the Olympic Stadium in Munich for the 1972 Summer Olympics. Otto won the RIBA Royal Gold Medal in 2006 and was awarded the Pritzker Architecture Prize in 2015, shortly before his death.

ANDRÉS F. RAMIREZ (1985) is a writer, curator and manager, working in the realm of architecture, engineering, urban planning and design. Challenging conventions in cultural communications, he explores the semantics of space and its socio-cultural implications. He is the co-founder and Managing Director of PLANE—SITE, an agency devoted to the production and dissemination of original content for architecture and the built environment.

DIETER RAMS (1932) is a German industrial designer and retired academic closely associated with the consumer products company Braun and the functionalist school of industrial design. His unobtrusive approach and belief in 'less but better' design generated a timeless quality in his products and have influenced the design of many products, which also secured Rams worldwide recognition and appreciation.

MATTHIAS RICK (1965-2012) was an architect based in Berlin. He was a musician in the crossover band Moorpaul, co-founder of the Institute of Applied Building Arts in Berlin before becoming a member of Raumlabor. As such he realised numerous projects around the world and was a requested lecturer, cook and moderator. He liked talking about potentials, self-enabling architecture, appropriation of space and squatting. He was Professor of Architecture at the Academy of Art, Architecture and Design in Prague (VSUP) and at the University of Aalborg.

TOM SACHS (1966) is an American contemporary artist and sculptor, probably best known for his elaborate recreations of various Modern icons, all of them masterpieces of engineering and design of one kind or another. In an early show he made Knoll office furniture out of phone books and duct tape; later, he recreated Le Corbusier's 1952 *Unité d'Habitation* using only foam core and a glue gun. Other projects have included his versions of various Cold War masterpieces, like the Apollo 11 Lunar Excursion Module, and the bridge of the battleship USS Enterprise.

LISA SPELLMAN (1959) founded 303 Gallery in New York City in 1984. She's launched the careers of numerous major artists such as Doug Aitken, Karen Kilimnik, Hans Peter Feldmann and Collier Schorr. Her current stable includes Stephen Shore, Kim Gordon and Larry Johnson. She showed Richard Prince, Vito Acconci, Robert Gober and Christopher Wool in the 1980s.

DENISE SCOTT BROWN (1931) is an American architect, planner, writer, educator, and principal of the firm Venturi, Scott Brown and Associates in Philadelphia. Scott Brown and her husband and partner, Robert Venturi, are regarded as among the most influential architects of the 20th century, both through their architecture and planning, and theoretical writing and teaching.

FARIDA SEDOC (1980) is a contemporary artist based in Amsterdam, The Netherlands. She uses diverse artistic mediums like silkscreen, graphic design, printmaking, patchwork and fashion to create colourful narratives. Her work is deeply rooted in hip-hop and street culture. She explores and questions contemporary cultural identity and the influence of economics, heritage and politics on the future of urbanism.

ALEXANDER SMALLS (1952) is the visionary of the award-winning restaurant The Cecil and its sister restaurant Minton's, serving as its co-owner and Executive Chef. Smalls has been honoured with the Legacy Award in 2014 by *The Amsterdam News*, which is one of the oldest African American newspapers in the country. Alexander is also a world-renowned opera singer and the winner of both a Grammy Award and a Tony Award for the cast recording of *Porgy and Bess*, by George Gershwin, with the Houston Grand Opera. Passionate about his involvement with non-profit organizations, he is on the Advisory Board of The Union Food Lab at Columbia University, and through his restaurants, he is involved in C-CAP (Careers through Culinary Arts Program). Alexander is also a former board member and Artistic Director of Opus 118 at the Harlem School of Music.

JERSZY SEYMOUR (1968) is a designer working in the most expanded sense of the field. He sees design as the creation of situations, as the general relationship we have with the built world, the natural world, other people and ourselves, and as much about the inhabitation of the planet as the inhabitation of the mind. The goal is the transformation of reality guided by constant humour and a tainted sense of poetry and the idea of the 'non-gesamt gesamtkunstwerk'. His work spans from playing with the industrial and post-industrial produced object, actions, interventions and installations, covering a range of mediums and materials, objects, film, performance, music and writing.

AHMIR KHALIB THOMPSON (1971), known professionally as Questlove, is an American percussionist, multi-instrumentalist, DJ, music journalist, record producer, and occasional actor. He is best known as the drummer and joint frontman (with Black Thought) for the Grammy Award-winning band The Roots. The Roots have been serving as the in-house band for The Tonight Show Starring Jimmy Fallon since February 17, 2014, as they have for the entire run of the show under Jimmy Fallon. Questlove is also one of the producers of the Broadway musical *Hamilton*. He is the cofounder of Okayplayer and Okayafrica. Additionally, he is an adjunct instructor at the Clive Davis Institute of Recorded Music at New York University.

EINAR THORSTEINN (1942-2015) was an Icelandic architect with an interest in geometrical structures. Thorsteinn was a follower of Buckminster Fuller and he worked with polyhedral and spherical shapes. He graduated from Technical University of Hannover. He worked with Frei Otto from 1969-1972 helping to design the Munich Olympiapark for the 1972 Summer Olympics. He then started the Constructions Lab in Iceland and experimented with tensile structures. He started a long collaboration with artist Olafur Eliasson. Early results from the collaboration included geodesic dome structures and he also worked with cells with fivefold symmetry used in the Harpa Reykjavik Concert Hall. He also worked with Guillermo Trotti to design mobile lunar research laboratories for NASA.

MADELON VRIESENDORP (1945) studied in Amsterdam at the Rietveld Academy and Central Saint Martin's School of Art in London. Her work was shown in the Serpentine, Guggenheim and MoMA in NY, and Stedelijk Museum in Amsterdam among others. She received an Honourable Fellowship from the RIBA in February 2009 'for the general advancement of Architecture', an Honorary Diploma from the Architectural Association in June 2017 'in recognition of her extraordinary contribution to the imagination of architecture', and the Ada Louise Huxtable Prize in March 2018.

AI WEIWEI (1957) is a Chinese contemporary artist and activist, famed for his tongue in cheek criticism. His work encompasses sculpture and mixed- media installation, photography, film, architecture, curation, and social criticism. He is renowned for his political activism and social media activity almost as much as for his social interventions, approach to the ready-made, and knowledge of Chinese traditional crafts.

LEGACY
Generations of Creatives in Dialogue

PUBLISHER
Frame Publishers

EDITOR
Lukas Feireiss

GRAPHIC DESIGN
Barbara Iwanicka

COPY-EDITING
Emma Lucek

PRODUCTION
Lucie Ulrich

PREPRESS
Edward de Nijs

COVER PHOTOGRAPHY
Front cover top to bottom, left to right: Tom Sachs, Photo by Mario Sorrenti; Zamp Kelp and Ludwig Engel, 2018; Andres Ramirez and Denise Scott Brown, Photo by Plane–Site, 2017; Ai Weiwei and Lukas Feireiss, Photo by Lukas Feireiss and Ai Weiwei, 2018; Rem Koolhaas, Photo by Charlie Koolhaas; Kerry James Marshall, Photo by Felix Clay. Courtesy of the artist and David Zwirner; Rachel Libeskind and Daniel Libeskind, Photo by Christopher Lane, 2016; Dieter Rams and Sophie Lovell, Photo by Gary Hustwit, 2018; Chermayeff family and friends, Photo by Daniel Salemi, 2016; Arata Isozaki, Photo by Keizo Kioku; Phyllis Lambert, Photo by Center for Canadian Architecture (CCA); Tuba Candar, Defne Ayas and Elâ Tara, Photo by Christoph Loeffler, 2015; Alexander Smalls, Photo by Beatriz da Costa; Ahmir Questlove Thompson and George Clinton, Schomburg Center for Research in Black Culture, The New York Public Library, 2015.

Back cover top to bottom, left to right: Olafur Eliasson and Einar Thorsteinn, Photo by Carol Diehl and Terry Perk, 2003; Bill Drummond, Photo by Thomas Ecke, 2010; Hans-Ulrich Obrist and Yona Friedman, Photo by Aedes Architecture Forum, 2004; Greg Lynn and Frank Gehry, Photo by Center for Canadian Architecture (CCA); Kristin Feireiss and Lukas Feireiss, Photo by Regina Schubert, 1992; Fabiola Alondra, Photo by Rafael Rios; Bob Dylan, Photo by F. Antolín Hernandez Con; Charlie Koolhaas, Photo by Jan Suklennik; Sir Ken Adam, Photo by Valerie Bennet.

PRINTING
IPP Printers

Trade Distribution USA and Canada
Consortium Book Sales & Distribution, LLC.
34 Thirteenth Avenue NE, Suite 101
Minneapolis, MN 55413-1007
T +1 612 746 2600
T +1 800 283 3572 (orders)
F +1 612 746 2606

Trade Distribution Benelux
Frame Publishers
Luchtvaartstraat 4
1059 CA Amsterdam
the Netherlands
distribution@frameweb.com
frameweb.com

Trade Distribution Rest of World
Thames & Hudson Ltd
181A High Holborn
London WC1V 7QX
United Kingdom
T +44 20 7845 5000
F +44 20 7845 5050

ISBN: 978-94-92311-30-6

Printed on acid-free paper produced from chlorine-free pulp. TCF ∞

Printed in Poland
987654321